PENGUIN BOOKS

THE NEW PELICAN GUIDE TO ENGLISH LITERATURE

8

Boris Ford is the G[...] [...]ide to *English Literature* (in [...] [...]ginal form was launched in 1954. At the time it was being planned he was Chief Editor and later Director of the Bureau of Current Affairs. After a spell on the Secretariat of the United Nations in New York and Geneva, he became Editor of the *Journal of Education* and also first Head of Schools Broadcasting with Independent Television.

Following a period as Education Secretary at the Cambridge University Press, Boris Ford, until he retired in 1982, was Professor of Education at the universities of Sheffield, Bristol and Sussex, where he was also Dean of the School, of Cultural and Community Studies. He edited *Universities Quarterly* from 1955 until 1986. He is General Editor of *The Cambridge Guide to the Arts in Britain* (in 9 vols, 1988–91), and of a forthcoming series of 8 volumes on the arts and civilization of the Western world.

The Present

VOLUME

8

OF THE NEW PELICAN GUIDE TO
ENGLISH LITERATURE

EDITED BY BORIS FORD

PENGUIN BOOKS

PENGUIN BOOKS

Published by the Penguin Group
Penguin Books Ltd, 27 Wrights Lane, London w8 5tz, England
Penguin Books USA Inc. 375 Hudson Street, New York, New York 10014, USA
Penguin Books Australia Ltd, Ringwood, Victoria, Australia
Penguin Books Canada Ltd, 10 Alcorn Avenue, Toronto, Ontario, Canada m4v 3b2
Penguin Books (NZ) Ltd, 182–190 Wairau Road, Auckland 10, New Zealand

Penguin Books Ltd, Registered Offices: Harmondsworth, Middlesex, England

First published in Pelican Books 1983
Reprinted in Penguin Books 1990
3 5 7 9 10 8 6 4

The acknowledgements on pp. 592–3 constitute an
extension of this copyright page

Printed in England by Clays Ltd, St Ives plc
Filmset in Monophoto Bembo

CONTENTS

CONTENTS

CONTENTS

PART IV

COMPILED BY FRANK WHITEHEAD

GENERAL INTRODUCTION

The publication of this *New Pelican Guide to English Literature* in many volumes might seem an odd phenomenon at a time when, in the words of the novelist L. H. Myers, a 'deep-seated spiritual vulgarity ... lies at the heart of our civilization', a time more typically characterized by the Headline and the Digest, by the Magazine and the Tabloid, by Pulp Literature and the Month's Masterpiece. Yet the continuing success of the *Guide* seems to confirm that literature – both yesterday's and today's – has a real and not merely a nominal existence among a large number of people; and its main aim has been to help validate as firmly as possible this feeling for a living literature and for the values it embodies.

The *Guide* is partly designed for the committed student of literature. But it has also been written for those many readers who accept with genuine respect what is known as 'our literary heritage', but for whom this often amounts, in memory, to an unattractive amalgam of set texts and school prizes; as a result they may have come to read only today's books – fiction and biography and travel. Though they are probably familiar with such names as Pope, George Eliot, Langiand, Marvell, Yeats, Dr Johnson, Hopkins, and the Brontës, they might hesitate to describe their work intimately or to fit them into any larger pattern of growth and achievement. If this account is a fair one, it seems probable that very many people would be glad of guidance that would help them respond to what is living and contemporary in literature, for, like the other arts, it has the power to enrich the imagination and to clarify thought and feeling.

The *Guide* does not set out to compete with the standard Histories of Literature, which inevitably tend to have a lofty, take-it-or-leave-it attitude about them. This is not a Bradshaw or a Whitaker's Almanack of English literature. Nor is it a digest or potted version, nor again a portrait gallery of the Great. Works such as these already abound, and there is no need to add to their number. What it sets out to offer, by contrast, is a guide to the history and traditions of English literature, a contour map of the literary scene. It attempts, that is, to draw up an ordered account of literature as a direct encouragement to people to read widely in an informed way and with enjoyment. In this respect the *Guide* acknowledges a considerable debt to those twentieth-century writers and critics who have made a determined effort to elicit from literature what is of living value to us today: to establish a sense of literary tradition, and to define the standards that this tradition embodies.

The New Pelican Guide to English Literature consists of eleven volumes:

1. Part One. *Medieval Literature: Chaucer and the Alliterative Tradition* (with an anthology)
1. Part Two. *Medieval Literature: The European Inheritance* (with an anthology)
2. *The Age of Shakespeare*
3. *From Donne to Marvell*
4. *From Dryden to Johnson*
5. *From Blake to Byron*
6. *From Dickens to Hardy*
7. *From James to Eliot*
8. *The Present*
9. *American Literature*
   A Guide for Readers

This particular volume, *The Present*, deals with the literature written since about 1940. The writers of this period are very much part of our own time and this can give their writing immediate life and interest, even though one may come to the conclusion that much of it will be comparatively short-lived. Creative writers and critics are subject to all the pressures of changing fashions and tastes, and this makes it harder to write about them with the critical assurance that is possible when discussing writers of earlier ages. Nonetheless, it has been imperative to make the effort, for the writers of today deserve to be read and enjoyed and evaluated with the same kind and quality of attention as their well-established forebears.

Though the *Guide* has been designed as a single work, in the sense that it attempts to provide a coherent and developing account of the tradition of English literature, each volume exists in its own right. This is particularly true of this final volume, in that it includes writers from the Commonwealth, some of whom are among the most interesting contributors to 'English' literature in the wider sense. On the other hand, a number of writers like Eliot, Auden, Orwell, Waugh, Leavis and others span the period covered by this and the previous volume. For this reason the boundary between the two volumes is not at all rigid; and John Holloway's two literary surveys have ensured a large measure of continuity between the two twentieth-century volumes.

Each volume of the *Guide* sets out to provide the reader with four kinds of related material:

(i) *A survey of the social context of literature* in each period, providing an account of contemporary society at its points of contact with literature.

(ii) *A literary survey* of the period, describing the general characteristics of the period's literature in such a way as to enable the reader to trace its growth and to keep his or her bearings. The aim of this section is to answer such questions as 'What *kind* of literature was written in this period?', 'Which authors matter most?', 'Where does the strength of the period lie?'.

(iii) *Detailed studies* of some of the chief writers and works in the period. Coming after the two general surveys, the aim of this section is to convey a sense of what it means to read closely and with perception; and also to suggest how the literature of a given period is most profitably read, i.e. with what assumptions and with what kind of attention. In addition this volume includes chapters on a few wider topics, such as writing for and by children, the loss (for most people) of the Bible, philosophical and political writing, and language. It also includes a chapter on the music drama of Britten and Tippett as providing an invaluable comparative landmark in relation to the literature.

(iv) *An appendix of essential facts for reference purposes*, such as authors' and general bibliographies, books for further study, and so on.

BORIS FORD

PART I

THE SOCIAL AND CULTURAL SETTING

KRISHAN KUMAR

Introduction: Towards 'One England'?

One ought, if one is a historian, to be very grateful to the Second World War: it provides such a convenient dividing line in the history of Britain – as of the world – during the twentieth century. Before it – the slump, the economics of the gold standard, and the politics of a Conservative hegemony; after it – full employment, the economics of Keynes, and the politics of a welfare state constructed by Labour. The contrasts run equally strong at the social and cultural levels. Before the Second World War, the British class system seemed more than ever firmly set in its grim contours of privilege and privation, upper-class glitter and working-class endurance, 'them' and 'us'. The line was sharply drawn between the culture of the masses, based largely on the dance hall and the cinema, and that of the elite, rooted in the traditional 'high culture' of painting, music, drama and literature. After the war, it seemed for a while at least as if egalitarian philosophies might effect fundamental changes in the structure of society; while the stimulus provided by the war to the national organization of the arts, and the arrival of the classless medium of television, seemed to hold out some promise for the radical dream of a 'common culture'.

Everyone will readily recognize both the force and the weakness of the contrasts thus drawn. To frustrated reformers and radicals, British society must at times seem explicitly designed as a text-book testimonial to 'history's seamless web', and the impossibility of achieving genuinely new departures in society. That this involves a caesura in the collective consciousness – the English chopped off a king's head in the seventeenth century and so set English political development on an entirely different course from its Continental neighbours – is not an unnatural phenomenon. It is perfectly

15

reasonable for the British to feel, in the light of their recent history, that abrupt social change does not happen, not here, anyway. From the perspective of the 1980s, certainly, it is as easy to see continuity as change in twentieth-century British society. Class and culture seem in many ways to be set in much the same split mould as in the earlier years of the century.

We shall see later how the balance stands. At the outset, however, the idea of the Second World War as the great divide is as plausible and helpful a starting point as any. War in the twentieth century has been the great engine of social change: more than mass unemployment, more than the activities of political parties. It would be odd if Britain were a complete exception to this general rule. The war, in a characteristic way, concentrated and consolidated ideas and movements which had been brewing in the previous decades, especially in the 1930s. As it drew to its close, it threw up the possibility of a far-reaching reconstruction of British society. And as so often, it was the enemies of change who, Talleyrand-like, saw things most clearly. What was for the radicals the scent of success was for them the warning sign of danger. Angela Thirkell spoke for all the middle and upper classes of her latter-day 'Barsetshire' when she pronounced in her novel *Peace Breaks Out* (1946) that, with the Labour victory of 1945, 'the Brave and Revolting New World came into its own'.

The Making of the Consensus

The politics of 1945–50 were the continuation of the war by other means. The idealism and the radicalization of the war years spilled over, with declining force, into the post-war period. Labour's peacetime policies were an extension of the torrent of 'progressive' propaganda and activity launched by the outbreak of war in 1939, and intensified following the Dunkirk debacle of June 1940. Men who had vacillated over the extension of state control over the economy and full-blooded policies of nationalization were quickly converted by their wartime experience. William Beveridge, who can fairly be regarded as one of the two patron saints of post-war reconstruction – the other is Keynes – had during the 1930s expressed serious doubts about his youthful enthusiasm for centralized social policy.

He had rejected the radical interventionist ideas of Keynes' *General Theory of Employment, Interest and Money* when it appeared in 1936. In the year of Dunkirk he abruptly came out with a comprehensive scheme of collectivist and egalitarian social reform. Early in 1940 he was writing to Beatrice Webb: 'I don't think Communism as such is an evil; I would very much like to see Communism tried under democratic conditions.' 'Beveridge is today a Socialist,' wrote Mrs Webb in her diary a few months later. 'He agrees that there must be a revolution in the economic structure of society.'[1] As Paul Addison comments, 'the home front organized for war was becoming a model, and an inspiration, for the reorganization of the peace'.[2]

Most of the ideas for reconstruction were, in any case, ready and waiting in the wings. The First World War had delivered a more or less mortal blow to the already fading nineteenth-century concept of the *laissez-faire* economy and the 'nightwatchman state', to use the familiar catch-phrases. A powerful groundswell of 'middle opinion' built up in the thirties, rejecting alike the positions of the extreme Left and the extreme Right, but committing itself unequivocally to state planning and state control of the economy on a large scale, together with a commitment to welfare that was seen by all as a necessary concomitant. The movement was quite promiscuous as to the source both of its ideas and of its participants. It drew upon the socialist writings of the Webbs, G. D. H. Cole, Oswald Mosley, and Barbara Wootton. It was particularly indebted to the contributions of interwar liberalism: the Liberal Party's manifesto of 1928, *Britain's Industrial Future* ('the Yellow Book'), instigated by Lloyd George and inspired by Keynes, has been said with truth to be the most important single influence behind the collectivist policies of the post-1945 period. Conservatives played their part in the persons and pronouncements of Robert Boothby, Oliver Stanley, Lord Eustace Percy, Winston Churchill (erratically), and especially Harold Macmillan, whose *Reconstruction* (1934) and *The Middle Way* (1938) were powerful and influential syntheses of 'middle opinion'. Then there were the non-party and all-party groups – the Industrial Re-organization League, Political and Economic Planning (PEP), the Next Five Years Group – in which the same names cross and criss-cross: Macmillan, Clifford Allen, Arthur Salter, Israel Sieff, Seebohm

Rowntree, Julian Huxley, and many other eminent scientists and industrialists. Lying behind much of this new thinking, apart from the calamity of the slump, was the challenge posed by the contemporary Fascist and Stalinist experiments in planning: a stimulus as much as a warning. The moral – adapt to the new conditions or perish – was in any case succinctly drawn by two powerful and influential books which arrived in England about this time: Peter Drucker's *The End of Economic Man* (1939) and James Burnham's *The Managerial Revolution* (English edn 1942). Certainly Arthur Marwick seems amply justified in his view that it was from the groundwork established by the planning movement of the thirties that

there arose the ideological structures which took Britain safely through the forties and brought her to rest in the fifties. That is to say, the mixed economy, 'Butskellism' (in all but name), all-party acceptance for a welfare state, all-party rejection of the nineteenth-century vision of state planning as a horrible evil, were concepts which received their vital nurture in the nineteen-thirties.[3]

But the Second World War was still the necessary and decisive catalyst. It was not simply that, as with the First World War, the state was once more forced to step in to mobilize the economy and society in an even more comprehensive case of 'total war'. The context of that intervention had now changed, making it impossible to conceive of a return to pre-war practices once the war was over. The scale and complexity of the operation meant that, for instance, the trade unions had to be brought directly into the government, as they were in the person of Ernest Bevin. The same thing applied of course to businessmen – and scientists, and economists, such as Keynes. Kingsley Wood's budget of 1941 was the first truly Keynesian budget ever, making possible 'macroeconomic' regulation of the economy. Like the incorporation of important 'functional' groups – trade unions, businessmen, doctors, farmers – it was to become a permanent feature of British government.

The stage was set for the typical tripartite – even 'corporatist' – form of decision-making that was to shape political practice for the whole of the post-war period. British government became largely a matter of an array of consultative and supervisory bodies. It moved from 'the government of men' to 'the administration of things': a victory for the planners, even though not quite in the terms that some such as Cole would have wished.

At the same time, the Second World War demanded a mobilization of moral resources every bit as much as of physical resources. Morale was crucial, and this called for a major and unprecedented effort of 'education for citizenship' – an effort applying as much to the largely conscript army as to the civilians of the home front. The Coalition Government, despite the fears of some of its members at the radicalizing potential of the venture, put its weight behind a programme of cultural mobilization the like of which had never before been seen in this country.

The arts were encouraged and propagated on a wide scale through ENSA, the Entertainments National Service Association (for the troops) and CEMA, the Council for the Encouragement of Music and the Arts (for the civilians). The cinema was given a much-needed boost through the sponsorship of the Crown Film Unit, a division of the Ministry of Information. Wide-ranging political and social discussion took place among the troops through the activities of the Army Education Corps and the Army Bureau of Current Affairs (ABCA). The BBC was encouraged to become in effect a Ministry of Culture. Its scope expanded dramatically, as reflected most obviously by its growth in size. In 1939 it had 4,000 staff, by the beginning of 1940, 6,000, and by November of that year nearly 11,000. More importantly, it widened its coverage to include not simply 'high culture' but a much larger range of 'light entertainment', giving rise to such wartime, and post-war, successes as the comedy programme ITMA (*It's That Man Again*), with Tommy Handley. From light entertainment – the Forces Programme – also came a current affairs programme, *The Brains Trust*, which somewhat to the surprise of its own producer proved to be as successful as the most popular variety shows, attracting a regular audience of ten million listeners. Equally popular were J. B. Priestley's 'Postscript' talks after the news on Sunday evenings – 'the biggest regular listening audience in the world', the BBC claimed for him – although their radicalism upset several Conservative members of the Coalition, including Churchill, and considerable pressure was put on Priestley to moderate or discontinue the talks. More acceptable was that the audiences for serious music increased sharply, and drama ratings doubled between

1939 and 1941, again, against initial expectations in the BBC. Already a national institution, the BBC consolidated its position in the war years as the cultural spokesman of the nation, although there were doubts then as later as to exactly whose voice did the speaking.[4]

The BBC became, not altogether happily for it or them, a refuge for many radical intellectuals during the war. Priestley, George Orwell, William Empson, Louis MacNeice, and Herbert Read all found a berth here. The most celebrated members of *The Brains Trust* – Julian Huxley, C. E. M. Joad, and Barbara Ward – were left-wing luminaries. Orwell wrote in 1943 that

the British Government started the present war with the more or less openly declared intention of keeping the literary intelligentsia out of it; yet after three years of war almost every writer, however undesirable his political history or opinions, has been sucked into the various Ministries or the BBC and even those who enter the armed forces tend to find themselves after a while in Public Relations or some other essentially literary job. The Government has absorbed these people, unwillingly enough, because it found itself unable to get on without them.[5]

But Orwell knew that this was only one side of the story. The government did not engage in cultural activities purely for Machiavellian reasons of state, out of its own need for propaganda. It is just as true to say that it was pushed into action by the popular feeling unleashed by the war, to which it was compelled to respond and to harness as best it could. Orwell himself put the strongest statement of this case in an earlier essay of 1941:

The English revolution started several years ago, and it began to gather momentum when the troops came back from Dunkirk ... If one wishes to name a particular moment, one cay say that the old distinction between Right and Left broke down when *Picture Post* was first published. What are the politics of *Picture Post*? Or of *Cavalcade*, or Priestley's broadcasts, or the leading articles in the *Evening Standard*? None of the old classifications will fit. They merely point to the existence of multitudes of unlabelled people who have grasped within the last year or two that something is wrong. But since a classless, ownerless society is generally spoken of as 'Socialism', we can give that name to the society towards which we are now moving. The war and the revolution are inseparable.[6]

Orwell fairly soon despaired of 'the English revolution' and the prospects for socialism. But he had pointed to the essential phenomenon, the rise of a radical egalitarian spirit which cut across party lines and even for a while across the lines of class and culture. It may have been Tom Wintringham, the ex-Spanish Civil War veteran and *Picture Post* journalist, who coined the term 'a People's war', a direct echo in any case of the 'People's Front' slogans of the late thirties. But the concept was in the air right from the start, and in the course of the war it crystallized the activities of a very diverse group of reformers. The idea of a people's war generated a powerful chorus of voices calling not simply for radical social change once the war was over, but for an acknowledgement that such changes were part of the very aims of the war.

Perhaps the most consistent campaigner, and certainly among the most influential, was *Picture Post* itself, edited for most of the war (and up till 1950) by Tom Hopkinson. In its combination of arresting pictures, direct, forceful writing, and social commitment, it epitomized the mood of 'the people's war'. At the height of the war it was selling over a million copies a week. As early as January 1941 it devoted a special issue to 'A Plan for Britain', supervised by Julian Huxley. Almost all the proposals were put into effect during the war or by the post-war Labour government. It campaigned vigorously on behalf of the Beveridge Report on social security (1942), and helped finance the later study by Beveridge on full employment. Among its regular contributors were Shaw and Wells, the young Quintin Hogg, Robert Boothby, Tom Driberg, Thomas Balogh and Bertrand Russell. At the 1945 election many a bitter Conservative blamed 'the bloody *Picture Post*' for the Labour victory; Tom Hopkinson's riposte was that 'the bloody *Daily Mirror*' carried greater responsibility.[7]

'Cassandra's' biting articles in the *Mirror* during the war certainly contributed greatly to the mood of sharp criticism and fervent idealism, and got Cassandra (William Connor) posted to the army by a disgruntled Churchill. But similar attitudes extended well beyond the classic populist radicalism of the *Daily Mirror*, *Picture Post*, and Priestley's 'Postscripts'. There was the 'people's Archbishop', Archbishop Temple, with his powerful advocacy of a new social order in his Penguin Special, *Christianity and the Social Order* (1942). There was the stream of Penguin Specials themselves, under Allen Lane's guidance, and the publications of the Left Book Club directed by

Victor Gollancz. There were the documentary films of Humphrey Jennings and Harry Watt (*Listen to Britain, London Can Take It, Fires Were Started, Target for Tonight*), made for the Crown Film Unit. Perhaps most significant of all, as a sign of the times, was the leader that appeared in *The Times* on 1 July 1940: 'The new order cannot be based on the preservation of privilege, whether the privilege be that of a country, of a class, or of an individual.' The Coalition Government was made well enough aware of the popular mood by a remarkable series of by-election victories by independents between 1941 and 1944, standing against Coalition candidates. Many of these independents fought under the banner of the newly-formed Commonwealth Party, representing what its historian Angus Calder has called 'the refined essence of "Beveridgism" – the revolutionary zeal, the millenarian dream, the unselfishness'. The Beveridge Report itself, with its programme of social security 'from the cradle to the grave', was greeted by a volume of popular acclaim which surprised not only the Government but Beveridge himself, never one to under-estimate his own importance. Similar enthusiasm accompanied the publication of Beveridge's independent study, *Full Employment in a Free Society* (1944).

The Coalition Government was in any case moving towards an acceptance of economic planning and a welfare state, although the intensity of the public response to Beveridge undoubtedly spurred it on. In a broadcast of March 1943, Churchill committed him-self and any future government he might head to 'national compulsory insurance for all classes for all purposes from the cradle to the grave', an end to unemployment, a National Health Service, equal opportunity in education, and a national housing programme. He also envisaged a 'broadening field for state owner-ship and enterprise, especially in relation to monopolies of all kinds'. Various measures quickly followed in an attempt to pre-empt more radical proposals. 1944 might almost be called the first year of the Labour government. Important White Papers proliferated: on social insurance, on employment policy, and on a National Health Service, which envisaged a scheme hardly less ambitious than that introduced in 1948 by Aneurin Bevan. To crown this remarkable year came R. A. Butler's Education Act, which guaranteed (and made compulsory) free secondary education to everyone up to the age of fifteen. Butler's Act has been called 'the most impressive ever passed in the field of British education'. It was, moreover, 'the most important single measure of social reform which became law during the war itself; indeed it was potentially the most important gesture towards democracy made in the twentieth century, a fitting product of the People's War.'[8] It was certainly a fitting tribute to the truth of Asa Briggs's remark that, in the twentieth century, 'warfare has necessitated welfare'.

The Labour Party was the natural beneficiary of the egalitarian and democratic mood of the people's war: in that sense there is no mystery about the electorate's rejection of Churchill and his party in 1945. The significant thing was the acceptance by all parties of permanent and continuous state intervention in the economy, whether through ownership, control, or regulation. Labour might talk more of nationalization, Conservatives of 'rationalization'. There might be an emphasis more on 'the mixed economy' (in the 1950s) or on 'the managed economy' (in the 1960s) or 'the regulated economy' (the 1970s). The instruments switched from direct 'micro-economic' control – as in the forties and sixties – to more remote 'macro-economic' control, as in the fifties and seventies. But not even with the coming of the Conservative Government of Margaret Thatcher in 1979 is there any real prospect in sight of a rejection of the Keynesian mixed economy. Nor, despite periodic nibbling by both Labour and Conservatives, has there been a fundamental assault on the Beveridgian welfare state, that other pillar of the postwar consensus.

In other ways the war years and the Labour government that continued it set the terms of the debates of the fifties and sixties. The 1940s brought about a degree of 'equalization' of experience and condition that was greater than any before. To an unprecedented extent the society was forced to take cognizance of itself, to become aware of all its members as sharing in a common struggle and working towards a common future. Typical was the experience of the young William Whitelaw, later Home Secretary in Margaret Thatcher's Government. Being teased once by some right-wing friends for his liberal views, he recalled with feeling:

Look, I'd had a safe and easy life. I'd never seen any members of the working class and therefore didn't like them very much. Then came the war and I saw how these desperately poor and disadvantaged people fought their guts out to save *my* England rather than theirs and I've never forgotten it.[9]

It was emotions such as these that supplied the essential energy for the regeneration of the Conservative Party after 1945. Conservatives had been slow to grasp the wisdom of the pronouncement of a former leader, Arthur Balfour, that 'social legislation is not merely to be distinguished from Socialist legislation but it is its most direct opposite and its most effective antidote'. Now the message was hammered home by R. A. Butler and others. Together with the refashioning of the party machine by Lord Woolton, they ensured that the Tory party would stop being 'the stupid party' – or at any rate stupider than any other. The new liberal Toryism was to give the Conservatives thirteen years of uninterrupted rule after 1951; and it was fitting that for half of these years the party should be led by Harold Macmillan, the great advocate of 'the middle way'.

It was clear from this general ideological reorientation that 'equality' would become a central term in the political vocabulary of the post-war decades: although whether equality of condition, or merely of opportunity, and whether these two could in fact be separated, were to remain contentious issues throughout. There is no doubt that, as a consequence of the new political framework, all groups were now made very much more aware of each other's contribution and rewards, and each sought to measure them by the common standard of social justice. The worse-off clearly felt they had a lot of catching up to do and, through the unions especially, fought hard to improve their condition, in material terms at least. 'Relative deprivation', rather than absolute need, was the motor of that struggle. The war had brought about one of the few significant shifts of the century in the distribution of income, by narrowing the difference between working-class and middle-class incomes. It was inevitable that the working classes should attempt to go further, just as the middle classes would fight to maintain their 'differentials'. Similarly with the relation between the sexes. Women had participated on a massive scale in the war economy and the war effort generally. After the war, following a brief (involuntary) withdrawal, women re-entered the economy in increasing numbers. Within twenty years more than half of all married women were at work. Few of them were 'feminist' in outlook; nevertheless the social phenomenon of women workers on a permanently large scale was the necessary prelude and prerequisite for the feminism of their daughters in the sixties and seventies.

The Nationalization of Culture

The war also did more than anything else in the century to stimulate 'the nationalization of culture' – if the phrase is not thought too gruesome. It brought the state into an active involvement with culture – in the Arnoldian sense – to a degree far surpassing any earlier concern. In the broader context, this posed enormous questions about control and creativity, about censorship and 'permissiveness', and about the relationship of the centre – which in practice meant London – to the parts, the provinces and regions. In the narrower sense, which will be considered first, it involved a dramatic increase in a state patronage of the arts.

'In a single decade, during and after the Second World War, the British Government did more to commit itself to supporting the arts than it had in the previous century and a half.'[10] There could no longer be any question about the importance of the state as the chief patron of the arts. Policies for education led the way, as in the past. In the two decades before Forster's Education Act of 1870, Henry Cole at the Department of Science and Art was putting the profits from the Great Exhibition to good use in building the Victoria & Albert Museum, and establishing the great museum and art complex in South Kensington. His arguments for public support for the arts were unashamedly utilitarian, and very much in keeping with the similar theme in education. In a democratic and industrial age, 'we must educate our masters', as well as instruct them in the 'useful arts' so that Britain could keep pace with its industrial competitors. Cole's achievement, highly controversial at the time, remained isolated and virtually unique. In the following half century, the state reverted to its traditional attitude of distaste and distrust. This position was powerfully reinforced by the growth of the 'fleshly school of poetry' and the 'decadent movement' in the arts, which suggested that state subsidies would support only immorality and subversion; while the doctrine of 'art for art's sake' knocked away the utilitarian argument that was the main prop of the case for government support.

Utilitarian arguments were around in the 1940s, of course, as they always are in the case of public spending on anything. For a government based on a mass electorate no other kind of appeal in the end can really signify, as Tocqueville pointed out long ago. And once more a major educational reform – Butler's 1944 Act – pointed up the traditional connection. But the advocacy was now made more subtle with the urging of the more rounded and attractive concept of citizenship. In order to play a full part in the life of society, the citizen needed to cultivate his mind and spirit as much as he needed the security of a job, a home, and a healthy body. The creative use of leisure was as important a concern for the citizen, and as fit a subject for public attention, as the striving for satisfying and remunerative work. It is indeed not simply a personal accident that the man most responsible for full employment in the post-war period, John Maynard Keynes, was also the first chairman-designate of the Arts Council, as he had been of CEMA during the war.

The establishment of the Arts Council was made more or less inevitable by CEMA's success during the war. CEMA both uncovered and stimulated the public appetite and audience for the arts (as the BBC had been doing throughout the thirties, and continued to do during the war). 'At the start,' Keynes told a radio audience in 1945, 'our aim was to replace what war had taken away; but we soon found that we were providing what had never existed even in peace time.' On that rising tide the idea of a permanent public body for the arts was conceived. Keynes, who would have been first chairman but for his death, inaugurated the Arts Council in suitably elevated tones:

> The purpose of the Arts Council of Great Britain is to create an environment, to breed a spirit, to cultivate an opinion, to offer a stimulus to such purpose that the artist and the public can each sustain and live on the other in that union which has occasionally existed in the past at the great ages of a communal civilized life.

The reality of the future was unfortunately more accurately anticipated in the more prosaic rendering of the first chairman, Sir

Ernest Pooley, when he announced the aim of the Council as being 'to support, encourage and advise' artistic ventures. The modesty of this objective has not by any means been the fault solely of the Council. Despite a steady bi-partisan policy of government support for the arts throughout the post-war period, neither political party when in power has been prepared to be particularly lavish with public spending on the arts. 'We get an Arts Council grant of five million plus for opera and ballet,' says Sir John Tooley, general administrator of Covent Garden, 'but that's nothing to the European opera houses. It's less than half of the subsidy for the Paris opera, or for one opera house in Germany.' The total amount given by the central government to the arts – about £100 million in 1982 – is less than the VAT received by the government for the sale of long-playing records, less than the sum spent by most county councils on education. The British public through its taxes pays out for the arts annually about £2 a head; in West Germany it is more like £25 a head.

Still, money isn't everything, and there have been other grounds for concern about the Arts Council's cultural influence.[11] Like other 'intermediate' institutions – such as the BBC – founded on the cherished 'arm's length' principle of British public administration, the Council has often been smug about its non-political, neutral, culturally-open stance. Policies are effectively determined by Panel Chairmen and their departmental officers, in consultation where necessary with the Council's Chairman and its senior officers. Taken with the overwhelming preponderance of members of the cultural 'Establishment' (which overlaps but is not identical with the political Establishment) on the Council and its Committees, the scene is set for the mood of 'bewildered consensus' that characterizes the operations of the body as a whole. 'What begins, from a Department of State, as a process of selective and administered consensus, cannot become at any of its lower levels an open and democratic public body and procedure.'[12]

The oligarchic and Establishment character of the Arts Council seems inseparable – whether as cause or effect – from its excessive metropolitan orientation: the second of the main charges it has faced throughout its thirty-five-year existence. It is fair to say that the Council is acutely sensitive to this, and in the last decade has expanded its regional activities considerably, noticeably in its support for the

27

dozen or so Regional Arts Associations, and in increased touring. In 1979/80 it allocated about £12 million (one-fifth of its grant) to regional activities, half of which went to the Regional Arts Associations. But this still has to compare with the nearly £19 million (thirty per cent of its total grant and nearly thirty-seven per cent of its spending in England) given to the 'Big Four' London-based national companies alone: the Royal Opera House Covent Garden, English National Opera, the National Theatre, and the Royal Shakespeare Company. Undoubtedly a good case can be made for concentrating one's limited resources in this way.[13] As the Council constantly points out, it is unlikely that without this degree of support the national opera or theatre companies could survive. Their demise would mean a heavy loss not simply to London but to the nation as a whole.

This, however, is naturally small comfort to the culture-starved regions. London houses not only the principal opera, ballet, and theatre companies, but also the principal museums, art galleries, and orchestras, not to mention the British Film Institute, the National Film Theatre, and the glittering new arts centre, the Barbican. (Compare this situation with, say, Germany or the United States.) Most of these are also funded by the Arts Council or directly by the government: that is, by the nation as a whole. The injury is compounded by the equally powerful centralization and concentration of broadcasting, publishing, and the press,[14] all of which are predominantly London-based and take the political and cultural life of the metropolis as their main point of reference. Northcliffe's ambition for his newspapers, to build up a national readership 'centring on London and looking to London for its news and opinions', has been realized over the whole span of the national culture. Thus not only is it the case that cultural initiatives from the provinces only gain significance if they are 'rerouted' through the metropolis, by making it to the West End or getting a hearing in the capital's newspapers or broadcasting networks. It also works, sadly, the other way round: the provinces are only interested in what London selects for them. As Anthony Smith, Director of the British Film Institute, says in justifying his decision to expand the Institute's London activities at the expense of the regions: 'nothing gets to the provinces without a London launch. It's the best help to provincial audiences to see new work being written about in the national Press.'

The causes of the extraordinary centralization of British culture are complex, and point to more powerful historical and social forces than the Arts Council, however constituted, could hope to deal with.[15] It is not surprising that most of its efforts to stimulate regional arts have been unsuccessful. The Regional Arts Associations – with one or two exceptions such as Northern Arts – have been palsied instruments in the main. Subjected to conflicting pressures from the Arts Council and the local authorities, they have generally succumbed to the philistine propensities of the local authority representatives who tend to dominate, and who resent their implied criticism of the local authorities' own efforts in the arts field. If regionalism is to be a genuine cultural force and not simply token window-dressing, a much more fundamental reordering of the political and financial relations between London and the provinces will be necessary.

There is less reason to excuse the Arts Council for a central ambiguity in the way it interprets its chartered duty to support, encourage, and increase the arts. 'The Best for the Most' was CEMA's slogan, somewhat less happily rendered as 'to raise and to spread' in the Council's version. This is certainly one understandable objective; and at a very general level the Council has spoken unequivocally. It has constantly and emphatically proclaimed its belief in standards of excellence in the arts, and its rejection of the view that all judgements in the arts are wholly and purely subjective.[16] This has carried the acknowledged implication that a clear line can be drawn between 'the arts' and 'entertainment' or 'mass culture', and that the Council's business is solely with promoting the first. But looking at the matter more closely, from the point of view of evaluating the Council's performance, two economists in a survey of the Annual Reports of the Council up to 1973 concluded that 'it is not too much to say that in 26 years of official reportage they have failed to produce a single coherent and operational statement of their aims'.[17] More significant have been the inconsistencies of practice, giving rise to the suspicion that the Council does indeed act 'politically' on many occasions; and that, at the very least, it is subject to the fashions and changes of mood which are traditionally more the province of the politician than the guardians of artistic standards.

Thus during the sixties and seventies its new-found fondness for the regions seemed to have a lot to do with the currents of regionalism and devolutionism that were running strongly at the time, expressed most visibly in the nationalist movements in Scotland and Wales.[18] Similarly, having for most of the fifties and sixties maintained a consciously conservative stance in distinguishing between the 'fine arts' and the 'popular arts' such as jazz, it abruptly shifted its emphasis in 1969 to 'throwing a bridge across to the young'. The vigorous youth culture of the 1960s seemed finally to have become too clamorous to ignore, and the Council manifested a sudden consciousness of whole sectors of peripheral artistic activities hitherto ignored. Even more striking a departure was the decision in the early seventies to subsidize the Theatre Investment Trust, a commercial initiative aimed at promoting provincial tours of successful London productions of musicals, comedies, and other forms of 'entertainment'. In line with this was the move in 1978 to collaborate with a commercial management in presenting a production of *My Fair Lady* in the regions. The Council may have been correct to insist, in the face of criticisms, that the venture 'brings pleasure to tens of thousands of taxpayers who would be unlikely to visit opera and ballet'. But this has always been thought to be a truth that commercial enterprises are fully apprised of, and to have exploited more or less successfully for a long time. It seems a little odd for the Arts Council, concerned with the diffusion of 'the best in the arts', to go into partnership with Old Nick.

The most difficult and frustrating development for the Council, as for all official custodians of the culture, has undoubtedly been the steady growth of 'community arts'. This is a cultural movement of the sixties and seventies marked by the advocacy of 'alternative' theatre, film, painting, music and dance. It mixes all the arts, popular and 'high', in a self-conscious effort to raise community awareness and involvement, especially among social groups hitherto culturally and politically excluded. The demands of the community arts activists have raised in the most acute form questions about the Council's conception of the arts and its commitment to broadening the audience for them. It is normal for artists to bite the hand that feeds them, but the Council has repeatedly had the painful experience of handling clients who openly repudiate the very premise of its

Charter, as it understands that. Thus the Council in 1979 was faced with this 'extraordinary statement' from a community artist:

> It must be understood that the so-called cultural heritage which made Europe great – the Bachs and Beethovens, the Shakespeares and Dantes, the Constables and Titians – is no longer communicating anything to the vast majority of Europe's population ... It is *bourgeois* culture and therefore only immediately meaningful to that group. The great artistic deception of the twentieth century has been to insist to *all* people that this was *their* culture. The Arts Council of Great Britain was established on this premise.

The Council has always stood firm against this challenge in its extreme form: it is difficult to see how it could do otherwise. And reading the Annual Reports one senses that most Council members and officers wish that community arts would simply decline and disappear. But they have not; and the Council – or those behind it – have clearly felt that it would be politically unwise to ignore the movement. The Reports towards the end of the 1970s begin to stress that community arts and 'the established arts' are complementary, and that both have their part to play in raising the cultural level of the population as a whole.

Naturally this has attracted criticism from the opposite camp. The Council is accused of rampant 'trendiness' and capitulation to modernist fads.[19] It clearly can't win. One might say that the Arts Council has done the best it can, within its political constraints and its limited means. But the achievement is a very long way off the goal of a real democratization of the arts – 'the Best for the Most' – conceived in the heroic years of the 1940s.

What of the BBC – that other great instrument of the national culture and self-professed cultivator of the middle ground? The BBC emerged from the Second World War covered in glory. 'It became, in the eyes of many, an additional established church, a source of authority over the language, an arbiter of cultural taste, a national musical impresario and a re-invigorator of national drama and song.'[20] It was the chief means by which the nation was infused with the sense of collective struggle and collective purpose. In 1945, nationally and internationally the BBC was at the peak of its prestige, as unassailable as the monarchy.

This status was the springboard for its rapid development in the later forties. To complement the Home Service, in 1946 the wartime General Forces Programme was retained on a permanent basis as the new Light Programme, and a completely new channel, the Third Programme, was established with an unqualified commitment to 'the highest possible cultural level' – the best in music, drama, poetry, and documentary features, 'corresponding in outlook to a *Times* of the air'. The reorganization of radio on a tripartite and apparently culturally divisive pattern provoked anxieties within and outside the BBC at the abandonment of the earlier policy as propounded by Lord Reith of 'mixed programming'. This had followed the strategy of 'culture by stealth', with the cunning idea that the innocent listener, encountering as it were automatically throughout the day both light and serious matter, would gradually and imperceptibly 'improve'. The criticism was countered by the Director-General, Sir William Haley, with a curious and remarkable image of the British people as a cultural pyramid slowly ascending:

> The pyramid is served by three main Programmes, differentiated but broadly overlapping in levels and interest, each Programme leading on to the other, the listener being induced through the years increasingly to discriminate in favour of the things that are more worthwhile. Each Programme at any given moment must be ahead of its public, but not so much as to lose their confidence. The listener must be led from good to better by curiosity, liking, and a growth of understanding. As the standards of the education and culture of the community rise so should the programme pyramid rise as a whole.

The Reithian conception was retained, but over the radio networks as a whole, rather than within each of them. There were Light Programme devotees, and there were Third Programme devotees, and both seemed happy to go their own way in relative ignorance of each other. The Third Programme listener attended to Britten's *The Turn of the Screw* and Goethe's *Faust*, the Light Programme to *Family Favourites* and *Housewives' Choice*. The Home Service valiantly held aloft the Reithian banner with such features as the annual Reith Lectures, launched by Bertrand Russell in 1948. It still saw itself as 'the real Home programme of the people of the United Kingdom, carefully balanced, appealing to all classes . . . and generally so designed that it will steadily but imperceptibly raise the standard of taste, entertainment, outlook and citizenship'.[21] Some excellent programmes were made in this spirit, such as Charles Parker's Radio Ballads. The best offerings tended to be in the lighter vein. The fifties were the golden age of radio comedy, with such sparkling series as *Take It From Here*, *Educating Archie*, *The Goon Show* and *Hancock's Half Hour*. But overall, the sense of the persistence of an old pattern, established during the war or soon afterwards, was very strong. Programmes started in the forties – such as *Mrs Dale's Diary*, *Desert Island Discs*, *Any Questions*, *Woman's Hour*, *The Archers* – ran for decades, setting up familiar and cosy points of reference on the broadcasting map that encouraged routine and formula radio.

In the end it was television that forced the BBC to follow through the ultimate logic of the Haley policies. By the end of the sixties television had clearly become the main medium of entertainment and information for the bulk of the population. Radio had to adapt by aiming for the remaining 'spaces' in people's lives – by providing the sort of thing suitable for listening to in the bath, doing household chores, or driving to work in the car. (The coming of the portable transistor radio greatly aided this strategy.) In a plan entitled *Broadcasting in the Seventies* (1969), the BBC proposed streamlining its radio services in an entirely functional way. To meet the demand for continuous 'pop music' revealed by the commercial 'pirate' radio stations of the sixties, Radio One, a new channel entirely devoted to pop music, had been set up in 1968. Radios Two, Three, and Four now took over the main functions of the old Light, Third, and Home, but with a much sharper separation of materials and interests. An ambitious programme of local radio stations was announced, together with the development of educational radio through the 'University of the Air' (and later the Open University). It was clear from *Broadcasting in the Seventies* – which stirred up much controversy within the BBC itself – that radio had abandoned the attempt to provide a comprehensive, integrated, national cultural service. It fragmented itself socially, culturally, and geographically. Programmes were now compartmentalized to fit different times of the day, different activities, different interest groups – 'youth', 'mature students', classical music lovers, local communities. It was the promiscuous supermarket system, leaving the choice entirely up to the listener rather than attempting to guide it through a sense of cultural purpose. So far as radio was concerned, Reith was firmly buried, a passing confirmed by the coming of commercial radio in the early seventies.

This left television, willy-nilly, with the task of providing a common cultural skin for the nation. No other institution could compete with it in the comprehensiveness of its social embrace, nor in the universality of its appeal. It had spread with astonishing rapidity. At the time of the Coronation in 1953 – the televising of which is generally held to have inaugurated the television age in Britain – scarcely ten per cent of homes had television sets. By 1963 only ten per cent of homes were without one, and by the end of the sixties virtual saturation point was reached, with homes now beginning to acquire a second, portable, set for the bedroom or bathroom. Moreover the mass audience for television was remarkably heterogeneous and representative. All ages, all classes, all faiths consumed it avidly – the middle classes joining in the national orgy after an initial disdain, just as with the welfare state. By the end of the seventies the English people were spending an average of twenty-five hours a week watching television (over the whole life span, more time than they spent in formal education or at work). As a 'leisure pursuit' it crowded out everything else, cinema-going in particular but also sport and other outside activities. As an institution and an activity, television established itself as the most representative emblem of the national culture. It was classless and culturally universal in a way and to an extent barely approached by the press, the traditional arts, educational institutions, and political groupings.

The rise of television did not simply mean the entrenchment of a new national medium. It symbolized – many said, it largely effected – a major change in the ethos and style of British society. The great age of radio was inescapably associated with struggle and sacrifice, however stoutly endured. It breathed in particular the atmosphere of the war and post-war austerity, and the collectivist ethos inspired by that. Television announced that the war, and all that went with it, was finally over. Its expansion took place in an era of unprecedented economic growth and rising standards of living. Its associations are with plenty rather than want, leisure rather than work, choice rather than necessity. It belongs to the Macmillan years of consumerism, 'individualism', hedonism, the time when the British people 'never had it so good'. The start of commercial broadcasting in 1954 strongly confirmed these associations. It finally broke the BBC's cultural monopoly, its right and power to speak for and to the nation as a whole, as it had supremely done in wartime. Broadcasting might still aspire to create 'one nation'; it could no longer claim to speak with one voice.

Commercialism and competition were to be the mainspring of change in the long-run. But the immediate effect was both less gratifying than the profit-seeking proponents had anticipated, and less dire than the cultural critics had prognosticated (Reith compared the coming of commercial television with the introduction of bubonic plague and the Black Death). This was largely because commercial television – ITV – was never given its head, to follow the American pattern of pure commercialism, but from the start was under the guidance of a public corporation. The Television Act of 1954 set up a supervisory body, the Independent Television Authority (later the Independent Broadcasting Authority) whose powers and functions were closely modelled on those of the Board of Governors of the BBC. There were to be no 'sponsored' programmes of the American kind, merely 'spot advertising' whose frequency, duration, and content were closely monitored by the Authority (currently, for instance it allows no more than seven minutes of advertising in any one hour). The Authority has wide discretionary powers, on pain of not renewing or even revoking the franchises of the commercial companies, to ensure that 'programmes maintain a proper balance in their subject matter and a high general standard of quality', and that 'due impartiality' is preserved, especially in the treatment of 'political or industrial controversy'. That these are not merely paper powers was shown in 1967, when three of the original fourteen commercial franchises were not renewed, most notably that of the London company, Associated Rediffusion. The Authority also from time to time lays down specific guidelines for programme schedules, as that one-third of all material broadcast by the ITV companies should be 'serious non-fiction, sensibly distributed over the week as a whole in appropriate times' (IBA *Report* 1978). One result of this is that 'serious programming' has increased from accounting for nineteen per cent of the companies' schedules in 1956 to thirty-six per cent in 1965, a proportion which has since been maintained.[22]

It was not, therefore, altogether far-fetched for a Director of BBC Television, Sir Gerald Beadle, to describe the British television structure as 'two state-owned networks', one run by the BBC, the other by the ITA. Over the years, and no doubt partly as a result of the competition for viewers, the programme schedules of the BBC and ITV came to look remarkably alike.

ITV might be more innovative and combative in political documentary and interview style, never the BBC's forte; and certainly the success of Independent Television News forced the BBC to reconsider its attitude to news gathering and presentation. But the BBC countered in the field of comedy – always a strong area – and under the stimulating regime of Sir Hugh Greene in the 1960s discovered a fertile vein of political satire as well. The sixties were the golden age of television comedy and satire, with such programmes as *Till Death Us Do Part*, *Steptoe and Son*, *That Was The Week That Was*, *Not So Much A Programme, More A Way of Life*, and *Monty Python*. But there was also a great growth of 'serious' arts and features programmes, shared equally by ITV and BBC. The BBC excelled at the grand cultural edifices – Kenneth Clark's *Civilisation*, Alistair Cook's *America* – but ITV produced perhaps the best documentary series in *The World At War*, a 26-part history of the Second World War. Both produced some excellent and challenging plays, as in *The Wednesday Play* series, transforming television drama from a pale imitation of stage plays into a new creative form, with its own themes and treatment.

Something of the richness of the offers from both sides in the field of the traditional arts can be seen from a week's television taken at random during April 1982. In that week one could see a complete performance of Wagner's *Parsifal*, filmed at Bayreuth, a three-hour film biography of Stravinsky (ITV's *South Bank Show*), a performance of a modern operatic *Passion* from Winchester Cathedral (BBC's *Omnibus*), a live relay of a complete Leonard Bernstein concert from the Royal Festival Hall, five parts of the series *One Hundred Great Paintings*, first episodes of dramatic adaptations in several parts of Wilkie Collins's *The Woman in White* (BBC) and Stan Barstow's *A Kind of Loving* (ITV), and the first in a series of new plays, *Play for Tomorrow*. This leaves out, from the same week, a three-hour documentary *The Trials of Alger Hiss*, films about Tibetan art and culture, several episodes from regular drama series, and about a dozen first-rate films, including a Greta Garbo season and some classic Hollywood musicals.

Some anxieties as to the content and quality of broadcasting were, therefore, stilled in the event. This was partly due to the vigilance of the cultural critics, who acquired a particularly influential voice in the deliberations of the 1960 Pilkington Committee on Broadcasting. The Pilkington Report (1962), widely thought to have been largely written by Richard Hoggart, author of *The Uses of Literacy* (1957), expressed the characteristically fifties concern at the deleterious cultural potential of television, especially commercial television. The broadcasting organizations suitably heeded these signals from on high, only to find themselves in trouble with the politicians in the 1960s on account of their very adventurousness and independence. At the same time, left-wing critics – some of them, such as the *Open Secret* group, within broadcasting itself – were accusing the broadcasting companies of being elitist and Establishment in their handling of problems affecting the working class, such as industrial disputes, and in their exclusion of minority groups from the air. Finally, in the later sixties and seventies, came a broad-based attack from conservative moralists led by Mrs Mary Whitehouse and her National Viewers' and Listeners' Association. This charged broadcasters with responsibility for undermining the whole fabric of Christian Society, and with wanton subversion especially in the spheres of family and sexual relations.[23]

The broadcasting organizations, therefore, like the Arts Council but with a greater intensity appropriate to their more central position, found themselves at the end of the seventies under continuous crossfire. Like the Arts Council, they tried to keep their heads down and proclaim their neutrality. Many observers saw a tendency for broadcasting to retreat into the 'safe' areas of entertainment and sport. But the greatest threats to broadcasting culture lay in the future, not the past. The rivalry between the BBC and ITV was conducted on the basis of a common acceptance of commitment to the culture as a whole. Now new developments in cable, video recorders, and satellite broadcasting threatened to blow that framework apart.

Commercial concerns were pressing for the 'wiring of Britain', so that the 100-channel capacity of the optic fibre cable could be exploited. A whole host of entertainment and consumer services were promised, ranging from a continuous stream of feature films to home shopping. Video recorders implied the by-passing of the elaborate programming schedules of the broadcasting organizations. Viewers could watch what they wanted when they wanted, or they could opt out altogether in favour of their own prepackaged hired or bought cassettes. Any policy of cultural 'mixing' or 'improvement' was now seriously vulnerable. Both the BBC and the ITV companies were faced with a future in which they were simply a few of the voices in the new tower of Babel; and given the power and persuasiveness of the forces behind the new technologies, there was a real prospect that theirs would be the voices that were drowned.

Class and Culture in the Fifties and Sixties

Television became the new potent ingredient in that heady 'mass culture' which had for long alarmed cultural critics by its intoxications. Richard Hoggart's *The Uses of Literacy* charged the new mass arts with undermining an authentic working-class culture and community, and replacing it with the false 'chumminess' and spurious values of the ad-man. Others in these years were also proclaiming the end of the traditional working class. As the Conservatives swept to victory with ever-increasing majorities in 1951, 1955, and 1959, many thought that the Labour Party was doomed to permanent opposition so long as it continued to base itself on a shrinking working class. Anthony Crosland's *The Future of Socialism* (1956) launched a bitter debate within the Labour movement over a 'revisionist' philosophy which involved abandoning the commitment to all-out nationalization and other Labour shibboleths. At the same time, and in the wake of the profound disillusion caused by the suppression of the Hungarian Rising of 1956, the radical left also regrouped under the banner of the *Universities and Left Review* (later the *New Left Review*), and called for a fundamental rethinking of socialist philosophy.

The sociologists stubbornly continued to insist that not much had really changed in British society. A wide-ranging Cambridge study, published as *The Affluent Worker* volumes, showed that the working class had neither disappeared nor merged into the 'endless Middle' of the society. At most it had shed some of its past communal solidarity and, joined now by a more combative, organized, middle class, rivalled it in hard bargaining for a greater share in the fruits of the new consumer society. Nor had the working class abandoned its traditional structures and values to the extent feared by Hoggart and others. In the late fifties Peter Willmott and Michael Young found the old 'extended', 'mum-centred', working-class family thriving in the heart of the East End of London. Social mobility out of a working-class milieu had in fact turned out to be far harder than had been hoped in the brave days of the 1944 Education Act. Buttressed by deep-seated cultural differences in the home, the new tripartite system of education divided the social classes almost as rigidly as in pre-war days, causing a particularly acute personal problem for those few bright working-class children who escaped through the grammar schools and universities. On the other hand, the success of the tripartite philosophy seemed in many ways even more threatening than its practical failure. Michael Young's satirical *The Rise of the Meritocracy* (1958) envisaged a future ruling class or caste based solely on educational achievement, like the Chinese mandarinate, condemning all academic failures to a permanent state of subordination.[24] Quite apart from that, by the mid seventies the bottom 50 per cent of the population still received less than a quarter of total personal incomes (barely changed since 1949), while the top 20 per cent held over 85 per cent of the total wealth (in 1923 it was 94 per cent). Despite the welfare state and 'progressive' taxation, 'what redistribution there has been is not between rich and poor, but between the very rich and the rich'.[25]

But sociology, as so often, protested too much in the vein of *plus ça change, plus c'est la même chose*. If basic aspects of social structure remained remarkably stable, the same could not be said for the culture and values of the fifties and sixties. Even discounting the more apocalyptic and absurd pronouncements of these years ('This is the dawning of the Age of Aquarius'), it is clear that profound changes occurred, amounting to something not far off a revolution in values and attitudes. The British for the first time threw off the mantle of Victorian morality that had shrouded them up to the Second

World War and beyond. Young people in particular sought and found a new cultural and moral independence of their elders. The family, sex, and marriage would never be the same again. The sights and sounds of British life changed immeasurably.

The year 1956 symbolized and summarized the important developments to date, and heralded new ones to come. It brought to a wider public awareness the 'Movement' of 'Angry Young Men'. Novelists, poets, and dramatists evoked a mood, rather than proffered a programme or a consistent philosophy. It was a combative, irreverent, defiant, edgy and ironic mood. The hero – or – 'anti-hero' – of the plays and novels were made, as Walter Allen suggested, as much by the Services as by George Orwell and F. R. Leavis.[26]

The Movement had a serious purpose. It sought a new moral and social centre for English society. But it did so largely through invective and ridicule than by constructive comment. In this it squared well with the other startling literary success of the year, Colin Wilson's *The Outsider*, a pot-pourri of Existentialist themes and personalities. A more fateful event of the year was the launching in Britain of rock 'n roll music. Bill Haley's film, *Rock Around the Clock*, played to frenzied audiences of teenagers, causing riots in numerous cinemas up and down the country. Prominent among the rioters were the 'Teddy Boys', the first real post-war working-class youth culture in Britain and the first fruits of the new economic power of the teenager. Later there were to be a stream of successors to the Teds: the Mods, the Rockers, the Skinheads, the Punks. Teenage cultures, originating usually in the working class, spread out to all ages and all classes. Their distinctive blend of gaiety and suppressed menace found an echo in the music, clothes, and speech of social groups of all classes, young professionals and executives being among the most susceptible. For middle-class youth specifically there was, from 1958, the Campaign for Nuclear Disarmament. Its annual Easter marches to or from the nuclear research establishment at Aldermaston, and the activities of its more radical off-shoot, the Committee of 100, provided the model for the marches, demonstrations, and occupations of the student radicals and the 'direct action' activists of the sixties.

The Movement of the fifties also momentarily revived the ailing body of the British cinema. The British film industry had really had only one decade of life and creativity, the forties. Overwhelmed by Hollywood before 1939, it found in the war an inspiration and a theme sadly lacking in the parade of comedies and historical romances that had been its staple fare before. During the war the documentary realism of John Grierson and Edgar Anstey fused with the more traditional strain of English whimsey to produce some powerful dramas, impressive as much for their technical and aesthetic virtuosity as for their atmospheric evocation of the mood of the 'people's war' (*Western Approaches, One of Our Aircraft is Missing, The Life and Death of Colonel Blimp, The Way Ahead*). After the war the same combination of documentary realism and fantasy was brilliantly employed in a lighter spirit in the Ealing comedies. In six years, 1945–51, 'British films rose to an apogee, then fell to an apology'. One glorious year, 1949, saw the premières of three of the best comedies: *Passport to Pimlico, Whisky Galore*, and *Kind Hearts and Coronets*. The Ealing comedies still drew on the democratic and egalitarian temper of the war years, but with a confidence that allowed them to subvert the bureaucratic solemnity and over-inflated idealism of 'the age of austerity'.

In the fifties came a rapid decline, as the industry continued to exploit, in a series of stock war films and vapid comedies, the formulas of the forties. Cinema audiences plunged precipitately, although admittedly more as a result of the competition from television than from a well-judged response to the quality of the films. By the end of the fifties, the number of admissions was less than a third of its post-war level, and the number of cinemas had more than halved. The audiences were not to return in any great numbers: generally both admissions and cinemas continued their steady decline throughout the sixties and seventies. But at least the artistic quality of British films rose for a time at the end of the fifties. Largely out of the plays and novels of the 'Angry' writers, a new generation of film directors – such as Lindsay Anderson, Karel Reisz, and Tony Richardson, the moving spirits of the 'Free Cinema' documentary movement – made a number of well-scripted and sharply-observed films in the style of 'social realism'. Many of these focused, with fresh insight and a striking use of locations, on working-class life and aspirations (*Saturday Night and Sunday Morning* 1960, *The Loneliness of the Long Distance Runner* 1962, *This Sporting Life* 1963, *A*

Taste of Honey 1961). In a similar style, and similarly based on successful plays and novels about working-class life, were Jack Clayton's adaptation of John Braine's *Room at the Top* (1958), and John Schlesinger's adaptation of Stan Barstow's *A Kind of Loving* (1962), and Keith Waterhouse's *Billy Liar* (1963).

But the inherent weakness of the British 'new wave' is apparent simply from this list of titles. It was essentially parasitic on a literary movement outside the cinema. The new film makers were heavily dependent on the originality and artistic talents of the playwrights and novelists whose works they adapted for the screen. The film critic Alexander Walker laments

the inability or disinclination of even established-name directors in Britain to articulate a view of life and society in freshly conceived and individual terms, and to translate these aesthetically to the screen with an unmistakable signature.

The failure is underlined by a comparison with the Italian and French 'new waves' of the same period, and the work of directors like Antonioni, Fellini, Visconti, Godard, and Truffaut.

At any rate it rapidly became clear that the signs of life in the British cinema were no more than the usual post-mortem tremors, not a true resuscitation. The films of the sixties took off into a dream world of technicolour fantasy that was an overblown and incoherent reflection of what many saw as another dream, sixties England. There were the Hammer horror films, the James Bond series, the Beatles films, and the films which reflected and celebrated the 'Swinging London' of the Sunday newspaper colour supplements. Not all the films were awful. Most had a glitter and a glamour that made for agreeable, escapist viewing. Some had a wry or anarchic humour that were nice send-ups of their subject. But on the whole they were as transient as the times that made them. It was left to a foreigner, Antonioni, in his English film *Blow Up*, to dig beneath the glossy surface and see something of the callousness and emptiness there.

Was 'sixties Britain' a dream, a 'collective fantasy' or 'psychic epidemic', as Christopher Booker argued in his biting jeremiad, *The Neophiliacs* (1969)? It must be obvious that we are referring to a very specific phenomenon here. We are talking not about the life of the whole society, but of the activities of particular groups and individuals who for a time achieved a special prominence and influence within the culture. It was, nevertheless, an extraordinary influence, ramifying through all levels and regions of the society, and even extending out to affect the peoples of America and Continental Europe. For a while the tide of 'Americanization', running so strongly since the war, seemed to be turned back. English music, English fashions, English television, English theatre, even English morals, became all the rage. Tourism boomed, and a good part of the appeal to visitors was to see the 'Swinging London' featured in a celebrated issue of the American *Time* magazine in April 1966.

A composite image or mosaic of sixties Britain, in this special sense, would include the following elements. However disparate, what marks them with the sixties label is some aspect of the mood of irreverence, ridicule, rebellion, novelty and of the general effort to throw off all 'artificial' and antiquated constraints, and to 'do your own thing'. Pop music: the music of the Beatles above all, but also the Rolling Stones, The Who, and many other British groups; the clothes and designs of Mary Quant and John Stephen, who set up their boutiques and bazaars, respectively in King's Road, Chelsea, and Carnaby Street. Terence Conran's Habitat furniture. The works and perhaps even more the lives of photographers and interior decorators such as David Bailey, Terence Donovan, Lord Snowdon, David Hicks. Models and actresses such as Jean Shrimpton, Twiggy, Julie Christie. Actors and pop artists – through their work or their lives, where they could separate them – such as Albert Finney, Michael Caine, Terence Stamp, David Hockney, Peter Blake. The satire boom, heralded by *Beyond the Fringe* (with Jonathan Miller, Alan Bennett, Peter Cook, and Dudley Moore), and continuing with the magazine *Private Eye*, *The Establishment* club, and BBC's *That Was The Week That Was*. Television personalities such as David Frost and Bernard Levin. The spy stories of John Le Carré and Len Deighton. Plays such as Peter Brooks' production of *Marat/Sade* at the Aldwych, and Edward Bond's *Saved* at the Royal Court. Films such as *Alfie* (Michael Caine) and *Darling* (Julie Christie). Television plays and documentaries such as *Cathy Come Home* and *Up The Junction*, and drama series such as *Z Cars* and *The Avengers*. Magazines such as *Queen* and, especially, the *Sunday Times* and *Observer* Colour Supplements, and the work there of journalists such as Kenneth Tynan,

Francis Wyndham and Mark Boxer. Drugs and discotheques. 'Permissiveness' in films, plays, magazines, and in sexual attitudes and behaviour. 'Progressiveness' in educational theories and practices. One can even, without any more incongruity, add such things as the gastronomic revolution led by Elizabeth David's cookery books and the *Good Food Guide*; the establishment of the new universities, such as Sussex and Essex; and the 'classless', 'progressive', 'dynamic' style in politics advanced by Harold Wilson and Edward Heath.

The striking thing about this cultural farrago is not so much its evidently chimerical quality as its familiarity to so many people – to practically any one over thirty, for instance. These names achieved a certain mythic quality for their times. Undeniably the main agents and participants were young, affluent, middle-class men and women. Undoubtedly, too, London featured disproportionately (but then that is hardly new in British society). But the working- and lower-middle class contribution was highly significant: both in the form of actual individuals, as with the Beatles, David Bailey, and Len Deighton; and, more generally, in the vitality of working-class youth cultures which originated the chief developments in music and fashion. The 'lifestyles' and values of the 'Sixties People' in Britain spread wide, encompassing all ages, classes, and regions.

It was true, as the sociologists again were at pains to point out, that many of the effects were superficial; that young people, for instance, expressed 'permissive' sexual attitudes more readily than they practised them; that the further you went from London, the less 'swinging' Britain seemed to be. The self-regarding myths about the sixties constructed by the media, whose role was central throughout, are only too patent to a later generation more concerned with the grimmer matter of a world recession and rising unemployment. But that leads easily to an opposite error, the playing-down of the very real cultural and moral changes launched in the sixties. It is partly because the revolution has been accomplished, and become a familiar part of society, that we are apt to discount it. It is possible now, as it was not before, for men and women to live together respectably without marrying, and to have children outside marriage without the stigma of 'illegitimacy'. One-parent families, though still suffering considerable hardship, are accepted publicly and even supported to a reasonable degree by public services. 'Premarital' sex is common among all classes, aided by the spread of the contraceptive pill and family planning clinics. Homosexual couples openly set up house. In all the print and electronic media, on stage and on screen, the range of topics handled and the manner of their treatment is more extensive and freer than ever before. The distinctions of dress, and to a lesser extent of speech and demeanour, coincide with social divisions to a lesser extent than at any time in the country's history. The same is true of cultural and leisure pursuits. Although the 'fine arts' still remain largely a middle-class preserve, the cultural overlap between the middle and working classes – in music, broadcasting, sport, holidays – is greater than at any previous time.

What all this amounts to is saying that something like a 'status revolution' has occurred in British society since the sixties.[27] The inequalities of class, and the differential structuring of opportunities, remain marked. The new comprehensive schools reproduce class differences almost as finely as the old tripartite secondary system. The public schools and Oxbridge retain their stranglehold on the top positions in the professions, public service, and industry. Social mobility, as the Oxford studies at the end of the seventies showed,[28] has increased since the war, but largely as the result of the rapid expansion of white-collar and service occupations in the lower and middle levels of the large corporations. This still leaves the majority of men in manual work, and the majority of their sons to succeed them there: it is their wives and daughters who make up the new 'white-bloused' workers.

But what have changed are social and cultural attitudes and behaviour: the way people regard themselves and each other. This shows both convergence and divergence. Young people of all classes have moved furthest towards a common culture. So too, in a more general and less complete way, have the older generations in matters of personal consumption, family life, and moral attitudes. (The continuing decline in church membership and attendance, and in church baptisms and weddings, is one index of the change.) But the cultural changes of the sixties have pressed further in a more disruptive direction. The deferential structure of British society has been cracked wide apart. Authority has no prerogative right in any sphere. The old can no longer expect automatic respect for their experience and knowledge from the young, especially as so much of that manifestly dates very rapidly, in an era of accelerated technological change. In asserting their right to personal, economic, and cultural equality, women have thrown down what is perhaps the most fundamental challenge of all, aspiring as it does to reverse the pattern of some thousands of years of human history. Working-class groups too since the late sixties have shown a militancy and a determination in their economic struggles that go beyond anything experienced since the beginning of the century. In 1973–4 a miners' strike in effect brought down Edward Heath's Conservative Government. This is hardly Marxist class struggle – the workers do not want to run the society or abolish classes – but it shows a clear refusal to be bound by the traditional conventions of 'collective bargaining'. Increasingly in the seventies has come the evidence that racial minorities are no longer prepared to tolerate the second-class status assigned to them. In the summer of 1981 there were scenes in many English cities reminiscent of the American race riots of the sixties. Finally even the constituent parts of the United Kingdom showed themselves restless at English tutelage. Ireland had for long been a special case, but the renewal of sectarian violence in Ulster in the late sixties coincided with the revival of nationalist movements in Wales and Scotland. What had started as the consensus of 1945 threatened, after the changes of the fifties and sixties, to end in 'the break-up of Britain' itself.

In the event, of all the centrifugal forces that of race has increasingly come to seem the most intractable. This can hardly be because of the novelty of immigration itself. At least since the Huguenots of the seventeenth century, British society has with varying degrees of smoothness assimilated immigrant groups, the Irish and Jews of the nineteenth century being the most prominent. Nor too should we forget that in the mid eighteenth century there were said to be over 20,000 negro servants in London alone. But something in the experience of Empire, both for the British and for the subject races, seems to have made a decisive difference to the fortunes of the Asians and West Indians who settled in Britain in the 1950s and 1960s. Again, the problem seems hardly one of numbers. 'New Commonwealth' immigrants, settled or born here, make up no more than about three per cent of the total population, although they are heavily concentrated in a few urban areas. They are also a markedly heterogeneous grouping, with different cultures and traditions which they no more wish to see merged into each other than into native British culture. Integration, not assimilation, is the watchword. But they are, by virtue of their colour, an easily identifiable minority. More to the point, they have experienced negative discrimination out of all proportion to their numbers in the fields of housing, employment, and education. British society has always been multi-racial, in the strict sense; but the addition of coloured races from the ex-colonies has so far proved a more difficult matter of integration than at any time previously. Much of the success in the future is likely to turn on the extent to which black Britons are seen as a 'problem', to be contained and treated as some sort of social lesion, or as an opportunity, as with other immigrant groups, for the diversification and enrichment of British culture as a whole.

Intellectual Currents and Cross-Currents

At the end of the seventies, the threat to the consensus seemed as much intellectual as cultural and political. Ideological divisions had developed in British society of a kind not known since the thirties. A Conservative Government under Margaret Thatcher was elected on the promise to 'roll back' the tide of welfare provision and social services that had been steadily rising throughout the post-war period. The Labour Party, in a bout of bitter internal feuding that recalled the 'revisionist' controversy of the late fifties, found itself split between the moderate leadership of Michael Foot and the uncompromising radicalism of a Left wing led by Anthony Wedgwood Benn. An even more uncompromising group of moderate Labour members had quit the Party to set up a new party, the Social Democratic Party. In alliance with the Liberals they became an increasingly powerful force. Not since the parliamentary debacle caused by Ramsay MacDonald in 1931 had British politics been in such ideological disarray.

The intellectual consensus had in fact throughout the post-war period been more fragile than the social and political consensus. It was nevertheless a particular irony that a series of powerful attacks on the reigning philosophy of planning and social democracy should come between 1945 and 1951, when that philosophy was at its most confident, backed by a sweeping victory at the polls. The most moving statement of 1945 was probably H. G. Wells's *Mind At The End Of Its Tether*, his last work. This foremost apostle of progress, science, and socialism now recanted half a century of public exhortation in the light of recent events, political and intellectual. 'The attempt to trace a pattern of any sort is absolutely futile ... The human story has already come to an end.' This expressed the mood of a good deal of the literary and cultural response to post-war Britain, seen at its blackest perhaps in the post-war novels of Evelyn Waugh (*Brideshead Revisited*, *The Ordeal of Gilbert Pinfold*). From Wells's cosmic despair and 'stoical acceptance' one descended to the brisker and more combative attacks on the orthodoxy of social planning. F. A. Hayek's *Road to Serfdom* (1944) argued the case against planning. Arthur Koestler's *The Yogi and the Commissar*, and Karl Popper's *The Open Society* and *The Poverty of Historicism* (all 1945) emphasized the basic, almost metaphysical, intractability of the sphere of politics and the logical impossibility of arriving at any scientific notion of 'truth' there. In 1949 came Orwell's *Nineteen Eighty Four*, the most ambitious and influential onslaught on state socialism, reworking in a nightmare mode his satiric fable on Stalin's Russia, *Animal Farm* (1945).

More strictly academic political philosophy also threw cold water on the idealistic hopes attached to collectivist planning. Michael Oakeshott's 'Rationalism in Politics' (1947) attacked the whole Enlightenment tradition – to which the Labour movement was heir – of conceiving society as amenable to rational understanding and rational political transformation. In 1951 he succeeded Harold Laski to the Chair of Politics at the London School of Economics, and Burkean conservatism displaced radical socialism as the reigning influence there. Oakeshott's inaugural lecture 'Political Education' roundly dismissed the idea of politics as the pursuit and achievement of specific social goals:

> In political activity ... men sail a boundless and bottomless sea; there is neither harbour for shelter nor floor for anchorage, neither starting-place nor appointed destination. The enterprise is to keep afloat on an even keel ...

All that a society could do was to pursue the 'intimations' of its particular political tradition; which in England's case apparently excluded active state intervention to remedy social injustice.

The elegance and power of Oakeshott's 'philosophic conservatism' won him many adherents in the universities, although the Conservative Party itself was busily whoring after the false god of 'Butskellism'. But liberal academic philosophy also counselled the abandonment of 'grand ideas' in politics, and the delusion that rational truths were available there. Using the tools of logical positivism, T. D. Weldon's *The Vocabulary of Politics* (1953) sceptically undermined the alleged rationale of 'democracy', 'communism', and any and all political ideologies since Plato. Further scepticism was induced by Isaiah Berlin's *Historical Inevitability* (1954) and *Two Concepts of Liberty* (1958), which treated with sparkling irony the attempts by European thinkers such as Marx to discern historical 'laws' and, under their guidance, to aim to force freedom or happiness upon society. Increasingly it seemed as if political philosophy had little to do with the politics of actual societies. In a glum preface to his collection *Philosophy, Politics and Society* (1956) Peter Laslett confessed that 'for the moment, anyway, political philosophy is dead'.

In the early sixties the academics rallied, partly under the stimulus of Peter Laslett himself, in successive volumes of the series *Philosophy, Politics and Society*. The move reflected an increasing distaste among social theorists for Oxford chop-logic, and a greater receptivity to Continental philosophies of existentialism and phenomenology, and to the implications of the later philosophy of Wittgenstein (e.g. Peter Winch's *The Idea of a Social Science*, 1958). But already there had come a strong revival of traditional political theory, in the regeneration of English Marxism after 1956 under the banner of the New Left. Basing themselves on the rediscovery of Marx's early humanistic writings, especially the so-called *1844 Manuscripts*, the New Left launched a wide-ranging critique of consensus politics and 'the affluent society'. It attacked the bureaucratic sterility of Labour's programme as much as the unprincipled adventurism of the Conservative 'never had it so good' philosophy. The Marxist concept of 'alienation' gave it unusually powerful access to areas normally ignored by traditional political theory: the routine and boredom of much work, the dehumanizing ethos of the mass culture, the strains and frustrations of contemporary family life, and of the relations between the sexes. In the writings especially of the social and literary

49

PART ONE

critic Raymond Williams (*Culture and Society 1780–1950*, 1958, *The Long Revolution*, 1961), and the historian E. P. Thompson (*The Making of the English Working Class*, 1964), the demand was made for a fuller, more 'participatory' democracy, one which paid as much attention to work, culture, and community as to the organization of the state. In achieving this, they showed, as much inspiration could be found in the values and practices of the native English radical tradition as in European Marxism.

The New Left's relationship to actual social and political movements always remained fitful and fragmentary. Its influence was strongest in higher education, especially in the sixties among the young university-educated media professionals in television, film, the theatre, publishing, and the community arts movement. Certain cultural institutions, like the Institute of Contemporary Arts and the British Film Institute, seemed for a time to be dominated by Marxist intellectuals. New journals and magazines appeared with a strong Marxist flavour: *Screen* (from the BFI), *The Socialist Register*, *Radical Philosophy*, *Radical Science Journal*, *Working Papers in Cultural Studies*. Many of them made for very difficult and frustrating reading. The writers often seemed incapable of naturalizing the concepts and vocabulary of European Marxism, of giving them meaning within the concrete terms of British history and culture. As compared, say, with George Eliot's 'Englishing' of Comtean Positivism in *Middlemarch*, the New Left served up chunks of Parisian Marxism raw and undigested. As a result they often condemned themselves to sect and coterie status.

Only E. P. Thompson and Raymond Williams escaped this fate. Their intellectual origins in English literary criticism, always a strong influence in their work, may have had something to do with this. They provide a bridge to the fourth group of dissidents of the post-war period, the cultural critics. This was a persistence of a form of criticism developed in the thirties in periodicals such as *Criterion* and *Scrutiny*, and in the writings of T. S. Eliot, W. B. Yeats, D. H. Lawrence, and F. R. Leavis. Behind that too was the longer tradition of the critical response to industrialization contained in the works of Coleridge, Carlyle, Dickens, Arnold, and Ruskin. In 1948 there appeared Eliot's *Notes Towards the Definition of Culture* and Leavis's *The Great Tradition*. Eliot's position was the more radically conservative. He believed that culture was the creation of elites nourished by their membership of 'the higher social classes', and that modern politics, with their levelling tendencies, threatened the basis of European culture and civilization.

> Complete equality means universal irresponsibility ... A democracy in which everybody had an equal responsibility in everything would be oppressive for the conscientious and licentious for the rest.

Leavis's more liberal vision emphasized the importance of 'centres of excellence' in the cultivation and diffusion of the highest values in the culture, the values explored and endorsed by the great English writers of the past. He looked to the universities, and especially the schools of English within them, to become such centres. In his later writings – e.g. *Nor Shall My Sword* (1972) – he expressed with rising fury the sense that politicians, businessmen, and intellectuals were engaged in a vast conspiracy to debase the culture, by their philistine and cynical advocacy of an indiscriminate mass culture.

One of Leavis's more explosive encounters was with the scientist and novelist C. P. Snow. In 1959 Snow gave the Rede Lecture at Cambridge on *The Two Cultures and the Scientific Revolution*. Despite Leavis's savaging ('The intellectual nullity is what constitutes any difficulty there may be in dealing with Snow's panoptic pseudo-cogencies, his parade of a thesis: a mind to be argued with – that is not there ...'), Snow's theme clearly struck a chord in many people. Already the signs were evident of the weakness of the British economy relative to the more dynamic economies of France, Germany, and Japan. Snow's diagnosis suggested that the backward-looking nature of the dominantly traditional, literary culture in Britain, its nostalgic pastoralism and its hostility to the machine and other manifestations of science and technology, would make that weakness even more serious in the years to come.[29]

The 'two cultures' debate stimulated by Snow's lecture showed that the critics of the post-war consensus did not make all the running in these years. Many thinkers accepted the basic framework of the 1945 settlement, but complained that things had not gone far or fast enough. Education was a key issue here. Not only had the tripartite secondary system proved socially divisive and wasteful of ability, ignoring in particular the needs of the 'non-academic' groups. Higher education, it was charged, was even more backward, dominated by the elitist ethos of Oxbridge and geared largely to careers in the traditional professions and in public service. A series of reports – the Crowther Report (1959), the Newsom Report (1963), the Plowden Report (1967) – urged radical changes in primary and secondary education. The school-leaving age was to be raised to sixteen (effected in 1972), and an effort made to increase the proportion of the age group continuing in full-time 'higher' or 'further' education. The Robbins Report on Higher Education (1963) recommended a doubling of the university population by 1980, the creation of six new universities in addition to the eight new ones already founded or contemplated, and the conversion of the Colleges of Advanced Technology into universities. Few of the reports' recommendations were actually carried out, at least as their authors intended them; but they played an important part in creating the mood of hopeful expectation that was so characteristic of Britain in the sixties.

A central role in the debates of these years was played, somewhat surprisingly, by a highly intellectual political and literary magazine, *Encounter*. During the fifties and early sixties it was precisely tuned to the mood and needs of the consensus. Founded in 1953 under Anglo-American editorship, it denounced the 'rhetoric of messianic arrogance' contained in the creeds of Marxism–Leninism as much as in Fascism, and pronounced 'the end of ideology' in the West. It devoted itself to building upon the political and economic achievements of the post-war consensus, on the view that all fundamental conflicts and divisions in society had now come to an end. In its columns in these years were to be found many of the people and ideas prominent in the reform movement: Noel Annan and John Vaizey on education, Richard Titmuss and Andrew Shonfield on welfare and economic growth, the American sociologists Edward Shils and Daniel Bell on intellectuals and the national culture, Anthony Crosland, Hugh Gaitskell, Roy Jenkins and other Labour intellectuals on the reform of the Labour movement. *Encounter*'s contribution to the thinking of these years reached a culmination in two symposia of 1963, 'Going into Europe' and 'Suicide of a Nation?', in which Britain's present position and future prospects were critically scrutinized

'Suicide of a Nation?' sounded the keynote of the debate: that

Britain had to 'modernize' or perish. It was a theme that grew and reached a crescendo in the decade of the mid fifties to the mid sixties. A stream of publications, many of them Penguin Specials, raked British society from end to end and found it wanting in almost every respect. Britain was class-ridden, antiquated, anti-technological. It was living on the depleting material and moral legacy of the Industrial Revolution and the Empire. No attempt had been made, economically and politically, to adjust to the rapid decline and end of empire, by any measure of historical significance the overriding fact of post-war British history. All the institutions of British society were in urgent need of overhaul: Parliament, the Civil Service, the law, local government, the unions, the educational system, the Churches, and much else. All was to be reformed.

A volume of essays edited by Hugh Thomas under the title *The Establishment* (1959) pointed to one source of the distemper, the domination of British society by an archaic elite. Other titles were equally self-explanatory: Eric Wigham's *What's Wrong with the Unions* (1961); A. Hill and A. Whichelow's *What's Wrong with Parliament* (1964), and Bernard Crick's *The Reform of Parliament* (1964); W Stankiewicz (ed.) *Crisis in British Government* (1967) and H. Thomas (ed.) *Crisis in the Civil Service* (1968). Michael Shanks's *The Stagnant Society* (1961) and Andrew Shonfield's *Modern Capitalism* (1965) analysed the economic malaise. Anthony Sampson's *Anatomy of Britain* (1962) and *Anatomy of Britain Today* (1965) forcefully combined campaigning journalism with judicious analysis. Max Nicholson's *The System* (1967) drew upon a lifetime's experience of economic planning and government service to castigate the whole tradition of British public administration. An important influence on much of the 'progressive' thinking of these years were the works of the American economist, John Kenneth Galbraith, such as *The Affluent Society* (1958) and *The New Industrial State* (1967). These pointed to the transformed nature of industrial capitalism since the Second World War, and indicated the extent to which Britain would need to tap all its resources of skill and energy in order to compete in the new world economy. High hopes – misplaced, as it turned out – were attached to Harold Wilson's new Labour government of 1964, with its promise to forge the new society in 'the white heat of the technological revolution'.

The 'What's Wrong With Britain' commentators were highly critical of their society, but they also remained on the whole confident that reform was possible and practicable. In the wake of deepening economic recession and the continued poor performance of the British economy, their successors in the seventies were far less hopeful. The tone of the inquiries became more sombre, more couched in apocalyptic terms. Something like the last rites began to be performed over the body of British society. Britain was 'the sick man of Europe'. Articles began to appear on the 'de-industrialization of Britain', and to sketch a future of ever more declining industries and, for the first time since the war, declining standards of living for the bulk of the population. Many found the closest parallel with the ailing economy and society of seventeenth-century Spain, and quoted the British Ambassador to Madrid in 1640:

> Concerning the state of their kingdom, I could never have imagined to have seen it as it now is, for their people begin to fail, and those that remain, by a continuance of bad successes, and by their heavy burdens, are quite out of heart.

In tune with this foreign criticism, and in response to manifest failures internally, ideological controversy revived in Britain in the seventies on a greater scale than at any time since the war. The whole 'received wisdom' of the post-war consensus came under attack. The attacks were naturally the sharpest from the traditional Right of the political spectrum, as the main victim of the consensus. Progressive educational philosophy and practice were scourged in a series of *Black Papers* on education, starting in 1969. They called a halt to comprehensivization, and to the expansion of higher education. 'More means worse', warned the authors; the Robbins assumption of a pool of untapped ability was declared to be typical of wishful 'progressive' thinking.

In other areas, spurred on especially by publications from the right-wing Institute of Economic Affairs, and the Conservative Party's Centre for Policy Studies headed by Sir Keith Joseph, the Right launched its increasingly influential counter-attacks. The market principle of private provision and 'free' consumer choice was strongly reasserted in the spheres of education, health, and other social services. State intervention and control were deprecated. The nationalized industries should be sold off to private enterprise or closed down where that was not possible. There was vigorous support for the widely publicized view of two Oxford economists, Robert Bacon and Walter Eltis, in their book *Britain's Economic Problem: Too Few Producers* (1976). Bacon and Eltis argued that the rapid expansion of the 'non-productive' public sector had eaten up scarce national resources of capital and labour sorely needed in manufacturing industry, and that this movement would have to be reversed if British industry were to recover its prosperity. Added to this were the arguments of Sir Keith Joseph and other proponents of 'monetarist' theory, that public spending had to be curtailed to contain inflation, and the resulting unemployment accepted as the regrettable but necessary blood-letting of a diseased economy.

Such philosophies were, after 1979, entrenched in government. The Left countered by an equally radical movement away from the centre. Stuart Holland's *The Socialist Challenge* (1975) called for a much greater degree of socialization of the economy, as the only means of curbing the activities of the multinational corporations, whose machinations were the main cause of the instability of the British economy. Banks, building societies, and insurance companies would have to be nationalized. The Institute for Workers' Control, founded in 1968 and backed by the radical wing of the Labour Party and the TUC, pressed for workers' control in industry both as a short-term solution to the problems of British economic management and as a step towards a socialist society. By the 1970s this had broadened out to the demand for participation and 'self-management' in all spheres of society. The brief French experiments with *autogestion* in May 1968, and the longer-lived Yugoslav examples, were studied for the lessons they might offer. Finally, the analyses and activities of feminist groups, and other 'direct action' groups such as the squatters in housing and the Claimants' Union in welfare, stimulated the Left to resort once more to its traditional support for an extraparliamentary opposition, to break or bypass the power of the 'capitalist state'.

Neither in the case of the Right nor the Left were the ideas new; but the vehemence and bitterness of the utterance were, at least within recent times. In politics as in culture, the middle ground, so laboriously cleared and staked-out in the forties and fifties, began to quake and crumble. The new Social Democrats came forward as champions and together with the Liberals stoutly offered to hold it. But, as fresh strains were imposed by rising unemployment and a continuing world recession in the early eighties, their success seemed highly uncertain.

Admass or Common Culture?

When J. B. Priestley made his *English Journey* in 1934 he discovered three Englands. There was 'Old England, the country of the cathedrals and minsters and manor houses and inns, of Parson and Squire'. There was 'Nineteenth-Century England, the industrial England of coal, iron, steel, cotton, wool, railways'. And there was 'New England', appropriately enough influenced by American civilization, the dominant force of the age. New England was to be found in the new towns and suburbs of the inter-war period. It was based on mass-production techniques and cheap goods ('You could almost accept Woolworths as its symbol'). It was essentially democratic and egalitarian, 'as near to a classless society as we have got yet'.

In this England, for the first time in history, Jack and Jill are nearly as good as their master and mistress; they may have always been as good in their own way, but now they are nearly as good in the *same way*.

Priestley did not entirely like this New England. It was imitative, standardized, lacking in spontaneity. But he welcomed it because for the majority of the population it was infinitely preferable to the other two Englands; and it was the wave of the future. During the Second World War he himself did much to urge it further into being, with his *Postscript* talks on the BBC, and his involvement in the Commonwealth Party. The post-war settlement, heralded by Labour's victory in 1945, was fundamentally a commitment to this New England. Nor was there any reason to suppose that the new society would necessarily be lacking in originality or spontaneity. There was the evidence of British films and British broadcasting in the forties to suggest that a truly common culture might be made out of the life of a democratic society.

In the 1950s Priestley's fears about the New England came to outweigh his hopes. The effects of the rapid spread of American culture after the war made him think that he had been too optimistic about it. 'Admass' had arrived:

... my name for the whole system of an increasing productivity, plus inflation, plus a rising standard of material living, plus high-pressure advertising
and salesmanship, plus mass communication, plus cultural democracy and the
creation of the mass mind, the mass man ...

The society of Admass still had to be accepted as preferable to one where many people had no jobs and no prospect of one. But basically it was 'a swindle', promising fulfilment through the mindless consumption of goods and pursuit of status symbols.

Has the post-war achievement been so empty? Has the promise of the 'people's war' and 1945 come simply to a soulless materialism and the rat race? What of equality and the aspiration to a common culture? Certainly the persistence of deep social and economic inequalities has, despite substantial general increases in material standards of living, caused the continuation of a muted class war. This has flared up fitfully since 1945, and in the era of high unemployment that started in the late seventies it seems destined to intensify, compli-cated now by racial conflict. Whole sections of British society have come to feel cheated – the old, the poor and unemployed, the young, especially those in the black ghettoes of the inner cities. The failure of educational reform has been particularly critical. It has condemned more than three quarters of all young people to low-skilled, dead-end jobs, and then removed even that prospect from them as such jobs were automated, while not preparing them for the newer oppor-tunities offered by the new technologies. The persistent inability of the educational system to offset home and class disadvantages – where that was attempted – has led some educators to despair of schools altogether as agencies of progress towards a fairer and more egali-tarian society. The alternatives however – 'community education' and 'learning centres' – do not seem any more promising. The educational system remains central to any attempt to create an informed, participant, democratic society.

It is true, then, that 'too much of the reconstruction of the Era of Consensus was in rhetoric rather than reality'.[30] But some things have changed. Some of the promise of 1945 has been realized. The outward and often humiliating symbols of class differences have all but disappeared. Social groups in British society no longer confront each other as different social species. Many changes in material conditions, dress, speech, food, have contributed to this relative class convergence – more accurately put, to the erosion of differences of social status. The motor car has perhaps been the prime symbol of this classlessness. So too, and more significantly in the long run, is television. It is indeed in the sphere of culture, broadly conceived, that both achievements and aspirations seem most hopeful. Cultural institutions and cultural changes since the war have not produced a common culture but they have enormously reduced the cultural distances between social groups. They have broadened horizons and raised aspirations, throughout society, beyond anything achieved before the war. There are more common values, attitudes, and beliefs in British society now than at any time in its history. This always runs the danger of succumbing to Admass, and no-one can feel any complacency on this score. But British society has proved remarkably resilient to many of the worst aspects of Admass. It has also shown a capacity for cultural renewal and creativity that has at times surprised even itself. There is no reason to think that this has vanished.

This can perhaps be put more strongly. The British have not lacked native critics, fro ... oth Right and Left, who have poured scorn on the society's seemingly inexhaustible ability to convert radical challenges into a pragmatically comfortable consensus. Complacency has always seemed the root of 'the British disease'. But for many commentators, especially those from abroad, this attitude is simply the other side of the continuing strength of British society. A practice of tolerance and civic concern, a 'pre-industrial' preference for the activities of leisure over the material rewards of greater efforts at work, are values which can go with an apparent indifference to more immediate questions of economic growth and social equity. This poses serious threats to the social order in the short run, and may even undermine efforts to redirect the society in accordance with longer-term goals. But such a cultural legacy gives reasonable grounds for hoping that British society may be better prepared to enter the 'post-industrial' future than societies which are still dominated by more narrowly commercial values.[31] Whether or not this diagnosis is over-optimistic, it serves to remind us that whatever the future prospects we shall always need our Coleridges, Arnolds, and

Leavises to make us attend to the things which give our efforts meaning.

NOTES

1. José Harris, *William Beveridge: A Biography* (Oxford, 1977), 366.

2. Paul Addison, *The Road to 1945. British Politics and the Second World War* (London, 1977), 118.

3. Arthur Marwick, 'Middle Opinion in the Thirties: Planning, Progress and Political "Agreement"', *English Historical Review*, Vol. 79 (1964), 285. The term 'Butskellism' was coined by *The Economist* in its issue of 13 February 1954 to express the convergence of politico-economic doctrine across the Labour and Conservative parties. It is a compound of the names of R. A. Butler, then Chancellor of the Exchequer, and his Labour predecessor and Opposition 'Shadow', Hugh Gaitskell.

4. For the BBC during the war, see Asa Briggs, *The History of Broadcasting in the United Kingdom*, Vol. III: *The War of the Words* (Oxford, 1970); and James Curran and Jean Seaton, *Power Without Responsibility: The Press and Broadcasting in Britain* (London, 1981), 159–204.

5. George Orwell, 'Poetry and the Microphone' (1943), in *The Collected Essays, Journalism and Letters of George Orwell*, Vol. 2: *My Country Right or Left 1940–1943* (Penguin, 1970), 381.

6. George Orwell, 'The Lion and the Unicorn' (1941), in *The Collected Essays*, Vol. 2, 112.

7. For a selection of *Picture Post* journalism in these years, see Tom Hopkinson (ed.), *Picture Post 1938–50* (Penguin, 1970). See also Stuart Hall, 'The Social Eye of *Picture Post*', *Working Papers in Cultural Studies*, No. 2 (1972), 71–120.

8. Angus Calder, *The People's War: Britain 1939–1945* (London, 1971), 628–9.

9. 'Wily Willie', *Sunday Times*, 28 March 1982.

10. Janet Minihan, *The Nationalization of Culture. The Development of State Subsidies to the Arts in Great Britain* (London, 1977), 215.

11. The Arts Council is not of course the only public patron of the arts in Britain, although it is the most important single one. Of total central government grants to the arts of about £100 million in 1980, it received £65 million (*Annual Report*, 1980/81). Local authorities spend on the arts in total about half as much as the Arts Council, as well as making provision for 'leisure and recreation' in a more general way. The Government makes direct grants to the British Film Institute, as well as to the main London museums and art galleries – the British Museum, the Victoria & Albert Museum, the National and Tate galleries, etc. The National Trust (founded 1885) and the National Heritage Fund (founded 1980) play an important part in arts patronage through their work in purchasing and preserving historic houses and their contents. And then there is, in a somewhat different category, the BBC (and

to a lesser extent ITV), whose patronage of the arts is diffuse but by any measure enormous. Stephen Hearst, former head of Arts Features at the BBC, estimates that the BBC spends over twenty per cent of its total income, or over £100 million, on artistic patronage: Hearst, *Artistic Heritage and its Treatment by Television* (London, 1981), 22. It remains true, however, that the Arts Council has always been seen symbolically as the most important patron, and its decisions, as well as decisions about it, have been subject to public controversy of an intensity little related to its actual (relatively modest) budget.

12. Raymond Williams, 'The Arts Council', *The Political Quarterly*, Vol. 50, No. 2 (April–June 1979), 162. For the social composition of the Council and its Panels, see John S. Harris, *Government Patronage of the Arts in Great Britain* (Chicago, 1970), 45–61.

13. The case is argued in the PEP report, 'Public Patronage of the Arts', *Planning*, Vol. 31 (November 1965), 315–30.

14. See Royal Commission on the Press, *Final Report and Appendices* (London, 1977). For overlapping ownership and concentration in the media in general, see G. Murdock and P. Golding, 'For a Political Economy of Mass Communications', in J. Saville and R. Miliband (eds), *The Socialist Register 1973* (London, 1974), 205–34; and the same authors' 'Capitalism, Communication and Class Relations' in James Curran, Michael Gurevitch and Janet Woollacott (eds), *Mass Communication and Society* (London, 1977), 12–43.

15. I have considered some of these causes in my 'The Nationalization of British Culture', in S. Hoffmann and P. Kitromilides (eds), *Culture and Society in Contemporary Europe* (London, 1981) 117–31.

16. See, e.g., Sir Roy Shaw, 'Problems of Evaluation', *New Universities Quarterly*, Vol. 35, No. 1 (Winter 1980/81), 33–6.

17. Karen King and Mark Blaug, 'Does the Arts Council Know What It Is Doing?', *Encounter*, Vol. 41 (September 1973), 6–16.

18. This allowed the Council to welcome a strongly devolutionist independent report by Lord Redcliffe-Maud, *Support for the Arts in England and Wales* (Calouste Gulbenkian Foundation, 1976).

19. See, e.g., Janet Daley, 'Cliques, Coteries and the Visual Arts', *New Universities Quarterly* (Winter 1980/81), 57–65.

20. Anthony Smith (ed.) *British Broadcasting* (Newton Abbot, 1974), 62.

21. Asa Briggs, *History of Broadcasting in the United Kingdom, Vol. IV: Sound and Vision* (Oxford, 1979), 63, quoting an internal Director-General's memorandum of 1944.

22. Curran and Seaton, *Power Without Responsibility*, 235.

23. For the politics of broadcasting in this period, see Anthony Smith, *The Shadow in the Cave. The Broadcaster, the Audience and the State* (London, 1973); Milton Shulman, *The Least Worst Television in the World* (London, 1973).

24. Michael Young and Peter Willmott, *Family and Kinship in East London* (London, 1957); J. W. B. Douglas, *The Home and the School* (London, 1964); B. Jackson and D. Marsden, *Education and the Working Class* (London, 1962).

25. Frank Field (quoting Prof. Atkinson), *Inequality in Britain* (London, 1981), 27.

26. On the 'Movement' and the 'Angry Young Men' see Kenneth Allsop, *The Angry Decade* (London, 1953); Blake Morrison, *The Movement: English Poetry and Fiction of the 1950s* (London, 1981); Robert Hewison, *In Anger: Culture and the Cold War 1945–60* (London, 1981).

27. This is the argument of A. H. Halsey's Reith lectures, *Change in British Society* (Oxford, 1978). 'Status' refers to the non-economic aspects of a person's position and behaviour.

28. J. H. Goldthorpe, *Social Mobility and Class Structure in Modern Britain* (Oxford, 1980).

29. On the longstanding nature of these attitudes, see Martin J. Wiener, *English Culture and the Decline of the Industrial Spirit 1850–1980* (Cambridge, 1981).

30. Arthur Marwick, *British Society Since 1945* (Penguin Books, 1982), 277.

31. See my 'Thoughts on the Present Discontents in Britain', *Theory and Society*, Vol. 9 (1980), 539–74.

PART II

THE LITERARY SCENE

JOHN HOLLOWAY

'Advance, Britannia!'

Even after a lapse of over forty years, the present writer vividly recalls hearing, in a requisitioned German farmhouse and along with the rest of his Army unit, those closing words of Winston Churchill's May 1945 victory broadcast; and equally vividly, the unanimous impression of anachronism and irrelevance that the speech as a whole called forth from those in the room. In 1945, Churchill still broadcast in the language that had so much moved and strengthened his listeners in 1940; but by the end of the war in Europe, a new spirit, not so much hostile to heroics as indifferent to them and dismissive of them, had supervened. It was this new spirit which led to the sweeping defeat of Churchill's party in the 1945 election, and it was strengthened by various things that followed the election. Writing in Britain for upwards of a generation was shaped by it and must be understood in terms of it.

At the time, many found this new spirit and attitude sudden and surprising: in reality it was neither of those things. In some respects, there were deep continuities with attitudes before the war. During the war years, Britain had pursued an international, a world role, altogether in excess of her resources. By the end of the Japanese campaign she had been at war longer than any other belligerent, and she was the only European country, save the neutrals, not to suffer occupation and its unprecedented horrors. From 1940 to 1941 she had waged war alone against virtually the whole of Europe. Yet by the closing months of the war the anomalous truths of this fact had begun to sink deep into people's minds. The scale of the American contribution to the 1944 'Second Front' in France, the confusions of the 'Falaise Gap' and the British adventure at Nijmegen and Arnhem, the enormous scale of the war in Eastern Europe, and even the magnitude of the German Ardennes offensive in the winter of 1944-5, all came together to show Britain as a highly-organized and indeed remarkably effective small nation for which a world role now made no sense.

By and large the population of Great Britain, and those in the armed forces abroad, realized this. There occurred one of the more significant changes of public opinion in our recent history, though it seems to have made itself felt among voters more than it did in some of the inner circles of politics. The British now began to preoccupy themselves with internal problems – nationalization of industry, social welfare, education, the removal of wartime shortages and drab austerity and, by the middle 1950s, the cult of affluence. Moreover, this change of interest and outlook, already in existence before the war ended, was soon strengthened by certain post-war events in the international field. The abrupt termination in late 1945 of American 'lend-lease' aid to Britain probably made as deep and disillusioning an impression as the relative breakdown of relations with the USSR and the Russian blockade of West Berlin. The latter inevitably revived traumatic memories of the surprise Russo-German Pact of the eve of war in 1939, and the disillusionment that it had brought to so many. Continued American and Russian testing of fission, and later fusion, bombs added to the picture. The large-scale violence and rioting in the Indian subcontinent during the transition to Independence and Partition (1947), and still more after the departure of the British, also made for disillusionment with the international, imperial role and increasing preoccupation with affairs at home.

Ford Madox Ford's tetralogy of the First World War (published 1924-8: see *The New Pelican Guide*, Vol. 7, pp. 83-4) leaves a most lasting impression, of the way major public events can torment and break up individual life and its genuine humanity; but Evelyn Waugh's trilogy on the Second World War (*Men at Arms*, 1952; *Officers and Gentlemen*, 1955; *Unconditional Surrender*, 1961) says something different. Already, in sometimes riotously funny pre-war novels like *Decline and Fall* (1928), *Black Mischief* (1932), *Scoop* (1938), Waugh had embodied a powerful sense of the empty absurdity of one traditional British institution after another – public school education, the judiciary, the Empire, the British diplomat, the press – and, moreover, had conveyed the clear impression that he had seen these absurdities from the inside, from the standpoint and experience of a member of the traditional élite. The trilogy does that for Britain at war: what Churchill and others presented as heroic – as, for example, the unavailing defence of Crete – Waugh offers to his readers as a designless charade of muddle, accident and posturing.

Along with Waugh's trilogy, one might consider Richard Hughes's later and less well-known chronicle – written in old age and after a long silence – of the years preceding the war (*The Fox in the Attic*, 1961; *The Wooden Shepherdess*, 1973). With its breadth and range, vivid variety of material, deep thoughtfulness and sophisticated narrative technique, this projected multi-volume novel, even uncompleted as it is, surely stands among the most important of post-war works of fiction in English. It is representative of the trends of the time especially in the way that it portrays the life and place of the English country house. While James had seen the great house as self-evidently the heart of English society or very near to that, Hughes is interested in its falsities, its tottering instabilities, its inadequacy to the political life of the time: fundamentally, the 'anachronism and irrelevance' of one of our great surviving institutions from the pre-war years.

As a Welshman, Hughes also links up with a quite different aspect of post-war changes, one to which the discussion will return (see below, pp. 109ff.). But Ivy Compton-Burnett, another novelist writing about the pre-war years, is also relevant here. More than any other novelist active over the post-war years, Ivy Compton-Burnett confined the setting of her novels to the south-of-England country house, the traditional milieu of the English ruling class. Yet in two ways her presentation of that suggests something of a world in decline. In the first place, while her central values had always been those of affection and loyalty, not between the sexes but within the family, and especially as that could involve its oldest members, in her later novels particularly the heads of families or their leading figures prove on balance to be monsters of destructive, disintegrative egotism. This was true already of Aunt Matty in *A Family and a Fortune*, her last pre-war novel. It is more conspicuous with Cassius in *The Present and the Past* (1953), and even more with Hereward in her last novel, *A God and His Gifts* (1963), almost a brilliant, esoteric parody of herself. What she depicts is a hard-up sub-aristocracy in self-destructive terminal decay.

The texture of her work derives from the continual driving force of the books, a ruthless if suave logic of dialogue that largely submerges characterization and even narrative event; and what distinguishes this logic is 'speaking with a sting', as she herself once called it, which comes always through recognizing falsity, and achieving a disillusioning clarity in the place of it ("". . . between Miss Griffin and myself there is our own relation" "I am afraid there is, Aunt Matty." There was a long silence.'). It is remarkable that such scepticism and disillusionment should lie at the heart of the post-war writer who, perhaps more than any other, preoccupied herself with the world and values of the past.

There are other points at which one may see, in the work of older writers of the time, reflections of some sort of retreat from the assumptions prevalent between the wars. John Cowper Powys withdrew from the style of his earlier panoramic novels of near-contemporary English provincial or rural life (for example, *Wolf Solent*, 1929; *Weymouth Sands*, 1934), to the obscurities of medieval Wales (*Owen Glendower*, 1941) and then even further, to that supremely enigmatical locale of the Welsh Marches after the end of Roman Britain (*Porius*, 1951). It is as if the author, while retaining his gift for sophisticated, sometimes almost surrealist narrative presented with apparent, almost disarming, amateurishness, felt now a need to move further and further from contemporaneity, in order to find a society which freed him to innovate independently of the long-established 'realist' tradition. Powys's last novels carry this retreat from contemporaneity still further (see below, p. 100). Rather similarly, Wyndham Lewis, after his detailed satirical portraits of London society of one kind or another (*The Apes of God*, 1930; *The Revenge for Love*, 1937) withdrew to depict a life of isolation in a wartime Canadian hotel (*Self-Condemned*, 1955) or to renew and extend the vast inferno-purgatorial settings of his earlier *Childermass* (1928) in *The Human Age* (1955). David Jones, again, went on from the vivid First World War realism of *In Parenthesis* (1937) (see *The New Pelican Guide*, Vol. 7, p. 211) to the recondite historical and mythological intricacies of *The Anathemata* (1952).

In all these cases it is persuasive to see movements backward in time, or outward from the centre of society to its periphery, or to fantasy, as attempts to find acceptable settings for fiction in a period when the structures of contemporary society were somehow failing to carry conviction. A younger writer, Nigel Dennis, in his remarkable *Cards of Identity* (1955), shows something of this but in another way. This novel depicts, literally and in detail, the collapse of the traditional 'great house' and its owners, now 'crushed, defeated men' (or their derelict spouses) full of 'laments for the old days': 'where once they had toiled to beautify the landscape, they now laboured to estimate its commercial worth'. Traditional society and its bases of power have ceased to supply men with a foundation for their personal integrity or 'identity'. In this book, the great house of the past is taken over for a conference of the 'Identity Club', which affords at least some kind of fantasy-recognition of the need to supply a new basis for personality, now that the traditional one has gone.

The upshot, in the case of Dennis's novel, may be left in abeyance. As late as 1967, Andrew Sinclair sought to establish, in his novel *Gog*, the identity and integration of his hero, an invalid wartime serviceman, through a medley of English historical perspectives from earliest times. This medley invoked not only the facts and fantasies of history but also, in Rabelaisian or Joycean fashion, the literary styles of the past. But a new basis for the integrations that were lost when 'Advance, Britannia' came to sound hollow was not so easily to be come by. In the post-war years it was not simply the international and imperial roles that had ceased to satisfy. Immediate post-war essays by George Orwell such as 'The Prevention of Literature' (1945–6) show that, while passé patriotism obviously now meant nothing to him, disillusionment with Stalinism and with what he saw as the willingness of the Marxist Left to accommodate integrity to tactics was an equally sharp sensation, if one more recently acquired, Spender records a similar response on Auden's part:

He had shed all preoccupation with politics ... he explained to me that his politics in the 1930s had been based on the conviction that the anti-Fascists could really stop the war. When he realized that this view was mistaken, he had dropped the ideas which went with it.[1]

A particularly full and significant illustration of this trend, and of the state of dilemma into which it came to a focal point, is a notable but largely forgotten book, Leslie Paul's *Angry Young Man* (1951). Paul's anger was not a simple kind. In the first place, it was a straight-forward anger aimed at the interwar capitalist society and its betrayal, as Paul saw it, of the working class in the matter of the 1926 General Strike. But as the years passed, another anger came to be super-imposed upon that, an anger much deeper than the first because it had no remedy. This was prompted by Paul's disillusioning visits to the USSR in the 1930s, and by the rise of Nazism, which with some reason Paul saw as not simply an ugly fact of history, but as a genuine breakdown of the predictive dimension of Marxist historical theory. Paul's left-wing politics had in fact been naïve. He had supposed that communist politics could go easily with the enjoyment of rural scenery and belonging to the 'woodcrafters'; with admiring Hazlitt, being interested in literature for its own sake, and writing in a rich, evocative descriptive style. Such things went, if anything, more easily with the politics that Paul the Marxist despised. The 'anger' bit deeper as time revealed to him that the remedy was, as much as anything, like another disease.

Precisely this kind of 'double-bind' impasse lies behind much of the writing of the post-war years. 'The present day is disastrous and the alternative riotously absurd,' Dennis wrote in *Cards of Identity*; and in their own way those words sum up something both distinctive and characteristic of attitudes in post-war Britain. The time was certainly out of joint, but for that to seem so is no uncommon thing. The uncommon thing was that any remedy came to seem out of joint too. Under these circumstances it is not surprising that the period seems far from one of the great periods of English literature. It should be remembered that some of the authors mentioned in this chapter are of particular interest because, being writers of some repute in the first place, they are of interest less for their already substantial merit than for the fact of their illustrating some trend of the time.

The clearest literary reflection of the end of Empire was Anthony Burgess's 'Malayan trilogy' (*Time for a Tiger*, 1956; *The Enemy in the Blanket*, 1958; *Beds in the East*, 1959); though in other works there are also important, less direct reflections. The central character of the trilogy is the outdated, ineffective idealist Victor Crabbe, and both his names are meaningful: the first is direct irony, and with the second the literary-minded Burgess is doubtless thinking of Hamlet's '... if *like a crab* you could go backward'.* Crabbe is a complex figure to the extent that his by now irrelevant notions of service to the native peoples of the colonial Empire are entangled with communist ideals from his earlier years. He successively loses his first and then his second wife, and finally his life, all through 'death by water': which may represent the sea-power which burdened Britain with its millstone Empire. At the same time, Burgess is far indeed from depicting life at home in Britain as a joyful alternative to colonialism. Fenella Crabbe, Victor's second wife, longs for 'the art galleries', and London on a wet day, river fog, the country in autumn and so forth: the novel depicts her as a spineless, self-pitying sentimentalist. The outdated scion of a traditional old-English family who ought to have been her partner in life is aptly if derisively named Costard. Burgess chronicles the end, in one context, of the imperial conception. He sees colonialism as, to say the least, a worn-out way of life. But the alternatives are also worn-out, or half worn-out, before they start. The result is that a distinctive relation seems to develop, as between the author and his characters.[2] To some extent they seem to be the tortured pawns of a man ultimately at a loss (see below, p. 84). Paul Scott's *Raj Quartet* (1966–75), set in post-Independence India, makes a detailed and sustained effort to avoid blinkering itself within post-colonial attitudes; but even so, there is a tendency for the work to dissipate itself in the peripheral and melo-dramatic, as if the task the writer had set himself were impossibly difficult to carry out in the event.

Lawrence Durrell's *Alexandria Quartet* (*Justine*, 1957; *Balthazar*, 1958; *Mountolive*, 1958; *Clea*, 1960) has attracted notice for its colour-ful settings, or alternatively for its alleged experimentation with relativity and space-time in fiction. Reflection on this series of books, however, suggests that what most significantly emerges from its 'interlineations' and palimpsests is a fable of the emergent Arab world and the decline and disappearance of British neo-colonialism in Palestine and Egypt. Little by little it transpires that the intense but restless and unsatisfying 'love'-relationships in the novels are, in large part, something like mere arabesque or smokescreen – and

---

* Italics here and elsewhere are the present writer's, unless otherwise stated.

this quite intentionally on the part of the author – over other more substantial and more public-life realities. At one of their encounters, Justine and Darley think that they see Justine's wronged husband outside their glass door, about to burst in on them; but whoever it is turns away. Really it is a British brigadier on a fruitless security mission on behalf of what he always refers to as 'the Raj'. In *Balthazar* Nessim's 'proposal' to Justine is not fully explained to us. Later, when the scene is replayed in *Mountolive*, we find that that proposal was not merely a marital one: it was for 'seeing further into history', and gunrunning to prepare for the British exit from the Near East.

Moreover, in this whole work, because of its unique setting in the great cosmopolitan city of Alexandria, the end of the Raj can be in part assimilated with a fable of contemporary city-alienation. 'We are observing the fall of city man,' we read (somewhat ponderously, no doubt) in *Clea*. Alexandria is the metropolis of terminal colonialism. Maskelyne, the Raj-dedicated brigadier, in the end dies without relatives or estate. Moreover, what is salvaged from the termination of the Raj is also significant. The various racial communities which had once lived in Alexandria in lively if precarious co-existence now stabilize themselves into a kind of segregated vitality; and the lovers Darley and Clea find their creativity as artists at last asserting itself, in the lyricism and isolation (compare the 'segregation' just mentioned) of a Greek island. In other words the apparently complex solution to life is replaced by the relatively simple and minimal. There is a deeper positive note in the way Durrell resolves the novel for his central characters than anything in Burgess's trilogy; but such a settling on the simpler solution has a point to which this discussion must return (see below, pp. 82ff.).

With Mervyn Peake's *Gormenghast* trilogy (*Titus Groan*, 1946; *Gormenghast*, 1950; *Titus Alone*, 1959) one moves into an area of the fantasy-novel which not all will be disposed to take very seriously, but which again must be considered more fully later. From one point of view, though, Peake's fantasy-trilogy is a deeply suggestive allegory of the Imperial theme. His image of a castle immeasurable in extent and immeasurably remote doubtless owes something to his early years in the great sea-girt rock-fortress of Sark or, still more, to the years he spent in Imperial China in its last days. But the work turns out also to be a fable for our own time. Its endless gradations of caste, its proliferating bureaucracy, reliance on half-written 'British-constitution' tradition, anachronistic paraphernalia everywhere, and almost ignored, down-trodden, prematurely-ageing 'natives' outside the Pale, turn the whole work into the fullest and most compelling allegory of the traditional-anachronistic in post-war British society. Peake's work, it is true, leaves one ill-satisfied. It threatens always to lapse into something sketchy, even a trifle juvenile. Yet its amplitude and drive make it memorable; and the aimless malignity and uncertain life-affirmingness, respectively, of its two principal characters (Steerpike and Titus) will warrant further comment later (see below, pp. 100–101).

Literary Institutionalism

Victor Crabbe's wife Fenella, quitting Malaysia and her husband, returned to England and made herself a name (a spurious one, Burgess intimates) in the poetry magazines. What sort of literary scene, in institutional terms, would she have encountered during the post-war years?[3] Official and semi-official patronage was significant throughout the period, and its motives were mixed, as were its effects, even from the war years themselves. The 'Council for the Encouragement of Music and the Arts' (CEMA) was founded in December 1939. The 'Entertainments National Service Association' (ENSA) had been founded the year before, at first as a voluntary society. These bodies reflected a governmental awareness that arts and entertainment had a practical, war-winning importance for both morale and industrial production. The attempt at a joint fostering of both light and serious entertainment went on into the 1951 Festival of Britain, with its lavish Battersea 'Fun Park', and at the same time over twenty provincial festivals (later, there were as many as four hundred, large and small); one of these, at York, produced some of the medieval mystery-cycle plays for the first time since the sixteenth century.

The same attempt at amalgamation – not altogether an easy one – appears again in Jennie Lee's Government White Paper (1965) called 'A Policy for the Arts'; in it the phrase 'arts and *leisure*' repeatedly catches the eye. The same admixture reappears everywhere, in fact. Study of prize-winning poems over the years at Cheltenham, one of the major annual festivals of the arts, shows a complex inter-relation of the slight and serious. 'Increasingly the writer is becoming a part of show business,' wrote R. Findlater in 1963. On the other hand, the 'extension' work of the British public library service is one of the striking features of the period, and it has created, through-out the country, a serious place for the arts. 'The work of a modern public library is predominantly educational, cultural and infor-mational, with leisure reading as a very minor activity.' Those words are to be read in the Gateshead Public Librarian's Annual Report for 1970. On the other hand, the local context was the replacement of the Libraries Committee by a Leisure Committee, a change which the librarian viewed with limited enthusiasm; and the two sides of the general picture are embodied there.

The 'Green Shield' and 'Habitat' catalogues of the 1960s contribute to a less favourable picture: 'book' seems to mean only 'reference book', like *A Pictorial History of Soccer* or road atlases – or indeed, classics, but for children. When shelves are shown in such catalogues, they are usually filled with long-playing records, toys, bottles or arty dinner plates. By 1959, average television viewing time throughout the nation was already $2\frac{1}{2}$ hours per person per day. On the other hand, by the 1960s, independent commercial television companies had begun to give substantial support to drama and theatre, and research in public libraries had shown that radio serials of classics like *David Copperfield* regularly led to substantially in-creased calls for the book itself, in the unabridged form.

Within this complex picture, certain other developments charac-teristic of the time may be noted. One is an increased institutionaliza-tion in the world of writing. In addition to PEN, the Society of Authors and others, the post-war years saw the founding or notable development of societies like the Radiowriters' Association, the Writers' Guild of Great Britain (to promote the interests of screen, television, radio and advertisement writers), the Critics' Circle, the Guild of Travel Writers, and more recently the London, and the National, Poetry Secretariats, to promote the material interests of poets (and would-be poets). Of Societies devoted to particular authors like Dickens, Hardy, Hopkins, Shaw, Byron and others, some were new, some (as were the English Association, or the Poetry

Society, active notably for the speaking of verse) already long-established.

A particular feature of the post-war years has been the strength and variety of local societies, either for readers or for writers. The London Writers' Circle, or the Poets' Group for example, has had counterparts all over the provinces – Canterbury, Essex, Somerset, Lincolnshire, Kent, Sussex, Nottingham, East Anglia, Suffolk and Newcastle are merely a few. Some, like the Calder Valley Poets Society (founded 1915) date from an earlier time, but such groups .frequently do not. Many of them cater not only for writers and would-be writers, but also for those interested in listening, reading or discussing. Among these, and in addition to some of the societies listed above, might be mentioned the Association of Yorkshire Book-men, or the London Contemporary Poetry and Music Circle. That these societies may vary in terms of learning, seriousness or permanence is an intrinsic part of the whole picture.

The prominence of north-of-England organizations in these fields is noteworthy (see also below, pp. 108–9), and quite probably it should be related to the long period of post-war prosperity and full employment which brought a new prosperity to the North; similarly related should be the widening effects of the 1944 Education Act, the later growth of comprehensive education, and the increasing literary importance of the northern universities. Among literary societies the Critical Society was based on the English Department at Manchester; so was the *Critical Quarterly*, probably the most influential English literary-critical journal in the academic field over the post-war decades. With it should be mentioned *Stand*, which was concerned with criticism and (especially) new writing in prose or verse, and long published in Newcastle-upon-Tyne; *Listen* was also one of the influential and most characteristic poetry magazines of the 1950s (followed some years later by the rather similar *Wave*), published by the important Marvell Press at Hull. *Lines Review*, appearing from Edinburgh but printing much English verse from England, should also be mentioned.

The trend has been much the same in the matter of patronage of the arts, including literature, by bodies of an official or semi-official kind. The Arts Council received its Charter in August 1946, and from its early years sought (though not to everyone's satisfaction) to avoid overendowment of the arts in London at the expense of the regions. In the course of time it developed subsidies to many provincial repertory companies, and also subventions to enable London companies to tour outside London (the DALTA Scheme). In addition, the Arts Council launched a system of travel subsidies to draw audiences in from country districts. Parallel to this should be mentioned the Local Government Act of 1948, which permitted local authorities to allot up to $2\frac{1}{2}$ per cent of their revenue specifically to the arts. By 1970 the average expenditure over the whole country was in fact far short of that, and was only about 0·1 per cent; but some authorities had been active, and again the North of England figures prominently.

This is particularly clear in respect of the rise of provincial theatres in the post-war era, a development which has related directly to the writing of important new plays (see below, pp. 114ff.). In the sixties, for example, the local municipality took over theatres, or supported new ones, in Watford (Civic), Liverpool (Everyman), Bradford (Alhambra), Edinburgh (Royal Lyceum), Glasgow (King's) Worthing (Connaught), Norwich (Royal, which also became an Arts Centre) and Kidderminster. In a related context the work of the civic universities should be noted. Southampton University opened the Nuffield Theatre in 1964, Manchester the University Theatre in the following year. The National Council of Civic Theatres held its first meeting in Sunderland in 1963: by 1970, it had 100 members, and in that same year about 400 civic authorities owned theatres or halls (needless to say, of widely differing standards) provided for entertainment (see the National Council of Civic Theatres Directory). In the North there were also other developments. Joan Littlewood's vitally important Theatre Workshop Company began in Manchester in 1945 before moving to the Theatre Royal, Stratford East, London, in 1953; and the Studio Theatre Company for 'theatre in the round' operated, from 1955, especially from Scarborough. The first of the Regional Arts Associations was the Northern Arts Association, founded in 1960. A network of Regional Arts Associations now covers the whole of England, the last to be formed being in the south-east, which has been somewhat overshadowed by London. Finally may be mentioned such developments as the 'Theatre for Young People' at Harrogate, the Coventry 'theatre education scheme' which involved teams of full-time drama specialists visiting schools in the region, and the Youth Theatres in Birmingham and Liverpool.

Since, by its nature, metropolitan is related to cosmopolitan, the growing prominence of regional and provincial cultural activity in Britain may link with certain facts which point to an increasing insularity, and a decline in world cultural contacts or cultural influence. Technical publications much obscure the book market picture, but all the same, in 1965, when the *world* percentage of translations to total published works was about 10 per cent, the figure for the United Kingdom was 2·4 per cent – below the USSR, the USA, or Ireland. In the same year, Britain's book exports were 0·8 per cent of total exports, the highest figure for any country. We exported our own culture, but did less to import that of others. In non-literary fields, the growth of English as a 'world language' is an important aspect of these developments. Over the post-war years generally, English has been the first of the so-called 'international' languages, understood by about one-fifth of the world's population, and easily foremost in the international political, economic and technical fields. At the same time, however, Britain's own role as one of the users of the English language in book form diminished. The United Kingdom published nearly half of the world's titles in English in 1950, not much over a quarter of them in 1965. Increasingly, the USA has come to dominate the scene. Not conspicuous, this major change nonetheless indicates yet another respect in which Britain's place in the international cultural scene has been recessive. With regard strictly to translations of literary works, the United Kingdom was thirty-fourth among listed countries in 1965, as compared with twenty-second in respect of translations of all kinds.

Le caractère autarcique, conséquence de la puissance du marché du livre britannique, est ainsi, pour l'avenir, une des plus grandes faiblesses de la littérature anglaise. (This self-dependent quality, which results from the strength of the market for British books, is one of the greatest weaknesses, so far as the future is concerned, for English literature itself.)[4]

Aspects of the Media

This subject is resumed, in a more specifically theatrical context, on p. 114 below. More generally, one must have in mind how the difficulty of diagnosing the literary scene is increased by the fact that most of the forces acting upon it are mixed and even what might be termed self-antithetical in their effects. There has been a great increase, for example, in reading; but predominantly, it would seem, of reading to a greater or lesser degree 'popular' in taste. Between 1937 and 1947, the circulation of newspapers increased by about 50 per cent, and of Sunday newspapers by 100 per cent; while in something like the same period the annual sale of magazines rose from 26 million to about 40 million copies. At the same time, though, publishing conditions have changed so as to favour what might be termed middlebrow work. A. P. Herbert recorded that of a new novel in 1970 selling three thousand copies, no less than 80 per cent would go to libraries; obviously, such a fact must influence publishers, and through them is likely to influence writers also. The Arts Council has sought to exercise a contrary influence, but until the mid sixties its subventions to new writing were on a small scale, and until more recently still they chiefly went (drama apart) to verse, not to fiction. In drama the recent main development has been the growth of the 'second list' of grants to small experimental, 'Off-Fringe' workshop groups: this policy barely existed in the mid sixties, but by 1974–5 the 'second list' included about eighty names. Even here, the exact workings-out of the scheme are uncertain, and the Council's attempts to foster 'community art' have occasionally provoked resignations and ridicule,[5] and seemed to encourage gimmicky novelties without much regard for serious interest. For all that, between 1956 and 1970 the Council increased its funding of art and literature from about 4 to 11 per cent of its total budget, at the same time as, most laudably, it reduced its administrative costs in very much the same proportions.

Likewise, the influence of the media on new writing has been noteworthy, and mixed in its effect. Television and radio have of course evoked some fine work in drama (see below, p. 116), but for the present it is their influence on the literary language which is at issue. One writer speaks of 'the gradual absorption into contemporary writing-style of some of the techniques of film expression'[6]; and specifically mentions a reduction in detailed descriptive writing, a staccato style, and 'heavy dependence on dialogue'. 'To compete with TV the serious novel had to choose topics formerly exploited by trash fiction,' wrote George Steiner.[7] Radio has 'pioneered the concept of "packaged" information and entertainment where the necessity for selection and preconceived choice can be eliminated'. In radio, there was a significant difference after the death of Lord Reith in 1971, and later the transformation of the Third Programme into Radio Three with more winter-gardens music and more catchy features in the place of serious talks; though at the same time, it could be argued that these changes made for social homogeneity, and for the preservation, on a wider scale, of values in a changing society. One aspect of these matters which has been insufficiently studied is how far the influence of the media has led to a reduction in range of vocabulary and variety of syntax:[8] the assimilation of English to the world-language pattern has certainly operated in that direction. Even the decimalization of 1968, and again in the late seventies, has done something to impoverish literary resources: consider the fate of idiomatic words and phrases like 'to inch forward', 'yardstick', or 'bob a job'; or the traditional song 'I have sixpence . . .'

In the theatre, John Osborne's *Epitaph for George Dillon* (written with Anthony Creighton: first performed at the Royal Court Theatre in 1958) celebrates the destructive side of media-influence. For its central character, the story is one of profound inner inadequacy which achieves a false release in commercialized pseudo-success. Ruth's ex-lover in the play is the same: his new mistress gets his book published, and rave reviews are enough to set him on top of the world. Ruth herself is a person of integrity. What is the result? That the only course open to her is one of successive rejection and withdrawal. She turns away, first from the Communist Party, then from her lover, then from George, then from the hideous closing epiphany of 'the cocktail cabinet in all its glory'; and exits, quite alone in the world. Society is alien to creativity.

The same shows elsewhere, as in, for example, John Arden's *Live Like Pigs* of the same year (see below, p. 107). Terson's *Zigger Zagger* (1964) is comparable for its picture of the media-backed juggernaut of the commercialized football-world. For poetry there has been one quite distinctive effect of the influence of the media; that is, the remarkable prevalence of what might be termed the news-item lyric: the staple of the poem is to recount some brief anecdote, made as vivid as possible, and often rounded off with a 'punch-line'. In other words, the poem follows a journalism-pattern, and in effect bases its achievement on the creation of a good 'story'. An alternative has been something like a 'feature item' or documentary piece: what comprises the poem in this case being simply the presentation of a catchy character, scene or object; again, made as vividly as possible.

Literary Criticism: F. R. Leavis

Much of what has been said so far has touched in various contexts on the new importance in the literary scene of the North of England; and it seems reasonable to suggest that the developing literary and cultural importance of the North ought to be related to certain features of post-war literary criticism. Indeed, the literary criticism of the time has been an integral and not uninfluential side of the literary scene. Throughout the 1970s quite new approaches and interests will prove to have come in from the Continent (and to some extent America: see below, pp. 119ff.); but there is little doubt that in the earlier years the most widely diffused and telling influence in criticism was that of F. R. Leavis at Downing College, Cambridge. Leavis's pupils, going more into schools and other forms of higher education than to positions at the ancient universities in fact contributed not a little to changes in attitude in the post-war scene.

This is not the place to expound or assess Leavis's criticism: the question is simply of how it seems to have become integrated into the general scene. In this respect, it must be emphasized that in many instances the question is of Leavis's critical work in some crudified or indeed tabloid form which he himself would hardly have endorsed. In such a context, it is legitimate also here to simplify Leavis's notably seamless and unitary critical approach into, as it were, certain nodal ideas. Leavis's stress on verse 'embodying' or 'enacting' its meaning, as upon 'concreteness' and 'full realization' in the detailed use of language, is reflected – again, in tabloid form, doubtless – in a widespread and concentrated seeking after vividness and 'body' in much recent verse. This will be discussed in more detail below (pp. 93–7).

Again, and even more obviously, Leavis's drily, sometimes caustically sceptical dismissal of the sentimental, the too-easily 'romantic', and the 'literary' was widely reflected in both the verse (Davie, Larkin, Gunn) and the prose of the 1950s (Amis and others). The implications extend more widely. That response, and its turning away from the traditional attitudes and centres of 'belles-lettrisme', makes a loose conjunction with the new features in the educational system, with class patterns, with the increasing prominence of the North, and with movement away from anything like lofty cosmopolitan stances.

Leavis's more essentially Lawrentian, and in his own writings certainly more elusive, sense that truly valuable writing comes from the deepest springs of creative life and therefore of necessity also of life taken and responded to in its widest and deepest totality, is nearer to the heart of his thinking about literature. Self-evidently also, it is nearer as well to what is essential in any major literary work. This profound and intense conviction on Leavis's part, which he always found it hard to be lucidly explicit over in his writings, is central to his own value as a writer on literature, and for the most part it makes one set aside the less rewarding aspects of his work – the ill-humour and animosity that sometimes distracted him, the not infrequent wearisome insistence, the inability sometimes to analyse with enough sympathy and so to conclusive effect. Moreover, it is this central conviction which unites Leavis's work as a whole: the earlier writing which concentrated largely on verse and its analysis, and the later which turned much more to broader though by no means less forthright discussion of prose fiction. That central conviction, obviously enough, does not lend itself to encapsulation. If one believes that, difficult as it may be to write with explicitness on such a matter, what is essential to greatness in literature indeed lies here, then it must be said that this aspect of Leavis's work has borne little fruit in the writing of the period. Few of its writers could even lay claim to what has, on that view, been central to the major works of the past. From this crucial standpoint, the Australian novelist Patrick White seems on the whole to be in a class apart from any British writer of the period (see pp. 147–63, below).

Responses to the Post-war World

To collect all the above points together, and create an integrated picture of how the scene in Britain has developed since the war, requires one to supplement the reference to full employment and all that that implies by recalling the substantial growth of population and what might, rather clumsily, be called the 'de-ruralization' of the countryside. This has taken place not only through large-scale suburban and village-estate development, but also through the growth of the motorway network and the spread of industrialized, hedgeless, insecticide-drenched farming and battery fowl-rearing. In those environmental conditions, there have been educational and linguistic changes, and changes through the media, which have drawn both authors and readers from new social milieux, have modified their language resources, and perhaps also made their literary attitudes and discriminations in some respects coarser and in others more robust. The influence of the wide range (noted above) of bodies and institutions both public and voluntary which have grown up to further patronage of, participation in, or discussion of literature, has not been a straightforward influence. But if one tries to penetrate to the heart of the matter, and consider the attitudes and convictions out of which writing has come, one finds a noteworthy combination of a loss of belief in traditional positions and roles, with at the same time perplexity, scepticism or near-indifference over what might replace them. 'The present day is disastrous and the alternative riotously absurd.' In the abstract, such a condition might be diagnosable by the psychiatrist; and schizophrenia, violence, nostalgia or throw-away resignation might be predicted as being among the outcomes.

'Minimal Affirmation'

In fact, there seem in contemporary writing to have been four or five principal distinguishable responses to conditions between, say, 1945 and 1965. First, one notices the writings which engage with the difficulties of the time through some kind or other of *minimal affirmation*. If (to recall Meredith) the soul hot for certainties gets a dusty answer, whichever way it turns – the typical post-war 'Catch-22' situation – perhaps even so, runs this way of thinking, there can be located some limited area of experience that has value, or some modest and unambitious conception of goodness which can as it were be insured against undermining.

Writer after writer has in fact pursued this possibility, this hope for a secure even if limited 'solution'. John Osborne's *Look Back in Anger*, the well-known play which is usually taken as having sparked off the theatrical revival of the fifties, is almost a caricature of the position. Its dilemma is first that the older and traditional loyalties of patriotism, family, 'manners', public service and so forth have come to seem absurd to a post-war generation. One recalls that this play was written in the year when Britain's traditionalist foreign-office outlook kept us from taking a leading role as founder-member of the Common Market, and first performed in the year of the great traditionalist show-up and let-down of the Suez Crisis. Second, and over against that, comes the complementary conviction in the play that no new values and allegiances have taken or can take the places of those empty shibboleths: certainly not Jimmy Porter's own provincial 'white tile' university and all that went with it. Hence the 'anger' he feels: that of a double and self-sealing frustration, though one quite different from Leslie Paul's (see p. 70 above). But that sense of frustration must be based on an underlying conviction that life, as we have to live it, cannot be absurd and meaningless. It absolutely must be important, significant and real. Only, the significance cannot be identified, or is identified (but ironically?) only in the pathetic, atavistic, trifling, private happiness that the 'hero' and heroine manage to get from their amorous baby-talk and baby-games at the end of the play.

There is a revealing contrast with certain popular plays of a generation earlier, Noel Coward's West End successes like *Hay Fever* (1925) or *The Young Idea*. Coward's plays are based upon patterns of thought and feeling which are more or less the opposite of Osborne's. Osborne's play is written as if life must be meaningful, but the meaning cannot be found. Coward's near-farce comedies, on the other hand, cheerfully present the life of their upper-middle-class nonentities as 'riotously absurd'. But something in particular is not absurd. This is the pattern of values – affection, family loyalties, being 'straight' – that admittedly work out absurdly in practice, but that as principles are perennially meaningful and wholly beyond question. That Jimmy Porter can find no alternative is true in quite another sense. He is convinced that there must be one somewhere, but he cannot find it.

William Cooper's *Scenes from Provincial Life* (1950) offers a minimal affirmation in quite another way; and that way is of particular interest as both foreshadowing, and going beyond, much of the better-known fiction of the middle and later fifties. This book gently brushes aside many of the principles and taboos of the Establishment and the world-before-the-war. With the words, 'I forgot that Sir Nevile Henderson had been to Berlin to explain the British plans before Parliament heard them', the central character dismisses both the momentous political crises of the time and the whole edifice of Parliamentary democracy. Likewise with a later reference to the characters' going to America to avoid the holocaust of the European war. All that is at the level of the boring and peripheral. Likewise again with more individualizing aspects of the book: that Steve and Tom are homosexual lovers; that virtually the opening scene between (unmarried) hero and heroine is of them in bed together; that the heroine combines an instinctively innocent meekness and 'sly smirking lubricity'; that the opening sentence of the book implicitly and quite casually records how the grammar-school boys frequent the local pub – all these things are presented with studied nonchalance. What 'surely' the reader cares about, just doesn't matter. Where then is the minimal, vestigial affirmation? It resides in nothing more than a relaxed, but pervasive, sense that, when everything is a kind of insignificant joke, some sort of simple, basic but positive sense of life remains, and is reflected, one begins to feel as one reads, in the easy buoyancy of the style.

Cooper's easy-going casualness about his characters has more marked parallels elsewhere. Burgess's trilogy, discussed above, left the reader with a stronger sense of the author's callousness towards his creations: they experience disasters but are not tragic; in the last analysis they seem expendable (the contrast would be with Hardy). Graham Greene seems almost to create characters in order to display them in conditions of torture. This is true of pre-war works (*Brighton Rock*, 1938; *The Confidential Agent*, 1939: this, against all likelihood, turns out to have a 'happy' ending); and still truer of post-war ones like *The Heart of the Matter* (1948) and *The End of the Affair* (1951). The same trend shows in John Fowles's *The Collector* (1963) and *The*

French Lieutenant's Woman (1969; see also below, p. 101), and in novels by Iris Murdoch like *A Severed Head* (1961) or *An Accidental Man* (1971). There are other examples, too, several of Muriel Spark's novels (see below, p. 123) being among them. The tendency for an author to victimize or even torture his characters is no more than one of several which suggest how writers have found it difficult to embody human values freely in their work over recent decades.

Minimal affirmation shows also in much of the verse of the 1950s. Remarkably, indeed, it does so sometimes in Eliot's late plays. After the soaring close of *Little Gidding*, it is astonishing to hear the note upon which *The Cocktail Party* ended in 1950: '... if this was right ... something else ... is terribly wrong'; or again, 'It isn't much that I understand yet! But ... every moment is a fresh beginning' (see also p. 92 below).

Among younger writers of verse there is something akin, at least, to a minimal affirmation in some of the wartime poems of Keith Douglas:

> *Lay the coin on my tongue* and I will sing
> Of what the others never set eyes on

are the closing lines of *Desert Flowers* (1943): and another poem begins:

> I praise a snakeskin or a stone:
> a bald head or a public speech
> I hate ...

Douglas has a dry, restrained style, with curt shifts of tone (from cool to icy in the main) and above all, a remarkable sinuosity of invention, so that his best poems read as a constant, sustained taut surprise. Had he not been a casualty of the war, English poetry in the post-war period would probably have been different and better. Something of his virtues show in the cool but vivid subtleties of Charles Tomlinson, and the powerful, dry and sometimes elusive work of Geoffrey Hill. Both poets are discussed at length elsewhere in this volume (pp. 281ff.).

The theme of minimal affirmation shows more plainly, however, in many of the poems included in the representative anthology *New Lines* (1956), a collection which, amid some controversy, was hailed at the time as sign of a new movement in post-war verse. Donald Davie's *Cherry Ripe* celebrated the 'pure' and minimal as against 'opulence'. Since the 1950s, Davie's verse, while never departing from his early allegiance to eighteenth-century ideals of order, tact and exactitude, has pursued a steadily individual course of constant development and innovation. His combination of wit, easy freshness of style, and often strong feeling is highly distinctive, and his work cannot fairly be considered briefly and in terms of the 'Literary Scene'. For Kingsley Amis, 'the word love, the word death, the word life' were the 'rhyme-words of poets in a silver age' (Amis was silent about the fact that, so far as rhyme goes, poets have found all those words singularly recalcitrant). Thom Gunn, in his widely-known poem *On the Move*, speaks of how anyone like his motor-cyclists 'joins the movement in a valueless world' and 'moves ... always toward, toward':

> In gleaming jackets trophied with the dust,
> They strap in doubt – by hiding it, robust –
> And almost hear a meaning in their noise.

Or again:

> At worst, one is in motion; and at best,
> Reaching no absolute, in which to rest
> One is always nearer by not keeping still.

Some might be inclined to see these passages as wholly cynical, wholly without sense of values. That is exactly what they are not. Over the course of the poem, Gunn traces a great deal of pointlessness and emptiness. But he senses *something* valid as well: and the curiously recurrent alternate sharpness and vagueness of the style well mirror this sense of some genuine good somewhere, although one can hardly say where or what it is.

Philip Larkin's novel *A Girl in Winter* (1957) is aptly named. The landscape of the novel is wintry in more than a seasonal sense. In this featureless provincial town in wartime, not only Katharine the refugee-heroine, but all the other characters also, are 'wintering out' in a world where family ties are either missing, or else summed up in the words: 'they tried to be good and yet we just *hadn't anything to say to each other*. I mean, we were quite friendly and all that ... but

... I can't explain it quite.' Affection between Katharine and the young man who spoke those words takes the same turn:

> If her mind had not been tired out so that it could be swept along unheeding, his sudden appearance might have moved her. As it was, it *failed to connect*. There were, she knew, things she should feel, things she should say, but whether through his fault or hers she had no command of them.

When they spend the night together aimlessly and pointlessly, the novel simply concludes. Yet there is a certain vestigial optimism. Most of the people in the novel are seen as likeable in a rough-and-ready, even if ineffective, way. Human life offers little enough, the book says, but those who live it have some worth, and on the whole they deserve better rather than worse. Also, at the end, there is another kind of gesture towards the positive, though not a particularly convincing one. As the winter snowflakes fall endlessly, we are told, all around the drowsy non-lovers in their drab garret:

> Yet their passage was not saddening. Unsatisfied dreams rose and fell about them, crying out against their implacability, but in the end glad that such order, such destiny, existed. Against this knowledge, the heart, the will, and all that made for protest, could at last sleep.

That muted note of optimism is inadequately prepared for and fails to carry conviction; but that Larkin chose to end the book on such a note confirms one's sense that *A Girl in Winter*, bleak and joyless as it is, for all that embodies a certain limited and muted affirmative trace.

The interest of that is largely, of course, such affinity as will prove to exist with Larkin's verse. Almost from the start, the novel does not always strike a reader as coming from a practised hand; but from the beginning too the verse leaves a contrary impression, one of quite exceptional, seemingly intuitive deftness, economy, precision. Be that as it may, the general point of this discussion is illustrated in his verse repeatedly, and with great exactitude and lucidity. Larkin's verse strategy in poem after poem seems to be to *insure* against anything that might come into his work on too easy terms, anything that could possibly be seen as a lapse into soft-centredness or sentimentality. Conventional conceptions of experience and the incidents that comprise it are held up to a dry, sceptical, and what might be called *subtractive* scrutiny. The formula for a poem might be said to be 'x minus y', where x is the corpus of conventionalities that would lead to the familiar kinds of bad poem, and 'y' is Larkin's disillusionary deflation of it.

But such a formula for the characteristic Larkin poem is not quite complete. It should be added that 'x minus y' does not equal zero. The 'answer' of the poem is always a small quantity, but it is, too, always a positive quantity. Hence the title of Larkin's first widely-known collection: *The Less Deceived* (1955). The poet's first move is to reject the stance of Ophelia. When Hamlet says, 'I never loved you', all she can reply, abjectly, is 'I was the more deceived.' The poems grimly – almost self-mutilatingly, one sometimes wants to say – sustain a high-premium insurance against any such dereliction. *Not to be taken in* seems to be the major aim of one poetic experience after another; in a world where, indeed, it seems as if we ought once more to recall the words, 'the present day is disastrous and the alternative riotously absurd'.

Yet not quite. These poems search out the modest positive quality that survives. The 'accoutred frowsty barn' of the church in *Church Going* was 'not worth stopping for': but the poem, having deflated conventionality, has something to add:

> Yet stop I did ...

By the end of the poem the valid if exiguous reason for that transpires:

> Someone will forever be *surprising*
> A hunger in himself to be more *serious* ...

The 'surprise' is not, one should see, only at finding that 'x minus y' does not after all equal zero, it is also that the small positive quantity remaining is among the most traditional and deeply established of our indigenous, insular, Protestant virtues. Even more so is that true of another poem, *Reasons for Attendance*. Here, the sceptical poet–observer begins with a disillusioned rejection of the too–easy–terms 'boy meets girl' legend. The poem soon tells us, by a word to which, in its beautiful, easy, relaxed movement, it gives the great prominence of a phrase bridging to the first word of a new stanza, where it is more important to focus attention:

> Sex, yes, but what
> Is sex? Surely, to think the lion's share
> Of happiness is found by couples – sheer
>
> *Inaccuracy*, as far as I'm concerned ...

Truthfulness, the most traditional of traditional Protestant virtues, is what the poem finds valid when the rest is exposed. Yet that also, not on too-easy terms: the distrust in the poem swiftly modulates into self-distrust:

> both are satisfied
> If no one has misjudged himself. *Or lied.*

Maybe the amorous dancers have done the first of those, but only the speaking poet can have done the second; and the strong if minimal endorsement of the last line comes out all the more, because with Larkin's characteristic if inconspicuous technical brilliance, only now do the concluding half-rhymes of the earlier stanzas focus at last into a full and perfect rhyme.

Space must set a limit to how far one can explore here these moves and attitudes in Larkin, or for example how they are reinforced by the constant witty dryness of the verbal texture ('... wind *distresses* tail and mane' is a well-known example in *At Grass*) or by the frequent 'un-poetical' use of quietly colloquial idiom. But a poem like *An Arundel Tomb* should be noticed as an outstanding example of the strategy of the 'residual positive', as also because of how we shall often find the same position elsewhere (the last line of the poem is 'What will survive of us is love': see below, pp. 92–3). Of Larkin's exceptional skill in utilizing poetic form to reinforce his technique of deflation followed by ultimate resistance to deflation, *Lines on a Young Lady's Photograph Album* is another striking example. Nearly every stanza closes on the characteristic note of dryness: 'I choke on such nutritious images'; '... lifting a heavy-headed rose/Beneath a trellis, or in a trilby hat'; ' ...you/Contract my heart by looking out of date' are examples. With one exception all the stanza-endings of the poem are so, more or less. But not the last one. By this point the pattern is deeply established for us that the close of a stanza, because it is dry and deflationary, is *valid*. It stands up against the 'scrutiny' of the disillusioned and sceptical, of the 'less deceived'. Then we read:

... you lie
Unvariably lovely there,
Smaller and clearer as the years go by.

A modest nucleus of nostalgic, poignant feeling is rescued from sentimentality (rescued, anyhow, if anything can rescue it) by the form of
the whole.

The unmistakeable continuity of this with Auden and with Hardy
also should not be overlooked (Larkin's respect for the early nineteenth-century poet W. M. Praed is also noteworthy). Larkin's first
collection of verse, *The North Ship* (1945: the choice of title for the
book should not go unnoticed) shows everywhere the influence of
Yeats. In the Preface, however, the poet writes of how he gave Yeats
up: 'the reaction, when it came, was undramatic, complete and
permanent.' Larkin speaks in the same place of his early admiration
for Auden – the rest of modern poetry was 'old-fashioned' by
comparison – and of the decisive influence of Hardy; mentioning
Hardy's *Thoughts of Phena ... at News of her Death* (c. 1898). The gist
of Hardy's poem is crucially to the point for Larkin: it is that Hardy
has absolutely nothing left by way of relic or memento of Tryphena
Sparks, his early love. But, says the poem, in just that great zero there
is perhaps hidden a small positive quantity: perhaps, Hardy suggests, I
retain her memory, the real her, all the better precisely on account of
that. 'Smaller and clearer ...'

Larkin also refers in that Preface to Auden's poem *Fleet Visit*, of
about the very year as *The North Ship* was being put together.
Curiously enough, the train of thought in *Fleet Visit* is very much
like that of *Thoughts of Phena* ... The poem contemplates some
American warships in harbour. They are neutral, they are doing
nothing, all the conventional or traditional interest or excitement
attaching to warships is missing from them. But, Auden says, they
look the better, they are more interesting not less, precisely because
of that. In both poems we have the characteristic Larkin pattern of
thought. The poems relinquish the conventional, too-easy-terms
sources of feeling, but the result is not a zero. A nucleus of feeling,
modest, traditional in fact in its own way, but insured against
deflationary collapse exactly through the stress on how conventionalities have been discarded, remains intact and can be accepted.

If in the fifties Larkin is thus a representative of insular and limited traditions, so, after her early work, is Iris Murdoch, though in other ways. After *Under the Net* (1954), hailed with plausibility as an Existentialist novel, and her incisive book on *Sartre* (1953), there begins to show in her work, though of course in twentieth-century terms, a certain Dickensian affinity. At a simple level, this shows in the vein of melodrama – less limited by convention, of course, than in Dickens – that runs through one novel after another. *The Unicorn* (1963) offers us attempted murder and hideous, accidental near-death; *The Italian Girl* (1964) registers hints of homosexuality, flagellation, and incest, to say nothing of fights, abortion, adultery, fornication and drunkenness. *The Nice and the Good* (1967) ranges through blackmail, murder, girl-swapping, prostitution and black magic; and *An Accidental Man* (1971) covers violence, murder, suicide, accidental death, blackmail and both kinds of homosexuality. Closer study of key scenes in the novels (Ducane's meeting with Judy McGrath in *The Nice and the Good*, ch. 13, or Mareus's attempted visit to Carel in *The Time of the Angels*, ch. 7, are examples) shows that this tendency away from, let us say, the humdrum realism of a Wells or a Bennett, and towards the melodramatic and bizarre, albeit most sophisticatedly so, reveals itself also in the detail of the writing. Every move in such scenes strikes one on reflection as just slightly improbable; all the time there is a sense of interweavings, of some kind of indefinite symbolism, suggestive simply of the open fecundity of experience rather than settling into any crystalline structure, over-orderly array. Alice in the rockpool (*The Unicorn*, 1963) is purification by water, or return to the sea, the giver of all life, or to the womb, or all and none of these and doubtless other things, by adumbration, as well. Pierce entering the cave at the end of *The Nice and the Good* is substituting for the sexual act (his name of course has its point), but Ducane (so no doubt has his, a son of Cain, a man) going after him is being reborn through the sea into finally confirmed goodness. At the same time, the scene is simply a vivid, melodramatic climax to a novel as conventionally understood. Writing which in some ways has merely the qualities of the middlebrow popular novel strives also to express something deeper: a distinctive sense of life, its rhythms and bizarre ebb-and-flow, its idiosyncrasy, its power of continuance and renewal.

All of this is a far cry from the way Larkin was being seen

PART TWO

as representative of a trend, in a time of evanescing values and many-sided uncertainty, towards a merely vestigial or residual kind of affirmation. When one turns, however, from Iris Murdoch's representation of the way experience is organized to her contribution in respect of what makes it significant, the change is great and the likeness with Larkin is immediate. Larkin's *Arundel Tomb* had as its modest message, 'What will survive of us *is love*'; and *Bruno's Dream* (1969), in one of its closing scenes, resolves into: 'love still existed and it was the only thing that existed'. One is wise to recall the climactic speech of Eliot's *The Elder Statesman* (first performed 1958):

> I've only just now had the illumination
> Of knowing what *love* is ...
> ... and now I feel happy –

but again, what that play has to say about such an 'illumination' is minimal indeed.

Iris Murdoch began her professional life as a philosopher, and in *The Nice and the Good* (1967) there is indeed, through the medium of a comparatively rich novel, almost a philosophical examination of what might be meant by 'good but not nice', 'nice but not good', 'not-good and not-nice', and so on:

> That's right, Mr Honeyman ... We're getting to know each other, aren't we? Isn't that nice ...?
> – I wouldn't call it nice exactly ... Whatever it is, it isn't nice,

Goodness, we find, lies simply in kindness and also in dignity. The movement of thought is something like that in the author's ambitious philosophical essay, *The Sovereignty of Good* (1970), which begins by repudiating the 'Romantic' Idealist conception of 'Kantian Man', but seems to conclude almost by endorsing it with the simple, traditional (and Romantic) quality of *humility*. Once again, moreover, in *The Nice and the Good* comes the simple stress on love. 'She knew perfectly well, with her heart's blood as well as her mind, that loving people were the most important of all things.' *Bruno's Dream* ends on a similar note: 'being kind and good ... nothing else matters at all.' In *An Accidental Man* we are told, 'try to find a few small things that are clear'. In *Time of the Angels* (1967) this approach is by way of being made systematic. The implication of the title is that God does not exist, and so no single source of all goodness exists. There are only fragments of goodness, like isolated individual angels. These fragments are all that we can collect for ourselves: scraps, in the end, of almost proverbial wisdom about the goodness of dignity, of uprightness, of kindness. And 'the greatest of these is *caritas*' – love.

So much for 'minimal affirmation' in a time of universal uncertainty.

Intensity and the Primitive

There is another line along which writers have responded to – or perhaps against – the conditions and qualities of life over the period. As a first approximation, one could see this as a cultivation of intensity; but to a considerable extent, it has involved a distinctive kind of intensity. One might term it the intensity of the minuscule, the limited, the primitive. One can see how this reaction could develop; and once again, we are in part not looking simply at a reaction, but also at a continuity. Before the war, Dylan Thomas in his youth began one of his poems:

> The force that through the green fuse drives the flower
> Drives my green age

– the intensity simply of growth down in the world of plants. One of his last post-war pieces, *Poem on his Birthday* of about 1950, expresses a similar sense of the violent intensity of the energies of the natural world as they are reflected in the poet himself:

> He sings towards *anguish*; finches fly
>
>   In the claw tracks of hawks
> On a seizing sky; small fishes glide
>   Through wynds and shells of drowned
>
> Ship towns to pastures of otters.

Those last lines are equating energy and destructive violence. They are typical of how it is the predatory energies of Nature that the writer is drawn towards; and one may see this as not only a reaction against more indulgent (or self-indulgent) attitudes in much early twentieth-century verse, but also as a response to the unprecedently violent historical dimensions of the period. Besides this, it should surely be related to the dissemination of an outlook informed, indirectly at least, by the biological sciences and the picture that they have given us of the non-human world.

In these matters, however, one is by no means concerned with something that leaves its mark merely in the 'Dylanesque' poets of the period. Poets at almost the opposite pole of verse-writing show something of the same; and that this should be so is surely the most significant part of the story. In Gunn, for example, despite his links with coolness and rationality, these patterns of feeling are easily seen. It is actually in his 1955 poem *To Yvor Winters*, archpriest of those very qualities, that Gunn writes of:

> *Ferocity* existing in the fence
> Built by an exercised intelligence.

A similar thought comes in the later *The Annihilation of Nothing*, published in *My Sad Captains* (1961):

> ... images burst with fire
>
> Into the quiet sphere where I have bided ...

Often enough, even in Gunn's work, it is the most basic, even primitive simplicities of the natural world which manifest abundancies and energies:

> And here the mauve convulvulus falls in
> Its narrow stalk as fat and rich in sap
> As I was rich in lusting ...
> (*Merlin in the Cave* ...)

The Scots poet Norman MacCaig is a writer whose work is also often marked by a certain dry, almost philosophical austerity ('... Tree/ And star are ways of finding out what I/Mean by a text composed of earth and sky': *Ego*, in *The Sinai Sort*, 1957). But for him too, the natural environment is often of interest precisely because of its Dionysiac energies:

> I have a Spring where no flowers yawn desire
> Nor birds make bright *explosions* in the green ...
> (*In No Time at All*)

> ... the rosebushes
> Whose useless flowers get on with their
> Three weeks' *explosions* in the air.
> (*Botanic Gardens*)

> Yet the bell's voice rings clear, the fruit *explodes*
> Oddly, into fruition.
>
> (*Spring in a Clear October*)

R. S. Thomas not infrequently depicts the natural environment with a similar 'ferocity', something that implies the violent, predatory, or sexual:

> ... the sun that cracks the cheeks
> Of the gaunt sky ...
>
> (*A Peasant*)

> Lost in the world's wood
> You cannot staunch the bright menstrual blood.
> The earth sickens.
>
> (*Song at the Year's Turning*)

Four very different poets: yet this same tendency shows in them all.

Poets such as Gunn, MacCaig and R. S. Thomas are of special interest when they manifest such a tendency, because it is not typical of their work as a whole. They therefore help the reader to see he is noticing something that pervades the period, and has some point of origin deeper than what is personal to any of them.

There are, however, two notable poets who manifest this kind of writing directly and constantly: Ted Hughes and Peter Redgrove. This is not the place for a full diagnosis of Hughes' remarkable verse: but from the beginning, even the titles of his poems (*Roarers in a Ring*, *Vampire*, *Bayonet Charge*) point along the line at issue here. The first, and title, poem in Hughes' first book, *The Hawk in the Rain* (1957) immediately strikes the note of intensity, perhaps of hypertrophy:

> ... banging wind kills these stubborn hedges

> Thumbs my eyes, throws my breath, tackles my heart,
> And rain hacks my head to the bone ...

Then the poem offers a contrast to this reality: but it is simply another mode of the same thing, it is:

> the master-
> -Fulcrum of *violence* where the hawk hangs still.

The poem is not a polarity between violence and its opposite; and immediately following those lines, it imagines that the hawk:

> ... meets the weather
>
> Coming the wrong way, suffers the air, *hurled* upside down,
> Fall from his eye, the ponderous shires *crash* on him,
> The horizon trap him; the round angelic eye
> *Smashed*, mix his heart's blood with the mire of the land.

Such, in fact, are the responses repeatedly dramatized in Hughes's work:

> Love struck into his life
> Like a hawk into a dovecote.
>   (*The Dove Breeder*)
>
> I kill where I please because it is all mine
> ... my manners are tearing off heads –
>   (*Hawk Roosting: Lupercal*, 1960)

Crow (1972) is the clearest example in Hughes's writing of the poetry of intensity sustained over a considerable length, and a clear example also of how such poetry has been linked to a preoccupation with the primitive, with what might be termed *ur*-experience. The protagonist in *Crow* is a kind of primal man that is also primal life and primal fiend. Examples like the following, in every case the opening lines of individual poems in the collection, come merely from the first few pages:

> In the beginning was Scream
> Who begat blood ...
>   (*Lineage*)
>
> Flogged lame with legs
> Shot through the head with balled brains
> Shot blind with eyes
> Nailed down by his own ribs ...
>   (*A Kill*)
>
> There was this terrific battle.
> The noise was as much
> As the limits of possible noise could take.
>   (*Crow's Account of the Battle*)

There is really no need to examine the point further.

Peter Redgrove's work (Philip Hobsbaum is reputed to have called Redgrove 'the great poet of our time') has very much its own character, but there is a clear similarity to Hughes:

> I see *boiling* eyes
> And a puckered mouth *shouting* silence as I razor
> (*The Wizard's New Meeting*)

> The roses have learnt to thunder,
> They spread petals like peals of red thunder echoing,
> The sky looks like blue boxes of white powder being
> *smashed* by grey fists.
> (*Dr Faust's Sea-Spiral Spirit*)

Marie Peel, Redgrove's editor, wrote, in her introduction to his *Selected Poems* (1975): 'his mind, his whole psyche, knew with appalling intensity ...'; 'every part of him ... recorded ... with extraordinary energy'. She also saw, and stressed, the 'primal' quality in Redgrove's work: 'the poet sees and feels with small ground creatures, inhabits trees and woods and stones as well as knowing power in the deep strata below'. That in much of Hughes's writing an endless *fortissimo* becomes wearisome, that Redgrove's verse often seems prolix in content and rhythmically drab, are matters not for the moment particularly relevant. But writing of this general kind is not only very widespread: at another level one could illustrate the argument just by passages from minor writers in minor 'Little Magazines'. Also, it accords with and it manifests some significant tendencies of the time. To expand this point, one might mention a reaction against, or at least an unease with, the too-easy-affluence society (of the fifties and earlier sixties that is to say); a deep disquiet at the manifold potentials for violence visible even within a long period of general peace; and an awareness of how the natural environment is at one level profoundly different from and alien to contemporary urbanized society, while at the same time humanity itself, superficially so different, seems at heart to be just as primitive, primal, predatory, as anything in that environment.

Violence and the primitive have assumed new and special prominence in the contemporary theatre. The discussion must return to this matter, for the moment perhaps it is enough to note how Ann

Jellicoe wrote, in her Preface to the revised *The Sport of My Mad Mother* (1958; revised 1964) of how the play creates rituals, and 'a ritual generally ... excites us above a normal state of mind ... the insecure and inarticulate group of people who figure in the play depend on them so much'. This original and striking work is then full of passages like:

FAK: I'm gonna get me a great red ruby!
            Rich and bulging and bold like blood.
            Sweet thick pleasure is guttering through me
            Red! Red! Red! 'll make me feel good.

CHORUS: Killer! Killer! Killer!
            Killer! Killer! Killer!

FAK: Flash 'em in the looker and stab and sting
            Send them solid and clutch in the mick.

In the field of prose fiction, Andrew Sinclair's *Gog* (1967) amalgamates attempted intensity of response and preoccupation with violence, with a deep underlying desire to present Everyman also as Primal Man, as *Urmensch*. The sick ex-serviceman Gog's fantastic journey of native-land-discovery and self-discovery from Edinburgh to London takes him through a series of violent but often absurd incidents. He attacks female mental nurses and tries to release the patients; finds hundreds of small moles, each one impaled by the farmer on barbed wire; watches old men playing dominoes in a pub – 'the sharp click of the pieces has all the *violence* of snapping teeth'; is battered by soldiers; meets a tramp who kills a ram and eats the raw flesh which he is forced to share ('he expects to vomit, but instead he tastes a curious pleasure, flesh still warm with blood'); is forced to join a double rape; is repeatedly nearly murdered by his wife; wins a murderous forty-round prizefight; battles with the police; is keelhauled; and much else of the kind. That the cult of intensity and violence penetrates intimately into the texture of the writing is easily shown:

... running through the shivering streets with the air *sharp as a mincer* ... coarse grass with edges rough as *rusty bayonets* and beaded with the *gory dew* ...   (p. 214)

Many readers (the present writer is one) will find this continual

'Asiatic style', as Arnold would have called it, and likewise the incessant violence of incident, soon begins to pall. But in some ways *Gog* is a book of central importance; and one of these ways is how it links style and substance: what might be termed a miniaturized but hypertrophied 'Baroque' as regards style, and in substance a pre-occupation with 'primitive' sexuality or universal violence. Is it not reasonable to suggest that such a tendency to intensify, anyhow, *something*, may be one form of response to uncertainty and lost bearings?

Trends towards Fantasy

There is another respect in which *Gog* is a significant, if perhaps dubiously inviting book. Many, perhaps in the end all, of its fantastic episodes might be interpreted as dreams and nightmares rather than waking life. But even so it is a prominent example of the trend towards fantasy in post-war writing. One can of course identify fantasy-writing earlier in the century. But its prominence and importance over the present period is new, and in an allegedly great age of technological advance and materialist preoccupation this is a remarkable fact.

Unquestionably the great archetype of the work of fantasy is Wyndham Lewis's trilogy beginning with *The Childermass* published well before the Second World War, in 1928 (see *The New Pelican Guide*, Vol. 7, pp. 88-9). This immense, macabre, grotesque parody of something like the Earthly Paradise cantos in the *Divine Comedy* ends up (appropriately for the Swiftian, Menippean satire-fantasy genre to which it belongs[9]) as an elaborate, ironical portrait of various political types and forces, and is closely related to Lewis's directly political writings during the 1930s, and his conviction of the in-adequacy of 'civilized' values in a conventional sense. One of the more memorable services that the BBC Third Programme per-formed for literature was that, through the offices of Donald Bridson, it encouraged and sponsored the by now blind Lewis, and made it possible for him to write a second and third part to the work, *Monstre Gai* and *Malign Fiesta*, both of these being presented in broadcast versions, and then published together in 1955 under the title of *The Human Age*. In these later parts of the work Lewis continued the fantasy-setting of *The Childermass*, and extended it into a prolix but always powerful rendition, in contemporary terms, of Dante's *Inferno*. The traditional Limbo of the Dead becomes 'Third City', a sinister fantasy of the spacious aridity, endless vapidity and vicious manipulative politics of the modern welfare-and-affluence metropolis at its worst. As the book proceeds, its picture broadens to take in, in fantasy terms, the enduring post-war nightmare of the atomic holocaust, and the wartime nightmares also of ruthless armed violence and the long-drawn-out sadism of the concentration camps. All this is presented with vivid power and insistence, though without the relish occasionally still attributed to Lewis.[10]

Probably there is deep significance in the fact that, so far as British writing is concerned, outstandingly the most notable reflection of the Second World War is this elaborate nightmare-fantasy set in an imaginary world (though fantasies by Camus and Gunter Grass should also be borne in mind in this connection). A minor point about *The Human Age* – that it must be seen in respect of some of its incidents as a forerunner of the space-travel or indeed science-fiction vogues of the post-war years – must be mentioned; and in that context it is worth while recalling how John Cowper Powys's last books, written in his late eighties (*Up and Out*, 1957; *All or Nothing*, 1960), count at least in part as early examples of the same genre. The third part of Peake's 'Gormenghast' trilogy, *Titus Alone* (1959) is another work, by a much younger writer, reflecting in fantasy-narration some of the horrors of the time or the recent past: this disjointed farrago – Peake's illness was severe by the time he wrote it – also has clear reflections of the wartime concentration camps, and more particularly of the sewer-world of the 1944 Warsaw Rising. Nigel Dennis's *A House in Order* (1966) is another and later work of fantasy which continues to draw on the Second World War (and perhaps some of its aftermaths): this time the terrors, absurdities and vacuities of prisoner-of-war camps and interrogations.

Peake's earlier fantasy-novels have already been discussed (pp. 72–3, above), and clearly they make a contrast with *Titus Alone* in that, more traditionally, they create, in the tumbledown ramifications of the immense other-world castle in which they are set, something of a traditional fairy-tale romance landscape. On this account they may be set beside the most widely-read of all post-war fantasies,

J. R. Tolkien's *Lord of the Rings* (1954–5), with its elaborately detailed landscape, mapped out Treasure Island style. But the first two Gormenghast books and *The Lord of the Rings* also fit tellingly into other patterns of the period; for in each case, these works resolve themselves into a struggle between good and evil seen (especially, perhaps, Tolkien) in the broadest, most abstract, most simplified terms. Both reflect, therefore, that representative uncertainty in respect of values, and tendency towards minimal affirmation, which has been discussed already. At this point it is right to mention the fantasy-element in a number of Edwin Muir's late poems, and how this is also clearly a result of meditation upon the wartime world.

William Golding's novels are a special and especially interesting case, but they certainly fall within the scope of post-war fantasy-fiction. *Lord of the Flies* (1954) turns the long-established boys'-romance desert-island tale into an intense, compelling allegory of the growth and corruption of political power. *The Inheritors* (1955) is a myth-rendering of the emergence of the crude, coarse, but effective homo sapiens through genocide against the 'humane', responsive, imaginative Neanderthalers. *Pincher Martin* (1956) sees a whole life within the drowning man's moment of total recall together with nightmare-delirium (and is another work that draws for its setting on experiences of the 1939–45 war). In *Free Fall* (1959), a more realistic study of corruption, there are prominent elements of at least near-fantasy and nightmare in the prisoner-of-war sections, and *The Spire* (1964) is a legend of hubris and nemesis in the world of medieval cathedral-building. Golding's imaginative sweep (sometimes over-written) and carefully planned structuring make his work especially noteworthy; but viewed as a whole, it fits clearly into the fantasy dimension of the period.

John Fowles's *The Collector* (1963), it could be argued, keeps just within the boundaries of realism; but *The Magus* (1965) is clearly a fantasy-novel, and one also that reverts to the war years: the 'god-game' that is supposed to mature the protagonist Nicholas draws fairly extensively on the atrocities of the Nazi occupation of Greece. One may add that this novel, almost as much as any other, reflects the moral uncertainty of the period. The 'Magus' himself, Conchis (= conscience? we are told that the 'c' is soft) is alleged to be manipulating Nicholas's whole environment for profound moral ends. In fact, he quite fails to achieve any meaningful moral status himself, the whole 'god-game' fantasy turns out on reflection to be pointless and a little unsavoury, and insofar as selfhood and moral reality are indicated at all, that seems to be only in gestures of crude, primitive assertion or defiance – another form of minimal positive.

It would be easy, thinking in general terms about the vein of fantasy in the period, to connect it only with the earlier widespread desire to depart from Zola-like realism in the novel. A further factor, however, ought to be adverted to once again, and this is the abiding if often indirect presence, through almost all the fantasy-writing of the period, of the giant traumas of the Second World War. In large part, those traumatic experiences (occupation, secret police, mass terror, refugees, use of 'ultimate weapons' like the fusion bomb) became familiar horror-legends; but for the British, over the war- and post-war years, vicariously so. Their reappearance in the forms of fantasy or near-fantasy in the fiction of the time need cause no surprise. Lastly, it should be mentioned that Orwell's late fantasy-novels obviously fit in with this general account, but they are discussed at length below (see pp. 129ff.).

It is clear also that there is a dimension of fantasy in much of the dramatic writing of the period, Tom Stoppard's *Jumpers* (1972) being one example, Peter Shaffer's *The Royal Hunt of the Sun* (1965) and *Equus* (1973) being others, and *The Sport of My Mad Mother*, already referred to in another context, being yet another. So is Beckett's *Waiting for Godot* (*En Attendant Godot* was published in 1952 and first performed, in Paris, in February 1953; the English version was first published in 1954, and performed in 1955). This was in some ways the most influential play to be staged during the period. The fantasy-element in all Beckett's work, both for the theatre and in fiction, cannot possibly be overlooked, and it too manifests its close relation to the grim experiences of the war. That being said, however, with all necessary emphasis, Beckett remains to be discussed more fully at a later stage.

The Fiction of Work and the Working Class

To turn from the fantasy-writing to the realistic fiction of the post-war years is to find that this fiction assembles itself in two major dimensions; which might briefly be indicated as the fiction of work, and fiction of locality. Both are in certain respects innovations, and both are distinctive of their time.

The subject of work in fiction is of course not new. But there have been two noteworthy changes. In the first place, at least, a great deal of the fiction of earlier periods dealt with the lives of people of leisure. This is true almost entirely of such writers as Virginia Woolf, James and, one must add, Lawrence. Further back, Meredith, Thackeray and Emily Brontë are other examples. On the other hand, Hardy, Conrad and, in several of her most important novels, George Eliot, dealt largely with work as it related to their characters. Yet such a diagnosis is insufficient. The work of millers, weavers, country doctors, ship-captains, yeomen farmers and even field-workers or dairy-maids in a traditional rural society is of a distinctive kind. It is to a large extent isolated, and it is self-employed or not far short of that. Also, to a large extent, it is as good as home-employed. But in the years after 1945, a significantly new kind of work-fiction becomes prominent in the literary scene. Its newness is indicated even by the title of one of William Cooper's novels: *Memoirs of a New Man* (1966); and its character shows also in his *Scenes from Married Life* (1961), because the non-marital, working life depicted here lies in the great bureaucratic institutions of the modern city-government, the law, and also higher education. Chiefly, too, it is the institutions of the metropolis; though from Amis's *Lucky Jim* (1954) and Wain's *Hurry on Down* (1953), through C. P. Snow's *The Masters* (1951) to Malcolm Bradbury's *The History Man* (1975) and in part anyhow, Angus Wilson's *Anglo-Saxon Attitudes* (1956), the 'University Novel' has reflected another characteristic development of the time (compare also Tom Stoppard's *Jumpers*, mentioned above).

There are certain somewhat remarkable similarities running through most or all of the novels which concern themselves with the life of work in the great bureaucratic institutions. One must except Angus Wilson (*Hemlock and After*, 1953; *Anglo-Saxon Attitudes*; *The Old Men at the Zoo*, 1961; and later novels). He writes on the edge of this world, but with a range and variety, and with a sense of humour and fantasy, that mark his work out from the others. Wilson aside, one may say that these pervasive similarities seem to emerge from the fundamental nature of the subject-matter. First, since the actual work done by senior civil servants, for example, is too intricate, too confidential (at least in wartime) and simply too boring, to display at large to the general reader, the novelist writes about the personal relations between colleagues at work, rather than about the detail of the work itself, or about its long-term ends. The result is that the 'New Men' seem involved predominantly in endless half-explained negotiation or intrigue. The free play of selfhood is constantly subdued or disguised, characterization tends to become progressively more colourless, and individuals progressively find themselves absorbed into the inexorable movement of 'the System'.

These generalizations take on substance as soon as one turns to the two *romans fleuve* of this kind in the period: C. P. Snow's *Strangers and Brothers* series, from the work of that title published in 1940 to *Last Things* of 1970; and Anthony Powell's *A Dance to the Music of Time*, running from *A Question of Upbringing* (1951) to *Hearing Secret Harmonies* (1975). Snow had considerable knowledge of the workings of bureaucratic institutions, and also had a very considerable talent for vivid, varied and quite complex characterization. But repeatedly in his work there is a sense of deflation, of genuine human potential somehow cut short by the impersonally-directed milieu within which it has to live and develop. Hence, one feels as one reads, the failed or fragmentary relationships, the pervasive sense of some inability to connect, as between the private life and the public life of work. Snow's fiction reads a little like the work of a man who has deliberately, almost conscientiously, chosen to write of a milieu which is likely in part to mute some of his gifts, to leave the impression of a certain arid fragmentariness in the whole. There is a contrast with Waugh's wartime trilogy (see above, pp. 66–7), where the characters have an abundance of life (often enough, to be sure, somewhat slight in substance), perhaps actually because what they have to do is reduced to near-farce.

A Dance to the Music of Time concerns itself with the 'New Man' chiefly in its later volumes, centring on the world of wartime Whitehall; but these make the climax of the book. Powell's immense narrative, a good deal more continuous and integrated than Snow's, is by way of being a *tour de force* of a curiously negative kind: a sort of anti-Proust *roman fleuve* of deliberately Proustian dimensions, arrangement and title. In every material respect, Powell seems to intend a memorable effect by means the direct converse of all the things that are taken to secure effect in fiction. The style is unrelievedly flat, it even seems sometimes clumsy; the characters, with few exceptions, are the same, loosely integrated and colourless, the events are trivial or simply tedious, their concatenation loose and shapeless, any overall design, direction or conviction almost ostentatiously lacking. The reader becomes inclined to think that this writer aspires to hold the attention, despite a deliberate relinquishing of established means of doing so. Moreover, there is a curious way in which the endless interweavings and what might in brief be called the rich banality of the work succeed in doing exactly that. Only in the last volume does a less prosaic approach unexpectedly begin to invest the narrative with a deeper sense of the individual and a more poetic atmosphere and integration. Otherwise, both Snow and Powell show once again something spiritually drab and uncreative in their pictures of professional city life. It is not without point that a substantial body of fiction so directly concerned with a very characteristic feature of the period, the life of what has been termed the 'meritocracy', should manifest, for all its interest, this relative lack of inward life; and it accords with much that has been said already.

The Labour victory of 1945 was intimately connected with the 'Rise of the Meritocracy',[11] but another side of the same story is the increased prominence of writing 'about the working class'. It is commonly thought that much of the best-established fiction of the fifties was in fact on this theme. On closer examination, that proves to a surprising degree questionable. What repeatedly proves to be the case is that the writing is ostensibly about working-class life, but that in reality it keeps turning into studies of withdrawal from that: as if such life were lacking in intrinsic interest. Many will know that that cannot be true. But, as with the detail of work in the higher civil service, a problem arises for the writer. The constant challenge and skill collectively encountered in much proletarian labour is something not easily known about in detail, nor easily presented to the reader, by one who becomes a writer. Moreover, the very distinctive men's-world humour (at least until very recently), and the raillery and racy language of manual workers, runs athwart the love–sex–marriage tradition of the novel; and the great part played by reminiscence, anecdote and childhood memories, often linking the city working-man back to quite other and more traditional environments, would not have suited the 'tough' and polemical stance in general taken up by the new novelists.

Be that as it may, the fact remains that the working-class fiction of the fifties recurrently deals, in the end, with one mode or another of *release* from, or evasion of, working-class life, rather than with the staple of it. Alan Sillitoe's *Saturday Night and Sunday Morning* (1958) is a vivid if very negative picture of drab squalor in a grimly hostile working-class environment; but the resolution of the novel is the way in which its (odious) 'hero' begins to move away from that jungle-like milieu through marriage and through becoming a charge-hand. John Braine's artisan hero Joe Lampton in *Room at the Top* (1957) makes a similar transition, and finds his working-class dis-satisfactions resolved by marrying the boss's daughter – a traditional escape-route. In Stan Barstow's *Ask Me Tomorrow* (1962), the young hero begins in a typical working-class household, but soon moves out of it because he is trying to become a writer. Arthur, the central figure in David Storey's *This Sporting Life* (1960) declines, when he reaches a corresponding point of success, to quit the working-man's life for a job in business; but this time the situation is different, or rather, it never was a characteristic working-class situation after all. Arthur is a Rugby League professional, someone in a peculiar and violent kind of 'show-biz', another and distinctive kind of near-fantasy-world. One novel of the period, Keith Waterhouse's *There is a Happy Land* (1957) actually rehearses this 'passage rite' in symbolic terms: the novel's working-class housing-estate children find a long conduit under the road, and the novel ends when, exploring this, they at last climb out at the other end and find themselves in a comfortable middle-class estate.

Sillitoe's short stories display the trend in another way. The 'long-distance runner'[12] himself is a working-class Borstal boy who becomes a criminal . . . but also a writer. Other stories in the collection depict working-class men locked in untypical isolation ('Uncle Ernest', 'Mr Raynor'), a suicide ('On Saturday Afternoon'), or a mental defective ('Frankie Buller'). Stan Barstow's short stories (*The Desperadoes*, 1961) follow a similar course: a workman and a gipsy fortune-teller ('Freestone at the Fair'), a life-long brass band enthusiast, a pathological gambler ('Gamblers Never Win'), someone with a strange power over the local bull, amateur dramatics, a rabbit-breeding enthusiast, another mental defective, and so on. Once again, in the majority of cases the central characters are deeply untypical of working-class life, because they are peripheral to it or have escaped from it or are 'drop-outs' from it.

'Working-Class' Drama

This tendency for writing to begin in a working-class context but then to move out from it, or to take not typical but peripheral working-class settings as its subject-matter, shows also in the dramatic writing of the period. John Arden's *Live Like Pigs* (Royal Court, 1958) is set in a working-class housing estate, but the mass of society is depicted as arid and destructive, with the real qualities of life to be seen only in the outsiders – tinkers, gipsies. Wesker's trilogy (*Chicken Soup with Barley*, 1958; *Roots*, 1959; *I'm Talking about Jerusalem*, 1960), one of the most celebrated theatrical achievements of the late fifties, and also another landmark of provincial writing and theatre, since all its parts were first put on at the Belgrade Theatre, Coventry, moves in the same direction. In *Roots*, Wesker's basic idea is of the atrophying horrors of the unimproved, uneducated, 'mindless' life of lower-class people, and the value and indeed nobility of those who (like Beattie in the play) struggle to become self- and also politically-conscious. This is what we are invited to see in Beattie, helped as she is by the articulate and aware working-class élite figure, Ronnie, in the background. But after the lapse of time, Beattie's uplifting affirmations now seem pompous, meddling and vacuous; and the characters who have wit, good sense, command of language and a genuine group life are the uneducated and unambitious 'locals' of the (doubtless slightly sentimentalized) rural society that Beattie moves into.

Lawrence's plays of *c*. 1910 are of great significance here: they offer a reader the decisive contrast. *A Collier's Friday Night*, or *The Widowing of Mrs Holroyd*, were plays set in typical working-class environments, not peripheral ones; and what they focus attention on is the direct and strong emotions of typical characters in times of crisis for them, and the way that such crises transform and deepen those who pass through them. Wesker's picture, with Beattie's insistence on 'love [i.e., making love] in the afternoon', and with the house that was originally to be a place of back-to-the-land subsistence and self-emancipation being eventually salvaged as a holiday home, is in reality deeply middle-class, not genuinely working-class at all.

Doris Lessing's *Each His Own Wilderness* (Royal Court, 1958) illustrates the point another way. All but two of the characters are once again not typical working-class: they are intellectuals, whether working-class ones on the international left-wing conference circuit or not. It is the two younger-generation characters who want to settle for 'being an electrician' instead of travelling around or getting degrees, who want to settle for life on (as they themselves call it) 'ordinary' terms; and the play ends with precisely this being made to seem the difficult thing. Peter Terson's *The Mighty Reservoy* (Victoria Theatre, Stoke-on-Trent, 1964), one of the finest of all post-war plays, has in it only a somewhat unstable office-clerk, son of a miner, and a lonely, heavy-drinking nightwatchman. The play is set entirely at the nightwatchman's isolated shack on top of the reservoir; and once again, it sounds the note at least of near-fantasy. Giles Cooper's *The Object*, which was originally a Third Programme radio play (1964) deals with an extremely poor, Beckett-like elderly couple, outcasts from society, living in a shack by a railway line where a spacecraft unexpectedly lands. Both of these works again illustrate the tendency to select peripheral or anomalous rather than typical proletarian settings. Pinter's *The Caretaker* (1960) also moves into the world of drop-outs or near drop-outs, and displays its author's characteristic powers of investing the drabbest realism with fantasy and strangeness (see also below, p. 117).

The Provinces: and the 'Periphery'

All in all, it is not easy to conclude that taking provincial life, or more particularly working-class life, as genuinely and funda-mentally the material for fiction over the post-war years has been wholehearted. John Braine's *Life at the Top* (1962) has a chapter in which the 'hero' expresses, at length, his deep intuitive attachment to his native (northern) town; but one cannot claim that the place itself and its regional distinctiveness play any substantial part in the novel. Often, there seems to be a much deeper attachment, of a nostalgic kind, to the time of *childhood* – on which northernness is merely superimposed. In Barstow's *Ask Me Tomorrow* the heroine returns, but with a certain arbitrariness, from her smart London job to the northern town where she was born and where she spent her childhood. *Life at the Top* in fact closes with the hero, when other relationships have failed him, finding fulfilment in the deep bond that he enjoys with his infant daughter. Waterhouse's *There is a Happy Land* is a book-length celebration of childhood nostalgia. Snow's *Strangers and Brothers* series starts (as did its author) in a Northern town, but moves on to life in London. Then, in *Homecomings* (1956) the warring adults are brought finally together in the healing of a sick child. Barry Hines' *Kestrel for a Knave* finds only barrenness in the adult life of a northern working-class housing-estate, but beautifully evokes the deep, secret, archaic relation that a solitary boy might create, Richard-Jefferies-wise, with a 'pet' hunting-hawk. All these works, and others, display in one way or another the sense of an escape into childhood out of an unrewarding adult environment. (One must note, of course, that there are books like Susan Hill's *I'm the King of the Castle*, 1970, or Muriel Spark's *The Prime of Miss Jean Brodie*, 1961, which present childhood in quite different terms.) All the works which have just been discussed recall the closing sequence of *Look Back in Anger*; and these celebrations of childhood are also part of how, over this period, writers have found fully adequate affirmations of life difficult, and have looked about for palliating, limited solutions instead.

From the point of view of sheer quality in writing, there has been a more important development than the fiction about the North of England. In the United Kingdom as a whole, there are probably greater differences of life and culture (at least until very recent decades) between the metropolis and its environs, or the large cities, and the extreme periphery of the north and west and their islands, than in any other European country save the USSR. Few recent literary developments have been more striking than the emergence of distinguished writing from the remote rural north of England, from the Highlands, the Northern Islands or the Western Isles, and rural Wales or Ulster. One may relate this to improved communications or to educational changes; but it seems also to reflect the increasing cultural uncertainties of metropolitan-centred experience, or – more perhaps – the strength and distinctiveness of life and work today, as well as the traditions of the past and the relative integrity of the environment, in what retains links with the archaic periphery of the country.

This has chiefly shown in respect of poetry. Basil Bunting has no doubt been deeply indebted to Pound in matters of style; but his terse, anfractuous free verse largely gains its textured stoniness from fidelity to the experience of his native Northumberland:

> Silver blades of surf
> fall crisp on rustling grit,
> shaping the shore as a mason
> fondles and shapes his stone.
> Shepherds follow the links,
> sweet turf studded with thrift;
> fell-born men of precise instep
> leading demure dogs
> from Tweed and Till and Teviotdale.

Briggflatts, the long poem from which those lines come, was not published until 1966, though begun earlier. It is the hard lines of that northern landscape, enriched by the poet's sense of its continuities with the sixth-century saints of the Farne Islands, or with Welsh poetry of the 'Dark' Ages and with the Vikings, that created the style in which Bunting wrote, with comparable distinction, of Italy or Japan.

The Orkneyman Edwin Muir was writing verse before the war, but most of his best work was produced only in the 1950s. The pure, austere lyric verse of this last decade of his life fuses an Orcadian scene such as had often appeared in his early verse, with a vision of war-haunted archaic pastoralism that united the Orkneys with Odysseus's Ithaca and with the mythology of Heroic Greece. Larkin's stanzas, recurrently closing with a movement of deflation, self-insurance, limitedness, were mentioned earlier. Muir's almost visionary hope-fulness and exploratory imagination focuses itself exactly otherwise: in the poems of his later years, the closing lines of stanzas, paragraphs or complete poems follow an opposite pattern:

> Past every choice to boundless good.
> (*Orpheus' Dream*)

> Saw far and near the fields of Paradise.
> (*Milton*)

> ... the great Roman roads that go
> Striding across the untrodden sky.
> (*Day and Night*)

> Standing on earth, looking at Heaven.
> (*Outside Eden*)

What the reader finds here is less a closing, than something that opens out into new, deeper, wider experience.

Muir's visionary limpidity is by way of being a rare sport among the writing of the period; and something of this may be easily seen by comparing him to George Mackay Brown, the other Orcadian, a generation younger, who also illustrates the importance of writing from the periphery of the United Kingdom. Brown, too, is very much conscious of the Orkney life of toil on the farm or the sea and, like Bunting, he vividly sees the continuity of that life with the saga-world of the Vikings. But his work also instantiates, forcefully, the drive towards a sometimes almost strained intensity. He writes:

> ... in the *fire* of images
> Gladly I put my hand
> (*Hamnavoe*)

Hence, such phrases as 'steel-kissed cobbles', 'gale of psalms', 'black-tongued bells'. Close study of Brown's renderings from Old Norse Saga-verse shows him steadily moving away from the terse reserve and dignified plainness of the original, towards a vivid, even sometimes galvanically sensuous concreteness. It is no surprise to find an admiring reference to Leavis (see above, p. 80) in one of Brown's occasional prose pieces, and his work as a whole – poetry, short stories, the novel *Greenvoe* (1972) – integrates with wider influences pervading the period also in this way: that Brown is clearly thinking in terms of *documenting* the distinctive society of which he writes. His vivid individualization is in part a kind of social study or very superior kind of literary reportage, with analogues in the fields of journalism, the TV or radio feature, and the documentary film. In this context it is worth recalling that the first British documentary film, *Man of Aran*, in the thirties, indeed depicted life in the island-periphery of the Irish North-West.

There is no need to discuss in detail all the poets of the periphery. Suffice it simply to mention the Highland poets Ian Crichton Smith and Sorley MacLean (the latter's poems are translated from the Gaelic); the way in which Ted Hughes has also celebrated the harsh life of the rural north and also west of England in *Season Songs* (1976); the earlier verse of Seamus Heaney, with its rich though cold evocation of labour and hard living in rural Ulster (Heaney's later, more political verse on the situation in the North of Ireland is discussed elsewhere, see below, pp. 380ff.); and along with Heaney, the work of another Ulster poet, Derek Mahon. Finally, one should notice the distinguished verse (in English) evocative of rural Wales, written by Anglo–Welsh poets like R. S. Thomas (see pp. 209ff.), or the modest, crisp elegance of Raymond Garlick (e.g., *Incense*, 1976); the magazine *Poetry Wales* is another pointer in the same direction.

David Jones's position is more complex. Speaking generally, his position in relation to Joyce is comparable to that of Bunting to Pound (Jones says that he became familiar with the work of Pound and Eliot after he had formed his own style); *The Anathemata* (1952), probably the most ambitious poem to appear in the United Kingdom since the war, covers a field altogether wider than Wales alone, but in its (excessively) elaborate attempt[13] to retrieve earlier Celtic mythology and history as background to the Great Britain of the present, Jones's position is to a certain extent comparable with that of Bunting or, more fundamentally though his verse forms are so different, with Muir. In this Welsh context, one should also recall Richard Hughes's late fiction, (see p. 67, above).

Samuel Beckett, (see also above, pp. 114–15) whose earliest work is of course pre-war, has spent most of his active writing life in France, and his disturbingly absurdist, experimental, avant-garde achievement will need to be considered later. His black portraits of poverty, meaninglessness and dereliction could well have been discussed along with other writing that is more obviously in the fantasy-genre. Beckett directly or indirectly recalls the European horrors of 1939–1945 (and before, and after). But Beckett's material is profoundly such that there is justice in thinking of him along with writers of the northern and western 'periphery'. This is not of course to deny that, seen *in toto*, his work is a notable cosmopolitan and avant-garde creation; but Beckett's world in novels like *Molloy* (1955) or *Malone Dies* (1956) is not Irish through the characters' names alone. Rural Ireland of the earlier twentieth century, with the 'Troubles' and the economic war, and with its rural destitution of the inter-war years – or later, it could well be argued – makes up their staple. This appears unmistakably in their treatment of old age, indigence, physical disablement, aimless misery and endless verbalization, whether in isolated dialogue or in solitude. *Malone Dies*, studied closely, shows that no one could be intended to overlook the Irish world it is based upon ('hills ... raise themselves gently, faintly blue, out of the confused plain. It was there somewhere he was born'; 'a summit called the Rock ... From here a fine view was to be obtained of the plain, the sea, the mountains'; 'the wind blew almost without ceasing'; 'a genuine English park, though far from England'; 'in the hope of chancing ... on a tree, or a ruin'; there is also the recurrent refrain-phrase 'caught by the rain far from shelter'). *All that Fall* (1957) is explicitly rural-Irish; and in general, more than the landscape, it is the human (or inhuman) predicament of the characters that epitomizes, again and again, the self-caricaturing wretchedness and isolation of the old and lonely in pre-affluent rural Ireland. There, ready made, Beckett could find material for his black comedy and his endless games with language.[14] Nor is Beckett the only example of rural Irish material providing the basis for sophisticated literary experimentation. Flann O'Brien's very different fiction also reflects other aspects of a similar reality.

Among writers of the 'periphery', Beckett certainly stands out for his originality, inventiveness and an almost terrifyingly cumulative power. But a number of the writers discussed have been, in one way or another, figures of distinction; and one sees at once how novel is their position, if one thinks back even to the 1920s, still more the 1900s, and considers who might be the corresponding figures of those decades.

It is time briefly to recapitulate the several literary trends which have been traced in this essay as responses to the challenge and perplexity of the post-war years. These have included the attempt to safeguard and assert some *minimal* area of experience or insight; the *intensification* of some small and limited area so that it assumes a new or fundamental potency; substitution of *fantasy* for reality, either as a complete substitute, or as creating a manageable surrogate for it and its interpretation; realism in attempts to develop for writing hitherto *neglected areas* of experience (say, working-class life) – attempts that have often proved self-defeating or atavistic; and the greater prominence of writing from, or at least representing, the geographical *periphery* of this country. Those are five trends which the preceding pages have summarily explored, and they may all be seen, in their various ways, as pointers towards the indeterminateness, fluidity and uncertainty of a great deal of the post-war scene.

Experiments in Drama

Some of the developments reviewed above may be traced in especially interesting forms in the drama and theatre of the period. From the middle fifties on, the theatre has manifested quite distinctive features of its own, which in part have set it in a position of contrast to other forms of writing, and have made theatre a natural bridge towards the new tendencies coming into English writing generally, from the later sixties on. In this context, the sensational success of Beckett's *Waiting for Godot*, played in London in 1955 shortly after its first performance in Paris in French, was a landmark. *Waiting for Godot* happened to bring together several hitherto independent trends. It established on the English stage the Continental Existentialism that had already attracted much respectful interest-at-a-distance from English readers. Its non-realist mode of presentation called at one and the same time on the more academic, history-based interests in theatrical possibilities of non-illusionism, and on the more politically or socially inspired reaction in the fifties against earlier dramatists like Coward or Rattigan. Certainly in *Waiting for Godot* may be found several of the responses which have been surveyed, across the post-war scene above. There is fantasy in the almost lunar landscape and the endless recurrence of action; there is Beckett's own very distinctive 'peripheralism' in the poverty, isolation, narrowness, and occasional hypertrophy of talk; there is a kind of intensity-reaction in the constant threats of violence or resorts to it; and in sequences like the following there is a certain clear if minimal affirmation, though of course some terrible indictment and perhaps a mocking disillusion as well:

VLADIMIR : We've arrived.
POZZO   : Who are you?
VLADIMIR : We are men.
           Silence.
ESTRAGON: Sweet Mother Earth!

But *Waiting for Godot* must be seen as one prominent landmark in a whole theatrical landscape.

The London 'Fringe' theatres have made a noteworthy contribution to the post-war scene, both for quality and for experimentalism (Fringe theatres also existed between the wars), and they well illustrate how avant-gardisme in theatre can come into being for practical, as easily as for strictly dramatic reasons. Over a pub (the King's Head Theatre), in a basement (the Basement, the Open Space Theatre), a converted synagogue (the Half Moon) or train-shed (the Roundhouse) – those are all locations making proscenium-arch theatre impracticable, and flexible layouts, varied for each production, as well as active audience participation, not only easy but natural and almost unavoidable.[15]

One striking thing about post-war theatre, in fact, is the many ways in which staging and practical problems integrate themselves with more far-reaching matters of attitude or psychology. Thus the violence of the incestuous rape scene in David Mowat's *Phoenix and Turtle* (Open Space Theatre, 1972) is far more savage and convincing in the confined space and non-illusionist decor ('Bare stage. One chair. Unvaried lighting throughout') than it would seem before a typical pre-war West End set. The homicide and suicide in Edgar's *Two Kinds of Angel* (Basement Theatre, 1971) together make the culmination of fantasy-sequences where the two young women characters are momentarily transformed into, respectively, Rosa Luxemburg and Marilyn Monroe.

Those transformations may at the same time be seen as metaphors of post-Freudian psychological (psychiatric) analysis. That is so because the play is representative of a great deal of the character-study of recent drama, where the individual's inward-turning fantasy-world takes over from reality and in the end frustrates communication. Dialogue becomes predominantly a manifestation of how characters are isolated from their fellows. William Trevor's 'Fringe' play *A Perfect Relationship* is an example; John Whiting's *The Devils* (Aldwych, 1961) depicts, ostensibly as diabolic possession, split personality, schizophrenia and the private fantasy-world as well as manifesting a dimension of violence in its hideous torture-scene. Harold Pinter's *Landscape* and *Night* (first performed 1968, 1969) are other studies in non-communication and private fantasy; the former, since its first performance was on the BBC, is a reminder that radio drama with its greater and more fundamental departures from illusionist stage presentation has contributed substantially to the dramatic innovatoriness of the period. The almost total darkness throughout Barry Bermange's *No Quarter* (1962), the anonymous voice parts ('they have a stylized, bodiless quality and should give if possible the impression of one composite mind', wrote the author), as likewise the disembodied piano-playing in Alan Sharp's *The Long-Distance Piano Player* (1962) are other examples.

Innovation in television drama naturally depends more upon use of the camera, as in the space-travel sequences presenting David's dreams to us in John Mortimer's *David and Broccoli*, or the panoramic shots depicting youthful vice or violence punctuating the domestic interiors in John Hopkins's *A Game – Like – Only a Game*.[16] The distinctive possibilities of radio drama had of course been exploited somewhat before these plays in Beckett's *All that Fall*, where much of the humour results from sound effects requiring to be interpreted by the audience in the absence of either visual or, often enough, even dialogue-information; and the constantly rising wind and rain, supplemented only by our imaginations, contribute to a typical sense of harsh remoteness and hostile environment.

Also it is easily possible to over-estimate Beckett's originality as an Expressionist or Absurdist dramatist in English. Stark horror, violence, anti-realism and black Expressionist fantasy are to be found, much along Beckett lines in fact, in the figures of Hanp, Arghol and Hotshepsot (the names are eloquent) in Wyndham Lewis's *Enemy of the Stars*. The dialogue version of this dates from 1932 (it was not, of course, broadcast), and a prose fantasy-version from as early as 1914. All the same, *Waiting for Godot* was not a forgotten work like Lewis's, but a major commercial success, and a major landmark in a whole theatrical scene that followed it and its lead.

The two most interesting British dramatists of the past twenty-five years both show continuities with Continental drama, but also show a movement away from the insular preoccupations and traditions that characterize, as with verse and fiction, much writing for the stage over the course of the fifties. Harold Pinter has opted for a terse, minimal language in his dialogue, contrasting with the often florid, copious, language-game dialogue of Ionesco; but his work often recalls Ionesco's in other respects. From his earliest plays (*The Birthday Party*, 1958, first produced in Cambridge, and *The Caretaker*, 1960, first at the near-Fringe Arts Theatre Club), Pinter's plays have been remarkable for their unnerving repetitions, flair for switching dialogue into absurdist ritual with undertones of violence, bewildering inconsistencies in what the characters say, scenes where non-communication between the actors is more significant than communication, and kaleidoscopic transitions between dialogue, half-soliloquy and dream-world isolation. *A Night Out* (1961) was particularly striking for its interweaving of fantasy, decorousness and brutality. *Landscape* and *Night* are both at first sight near-absurdist fugues of schizophrenic daydream and isolation, but the absurdism modulates into hauntingly convincing pictures of the irremediable horrors of long-continued unsuccessful intimacy. The all-male *No Man's Land* (1975) is a near-comic version of much the same dramatic and linguistic procedures. Pinter, here and elsewhere, exploits and celebrates cliché so as to make of it, in the first place, effective verbal pyrotechnic, but then behind this, something that leaves a memorable sense of human reality and suffering. With Pinter's work in general, the literary scene in Britain went a certain distance towards resuming the path of internationalism, experimentalism and non-realism of the earlier part of the century. Pinter's plays have more solidity than Ionesco's to the extent that, repeatedly, their unrealism turns, Dostoyevsky-like to a certain extent, into a deeper representation, schematic but searching all the same, of the strangeness of reality.

In Edward Bond's plays, also, there is a seemingly loose, episodic and far from rigidly consistent 'story-line'; and the individual characters often display something like the 'allotropic states' that Lawrence described as more real than conventional realism (see

The New Pelican Guide, Vol. 7, pp. 94–8). Such qualities serve very different purposes from anything to be found in Pinter, and while Bond too has roots in Continental drama and thought, his plays do not take us back towards Ionesco and the Theatre of the Absurd, but to the contemporary European Socialist consciousness and to the 'epic theatre' of Berthold Brecht. Bond's plays are probably the first literary works in English to display not a working-class but a thoroughly politicized and whole-heartedly socialist, essentially revolutionary consciousness. 'Like most people' (the words are consciously polemical of course) 'I am a pessimist by experience, but an optimist by nature', he writes in the 'Author's Note' to *Saved* (1965). The notorious stoning of a baby in its pram in the course of this play; the ravages, grim punishments, and executions of *Narrow Road to Deep North* (1968) and its retelling in *The Bundle* (1978); the girl driven half-insane by public flogging and finally hanged in *Bingo* (1971); and the endless persecutions of *Lear* (1972), all testify to Bond's near-obsessive preoccupation with violence.

But above all he is preoccupied with political violence, the outrages of those in power against the poor and helpless (whether peasants, women, children or victims of whatever kind). Over and over, Bond sees organized society as gigantic legalized brutality sustained throughout history, and resisted only by the simple, bedrock, minimal affirmation of human goodness. 'Len, the chief character, is naturally good ... but ... not wholly good or easily good', Bond writes of *Saved*. For Bond, realism in the older sense is not enough. 'Effect no longer follows cause, judgement no longer assesses deed, as they did in the past. The interpretation is counterfeited by society' ('A Note on Dramatic Method', *The Bundle*, 1978). 'This means' (he goes on) 'that our moral sanity is at stake ... it is simply that we have to rewrite human consciousness.' That such views, in all probability, can as easily be destructive as salutary, that Bond's politics are utopian and his moral affirmations deeply felt but essentially minimal, are points clear enough.

We live in a time of great change. It is easy to find monsters – and as easy to find heroes. To judge rightly what is good – to choose between good and evil – that is all that it is to be human

is the final speech of *The Bundle*. 'There is a counter-culture ready

and it's been developing for hundreds of years: it is democracy':
those are the closing words of the Introduction to *Bingo*. One cannot
but be reminded of the devoutly held but minimal value-assertions
of works as remote from Bond as *Bruno's Dream* and the rest (see
above, pp. 92–3).

Bond is a significant figure not only because of the intrinsic interest
of his deeply-felt and humane work, but because he embodies, as
perhaps no other writer of the sixties and seventies, some of the
distinctively insular traits of the writing of the time, along with
qualities that represent the growing strength of Continental influences and traditions, as they begin to return to the literary scene in
Britain in the later years of the post-war period. There is no need to
stress how this development coincides in time with Britain's entry into
the EEC, abandonment of the roles that many had wished for in the
fifties, and general decline from the 'never-had-it-so-good' epoch into
the growing inflation and evanescing affluence of the 1970s.

The 'Literature of Language': Post-Critical Criticism

The anti-cosmopolitan trends of the 'fifties went parallel with
Britain's years of disillusionment, withdrawal from Europe, and
apparent conviction of insular (if not imperial) self-sufficiency in the
political field. The debacle of Suez (1956) and retreat from Cyprus
in the later 1950s were turning-points, and the slowly growing British
awareness of how other Western European nations were, of all things,
proving to be better organized in respect of industrial production
and economic organization, tended in the same direction. In the early
'sixties Britain tried to enter the West European Common Market,
and was rejected. She succeeded in doing so at a second attempt
some years later, and the end of an era of would-be material self-
sufficiency not unnaturally coincided, more or less, with a period
during which the literary scene showed clear signs of returning
Continental influences.

The same trends as have already been discussed in respect of Pinter
and Ionesco, or Bond and Brecht, have shown in recent years in
the field of the novel, and more recently still in literary criticism.
The most fundamental and pervasive shift has been, at one and the
same time, a shift away from traditional modes of fiction purporting

objectively and reliably to record, chronicle-fashion, an external reality; and a growing interest in language for its own sake, with its own inner hierarchy of sub-languages and its own system, self-generative and not determined by an external world, of conventions. Moreover, this latter shift of interest has reinforced, as it has seemed to explain and to justify, the former one. Christine Brooke-Rose's *Such* (1966) projects the fantasy-trend in recent fiction to a dazzling extreme of science-fiction ideas mingled with endless wordplay and linguistic (or indeed diagrammatic) virtuosity; her *Thru* (1975), an even more remarkable linguistic pyrotechnic, flashing in all directions the influences of Saussure, Barthes, and other recent linguistic-critical thinking in France (where the author has lived for many years). Alan Sheridan's *Vacation* (1972) shows affinity with recent French fiction (Robbe-Grillet in particular) and manifests its author's interest not only in contemporary French theoretical writing but also in 'chosiste' developments in fiction which have contributed to the 'documentary' novel: B. S. Johnson's *See the Old Lady Decently* (1975) allegedly deploys authentic letters and documents to part-constitute its narrative, his *House Mother Normal* (1971) depicts the lives of inmates in a geriatric home in the form of a series of dossiers on the occupants and finally one on the matron, who wrote up the others. Alan Burns's *Dreamerika* (1972) conducts its narrative through newspaper headlines and news items. Ann Quin's *Passages* (1969) juxtaposes the events of a fantasy- and torture-riddled experience in a country rather like the Greece of the 'Colonels' with notes of classical Greek painted vases that, in generic form, mirror the events of the novel. Her *Tripticks* (1972) uses headlines, statistical data ('520 muscles ... $18\frac{1}{2}$ inch big arms ... 52 inch heroic chest', the hero enjoys) and illustrations, intimately integrated into the text, which are in the style of a sex or thriller strip-cartoon – or perhaps one should say, caricaturing such styles, but the reader really has a free choice in that matter. In works like these, the 'media' influence of the popular press and of film and radio and T V are of course clearly to be seen.

In poetry, there has been a very different but nevertheless related development, one based also on a new predominance of concern for the language of the work: concrete verse. Of this international movement Ian Hamilton Finlay and Edwin Morgan, active at least since the early 1960s, have probably been the chief exponents in Britain. Concrete verse may be compared to film or TV in one respect, since it effects a kind of marriage between the visual and the lexical: sometimes by collage, sometimes by experimental typography, sometimes, indeed, by utilizing the technical resources of the typewriter for purely visual patterning where lexical meaning is blurred or even absent. It has also utilized the potentialities of, for example, the cassette recording, to effect a similar link between spoken language and non-vocal sound; the result being known (in a phrase appropriating rather too much) as 'sound poetry'. Morgan's concrete verse has certainly succeeded, from time to time, in evoking deep feeling from what at first sight could be taken merely for ingenious pattern-making.

It is easy, maybe too easy, to relate these various forms of writing to a broad social and cultural picture; as also, more specifically, to recent influences in criticism or rather in critical theory. A trend towards what might well be termed 'the literature of language', a verbal copiousness and ingenuity that demand to be liberated from notions of chronicling 'reality', is one not unnatural response both to ampler technical resources (typewriter, audio equipment, offset-litho printing and much else of the kind) and to an external world that seems over-complex, baffling and dispiriting. B. S. Johnson's remarks about his own writing are sometimes enigmatical, but when he says, 'I am not trying to set a puzzle ... but randomness, chaos is not neat and tidy', or again, 'It may be that all is chaos', one sees signs of that kind of response. Again, it could be said that rather as 'Art for Art's Sake' in the 1880s and 1890s was a reflection of late-Victorian prosperity and opulence, so the 'literature of language' of the past decade or so is a reflection of the affluent society and of Welfare State security. After nearly forty years, some of the horrors of the war period have in a sense been assimilated: enough at least for them to serve now, in the first place, as material for sophisticated literary experiment. The language in which humanity once recorded one of its most terrible convulsions loses its reference, and comes to enjoy an intrinsic validity, in the linguistic games and manoeuvres that may be executed within it. Some may find this cause for sorrow or even a certain outrage, but it may also be seen as a sign of self-renewing human vitality.

'Deconstructionist' criticism, stemming largely from the work of Jacques Derrida (French by origin, but long chiefly resident in the USA) also rejects the idea of a definitive meaning or message in the literary work, a meaning under the control of the author and sent by him, about external reality, to the reader. Rather, he asserts that criticism invites the reader to create meaning, *ad lib.*, in a joyous and endless play-encounter with the text. Again, it is easy to connect this with the security of university life in the expansionist period of the sixties and earlier seventies, and to see how overturning the decisive authority of either the author, or his subject in reality, or indeed the interpretative critic, could be welcome to those wishing to reject the paternalistic dominance of capitalist society, the male gender, traditional morality or literary convention.

Two things, however, are likely to leave the reader with a certain disquiet. The first is that anything in the nature of game within the world of language, brilliant, dazzling and engrossing as it may be, is also, necessarily, self-sealing. That is a fundamental of the case. It is why game-playing is inexhaustibly available to us – the more a game offers inexhaustible variety, the better – but also why even the most momentous game is momentous only as it is being played or perhaps replayed. Maybe this is ultimately why the 'literature of language', even at its best, leaves in the end a certain feeling of triviality, a peripheral quality in respect of values (not in the sense in which that word was used earlier, for the geographical perimeter). Even the endless sardonic deflations and logical *bouleversements* of Beckett's *The Unnamable* (English version 1958) leave, once one is familiar with them, a feeling of strange and distressing near-triviality.

The other matter to consider is how an insistence on ostentatiously dismissing traditional values as empty, can in the end obliterate all sense of value whatever; even in writing which contrives to aim at social comment or which combines that with literature-of-language interests. On the whole this is so of the interminable formalized sex in Ian McEwan's novels or short stories (e.g., *First Love, Last Rites*, 1976; *In Between the Sheets*, 1978), or the four-letter-word and skit-strip-cartoon preoccupations of *Tripticks*. Johnson's *House Mother Normal*'s climactic pornographic pyrotechnics for the benefit of the matron and on a stage in front of the senile inmates effaces the real plight of old age in a furore of black farce; if we are told that to say this is to miss a powerful metaphor, an allegory of capitalist brutality, we have to reply that some allegory deflects more than it directs, and if we are told that we are failing to respond to a language-game, there remains the problem of art that trivializes the serious affairs of life. To turn from such works as those to, say, Jean Rhys's *Wide Sargasso Sea* (1968), is to find how the experimentalism of the twenties and thirties, used again after long silence by this writer of genius at the end of her life, and of as remote a subject and setting as the West Indies in the 1830s, can still fuse linguistic brilliance with hauntingly yet richly topical reference back to 'reality'. Something of the same could be said of Muriel Spark's later books: *The Public Image* (1968); *The Driver's Seat* (1970); *Not to Disturb* (1971), being among them. In these works there is sexuality, violence and social chaos, but it does not obtrude and monopolize because of a rapier-like precision and economy of style: not 'deconstructive', but constructive of a decisive total effect and meaning.

As this account of the 'literary scene' draws to a close, the writer finds himself most conscious of its omissions. More needs to have been said about developments in the 'literary language' – English has not, on balance, gained through having become the medium of world bureaucracy and commercialism – and about the use of the spoken language on radio and television and the changes that have resulted. That would also call for a discussion of the growing institutionalization of the speaking of poetry, the growth of the 'reading circuit', and the effects of these changes on recent verse and in turn upon 'little magazines'. More needs to have been said about para-literary forms like science fiction, the detective story, and the impact of the latter, at least, on certain aspects of critical theorizing and also practice. More certainly needs to have been said about the writing (to a noteworthy extent, in the form of fiction) which has come out of the recent Women's Movement: in fact, the writer has reluctantly left this aside, precisely because his own limitations and the space available would have foredoomed his comments to a seemingly 'patronizing' brevity. Above all, perhaps, there is an omission in regard to the many important writers who have appeared, and in some cases acquired high reputation, in Commonwealth or ex-Commonwealth countries (Patrick White is discussed at length, in a later chapter, by the present writer, pp. 147ff.). This seems inevitable, however, if condensation is not to be taken to the point of absurdity. Writers of the stature of White, Naipaul, Soyinka and others can in no way be seen as part of the 'literary scene' of the United Kingdom: their setting is largely or entirely elsewhere, and they must be so considered. Here it is possible only to notice the immense richness, variety and indeed vitality of this great body of overseas writing in English, and to note that there is no reason why, in the future or indeed in the present, it should not offer, in its entirety, greater interest and value than what emerges 'at home'.

All in all, it is not easy – no, it is not possible – to see the period of this review as one of the major periods of English writing; or to set it on any kind of parity with the earlier years of the century. There is no need to stress that there has been much originality and inventiveness, nor how most notable works in fiction, theatre and poetry have seen the light. For all that, to recall the great figures of the early years of the century is to decide that something has been generally wanting in the later years. In brief, it seems fair to sum up by saying that the period leaves the student with a growing conviction that while the need has been felt for fundamentally new starts – a new use of language, a new sense of values and of the literary work, a response to profoundly if evasively new general conditions of experience – all the same, that has gone along with uncertainty, with an inability wholly to adapt or to solve the problems and difficulties, as if these have been just too great for those who confronted them. The result has been a fairly pervasive disposition to settle for some partial solution or to be preoccupied with what has in some way, unobtrusively, been a partial retreat from experience or a simplification of it. If one further, but crucial, instance is called for, perhaps it is Angus Wilson's *The Old Men at the Zoo* (1961). This is a book which displays truly brilliant powers of irony, characterization, dialogue, descriptive writing, and much besides. Yet the reader lays it down with an uneasy feeling that these powers have somewhere wanted fundamental direction; and that towards the end of the book they have dissipated themselves in accelerating fantasy and ultimate inconclusiveness.

'*Advance, Britannia . . .*' Is the 1940–80 period some transition, not yet wholly in focus, towards a fundamentally new society and sense of life, and the writing which would go with that? It is at this point that a writer attempting to survey such matters comes to believe that his best course is to leave speculation to his readers. The younger ones amongst them will doubtless be able to find out, firsthand, in time. Certainly, there are few today who would speak, in the opening words of this discussion, about 'Britannia'; and few indeed (save merely at the level of practical, organizational matters) who would use the term 'advance', or would know what it meant for them if they did.

NOTES

1. Stephen Spender, *World Within World* (London, 1953), 258.

2. Contrast the tendency among some rather earlier novelists to put first the exploration and depiction of their character's self-realization (see *The New Pelican Guide to English Literature*, Vol. 7).

3. Much of the detail which follows here is taken from a wide variety of documents, some published and some unpublished, issued by cultural societies or institutions, and assembled together by John and Joan Holloway in Cambridge over the period 1970–81. This is now a special Collection in the University Library at East Anglia.

4. R. Escarpit, *La Révolution du livre* (Paris, 1965); English translation, 1966.

5. See for example Roy Fuller, 'Taxpayers, the Arts and Big Balloonz', *Encounter* (October 1977) and subsequent correspondence.

6. See S. Holmes and T. Rix, 'Beyond the Book', in *Essays in the History of Publishing*, ed. A. Briggs (London, 1974).

7. *Language and Silence* (London, 1967).

8. See *The Quality of Spoken English on BBC Radio*, by R. W. Burchfield, D. Donoghue, and A. Timothy (London, 1979).

9. See A. Munton, 'A Reading of the Childermass', in *Wyndham Lewis: A Revaluation*, ed. Jeffrey Meyers (London, 1980).

10. See, however, F. Jameson, *Fables of Aggression* (Univ. of California Press, 1979), 4 n.: 'This is perhaps the place to say that it strikes me as disingenuous to read Lewis's work, as John Holloway does ... as the *critique* of violence rather than its expression.' Italics in the original.

11. M. Young, *The Rise of the Meritocracy, 1870–2033* ... (London, 1961).

12. A. Sillitoe, *The Loneliness of the Long-Distance Runner* (London, 1959).

13. See the present writer's 'David Jones: A Perpetual Showing', in *Hudson Review* (Spring 1963: reprinted in *The Colours of Clarity*, 1964).

14. See François Martel, 'Jeux formels dans "Watt"', in *Poétique*, No. 10 (1972).

15. See *The London Fringe Theatre*, ed. V. Mitchell (London, 1975).

16. For these plays see *Five Television Plays*, ed. M. Marland (London, 1968). The plays are undated here.

PART III

THE FATALISM OF GEORGE ORWELL

D. S. SAVAGE

George Orwell (pseudonym of Eric Arthur Blair, 1903–50) presents
something of a problem for the literary critic. At first a dissident
'minority' writer with a readership of moderate proportions, Orwell
suddenly achieved wide fame with the publication of two books
which touched the nerve of the wider public both in Britain and
the USA – *Animal Farm* (1945) and *Nineteen Eighty-Four* (1949).
Released at a time when world power relationships, and popular
opinion with them, were suffering a painful change, Orwell's books
played an important part in effecting a reversal of attitudes towards
the West's wartime Soviet ally. Their author's hitherto uncomfortable anti-Stalinism became all at once not only acceptable but
fashionable, and the way was opened for his subsequent gradual
elevation into a cult figure, a hero of our times, a secular saint.

Criticism, however, is concerned not with the factitious heroism
or sanctity of literary cult figures but with the quality of the writer's
work; and considered simply as an artist it must be said that Orwell
does not in fact rank very high. Less a *writer* pure and simple than
a puzzling hybrid of *littérateur* and publicist, Orwell fails as an artist
because of a general inability to transcend and so fully to possess
and master his material – ultimately, his own experience. He is not
a mere propagandist, but his books, rather than having their end
in themselves, tend to point to some not always very clear external
intention. Orwell's works do not have the integrality of art because
the man himself did not have the integrity of the true artist. When
he wrote well, it was plainly, without grace or sensitivity; when
he wrote badly, it was crudely and vulgarly. It is fair to say that
in his production as a whole one is confronted piecemeal with the
picturesque life-history of an English eccentric, an upper-class social
dissident or misfit whose vagaries and oddities, with his insights and
forthright opinions, come together to make up a somewhat bizarre

extended self-portrait. In a case like this it seems to me that the second task of the critic is to piece the fragmentary portrait together in an intelligible way, even if this means widening the bounds of criticism into the territory of biography, psychology and politics. To do this, one does not have to go beyond the texts themselves; and fortunately for the investigator, towards the end of his life George Orwell produced, in *Such, Such Were the Joys*, a confessional document of the first importance. I shall draw upon this revealing source in due course.

In the thirties Orwell wrote five novels widely different as to their subjects and settings but unified by their close adherence to a single theme, a theme which it so happens they share with *Nineteen Eighty-Four*. Each tells the story of a single lonely individual's disaffection from his society, his partially successful retreat or escape from it, and his final return, leading either to resigned conformity or death. The philosophy is fatalistic. Flory, the jaundiced timber-merchant hero of *Burmese Days* (1934), the first – and best – of the novels, is doomed from the start to misery and failure:

> Flory had been fifteen years in Burma, and in Burma one learns not to set oneself up against public opinion. But his trouble was older than that. It had begun in his mother's womb, when chance put the blue birthmark on his cheek.

Gordon Comstock in *Keep the Aspidistra Flying* (1936) is condemned to futility by his mere ancestry:

> 'Gordon Comstock' was a pretty bloody name, but then Gordon came of a pretty bloody family ... The Comstocks, as Gordon knew them, were a peculiarly dull, shabby, dead-alive, ineffectual family.... One and all they turned out listless, gutless, unsuccessful sort of people.

Penalized from birth, the Orwellian man, so far from defining the outlines of his spiritual world through successive acts of moral choice, sees no option but to submit querulously to the mechanical course of events. 'But you see the way things happen, the kind of dull, pointless way,' complains the middle-aged George Bowling in *Coming Up for Air* (1939), when he meets again the now faded, blowsy woman he had courted in his youth. '... Who'd have thought the time would ever come when there would be just no feeling whatever between us?' And Flory while still a young man, baulked by a decision of his remote superiors of his hopes of escape from soul-deadening Burma, submits apathetically to his own undoing:

> Something turned over in Flory's heart. It was one of those moments when one becomes conscious of a vast change and deterioration in one's life. For he had realized, suddenly, that in his heart he was glad to be coming back. This country which he hated was now his native country, his home.

Invariably with Orwell conscious decision is pre-empted by the influence of unconscious determinism, signifying a failure to rise psychologically from a sub-personal to a personal level of existence.

As a novelist Orwell is severely limited by his obvious inability to transcend the viewpoint of his central character. Empathizing with naïve directness with his heroes, he implicitly invites his readers to do the same. Yet these Orwellian figures must be shown not only as sensitive and well-meaning beings, but as loutish, splenetic and abject ones – and this not because Orwell has unusually subtle insight into the grey areas of human nature, but because of his depleted ability to distinguish between the normally 'good' and the 'bad' in character and behaviour. That this might well be connected with a degree of moral ambiguousness or indifference is not difficult to see.

So thoroughly does Orwell identify with his central character that one can hardly inquire into these characters without probing the human qualities of their author. Such probing yields discomfiting results. For instance, the *moral character* of the would-be jovial George Bowling may be gauged from his family feelings: 'Well, Hilda and I were married, and right from the start it was a flop ... during the first two or three years I had serious thoughts of killing Hilda.' His *peaceableness* is underlined in his indignation over the accidental dropping of a bomb by an airplane over Lower Binfield, the revisited village of his youth; yet the fake-Tudor houses in Upper Binfield '... made me wish I'd got a hand-grenade in my pocket'. His *gentleness* appears in his ruminations upon his rural boyhood:

> It's a wonderful thing to be a boy, to go roaming where grown-ups can't catch you, to chase rats and kill birds and shy stones and cheek carters and shout dirty words. It's a kind of strong, rank feeling, a feeling of knowing everything and fearing nothing, and it's all bound up with breaking rules and killing things ... Thank God I'm a man, because no woman ever has

that feeling ... There was another game we had when the toads were spawning. We used to catch toads, ram the nozzle of a bicycle pump up their backsides, and blow them up till they burst. That's what boys are like. I don't know why.

Yet it is just this uncomprehending torturer of toads who, without seeing any connection, anticipates with anxious dread (the date is 1939)

...The world we're going down into, the kind of hate-world, slogan-world. The coloured shirts, the barbed wire, the rubber truncheons... And the processions and the posters with enormous faces, and the crowds of a million people all cheering for the Leader till they deafen themselves into thinking that they really worship him, and all the time, underneath, they hate him so that they want to puke.

While a great deal of what Orwell writes has genuine objective relevance, the springs of his work lie not in disinterested social observation and concern but in unacknowledged feelings, chiefly of self-hatred and contempt, which find objective expression and justification through their projection on to the external scene. The failure of self-knowledge which this entails results in a degree of confusion between fantasy and reality, feeling and fact. It also implies a loss of control over one's own experience. Like Flory in the earlier novel, Gordon, in *Keep the Aspidistra Flying*, is mortified by his sexual experiences:

The faces of women flowed through his memory. Ten or a dozen of them there had been. Tarts also. *Comme au long d'un cadavre un cadavre étendu.* And even when they were not tarts it had been squalid, always squalid. Always it had started in a sort of cold-blooded wilfulness and ended in some mean, callous desertion.

Sexual experiences here seem less something willed, desired or consented to than an injury or indignity done one by uncalled-for circumstance. It is not his *fault* if the encounters have ended in mean, callous desertion, for neither he nor anyone can be held accountable for the wretchedness of a world in which things 'just happen' in a dull and pointless way beyond choice or evasion.

A flood of light is cast on Orwell's fatalism by the account of his critical adolescent years in *Such, Such Were the Joys,*[1] already referred to. At his preparatory school, 'St Cyprian's', the already

self-mistrustful Eric Blair had been intimidated to the point of terror,
Orwell would have us believe, by those surrogate parents, the man
and wife teaching team nicknamed 'Sambo' and 'Flip'. This dreaded
pair, claiming to befriend him and to act entirely for his wellbeing,
included in their friendship '... canings, reproaches and humiliations,
which were good for me and saved me from an office stool' – i.e.,
from an inferior status in later life. Partly because of this wounding
treatment (but both social inferiority and sexual guilts and shames
came strongly into the picture) the boy became utterly perplexed
between false values genuinely believed in, and genuine feelings
falsely denied: in particular, between the gratitude, affection and
respect which he *knew* he owed his benefactors and the actual
fiercely suppressed feelings of hatred and contempt which he really
felt for them:

A child accepts the codes of behaviour that are presented to it, even when
it breaks them. From the age of eight, or even earlier, the consciousness of
sin was never far away from me. If I contrived to seem callous and defiant,
it was only a thin cover over a mass of shame and dismay. All through my
boyhood I had a profound conviction that I was no good, that I was wasting
my time, wrecking my talents, behaving with monstrous folly and wickedness and ingratitude – and all this, it seemed, was inescapable, because I lived
among laws which were absolute, like the law of gravity, but which it was
not possible for me to keep.

The more subtly dominating of the two tyrants was Flip, and:

I think it would be true to say that every boy in the school hated and
feared her. Yet we all fawned on her in the most abject way, and the top
layer of our feelings towards her was a sort of guilt-stricken loyalty ...
Whenever one had the chance to suck up, one did suck up, and at the first
smile one's hatred turned into a sort of cringing love.

This numbed ambivalence of feeling worked in the young Eric
Blair towards the erasure of all sane and sound values, beginning
with his religion. For the essay leaves no doubt that his warped
responses to the two adults were directly transferred to the Deity
whose representatives they doubtless were. Though up to the age
of fourteen he, Blair, had *believed* in God, he did not love him:

On the contrary, I hated him, just as I hated Jesus and the Hebrew
patriarchs. If I had sympathetic feelings towards any character in the Old

Testament, it was towards such people as Cain, Jezebel, Haman, Agag, Sisera: in the New Testament my friends, if any, were Ananias, Caiaphas, Judas and Pontius Pilate.

These 'friends' of the thirteen-year-old boy might give a contemporary theologian cause for a mighty headache: especially the last. God as a tyrant who has framed the iron Necessity of a cosmic order in which the strong, handsome and well-heeled have a predestinate right and obligation to ride roughshod over the weak, ugly and unendowed (and precisely this was the young Eric's view of God and the universe) might perhaps not ignobly be hated and defied; but what is surely strange is that the revolt should stop short half way and bend back on itself, so that Caesar, the god of this world (or Pilate his vicegerent), is ambiguously included among the 'friends'. Significantly, in view of his later life, the boy's rebellion failed to complete itself, and his resentment smouldered darkly without ever bursting into flame. Yet rebellion in the adolescent is not an evil, and perhaps only wholehearted revolt could have delivered Eric Blair once and for all from the never-to-be-outgrown constrictions of his early conditioning. As it is, anyone who is puzzled by the alternations in George Orwell's later attitudes between sadistic and masochistic identifications, i.e., between Power and Authority typified by the police and military on the one hand, and Weakness and Revolt typified by the rebel and the social outcast on the other, need look no further than this aborted half-revolt of the intimidated child.

What, then, of the political actualities which seem to have featured so largely in Orwell's career? It is a striking fact that the early writings, up to the year 1937, are altogether devoid of political concern. The rather implausible account given in the *Down and Out* volume of the motives for his aberrant behaviour in dressing like a workman in order to mix romantically with 'dirty' and 'smelly' men in doss-houses and casual wards can hardly be other than a rationalization of a strong unconscious compulsion. In the novels too, the desire of his heroes to escape from their loneliness, to find love or sexual comfort and to fraternize generically with others, only to be thwarted by the impassable nature of things is again innocent of political motive. This hardly applies, it is true, to *The Road to Wigan Pier*

(1937); but the book is a special case. Commissioned by Orwell's publisher, Victor Gollancz, for the Left Book Club, this book from the pen of a man of professed proletarian sympathies was tailored for a left-wing readership. But even so Orwell's ideas and sentiments were so little in accord with the current orthodoxy that the volume had to be issued with an embarrassed disclaimer by the publisher. It is only after the newly-married author,[2] leaving his wife in England, had departed for war-torn Spain on a newspaper assignment – and while in Barcelona had on pure impulse joined the POUM militia – that he declared for socialism and, returning to England in 1938, enrolled as a member of the Independent Labour Party.

An unbeliever, in Spain Orwell underwent an emotional upheaval or convulsion resembling a conversion. The deeply-moving experience of comradeship with a band of brothers fighting a common foe in the filthy conditions of the battlefield (a detail which is particularly dwelt on in *Homage to Catalonia*, 1938) enthused the despondent loner with a quasi-religious belief in the possibility, or necessity, of a socialist Utopia, a barrierless brotherhood in which Old Etonians like himself could fraternize on equal terms with newsvendors, peasants and factory-hands. This new-found political faith, not being grounded in any prior religious or ethical principle or commitment, took the field of politics to be the summation of all human activity and value; its objective, the socialist commonwealth, was the final human goal.

Clearly, such chiliastic collectivism takes a much oversimplified view of the nature of man and of social institutions. Orwell, however, who remained always at an infra-personal level of development, was constitutionally incapable of conceiving of a more wholesome approach, viz., the unity of an inward commitment of the person, in which means and ends are integrally related, with its proper, universally valid political objective, the realization of justice among men in society at large. To him as to many of his contemporaries it appeared that moral issues belonged to a discarded 'bourgeois' period of the past; in modern times they had been 'replaced' by political ones. Morality being abolished, politics ceased to be relative and conditional and became in a false way absolute. Unconscious emotional exigencies – George Orwell's among them – could be projected blindly into the political field, with lamentable results.

Socialists are not necessarily humanists, and the roots of Orwell's own humanism did not go deep. His avowals of belief in 'decency' and 'freedom of speech', while not insincere, implied no hard-core of moral principle and no profound belief in freedom *per se*. In a review of *Russia Under Soviet Rule* written early in 1939, he takes it as given that man is an animal whose inner being can in principle be permanently altered by external pressure:

In the past, every tyranny was sooner or later overthrown, or at least resisted, because of 'human nature', which as a matter of course desired liberty. But we cannot be at all certain that 'human nature' is constant. It may be just as possible to produce a breed of men who do not wish for liberty as to produce a breed of hornless cows.[3]

Since Orwell himself shared in 'human nature', it seems likely that he held himself, too, to be susceptible to such conditioning.

With such shifting foundations, it would be vain to look to Orwell for consistency. His single claim to political prescience is his timely and outspoken anti-Stalinism, and this rests in part on the psychological revulsions laid bare in *Such, Such Were the Joys*, and in part on the accident of his experience in the POUM militia, when he had made the disconcerting discovery that the cadres of the Revolution sheltered a contingent of dedicated Stalinists under orders to subvert the Revolution in the Russian interest by eliminating its leading spirits. Here the subjective and the objective factors fused to reinforce one another: Stalin became the archetypal tyrant-figure. Although *Homage to Catalonia* contains as much grist for the psychiatrist as for the historian, Orwell deserves the credit for his honest reporting of the facts, on his return to England, to unheeding leftist ears. His belated political education began from this point. It was then that he joined, not the Communist Party, but the ILP.

The ILP was an elite company of Marxist and near-Marxist workers and intellectuals which aspired to ideological leadership of the British working-class movement. While supporting the militant revolutionaries in Catalonia, it staunchly opposed both the Russian-engineered Popular Front and the rearmament programmes of the capitalist democracies, now preparing for Hitler's war. In conformity with the ILP's pacifist–socialist policies and principles, in 1938/39 Orwell wrote numerous anti-war, anti-rearmament letters and articles.[4] Consistency required that, should war come, he would hold to his declared principles and support the ILP in opposing it, however unpopular this course might prove. This was not to be. Shortly before the war broke out he went into reverse, denied his pacificism and reverted to the Kiplingesque militarism of his early upbringing or conditioning. At this further life-juncture, which can hardly be called a decision, he did not reason with himself but, rather, dreamed a dream:

> It was one of those dreams which, whatever Freudian inner meaning they may have, do sometimes reveal to you the real state of your feelings. It taught me two things, first, that I should be simply relieved when the long-dreaded war started, secondly, that I was patriotic at heart, would not sabotage or act against my own side, would support the war, would fight in it if possible.[5]

And as for socialism and the brotherhood of man, these ideals could be retained if they might be combined with patriotic nationalism, and the war-effort taken out of the hands of right-wingers and somehow directed to socialistic ends. Committed to a theory which held that socialism was to be attained through the impersonal collaboration of individuals with overriding Necessity – 'History has to move in a certain direction, even if it has to be pushed that way by neurotics'[6] – Orwell held still to the disjunctive view that in the fleeting, crucial present the marvellous but unborn utopian future was engaged in a deadly struggle with the evil past. In a curious wartime pamphlet, *The Lion and the Unicorn* (1942), he exhorted his readers:

> We cannot establish anything that a western nation would regard as Socialism without defeating Hitler; on the other hand we cannot defeat Hitler while we remain economically and socially in the nineteenth century. The past is fighting the future and we have two years, a year, possibly only a few months, to see to it that the future wins.

Military conscription and mobilization must be followed by in-dustrial and political conscription and centralization – by democratic consent, of course.

The statement, meaningless enough at the time, conveys some-thing of the nature of the impasse into which Orwell had walked. People and events refused to take the course he mapped out for them, and he had to pay a costly penalty for self-deception and wishful thinking. His published papers for 1942/44 reveal his deepening dismay as the war intensified, extended itself and dragged ruinously on. By 1945 the world situation had become too dreadful to contemplate and for a while he retreated in fancy into the childhood world of Beatrix Potter.[7] *Animal Farm*, when at length it found a publisher, performed two services for thousands of readers. By cocking a snook at the Soviet colossus at a time when it was yet barely permissible to do so it gave pleasurable release to their suppressed feelings of fear and hostility; and by reducing Stalin, Trotsky and Co., to nursery-animal proportions in its simple-sardonic way, it presented them with an acceptably homely and comical image of a frightening reality. The pessimism of the fable is not in doubt; but its message that revolution is futile and Utopia a pipedream could be taken in more than one way.

By 1948, when he came to write *Nineteen Eighty-Four*, Orwell's utopianism had shot its bolt and his innate fatalism arose desolatingly to possess the now sick and dying man. The 'Ingsoc' of Big Brother (Stalin) is a system of absolute tyranny grown out of the twin resolve to wage total war and to establish socialism which Orwell himself had urged in 1940/42; but now the weakly rebellious Orwellian man – who in previous fictions had declaimed against a callous society which, despite its indifference to human brotherhood, at least left him free to fulminate – is oppressed to extinction by the society of organized brotherhood itself. Yet Winston Smith, who begins by fearfully writing dangerous thoughts in his diary, and who then goes on to form an illicit love-relationship with Julia, a fellow rebel and a colleague in the Ministry of Truth, is condemned at the last by nothing more than his inability to believe in his own human worth and his *right* to rebel.

The prison scenes of *Nineteen Eighty-Four* patently derive from a work which had deeply impressed Orwell after its publication in 1940, Arthur Koestler's *Darkness at Noon*, and it may be instructive briefly to compare the two works. It should be noted that the central situation of the two novels is by no means the same. Koestler's Rubashov is not, like Winston Smith, a lukewarm libertarian in half-hearted revolt against a social system to which he has yet fully to capitulate, but an ageing member of the first generation of committed Russian revolutionaries who, having dedicated himself in youth to the Communist cause and accepted without demur the maxim that the end justifies the means, now finds himself a victim of the amoral, arbitrary political machinery he has himself helped to set in motion. Having sent others without compunction to their expedient deaths, he finds himself, at the time of the Stalin treason trials, without grounds for objection to his own expedient consignment to the rubbish-dump of history. The full ambiguous irony of his situation emerges with the realization that his own consent to his degradation and disposal is the final service he is asked to render the deified Party in whose infallibility he can no longer believe.

Darkness at Noon may not be a great novel, but its authenticity is beyond doubt. The same cannot be said about *Nineteen Eighty-Four*. Where Koestler writes with convincing imaginative objectivity about realities of which he has actual experience, Orwell, forced to rely upon invention, cannot prevent the disturbing emergence into his work of repressed materials which, not integrated with consciousness through the act of composition, weaken the authority of the writing and detract from the novel's artistic worth.

Orwell has been praised for his plain prose style. He did indeed employ an idiomatic, saloon-bar style exactly suited to such fatalistic anecdotal material as is to be found in 'Shooting an Elephant', 'A Hanging' and 'How the Poor Die'. It is when he departs from reminiscence and reportage and employs a similar cloth-capped prose for the ventilation of opinion and discussion of ideas (with Orwell the two are much the same) that he is prone to fall into malpractice and set traps for the too trusting reader. Perhaps his invention of *Newspeak*, the truncated language of Ingsoc, is relevant here. It arose out of his concern in his last years with the relation of writing to politics, and it is in part an ingeniously perceptive *reductio ad absurdum* of totalitarian linguistic trends; but its central concept, *doublethink*, it owed to an ambiguous quirk in his own mentality, to which I shall return.

Orwell's failure to attain personal maturity, to move out of egoistic isolation into the realm of persons-in-relation which constitutes the human community, meant that he was unable to see the world other than in terms of a bare opposition of the isolated ego to the sub-personal collective. In literary matters he was obliged, in parallel, to oppose aestheticism to propagandism. Unhappy with either extreme, he could find no tenable ground between them, and was forever unable to tie together those dangling ends, literature and politics. In 'Why I Write'[8] he declares:

> Every line of serious work that I have written since 1936 has been written, directly or indirectly, *against* totalitarianism and *for* democratic socialism, as I understand it. It seems to me nonsense, in a period like our own, to think that one can avoid writing of such subjects.

Setting aside the point that democratic socialism as Orwell understood it is hardly the antithesis of totalitarianism, and might be its preparatory stage, this is clearly a declaration of literary politicism which, however, stops short of crass propagandism. Its inutility as a halfway house between two extremes repeatedly shows itself in Orwell's literary essays. In 'Politics and the English Language',[9] for instance, he first asserts that contemporary English usage has become corrupt, and then goes on to say that this cannot be due to the bad influence of individual writers but must ultimately have political and economic causes. But where a propagandist Communist would, consistently, explain what these are and propound a political remedy, Orwell inconsistently veers off on an aesthetic tack and proposes that the disease be remedied through the individual writer's deliberate cultivation of a plainer prose style. Good, clear English will enable its practitioner to think more clearly, '... and to think clearly is a necessary first step towards political regeneration'. But that plain prose does not of itself generate clear thinking is shown by Orwell himself, who fails to explain how, if that supposition were true, the corruption of language could have come about in the first place not through the influence of bad writers but through detached political and economic causes. What Orwell leaves out of account, of course, is that clear thinking cannot proceed of itself, irrespective of the psychological condition of the thinker, but depends first of all upon a fundamental personal dedication to truth. But truth, like goodness and beauty, is a value; and neither persons nor values can exist in a politicized world which admits only isolated individuals and abstract collectives.

Lack of commitment to value leaves a hollowness, a hiatus at the centre of Orwell the man which deprives such assaults upon totalitarian regimes as 'The Prevention of Literature'[10] of all force or point;

for the pose of liberal humanism he tacitly adopts in that essay must be dismissed as fraudulent. But the essay which most thoroughly exposes Orwell's split personality is the very late 'Writers and Leviathan',[11] with its despairing counsel to the creative writer that he 'split his life into two compartments', in the political part acting as violently and insanely as necessity may dictate, while in the literary part standing aside and writing without factional bias, in disabused aesthetic detachment.

Truth for Orwell meant only fidelity to fact; his failure as a would-be thinker to commit himself to truth as value was linked with that characteristic refusal of the neurotic to look within and know himself. This kept him in fixed ignorance of his divided condition and allowed him to discharge his hidden preoccupations into his public pronouncements and to project on to others faults and failings which he could not admit in himself. The quirk in his mentality to which I referred above can best be detected in his essay on 'Lear, Tolstoy and the Fool',[12] in which he makes the apparently disinterested point that the ageing Tolstoy, when attacking the poetry of Shakespeare, selected King Lear in particular as a target for ridicule because, without permitting himself consciously to know it, he recognized the situation it presents as reflecting his own tragic enough domestic predicament. The argument is both arresting and convincing, but it points to the almost certain conclusion that Orwell singled out Tolstoy for attention and lay bare the knowing-not-knowing mechanism in the old moralist because it corresponded uncannily to his own obscure mental functioning, which he, too, could admit to consciousness only in alienated form.

Such ambivalent awareness is very close to the doublethink of Newspeak. Once one has grasped the lack of a core of personal integrity in Orwell, and the ambiguousness in which it resulted, one can find evidence everywhere in his work that he was well versed in doublethink: a practice which, again, he was able to confess to only indirectly: by formulating it as a theory! I cannot here give chapter and verse in any detail, but I would point to a particularly flagrant example of doublethink in an article of 1946, 'In Front of Your Nose',[13] where Orwell first dilates upon the harmful twin faculties seemingly possessed by many people, of 'holding two or more contradictory ideas in their heads at once', and of 'ignoring obvious and unalterable facts', and then goes on to give as an example the case of those 'enlightened people' who, before the war, were 'in favour of standing up to Germany', while contradictorily, being 'against having enough armaments to make such a stand effective'. By giving his readers to understand that he was himself among these 'enlightened people', and implying without directly stating that he had been in favour of pre-war rearmament, and so drawing a veil over his actual pre-war pacificism (which by this time had become a distinct embarrassment to him) Orwell himself succumbs to the very kind of self-deception he castigates in others. All in all, Orwell's was a most unhappy psychological condition to be in, the full misery of which was only to appear in the pages of *Nineteen Eighty-Four*.

The ambiguousness already discernible in the early novels has in *Nineteen Eighty-Four* widened to take possession of the entire work. Riddled with ambivalence, the novel hinges upon the equivocal. Good is bad, and bad good. Right is wrong, and wrong right. This is not at once obvious, for no novelist can expect to establish connection with his readers without some recognition of those normative values which, as participators in the same cultural milieu, both parties must be supposed to acknowledge, and Orwell is obliged at least to seem to posit such values. But he does so, only immediately to twist them around. Sexual love, for instance, is a normative value. But Winston Smith's apparently normal love for Julia, once asserted, instantly turns into its contrary, and Winston demands of the girl not that she shall be faithful, loving and true, but that she be promiscuous, disloyal and corrupt, for only these qualities it seems are able to 'rot' and 'poison' the fabric of the puritanical Ingsoc society: 'I hate purity, I hate goodness! I don't want any virtue to exist anywhere. I want everyone to be corrupt to the bones.' And Julia at once assures him that she is as delectably corrupt as he demands. Thus it turns out that the oppressive Party is the guardian of purity, goodness and virtue, while its bemused opponents not only exult in their corruption but, at the behest of the bland double-agent O'Brien, solemnly undertake to perform acts of savage cruelty should this be required of them by the fictitious counter-revolutionary (Trotskyist) Brotherhood. Winston, when arrested by the Thought Police, jailed, and at last brought before the torturer-inquisitor, O'Brien, has deprived himself of any claim to moral superiority to the system he detests and placed in his opponent's hands the very cards he needed to win the game. Convinced by the flawless logic of O'Brien's arguments for the State's pursuit of absolute Power, the worn-out prisoner at length breaks down and submits to the oppressor; but his submission is not only compelled from without, it is evoked from within. The subjugated Winston is released, and the story ends:

He gazed up at the enormous face of Big Brother. Forty years it had taken him to learn what kind of smile was hidden beneath the dark moustache. O cruel, needless misunderstanding! O stubborn, self-willed exile from the loving breast! Two gin-scented tears trickled down the sides of his nose. But it was all right, everything was all right, the struggle was finished. He had won the victory over himself. He loved Big Brother.

What is truly remarkable is that the pattern of the novels should reflect so faithfully the larger pattern of Orwell's life. From childhood onwards an embittered fatalist, Orwell yet struggled fitfully against his crippling despondency in vain attempts to escape into some freer, happier ambience. The peak period of his life was undoubtedly that which embraced both the Spanish adventure and the brief subsequent period of ILP socialism. But the Spanish debacle, followed by his own desertion of principle and then the wartime collapse of his national-socialist hopes, and the dumbfounding rise of the world superpowers, robbed him of his illusions and drove him back upon the bleak determinism of his adolescent years. For in essentials there is absolutely no difference between the predicament of Winston Smith in *Nineteen Eighty-Four* and that of the dismayed and petrified Eric Blair as portrayed in *Such, Such Were the Joys*.

George Orwell has been much misunderstood. Rather than a man of courage and insight who in his last novel issued a timely warning to humanity, he was himself the warning. Besides its overt tidings – 'this is what the world may well be like in the year 1984' – the cryptic message actually conveyed by the underlying complex of fears, revulsions and obsessions in the novel is rather: 'this is what my inner world is really like in 1948.' The misinterpretation of Orwell has been assisted both by his deceptive pose as the outspoken, no-nonsense George, self-appointed mouthpiece of the common man, and by the convergence of his own neurotic fears and fantasies with the general mood of the times. As a one-eyed man in the country of the blind he has been elevated to a position of eminence from which, with a change of mood and circumstance, he is bound to be dislodged. In any case his reputation will find its proper level when his writings come to be judged in due course not by their flattering acceptability as tracts for the times but by their quality, which will be seen not to be high, as works of the literary imagination.

NOTES

1. George Orwell, *Such, Such Were the Joys* (New York, 1953). Included in *The Collected Essays, Journalism and Letters of George Orwell*, ed. Sonia Orwell and Ian Angus (London, 1968), Vol. 4, 411. (Page references are to the Penguin edition.)

2. In a letter to an Old Etonian friend, Denys King-Farlow, dated 9 June 1936, Orwell excuses himself for his inability to meet him '... because like the chap in the *N.T.* I have married a wife & therefore cannot come. Curiously enough I am getting married this very morning – in fact I am writing this with one eye on the clock & the other on the Prayer Book, which I have been studying for some days past in hopes of steeling myself against the obscenities of the wedding service', *Collected Essays*, Vol. 1, 253. Orwell's misogyny appears frequently in his writings, in which there is throughout abundant support for the conclusion that he was, in fact, a repressed homosexual.

3. Review by George Orwell of *Russia Under Soviet Rule* by N. de Basily, in *The New English Weekly* (January 1939). Included in *Collected Essays*, Vol. 1, 419.

4. In September 1939 Orwell was writing in *Left Forum*: '... But we happen to be at a moment when the rise of Hitler has scared the official leaders of the Left into an attitude not far removed from jingoism. Large numbers of left-wing publicists are almost openly agitating for war. Without discussing this subject at length, it can be pointed out that a left-wing party which, within a capitalist society, becomes a war party, has already thrown up the sponge, because it is demanding a policy which can only be carried out by its opponents', *Collected Essays*, Vol. 1, 444.

5. George Orwell, 'My Country Right or Left', in *Folios of New Writing* (Autumn 1940). Included in *Collected Essays*, Vol. 1, 592. Something of the flavour of Orwell's national socialism at this time may be discerned in the following extract from the same article: '... It is exactly the people whose hearts have *never* leapt at the sight of a Union Jack who will flinch from revolution when the moment comes. Let anyone compare the poem John Cornford wrote not long before he was killed ('Before the Storming of Huesca') with Sir Henry Newbolt's 'There's a breathless hush in the Close

tonight'. Put aside the technical differences, which are merely a matter of period, and it will be seen that the emotional content of the two poems is almost exactly the same. The young Communist who died heroically in the International Brigade was public school to the core. He had changed his allegiance but not his emotions. What does that prove? Merely the possibility of building a Socialist on the bones of a Blimp, the power of one kind of loyalty to transmute itself into another, the spiritual need for patriotism and the military virtues, for which, however little the boiled rabbits of the Left may like them, no substitute has yet been found.'

6. 'With such a history as he has behind him, he [Arthur Koestler] would be able to see that certain things have to be done, whether our reasons for doing them are "good or "bad". History has to move, etc . . .', George Orwell, 'Arthur Koestler', in *Focus* 2, (1946). Included in *Collected Essays*, Vol. 3, 243.

7. A childhood friend of Eric Blair writes, in an article entitled 'The Young Eric': 'We had in our house a copy of Wells's *Modern Utopia*, which was so greatly fancied by Eric that it was eventually given to him. He said he might write that kind of book himself. Broadly, *Nineteen Eighty Four* is classifiable as 'that kind of book'. And the genealogical tree of *Animal Farm* has its roots in *Pigling Bland* by Beatrix Potter. *Pigling Bland* was Guiny's [younger sister's] book: Eric and I were far too old for it, but we adored it all the same. I remember him reading it through to me from beginning to end, to cheer me up one time when I had a cold. The heroic Pigling Bland was a white pig, and in *Animal Farm* the white pigs Major and Snowball are the *good* pigs. But it is a sorry metamorphosis for the delicious black Berkshire Pig-wig to be displaced by the dreadful black Berkshire Napoleon. Mr Pilkington is a relative of Mr Piperson, I think.' To turn human characters into animals came easily to Orwell, whose minor characters in the early novels are frequently described in terms of their beastlike features.

8. George Orwell, 'Why I Write', in *Gangrel* (1947). Included in *Collected Essays*, Vol. 4, and also *Decline of the English Murder and Other Essays* (Penguin Books, 1965).

9. George Orwell: 'Politics and the English Language', in *Horizon* (April 1946). Included in *Collected Essays*, Vol. 4, 167, and in *Inside the Whale and Other Essays* (1962).

10. 'The Prevention of Literature', in *Polemic* No. 2 (1945/6). Included in *Collected Essays*, Vol. 4, and in *Inside the Whale and Other Essays*.

11. George Orwell, 'Writers and Leviathan', in *Politics and Letters* (Summer 1948). Included in *Collected Essays*, Vol. 4, 414. The essay should be read in its entirety. In it Orwell writes: 'To suggest that a creative writer, in a time of conflict, must split his life into two compartments, may seem defeatist or frivolous: yet in practice I do not see what else he can do. To lock yourself up in an ivory tower is impossible and undesirable. To yield subjectively not merely to a party machine, but even to a group ideology, is to destroy yourself as a writer. We feel this dilemma to be a painful one, because we see the need of engaging in politics while also seeing what a dirty, degrading

business it is ... If [the writer] refuses [to debase his work in the service of a political faction], that does not mean that he is condemned to inactivity. One half of him, which in a sense is the whole of him, can act as resolutely, even as violently if need be, as anyone else. But his writings, in so far as they have any value, will always be the product of the saner self that stands aside, records the things that are done and admits their necessity, but refuses to be deceived as to their true nature.'

12. George Orwell, 'Lear, Tolstoy and the Fool', in *Polemic* No. 7 (March 1947). Included in *Collected Essays*, Vol. 4, and in *Inside the Whale and Other Essays*.

13. George Orwell, 'In Front of Your Nose', in *Tribune* (1946). Included in *Collected Essays*, Vol. 4.

PATRICK WHITE

JOHN HOLLOWAY

An important article could be written on Patrick White's fiction which discussed nothing on a larger scale than the construction of individual sentences or the handling of dialogue and of the continuing movement of narrative or description. This is true of White because the distinctiveness and individuality of contour of his writing is something that works its way down into the smallest features of the prose:

> ... The duck made straight for Glastonbury, to *stalk* and hide in its wilderness, and to endure all kinds of *frights and elements* in order to preserve its illusion of freedom. Stan Parker went up the hill in pursuit, parting the tall weeds, so that *the seed flew from them*, and the dusk was *floating* with a fine down. There was a cabbage gone wild in one place. It had a rank smell *beneath the foot* ...
>
> (*The Son of Man*, p. 216)

In this passage[1] (taken almost at random) the sinuous contour of the prose, so full of observation and recollection, so succinct with condensed implication and poetic depth of suggestion, never falters for an instant in its tensed grasp on the reader's mind. The whole paragraph needs to be studied at more length than is possible here.

Such alert density of texture is characteristic of White's prose almost from the beginning of his work:

> ... You were always dismissing people. It was seldom you came any closer. You dug the ferule of your umbrella in the pavement with a cool metallic hatred, walking *homeward*, as if you wanted also to *deny* the cold, *answering* sensuality of Muriel Raphael.
>
> (*The Living and the Dead*, 1967, p. 214)

There the second person, as not infrequently in White, is marker for a passage of free, indirect style which tersely kaleidoscopes the author's awareness, and his character's limited and partial resources of the same. Here is a rather more complicated example:

> ... Muriel has a handsome figure, said Mrs Standish, in a tone of voice that suggested she was just about to take back what she had given. If only, she added, someone would teach her where it begins.
>
> Muriel moved in the oblivion of a woman getting to her table, of the chic woman, in a non-existent situation, in an almost non-existent room. Browner against her dress, she had she knew, that *amusing* cachet, she had paid for it at Schiaparelli's ...
>
> (*The Living and the Dead*, p. 259)

White's constant dry wit only in part masks the often slightly manipulatory quality of his characterization ('a tone of voice that suggested ...'), but it would be a pity if both of those qualities were to mask from the reader the constant touches of subtle imagination and acute psychology ('in a non-existent situation, in an almost non-existent room'), and how, from the technical standpoint, those words introduce a kind of free, indirect style that seems to speak almost from the character's unconscious.

Local transitions in White's narratives might also be discussed. When, in *The Aunt's Story* (1948), the plain, middle-aged spinster Theodora Goodman settles in a modest Riviera hotel, the guests one after another lay bare before her their respective private-fantasy worlds. The White Russian 'General' (really a refugee major) calls her 'Ludmilla', after his long-lost sister, and speaks to her of Varvara, a former mistress, as if she were in the present. Then, she becomes so:

> 'I am expecting Varvara,' he said.
>
> 'Oh,' said Theodora. 'Varvara.'
>
> 'You speak of her with contempt,' said Alyosha Sergei. 'Because I love Varvara ... Varvara comes to me in the morning, when I am young.'
>
> Theodora knew that this was true ... Varvara swam against the waltz, and they stood in the open doorways, applauding ... she stood in the doorway, with her muff, on which little crystals of snow had not yet melted. Her breath was still silver in the stovey room.
>
> 'Alyosha Sergei,' said Varvara, 'it is morning ...'
>
> (*The Aunt's Story*, p. 169)

With the pathetic if odious Mrs Rapallo it is soon the same:

'Most evenings I walk as far as the *poste restante*. Just in case ...'

'Does she write often?' Theodora asked.

'One must expect women of rank to make certain sacrifices,' Mrs Rapallo said ... 'It was only to be expected that Nino ... if we stand right here, we shall see ...'

'We shall see?' asked Theodora, for whom the *transition from asphalt to marble* was too abrupt.

'Don't be absurd,' said Mrs Rapallo. And it was. It was obvious that Cardinals would pass ...

'There is Nino – my son-in-law, the Principe ...'

A few lines later, and that hallucination of the dream past is conjured away as deftly and smoothly as it was conjured up.

I have deliberately illustrated these narrative sophistications, from White's earlier works. Another characteristic technique is to sectionalize the narrative, sometimes explicitly, sometimes by half-concealed fade-ins, so that the vivid opening scene of the novel is replenished in the reader's mind with the backgrounds of whole life-histories. But it is at this point that one becomes aware of how much would be lost by concentrating too much on White's local technique. The very fact that novel after novel follows the same pattern of the vivid opening scene which then unfolds complexly into whole life-histories, told now retrospectively, shows that White has a range of concern that considerations of technique are unlikely to reveal. Recurrently and profoundly he is that somewhat old-fashioned artist, the writer of the *life-history* novel. Why? Why this great, and traditional, comprehensiveness of scope?

The answer begins to reveal itself (though only begins) if one calls to mind that most notable of nineteenth-century Australian novels, with its title inevitably suggested by the present train of thought: Marcus Clarke's *For the Term of his Natural Life* (1874). This novel about the hideous transportation prisons of Tasmania (Van Diemen's Land) and the still more isolated Norfolk Island is quite different from anything that White has written; it strikes the modern reader as endearingly amateurish, and somewhat less endearingly diffuse. Yet White's novels recall it (and I am not thinking of the actual presence of transport convicts in *Voss* or *A Fringe of Leaves*) in two ways. White's novels, like Clarke's book, depict and strive to unite two profoundly different, indeed antithetical modes of life, and to do that in the context of two contrasting, almost unrelated terrains. The former contrast might be available to a British novelist, but far less so the latter: today perhaps it is a resource peculiar to the Australian continent. These continuities back to Marcus Clarke, writing so much earlier and in a different style, are a major clue to White's essential interest.

The convict settlements in *For the Term of his Natural Life* include the 'polite' society of prison or military officers and their families and servants. One 'educated' prisoner (a clerk, transported for ill-proved embezzlement) is employed as butler in the house of the Commandant in the Port Arthur prison. Mr Meekin, the aptly-named, canting prison chaplain, experiences a moment of 'genuine compassion' when he witnesses the animal-like inspection of convict fetters, but recovers himself: 'bless me, it is one o'clock, and I promised to lunch with Major Vickers at two. How time flies, to be sure.' Even on the hideous Norfolk Island there is wine for dinner, French novels, and napkin rings 'daintily carved' by the prisoners. Contrasting with that life is the convicts' life of unbelievable hardships and horrors, and of desperate loyalties.

Then there is a further antithesis: beyond the flowers and gardens of the staff lies the savage, virgin terrain outside the penitentiary. Clarke depicts it at some length in a chapter pointedly entitled 'The Power of the Wilderness':

... he lay in a thicket of the thorny melaleuca, and felt at last that he was beyond pursuit. The next day he advanced more slowly ... Dense scrub and savage jungle impeded his path; barren and stony mountain ranges arose before him ... Above him rose the iron hills, below him lay the panorama of the bush.

If there is a prison break-out the authorities feel little alarm. No prisoner escapes. They die of starvation in the bush, or they give themselves up to renewed torture. Some are able to prolong the agony a little by cannibalism amongst themselves.

Save in *A Fringe of Leaves* (1976), the polarities in White's fiction, insofar as the setting is Australia, do not involve the convict world; but basically they are much like Clarke's and they lie with surprising starkness below the endless variety of character, incident, situation and dialogue throughout the novels. In, for example, *The Tree of*

Man (1956), there is the frugal, subsistence domesticity of the Parkers on their outback farm:

> They sat dashing the milk, and an anxious froth began to fill the bucket ...
> Not long after, her husband came in for a quick breakfast ... there were the
> frilly fried eggs, and the red tea ... in a blue enamel pot.   (p. 97)

Subsistence domesticity has its darker side: not only in the sudden, animal-like sensuality of Amy Parker in middle-age with her paunchy, easy-going commercial traveller in 'frills', but in the latent violence and sensuality of domesticity itself:

> Ah, she sighed, sitting on the edge of the well, and her skin drank the
> cool.
> She watched the knife in her husband's hands, that he pressed against the
> stone. She held her throat up, in the dim cool light of the tree above the
> well, offering it almost to the gleaming knife, that she would have received
> with what cry of love.
> Then when he had finished he felt the knife with his thumb, and looked
> at her at last ... Outside ... were his cleared paddocks, burnt to a white-grey
> by the heat of the summer, and the house he had knocked together ... even
> pretending a bit between the tendrils of vines and a shower of roses ...
> And he was pleased at the strong throat of his wife.

The Armstrongs, however, are a local rich family, and have a different kind of life, with sarcastic servants in the kitchen, silver candles, wine, opulent, bejewelled women. Their house is much more than 'pretending a bit':

> ... the Armstrongs' gateway, which had cost a great deal of money, and
> showed it, in volumes of iron and brick, and on each pillar of red brick
> the name was printed in white flints.

This rich ex-butcher's house is called Glastonbury – Glastonbury, Meroë, Xanadu, White has a skill over the unconvincing names of high-caste Australian *nouveau-richesse* – and the expanses of laurel, 'shrubberies and lawns', grove of gardenias, summer-house, articulate a terrain of opulent display. But the polarity returns, because that opulence is uncomfortably close to something other than itself. Hot summer brings the first distant smokes of the bush-fires; and then, the burnt woman 'twitching' on the dried mud, the scorched

chickens, 'their wattles gone black', the trees falling, the screaming
fox, the bird 'flaming from the beak upward' that falls 'into an agony
of writhing *twigs*'. In the end the 'jaunty tongues of flame' make
for the grand house; and before rain dowses it, fire destroys all
there is, and scorches the hair off the head of the beautiful rich girl,
rescued just in time, so that one thinks of how she looks like a
convict as in her agony she 'fell on her knees and began a kind of dry
retching'.

Another incursion into domesticity from the terrain of the Other
is the gale:

... Fowls flew, or handfuls of feathers. The wind peeled off a sheet of iron
and flung it with a brittle tinkling of silver paper.

Ahhh, cried the woman against her husband's neck, which had once been
strong.

'The great trees had broken off. Two or three fell. In a grey explosion.
Of gunpowder it seemed.' (p. 48)

This whole account of the storm is very representative of White,
and hints at something that must be discussed more later. Not only
does great descriptive power manifest itself in a prose style idiosyncratic at every turn, though clipped and dry enough never to lapse
into posturing or melodrama; but also, as the wind drops because
torrential rain arrives, the settler and his young wife build their
wordless and half-sexless communion anew, from the sense of each
other's nakedness, their primordial reality, under drenched clothes,
and in the resumption of work and normality (she 'wrung the water
from her hair ... chafing her skin before the fire').

Voss (1957) also reflects the Marcus Clarke polarities of social
milieu and terrain – in some ways more precisely, indeed, though
there is also more variety. One senses more than in the previous
novel White's fertility of invention not only in greater variety of
character, but also in the way his polarities interact or grow out
of each other. Voss, it is said, was suggested to White by the life of
Ludwig Leichart, who in 1846 changed the face of the exploration
of Australia by suddenly breaking out from the relatively slow-
moving opening-up of central Queensland, which had been proceeding since the 1830s. Leichart struck right across what is now
the upper part of the Northern Territory, to reach the Indian Ocean

along the topmost section of the Australian West Coast. The inspiration of the novel is exactly contemporary with the date that Marcus Clarke ascribed to the final part of his story. Two years later Leichart set out to cross the Central Desert, and was never seen again. This final phase of his life provided the germ of White's *Voss*.

Once again there is a polarity between the dreadful hostility of life in the outback, and the luscious rose-garden of Mr Bonner, the merchant who in a sense is Voss's patron; only in a sense because there is a predatoriness about his patronage. As one of the comfortably settled burgers of early Sidney, Mr Bonner is happy to bask amiably in the reflected glory of the exploration, but his servant wonders whether the strange German visitor, left alone in a room on his first call at the house, may filch something. His niece offers the visitor the second-best port, and Mr Bonner's material help is limited, more or less, to what he can supply from his own emporium. Sydney's George Street, full of 'the wives of officers and graziers, in barouche and brougham', is one polarity of terrain, but the other is the 'valley sculptured in red rock and quartz', the wild dogs that howl in the dark, and the aborigines of the outback, appearing 'first as shreds of bark glimpsed between the trunks of trees', who treat the precious gift of a bag of flour as a toy.

White's satire has a good deal more to say of the prosperous Sydney middle class; the Governor who 'was confined with a severe cold' the day the expedition started for the interior; his stand-in, Colonel Featherstonehaugh, with his speech for that occasion full of 'Our Illustrious Young Queen'; the young Lieutenant 'of sterling origins and pink skin'; Mrs Bonner's beautiful and dutiful daughter ('Everyone ... was agreed that Belle was the belle') and her even solider fiancé, Lieutenant Radclyffe, 'blazing in scarlet' ('Dear me, if these educated young ladies are not the deuce', he says of the odd-one-out expatriate niece in the Bonner family). At the other extreme are people such as Voss himself, whom Belle's military inamorato dismisses as 'harmless mad'; Robarts, who is almost a ship's boy on the voyage out, devoted in stock Victorian fashion to the entranced explorer; and Judd the 'emancipist' convict, whose skills and practicality in the bush vividly call to mind Rufus Dawes, the resourceful convict-hero of Marcus Clarke's novel. Also with the Bonners is Ruth Portion who at first, as an 'assigned' convict, walks to and fro in her shackles with baskets of earth and stone which Bonner uses to lay out his garden rockeries. Later she is freed and becomes a skilful domestic servant, but remains, in her unmarried pregnancy, the procreant one, the life-giver.

White is drawn recurrently to such patterns (including, as we shall see, the emergence of the life-giving within them). Polite settled life, and the outback wild country that lies somewhere behind it, also make a crucial antithesis in *The Eye of the Storm* (1973). The book opens with an everyday domestic scene in the house of Mrs Hunter, the rich, elderly Sydney-society widow, attended by her servants and her three nursing sisters, working shifts in a rotation of head-spinning costliness. As the novel proceeds, other scenes, both from her own earlier life and, interlocking with those, from the separate lives of her celebrated actor son and newly aristocratic daughter, join the narrative and add to it their accumulating weight and receding densities. But crucial to the whole accumulative process are the scenes from Mrs Hunter's earlier married life, when her late husband had his big sheep ranch, 'Kudjeri', a place of remoteness and productive toil that his wife visits but never belongs to. More significant by far, though, is Brumby Island on the remote Queensland coast (a 'brumby' is an Australian wild horse: she encounters their savage beauty more than once) where she spends a holiday as a house-guest along with her grown-up daughter. Here, the terrain is one lonely coast-line, and densely massed rain-forest. The 'ramshackle rickety structure' of the house stands on the very spot where aborigines are supposed once to have wiped out the survivors of a shipwreck ('There's the oyster shells the blacks have left'). This is the scene of the violent, primordial cyclic storm that crumples the wooden house as if it were paper, and leaves the society woman, its sole occupant, to find shelter on a shelf in the concrete wine-cellar. She is an inexpugnable 'survivor', and she dwarfs all the other characters in the book.

These two landscapes, the over-civilized on the one hand, the almost destructively primitive on the other, stand out clearly in *The Twyborn Affair* (1979). Here, after the mock elegances of the 'Grand Hotel Splendide' and the chauffeur-driven excursions on the Riviera, and after the lapdog-infested opulence and lush gardens of Judge Twyborn's Sydney villa, the elusive hermaphrodite-hero of this novel finds himself the sole passenger for the remote outback railway station at 'Fossickers Flats':

> The landscape was ... was cold, and huge, undulating in white waves towards distant mountains of ink blue. Rocks, not strewn, but arranged in groups of formal sculpture suggesting prehistoric rites, prevented monotony taking over the bleached foothills. (pp. 174–5)

White seems to know exactly what he sees in the Australian outback landscapes, and exactly what he wants to do with what he sees (there is a significant contrast with Lawrence's – not unnatural – wondering uncertainty over comparable descriptive passages in *Kangaroo*). The Fossickers Flats country of 'rudiments and stone', with its 'string of sheds, together with a huddle of cottages' making the working quarters of the sheep station, is more than simply rural as against urban Australia. It is an assertively aboriginal landscape, an ultimate of the wild and primitive, within which a somehow tender but also savage dimension in human relationships, homosexual or other about equally, flourishes as the natural, ingrained thing that the book says it is. Don Prowse, the farm manager ('... he let you down. And now you want the bull again'), is the Rufus Dawes of the book even down to his great strength, red hair, and streak of sentimentality ('he was being won over, not by the orange brute so much as the poor old Prowse of the snapshots and meticulous white-ink captions'). Against this primitive background, the last section, when the hero–heroine has mutated again, this time to be the middle-aged madam of a high-class West London brothel, completes the strange and original picture that this book gives of mankind as, throughout, a deeply and wholly ambivalent sexual animal. That last word carries its full weight: amid the gross pearls, golf-clubs, garden-trowels and 'creamed sunburn' (White's satire is crisp as ever), as much as amid the jewels, hothouse flowers, long rolls of carpet, beckoning mirrors, Fabergé cigarette-boxes, and men's unbuttoned 'formal black' in the London brothel, the animal beneath is what White's steely gaze reveals.

That outback extreme of primitiveness versus 'the established Australian rich' (the phrase comes in the novel last mentioned) occurs in the other works, if less directly. In *Dead Roses*, the principal short story in the collection entitled *The Burnt Ones* (literal translation of a

Modern Greek idiom: I venture to think 'Victims' might have been a
good alternative title) there is another Queensland island where the
cosseted Anthea Scudamore spends summer as a house-guest. The
island has its stunted, wind-swept trees, mobs of turkeys, 'gold blur of
barley crops', and sun-drenched strand where the young ordinary
doctor-man so nearly becomes her lover. 'Not like animals' she
remonstrates. 'We are, aren't we? With instincts for decency thrown
in,' is his reply: it is apt for the point now at issue, though perhaps
less winning than is intended.

At the end of *The Aunt's Story*, there is the remote Southern-States
railway-station where Theodora Goodman impulsively alights to
encounter the 'perhaps an Indian woman, or a Mexican' from whose
house she strays further into wild country, ending up at a deserted,
half-derelict shack in the forests where she rehearses her own private
fantasy. In *The Vivisector* (1957) the painter Hurtle Duffield buys himself a 'strip of scrub upon which, he had begun to feel, his creative life
depended', and builds himself a crude 'house or shack on the edge of
the gorge'. 'Helped by its primitive nature, it soon settled into the
ironstone and eucalyptus landscape. The rocks might have been fired
on some *primordial* occasion.' Here, another night-time of storm and
wind rejuvenates the jaundiced lovers. When Duffield becomes a
successful painter and an affluent man, there is a superficial change but
the fundamental pattern is preserved. A corner of the city itself can
revert to outback, and bring with it its isolation and hard living.
The old, ramshackle house in Flint Street, with its derelict gutters,
pipes that 'gushed whenever there was a deluge' (the encroaching
wilderness violence), the sagging balcony, rust-stained bath, ruined
conservatory, make an island of primitiveness in the poor, crowded
Sydney suburb. Immediately following the ruined conservatory
comes Duffield's visit to his patroness and half-mistress, a pole star of
the other polarity. As ever, to read any single phrase lazily is to miss at
least one point:

> Of a period no longer fashionable, the house had been made desirable by
> wealth. There were glimpses of tame sea through clumps of bamboo and
> strelitzia, but a bed of salvia burning too fiercely spoiled to some extent the
> jade-and-tussore effects of the bamboo.
>
> 'Mr – Duffield? Oh, yes, Mr Duffield!' The parlour-maid gave him her
> whiskery smile. (p. 273)

The painter is ushered into a room where three ageing socialites are already waiting for the hostess. When at last they identify him, White's satire is at its cruellest: "I adore paintings," Mrs Trotter said as she had been taught. "I'm going to get one – when we're properly settled in." In *The Solid Mandala* (1976) the two brothers at the heart of the narrative spend the long later part of their lives in a 'brown weatherboard house' in 'Terminus Road' (again, White's proper names are pointed). As the years pass and the brothers, locked in their private world (one a kind of holy idiot, the other a hopeless, desiccated introvert) grow into old age and near-senility, the house ages too. We read of its 'dry-rotten tremors and wooden tick tick', its roof leaking into the basin in the scullery when again the rainstorm comes from Beyond, its overgrown 'rosethorn' scrub scraping at the window-panes, its dusty relics of the past everywhere, its broken gate, sinking foundation, plants invading the house from outside. The contrast with the trim, clean, always new-painted house of the elderly Poulters living nearby, is that of the terribly but creatively wild with the over-tame.

The most ambitiously depicted of these houses where bush and outback recreate themselves within the domestic scene, as characters age and age brings both hopeless sameness and a mysterious intensification of life, is 'Xanadu' in *Riders in the Chariot* (1961), in my view White's grandest and most moving novel (near to it I put *The Eye of the Storm*). 'Xanadu' starts off as a rich, egotistic sham-connoisseur's folly – a stately pleasure-dome, 'golden, golden, in a frill or two of iron lace, beneath the dove-grey thatching of imported slates', its marble stairs wide enough for the owner once to have ridden a horse up them. But as the years pass, and the plain, dull, solitary daughter of the house ages her life away in it, the house itself reverts from its over-civilization to be an archetype of the opposite. We read of its always dusty carpets, loose stair-rods, choked garden; of how the garden creatures migrate inside, and the climbing plants invade the rooms. An earthquake makes the main foundations subside. It reveals the moss on the damask curtains, the birds come in from the garden and nest. In the end, the ruined pleasure-dome falls before the bulldozers, and trim suburbia spreads its villas over what had reverted to wilderness.

I have given space to setting out this polarity, and in particular to the recurrent dimension of the anti-suburban and 'primordial' in White, because the less conspicuous but in the end more distinctive and valuable line in his work lies there, in that decayed or outcast or wilderness world. What is most conspicuous, though, on account of its forcefulness as well as its magnitude, is White, the social satirist.

Not everyone will admire that satire, or even enjoy it. The tone is harsh and sarcastic. 'I have to admit to a bitter nature,' White writes in his autobiography, *Flaws in the Glass* (1981). There is entertainment and humour, but especially, though by no means exclusively, in the satirical portraits of women, White seems to write out of a hard, almost Swiftian distaste. Moreover, there is often a sense that the characters don't stand a chance; we are not only shown what there is in them, with an ironic and condemnatory eye, but told in advance to see it, and then not so much nudged into compliance as brusquely ranked into line and given orders, as it were, to watch now. But no one can miss the magisterial range of the satire, from the fiendish if ineffective Mrs Jolley, housekeeper in *Riders in the Chariot*, to the Princesse de Lascabanes (*lascive, bains* perhaps) foremost of aristocratic life-deniers, and her actor-brother the greedy, ageing poseur Sir Basil, in *The Eye of the Storm*. Above all, though, it is the opulent business–law–suburbia world of Sydney that White castigates; though as *The Woman Who Wasn't Allowed to Keep Cats* reveals, White's long relationship with Manoly Lascaris, and all his consequent experience of Greece, enabled him to see rich Greeks with the same Rhadamanthine eye. His writings on the Sydney world have an encyclopaedic fullness and detail, and a dry, curt precision of style, which are hard to match anywhere else in fiction written in English. There are the eight long, major novels with this astonishing social satire running through nearly all of them to substantiate that claim. Throughout the discussion so far there have been illustrations of this satire from time to time, and space will barely allow further illustration because more remains to be said.

The most important thing to be said is how that satire, reminiscent of Flaubert's whole oeuvre or to some extent of Conrad's long, land-based novels, has combined with a great if more obscure movement of *anti-satire*. This second fundamental moment in White's work is every bit as profoundly affirmative as Lawrence's, though it issues forth with a most un-Lawrentian indirectness and reserve. And this is where the polarities that have been given so much space up to now in this discussion reveal their major potential. In *The Living and the Dead* the polarity of satire and anti-satire runs between, on the one hand, the exact, acute Elyot Standish ('You had chosen the dictatorship of the mind') or Muriel Raphael ('Muriel recognized the physical necessity. She ran her life along those lines. Any sign of unruliness annoyed her. It pleased her when the disappointed told her she had a masculine mind') or Mrs Standish the mother ('She was safe again behind the language she had learnt to speak on her afternoons'). These are the materially successful people in the novel. Against them are Elyot's sister Eden, unable to protect herself from her cringingly predatory lover, or Julia the plain, good-hearted servant, or Connie Tiarks, helpless, tactless, plain but with an elusive psychic generosity ('she sat there feeling herself overflow, her stupidity, clumsiness, into the room'), or Wallie Collins, the casually or perhaps callously open-spirited black saxophonist. In this early book the contrasts are a little laboured, perhaps (though always tersely, as is White's way), and the locale monotonously unvaried; but that White's relentless social satire also releases its opposite is clear.

The Aunt's Story 'accumulates' the life-story of 'Theodora' Goodman (like 'Eden', 'god-gift' has its meaning). She is the plain, clumsy child who grows into the awkward, inarticulate, almost idiot spinster; and the book ends with her being taken into care as some sort of mental defective. But it is she who understands the music she is too clumsy to play, it is she who perceives that 'there are certain landscapes in which you can perceive the bones of the earth', and she who releases the essential life-illusions of one after another of the benighted souls in the shabby Riviera hotel. 'I never thought about being anything in particular. One *lives*, and that is all.'[2] In *Voss*, the polarity over against Mr Bonner who did 'behave with jolly or grave precision, according to rule', is his unwanted expatriate niece ('it seemed to Laura Trevelyan, those moments of her *life* which had been of most importance were both indistinct and ugly. The incident with the German in the garden had been almost indescribably ugly, untidy, painful'); or Voss himself, or Harry, 'who was, of course, a lad, and a simpleton'; or Jackie the aborigine, or Judd the ex-convict ('It was easy in that landscape to encourage thoughts of death. But the thick Judd, whose soul had achieved fulfilment not by escaping from his body, but by returning to it, preferred to interpret the aboriginal illusion in terms of *life*.') White's sense of the wonderful life of Australia's vegetation, of the 'bones of the earth', provides a setting:

> ... So she would hurry on ... until, there at the end, in a circle of light, was the cabbage tree. According to the day, the miraculous spire did not stir from its trance of stillest, whitest wax, or shuddered stiffly on the verge of breaking free, or rejoiced simply in its jewels of innocent and tinkling crystal.

That side of suburbia, known to the niece, the suburban outcast, has its continuity with Voss and Harry in the fiendish desert:

> 'It would not be worth it. Not since you taught me other things.'
> 'What things?' asked Voss quietly ...
> 'Why, sir, to *live*, I suppose.'
> ... The German was shivering with the cold that blew from the immense darkness, and which was *palpitating with little points of light*.

Likewise in *The Solid Mandala*. Waldo the prim, autistic brother is the negative pole to Arthur the great lumbering defective who, however, can dance, make up poems and sing them (while Waldo in the end secretly destroys his own lifelong secret writings), and can even intuitively understand the ageing Mrs Poulter's pathetic maternal orgy with the naked plastic doll. 'This man would be my saint ... if we could still believe in saints,' she tells the police at the macabre end of the book. In *The Vivisector*, Duffield's 'creative *life* depended' upon his strip of scorched scrub. Later, it grows, in 'self-fertilization', amid the 'flaking plaster rust deposits, balding plush, and pockets of dust enriched with cobwebs', of his hideout in Flint Street: in its squalor and isolation, the painter's creativity burns on into a final, lethal blaze of always brightening colour. In *The Eye of the Storm*, there is a curious interpenetration of roles. The jumped-up princess, the 'great' actor, the nursing sisters, rapacious for sex or for material gain, the members of Sydney 'society' are the predators, and Mrs Hunter as rapacious society hostess is among them. Yet, even at the same time, there is something in this helpless, grotesque, half-senile invalid that intimidates and finally evades them all: a side of her that we saw, intact, in her early days, when on that Queensland holiday island she took over the cooking, enchanted the children, and, alone in the ruined house, 'survived'.

Finally, the four apocalyptic 'Riders in the Chariot' comprise an

PATRICK WHITE

inarticulate aborigine painter, a solitary, elderly Jewish refugee ('the
Jew must understand the essential mystery and glory'), the simple-
minded shack-dweller Mrs Godbole, and the ageing, retarded spinster
who is the last dweller in the disintegrating pleasure dome ('in her
equal relation with air and earth, and responding as she did to the
motion of leaves' ... 'her love for all *living* matter'). Dubbo the
aborigine, rejecting the insistence of the good rector's wife who
thinks she is teaching him 'art', paints not from, but into 'life'. Those
four among the 'despised and rejected' converge slowly upon each
other, over the massive course of the book, because in each of them
life struggles through to become out-going, creative, affirmative; and
it can do so precisely because in them it is rudimentary and of a primal
innocence which cannot comprehend, and in the world's sense cannot
resist, the emptily destructive conformist patterns emanating from
White's other polarity. Yet in the end, all four rise above that
conformism; because they belong to what White himself, drawing
aptly upon the esoteric Jewish conceptions that he mastered so readily
for this work, refers to as the 'hidden zaddikhim – holy men who go
secretly about the world, healing, interpreting, doing their good
deeds'.

   In *A Fringe of Leaves*, set in transportation times in the wilds of what
is now Queensland, the pattern of hollow civilization against the
brutal but somehow still deeply-human convict world, or again of
the thin strip of 'civilized' terrain (complete with triangles and endless
flogging) against the vast, beautiful but life-critical outback, are very
clear and are close indeed to Marcus Clarke. This is not among
White's greatest novels, but here too human reality lies with convict
and castaway, and the satire – unusually gentle this time – is reserved
for the 'civilized'.

   At the time of writing White's most recent novel is *The Twyborn
Affair*. This is also by way of being an anomaly among his works.
The strange, deeply original life-history of a man of totally herma-
phrodite tendency calls for reading in conjunction with White's autobiography, *Flaws in the Glass* (1981) where the author emphatically
affirms his own similar personality. One is inclined to wonder
(perhaps to no very significant purpose) whether feeling free, at last,
in 1980, to depict such a character and his sexual life in all its disruptive detail has in fact released some mechanism which, in the earlier

fiction, White drew upon covertly, and only by transmuting it into disguised forms. At all events, in *The Twyborn Affair*, the old polarities of terrain are present, but the polarities of character have as good as gone. Bisexuality turns up almost everywhere in the book; over and over, it seems in the end to be the key to character; and, with its universal dissemination, it rather seems as if the deep, intuitive life-affirmingness that has so much made one polarity of character hitherto in White, has now become more diffused, and moreover has lost something of its power and depth. 'Twyborn', yet another of White's pregnant proper-names, may mean 'Ambivalently Born', but it does not mean, what one encounters with such decisive significance elsewhere in this fiction, twice-born, re-born. I suppose it is possible that, as it were with the release of crucial facts about himself, the novelist might cease to be preoccupied with indirect or disguised versions of what has embodied for him his own creative power.

Certainly, one inclines to speculate that White's extraordinary succession of outcast figures — unwanted spinster dependent, coloured man, aborigine, Jew, near-idiot, Cinderella-figure but stupid and ugly, introvert artist, senile invalid, convict, castaway, mad idealistic foreigner — have been surrogate-figures for the 'outcast' creative personality in White's own life; and that the strange, peripheral, 'drop-out' relationships which have played such key parts in his novels — brother with idiot brother, penniless painter and whore, freak brother and sister deeply and ambiguously involved together, convict and castaway, whore and aborigine — have to some degree been surrogate relationships for some relationship, also socially peripheral or taboo, which the author did not find it convenient to write about until late in life. Writing of a time a generation ago, White speaks in his autobiography of his 'homosexual temperament, forced at that period anyway to surround itself with secrecy' (*Flaws in the Glass*, p. 80).

Such reflections suggest a persuasive cohesion and logic in White's work as a whole. Certainly there is a thought-provoking recurrence, even underlying repetitiveness, across the novels which more and more catches the eye of the attentive reader (a trifling incident in *The Eye of the Storm*, when a man and a woman fight over who is to carry the heavy luggage, is for example repeated between two men, six years later, in remarkably similar terms). But the literary interest of such reflections is limited. White's greatness of achievement – no other word comes into consideration – sets aside questions of motivation. It lies in a combination of the three great traditional achievements of major fiction. These are, an encyclopaedic range of social portraiture; a deep instinctive grasp of the springs of positive life; and a close, detailed mastery of style that, endlessly, fills the corners of every sentence with point and pith, and succeeds (in Johnson's words) in 'securing the first purpose of a writer, by ... compelling him that reads his work to *read it through*'.

NOTES

1. Quotations from White's works are from the Penguin editions, except for those from *A Fringe of Leaves*, *The Twyborn Affair*, and *Flaws in the Glass* (1981), which are from the Cape editions. Italics in quotations are added by the present writer.

2. In this and the quotations which follow, 'life' or its cognates are italicized simply to draw the reader's attention to their recurrence.

SAMUEL BECKETT: THE NEED TO FAIL

GABRIEL JOSIPOVICI

'I am only interested in failure,' Beckett told his friend Thomas McGreevey when he saw him again after the war. And this was not a boast but a simple statement of fact. In 1946 he was forty and his life seemed to have been a total failure. Born with remarkable gifts, as a sportsman, an intellectual, a poet, he seemed, by the end of the war, to have squandered them all. He had rejected a promising academic career which was his for the asking; he had cut himself off from his family in Dublin; and all he had to show for it were an eccentric volume of stories and a novel, a few poems and translations which had appeared in French literary journals in the pre-war years, and an extensive circle of acquaintance in the bohemian and avant-garde world of Paris. The novel, *Murphy*, had been rejected by forty-two publishers before it was finally accepted in 1938, and when the pattern started to repeat itself with *Watt*, the novel he had worked on throughout the war, with publishers justifying themselves by saying that at this point in time what they were looking for was something more positive and heroic, Beckett could say with feeling to McGreevey: 'I am not interested in heroism and success. I am only interested in failure.'[1]

Yet less than ten years later he had achieved success and recognition to a degree he cannot ever have dreamt of. *Waiting for Godot* (1954) and the publication of the Trilogy made Beckett, overnight, the most talked-of writer of his time, and his life, despite himself, had become the fulfilment of a Romantic fairy-tale: the struggling, solitary artist, refusing ever to compromise, suddenly hailed as the voice of a generation. Of course nothing in his work had fundamentally changed; only the public's recognition of it. And the extraordinary thing is that Beckett has been able to take success in his stride just as he took failure, and simply go on being himself. Now, at seventy-five, he seems younger than any other writer, and each new work is still a venture into the unknown, the taking of risks which nearly all writers would balk at. In fact, though Beckett could never stand the posturing of Yeats, it is of the old Yeats and the old Wallace Stevens, artists whose late work constitutes their greatest achievement, that he now most forcibly reminds us.

Yet, if Beckett became famous in the fifties, he has never been exactly popular. His plays have never been performed in the West End, his prose has been more talked about than read. Compared to a Hemingway, a Graham Greene, a Saul Bellow, his is clearly a minority following. In this he reminds us more of the great masters of modernism – Eliot, Webern, Mondrian – than of his contemporaries. The sociology of art cannot deal with such artists because there is no clear or simple correlation between their significance and their popularity. For some they have changed the history of art; for others they are nothing but charlatans. And, especially in the case of Eliot and Beckett, their work seems both to invite and to resist criticism. It invites it because it seems to suggest a mystery to be uncovered; and it resists it less because that mystery proves difficult to uncover than because criticism, no matter how sensitive and intelligent, never seems able to bridge the gap between the immediate impact of the least of their works and any subsequent explanation.

What is the nature of this gap? Why does it exist? Such questions clearly cannot be answered in the abstract. Let us look briefly then at the best of Beckett's early stories (published when he was twenty-six), 'Dante and the Lobster'.

'It was morning and Belaqua was stuck in the first of the canti in the moon. He was so bogged that he could move neither backward nor forward.' Belaqua is not Dante's slothful character but a Dublin intellectual and layabout. No explanation is given for his name, which engenders in the reader a curious unease: the details of his life and actions are too specific for this to be allegory or even Joycean replaying of myth, but the name is too odd, too literary, for us to feel entirely at ease within the fiction. As we will see, both the style and the content of the story will reinforce such feelings in the reader.

Belaqua's situation as he struggles with the opening canti of the *Paradiso* parallels Dante's own as he seeks enlightenment from Beatrice:

Blissful Beatrice was there, Dante also, and she explained the spots on the moon to him. She shewed him in the first place where he was at fault, then she put up her own explanation. She had it from God, therefore he could rely on its being accurate in every particular.

It is difficult to decide if 'he' in this last sentence is Dante or Belaqua, but it doesn't matter. They are both mortal, incapable of full understanding, driven by needs other than those of pure intellect or pure love.

Indeed, as midday strikes Belaqua triumphantly closes his book and prepares for lunch. In the afternoon he has to collect a lobster which he is bringing to his aunt for supper, and then have his Italian lesson. But first, lunch:

Lunch, to come off at all, was a very nice affair. If his lunch was to be enjoyable, and it could be very enjoyable indeed, he must be left in absolute tranquillity to prepare it. But if he were disturbed now, if some brisk tattler were to come bouncing in now with a big idea or a petition, he might just as well not eat at all, for the food would turn to bitterness on his palate, or, worse again, taste of nothing ... The first thing to do was to lock the door. Now nobody could come at him. He deployed an old Herald and smoothed it out on the table. The rather handsome face of McCabe the assassin stared up at him ... Now the long barrel-loaf came out of its biscuit-tin and had its end evened off on the face of McCabe. Two inexorable drives with the bread saw and a pair of neat rounds of raw bread, the main elements of his meal, lay before him, awaiting his pleasure. The stump of the loaf went back into prison, the crumbs, as though there were no such thing as a sparrow in the wide world, were swept in a fever away, and the slices snatched up and carried to the grill.

We may at first be tempted to see the prose as merely mannered and self-conscious, and conclude that Beckett is simply trying to be funny. He succeeds too, quite as well as Wodehouse and Waugh. But instinctively we feel that there is more to it than that. In a peculiar way, though it is only the cutting of two slices of bread that is being described, we feel that something much more serious is going on than in the two English writers. Serious, of course, does not mean solemn; on the contrary, seriousness here is obviously connected with laughter. But how? Provisionally we may say that it has something to do with the fact that here there is no way of establishing that comfortable distance between reader and story, author and character, which is one of the delights of Wodehouse and early Waugh. On the contrary, our laughter is tinged with panic because there is something excessive about the manner of both hero and writer, and we cannot easily perceive the reason for this excess. But, as with all the best fiction, these feelings remain latent and we read on.

McCabe the assassin, like Dante and the lobster, is mutely present throughout the story. In the pub where Belaqua finally settles down to eat his toasted sandwich, so lovingly prepared, and now filled with a mouth-burning mixture of salt, pepper, mustard and Gorgonzola, he learns that

the Malahide murderer's petition for mercy, signed by half the land, having been rejected, the man must swing at dawn in Mountjoy and nothing could save him. Ellis the hangman was even now on his way. Belaqua, tearing at the sandwich and swilling the precious stout, pondered on McCabe in his cell.

He is clearly still pondering when, having collected the lobster, in the course of his Italian lesson he asks the teacher to translate Dante's punning line: 'Qui vive la pietà quando è ben morta.' ' "Do you think," she murmured, "it is absolutely necessary to translate it?" ' Her reticence may seem puzzling at first. For after all a translation is certainly possible. Virgil is here rebuking Dante for feeling sympathy for the damned, and he says: 'Here *piety* lives when *pity* is quite dead.' But what the teacher senses and what it will take the rest of the story for Belaqua to grasp, is that what is at issue here is not translation *into English*, but *into reality*. For how can our liberal secular culture make any sense of Dante's distinction?

Belaqua finally arrives at his aunt's house and hands her his parcel. She undoes it and lays the lobster out on the kitchen table:

'They assured me it was fresh,' said Belaqua.
Suddenly he saw the creature move, this neuter creature. Definitely it changed its position. His hand flew to his mouth.
'Christ!' he said, 'it's alive.'

Unperturbed, the aunt bustles off to the pantry and returns with an apron on and her sleeves rolled up. 'Well,' she said, 'it is to be hoped so, indeed.'

'All this time,' muttered Belaqua. Then, suddenly aware of her hideous equipment: 'What are you going to do?' he cried.
'Boil the beast,' she said, 'what else?'
'But it's not dead,' protested Belaqua.

Gently she explains to him that lobsters are always boiled alive. 'They
must be.'

She caught up the lobster and laid it on its back. It trembled. 'They feel
nothing,' she said.

In the depths of the sea it had crept into the cruel pot. For hours, in the
midst of its enemies, it had breathed secretly. It had survived the French-
woman's cat and his witless clutch. Now it was going alive into scalding water.
It had to. Take into the air my quiet breath.

Belaqua looked at the old parchment of her face, grey in the dim kitchen.

'You make a fuss,' she said angrily, 'and upset me and then lash into it for
your dinner.'

She lifted the lobster clear of the table. It had about thirty seconds to live.

Well, thought Belaqua, it's a quick death, God help us all.

It is not.

Everything comes together here: the problem of God's mercy to
the damned, raised by Dante's punning line; the question of the fate of
McCabe the murderer; the reason for Belaqua's aggressive way with
objects and the writer's aggressive way with language. None of these
has been overtly dealt with so far, they have merely troubled the
stream of the narrative. In the face of the aunt's calm, 'They feel
nothing', we are forced to face them.

The aunt's attitude suggests a refusal to open oneself to another's
sufferings, and we naturally side with Belaqua's horror and disgust.
Though in the end he too tries to anaesthetize himself with a cliché,
'It's a quick death, God help us', the last three words, uttered not by
him, we feel, but by some absolute impersonal authority, show that in
the face of what he has witnessed clichés will have little effect: 'It is
not.'

Yet do Belaqua's horror and pity for both the lobster and McCabe
do anything for them? Is Dante not perhaps right? To feel pity is
meaningless. It only makes the pitier feel better. It could even be
argued that Belaqua's pity is worse than his aunt's realism, for he
wishes to salve his conscience, yet is not above tucking into the
lobster. And now we can begin to understand something about why
the story is written as it is. For is Belaqua's attitude very different from
that of the writer? By imaginatively conveying the lobster's agony
the writer puts himself on the side of honesty, sympathy, truth. But is
this sympathy not bought far too cheaply? Does he in fact really

understand the agony of McCabe or the lobster? Is there not even a monstrous presumption in imagining that he does?

Belaqua can ponder the fate of McCabe and the lobster but he will always be denied a full understanding of them because he, unlike them, can escape. And this is the case of Beckett as well. He is thus caught in an impossible situation. He wants to make us sense what McCabe and the lobster are suffering, *and* to make us recognize that, however much we project ourselves imaginatively into their situations, we will never have any conception of the horror of those last thirty seconds.

But there is a further twist. For McCabe and the lobster the time of imagining, of prevarication, of 'being stuck', is over. Now they are locked in their horrible reality. And for this they are to be envied as well as pitied. Imprisoned, hopeless, they await their end. Yet we, who think ourselves free, are also imprisoned. Our end too will come. But, because there are no bars we cannot imagine it, and live as though we were immortal. Now the reason for Belaqua's violence ('the crumbs . . . were swept in a fever away') and his masochism ('It was like eating glass. His mouth burned and ached with the exploit!') is clear: instinctively he tries to make himself feel the vulnerability of his own body, to prepare himself for his own impending death.

And again, behind Belaqua is his maker. 'The stump of the loaf went back into prison, the crumbs, as though there were no such thing as a sparrow in the wide world, were swept in a fever away.' Just because it is so easy to make a sparrow fly in fiction, fiction cannot convey the miracle of a sparrow's flight, of its freedom. Conversely, the reason why there is such an insistence on enclosure in Beckett, on the lack or loss of limbs, such a denial of generosity, such apparent cynicism, is that movement of the body or the spirit is felt by him to be bought too easily in words. Words can do anything; by the same token, they can do nothing. And so, since fiction is helpless in the face of reality, only the fiction of helplessness will be real. Here it is only the loaf that is maimed and pushed back into its box; later, it will be the protagonist himself.

The pleasures of the imagination are not *innocent* pleasures. This is the driving force behind all Beckett's work, from first to last. The very act of writing and of reading distorts reality, the central reality that we are imprisoned in our bodies and will soon be no more.

Beckett thus tries to use the imagination against the imagination. But each time we say 'I see', each time we are moved to feel for the suffering of McCabe or the lobster, Beckett has failed. Each time he has to add an 'It is not', but then that too becomes part of what we 'understand' and he has to start again. The more he succeeds then, the more he fails. But failure, of course, is not in its turn transmuted into success. It remains itself.

For the next fifteen years Beckett struggles to escape this contradiction. He struggles against himself, his gifts. The brilliance and bitterness of *Murphy*, *Watt*, and *Molloy* stem from this sense of unresolvable struggle. He senses reality forming under his hand as he writes, but what kind of reality is it?

Belaqua drew near to the house of his aunt. Let us call it Winter, that dusk may fall now and a moon rise. At the corner of the street a horse was down and a man sat on his head ... A lamplighter flew by on his bike, tilting with his pole at the standards, jousting a little yellow light into the evening.

Most writers would be more than satisfied with such gifts. But for Beckett the gifts themselves are a sign of damnation. 'One has to be very strong to deny oneself the luxury of such speculations,' Wittgenstein remarked to a friend who showed him a book of metaphysics. And Wittgenstein's constant attempts at flight from philosophy have much in common with Beckett's own attempts at escape from his art. For no horse was down, no lamplighter at his rounds, there was no aunt or even Belaqua, for that matter, only Samuel Beckett, whoever he might be, needing to write. But why? Where does such a need come from? How can it be satisfied?

He still has an uneasy conscience at the ease with which it is possible to conjure a world out of paper when he comes to the end of *Molloy* (1955). The second part of that book had opened in good classical first person style: 'It is midnight. The rain is beating on the windows. I am calm. All is sleeping.' It ends: 'Then I went back into the house and wrote, It is midnight. The rain is beating on the windows. It was not midnight. It was not raining.'

We have grown so used to this kind of thing that we dismiss it with glib remarks about Chinese boxes and novels about writing novels. As with all art, everything depends upon our sense of the artist's responsibility. In Beckett it is not a joke or a clever way to end, but a mute cry of despair: Why am I writing this? Why going through with this fraud?

The Trilogy grew out of the attempt to face this. For Beckett did not stop at the end of *Molloy* and look round for *another* novel to write. There seemed to be no way forward, yet he found he could go on moving. And he could do so, precisely, by reducing the fictional protagonist's own possibility of movement. And so he went from Molloy and Moran circling round each other in the forest to Malone dying alone in his room, and from Malone to that which can only be named in negative terms: not Molloy, not Malone, not Worm. The unnamable is the source of both light and dark, speech and silence, and it cannot be grasped as an essence, only seen in its operations.

In the earlier work, as we have seen, the sense of bitterness and anger stemmed from frustration at being locked in an impossibly contradictory enterprise: there seemed to be no way in which 'It is not' could detach itself from the fiction and acquire the unquestioned status of Beatrice's lessons to Dante in the *Commedia*. But now, with *Malone Dies* (1956) and *The Unnamable* (1958), we start to feel that Beckett's acceptance of impossibility frees him, releases new energies: he will not name and then point in derision at the name; instead he will show the operations of the unnamable.

Between these two novels came *Waiting for Godot* (1954), and the theatre was of course an important factor in this transformation. For the theatre is the real locus of illusion. In one sense it is a place of far greater reality than the library, since here flesh and blood figures speak directly to us. But for that very reason it is a place of far more dangerous illusion, since these figures are only apparently as free as we are; in reality they are doomed to repeat the same words over and over, every evening. What Beckett does is to use this greater appearance of reality in the theatre to force us into a recognition of the complex interplay of memory, imagination and desire in our own lives. The central question remains, as always: what does it mean to be alive? But in the theatre this question acquires a new sharpness and immediacy.

Not I, written in 1972, is the culmination of the Trilogy. Here a mouth, unattached to any body, talks to us or to itself from a darkened stage. We see the mouth, we hear it speak, but we also see that there is no body. We are thus forced to accept both its reality and its separation from the body. And so Beckett makes it impossible for us to avoid awareness of the fact that we too are never wholly where we are, that we can never speak what we know or know fully what we speak, can never attain a fullness of speech that takes account of our bodies.

Between mouth and audience stands a shadowy figure. What is it doing there? It reminds us that none of Beckett's stage monologues are ever quite that: Krapp has his tape, Winnie her Willie. We are never unified, never one even when most alone. Moreover, our voice is not attached to our body as our hands and feet are, while neither voice nor body is fully alive without the other. The theatre is the place where the inevitable distance between them can be demonstrated.

The mouth cannot say what it is, but it is present to us. And the more it cannot say the more aggressive it seems to become. The mouth is the body reduced to a minimum; it is a hole, but a hole only exists by virtue of what surrounds it. The mouth is the place of connection between sound and meaning, and it is the presence of the shadowy figure which saves it from falling back into either the one or the other. The unpleasant though powerful effect of the TV version, which dispensed with the figure and filled the whole screen with the mouth, was due to the fact that it left one with too immediate an identification of that organ with the vagina. The connection is there, of course, just as the tape is *Krapp*'s, but the space between Krapp and crap, between mouth and vagina is precisely the space where art can – just – exist.

The figure has its instructions:

Movement: this consists in simple sideways raising of arms from sides and their falling back, in a gesture of helpless compassion. It lessens with each recurrence till scarcely perceptible at third. There is just enough pause to contain it as MOUTH recovers from vehement refusal to relinquish third person.

Why will the mouth not relinquish third person? As so often in Beckett, there are two contradictory answers. (Art can contain such contradictions, but criticism has to fight its own tendency to dissolve.) The mouth will not accept responsibility for what it says, denying that it is attached to any body. But it also knows that to speak in the first person is to perpetuate a falsehood, since that which is the source of utterance is never a single 'I'. This is what constitutes the drama. Somewhere something which is not the mouth keeps wanting it to use the first person, to acknowledge that speech comes from a person, with the responsibilities we all share; but another part of the self knows that to say 'I' is to lock out major portions of the self. The only acknowledgement of the force that seeks to say 'I' is a violent denial, and this is followed by the figure's gesture: '... and she found herself in the – ... What? ... who? ... no! ... she! ... (*Pause and movement*).' Once this is grasped we can see that the compassionate figure is deeply ambiguous: father confessor but also judge; friend but also betrayer.

Beckett, since *Godot*, seems to have moved from stage to page and back as a way of unblocking, of keeping the forward momentum going in spite of everything. *Not I* was a kind of culmination, but since it was written he has published two long prose pieces which are more relaxed, lyrical and all-embracing than anything he has done, *Company* (1979) and *Mal vu mal dit* (1981).

In *Company* we once again have a narrator unable to say 'I'. 'A voice comes to one in the dark. Imagine.' The voice speaks, tells stories, but 'only a small part of what is said can be verified'. All that can be asserted is that someone is lying on his back in the dark, and that to this someone comes a voice, telling him stories:

> Use of the second person marks the voice. That of the third that cankerous other. Could he speak to and of whom the voice speaks there would be a first. But he cannot. He shall not. You cannot. You shall not.

Of course it would be wonderful if he/you could. 'What an addition to company that would be. A voice in the first person singular. Murmuring now and then, Yes, I remember.'

The entire tradition of novel and autobiography depends on just this sleight-of-hand. A voice murmurs: 'Yes, I remember,' but even the most truthful of autobiographers omits to ask himself: 'Even if the stories the voice tells me are familiar to me, how am I to know they are stories about myself?' It may be that repetition has made him imagine that they belong to him. And what is 'a story about myself' anyway? We say: 'This is how it was', or: 'This is what I did' – but in what sense is this 'I' oneself? Is it not a construct made up of social, psychological and literary clichés?

This does not mean, as some recent theorists have maintained, that there is no self, only that it is less an entity than a source of potential. For Beckett all that can be said is that a voice comes to one in the dark, and that to listen to this voice is to acquire a sense of company. All that can be said with certainty is: 'Devised deviser devising it all for company. In the same figment dark as his figments.' And so a kind of provisional truth is arrived at:

> Huddled thus you find yourself imagining you are not alone while knowing full well that nothing has occurred to make this possible. The process continues none the less lapped as it were in meaninglessness. You do not murmur in so many words, I know this doomed to fail and yet persist. No. For the first personal and a fortiori plural pronoun had never any place in your vocabulary.

Though *Company* is clearly there in embryo in the early stories, it was of course impossible to imagine it till Beckett had written it. And the tone has changed. Now there are no sudden jerks and shifts of register; the ambiguities concerning self, voice and imagination are explored, gently played with rather than aggressively butted against. The process continues, though lapped as it were in meaninglessness. But the important thing is that it continues, and that what reading it does to us is to make us sense that what lives in us and makes us live is less a history or a set of memories than a certain rhythm, which may, in the end, be simply the unique rhythm of our own breathing. But, curiously, we can only apprehend that rhythm by submitting ourselves to that otherness which is language and the language of another. It can never be grasped by introspection. And what Beckett's work leaves us with is a powerful sense of the rhythm of another's existence. To pay it the attention it deserves is to grow aware of our own rhythm. But the paradox is always there: we become conscious of who and what we are only in the moment that we recognize that that is what, once again, we have failed to be.

NOTE

1. For this and other biographical information I have drawn on Deirdre Bair's biography, *Samuel Beckett* (London, 1978).

F. R. LEAVIS AND 'ENGLISH'

GEOFFREY STRICKLAND

To describe F. R. Leavis's work without appraising it is to offer a
caricature and yet the task of appraisal is daunting, as anyone who
knew him personally or is already familiar with his writings will
agree. His influence on the study of English literature is well known
and unlikely to be challenged, even by those who may deplore it or
who think it has long since been superseded. Leavis belongs, in one
sense, to history; this can hardly be disputed. I can only hope that it
will emerge from my own account of the history that he does so in an
exemplary way; that is, as someone who cannot be imitated but from
whom, as well as about whom, the general reader and student of
literature can learn.

By Leavis's work I mean his collection of critical essays on what
might, for convenience, be called literature, society and education;
the supervisions and lectures he gave at Cambridge and later York
universities; and the quarterly review, *Scrutiny*, which he edited with
L. C. Knights, D. W. Harding, and his wife Q. D. Leavis, among
others (though her name never appeared on the title page) from his
house in Cambridge, the town in which he was born on Bastille Day
in 1895. He continued to live in Cambridge all his life until his death
in 1978, except for the First World War when, although a conscientious objector, he worked as a stretcher bearer on the Western Front
and was the victim of a German gas attack. The Leavises had been
local tradesmen and his father ran a piano shop in Cambridge, where
Leavis attended the Perse School and learned, as well as Latin, German
and French, Greek by the direct method from its famous headmaster,
W. H. D. Rouse. After the war, he read History and English before
writing a doctoral dissertation on political journalism in the
seventeenth century and before becoming Director of Studies at
Downing College, where most of his teaching career was spent, a
University Lecturer and finally a Reader in English. The title

'Reader' which, in plain English means 'writer', has never been more appropriately bestowed.[1]

It is the word 'English' which needs to be discussed at some length if one is to say where Leavis stands in any history worthy of the name. 'English' is the name given to an educational programme which was almost unheard of in England a hundred years ago, which has enjoyed enormous prestige since then and which was once advocated in fairly unanimous terms. It now, of course, holds by sheer right of occupation a prominent place in the school and university syllabus, though it can no longer claim to be justified by any view of its purpose which is shared by all or even a majority of those who teach it.

In the nineteenth century, English seems to have been in competition, among educational reformers, with natural science for the place of honour in the primary and secondary school syllabus, as compulsory universal education got under way. Those who, like T. H. Huxley, favoured science pointed to the apparent success of scientific teaching in Germany, which was already seen as a serious economic rival, and also to its virtues as an intellectual and moral discipline. Those who, like Huxley's friend, Matthew Arnold, favoured English adopted what is still the common view that the uncultured scientific spirit is Philistine. Arnold's advocacy met with considerable success; though the task of promoting English studies in universities and training colleges went on into the 1920s. The Cambridge English Tripos itself, for which Leavis was one of the first undergraduates to read, was not inaugurated until 1917. The arguments of Arnold, consequently, tend to be repeated with few variations over a period of half a century or more and with the same kind of reforming zeal. Poetry, more than anything else for Arnold, exemplifies culture. Its influence, he argues, could come to resemble that of religion and like religion it transcends all other interests, especially those of class:

Culture ... seeks to do away with classes; to make the best that has been thought and known in the world current everywhere; to make all men live in an atmosphere of sweetness and light, where they may use ideas as it uses them itself, freely – nourished and not bound by them.

'The men of culture' are therefore 'the true apostles of equality'.[2] This same belief that the study of literature can ennoble and refine and at the same time inspire social harmony (thus forestalling political

F. R. LEAVIS AND 'ENGLISH'

revolution) is expressed in the Newbolt Committee's Report of 1921 on *The Teaching of English in England*. English, it claims, could 'form a new element of national unity, linking together the mental life of all classes by experiences which hitherto have been the privileges of a limited section'. The university professor of literature has, therefore,

obligations not merely to the student but still more to the teeming populations outside the University walls, most of whom have not so much as heard 'whether there be any Holy Ghost'. The fulfilment of these obligations means propaganda work, organization and the building up of a staff of assistant missionaries.[3]

Possibly the most ambitious claims made for the teaching of literature at this time were, however, those of I. A. Richards. As he wrote in 1924 in *The Principles of Literary Criticism*:

The critic ... is as much concerned with the health of the mind as the doctor with the health of the body ... Bad taste and crude responses are not mere flaws in an otherwise admirable person. They are actually a root evil from which other defects follow.[4]

Two things will, I think, be obvious today as one looks back on this period. Despite the energy and conviction that went into the promotion of 'English', it was not an unqualified success – certainly not by the standards of its instigators. One has only to think what Matthew Arnold would say if treated to a few minutes of 'Tom and Jerry' or 'Starsky and Hutch'.[5] It would also be difficult today to find among the thousands of English teachers any unanimity regarding the purpose of English studies comparable to that which seems to have existed half a century ago. There are also few who would regard the idea of promoting social harmony as anything other than a naïve or mischievous delusion; few also who would not be embarrassed at the idea of being thought of as a 'missionary'. Some might be embarrassed only by the candour with which such a term expressed what is still their own idea of their function. The candour, however, is the candour of confidence and that confidence in a clear common purpose belongs almost certainly to the past.

Culture and Environment, which Leavis wrote with Denys Thompson (at the time, a public school teacher) and published in 1933, reflects some of that confidence. The book is original, in that it offers a detailed programme of study for schools, extending the English

177

syllabus to include the study of advertisements, newspapers and commercial fiction, in order to help young people resist conditioning by what we now call the 'media'. However, it is by no means representative of his work since then. The importance of English studies is something he never disputed. But his claims on their behalf are very different from those that were once commonly made. Leavis continued throughout his career to see 'English' as playing a crucial role in the life of the university and the nation as a whole. He continued to write like Richards also, to the extent that he saw the good or great work of literature as the manifestation of something both psychologically and ethically valuable.[6] But he was clearly less inclined as the years went by to speak of the teaching of English as self-evidently beneficial. Terms like 'apostles' or 'missionaries', used by the early propagandists for English, are absent from his vocabulary. The ideal of the university and of the 'English school', for Leavis, became increasingly divorced from the disappointing reality. 'The academic is the enemy,' he would often say, and he included among the enemy, especially, colleagues in his own discipline. This may make Leavis appear at first an enigma (or worse) and what he advocated is certainly far from straightforward or obvious. This is what he constantly reminds us himself. In fact, the famous difficulty of his style is partly due to the intrinsic difficulties of any answer that is neither complacent nor dismissive to the question: why English?

'English' matters for Leavis, it could be said, because poetry matters. And poetry matters, to quote from *New Bearings in English Poetry* (1932), 'because of the kind of poet who is more alive than other people, more alive in his age'. What, though, does 'more alive' mean? And how can one possibly know, even confining oneself to the population of the United Kingdom, who qualifies for the title 'most alive'? It does not mean, for example, that such a poet is necessarily wiser than other people about economics or foreign affairs; and the fact that the poetry of Auden and Spender in the 1930s was overtly political did not in itself, for Leavis, entitle it to be taken seriously. An answer, however, is to be found on the same page:

> He is unusually sensitive, unusually aware, more sincere and more himself than the ordinary man can be. He knows what he feels and what he is interested in. He is a poet because his interest in his experience is not separable from his interest in words.

The phrase 'to know what one feels' is crucial and bears the full weight of Leavis's argument. And it is further elucidated by a quotation later on from the *Autobiographies* of Yeats who remarks how many years it is 'before one can believe enough in what one feels even to know what the feeling is'. The long section on Yeats in *New Bearings* is worth quoting in this respect. It is also an example of the sophistication of Leavis's prose, the economy his respect for his readers' intelligence allows and the swiftness and ease with which he is able to relate the different aspects of a poet's experience, his limitations and strengths, to the particular conditions of civilization at a given time. Yeats, according to Leavis, became a poet at a time when poetry seemed doomed, if it was to survive at all, to create an imaginary world set apart from reality and constituting, if possible, a higher reality. Yeats, Leavis writes,

differs from the Victorian romantics in the intensity with which he seeks his 'higher reality'. This difference we have attributed to his being Irish; but it will not do to let this explanation detract from his rare distinction of mind and spirit ... Mr Yeats knew much of intellectual suffering ... he had a magnificent mind, and less than the ordinary man's capacity for self-deception ... Indeed, his dealings with spiritualism, magic, theosophy, dream and trance were essentially an attempt to create an alternative science. The science of Huxley and Tyndall he had rejected in the name of imagination and emotion, but he had an intelligence that would not be denied. He exhibits for us the inner struggle of the nineteenth-century mind in an heroic form. (pp. 40–41)

The poet once again contrasted with 'the ordinary man' unsure of what he feels or believes! This may still sound preposterous. A 'Paki-bashing' member of the National Front may know what he feels and believes. Yeats himself acknowledges as much:

> The best lack all conviction, while the worst
> Are full of passionate intensity ...

However, what Leavis writes (to return to my previous quotation) is, 'He is a poet because his interest in his experience is not separable from his interest in words.' And this 'interest' can be demonstrated; for Leavis's well-known insistence on judging every piece of writing by the highest possible standards turns out on examination to be a matter of judging the writer on his own terms and by his own standards. It amounts to a refusal to misrepresent.

This possibly paradoxical-seeming claim calls for some explanation. To judge something by its own standards or on its own terms is usually taken to mean judging it with studied forbearance, with a kind of willing suspension, when necessary, of one's feeling of boredom or distaste, and such forbearance was, surely, beyond Leavis's powers. Studied forbearance in itself is not, however, a surer guide to understanding than instinctive admiration, boredom or disgust, and a willing suspension of the latter may entail merely sharing a writer's own most hopeful and flattering view of what it is he thinks he has achieved. Almost anyone who has tried to write poetry will know that much of what is written, as Leavis reminds us in *New Bearings*, is

not so much bad as dead – it was never alive. The words that lie there arranged on the page have no roots: the writer himself can never have been more than superficially interested in them.   (p. 6)

The same fidelity to actual intention, on the critic's part, is apparent in what he says of poetry and prose in which we have every reason to believe that the words, which are 'alive', were and remain the focus of some intense interest. The extraordinary conviction, for example, conveyed by Yeats in his creation of a world of magic and myth, in defiance of Victorian science and materialism, is shared by Leavis to the extent that Yeats shares it himself and Leavis is clearly convinced too by Yeats' own admissions of futility and failure.

New Bearings is an early work and many of the judgements Leavis makes in it were to be radically modified later on, but it illustrates conveniently what was to remain a characteristic manner (he disliked the word 'method') of reading. It is obvious here as later, for example, that his interest in the poet goes with an extreme attentiveness to the poetry as such and especially to what is revealed by rhythm and what Leavis calls 'movement'. The best example of this is probably his commentary of 1952 on Emily Brontë's *Cold in the Earth* and Hardy's *After a Journey*, reprinted in *The Living Principle* (1975). But take also his commentary in *New Bearings* on another poem by Hardy, *The Voice*, which

seems to start dangerously with a crude popular lilt, but this is turned into a subtle movement by the prosaic manner of the content, a manner that elsewhere would have been Hardy's characteristic gaucherie:

> Can it be you that I hear? Let me view you, then,
> Standing as when I drew near to the town
> Where you would wait for me: yes, as I knew you then,
> Even to the original air-blue gown!

By the end of this second stanza the bare matter-of-fact statement has already subdued the rhythm; the shift of stress on the rhyme ('viéw you then', 'knew you thén') has banished the jingle from it.   (pp. 59–60)

For Leavis, 'movement' and 'rhythm' are not synonymous, though they are necessarily related and related also to another key term in his criticism, 'direction'. It is these terms which are used to describe what is positively affirmed in T. S. Eliot's *Ash Wednesday* (pp. 115–132), when contrasted with a poem like *The Journey of the Magi*: positively affirmed, even though so much of the poem is explicitly hopeless and though the positiveness of the affirmation has nothing to do with an assertion of belief on Eliot's part or a demonstration of logic.[7] 'Positively affirmed' needs of course, considerable qualification, since Leavis himself returned continually, especially in his later years, to this theme. His admiration for the *Four Quartets* when they were first published was almost unqualified, but he came increasingly to regard even this poetry as that of a great poet disabled by his 'fear of life and contempt (which includes self-contempt) for humanity' from recognizing the nature of his own all too human creativity. The implicit and often explicit contrast was with the achievement – literary and hence far more than literary – of D. H. Lawrence.

What calls for comment too is the all-important distinction, for Leavis, between intentions which are merely intentions and those that are 'realized' in a work of art and between works of literature which merely state or assert and those that 'enact' their meaning. Leavis seems, as a young critic, to have been impressed by the notion derived from Eliot and Santayana of an 'objective correlative' of emotion, which Eliot, in his essay on *Hamlet*, calls

a set of objects, a situation, a chain of events which shall be the formula of that *particular* emotion; such that when the external facts, which must terminate in sensory experience are given, the emotion is immediately evoked.

A rigorous examination of what Leavis himself means by 'realize' and 'enact' (terms that appear less often in his later than in his earlier criticism) would probably, however, reveal that this was a matter ultimately of the writer's 'interest in words' and that it was, for him, demonstrable only as such. The inadequacy, as he sees it, of Eliot's own terminology and arguments is pointed out in a lecture of 1967, 'The Necessary Opposite', reprinted in *English Literature in our Time*.

'English', for Leavis, matters because poetry matters and the English history of which it is part, the history of one's own time which it is impossible to understand if one sees it in isolation from either the past or the future. In his recommendations to under-graduates, works of history featured prominently and he was more concerned that they should read the works of Elie Halévy or the essays of Mill than the poems of Meredith or Rossetti. This doesn't mean that he thought of the study of history and literature as indistinguish-able but he certainly saw them as complementary; for the testimony of the poet who 'knows what he feels' tells us more (by definition) than that of the 'ordinary man' as described, for example, by the historian, Marc Bloch:

> As a student of the present instant, I apply myself to the task of sounding public opinion on the important issues of the day. I ask questions. I note and compare the answers. What do I have then but the rather awkwardly expressed ideas which my communicants have formulated as to what they believe they believe, or what they are willing to reveal?
>
> (*The Historian's Craft*, p. 51)

Joseph Conrad's young skipper in *The Shadow Line*, Leavis argues,[8] who gave up a safe berth because he refused to accept the tedium of security and the accompanying 'life emptiness', exposes himself to testing circumstances and thereby becomes humanly 'representative' – paradoxically in so far as he is thus far 'exceptional', just as the Conrad who was able to tell his story was exceptional. Leavis is not arguing that the only possible kind of history is history founded on real or imaginary testimonies of this kind. He is, however, arguing that such testimony is indispensable to the kind of history so often neglected by professional historians, the history of feelings and beliefs, and of life as lived consciously.

The study of history from this point of view is the opposite of antiquarian. Leavis was never a Marxist, despite his sympathy in the early thirties for the idea of 'some form of economic communism' and his qualified admiration for Trotsky and Hugh MacDiarmid.[9] By the time of Stalin's purges, Leavis had turned decidedly against communism in practice, but despite his outspoken anti-Marxist views, there are certain aspects of his approach to literature and history which Marxists could and often in fact still today find congenial.[10] Like the Marxists, Leavis insists that the act of understanding is not a passive reflection of the world as revealed to a disembodied mind but an act for which one bears an inescapable responsibility and which, on however small a scale, changes the world as well as reflecting it. 'We didn't need Nietzsche to tell us to live dangerously,' he writes in one of his retrospective moments, 'there is no other way of living.' In his famous Richmond Lecture of 1962 on C. P. Snow, when defining the 'nature of the existence of English literature', he calls it a

living whole that can have its life only in the living present, in the creative response of individuals, who collaboratively renew and perpetuate what they participate in – a cultural community or consciousness.

A Marxist might note approvingly too that for Leavis the work of literature is never merely an individual creation, as the Romantic tradition has assumed, but the expression of the life of a community and an exemplification of what it values and believes. In this other sense of the word as well, the genuine work of art is representative, something demonstrably true, for Leavis, in the case, for example, of Bunyan and Mark Twain. Where Leavis differs from most Marxists is in his account of the value of such works from the past, which lies not in what they reveal of the class struggle at a certain stage of evolution but in the 'renewal' and 'participation' of which he talks in the Richmond Lecture. When we read the great or authentic writers of the past, we read them as if they were 'contemporaries'.

'Great' and 'authentic' are not terms, however, that can be applied merely to any literature which has been popular for a time. And what Leavis says of poetry that 'matters' in *New Bearings* is taken, implicitly at least, to be true of other genres as well. Increasingly, in fact after *New Bearings* and his study of the Metaphysicals, the Augustans and the Romantic poets in *Revaluation* (1936), he came to think of the poetic life of the English language as finding expression in more recent times in the novels, or as he called them 'dramatic poems', of George Eliot, Henry James, Conrad and, pre-eminently, Dickens and D. H. Lawrence. All of these novelists are distinguished by their unusual moral seriousness, their sense of the 'possibilities of life', their intelligence and their representativeness.[11]

> Really distinguished minds are themselves, of course, *of* their age; they are responsive at the deepest level to its peculiar strains and challenges: that is why they are able to be truly illuminating and prophetic and to influence the world positively and creatively. (Richmond Lecture)

However, being *of* one's age can be a liability as much as an asset to the would-be novelist or poet. To quote from *New Bearings* once again, 'if the poetry and the intelligence of the age lose touch with one another, poetry will cease to matter much and the age will be lacking in finer awareness' (p. 14). (In conversation during his later years, Leavis often pointed out that in Russia literature still mattered, mattered enough to be persecuted.)

For Leavis, it is obvious that the writing of the period since the death of D. H. Lawrence and the last of Eliot's *Four Quartets* is that of an age lacking in 'finer awareness', in which literature has ceased to 'matter much'. Similarly it is obvious that the former culture of the people, in what he calls 'the organic community', has been destroyed by suburbanization, technology and the mass-media. In *Culture and Environment*, Leavis and Thompson recommended the writings of George Sturt, the wheelwright from Farnham in Surrey, chronicler of the lives of the local labourers and craftsmen in the years before Sturt's wheelwright's shop became a garage and Farnham a dormitory as distinct from a market town. Speaking of Sturt's evocation of a world in which the craftsmen knew where the trees they seasoned had grown and the roads and fields on which the wheels would turn, as well as the men who would use them, Leavis wrote, in the 1970s:

> We didn't recall the organic kind of relation of work to life in any nostalgic spirit as something to be restored or to take a melancholy pleasure in lamenting; but by means of emphasizing that it was *gone*, with the organic community it belonged to, not to be restored in any foreseeable future. We were calling attention to an essential change in human conditions that is entailed by the unrelenting technological revolution and to the nature of the attendant human problems. (*Nor Shall My Sword*, p. 85)

F. R. LEAVIS AND 'ENGLISH'

Leavis's insistence on the inevitably profound consequences of such changes would put him (if one were to call him a sociologist) among those who, like Peter Townsend, were among the first to see the appalling consequences of the post-war 'planning' of British cities, the driving out of the people of Bethnal Green into high-rise apartments and the destruction by 'local authorities' of Dickens's London. It is the uprooting of communities, the obliteration of folk memory and the disappearance at the same time of an educated public for literature that made the university for Leavis and the English School in particular what he calls in the Richmond Lecture 'a centre of human consciousness'.

This is not the place to consider whether Leavis was right and right to deny that he was in any way a 'Luddite' or a victim of mere nostalgia. But it is worth asking perhaps whether any such global judgements of society could ever be, in any literal sense, true. It is easy, of course, to say that they could not and to discuss any argument that depends on them as futile, though the implications of such a conclusion are no less far-reaching than those of the position Leavis adopts. If it is impossible to know enough about society to talk meaningfully about cultural deprivation and loss, then it is impossible to talk about progress, that is, advances in civilization too. It is, in fact, the belief that one can ignore the larger issues, including the question of human purpose and ends, and at the same time promote schemes of human welfare and happiness that Leavis sees as one of the absurdities of the age and one that has its origin in the version of Utilitarianism propounded by Jeremy Bentham. J. S. Mill's essay on Bentham which Leavis brought back into currency in 1950 is, he claims in his introduction, both definitive as a critique and prophetic. For Bentham, 'quantity of pleasure being equal, push-pin is as good as poetry'.

If there were only a little ascertainable truth, however, in Leavis's observation of cultural decline, the case for the English School, as he sees it, would not be invalidated. The more likely it is that Leavis is right, the stronger the claims, if not necessarily for the particular programme of studies he recommends, at least for one with a similar raison d'être. However, Leavis's concern is no less with literature than with the state of civilization and here what he says in New Bearings and subsequently is susceptible to a more precise kind of corroboration or refutation than his pronouncements concerning society as a whole. One has to ask, of course, whether the educated public of the past to which Leavis refers ever existed, and to consider part of the evidence he offers: namely, the quality of the criticism of the great nineteenth-century reviews and their successors in the early twentieth century, notably *The Nation and Athenaeum*, when its editor was Middleton Murry[12] and T. S. Eliot and Santayana were among its contributors. The evidence also, however, for Leavis lies in the literature itself of the period before 'poetry' appeared to lose touch with 'the intelligence of the age'.

Leavis's view of the relation between the writer and his age amounts to no more perhaps than the truism that no one ever writes merely for himself. The act of writing, even the writing of a private diary, presupposes a certain type of reader, if only oneself as one imagines oneself in years to come. For the poet or novelist especially, the sense of an audience is crucial and the creative act presupposes necessarily some kind of conscious pre-existing community. Leavis's comments on Blake, Hopkins and the later Henry James touch on the cost for each of them, for all their genius and originality, of losing the sense of contact with a public, the cost which is apparent in the writing itself. By contrast, a poet whose work gives direct expression to the intelligence of the society of which he is a member is Pope, in writing on whom Leavis was to demonstrate as cogently perhaps as any critic ever could what he meant by a poet's 'interest in words'.

In the Oxford journal *Essays in Criticism*, its editor F. W. Bateson had taken issue with Leavis over the latter's reading in *Revaluation* of the *Dunciad* and of the following lines in particular, in which Pope portrays a university graduate who goes in for politics and becomes a devotee of the goddess Dullness:

> From priest-craft happily set free
> Lo! ev'ry finished son returns to thee:
> First slave to words, then vassal to a name,
> Then dupe to party; child and man the same;
> Bounded by nature, narrow'd still by art,
> A trifling head and a contracted heart.
>
> (Book IV, lines 499–504)

Bateson was unimpressed:

> How is it that Pope, a master of language if ever there was one, has used his concrete terms with so little precision? In these lines, 'slave', 'vassal' and 'dupe' are virtually interchangeable. And so are 'bounded', 'narrow'd' and 'contracted'.
>
> *(Essays in Criticism,* January 1953, 12)

Bateson's argument is directed both against Pope and Leavis, who finds these lines superb. Leavis replied:

> Words should be servants – the servants of thought and the thinker; the badly educated child is made a 'slave to words' ... Such a child, grown to political years, naturally becomes 'vassal to a name'. The felicity of this expression takes us beyond cliché (the 'mastery of language' shown here is characteristic of Pope): the relation of personal subservience to a great patrician name (and a 'mere name', it is suggested) – a relation substituting for service of Principle – is with special point described contemptuously by the feudal term in an age in which feudalism is Gothick. And such an initiate into politics, expecting his reward for faithful service of Party, finds himself a 'dupe': he has been used, but can command no substantial recognition from 'Int'rest that waves on parti-coloured wings'. 'Vassal' and 'dupe' express quite different relations, and a moment's thought will show that they cannot be interchanged.
>
> *(Scrutiny,* XIX, 3, 1953, 171)

If it seems far more probable that Leavis is right than Bateson, this is because of what is implied by each of the two readings. If Bateson is right, then we must assume that not only 'slave' and 'vassal' are synonymous here but 'dupe' as well; that Pope was thinking only of the need to avoid repetition when he used them; that the subtly interrelated meanings of which Leavis speaks are merely the creation of a modern reader's ingenuity and their seeming appropriateness within the context of *The Dunciad* as a whole merely coincidental. All this is possible but not likely.

As an example of *reasoned* criticism, I like to think that Leavis's defence of his reading of Pope is unsurpassed. Its implicit appeal to probabilistic criteria can always be referred to if one finds oneself arguing against the view that literary criticism has no possible objective validity and is not therefore an intellectual discipline. Leavis himself, it has always been mistakenly assumed, was unaware of the problems of objective validation and was the victim of a disabling inability to handle even the simplest general ideas. René Wellek wrote to him in a letter published in *Scrutiny* (V, 4, 1937):

Allow me to sketch your ideal of poetry, your 'norm' with which you measure every poet: your poetry must be in serious relation to actuality, it must have a firm grasp of the actual, of the object, it must be in relation to life, it must not be cut off from direct vulgar living, it should be normally human, testify to spiritual health and sanity.

The description is, of course, recognizable. The best known instance of his approval of writers with a 'firm grasp of the actual' is his adverse commentary on Shelley's *Ode to the West Wind* in *Revaluation*. Yet it is a faithful reading of the poem, as Leavis sees it, a readiness to be 'swept along' in the 'poetic surge', that prevents any 'inconvenient degree of realization' when we come to the images of the 'clouds' like 'leaves that are shed' or the 'tangled boughs of Heaven and Ocean'. A more literal realization of these images would be incompatible with the mood and the 'sweeping movement of the verse'. As if to demonstrate his freedom from any such constricting 'norm' as Wellek sketches, Leavis's reply contains an appreciative commentary on one of the most boldly as well as subtly allegorical poems by Blake, 'Earth's Answer' from *The Songs of Experience*.

What Leavis wrote on this occasion shows anything but unawareness of principle; and it also throws considerable light on the question 'why "English"?' with which this chapter has been largely concerned:

That Dr Wellek should slip into this way of putting things seems to me significant, for he would being challenged agree, I imagine, that it suggests a false idea of the procedure of the critic ... By the critic of poetry, I understand the complete reader: the reading demanded by poetry is of a different kind from that demanded by philosophy ...[13]

Something like the same incomprehension betrayed by Wellek must have led Leavis's friend Wittgenstein to say to him 'Give up literary criticism' and has led some philosophers and philosophically-inclined critics to point out what they see as the mere dogmatism of his views on, for example, *The Golden Bowl* of Henry James and in particular its variations on the theme of adultery:

We remain convinced that when an author, whatever symbolism he intends, presents a drama of men and women, he is committed to dealing in terms of men and women, and mustn't ask us to acquiesce in valuations that contradict our profoundest ethical sensibility.

(*The Common Pursuit*, p. 228)

What those who object to this usually, however, fail to quote is the sentence which follows:

If, of course, he can work a revolutionary change in that sensibility, well and good, but who will contend that James's art in those late novels has that power?

The art that for Leavis does have this power (and anyone familiar with his writing at all will realize that quotation here is unnecessary) is, pre-eminently in our own time and more than that of Yeats or even Eliot, that of D. H. Lawrence.

If Leavis is an enigma, the clue to the enigma lies in that readiness to go where the 'poetry' takes him of which I have spoken already, that readiness to read the poetry on its own terms, whatever these terms may turn out to be. It is this which makes him the most adventurous as well as the least prescriptive of critics, the least concerned with a formal or ethical 'norm' of the kind Wellek offered to 'sketch' for him. If this is far from obvious to many intelligent readers, it is almost certainly because Leavis never pretends that the kind of judgement we make when we respond to a work of literature is any different in kind from that of any other human pronouncement or utterance. Implicit in Leavis's earlier and explicit in his later writings is the notion of a common human nature, which is not established in one form for all time or given to us simply as known, but which we discover in unexpected ways through the revelations of experience. (One of the plays by Shakespeare which seems to have meant most to him and in which he played the leading role at the Perse School was *Macbeth*.) To appeal to human nature, for Leavis, and in doing so participate in what Eliot had called 'the common pursuit of true judgement' is not, however – and Leavis never claimed that it was – a matter of denying one's own instinctive personal response or the particular social and historical factors which have, to a large extent, determined it. One cannot speak for one's fellow men unless one is speaking for oneself and speaking with total

candour. ('By the critic of poetry, I understand the complete reader.')
The seeming paradox in Leavis's writing of the judgement which
is both 'personal' and yet more than merely personal[14] is related
to that other paradox explored in his essay on Conrad's *The Shadow
Line* of the individual who is both 'exceptional' and 'representative'.
One thing has always surprised me and this is that Leavis's Marxist
critics, like Perry Anderson and Terry Eagleton, should not have
seen, apparently, in the candour of Leavis's moral judgements an
implicit acknowledgement of the fact that he is writing as an
individual with a specific background and education, living at a
particular time, 'petty bourgeois' no doubt in his origins at least,
as Eagleton, with implied superiority, calls him. To ask the critic
to write as if he had no class or background is to ask him to deny
his own historicity.

'All speech is art speech,' Leavis would often quote Lawrence as
saying and when the unexpurgated *Lady Chatterley's Lover* was
published in 1960, he turned down the invitation to go into the
witness box in its defence; though his absence was made up for by
a number of literary academics, one of whom claimed that the word
'shocking' was one that no literary critic should ever use and a leading
Churchman, who spoke of the sexual act as described by Lawrence
as an act of 'holy communion'. Among Leavis's principal objections
to the triumphant defence (he did not approve of the book being
banned) was the fact that it was, with all that this implied, 'a bad
novel', one that 'violates Lawrence's own essential canons as an artist,
serves as a foil to his successful and great art, and in that way may
be used as an aid to its critical appreciation'.

... the integrity we demand of an artist is a rarer thing than that which
we testify to (perhaps) in a politician. Lawrence himself, in postulating it
as the essential aim in both life and art, insisted on the most exacting conception and criteria. He is insisting on them in his caveats against 'will' and
'idea' (terms, in his use of them, intimately related).[15]

'Will' and 'idea' stand for Leavis, as for Lawrence, in opposition
to the spontaneity without which there is no creativity and whose
manifestations can only be unpredictable. It is because the philosopher
(*qua* philosopher) is concerned with what is or should be conceptually
predictable that 'the reading demanded by poetry', as he told Wellek,

'is of a different kind from that demanded by philosophy'. In the greatest and, for Leavis, the last great modern English poem, Eliot's *Four Quartets*, we have a clear instance of what, quoting D. W. Harding, he calls 'the creation of concepts'. And literature, for Leavis, is no more than language at its most compelling and alive. The most obvious illustration of this truism is the work of Lawrence, including as it does the unfortunate advocacy in *Lady Chatterley* on behalf of the 'four-letter words'. To advocate understanding of the great Lawrence and *The Four Quartets* is to promote understanding of the English language itself, with all that this implies. Leavis's lifelong and, for many, quixotic campaign on behalf of 'English' is that of a man who assumed a certain conscious responsibility.

NOTES

1. See Ronald Hayman's short but comprehensive and fair account of his controversial career, *Leavis* (London, 1976), a very well documented obituary article by John Harvey in *Encounter* (May 1979), and the entry on F. R. and Q. D. Leavis in the *Dictionary of National Biography* by Boris Ford.

2. *Culture and Anarchy*, Cambridge edn (1970), 70.

3. Quoted by Margaret Mathieson in *The Preachers of Culture* (London, 1975), 259.

4. *The Principles of Literary Criticism* (London, 1924), 62.

5. Interesting in this respect also is the confession of a soccer hooligan in a *Sunday Times* colour supplement: 'He got three O-levels out of six, including a grade A in English Literature, and remembers with particular affection *The Destructors* by Graham Greene. "You know, the one about these kids an' this old geezer an' when he goes on holiday they pull the house apart. Great book."' Leavis's term for young people of this kind is 'the disinherited'.

6. *Scrutiny*, however, published in 1933 (I, iv) an essay on Richards by the critic and psychologist, D. W. Harding, highly critical of the 'amateurishness' of Richards' attempts to find a justification in psychology for the importance attributed to works of art. As in many other respects, Harding's (frequently acknowledged) influence on Leavis may be relevant here. Leavis's own account of the fallacy, as he saw it, of Richards' attempts to extend to the understanding of literature the 'pleasure principle' of Jeremy Bentham is to be found in 'Dr Richards, Bentham and Coleridge', *Scrutiny*, III, iv (1935).

7. For Leavis's major and developing accounts of Eliot's later poems, see *Education and the University* (London, 1943), *Lectures in America* (London, 1969), *English Literature in Our Time and the University* (London, 1969) and *The Living Principle* (London, 1975).

8. In an essay on *The Shadow Line* of 1957 reprinted in *Anna Karenina and Other Essays* (1967).

9. See 'Restatement for critics', *Scrutiny*, I, iv (1933) and the review of MacDiarmid's 'Second hymn to Lenin' in *Scrutiny*, IV, iii (1935). MacDiarmid admired Leavis as well, whom he met while addressing the Downing College Doughty Society in 1960. 'He doesn't drink,' he told me afterwards, 'but I like him. He's aggressive.'

10. See Perry Anderson, 'Components of the national culture' in *The New Left Review*, 50 (1968), Terry Eagleton, *Criticism and Ideology* (London, 1976), and Francis Mulhern, *The Moment of 'Scrutiny'* (London, 1979).

11. Leavis's view, expressed in *The Great Tradition* (1948) that it was only in *Hard Times* that Dickens wrote a novel comparable in its seriousness and its appeal to the adult mind with those of the great English novelists, was completely revised in *Dickens, the Novelist* (1970), which he wrote with Q. D. Leavis. It was regretted by many that neither author admitted how much each had shared the generally disparaging view of Dickens which they both condemned in this later work.

12. Middleton Murry is, with T. S. Eliot and Edgell Rickword, among the strongest influences on his early criticism. Compare the passages chosen for special attention by Leavis when writing about Hardy and Edward Thomas in *New Bearings* and Pope in *Revaluations* with those picked out by Murry in his essays on Thomas and Hardy in *Aspects of Literature* and on Collins in *Countries of the Mind*.

13. Leavis's reply is reprinted in *The Common Pursuit* as 'Literary criticism and philosophy'.

14. 'A judgement is personal or it is nothing; you cannot take over someone else's. The implicit form of judgement is: This is so, isn't it? The question is an appeal for confirmation that the thing *is* so; implicitly that, though expecting, characteristically, an answer in the form, 'yes but –', the 'but' standing for qualifications, reserves, corrections ...' ('Two cultures? The significance of C. P. Snow', reprinted in *Nor Shall My Sword*, 1972).

15. See 'The Orthodoxy of Enlightenment', in *Anna Karenina and Other Essays*.

ANTHONY POWELL AND ANGUS WILSON

GRAHAM MARTIN

Anthony Powell (b. 1905) and Angus Wilson (b. 1913) first achieved reputation in the 1950s, and they share a satiric interest in the changes in English society over the last half-century. But the differences are more striking. Powell's social range is narrow, and he tends to view change ahistorically. Wilson ranges widely through the English class structure, and strives to analyse the social processes reflected in post-war and post-imperial England. Formally, too, Powell elaborates a highly idiosyncratic style, both in language and structure; while Wilson, a parodist and mimic, evolves a range of individual language styles according to the character, unified in complicated plots. Both novelists are witness to the range and variety of English fiction after 1950.

During the 1930s Anthony Powell published five novels, but in striking contrast with the relative balance between Waugh's writing in this and later decades, these early novels are overshadowed by Powell's *magnum opus*, the twelve-novel series *A Dance to the Music of Time*, appearing at intervals between 1951 and 1975. *A Dance* recounts aspects of the lives of the friends, acquaintances and relatives of the narrator, Nicholas Jenkins, from just before the First World War till the early 1970s. Jenkins' own mainly 'literary' life – reviewing, writing a book about Burton's *The Anatomy of Melancholy*, cultural conferences – offers little more than a capacious frame for what he recounts about some three hundred other people.[1] Perhaps a hundred of these recur with significant frequency, and we learn about the twenty or so expected to hold our sustained attention only in piecemeal fashion, their individual life-stories stretching over several novels, not always consecutive, each intricately woven into that of many others, of both central and marginal interest. As narrator – the only character to whom all the others (in *some* sense) matter –

Jenkins is appropriately delineated for his task. A minor literary figure, he has youthfully unhappy love-affairs, eventually a happy marriage, as well as children, nothing of this however being explored in any depth. Public school and university provide friends in business life and access to an upper-middle-class social milieu where he meets his future wife; his work adds 'bohemian' acquaintances. He has the talents for undemanding and varied friendship in these groups, together with exceptional powers of memory. From time to time, he is the voice for general reflections about life (the obscurity of human motives, the fragmentary character of our knowledge of others, mortality, friendship, marriage, war, art).

Widely read, knowledgeable about painting and music, he observes and listens, leaving argument to others. His meditative temperament and pertinacious curiosity about his fellow human beings repeatedly contrasts with the unreflecting self-absorption of many of those whose stories he recounts. Witty himself, he enjoys comic or grotesque juxtapositions of behaviour and in these various ways his sensibility permeates the whole sequence. Yet, *A Dance* is in no sense 'about Jenkins'. To adapt Yeats' phrase for literary realism, 'a mirror dawdling down a lane', Jenkins is more mirror than character. Self-discovery by means of memory plays no organizing part in *A Dance*. As narrator, Jenkins is evidently important to any effect of unity Powell strives for in *A Dance*, but this cannot derive from the exploration of his narrating consciousness. In this respect, the contrast with another near-contemporary 'saga-novel', C. P. Snow's *Strangers and Brothers* (1940–75), cumulatively dominated by its narrator Lewis Eliot, is emphatic.

Powell has described himself as 'a naturalistic writer ... [aiming] never to describe anything that could not have happened in everyday life', an aim realized in the distinctive narrative texture of Powell's novels which stems largely from the narrator's scruples about what he can personally vouch for. The narrative weaves together 'presented' episodes which include Jenkins, with reports by Jenkins of what he remembers from other occasions or other characters, the latter carefully graded for reliability. Narrative pace is therefore slow, often meandering, and though narrated time is usually short, it is strikingly elaborated by proleptic and retrospective interventions judged by Jenkins to have a bearing on the matter in hand. It is by

this means that Powell's preoccupation with Time is directly introduced into Jenkins' 'telling', and becomes both cause and effect of
another prominent feature of these novels. The construction of each
consists of a small number of set-piece episodes, usually involving
several characters, providing Jenkins with plausible occasions for
hearing their conversations as well as stimulus for his memory about
past – or future – incidents. Parties, meetings in pubs and restaurants,
more or less formal family occasions, provide the usual settings.
Details of work and career are of minor interest to Jenkins; and family
life is a mere background. Engagements, marriages, divorces, re-
marriages are the stuff of his narrative, 'gossip', as one critic has
remarked, 'given the condition and status of art'.[2]

Jenkins has thus no access to the inner consciousness of his 'subjects'.
Narrative is controlled by the need to place the main characters in
situations where self-revelation of some kind is 'probable' through
conversation, either with Jenkins, or in his presence, and the coincidental meeting becomes a heavily-worked device. Direct interchange
between the characters rarely achieves depth or complexity, unless
between Jenkins and a close friend, often a 'confession' by the friend
under the stress of some crisis. Dialogue, as a result, has typically
a 'public' character, matching the relative formality of the social
occasions. In this respect, we touch on a limitation in Powell's equipment as a novelist, an inability – certainly a reluctance – to 'show'
self-revelatory exchange in appropriate dialogue. Powell has a good
ear for South English upper-middle-class speech registers, which he
exploits to comic effect, but on the whole his characters speak at,
rather than to, each other. For 'innerness', we have to rely on Jenkins'
speculative interpretations.

The point may be illustrated from *The Valley of Bones* (1964). After
a long war-time absence from home, Jenkins is reunited with his
heavily-pregnant wife, among other family and friends. After six
pages of gossip about the latter, they move to the personal note, and
we get this threadbare exchange.[3]

> 'Anyway, it's nice to meet again, darling.'
> 'It's been a long time.'
> 'A bloody long time.'
> 'It certainly has.'

(p. 156)

Powell adheres, of course, to a class convention whose only language for overt feeling seems to be clipped, stoical understatement. There is too the question of relative emphasis. Jenkins' marriage is no part of Powell's substantive interest. Nevertheless, mechanical and colourless speech of this kind stands in sharp contrast to the lively caricatures realized in the 'public' exchanges. Jenkins' sister-in-law has just got engaged to Dicky Umfraville, a minor character already known to us as something of a 'wild man'.

'Look here, old boy,' he said, when I joined him, 'how do you think you and the others are going to stand up to having me as a brother-in-law?'

'A splendid prospect.'

'Not everyone would think so,' he said. 'You know I must be insane to embrace matrimony again. Stark, staring mad. But not half as mad as Frederica to take me on. Do you realize she'll be my fifth? Something wrong with a man who keeps marrying like that. Must be. But I really couldn't resist Frederica. That prim look of hers. All the same, fancy her accepting me. You'd never expect it, would you? All the business of her emptying the royal slops. She'll have to give up that occupation of course. No good trying to be Extra Woman of the Bedchamber with me in the offing. Not a bloody bit of use. You can just picture H.M. saying: "Why's that fellow turned up again? I remember him. He used to be a captain in my Brigade of Guards. I had to get rid of him. He's a no-gooder. What does he mean by showing his ugly face again at Buck House? I won't stand it. Off with his head." You agree, don't you?'

'I see what you mean.'

(p. 157)

Such writing illustrates a further general point about the narrative texture of *A Dance*. A combination of comic behavioural surfaces with Jenkins' probing but always unconfirmed analyses of what these might portend, both whets the reader's appetite for further 'significance', yet by shifting from one narrative strand to another, also denies it. Powell's skill in endlessly postponing both forms of satisfaction – narrative and interpretative – doubtless accounts for the addictive character of the sequence noted by many reviewers.

Jenkins has also a marked visual sense which contributes to the general externality of the characterization. Personal appearance gets a good deal of attention, often with effects amiably grotesque. People and places are usually registered in what Barthes calls the cultural code: mythological or literary allusion, 'correct' clothing, pictorial analogy.

A single oil lamp threw a circle of dim light round the dining table of the farm parlour where we ate, leaving the rest of the room in heavy shadow, dramatizing by its glow the central figures of the company present. Were they a group of conspirators – something like the Gunpowder Plot – depicted in cross-hatchings of an old engraved illustration? It was not exactly that ... Here was Pharaoh, carved in the niche of a shrine between two tutelary deities, who shielded him from human approach. All was manifest. Colonel Hogbourne-Johnson and Colonel Pedlar were animal-headed gods of Ancient Egypt. Colonel Hogbourne-Johnson was, of course, Horus, one of those sculptured representations in which the Lord of the Morning Sun resembles an owl rather than a falcon; a bad-tempered owl at that.

(*The Soldier's Art*, 36–7)

This is, in fact, an account of the General's Mess in Jenkins' regiment, lead-in to the kind of comic scene Powell delights in, routine public exchange between military men who know each other too well for liking, yet must live and work together day after day. The static frieze-like effect, the mixture of solemnity and send-up ('a bad-tempered owl at that'), conveys Jenkins' implicit pleasure in hierarchic ritual, in formalized emblems of order and control. Yet in the end such playful 'conceits' add nothing to our grasp of the characters, rather underlining the distance that Jenkins' view of them otherwise maintains.

In a sequence of such length, the question inevitably arises: where is the centre of interest? Powell offers one possibility in the opening pages of the first novel, *A Question of Upbringing* (1951). He describes a picture by Poussin, source of an image for the whole sequence.

The image of Time brought thoughts of mortality: of human beings, facing outward like the Seasons, moving hand in hand in intricate measure: stepping slowly, methodically, sometimes a trifle awkwardly, in revolutions that take recognizable shape: or breaking into seemingly meaningless gyrations, while partners disappear only to reappear again, once more giving pattern to the spectacle: unable to control the melody, unable, perhaps, to control the steps of the dance.   (p. 6)

Yet it has to be said that except in having followed the course of a number of human lives from youth to age or death, *A Dance* has no pattern to offer. Time passes; some hopes are fulfilled, some disappointed; friendship is important, but rarely sustained; love blooms and fades; marriages usually founder; family life persists, which is all that can be said for it; public affairs whether menacing or farcical, are temporary matters; and while for some it provides success, this is not much to be admired, the 'glittering prizes' an illusion even for the winners; only art offers a limited transcendence, and the struggle to create it commands an unillusioned respect. If Powell's sequence has a consistent emphasis it is that beyond providing comic, touching and grotesque examples of the Vanity of Human Wishes, the passage of time yields nothing significant. As Auden remarks, 'Time will say nothing but "I told you so"': the lesson of *A Dance* hardly differs.

We have seen that Jenkins himself cannot provide the centre of interest, however much this might seem to be promised by the quasi-autobiographical progress of *A Dance*, especially of the early novels. Despite the tests and pressures that Jenkins survives – of dutiful soldier, faithful husband, or loyal friend – we hardly know him better at the end of *A Dance* than at the beginning, and his virtues remain significantly unrealized. A more limited claim for the 'theme' of *A Dance* lies in Jenkins' interest in human relationships. In the fifth novel, *Casanova's Chinese Restaurant* (1960), the recently-married Jenkins, on his way to the hospital where his wife is recovering from a miscarriage, remarks that

... the difficulties of presenting marriage are inordinate. Its forms are at once so varied, yet so constant, providing a kaleidoscope, the colours of which are always changing, always the same. The moods of a love-affair, the contradictions of friendship, the fellow feeling of opposed commanders in total war, these are all in their way to be charted. Marriage, partaking of such – and a thousand more – dual antagonisms and participations, finally defies definition.   (p. 96)

Definition, the reader may be tempted to reply, 'is not the issue, but presentation, *mimesis*, "showing"; that is what we turn to novels for'. And to some extent, the first six novels of *A Dance* offer to trace the course of marriages begun, faltering, deadlocked, ended and begun again, an interwoven pattern of relationships which is the 'showing' to match Jenkins' general comment on marriage. Yet, given the 'public' method of characterization, none of these relationships, not even Moreland's, who is Jenkins' closest friend and of which we know most, is finally clarified, neither in themselves nor in their relationship to the success of Jenkins' marriage. The reader who searches beyond the narrator's refusal to generalize about the married state for the *novelist's* deeper grasp of causes, interactions and effects, remains unsatisfied. And this is characteristic of *A Dance* as a fictional record of human relationships.

The point may be illustrated more generally in terms of Kenneth Widmerpool, Jenkins' unpopular schoolboy acquaintance, who appears in every novel, and whose death is the main event of *Hearing Secret Harmonies* (1975). Power-hungry, self-absorbed, philistine and charmless, he is 'the villain' of *A Dance*, the 'man of will' repeatedly juxtaposed with Jenkins in his role as tacit spokesman for a cultivated and reticently humane view of relationships. Yet his evolution in these later novels, from ambitious Staff Officer, to fellow-travelling Labour MP, Labour peer, trendy pro-student Chancellor of a provincial university, then as an elderly man in the 'permissive' sixties joining a hippy commune in search of 'spiritual' powers, and dying in the attempt to defeat its sinister youthful leader, carries no final conviction. Powell's narrative method allows him to pass off as plausible 'development' a series of static impressions. Widmerpool's different appearances allow scope for some grotesquely comic episodes, darkening into menacing farce; but the man remains a mystery, an articulation of surfaces, a character to whose self-understanding we have no key.

In most of the novels of *A Dance*, public events are a background presence. The Abdication, Spanish Civil War, Popular Front politics, Munich, are variously brought into focus in the early group. In the trilogy about the Second World War, blitzed London, the V-bombs, the sense of exhaustion accompanying victory mark its different stages, and in the post-war, contemporary literary and cultural trends are sketched in. Unlike Waugh, Powell indulges no explicit denunciations of the 'modern age', no nostalgia for an idealized past. On the other hand, he registers no interest in the nature or sources of social change. (We may say that his abstract conception of Time rules out such discriminations and analyses.) This is strikingly the case in the war trilogy where an ahistorical perspective is brought to bear on the whole event. Joining his regiment in Wales, Jenkins thinks about his primitive Celtic forebears, the warriors who fought and killed in pre-Christian Britain, of the Napoleonic Wars, and Imperial struggles in British India (*The Valley of Bones*, pp. 6–7); visiting Normandy after D-day, in a deliberate displacement of the British military victory, he thinks of older battles like Zutphen and Maastricht (*The Military Philosophers*, p. 186). The effect is to disengage the Second World War from any bearing upon the immediate life of our times, save as a violent impersonal disruption, a recurrent feature of European civilization. To these explicit pointers from the novelist may be added the recognition that his conception of social existence as an endless criss-crossing of 'individual' lives denies 'society' any significant reality.

From this angle, it is then logical for *A Dance* to conceive left-wing political activity as comic, or sinister, or both, an arena in which malcontents, power-seekers, or mere self-indulgent egotists exercise their mischievous talents. Yet change comes about, and the social observer in Powell can only register the fact by displacing and condensing the intricate complex of social, economic and political factors into the notion of obsessional, threateningly disruptive characters, both fascinating and horrible. Only in this way can we understand Widmerpool's political leanings (politically without content), his final self-destroying effort to master demonic forces, or his marriage to Pamela – unequivocally an emblem for threatening female sexuality – who destroys her lover Trapnel, the creative writer, emblem of art's transcendence, of which *A Dance* itself is the achieved example.

Angus Wilson's fiction strikingly contrasts with Powell's in its restless experimentation, and it seems to me a more considerable achievement. Powell's sequence is long and voluminous, yet also substantially in the same fictional mode. Wilson's is varied in kind, in success, in scope; and in bulk too substantial to be easily discussed here, except by concentrating on aspects of his work with a general bearing on its characteristic methods and themes. The first such aspect arises from a central difference between his earlier and later writing. In the short stories and the first group of novels (*Hemlock and After*, 1952, *Anglo-Saxon Attitudes*, 1956, *The Middle Age of Mrs Eliot*, 1958, and *Late Call*, 1964), 'realism' – granting for the moment the slippery complexity of this term – is the dominant method; whereas in the second group of novels, 'realism' gives way to 'fable' or 'allegory' (*The Old Men at the Zoo*, 1961, *Setting the World on Fire*, 1981), or more emphatically to an explicit and extended emphasis on 'fiction-ality' (*No Laughing Matter*, 1967, *As If By Magic*, 1973).

The distinction is not absolute: signs of the conscious 'fabulist' are to be found in the early writing, as of the 'realist' in some of the later. Nevertheless, the contrast is unmistakable. In *Hemlock and After*, an impersonal sentence heading the list of characters assures the reader that 'the events of the novel take place in the summer of 1951', while in the course of the story we find a supporting network of contem-porary political and cultural references. *Anglo-Saxon Attitudes* has no pre-narrative dating, but opens with an invented extract from *The Times* from November 1912, and ends with an Appendix including dated fictional extracts from a learned journal (1931), scholarly books credited to characters in the novel (1930, 1950), and another extract from *The Times*, January 1955. The narrative spans the years 1912 to 1954, and contains references to such events as the Piltdown Man hoax, the first cultural impact of television, and the Bevanite split in the Labour Party. In *The Wild Garden* (1963), an account of his life and writing based on lectures delivered in 1960, Wilson insists that 'novels are lies', an opinion previously elaborated in a 1957 inter-view:

> All fiction for me is a kind of magic or trickery – a confidence trick, try-ing to make people believe something is true that isn't. And the novelist, in particular, is trying to convince the reader that he is seeing society as a whole.[4]

The early work is then 'realist' in a traditional sense, deploying speci-ficities of time, place and circumstance, in order to persuade the reader that the fiction faithfully reflects 'the real'. In the later work, this is no longer so. *The Old Men at the Zoo*, in the manner of prophetic fables, locates in a familiar 'real' place, the Regents Park Zoo, the main action of a confessedly fictional future. *No Laughing Matter*, whose list of characters is divided into 'Principal Players', 'Supporting Roles' and 'Additional Cast', opens with a prefatory section entitled 'Before the War' (i.e before 1914), details of which then concede its fictional status, while the novel alternates narrative and dramatic presentation, formulating several episodes as short plays, complete with extensive stage directions, *Setting the World on Fire* opens with a foreword about the history of Tothill House on which the novel will centre, linking it with the Glorious Revolution, only to end in the admission that 'house and garden are of course the inventions of the author'. In this later work, then, the conjuring artist presents the 'magic and trickery' of his procedures entirely in the open; in the earlier, he practises concealment of a traditional kind.

The key to this change of emphasis may be found in Wilson's attempt at convincing 'the reader that he *is* seeing society as a whole', a feature of his work prompting early commentators to notice the Victorian Novel as a distinctive influence. In the first two novels, the principal character's story is flanked by, and in some degree its thematic significance replicated in, several minor characters and lesser narratives. Such characters engage a range of social and cultural backgrounds, often differentiated in terms of class as perceived from the angle of an English middle class mainly located in London and the Home Counties. Wilson registers these distinctions primarily through manners and cultural reference, and especially through his command of speech-styles. (He remarks in *The Wild Garden* that a talent for mimicry is one of his chief resources as a novelist.) A further important contributor to the construction of this 'social reality' is Wilson's explicit rendering of historical change. In *Hemlock and After*, central characters like Bernard Sands and his sister Isobel, progressive left-wingers from the thirties linked by memories of opposition to Spanish Fascism, are shown grappling with the changed climate of 1951, Sands himself having lost the certainty of his earlier convictions. In *Anglo-Saxon Attitudes*, Gerald Middleton's lengthy examination of his own past conduct provides glimpses of Edwardian Liberal England, of Bernard Shaw's influence, and of the impact of Fascism in the thirties on a famous English historian; and the reader is permitted to speculate on the links between English cultural and social failings and Middleton's earlier moral cowardice and lack of determined self-scrutiny. Both novels turn upon a process of self-discovery in the main character, whose narrative construction also conveys the movement of a changing society. In each case, the fictional present becomes the basis for interrogating a past whose determinations are both personal and social.

Yet it is also true that the social fabric thus invoked lacks sub-stantiality. As narrator, Wilson maintains a certain distance between us and the varied locations of his stories, especially when these belong to the fictional present. We retain a stronger impression of how the characters talk, than of where they are; of what they are wearing than what they might look like; and of the significance of how they furnish their rooms, than of the felt presence of these rooms. Wilson's impressive grasp of speech-styles often has the effect of identifying characters with their voices, so that when they are not talking, they evaporate.

Then, the narratives are mainly presented through the conscious-ness of the principal characters, involving a play of irony, directed both inwardly on the character's own experience, and outwardly upon his contact with others. Its characteristic target is the playing of social roles, the degree to which the 'self' creates a superficial or wholly false existence by enacting socially- or culturally-given 'scripts', in order to escape the pain of humbling self-knowledge and the difficult effort to achieve it. It is this ironic dissolution of social life into the constituent elements of unadmitted and aggressive egoism, on the one hand, and a concealing behavioural mask on the other, that most strongly conveys the emptiness and insubstantiality of the society set before us.

Here, Wilson's perception of the role of *class* in English life is directly germane. It is, repeatedly, the rich repertoire of social per-formances offered by the signs and shibboleths of class-distinction that provides the characters with so many of their roles of evasion, of protection from self-knowledge and the genuine relationships which such knowledge makes possible. 'Virtue' consists in refusing such protection, in striving for an 'authentic' personal life of vulner-able solitariness to be defended in 'society' by a *conscious* tactic of skilled role-playing, and an ironic recognition of the always-potential treacheries of the inner 'self'. Auden's poem *1st September, 1939* ends by affirming those 'ironic points of light/[which] flash out wherever the Just/exchange their messages'. Through the narrator, and through the sensibility of the principal characters, such are the signals which are flashed to the reader. *Class* is thus observed, rather than analysed, from an 'outside' that has no social location. The false social occasions which, in different ways, *class* permeates – the opening ceremony for Vardon Hall, the cultural *salon* of Marie-Hélène – provide Sands and Middleton with their respective crises of recognition, prompting the first to neurotic isolation, the second to a lonely freedom, but neither to the realization of alternative relationships. Wilson's 'realism' in this early work, working through such assemblages of 'individual' characters, substantially excluding the presence of impersonal and institutional social structures, thus commits him to a dissolution of 'the social', to which ironic disengagement becomes the sole alternative. Only characters lacking ironic self-consciousness, whether from bad faith (Middleton's wife) or a deeper complicity with the false society (Mrs Curry in *Hemlock and After*), achieve the substantial identity of satirical 'grotesques'.

A second general aspect of Wilson's writing is the role of 'nature' as a source of stable values, a perspective from which 'society' can be securely judged. The 'fable' of *The Old Men at the Zoo* turns on this familiar Romantic opposition, but it will be convenient first to notice its central role in *Late Call*. The novel's theme is *class* as a structure of cultural and economic oppression. Narrated mainly through the consciousness of the heroine Sylvia Calvert (often rendered in free indirect style), the novel is set in a post-1945 New Town of East Anglia. The social milieu is 'classless' in a sense: schoolteachers, small businessmen, for whom 'status' has replaced 'class' as the significant social indicator. Sylvia Calvert, just retired from managing a hotel, married to an ex-officer badly wounded and semi-invalid since the First World War, has come to live with her recently-widowed son, headmaster of the local comprehensive school. The stress of adapting to this new environment, of the lack of a genuine relationship with her son, as with her husband, who depends wholly on her yet exploits her good nature and moral integrity, culminate in her nervous breakdown, a psychological retreat into escapist reading, TV watching, and miserable fantasy-ridden solitary walks in the surrounding country. A prologue to the story entitled 'The Hot Summer of 1911' provides both a historical dimension enabling us to measure the real social progress represented by the New Town, and the source and cause of Sylvia's 'wound'. Daughter of a poor East Anglian tenant farmer who takes summer lodgers to help make ends meet, 'the little Tuffield girl' (as Sylvia is called) is encouraged by Mrs Longmore, a middle-class Edwardian lady holidaying inexpensively at the farm with her two children, to make her own claims to life, freedom, and self-expression. Sylvia responds by going off one afternoon, Mrs Longmore's daughter Myra her only companion, to explore the fields and woods outside her usual routine, a touching, comic, memorable episode. The little girls pick flowers, paddle in a stream, get too hot; encouraged by Sylvia, they take off their dresses, and enjoy the freedom of wandering about in their underclothes. Discovered in this scandalous state by Mrs Longmore, Sylvia is angrily denounced for her low-class behaviour, then brutally thrashed ('till the blood run') by her father. The parents' angry resentment at their own hard life turns savagely against Sylvia, herself the mere innocent victim of Mrs Longmore's self-admiring liberalism. The outcome of her one 'selfish' escape from the premature adulthood forced upon her by her parents lays down the shape of her subsequent relationships: always 'responsible', always tending to self-blame, her capacity for spontaneous feeling permanently damaged.

Yet Sylvia is also strong. Wilson invites no easy sympathy for her either as victimized child or endlessly put-upon adult. Her life has been shaped for her, yet also she chooses it. Her bid for freedom in the prologue reveals a capacity for experiencing life on her terms, and here Wilson uses 'nature' both as occasion for releasing, and symbol for Sylvia's inner resources. Entering the allegedly fearsome Paddock Wood, Sylvia ignores her fears, and experiences a moment of pure release.

> Above her she could see the smooth flat underside of a giant yellow fungus that protruded from the tree trunk. She gazed up at this for a while, and then turned her attention to the ground, to some woodlice that in idly scratching away a piece of bark she had set in motion. But she was absorbed in neither the still fatness of the fungus nor the scaled scurry of the woodlice, they seemed merely objects helpful in crowding out thought or fancy. She was content, lying back in the warmth of the leaf-dappled sunshine, just to be; she could not remember such a thing before, she could only recall doing things or thinking about things to be done. (*Late Call*, p. 19)[5]

We contrast this undramatic 'wisely passive' attunement to natural objects with the histrionic fancies of Sylvia's companion Myra, for whom nature becomes a theatre for egoistic self-display. Moreover, it is a wood, uncultivated nature, and not worked farm-land, idealized as pastoral idyll, that provides Sylvia with her opportunity 'just to be'. As adult, the empty rural scenery stretching away from the New Town at first frightens Sylvia with its suggestion of formlessness. Yet this same landscape becomes the place of her recovery. On one of her depressed, solitary wanderings, she rescues a little girl from being struck by lightning, is doused by thunderous rain in a sort of baptism of renewal, and then made much of by the grateful parents (the mother is Canadian). An elderly woman, not in good health, Sylvia cannot look for much future life. She develops a better self-esteem, recovering a sense of her past in describing it to her new 'family'. Yet she remains a solitary, and the final impression is of loss, of what, in a different world, Sylvia might have become. And we sense the loss as characteristic, as generalized. In Wilson's evolution as a novelist, *Late Call* is unusual in its grasp of the invisible, never-recorded human cost of *class*. The novel invites us, not to a fascinated ironic recognition of its myriad social signs, but to an analytic understanding of continuing human damage. The 'classless' New Town will not be 'classless' long. Better than the society rendered in the prologue, it still has no place for the quality of life invoked in Sylvia.

Yet it is also true that the social fabric of the New Town is less strongly realized than the episode of the prologue; its 'realism' lacks the power of the opening 'fable'. In this respect, the 'fabulist' structure of *The Old Men at the Zoo* had already achieved a more consistent success, where Wilson's satirical gifts are used to render 'society as a whole', though from a particular angle. A fable of the future, the narrative is largely free of the conscientious demands of 'realism'. The Regents Park Zoo and its staff make up a composite symbol for post-imperial England (the novel coincided with the Macmillan era), and Wilson's concern is with the crisis in the relationship between 'man' and 'nature' brought about in industrialized urban-centred meritocratic societies by capitalist economic growth. (We learn that the West Country has been developed as a huge subtopia.) The zoo's animals represent all the forms of life threatened by such developments, including human life whose continuing health depends upon the recognition that we belong in 'wild Nature' as much as in 'society'. Simon Carter, zoologist turned efficient bureaucrat, discovers this truth the hard way when, in the wake of an English military defeat by European trade rivals, the social structure breaks down. Carter's real care is for nature-observation, especially of badgers. Pursuit of his duty to the system repeatedly intervenes between his efforts to make this genuine contact with 'nature', and when the anarchy and starvation caused by the war finally defeat him, he survives only by helping to kill and eat a badger, a traumatic experience which initiates him into a deeper understanding of our real dependence upon the world of natural life. These 'symbolic' episodes, together with others of more satiric note (such as the final destruction of the Regents Park Zoo, emblem of England's Victorian Empire), have a compressed imaginative force which, as a characterization, Carter lacks. Of all the characters, he alone is treated in a 'realist' mode, undergoing a process of self-discovery which is also a discovery of aspects of human nature beyond the normal ken of the efficient bureaucrat. But in its personal aspect this development is perfunctorily handled; the power of the 'fable' lies rather in its social and political acuity.

The third general aspect of Wilson's work, his later emphasis on 'fictionality', must be more briefly treated. Following the relatively limited compass of the two novels just discussed, Wilson returned in *No Laughing Matter* to a full-scale effort to see 'society as a whole'. This novel traces the lives of a family from just before the First World War till the 1960s, extending and elaborating the historical dimensions sketched in *Anglo-Saxon Attitudes* and *Hemlock and After*. Of particular interest are the different ways in which the Matthews children are presented both directly through their own individual consciousness (as in *The Waves*), and by means of short plays which convey the sense in which each character's identity is partly a performance for the others. None of the children is finally successful in escaping the mismanagement of their lives by their parents, practising in their own lives variants of the self-protective ruses whereby Mr and Mrs Matthews defend themselves from genuine human claims, as a married couple and as parents. The interweaving of personal, sexual, social and political narratives is an impressive accomplishment. To take a single example, the complex of motives that leads the eldest son, Quentin, sickened by his experience of trench war in 1914–18, to become first a pacifist, then an active Socialist journalist and ruthless womanizer, finally a TV personality eloquently inveighing against the spread of Western 'civilization', and also against contraception and the sexual morals of the sixties, the whole development is brilliantly set out without any suggestion that, as a development, it gives final and authoritative access to the character. What is presented to us, and what we more or less plausibly deduce from less direct sources, shades off into much that remains unknown.

For all these individual lives, and for the society they live in as creators as well as critics, authorial irony is replaced by a comic sympathy that makes no claim to final judgements. Narrative moves, not towards the harmonious resolutions of 'realism', but towards the openness of a future that the narrator does not pretend to foresee or foreclose. Story-telling, shaping the flux of events into narrative, is specifically questioned as a means to true insight, in the character of Margaret Matthews, a novelist whose consciousness is mainly presented to us through her struggles to write. Viewed as fictional history, this novel is Wilson's most successful and ranging attempt to follow, and in the degree that fiction *can*, to analyse the social and political 'decline' of England since the apogee of Empire. The conscious refusal to define the characters too distinctly, or to enclose them in a story which overtly proceeds from a narrator, gives the novel striking powers of implication. Explicitly a work of fiction, those complicated and (after all) modestly-understood historical *realities* against which we are repeatedly invited to measure it are rendered more compellingly than in any other contemporary novel.

NOTES

1. For a 'who's who' of the characters, see A. T. Tucker, *The Novels of Anthony Powell* (London, 1976), 41–76.

2. Stephen Wall, 'Aspects of the Novel, 1930–1960', in *The Sphere History of Literature in the English Language*, ed. Bernard Bergonzi, Vol. 7, 241.

3. Page references to this and later novels are to the paperback editions of the novels published by Fontana Books.

4. Cited in Peter Faulkner's valuable study of Wilson's work, *Angus Wilson: Mimic and Moralist* (1980), 77.

5. Page reference is to the Panther paperback edition of the novel.

WELSH BARDS IN HARD TIMES:
DYLAN THOMAS AND R. S. THOMAS

C. B. COX

The two Thomases use language in very different ways. R. S. Thomas's *The Word* (1975) reflects his own intransigent honesty:

> A pen appeared, and the god said:
> 'Write what it is to be
> man.' And my hand hovered
> long over the bare page,
>
> until there, like footprints
> of the lost traveller, letters
> took shape on the page's
> blankness, and I spelled out
>
> the word 'lonely'. And my hand moved
> to erase it; but the voices
> of all those waiting at life's
> window cried out loud: 'It is true.'

R. S. Thomas will never erase any word of the truth, however unpalatable. In contrast, Dylan Thomas's rhetoric is a device to control and render significant a disordered life, to combat his fear of death. His art is a force for survival, an adoption of compulsive rhythms whose energy can keep his nightmares within acceptable limits. R. S. Thomas is determined to look reality in the face, to confront his doubts. Dylan Thomas's aim is to conquer reality by a willed refusal to mourn, by creating through poetry an alternative style committed to affirmation.

Dylan Thomas's (1914–53) seductive language has provoked in some English poets a fierce resistance. Donald Davie has accused him of abandoning the task of articulation, so that the objects to which he refers, tumbled pell-mell together, can no longer be identified.

C. H. Sisson acknowledges that Thomas's obscurity was largely a willed effect, resulting from a deliberate revision of many drafts, but finds in the poems a lack of emotional and intellectual development which finally bores the reader, once the first surprise has worn off. Thomas is historically important, Sisson contends, as the prototype of much of the literary pretension of the 1940s. David Holbrook finds in Thomas a disabling amorality, 'leading towards the trivial and ultimately the inarticulate'. According to this extreme view, 'Thomas's verbal impotence goes with his own failure to grow up and accept adult potency'.

These seem extraordinary reactions to a poet who wrote some of the most passionate, courageous lines in the English language: 'I advance for as long as forever is', 'I sang in my chains like the sea', 'Do not go gentle into that good night'.

John Wain thinks that these hostile English critics of Thomas are often objecting to his Welshness, 'the open emotionalism, the large verbal gestures which seem to them mere rant, the rapt pleasure in elaborate craftsmanship, and above all the bardic tone'. The American poet Louis Simpson prefers this bardic tone to the dry impassionate discourse he associates with the Auden of the 1940s and 1950s. He considers that Thomas's American tours, his flamboyant readings, effected a transformation in American poetry. Thomas's physicality, his musical sounds and highly visual images, his contempt for rational meaning, helped to liberate American poets from the restraints of the impersonal; this process led to the enormous success of Ginsberg's reading of *Howl* in San Francisco in 1955.

Simpson is probably right to suspect that dislike for Thomas often derives from a puritanical fear of passion and the irrational, yet most admirers of Thomas must confess to moments of uneasiness. About half the verses in the *Collected Poems* do not come off, and at times Thomas strains language beyond possible limits. The ingenious word play disintegrates into baffling riddles. If we extract themes from his work they are very simple: a love of childhood, an obsessive concern with anatomy and sex, the interinvolvement of creation and destruction, a sacramental feeling for nature. These themes are expressed in repeated images of wombs and tombs, worms and seeds; progress in his poems is achieved not by intellectual development but through wit, verbal play and incantation. Those who search for ideas in the poetry are likely to be disappointed.

Thomas's rhetoric drives forward, often in anguish and rage, in a desperate attempt to overcome the fact of personal extinction. His bardic gestures are deliberate acts of defiance. In *And Death Shall Have No Dominion* he conducts a service for the dead, like a Welsh preacher asserting his confidence in resurrection:

> Though they be mad and dead as nails,
> Heads of the characters hammer through daisies;
> Break in the sun till the sun breaks down,
> And death shall have no dominion.

His own poetic handwriting, his 'characters', are part of the process of rebirth. His rhetoric will 'Break in the sun till the sun breaks down' because art will survive even until doomsday. The title, repeated in the first and last line of each verse, is taken from St Paul, Romans vi, 9: 'Knowing that Christ being raised from the dead dieth no more; death hath no more dominion over him.' In the Authorized Version the words move onwards with confident sonority. In contrast, there is a touch of hysteria in Thomas's rhythms and images. No Christ promises resurrection of the body. The thematic title, repeated like an incantation, becomes an assertion of what is obviously not true: no wonder the dead men are said to be mad. As so often in Thomas, the affirmations are put forward with such excess they call attention to their negatives. In the line 'Heads of the characters hammer through daisies', the violence of 'hammer' creates an awareness of the difficulty of rebirth, while the alliteration sweeps the reader on, like Thomas himself, towards suspension of belief in the power of death.

Thomas's villanelle for his father, confronted by blindness and death, depends on a similar kind of rhetoric:

> Do not go gentle into that good night,
> Old age should burn and rave at close of day;
> Rage, rage against the dying of the light.
>
> Though wise men at their end know dark is right,
> Because their words had forked no lightning they
> Do not go gentle into that good night.

Once more the repetitions work in an incantatory manner to force the reader into emotional compliance, yet here the double meanings draw attention to conflicts in Thomas which he could never resolve. 'Good night' is a prayer, yet also suggests that night is good, a natural ending which the father must both accept and rage against. In the second stanza we cannot be sure why the wise men know dark is right. Is Thomas saying that death is inevitable, or that because these men's words 'forked no lightning' death is a suitable end for their failures? In both stanzas Thomas is torn between anger that his father is dying and his desire for a saving belief that death is part of an inevitable process through which the life force will survive. The buoyancy of rhythm, alliteration and rhyme carries him forward, enacts the life principle, even when he is most in despair. The emotions are simple, contradictory, but the poem dramatizes his conflicts with compelling eloquence.

The same problems recur in the controversial poem, *A Refusal to Mourn the Death, by Fire, of a Child in London*. For some readers Thomas seems coldly aloof from the horror of the child burned to death. Is not his rhetoric sentimental, entirely inappropriate to such a shocking event?

> Never until the mankind making
> Bird beast and flower
> Fathering and all humbling darkness
> Tells with silence the last light breaking
> And the still hour
> Is come of the sea tumbling in harness
>
> And I must enter again the round
> Zion of the water bead
> And the synagogue of the ear of corn
> Shall I let pray the shadow of a sound
> Or sow my salt seed
> In the least valley of sackcloth to mourn
>
> The majesty and burning of the child's death.

The literal meaning (and Thomas often insisted his poems should be read literally) is that he will not mourn the child until the world comes to an end. The words from 'mankind' to 'humbling' compose a resonant adjective modifying 'darkness', the origin and end of life, genesis and apocalypse. Not until silence and stillness replace the movement of the tides, not until Thomas himself, like all men, becomes one with water and seed, will he put on sackcloth. The effect of these lines is to praise life, so this poem that refuses to mourn turns into a form of mourning. The Old Testament words, Zion and synagogue, celebrate the holiness of Nature. The argument implies that he will never abandon himself to grief, will fight on for a kind of celebratory pantheism, even when confronted by the worst. Yet the literal meaning seems faintly ridiculous, or at least unreal, with Thomas saying that he won't weep and wear sackcloth until doomsday. In the last stanza, the 'unmourning' water of the Thames suggests the indifference of Nature, but this does not accord with the central idea that the poet, like Nature, will not mourn. The last line, 'After the first death, there is no other' might imply that after the death of Adam and Eve, death is death. Or it might be interpreted as a Christian declaration that death is followed by eternal life. This ambiguity ends the poem.

Individual lines achieve a lyrical grandeur, particularly

> Deep with the first dead lies London's daughter,
> Robed in the long friends,

yet this rhetorical flourish cannot hide the ambiguities forced on Thomas by his refusal to mourn. It can be argued that his difficulties contribute to the honesty of the poem. The strain and excess are essential to the total effect, creating a dramatic sense that no conventional elegy is appropriate for the burning of a child. Certainly the last stanza invests the child with a tragic grandeur, but this remains under question as Thomas tries not altogether successfully to maintain his belief in the value of life.

That he had clear ideas about his art is shown by his letters. In a Christmas epistle of 1933 to Pamela Hansford Johnson, he tells his correspondent:

And if I can bring myself to know, not to think, that nothing is un-interesting, I can broaden my own outlook and believe once more, as I so passionately believed and so passionately *want* to believe, in the magic of this burning and bewildering universe, in the meaning and the power of symbols, in the miracle of myself and of all mortals, in the divinity that is so near us and so longing to be nearer, in the staggering, bloody, starry wonder of the sky I can see above and the sky I can think of below.[1]

In the early poems, with their occasional morbidity, this urge to praise wrestles against self-disgust. 'I want to believe,' he wrote in the same letter, 'to believe for ever, that heaven is *being*, a state of being, and that the only hell is the hell of myself. I want to burn hell with its own flames.' His choice of images owed much to his reading of poets such as Donne, Webster and Beddoes. He sought to treat the body honestly, even the ugliness of disease and death, as part of a divinity 'that is so near us and so longing to be nearer'. This led him to shock his readers with lines such as

> Some dead undid their bushy jaws,
> And bags of blood let out their flies; ...

In a letter of November 1933 he insists that his emphasis on the body should not be regarded as hideous, for the body 'is a fact, sure as the fact of a tree'. His own aim is to translate ideas, intuitive or intellectual, into 'terms of the body, its flesh, skin, blood, sinews, veins, glands, organs, cells, or senses'.[2]

Sometimes in pursuit of this aim he stumbles through grotesque, sensational images; in other poems his language attains an extra-ordinary physicality. He tries to participate imaginatively in every stage of the process of life, even beginning in the womb. Written about two months after the birth of his son, *If my Head Hurt a Hair's Foot* is a dialogue between embryo and mother. The embryo affec-tionately tells his mother he would rather stay in the womb if his birth should give her pain. The mother replies that nothing would persuade her to change 'my tears or your iron head'. This bizarre dialogue proved incomprehensible to its first readers, including Robert Graves, but like many of Thomas's poems it is really very simple once the basic idea has been grasped. Individual phrases are strikingly descriptive, as when the embryo says:

> Sooner drop with the worm of the ropes round my throat
> Than bully ill love in the clouted scene.

Unfortunately the poem fails because the idea of a talking embryo seems faintly absurd, too contrived.

This stricture does not apply to the much shorter *Twenty-Four*

Years, written for his birthday, which examines the process of life from womb to tomb:

> In the groin of the natural doorway I crouched like a tailor
> Sewing a shroud for a journey
> By the light of the meat-eating sun.

'Meat-eating' is too melodramatic, but 'crouched like a tailor' impresses with its vivid immediacy. In this poem the irony is deliberate; the body, the shroud of the spirit, is being sewn for its journey towards death. The irony is continued in the description of the young man's 'sensual strut'. In the last line, 'I advance for as long as forever is', the confident forward movement of the verb is counterbalanced by the hint that he does not know how long forever is. Here, as in *A Refusal to Mourn*, the doubts are part of the total effect.

Thomas's first book, *Eighteen Poems*, appeared in 1934, to be followed two years later by *Twenty-Five Poems*. These include some of the most difficult poems and images, whose reverberations defy rational analysis: 'Light breaks where no sun shines', or 'The two-a-vein, the foreskin, and the cloud'. At his best, as in the famous *The Force that Through the Green Fuse Drives the Flower*, his words are both vividly descriptive and symbolic of his pantheist convictions. As he explains in his fine poem, *Especially When the October Wind*, he is shut in by conventional words, seeking a new language which can bring the physical world alive:

> Shut, too, in a tower of words, I mark
> On the horizon walking like the trees
> The wordy shapes of women, and the rows
> Of the star-gestured children in the park.
> Some let me make you of the vowelled beeches,
> Some of the oaken voices, from the roots
> Of many a thorny shire tell you notes,
> Some let me make you of the water's speeches.

Thomas wants his verses to become part of the creative process. The architecture of his poems, their careful rhymes and image patterns, are intended to reincarnate the order and vitality of life, to act as magic rituals against the powers of dissolution.

In *The Map of Love* (1939), Thomas often seems to be imitating himself, but in the 1940s he developed a new serenity. *Deaths and*

Entrances (1946) and *In Country Sleep* (1952) include some of his most popular poems: *Poem in October*, *A Winter's Tale*, *The Hunchback in the Park*, *Fern Hill* and *Over Sir John's Hill*. He had not solved his personal problems, for his alcoholism grew worse, but in his verse he preserved his commitment to an alternative vision, a creativity undiminished by death.

Fern Hill is the farm of his aunt, Ann Jones, where Thomas spent holidays away from Swansea. In this poem the double impulse of his work is held in perfect balance. In every stanza the adult narrator laments the power of time, but for the boy, 'once below a time', the farm is paradise, an eternal moment of grace. *Fern Hill* stands in a tradition that looks back to Vaughan, Traherne and Wordsworth. Through transferred epithets, 'lilting house' and 'happy yard', we see how the boy's emotions transform every object, uniting him with creation. He is 'honoured among wagons' and 'prince of the apple towns'. On a first reading the magical language may seem out of control, the repeated 'and' sweeping the reader on breathlessly past half-understood images; but close attention reveals how carefully Thomas had worked out his effects. Why, for example, did he choose the word 'windfall' at the end of the first stanza?

> And once below a time I lordly had the trees and leaves
> Trail with daisies and barley
> Down the rivers of the windfall light.

The farm-carts brush against the trees leaving trails of daisies and barley. These hang from the branches in shafts of sunlight, 'rivers', as Thomas says, suggesting movement and power. The splendour of these rivers of light is a 'windfall', an unexpected prize; yet the word also recalls the green apples which fall before their time. The light is part of a natural process which includes decay. The wit includes the double impulse of the poem.

In the last line of *Fern Hill*, 'Though I sang in my chains like the sea', child and sea are imprisoned by time and the tides, but the child's joy is like the power of oceans, the noise of waves, which Thomas asserts is a form of song. It is instructive to compare this exuberance with Ted Hughes's black despair in *Pibroch*: 'The sea cries with its meaningless voice.' Some readers find Thomas's worship of life an evasion of the truth. Here once more the final image of the sea stands as a gesture of defiance.

Dylan Thomas will be remembered for his poetry rather than for prose or drama. In his popular play for radio, *Under Milk Wood* (1954), he develops more varied rhythms, and there are splendid sharp fragments of conversation. The play is still performed, in spite of bitter attacks on its sentimentality and necrophiliac obsessions, but it lacks the originality of language of his best poems. Whether this new development would have helped him to escape from his self-absorption we can never know.

After such magniloquence there could be no greater contrast than R. S. Thomas's (b. 1913) uncompromising honesty, his awkward, restless Christianity. A year older than Dylan, he did not achieve any kind of popularity until 1955, when *Song at the Year's Turning* was praised by Kingsley Amis and John Betjeman. In spite of this success, he has never suffered anything like the fervent adoration which plagued Dylan's career. In the late 1960s he changed his style towards a more personal idiom, a questioning of cosmic reality in broken rhythms and harsh, angry tones. These experiments led to many failures, but his later work includes some outstanding poems which confirm his status as a major poet. The sense of pain and isolation expressed in these poems goes far beyond anything to be found in Dylan Thomas's verse. This courageous development of a new style has attracted little attention, and he still has not received the acclaim he deserves.

His own concept of poetry is brought out in many poems, in *The Word*, as we have seen, or *Waiting*, included in *Between Here and Now* (1981). The poem begins by recalling youthful admiration for Yeats, now turned sour, and then continues:

> What counsel
> has the pen's rhetoric
>
> to impart? Break mirrors, stare
> ghosts in the face, try
> walking without crutches

at the grave's edge? Now
in the small hours
of belief the one eloquence

to master is that
of the bowed head, the bent
knee, waiting, as at the end

of a hard winter
for one flower to open
on the mind's tree of thorns.

The last lines are typical of many occasions in Thomas's verse when the linguistic austerity is suddenly illuminated by a simple but extraordinarily effective metaphor. The only eloquence to master is humility. In several poems he kneels before the Cross. His thoughts are often uncertain, ambiguous, anguished. In contrast to Dylan Thomas he will not use bardic rhythms to overcome his loneliness and despair. Instead he remains kneeling, probing his own responses to the silent God who gives no answer to his prayers. He is the poet not of Resurrection but of the Cross.

In Church (1966) describes the empty pews after the few worshippers have departed and the lights have been put out:

> There is no other sound
> In the darkness but the sound of a man
> Breathing, testing his faith
> On emptiness, nailing his questions
> One by one to an untenanted cross.

The Protestant cross bears no figure of Christ. The man in the dark church crucifies Christ once again, nails him to the Cross, by asking questions and resisting faith. This orthodox Christian interpretation of the poem is contradicted by the emotional quality of the last two lines. 'Emptiness' suggests that no God hears his prayer. The cross is perhaps untenanted because Christ no longer exists.

These ambiguities, held together in the final image, appear elsewhere in the form of dialogues with God. In *The Moon in Lleyn* (1975), as he kneels in a stone church, he sadly acknowledges that perhaps Yeats was right:

> Religion is over, and
> what will emerge from the body
> of the new moon, no one
> can say.
>   But a voice sounds
> in my ear: Why so fast,
> mortal? These very seas
> are baptized. The parish
> has a saint's name time cannot
> unfrock.

'You must remain Kneeling', the voice tells him, for, like the moon, 'prayer, too, has its phases'. In spite of all his doubts, his poems on occasions break out into moments of epiphany. *Pieta* (1966) is a great religious poem, quoted here in its entirety:

> Always the same hills
> Crowd the horizon,
> Remote witnesses
> Of the still scene.
>
> And in the foreground
> The tall Cross,
> Sombre, untenanted,
> Aches for the Body
> That is back in the cradle
> Of a maid's arms.

The first four lines suggest that 'always', throughout history, the Cross is at the centre of all natural phenomena. The living hills are turned into witnesses, their significance dependent on the Crucifixion. The poem ends with Mary's love, but the extraordinary idea that the Cross 'aches' for the lost body suggests that all creation, even the wood of the Cross, longs for the absent Christ. At the same time this 'aching' conveys the idea that suffering is an essential part of love. This is the meaning of Pieta. The question why the Cross aches for the Body cannot be finally resolved, for there is something disturbingly perverse in this desire, as if Nature prefers pain to love. The image resists paraphrase.

The same ambiguities are to be found in *Here* (1961), one of his best-known poems. Christ is on the Cross, presumably at the moment when he cried out: 'My God, My God, why hast thou forsaken me?' In the poem Christ speaks:

> Why are my hands this way
> That they will not do as I say?
> Does no God hear when I pray?

In the opening line Christ says 'I am a man now', and he ends with the line: 'I must stay here with my hurt'. In both *Pieta* and *Here*, Thomas explores the meaning of the Crucifixion, suggesting that man's destiny is to live like Christ on the Cross, torn by doubt, his love inextricably and mysteriously involved with pain.

His poetry uncompromisingly records the shifting moods of the believer, the moments of spiritual sterility as well as of epiphany. In *The Belfry* he describes his times of despair in a typically bold metaphor:

> There are times
> When a black frost is upon
> One's whole being, and the heart
> In its bone belfry hangs and is dumb.

There is none of Dylan Thomas's incantatory force which carried the reader forward across the obscurities. Instead the metaphors brilliantly enact the movement, from doubt to faith. 'But who is to know?', he continues, for prayers fall steadily through the hard spell of weather between him and God:

> Perhaps they are warm rain
> That brings the sun and afterwards flowers
> On the raw graves and throbbing of bells.

These very personal religious poems are usually set in the context of Wales. He resents the English tourists 'Scavenging among the remains of our culture', or the sentimental watercolour appeal of quaint villages. He is the poet of

> the smashed faces
> Of the farms with the stone trickle
> Of their tears down the hills' side.
>
> (*Reservoirs*, 1968)

In such poems the landscapes enact the pain of crucifixion.

In contrast to Dylan, R. S. Thomas is not self-absorbed. His poetry is full of compassion for his parishioners, Welsh hill-folk imprisoned in the daily routines of survival: 'the long queue of life that wound through a Welsh valley'. Thomas's conflicting responses to Iago Prytherch, the ordinary peasant, form the subject matter of several outstanding poems. He watches Iago's dark figure 'Marring the simple geometry/Of the square fields with its gaunt question'. His own refinement implies a superiority, not only because of his intelligence and education, but because he responds to spirit in Nature, the order and beauty of the world which apparently never touch Iago. For Thomas in his early poems Nature's beauty is sacramental. In *The Moor* (1966), 'the air crumbled/And broke on me generously as bread':

> It was like a church to me.
> I entered it on soft foot,
> Breath held like a cap in the hand.

In many poems he is angry because Iago does not share this vision, yet he is also ashamed to be so helpless. His compassion can do nothing to change Iago; it is a form of creative attention, a human care which acknowledges in the peasant his own prototype:

> There is something frightening in the vacancy of his mind.
> His clothes, sour with years of sweat
> And animal contact, shock the refined,
> But affected, sense with their stark naturalness.
> Yet this is your prototype ...

The 'impregnable' Iago both attracts and repels Thomas. He is appalled by the emptiness of his parishioners' lives, yet senses that in their endurance they exist in Nature in ways more fundamental than he can comprehend.

In the later poetry, particularly in *H'm* (1972) and subsequent volumes, there is increasing bitterness of tone. Institutional religion is dead, and Nature perverted by what he calls the Machine, 'singing to itself of money'. In new imagery of germs, molecules, corpuscles, bacteria, viruses, he introduces multiple pictures of God, now his confederate against the Machine, now incompetent (as in Ted Hughes's *Crow* poems, which influenced Thomas), now an Old

Testament avenger, as in *Soliloquy* (1972), where God threatens his people with extinction:

> Within the churches
> You built me you genuflected
> To the machine. Where will it
> Take you from the invisible
> Viruses, the personnel
> Of the darkness that do my will?

In this Job-like wrestling with God, Thomas retains his usual mixture of plain language with sudden metaphors of surprising brilliance. His concern is with the failure of language to express the paradoxes of God:

> We die, we die
> with the knowledge that your resistance
> is endless at the frontier of the great poem.
>   (*The Combat*, 1975)

In these astonishing later poems he conceives his own words reaching out towards unknown space, towards the secret writing of God. He is torn and divided by seen and unseen languages, perhaps only connected by the omnipresence of the Cross.

Both Thomases adapt the Welsh bardic tradition to modern problems. Dylan's high-flown rhythms invite his readers to repress their doubts, to lose themselves in pagan celebration. R. S. Thomas's poetry is not without metaphoric brilliance, but he prefers a plain style, spare, unflinching, honest. He is like an Old Testament prophet, calling his people to resist the temptations of urban materialism, the siren voices of the Machine. Both types of poetry have their flaws. Dylan's temptation is self-indulgence, rhetoric for its own sake R. S. Thomas can seem too dour, too ascetic. In spite of their many differences, both reject compromise and try to preserve religious forms of language. In retrospect, R. S. Thomas's love of truth, his desperate self-questionings, seem more relevant to these hard times when belief is so difficult. He deserves the last word:

> I am alone on the surface
> of a turning planet. What
>
> to do but, like Michelangelo's

Adam, put my hand
out into unknown space,
hoping for the reciprocating touch?
(*Threshold*, 1981)

NOTES

The dates of individual poems indicate when they were first published in
books.
  1. Constantine Fitzgibbon (ed.), *Selected Letters of Dylan Thomas* (1966),
83.
  2. *Selected Letters of Dylan Thomas*, 48.

IRIS MURDOCH:
THE LIMITS OF CONTRIVANCE

S. W. DAWSON

For more than a quarter of a century the novelist most likely to be cited by the average reader as representing intellectual weight and seriousness has been Iris Murdoch. She has occupied a position, similarly supported by the almost unanimous weight of literary journalistic opinion, in many respects equivalent to that of Aldous Huxley during the interwar years, though the dimension of social concern represented by *Brave New World* and the best parts of *Antic Hay* has, with the exception of a few half-hearted political gestures in the early novels, been strikingly absent from her writing. Nor is she, as he was, an explicit popularizer of current ideas, though she has been a professional philosopher and her novels provide ample evidence of a serious interest in psychology and anthropology. One is often reminded of Huxley's weaker sides – the social and cultural knowingness (though her social range is far narrower than his, and she moves unsurely outside the professional middle class), the lapses into sentimentality, and the desire to shock, though there are many significant differences in tone, and she strikes one always as more provincial than Huxley. But essentially the appeal of both is to a readership which seeks the pleasures of fashionable fiction tempered by a flattering sense of intellectual weight.

To begin here, and to categorize Miss Murdoch according to the nature of her audience, is to run the risk of considerable critical injustice. Yet she does present criticism with the kind of problem which arises in Huxley's case – the co-presence of intelligence and seriousness in novels which as imaginative writing, as aspirants to the realm of 'art', are radically unsatisfactory. There can have been no more striking demonstration since Huxley that, in art, cleverness is not enough.

To judge Miss Murdoch so severely is to invoke high standards, no doubt, and there is much in the early novels (up to, say, *An Unofficial Rose*, 1962) which earns the respect due to an individual minor talent. *Under the Net* (1954) her first novel, was an interesting attempt to use the neo-picaresque comic form of the time (Kingsley Amis's *Lucky Jim* being the best-known example) to provide the framework for a novel of ideas in the tradition of Peacock, Mallock and Huxley. It revealed a talent for creating farcical incident in a style primarily descriptive rather than dramatic. There are already signs in *Under the Net* of what has become a prominent characteristic of Miss Murdoch's manner, the painstakingly detailed descriptions of the appearance of her characters, their physical actions, and the physical world which they inhabit. This deliberate construction of the world of appearances has about it something almost obsessive. (Certainly a reader imperfectly acquainted with the capital would do well to equip himself with a street plan of London.) Localities, streets, houses and rooms are described in meticulous detail. Perhaps the most striking example of her determinedly descriptive manner are the feats of physical ingenuity, like the raising of the bell from the lake in *The Bell* (1958), or the rescue of Mor's son from the school tower in *The Sandcastle* (1957).

This obsession with particularizing what she calls in her writings on fiction the 'contingent', suggests a calculated attempt on Miss Murdoch's part to counterbalance a powerful opposite tendency in her fiction – that towards allegorical fantasy and what might be described as the 'mythic'. One might point here to the somewhat self-indulgent whimsical fantasy of the early *The Flight from the Enchanter* (1956) significantly dedicated to Elias Canetti, the role of magical rituals in a number of the novels, or the monster rising from the waves in the more recent *The Sea, The Sea* (1978). There is already developing a thriving Ph.D industry in the unravelling and laying bare of mythic patterns in Miss Murdoch's work, though in this case also objection might be made to the pointed deliberateness with which the clues are planted, and the predictability of the 'symbolism' (water, swimming, dogs, the taking off of shoes, etc). This impression of deliberateness extends to the characters themselves; they usually seem to be manipulated according to a predetermined pattern, and as one follows the often bizarre combinations which form and reform one seems to be observing the demonstration of a theorem in human algebra rather than a reflection of the rich and often disconcerting variety of human experience. It is as if Miss

Murdoch first conceives an idea in conceptual terms (which is sometimes expressed in the novel's title, like *The Nice and the Good* (1968)
or *The Sacred and Profane Love Machine* (1974)), then chooses a range
of moral types to act out this idea, and finally constructs a physical
world in which it is to be acted out. The selection of the 'world',
which often has the air of being, as one might say, 'swotted up' for
the occasion, is determined to some extent by the need for appropriate
'symbolism', like the roses in *An Unofficial Rose*:

> 'She doesn't directly discourage me from anything. It's what she is that
> does it. And it isn't just writing either. Can't you see me fading away before
> your eyes, can't everyone see it? "Poor Randall," they say, "he's hardly there
> any more." I need a different world, a formal world. I need form. Christ,
> how I fade!' He laughed suddenly, turning to face Hugh, and took the rose
> out of his hand.
>
> 'Form?'
>
> 'Yes, yes, form, structure, will, something to encounter, something to make
> me be. Form, as this rose has it. That's what Ann hasn't got. She's as messy
> and flabby and open as a bloody dogrose. That's what gets me down. That's
> what destroys all my imagination, all the bloody footholds. Ah well, you
> wouldn't understand.'   (ch. 3)

The objection to this is simply that the roses do not in the novel
ever suggest anything deeper or more subtle than what is here deliberately set out – this is merely the establishment of a formula.

'We are not isolated free choosers, monarchs of all we survey, but
benighted creatures sunk in a reality whose nature we are constantly
and overwhelmingly tempted to deform by fantasy.'[1] This extract
from one of Miss Murdoch's essays has been justifiably taken as
offering an essential clue to the tendency of her fiction. (The rhetorical over-emphasis in 'benighted' and 'sunk' is worth remarking.) The
egregious hero of *The Sea, The Sea* strikes a similar note in the novel's
closing pages:

> I have talked with Lizzie about Hartley and though nothing important
> was said my heart feels eased, as if it has been gently prised open. I accused
> Hartley of being a 'fantasist', or perhaps that was Titus's word, but what
> a 'fantasist' I have been myself. I was the dreamer, I the magician. How much,
> I see as I look back, I read into it all, reading my own dream text and not
> looking at the reality. Hartley had been right when she said of our love that

it was not part of the real world. It had no place. But what strikes me now is that at some point, in order to ease things for myself, I decided, almost surreptitiously, to regard her as a liar. In order to release myself from the burden of my tormented attachment I began, with the half-conscious cunning so characteristic of the self-protective human ego, to see her as a poor hysterical shrew; and this debased pity, which I tried to imagine was some kind of spiritual compassion, was the halfway house to my escape. I could not bear the spectacle of that whimpering captive victim in that awful windowless room which I still see in nightmares. My love's imagination, gave up the real Hartley and consoled itself with high abstract ideas of blindly 'accepting it all'. That was the exit.

His kidnapping of the woman who had been his childhood sweet-heart ('that whimpering captive victim') in order to recapture through her some of the purity of that childhood world is presented in terms of grotesque farce. This is not unusual – indeed most of Miss Murdoch's successful passages are entirely farcical.[2] This is hardly surprising since farce is usually generated by the collision of fantasy and reality. The farce becomes more grotesque as the fantasy becomes more abandoned and the reality more arbitrary (or as Miss Murdoch would no doubt put it, 'contingent'). The following con-versation from *Under the Net* clearly points out the direction her fiction was to take:

> I had a confused sense of something terrible raising itself up between us. Hugo saw it too, and added immediately, 'Jake you're a fool. You know anyone can love anyone, or prefer anyone to anyone.' . . .
>
> 'Well, I don't know what to say,' said Hugo. 'I'm terribly sorry about all this, Jake; it's like life, isn't it? I love Sadie, who's keen on you, and you love Anna, who's keen on me. Perverse, isn't it?'

The utter arbitrariness of love has become the driving force of Miss Murdoch's fiction, but it would be difficult to argue that she has taken the matter any further than the last-quoted passage in a quarter of a century of writing. Her characters are seized by erotic obsessions and driven by them into grotesque actions, making fools of themselves in short, and it is in describing the resultant violence and humiliation that Miss Murdoch's writing, in passages like chapters 20 and 23 of *The Bell*, rises above her customary level of deliberate competence. This is to say that the central thrust of her fiction (which is not to speak of her *intention* – 'Never trust the artist, trust the tale') is reductive.

It is true, as John Holloway argues earlier in this volume, that in this uncertain world of colliding obsessions we are periodically offered positive values, also associated with 'love' – goodness, kindness, the truth of art and so on. But in terms of achieved creation they hardly exist.

Dora stopped at last in front of Gainsborough's picture of his two daughters. These children step through a wood hand in hand, their garments shimmering, their eyes serious and dark, their two pale heads, round full buds, like yet unlike.

Dora was always moved by the pictures. Today she was moved, but in a new way. She marvelled, with a kind of gratitude, that they were all still here, and her heart was filled with love for the pictures, their authority, their marvellous generosity, their splendour. It occurred to her that here at last was something real and something perfect. Who had said that, about perfection and reality being in the same place? Here was something which her consciousness could not wretchedly devour, and by making it part of her fantasy make it worthless. Even Paul, she thought, only existed now as someone she dreamt about; or else as a vague external menace never really encountered and understood. But the pictures were something real outside herself, which spoke to her kindly and yet in sovereign tones, something superior and good whose presence destroyed the dreary trance-like solipsism of her earlier mood. When the world had seemed to be subjective it had seemed to be without interest or value. But now there was something else in it after all.

These thoughts, not clearly articulated, flitted through Dora's mind. She had never thought about the pictures in this way before; nor did she draw now any very explicit moral. Yet she felt that she had had a revelation. She looked at the radiant, sombre, tender, powerful canvas of Gainsborough and felt a sudden desire to go down on her knees before it, embracing it, shedding tears.

This (from the closing pages of chapter 14 of *The Bell*) is certainly intended to be a crucial passage in the spiritual development of Dora, the central character of the novel. Yet it neither evokes the picture itself, nor takes Dora's consciousness beyond the abstractions and generalities to which the inert rhythms of the prose impart no dramatic force beyond what one might have expected in one of Miss Murdoch's philosophical essays. 'Yet she felt she had had a revelation.' One cannot but comment that *we* don't feel this, we simply register it as something we are *told*, so that the end of the passage is forced and embarrassing. This is not the language of revelation, it is the language of disquisition.

'Achieved creation' – the phrase is a necessary reminder that it is by the standards of literary criticism that Miss Murdoch's novels are to be judged. Her conception of an arbitrary and finally incomprehensible world would be powerfully terrible if we could be possessed by it, as we are, for instance, by the panic dance of meaninglessness in the earlier novels of Evelyn Waugh, like the fate of Miss Runcible in *Vile Bodies*. We are not possessed by it, we are not disturbed by it, since Miss Murdoch remains for the most part at a comfortable distance from her action and characters. We cannot accept the motivating forces of her characters as other than absurd obsessions because as a writer she simply lacks the dimension of passion; she never fully enters into or lives the human experience to which she points. As one reviewer of *A Fairly Honourable Defeat* (1970) remarked:

> between the long and diffuse stretches of chatty and even jolly dialogues, apparently authoritative analyses of the characters are given. And the tone of these passages seems to imply that the author has thought of and thought about her creatures carefully, but that she has not lived them or been possessed by them.
>
> They are treated with the interested, speculative, but ultimately neutral attention that is given to acquaintances about whom one gossips but about whom one does not really care. However much the sympathies of the novel's total design are, as we should expect, on the side of love and intelligence, the quality of the author's absorption in the individual case lacks creative enthusiasm.
>
> Such handicaps are too fundamental to be compensated for by the kind of tit-bit snapped up by explicators ... however energetically such details of reference and such figures in the carpet are picked out and deployed, they seem unlikely to accumulate sufficiently to bring round the unconvinced reader.[3]

Henry James wrote

Catching the very note and trick, the strange irregular rhythm of life, that is the attempt whose strenuous force keeps Fiction upon her feet. In proportion as in what she offers us we see life without rearrangement do we feel that we are touching the truth; in proportion as we see it with arrangement do we feel that we are being put off with a substitute, a compromise, a convention.

The oddities of Miss Murdoch's novels are not the strangeness of life, and this is not to enter against her the vulgar complaint that 'people don't do such things', a delusion which a perusal of *The News of the World* would quickly dispel. What one rather finds oneself objecting is that such things don't happen like that, remarking with James again that 'Humanity is immense, and reality has a myriad forms; the most that one can affirm is that some of the flowers of fiction have the odour of it, and others have not.' Hence we follow her narratives out of curiosity, not concern; we are not usually moved by the fates of her characters, simply startled and intrigued by the unexpected turn of events, as if we were watching a game of snakes and ladders played with human beings for counters. Yet curiously the very arbitrariness of the events always carries with it a sense of contrivance, of subjection to the conceptual scheme. In *The Nice and the Good* there are extended passages which differ hardly at all from what we might find in one of the author's philosophical essays:

What Ducane was experiencing, in this form peculiar to him of imagining himself as a judge, was, though this was not entirely clear in his mind, one of the great paradoxes of morality, namely that in order to become good it may be necessary to imagine oneself good, and yet such imagining may also be the very thing which renders improvement impossible, either because of surreptitious complacency or because of some deeper blasphemous infection which is set up when goodness is thought about in the wrong way. To become good it may be necessary to think about virtue: although unreflective simple people may achieve a thoughtless excellence. Ducane was in any case highly reflective and had from childhood quite explicitly set before himself the aim of becoming a good man; and although he had little of the demoniac in his nature there was a devil of pride, a stiff Calvinistic Scottish devil, who was quite capable of bringing Ducane to utter damnation, and Ducane knew this perfectly well. (ch. 35)

The body of the novel is taken up with a succession of startling and bizarre adventures and discoveries, the interest of which is essentially that of the detective story, and culminates in one of those bouts of perilous swimming which are a fairly customary resource in her work. The effect of this action on her central character, Ducane, is communicated as follows:

I wonder if this is the end, thought Ducane, and if so what it will all have amounted to. How tawdry and small it has all been. He saw himself now as a little rat, a busy little scurrying rat seeking out its own little advantages and comforts. To live easily, to have cosy familiar pleasures, to be well thought of. He felt his body stiffening and he nestled closer to Mingo's invincible warmth. He patted Pierce's shoulder and burrowed his hand beneath it. He thought, poor, poor Mary. The coloured images were returning now to his closed eyes. He saw the face of Biranne near to him, as in a silent film, moving, mouthing, but unheard. He thought, if I ever get out of here I will be no man's judge. Nothing is worth doing except to kill the little rat, not to judge, not to be superior, not to exercise power, not to seek, seek, seek. To love and to reconcile and to forgive, only this matters. All power is sin and all law is frailty. Love is the only justice. Forgiveness, reconciliation, not law.

(ch. 35)

It is impossible to judge how one is to take this banal piece of writing – it doesn't, at any rate, seem to be ironic. Nor is it easy to see how Ducane's conclusion has emerged from his experience during the novel's action, or his more recent aquatic adventures. Yet it has the air of a kind of demonstration of the truth of a proposition, a demonstration which Ducane and his 'case' have been invented specifically to provide.

There has been no attempt made here to discuss Miss Murdoch's novels in terms of their ideas, and what she makes of Sartre, Freud, Simone Weil and others, nor to trace the 'patterns' and elucidate the symbolism. The question which poses itself first is simply this: to what extent is Miss Murdoch as a novelist worth our serious and sustained attention? The implicit claims her novels make, their increasing portentousness, bear no relation to the quality of the writing. The farcical liveliness has faded, and it seems that she has immersed herself so completely in the ludicrous that she can no longer see that it is ludicrous. Her novels have become a closed system in which, despite the intellectual trappings, it is possible to say with effect (the effect of art) little more than 'Lord, what fools these mortals be.' It is perhaps an achievement, if hardly a considerable one.

PART THREE

NOTES

1. Iris Murdoch, 'Against Dryness', *Encounter*, No. 88 (January 1961), 20.
2. See the present writer's 'Anyone for Incest?', *The Human World*, No. 2 (February 1971), 57–61.
3. *The Times Literary Supplement*, 29 January 1970, 101.

DORIS LESSING AND NADINE GORDIMER

ROBERT TAUBMAN

She was adolescent, and therefore bound to be unhappy; British, and therefore uneasy and defensive; in the fourth decade of the twentieth century, and therefore inescapably beset with problems of race and class; female, and obliged to repudiate the shackled women of the past.

So Martha sees herself at the start of *Martha Quest* (1952), the first of Doris Lessing's sequence of novels *Children of Violence*, four of which are set in Rhodesia before independence. As Martha grows up her problems change but do not go away. The particular form these problems take, in the mid twentieth century – political, sexual, psychological – is mercilessly recorded. They are never resolved, because at the heart of them is the typical Doris Lessing character cherishing her resentments: preserving her sense of herself at all costs – and not unlike other human beings in that; but peculiarly dependent on her problems and their inevitability in order to reach any definition of herself. By the time Martha Quest is ready to leave Africa, in *Landlocked* (1965), she is older and more experienced and yet no more mature.

The 'progressive' group in the town in 'Zambesia' is now breaking up; it is 1945, suspicion of Stalin is being voiced, African leaders are turning from socialism to nationalism. Martha, awaiting divorce from the German communist Anton, has an affair with Thomas Stern, 'a Jewish Polish peasant'. Her father dies, and Stern dies – probably crazy – of blackwater fever in the Zambesi valley. It is time to leave for England. These are the strong lines in the narrative, which together with the calm, cursory tone – 'Martha got up, the two young women kissed, and Martha went out' – might suggest that everything's exactly under control. Yet the real experience in the novel happens piecemeal and depends on mere contingencies: Martha, at a dance, examining her hand and being astounded by its cruelty, the garden shed where Martha and Thomas meet, the quite transitory divisions between people that give rise to: 'Go away, don't touch me.' Martha has a good deal of insight into her own condition, but the states she discerns in herself are discontinuous. She herself, drifting somnambulistically into and out of the affair with Thomas, seems to be looking for explanation wherever she can find it – in any dream or abstraction that has inevitability about it and will give a pattern to her life. One sees why, four years earlier, she became a Marxist.

In spite of these insights, one doesn't understand Martha, and they don't really help Martha to understand. Moreover, the author too is involved, reluctant to make anything clearer than it appears to Martha. With almost wilful honesty, what she sets down is the record of a failure to understand. And yet every scene becomes a skirmish provoked by Martha's irony or resentments – against men, or her parents, or the bourgeois or the 'progressives'. Such all-round criticism must imply, one would think, a scheme of values or at least some reference to a moral principle. But nothing so explicit emerges; Martha's discontents are rarely rational, they're simply *her*, or they're what she calls 'autonomous feelings'. Mrs Lessing has what the great novelists have, singular powers of appropriation. Her Africa is all her own (an impression of space, light, movement, hardly ever looked at in detail); most of her characters, for all their contained vitality, are hard to tell apart, self-absorbed, humourless; the whole novel is Martha-coloured.

The Four-Gated City (1969) is the largest and last of the Martha Quest novels. She is now in London, living through the fifties and the Cold War, and the novel is a bulky compendium of the discontents of the time. Doris Lessing's way with what she doesn't like is dismissive, as in her bad words for intellectual fashion:

There is a new phenomenon, or one conceived to be new: the creature, sullenly alerted, all fear, is concerned for only one thing, how to isolate it, how to remain unaffected. The process is accomplished, in this society, through words. A word or a phrase is found: communism, traitor, espionage, homosexuality, teenage violence – for instance. Or anger, or commitment, or satire.

But this is just the sort of creature Martha herself is: a woman living in a continuous present, without a memory (she now rarely even recalls her husbands or her child or Africa). What is wrong with the times shows indeed most clearly in Martha herself. She is shocked by her own discontinuous states of being:

> She walked, walked, fast, wanting to get away, till she came towards a sheet or expanse of gleaming substance and saw approaching her a creature wrapped in the fur of an animal, short, pale fur on its head, its eyes wide and horrified as if in flight from something, or looking for somewhere to hide itself. This she realized after a moment, was herself, Martha, who so lately had been dissolving in joy at the sight of a sunlit cloud above an airy mass of leaf.

The sequence of novels ends without any resolution of Martha's problems, pointing only towards possible solutions on another plane – in salvation on the other side of madness, or in release from personality in the prophetic world of 'space fiction'.

Meanwhile, Doris Lessing had given the disintegration of the self still closer attention in her most famous novel, *The Golden Notebook* (1962) and in a range of her shorter stories. The first inset in the novel is a narrative called 'Free Women', which shows us Anna and Molly in a London flat in 1957, and offers a provisional definition: they lead 'what is known as free lives, that is, lives like men'. This intermittent narrative frames four huge sections devoted to Anna's notebooks of the 1950s: the black notebook dealing with the African experience out of which she has written her only novel; the red for politics – the decline and fall of the communist myth; blue a record of relations with men, and of dreams and sessions with her analyst; yellow in which she 'makes up stories', mostly drafts of a novel in which 'Ella' re-enacts a large part of Anna's experience. In all this what it means to be a 'free woman' is thoroughly worked over. Not only the question of 'lives like men' – an illusion, for if Anna enters a sexual relationship as freely as a man, she nevertheless ends it in humiliating dependence – but also the freedom of choice that paralyses her as a writer, the freedom allowed by the irresponsible state of the world, and the ironical freedom of a woman haunted by the idea of integrity who is condemned to act at random to find out what her actions mean. Structure and scene are more complex than this suggests; but the book's striking quality is not that it is difficult in a profound or original way, but rather the reverse – the conviction it carries of being a close transcription of actual experience, in which most of the expected preoccupations of a writer in the mid twentieth century naturally find their place. Simply as a record of how it is to be free and responsible, a woman in relation to men and to other women, and to struggle to come to terms with one's self about these things and about writing and politics, it seems to me unique in its truthfulness and range. Its interest has been widely felt; it is the sort of book that determines the way people think about themselves.

Doris Lessing has one theme that puts a few of the stories collected in *A Man and Two Women* (1963) on a different level of intensity from the others, and is also the centre of interest of the novel. This is the theme of the couple or the 'affair'. What she deals with here is of course complex, but complex by nature, not because of anything very elaborate in her treatment of it; indeed an unusual directness on this topic is what we come to expect from her. The picture isn't encouraging: none of her women seems capable of a stable relationship, and none of her men worthy of one. They come together with little more than foreboding, and most of the time they struggle to get apart. She casts several glances of contempt at women who depend on men in the way that once was thought wholesome and now seems impossibly naïve. But one comes to recognize a woman in several of these stories and in the characters of *The Golden Notebook* (themselves evidently the projections of a single woman, Anna) who is certainly disturbing. This woman is frank about her sexual needs and satisfactions, yet clearly unhappy with them. She gives herself a role: it is to be thoroughly female, to turn herself into a love-object as naked and opaque as a stone; and she both wants this role and resents it; and still more resents the male who takes advantage of it. In the long run, though, Mrs Lessing doesn't let anyone off lightly. Her girls, sooner or later – this is the story of *The Golden Notebook* – collapse. And then they're at their most interesting. Not, I think, on account of anything that can be read into the collapse, in the light of the big ideas with which her novel is concerned, but rather the opposite, for Mrs Lessing seems to me admirable in being able to realize in her characters a despair devoid of any particular meaning. It is the shallowness of breakdown she conveys, a thing like, but worse than, the exhausted mental processes of someone who hasn't slept for nights. And having abstracted all else from them, she is now very honest about her characters. Nothing *deepens* them; they are truest at their most shallow; and like this they can be as frightening as Medea. The most explicit study of self-destruction is 'To Room Nineteen', in which Susan drifts away from her family into indifference, almost into non-being, practised like a religious discipline in hotel rooms, and then kills herself. Such hopelessness in a practically pure state has interested other modern writers, but most of them find it extraordinary; I don't think anyone else has made it quite as natural as Mrs Lessing. She sees it steadily as a kind of experience, and that's all. There are no overtones or promises; she doesn't strike one as a defeated romantic or a potential mystic. She is only writing about human beings and how they can still operate under near-zero conditions.

The prospects aren't good for them, obviously; and Susan dies, the *Golden Notebook* people are driven out of their minds. Mrs Lessing seems to want to push pessimism as far as it will go. But sometimes she surprises us with more than just pessimism. Her story 'Dialogue' shows, with no relaxation of rigour, that under such conditions human beings really can still operate, and that what they achieve, because it's so shorn of falsity and illusion, is worth something. Here the principle of solitary indifference is in the man; while the woman, after visiting this cold, unconnected man living at the top of a modern building, finds that a leaf from a hedge is enough to warm her and bring her back to life. Yet what we also feel is a tremendous force in the man's solitariness, and some justice in his claim: 'For all that, it seems to me I'm nearer the truth than you are.' They achieve no more, these two, than things like putting on a jazz record; looking at the view; or her realization that 'these men and women, the solitary ones, do give back, otherwise they wouldn't be so welcome, so needed'. And this alone wouldn't be much if it wasn't also a wonderfully *seen* story, in which colour and texture are all-important – vegetables and leaf, concrete, the ill man with close-cut reddish hair, his room like an exposed platform challenging him with its openness.

Since 1979 Doris Lessing has been occupied with 'space fiction'; this is neither science fiction nor free-wheeling fantasy but has something in common with the myth-making in Rousseau or William Morris that offers visions of hope or disaster for mankind. The myth-making in *Shikasta* (1979) seems, by comparison, unconvincing, being vague on the lost values of the past ('voluntary submission to the great Whole') and both vague and cranky on the continuing bond between earth and Canopus through the intermittent flow of SOWF ('Substance-of-we-feeling'). But these novels are not an escape from the themes of the realistic novels; colonialism is the subject of *The Sirian Experiments* (1981), and near-zero conditions of almost non-being occur again on the dying planet of *The Making of the Representative for Planet 8* (1982). The universe of Canopus, Sirius and Shikasta is a battlefield of good and evil: though in a still unfinished universe these are ambiguous terms, and what we know so far of the benevolent star Canopus, for instance, is not particularly seductive: its geometrical cities (an earlier one, the original four-gated city, appeared unpersuasively in *Martha Quest*) and its hideous bureaucratic jargon. By contrast, there are passages in Canopean archives that have Mrs Lessing's real touch about them – her particularly fine touch in rendering people just being themselves or walking dully along. But if they don't evade the problems that faced a Martha or an Anna, these space fictions make do without the insistent, resentful self that so dominated the earlier novels. They escape from personality by moving on to the level of fable. But they are also more than just fables. *The Marriages Between Zones Three, Four and Five* (1980) is a story of dynastic marriages between the Zones and makes use of polarities such as mountain and desert, light and dark, and male and female principles. The fable is simple enough, but the novel is more complicated, for much of it works against the fable. And this is where the real interest lies. Not content merely to recount a fable, what the novel does is to dramatize all along an opposition between fable and reality. 'This exemplary marriage' – in the chronicler's opening words – turns out in the telling to be not at all exemplary, but a tense, difficult relationship between two human beings who are aware of shifting senses of the self and are capable of both love and hate. Well, if it doesn't fit, so much the worse for the fable. What would have been proved anyway by a successful symbiosis of the male and female principles? And this is also a political novel with utopian tendencies. The people of Zone Three communicate with animals and know their thoughts, there's no guilt or jealousy, no law; 'everything was entwined and mixed and mingled, all was one, there was no such thing as an individual in the wrong, nor could there be'. As often with Utopias, it seems a bit ruthless, the way ideas – in this case the idea of feminine consciousness – appropriate everything, denaturing it, so that horses have friendly or sorrowful thoughts, or a mountain scene isn't simply and naturally itself but is pregnant with meaning. But here too a note of realism creeps in and undoes the fable. One of the Queen's last thoughts is about 'this dream she was dreaming, or idea she had stumbled into ...' – where stumbling into an idea has very much the effect of stumbling out of it, leaving it precariously poised on its own. Doris Lessing's own conclusions about Zone Three as a utopian vision are less stumbling, for clearly enough a criticism of this complacent Zone is implied. Ultimately the fable is there to evoke objection as well as assent. Equality, instinct, well-being, all the entwining and mingling, are not meant to blind us, as they do the inhabitants of the Zone, to the absence of individual responsibility and the possibility of guilt. The narrative, in being both direct and dream-like, works against itself with great subtlety.

Nadine Gordimer and Doris Lessing both grew up in Southern Africa, exposed to contradictions. One response was that of politics and radicalism. But unlike the young Martha Quest, with her sense of oppression by the illogicalities in and around her, they are creative writers; and this brings in further contradictions. They are English writers, but not naturally at home in any English tradition. Both have remarked on the cultural deprivation of their background. Their isolation, however, has exposed them to a wider range of influences than English literature supplies; and above all has given them their freedom to experiment with the novel. But there the resemblance between them ends. Experiment in Nadine Gordimer takes the form of concentration. Her work concentrates on a single subject, Africa; and is most powerful in single, exemplary scenes – *anagnorisis* scenes, revealing and destroying false assumptions. And the words on the page, from being somewhat loose and casual in the early novels, become ever more intense and rigorous. As her vision of Africa – indeed of life – gets bleaker, her art gets more meticulous and dominant, even oppressively so. One can talk of the art of Nadine Gordimer, as distinct from her subjects; and the two aren't always quite happily matched.

In *A World of Strangers* (1958), a picaresque novel about a young

Englishman's first experience of South Africa, and in many short stories, the joys as well as the contretemps of life are still in evidence. By *The Late Bourgeois World* (1966) the contradictions of society have given place as her subject to images of exhaustion and defeat – the suicide of a white activist, the disillusion of his former wife, the narrator. There is a vitality in this novel, however, that comes from the narrator, from her self-possession and her sexual freedom, and her ability to respond to a black African:

> He is immediately *there* – one of those people whose clothes move audibly, cloth on cloth, with the movement of muscle, whose breathing is something one is as comfortably aware of as a cat's purr in the room, and whose body warmth leaves fingerprints on his glass.

Yet any human response is in Nadine Gordimer only an aspect of a situation, and she sees all human beings as trapped in their situations. This applies no less in *A Guest of Honour* (1972), the novel set in a new independent African state, than in those about South Africa The menacing sense of history in her novels, and their cast of young revolutionaries and father figures of the old order, recall the scene reflected in political novels of the thirties. Nadine Gordimer often seems to be living through now, in South Africa, the European experience of Fascism, and to be experiencing the same loss not just of illusions but of hope. What once went with anti-Fascist attitudes, in Malraux or Auden for instance, a fascination with power, a recognition of the sinister attraction of the will to dominate, is found in the portrait of the capitalist Mehring in *The Conservationist* (1974). And the only counter-attraction to power that is offered in this story is not that of life but of art – the conscious art with which it's told, an art that therefore itself comes to seem willed and assertive: authorial intervention in the guise of interior monologues, or in the symbolism of a black African body that refuses to stay buried.

The magnificent and wide-ranging *Burger's Daughter* (1979) is a work of far more subtle and supple art, echoing the impulses of its heroine towards life and freedom. This is an art that doesn't connive with the inevitable but allows for the unpredictability of life. Rosemarie (or Rosa) Burger is a much-divided person, named after Rosa Luxemburg and an Afrikaner grandmother. The narration is in both first and third persons, and in the first person Rosa addresses three different imaginary interlocutors. A tremendous dialectic of attitudes is brought into play: liberal and Communist of the dominant whites; the mass movement of black consciousness; Afrikaner tradition and the sanctions of family, church, law; the claims of the private life, 'the closed circuit of self '; and those of delight in nature and art (as in paintings of mimosa by Bonnard, done during the Occupation, 'as if nothing had happened'). Nadine Gordimer's handling of political and philosophical argument among her characters – European and African – is something unique in the modern English novel; not only in particular scenes but in her fundamental interests she has brought the novel of ideas back into English literature, filling a place that had been vacant in living memory, and was never exactly crowded. At the centre of the dialectic is Rosa, who is as disturbed by the death of a white meths drinker on a park bench as by political injustice, and who looks for a meaning outside herself and her destiny as the daughter of a famous Communist. There are areas of numbness and obscurity in Rosa – a love affair with a professor in France, an under-examined affair that somehow just happened, offering an opportunity of escape; in fact, anything at all in her not directly concerned with South Africa – but that numbness too merges into the meaning of the novel.

July's People (1981) is her most unsparing novel, a wholly pessimistic account of the near future. With 'nothing else to do but the impossible', when revolution breaks out in South Africa, Bam and Maureen Smales accept their house servant's offer of refuge in his tribal village 600 kilometres from Johannesburg. They are all decent people – the two white liberals, their young children, the trusted servant, the peaceable villagers. All human instinct argues that this is not, after all, an impossible situation. Nadine Gordimer suggests otherwise. Set in a round mud hut in a village of round huts, 'its circles encircled by the landscape' as in the conventional view of 'the single community of man-and-nature-in-Africa', *July's People* reaches conclusions that are not just bleak but hopeless. Community of man and nature is only an irony in a book about the absolute failure of community between men.

There are few incidents: an awkwardness over the keys to the Smales's truck; the evidence of white practicality when Bam kills two young wart-hogs for food or builds a water tower for the village; the theft of Bam's shotgun. These merge with the routine of village life: the women foraging for plants or cutting grass for thatch; and with the evidence both of poverty and of indigenous culture, as in the black children's manners. But the situation is exceptional, and the Smales see it in all its social and political complexity, and discuss it with a fine conscience. What Nadine Gordimer can do, which is still finer, is to let the book itself enact their situation at a deeper level, putting itself alongside the black Africans – July the servant who is now the host, his wife and family – with a freedom and acceptance the Smales could never hope to match. To be able to do this is enough to justify her art in its intervention in politics. At this unspoken, undoctrinaire level, in its uncompromised attitudes to all its characters, the book establishes its right to be trusted.

It's a novel without warmth or sympathy for any one person or for any side. The subject is a situation in which all the characters are trapped. The traps are those of colour and class, the family, the relations of master and servant, and simply the human condition. Not that any of these terms has a simple meaning; for what Nadine Gordimer has specially set up for study are the anomalies and reversals the situation contains. It is anomalous for the role of dependent to pass from the servant to the master, as happens here: but this is further complicated by the fact that the Smales aren't typical whites – they left Johannesburg because they didn't accept 'the necessity to defend their lives in the name of ideals they didn't share'. For his part, July is by no means anxious to abandon the position of servant; and other black Africans show an equal reluctance to act out an appropriate historic role and assert their independence. And not only what the Smales don't believe in, but what they do – 'the absolute nature of intimate relationships between human beings' – is seen to disappear in their new situation. It is particularly Maureen Smales who suffers the progressive loss of certainty, even about herself:

She thought she heard him singing, way up in the bones of his skull, the hymns he breathed while he worked at something that required repetitive, rhythmical effort, polishing or scrubbing. But when he appeared he was merely coming over to her, unhurried, on a sunny day. Nothing sullen or resentful about him; her little triumph in getting him to come turned over inside her with a throb and showed the meanness of something hidden under a stone. These sudden movements within her often changed her from persecutor to victim, with her husband, her children, anyone.

In the end Maureen does come to trust herself, but – the final irony – it is at the cost of abandoning all responsibility. She runs towards a helicopter that may contain anyone: Americans? Frelimo? Cubans? – it no longer matters:

> She runs: trusting herself with all the suppressed trust of a lifetime, alert, like a solitary animal at the season when animals neither seek a mate nor take care of young, existing only for their lone survival, the enemy of all that would make claims of responsibility.

The terrible, Brechtian analysis subdues one with its intelligence; and there goes along with it a Brechtian impatience with anything suggestive of warmth (except perhaps towards animals – 'a bald fowl entered with chicks cheeping, the faintest sound in the world') or of individuality, nostalgia or expectation. It is part of the situation that people are trapped, not just in their colour or ideologies, but trapped in unpleasant ways by the innocent fact even of their bodies. The situation includes a zinc bath tub with Maureen in it, where she 'disgustedly scrubbed at the smooth lining of her vagina and the unseen knot of her anus'. Can anyone like another body, or their own, or feel friendly, in this unsympathetic world? When there's no human touch except boredom and irritation in the relations between Maureen and her husband, what chance do they stand in the test case: how to be friends with their servant July? There were tangible obstacles to friendship between black and white at the end of *A Passage to India*, but here there are none – no longer any real opposition, only a lack of human capacity. The book's austerity conveys a disdain for all its characters as mere products of their situation. And yet, in this respect, Nadine Gordimer's art isn't entirely to be trusted. She uses it sometimes to cheat and to blacken the picture: and where art and truth are as closely related as they usually are in her writing – clearly one of its distinctive virtues – this leaves open the possibility that she's not altogether right about the human situation. For instance, the austerity seems to relax at the end of the novel, on a fine day that calls forth an unwonted response: 'On such a morning, lucky to be alive.' Everyone is kind on this morning, and Maureen's children have begun to pick up African good manners:

'Victor is seen to clap his hands, sticky with mealie-pap, softly, gravely together and bob obeisance, receiving the gift with cupped palms.' But all this has been set up ironically; it serves only to provide a frame for Maureen's act of abdication and flight to the helicopter. It is an effective irony, this one redeeming glimpse of a possible Africa: but effective only as a triumph of art over hope – it diminishes things one would rather have seen taken seriously.

INDIA AND THE NOVEL

WILLIAM WALSH

To speak about India and the novel in the space of less than twenty pages requires unusual qualities of concision and inclusiveness, and one runs the danger of being abstract and arbitrary. So I will begin with one or two generalities. If literature is the most powerful, subtle and inclusive use of the language, then it is only when the language has been organically nourished that the life of art may be distilled from it. Shakespeare, as the philosopher Samuel Alexander averred, did not invent Hamlet but discovered him in the English language. In a more contracted and minor way, one can say that the English novel in India which began in the 1930s required, as well as the novelists, an idiom for its expression. All the more so must this be the case, when the medium is a second language which has to be learned from books and teachers rather than taken in with one's mother's milk. One Indian critic, Buddhadeva Bose, thought that this effort to express one's deepest human experiences in a foreign language was 'a blind alley, lined with curio shops, leading nowhere'. But as Nissim Ezekiel, a contemporary Indian poet in English replied, 'historical situations create cultural consequences'. There is nothing unnatural, since Indian English was introduced as the medium of higher education one hundred and fifty years ago, in the fact that some Indians naturally took to writing in English. But the idiom being prepared for Indian fiction in English was not elaborated by the rather feeble works of fiction written in the nineteenth century in India, for example Bankim Chandra Chatterjee's *Rajmohan's Wife* (1864) or Romesh Chunder Dutt's *The Lake of Palms* (1902) and *The Slave Girl of Agra* (1909), but rather by a line of notable Indian sages who from the end of the eighteenth century to well on in the twentieth wrote in India in a vigorous, Victorian English. The staple of this is an extensive vocabulary, slightly abstract diction, and long, supple, balanced sentences. One of the first of this line was Rammohan Roy

(1774–1833), whose purpose was to reform Hindu religious thought and practice by introducing into it a stricter, Protestant ethos, and to argue with energy and determination for women's rights, religious toleration, the freedom of the Press, and the radical improvement of the conditions of the peasant.

Another and grander sage was Vivekananda (1862–1902), a man of profound spiritual force, powerful intellect, great learning, and Franciscan candour, who wrote, given the period and a national bias towards the nebulous, in a remarkably strict and athletic way. He detested abstractions and his analysis and evocation of the ancient Indian spiritual tradition, which he wished both to recover and to revivify, is made with the utmost precision and concreteness. He resisted an undignified and philistine submission to Western, pragmatic thought, just as he had no sympathy with a simple nostalgia for the past. He was a moralist not just a moral philosopher, a thinker not just a theorist, a speculative critic not just a man of erudition deeply familiar with European philosophy. His intelligence, that is to say, had an active inclusive character; and it had, as well, an attractively sardonic sharpness: 'The Hindu man drinks religiously, sleeps religiously, walks religiously, marries religiously and robs religiously.' 'No single individual before Gandhi and Nehru ... did more to dehypnotize a complacent, slumbering people,' wrote the Indian critic C. D. Narasimhaiah.

A modern version of the Indian sage, a very different and even fanatically individual version, is Nirad C. Chaudhuri (b. 1897). The development so exhaustively detailed in his *The Autobiography of an Unknown Indian* (1951), which belongs incontestably to the line of Roy, Vivekananda and Aurobindo, is not just an evolutionary one in which a Western Protestant astringency displaces the warm appeal of an Indian past – although it certainly *is* that. It is also a more personal and strenuous achievement which involves, on the one hand, hacking out an area of freedom and manoeuvre from a choked jungle of inheritance; and on the other, constructing a fresh identity which would join a questioning Western mind to a temperament laced with Bengali fury. The instruments of demolition and of building, and the elements out of which the new self was to be made, were concepts and principles, usages and styles, which Chaudhuri found not in the imaginatively cramped local British population, or the restricted Anglo–Indian tradition, but in the immensely more inclusive source of the English language and its literature. It was an undertaking which required on the part of Chaudhuri not only intellectual energy and analytical skill but also courage, will, stamina and a quite unabashed interest in himself. The psychological composition or structure which results is a triumph of self-education and a model of the formative power of language, of its capacity to disturb and rearrange at the depths of the personality. It is also – like *The Autobiography of an Unknown Indian* itself and the whole literary production of which it is part – a monument to the creative clash of two civilizations.

It was in the 1930s, however, that the Indians began what has now turned out to be a substantial contribution to the novel in English, and one particularly suited to their talents. To three of these writers belongs not only an intrinsic distinction but the peculiar importance attaching to inaugurators. They are R. K. Narayan, Raja Rao and Mulk Raj Anand. It was these three who defined the area in which the Indian novel was to operate. They established the suppositions, the manner, the idiom, the concept of character, and the nature of the themes which were to give the Indian novel its particular distinctiveness. Each of them used an easy, natural if old-fashioned idiom, which they succeeded in freeing from the foggy taste of the British inheritance. The most economic way of suggesting the quality of each, it seems to me, is perhaps to concentrate on a single work.

Mulk Raj Anand belongs to the tradition of the nineteenth-century writer – not necessarily just the British tradition, for one is aware of a distinctly European set of influences operating on him, particularly French and Russian influences – in his approach to the novel, in his techniques, his weaving together of theme and event, in his sensibility and in his hope for what the novel may publicly achieve. He is particularly of this tradition in point of his fluency. Creation appears to be no agonizing struggle for him, communication something he engages in with an unstrained and vivid enthusiasm, and the facility of a Russian writer. He is nineteenth century, too, in his conception of the novel, seeing it as an organization strongly based on a double foundation of character and circumstance: character, I repeat, which has to be clearly defined and then developed, largely through the causality of the other constitutive forces, social circumstances and influences, usually of a harshly oppressive sort. He has, too, a natural disposition towards the picaresque. The trilogy, *The Village* (1939), *Across the Black Waters* (1940), and *The Sword and the Sickle* (1942), takes the peasant boy, Lal Singh, from his North Indian village and a life stifled by suffocating layers of custom and religion, into the ferocity of the 1914–18 war and the crass commercialism of Europe, and then back again to India to a new political stance towards life.

The defect which constricts his real creative capacity is the habit of allowing his moral and social purposes to become separate from the particular actuality of the fiction, so that they frequently lead a collateral rather than a unified existence. This is accompanied by a certain passivity on the part of the characters, apt no doubt when they are the victims of circumstances, which they so frequently are, but out of place in those parts of his work where the individual should be more energetically active in the working out of his own nature.

As a writer, Mulk Raj Anand lacks the concrete sagacity, the *finesse*, the 'appetite for the illustrational' – to use Henry James's phrase – which marks everything that R. K. Narayan writes; nor does he have that sense of the metaphysical nature of man we find in the other distinguished novelist, Raja Rao. But he has a deep feeling for the deprived, a grasp of the social structure of his society, and an extraordinary fluency of communication.

Mulk Raj Anand is passionately concerned with the villages, with the ferocious poverty and the cruelties of caste, with orphans, untouchables, and urban labourers. He writes in an angry reformist way, like a less humorous Dickens and a more emotional Wells, of the personal sufferings induced by economics – really economics, one feels, even when he is writing of caste. His sharpest, best organized novel is *Untouchable* (1933) which was very highly thought of by E. M. Forster. It is an interesting combination of hard material, narrow specific theme, and throbbing Shelleyan manner. The action, occupying a single day, is precipitated by a great 'catastrophe', an accidental 'touching' in the morning. Everything that follows is affected by it, even the innocent and vividly realized hockey match. Of the three solutions hinted at to the problem of the untouchable – Christ, Gandhi, and Main Drainage – it is the last which is most favoured by Anand. He is a committed artist, and what he is committed to is indicated by Bashir's mockery in *Untouchable*: 'Greater efficiency, better salesmanship, more mass-production, standardization, dictatorship of the sweepers, Marxian materialism, and all that.' 'Yes, yes,' is the reply, 'all that, but no catch-words and cheap phrases, the change will be organic and not mechanical.'

Mulk Raj Anand's semi-Marxist categories, his furious, and one must say well-grounded, indignation, and his habit of undue explicitness, together with a deficiency in self-criticism, make him a writer whose work has to be severely sieved. Like many writers impelled by social motives, however worthy, whose attitude to life is too patently dominated by theory, he has a habit of preaching at the reader. But when his imagination burns, and the dross of propaganda is consumed, as in *Untouchable, Coolie*, and *The Big Heart* (1945), there is no doubt that he is a novelist of considerable power.

How very different in every particular is Raja Rao, a member of an old Brahmin family, born in Mysore in 1909 and roughly a contemporary of the two senior novelists, Mulk Raj Anand and R. K. Narayan. He has, however, a completely different literary character. He is not, like Anand, a politically committed writer, and he is very different from Narayan in being poetic, metaphysical, Lawrentian. *Kanthapura* (1938) focuses on the intensity of Indian life, its physical immediacy, its traditional swaddling, and its religious murmurations. *The Serpent and the Rope* (1960), his most elaborate work, gives no impression at all of any constricted or meagre talent. On the contrary, it strikes the reader with its flowing, outgoing abundance. It is a meditation, but a dramatic one, on the nature of existence, profoundly 'philosophical', but not at all abstract or theoretical. Its tone is strikingly individual, a blend of Indian tenderness and French clarity. The action, or the meditation, since external events do not have high status in the novel, swerves from India to France to England and takes in an astonishing number of authentic, sharply realized characters. It is a novel in which the examination of human nature is done through the intense diagnosis of its hero, Rama – Southern Brahmin, tubercular, intellectually brilliant, spiritually sensitive, and profoundly sad.

A delicate and exact vehicle for Rao's talent is *The Cat and Shakespeare* (1965), a novella of patterned complexity and sardonic poetry. There is no vague wash of feeling round the edge of this book, no conceptual cloud floating in the air. The racial and poetic wisdom which is everywhere implicit is thoroughly absorbed into the details of the fable, and the cat, the rats, the wall, the ration shop, as well as the characters, Ramakrishna Pai, Govindan Nair, Abraham, John, Saroja, Shantha, can each be, in Henry James's terms, 'a strikingly figured symbol' because each is also 'a thoroughly pictured creature'. Moreover, the innumerable literary and philosophical hints, analogies, the muted quotations and obscure connections which echo and re-echo everywhere are used with a musical propriety quite different from any explicit or academic pointing.

If Anand is the novelist as reformer, and Narayan the novelist as moral analyst, Raja Rao is the novelist as metaphysical poet.

R. K. Narayan, now in his seventies, has produced a sizable body of work – more than a dozen novels and collections of short stories – which makes him one of the most respected novelists at present writing in the British Commonwealth. Over a period of forty years of composition he has built up a devoted readership through-out the world from New York to Moscow. The location of his novels is the South Indian town of Malgudi, an imaginative version of Narayan's beloved Mysore, and it is as familiar to his readers as their own suburbs, and infinitely more engaging. His writing is a distinctive blend of Western technique and Eastern material, and he has succeeded in a remarkable way in making an Indian sensibility at home in English art.

Let me take a single, a significant, and distinctively Indian example from among Narayan's novels. *The Sweet-Vendor* (1967) is centred, of course, in the familiar and by now well-loved Malgudi. But it does add a new note to the quietly complex tone of Narayan's fiction. Narayan's novels assert no tremendous faith, but as his work has matured, the manner in which he expresses his belief in the nature of whatever it is that supports a hope for humanity, becomes less diffident. What at the end of *The Guide* is only the most feathery intimation, became in *The Man-eater of Malgudi*, in spite of the fantasy of its context, a less oblique statement of his belief in the sustaining role of some other influence – the blessing of the gods or just the stubbornness of life itself. Certainly an explicit notation of this kind appears in the conclusion of *The Sweet-Vendor* where Jagan, the protagonist, suddenly determines to detach himself from 'a set of repetitions performed for sixty years', in order to spend the rest of his life helping the stonemason to carve a pure image of the goddess for others to contemplate. His decision, which is of course in the classical Indian line, requiring that 'at some stage in one's life one must uproot oneself from the accustomed surroundings and disappear so that others can continue in peace', is in Jagan's case charmingly freckled with an appealing human flaw. He doesn't neglect to take his cheque book with him. This touch is characteristic of Narayan's sensibility. His concept of spirituality is as precise and as stained with human fallibility as is his notion of the rest of life. The servant of the goddess with whom Jagan proposes to finish out his days explains that the perfection in stone which he is aiming at must still contain a deliberate fault:

I always remember the story of the dancing figure of Nataraj, which was so perfect that it began a cosmic dance and the town itself shook as if an earthquake had rocked it, until a small finger on the figure was chipped off. We always do it; no one ever notices it, but we always create a small flaw in every image; it's for safety.

Jagan's decision to retire from the world is not only part of the national tradition. It also follows the bias of his own nature. He is highminded, pious, attentive to the scriptures, observant of custom, scrupulous about ritual, a follower of Gandhi, and he has evolved a number of prim theories about diet, footware, toothbrushes and hygiene. But his character also includes the 'small flaw' making for safety. The largeness of his spiritual ambition is clipped a bit by a mercantile flexibility which enables him to count some of the money taken over the counter 'as free cash ... a sort of immaculate conception, self-generated, arising out of itself and entitled to survive without reference to any tax'. Moreover, he is – 'protected' is the word Narayan's account suggests – protected from too much voyaging into the ineffable by a certain appealing simplicity of intelligence. 'Conquer taste, and you will have conquered the self,' said Jagan to his listener, who asked, 'Why conquer the self?' Jagan said, 'I do not know, but all our sages advise us so.'

Jagan's renunciation of the world, then, is of a piece with the Indian tradition and the radical disposition of his own character in so far as it is a reflection of that tradition. But, of course, for Jagan himself his renunciation is a very big decision, too big in some ways for his surface or immediate personality, which is dry, fussy, narrow, commercial and self-regarding. What is necessary to make this Jagan into the world-renouncing Jagan is supplied by the Indian religious tradition. Even a nature as thin as Jagan's, it becomes clear, is able to be fed from deep and more than personal sources. Part of Narayan's gift as a novelist of a more inclusive life is the delicacy and firmness with which such depths are convincingly implied in the structure of his characters. This gift depends partly upon Narayan's own profound acceptance of it, partly, and as far as the reader is concerned, most, on Narayan's beautifully executed evocation of the actual presences and concrete specifications of the life of the town. The suggested halo of significance follows naturally on the meticulously defined detail.

Three areas of the life Jagan is to renounce are drawn with the crispest line and shade in *The Sweet-Vendor*. First the steady encircling routine of the community of Malgudi which laps Jagan round with the certainties of history and the stability of current relationships; while testing and proving him in a dozen ways, it still validates his function and confirms his identity and value. Next, there is his work as the proprietor of an establishment making and selling sweets. Narayan is much drawn to the truth of character shown in a person's work in which the stretched personality submits itself to impersonal ends, and he describes with tender and precise care the style and method, the rituals and satisfactions of Jagan's work. Then there is the ambiguous and dangerous ground of his relations with his son, the sullen westernized Mali, whose American–Korean wife turns out to be – dumbfoundingly to the conventional Jagan – only his mistress, and whose contemptuous explanations to his bewildered father of a scheme for manufacturing a fiction-writing machine include all the diversions which so maddeningly separate the two of them, the division of East and West, of young and old, of child and parent.

This triple structure makes a composition marked by the combined ease and authority of an artist in full control of his instrument; and it supports a world which has a background, a context, an immediate presence and a nervous individual centre, a

INDIA AND THE NOVEL

world which impresses the reader with the quality of its completeness.
Whatever happens in India, the reader feels, happens in Malgudi,
and whatever happens in Malgudi, he is persuaded, might well
happen in his own life. Malgudi is an image of India and a
metaphor of everywhere else.

When Jagan retires from life – 'I am going to watch a goddess
come out of a stone' – he does so unromantically, practically, like
a sound business man, arranging for his shop to be open and deciding
where he should leave his keys. He seems to be doing so for comparatively external reasons because of the hell which his son Mali
has made of his life at home, or because he can no longer face the
incomprehensibility of action deriving from motives beyond his
grasp. But the real reason is a more inward one. His life, or that
part of it, he realizes, is complete. It has achieved whatever shape
it is capable of. Enlightenment means realizing that one has come
to the point at which struggle and all the comedy of friction are
irrelevant: it means recognizing and accepting the bitter conclusion
of an early novel, *The English Teacher*, that 'a profound and un-
mitigated loneliness is the only truth of life'. This 'law' comes home
to one with force and clarity as one shares in a life like Jagan's, so
warmly surrounded by a community and so totally involved in work
and family. Mobility, shape, and the significance of completeness –
these are the values (and they are not only Indian ones) which animate
Narayan's pure, disinterested art.

It will not be possible to speak of the new novelists except in a
hurried, pell-mell fashion. Before one looks at the orthodox fiction
one should certainly mention the astonishing *All About H. Hatterr*
(1970) by G. V. Desani (b. 1909), the earliest example of the wild,
fantastic fiction of which Salman Rushdie's novel *Midnight's Children*
(1981), which I glance at later, is an even more remarkable instance.
Desani's prose-poem *Hali* was praised by Forster, and it is, after the
manner of these things, rhetorical, self-conscious, contrived. But *All
About H. Hatterr* is a remarkably different production, the account
of the weird self-education of the fantastic H. Hatterr. It is turbulent,
deflationary, bawling, magnificently irregular in its extraordinary
language. 'It is what may be termed,' said Anthony Burgess in his
Introduction to the novel, 'whole Language, in which philosophical
terms, the colloquialisms of Calcutta and London, Shakespearian

archaisms, bazaar whinings, quack spiels, references to the Hindu pantheon, the jargon of Indian litigation, and shrill babu irritability seethe together.'

Bhabani Bhattacharya's two novels, *So Many Hungers* (1947) and *He Who Rides the Tiger* (1954), are written in the manner of Mulk Raj Anand. They are flowing, fervid novels with big themes, too neatly discriminated characters, and a great flow of loose feeling which washes round the detail of event and character. If Bhattacharya is too innocent, Balchandra Rajan (who has been a Cambridge don and a distinguished diplomat) is too sophisticated. In *The Dark Dancer* (1959) there is a laboured straining after significance as well as a too deliberate awareness of how significance has been traditionally imported. All sorts of explicit and muted literary reference show – or betray – the author's intention of assimilating his novel to the great works of literature. The novel is full of quick, glinting insight, but is spoiled by its academic obliqueness and its mannered prose. Khushwant Singh's *Train to Pakistan* (1956), a study of the communal massacres of 1947, is, in spite of its theme, much drier and cooler. It is a tense, economical novel, thoroughly true to the events and the people. It goes forward in a trim, athletic way, and its unemphatic voice makes a genuinely human comment. Manohar Malgonkar has written *Distant Drum* (1960), a racy but rather indulgent account of the Indian Army from an officer's point of view, and *The Princess* (1963), a more perceptive, a more personal one of the withering of the Princely States.

Of the women novelists the best known is Ruth Prawer Jhabvala, whom I shall speak of later in another context; the newest is Attia Hosain; the most gifted is Kamala Markandaya. *Sunlight on a Broken Column* (1961) by Attia Hosain is not a 'case' against purdah but a well-shaped, genuinely felt reconstruction of life in such conditions, its collisions with the modern world, and the astonishingly tough-minded women it breeds. She writes from a Muslim point of view about the intense life of the Muslim family. Her study of Laila is very firm, clear and sympathetic, and she exhibits the sort of dilemma which the overwhelmingly claustrophobic life of the family in India tends to bring about – the character with a bias to independence and solitariness who becomes almost a solipsist in reaction to the smothering family. In Miss Hosain's sensitive novel there is an attractive Persian glitter. There is also a kind of strange dignity, a more masculine force in the character of the women than one often gets in Indian novels. Politics is the other great theme in her novel, and one has the sense of the way in which politics at that period became fused with religious feeling. This complicated and impressive novel keeps a number of different themes smoothly in play and firmly in order. The tense, bitter girl Laila evokes in her character and suffering a great section of life in the Indian sub-continent which has been rarely heard of from the inside – the woman in purdah.

Kamala Markandaya is one of the most distinguished of the generation of Indian novelists in English who succeeded the big three, R. K. Narayan, Mulk Raj Anand and Raja Rao. Her work has been notable for an unusual combination of range and intimacy. *Nectar in a Sieve* (1954) is set in a village and examines the hard agricultural life of the Indian peasant; *Some Inner Fury* (1956) which includes a highly-educated young woman and her English lover who are torn apart by the Quit India campaign of the time, has to do with the quarrel between Western and Indian influences, as they are focused in a marriage; *A Silence of Desire* (1960) deals with the middle class, and *A Handful of Rice* (1966) with the city poor; *Possession* (1963) moves from the West End of London to a South Indian village, and is centred on the conflict of Eastern spirituality with Western materialism; *The Coffer Dams* (1969) is a highly contemporary examination of the activities of a British engineering firm which is invited to build a dam in India. Karmala Markandaya has not the same intimacy and familiarity with all these areas of life, and she has indeed been criticized by Indian critics for a certain lack of inwardness with the life of the Indian poor. Her particular strength lies in the delicate analysis of the relationships of persons, especially when these have a more developed consciousness of their problems and are attempting to grope towards some more independent existence. She has, too, the genuine novelist's gift for fixing the exact individuality of the character, even if she is less successful at establishing it in a reasonably convincing social context. She has been most successful and at her best, an impressive best, in dealing with the problems of the educated and middle class, and she has a gift for delineating the self-imposed laceration of the dissatisfied.

One of her most achieved and characteristic works is *A Silence of Desire*. It is a subtly precise study of husband and wife, although the wife has less actuality than the husband, Dandekar, a wrought-up, conscientious, petty government clerk. He is rocked off his age-old balance by his wife's strange absences, excuses, and lies. It turns out that she has a growth and is attending a faith healer. The husband is by no means a westernized person, but he is to some degree secular and modern, and the situation enables the author to reflect on the tensions, the strength, and the inadequacies and aspirations of middle-class Indian life. The book is gentle in tone but sharp in perception, and the mixture of moods, the friction of faith and reason, the quarrels of old and young, are beautifully pointed. There are conventional, perfunctory patches in the novel but Kamala Markandaya shows very high skill in unravelling sympathetically but unflinchingly the structure of the protagonist's motives and the bumbling and stumbling progress of his anxieties.

The Golden Honeycomb (1977), her latest novel, is a historical examination of three generations of princely India, and it has both range and intimacy. The range has to do with the decline both of the princely order, a glittering British surrogate, and with the gradual enfeeblement of British power. The intimacy has to do with an inward and sensitive treatment of the life of a puppet prince in his relations with the contemporary British power, with his Indian civil servants, his lover and family. In earlier novels the balance between range and intimacy was imperfect. Markandaya has always had the genuine novelist's gift for fixing the exact individuality of a character but was less successful at establishing it in a wholly convincing social context. In this novel the equilibrium is poised and sustained. Moreover, she has the added merit of prose of great clarity and point, considerable metaphorical vivacity, and a gift for the nice discrimination of motive. *The Golden Honeycomb* is a novel in the grand manner, large in scope, constructing a world with authoritative ease, with a central figure, a biographical line, a multitude of grasped minor characters, people who are seen from within so that they possess an intrinsic and spontaneous vitality, and from without, so that they are located in time and place in a context of value and feeling. It signals the impressive maturing of an authentic talent.

As authentic, but even more remarkable is that of Salman Rushdie, the author of *Midnight's Children*, published in 1981. This novel, dramatizing the history of independent India in the person of the beak-nosed wildly extravagant Muslim, Saleem Aziz, who was born on the stroke of midnight bringing in India's independence, combines the rush and fluency of Mulk Raj Anand, the speculative and metaphysical habit of Raja Rao, the shrewd psychological acumen of R. K. Narayan with the linguistic wildness, inventiveness and fantasy of G. V. Desani. Its astonishing staple is composed of elements of magic and fantasy, the grimmest realism ('cripples everywhere, mutilated by loving parents, to ensure them of a lifetime's income from begging'), extravagant farce, multi-mirrored analogy and a potent symbolic structure. All this is indelibly stamped into unity by a powerful personality, which wrestles the language and the fiction down and masters it to serve a huge purpose, namely the personification of India and the realization of Indian life.

The novelist makes an extraordinarily successful hand at turning into a dense and palpable art the Indian instinct for absorption and inclusiveness. He can do this because he is able to make the mythic and hieratic impulses of his vision issue into a positively Dickensian sumptuousness of detail. If the Dickensian strength is at all weakened, it is by the occasional intrusion of a rather too marked, and irritating self-consciousness. Here is a passage from the middle of the novel in which scent becomes as vital and powerful as Dickens's fog.

Escaping, whenever possible, from a residence in which the acrid fumes of my aunt's envy made life unbearable, and also from a college filled with other equally dislikeable smells, I mounted my motorized steed and explored the olfactory avenues of my new city. And after we heard of my grandfather's death in Kashmir, I became even more determined to drown the past in the thick, bubbling scent-stew of the present … O dizzying early days before categorization! Formlessly, before I began to shape them, the fragrance poured into me: the mournful decaying fumes of animal faeces in the gardens of the Frere Road museum, the pustular body odours of young men in loose pajamas holding hands in Sadar evenings, the knife-sharpness of expectorated betel-nut and the bitter-sweet commingling of betel and opium: 'rocket-paans' were sniffed out in the hawker-crowded valleys between Elphinstone Street and Victoria Road. Camel smells, car-smells, the gnat-like irritation of motor-rickshaw fumes, the aroma of contraband cigarettes and 'black-money' the competitive effluvia of the city's bus drivers and the simple sweat of their sardine-crowded passengers. (One bus-driver, in those days, was so incensed at being overtaken by his rival from another company – the nauseating odour of defeat poured from his glands – that he took his bus round to his opponent's house at night, hooted until the poor fellow emerged, and ran him down beneath wheels reeking, like my aunt, of revenge.) Mosques poured over me the itr[a] of devotion; I could smell the orotund emissions of power sent out by flag-waving Army motors; in the very hoardings of the cinemas I could discern the cheap tawdry perfumes of imported spaghetti Westerns and the most violent martial-arts films ever made. I was, for a time, like a drugged person, my head reeling beneath the complexities of smell; but then my overpowering desire for form asserted itself, and I survived.

It is this 'overpowering desire for form', as warranted on the writer's as well as the character's part, that saves the novel from anarchy. Life in it sprawls, multiplies incessantly, flows hither and thither but is saved – sometimes it seems at the final instant – from collapse and dissolution by some ultimate appetite for shape. The friction of the two instincts for flow and control, looseness and tightness, generate the astonishing energy of a novel unprecedented in scope, manner and achievement in the hundred and fifty year old tradition of the Indian novel in English.

India has entered the English sensibility in another way, as the title of this chapter implies. For some 200 years it has figured in the English imagination as experience, theme, and lately even as a metaphor of human experience itself. Kipling (1865–1936) not only evoked the rash, self-confident attitudes of the English ruling class in India, but he also realized and expressed with uncanny fidelity and subtleties of insight the experience of the Indian folk themselves as well as the unique quality of the Indian landscape. At the other end of the scale from Kipling, E. M. Forster (1879–1970), representing the finest and most humane in the liberal spirit, began in *Passage to India* (1924) the tradition of using Indian life as an image of personal experiences. There is also L. H. Myers (1881–1944), almost as distinguished, although certainly less known, whose delicate and searching study of Indian experience, spirituality and landscape in the tetralogy set in the period of the great mogul, Akbar, *The Near and the Far* (1929), *Prince Jali* (1931), *The Root and the Flower* (1934) and *The Pool of*

[a] Unction, oil or juice

Vishnu (1940) is one of the most notable, if neglected achievements of the Anglo-Indian cultural connection.

Much later, Ruth Prawer Jhabvala, who though Polish married an Indian husband and lived in Delhi for many years, produced a series of novels which dealt with fluency and understanding with the problems of the middle and upper class European and his Indian neighbours and associates. She has been rather absurdly compared with Jane Austen, but is more like a gentler Mary McCarthy. Her characters are a trifle routine, her prose is sometimes pedestrian, but she is an expert analyst of domestic friction and the edgy differences of national sensibility.

J. G. Farrell, who died in a fishing accident in 1979, was another to use the Indian life and the Indian context to express in *The Siege of Krishnapur* (1973) and *The Hill Station* (1981) a certain reading of experience. Farrell writes of India and the Raj and of English men and particularly English women blending English sensibility and eccentricity with Indian suppleness and exoticism. Paul Scott, who died in 1978, was one of the latest and more able writers to locate much of his work in India. India for Scott is a metaphor of life rather in the way that Malgudi is a metaphor for Narayan. But neither Scott himself nor his characters, and not all are strongly defined, bring to their India or have expressed by it that serene, coherent personality which sustains Narayan's fiction. Scott brings to India the fractured and fractious personality of the Westerner. For Scott India, a lost Paradise, a living illusion, was that against which his characters defined themselves, their duties, their moral values. For the British who lived there, India was an all-embracing experience. It is the Englishman's India to which Scott has given density and animation, a feeling for the country animated by the sense the British had of the rightness of their presence.

In *The Corrida of San Feliu* (1964), Scott's most difficult novel, Patrick Swinden, one of Paul Scott's few and probably best commentators, discovers all Scott's main themes given disturbingly original treatment: the loss of Paradise, now glimpsed as an idea in the mind, which in lived reality must fall intolerably short; the deceptions men and women play on each other, in what must be far from ideal sexual relationships; the distortion of reality in the interests of both responsible and irresponsible functions of the imagination; and the ways in which men strive to exert power over one another. These themes distributed through the rest of the fiction, and particularly in the *Raj Quartet* (1978) as well as in *Staying On*, are the constituent insights of a novelist of increasing power, whose death was certainly a severe loss to English fiction.

THE ENGLISH STAGE COMPANY
AND THE DRAMATIC CRITICS

OLIVER NEVILLE

On 4 February 1982 the English Stage Company (in association with the Crucible Theatre Sheffield) presented G. F. Newman's *Operation Bad Apple*. The play, about alleged corruption in the Metropolitan Police, brought a social problem with widespread ramifications, and which had been handled tentatively by the press, into the public arena. The Board of Management, alarmed by adverse publicity and the possibility of a private legal action against them, tried to stop production; but after lawyers had vetted the script and Newman had made necessary alterations, Stafford-Clark and his staff insisted that the play should open. Newman's work, which with sharp wit anatomized the London police, went ahead to a moderately successful run playing to a limited audience including, it was said, members of the Metropolitan Police who enjoyed the show immensely. Here we have a typical episode in the life of the Royal Court Theatre, a serious attempt to bring theatre into the centre of public debate. Powered by a young articulate élite, the Court gives the impression of living dangerously near the centre of potential middle-class revolt.

From the beginning the Court's seen achievement (its whole programme of work and influence spreads beyond the main programme of plays) rested on specific and sporadic successes rather than on a consistent general policy. The theatre that George Devine had in mind, a permanent company of actors dedicated to presenting new English writers, was impossible in the British theatre governed by commercial principles. Forced to react to the day-to-day exigencies of theatre management, its policy has been infinitely flexible, sustaining its 'revolutionary' image with weapons of commercial theatre – stars and star vehicles, sex, violence, and contrived critical controversy. In the 1950s it faced, with notable exceptions, a generally unfriendly or non-committal critical press. The sixties saw the growth of television, and the expansion of the Royal Shakespeare

Company and National Theatre complex together with their small, experimental studios which then became the prime target for young playwrights. An important watershed was the censorship debate, which put the Court firmly in the public eye, but nearly resulted in the withdrawal of its Arts Council grant. The late sixties saw the rise of Alternative theatre, which came to regard the Court as an 'establishment' theatre playing to select metropolitan audiences. In the eighties, recession has caused audiences nostalgically to hark back to large-scale musicals and spectacle which can only be provided by the heavily subsidized Royal Shakespeare and National Theatre companies. These movements in the theatrical scene have all had their effect in Sloane Square. And yet the Royal Court Theatre still plays an important role in British theatre. It stands for intelligent thought-provoking theatre, firmly based in the text, and youthful in outlook. A visit to the Court is a special social event, put into focus by the size, proportion and resonance of that particular building which, unlike the new auditoria, is adapted to human scale, forcing concentration on subject-matter. Its Theatre Upstairs, Young Peoples' Theatre Scheme, and experimental workshops feed the London theatre, and offer opportunities for writers, directors, actors and theatre-workers in general to recreate their sense of purpose. For the theatre historian the Court reflects the changing map of British theatre from the mid fifties to the present day, not only by what it has achieved, but by what it has reacted against.

The political and social background during the fifties has been discussed earlier in this volume by Krishan Kumar (pp. 38–48). The sense of loss of direction in politics in which Britain had achieved, by contrast with the 1940s, 'an ignoble loneliness', as Aneurin Bevan so aptly described it, was reflected on the London stage in a similar kind of dislocation between actuality and fictional rhetoric. The thinking public had memories of the clarity and truth-to-life of wartime documentary films, and of the engagement, heightened naturalism and panache of the Irish players in Sean O'Casey, and of Italian and Japanese films of unfamiliar force and very dissimilar dramatic power. Also, there were still powerful forces at work in the classical theatre: Wolfit's *Tamburlaine* at the Old Vic (1951), and at Stratford, Anthony Quayle's season of *Histories*, Peter Brook's *Measure for Measure* and Olivier's *Macbeth* and *Titus* (1955). Those who lived near the old-style repertory theatres at Birmingham, Liverpool, Glasgow, Nottingham and Manchester had already seen the active formative years of Scofield, Badel, Porter, through to Finney, Robert Stephens, and the actors who were to become the 'new' wave in London. But mainstream London theatre was generally content with the pursuit of a false rhetoric ranging from deeply serious attempts by Eliot to form a new poetic language for his age, to the banalities of *The Manor of Northstead*. Writing at about this time, Kenneth Tynan stated bluntly:

The bare fact is that, apart from revivals and imports, there is nothing in the London theatre that one dares discuss with an intelligent man for more than five minutes. Since the great Ibsen challenge of the nineties, the English intellectuals have been drifting away from drama.[1]

He sought a prose drama about current events and involvements, enlivened by an appropriately gritty style of acting.

In 1955 a small group of people with widely different backgrounds and aims joined together to establish a theatre in London which would encourage new English plays and contemporary 'classics' from abroad, and build an interpretative team of actors, directors, designers and theatre technicians, together with an audience for a revitalized contemporary drama. Calling themselves the English Stage Company, they negotiated the lease on a small Victorian playhouse known as the Royal Court theatre in Sloane Square. From that time the English Stage Company became known to its theatre-going public as the 'Royal Court', or simply 'the Court'. The English Stage Company were fortunate in their choice of theatre: though located outside the main theatre district of the West End, and having an air of down-at-heel regality which sorts oddly with its reputation as a 'revolutionary' theatre, the proportion and scale across its proscenium arch provide a sensation of close contact between actors and an audience of 450 at the most. Fortuitously, the building happened to be large enough to do major works and yet it was able to totter along, even in lean times, without gross subsidies of the order demanded by the major national companies.

The English Stage Company appointed as its first Artistic Director George Devine, an experienced actor and teacher of acting whose artistic roots and principles, developed in pre-war experimental and establishment theatre, may be traced to the Oxford University Dramatic Society in the thirties, and beyond to the French avant-garde companies of Jacques Copeau. Devine brought with him as Assistant Artistic Director 27-year-old Tony Richardson, who had been working as a BBC television director. The idea was to match solid experience with what was called 'flair'. Richardson's interest was to promote new English playwrights, while Devine's genius was an ability to use basic clashes of principle within the Board of Management to his own and Richardson's creative ends. The working-world of the Court has been aptly described as 'a conflict of battling egos' for conflict, both internal and external, has kept the Court alive.

The first season opened in 1956 with a play by Angus Wilson, which was performed in repertoire with Arthur Miller's *The Crucible* (1953). In May John Osborne's *Look Back in Anger* was introduced into the repertoire, together with two full-length plays by Ronald Duncan, who was one of the founding fathers. Nigel Dennis's adaptation of his novel *Cards of Identity* and Brecht's *The Good Woman of Setzuan* followed, and Wycherley's *The Country Wife*. Devine's play list was tightly knit and a shrewd piece of planning, combining the known, half-known, and new. What was less shrewd was his letting slip their options on Beckett's *Waiting for Godot*, which was later directed by Peter Hall at the Art's Theatre, and on *The Threepenny Opera*. The unknown factor was *Look Back in Anger*. The script, by an unknown author, had arrived through the post along with 700 or more sent in answer to an advertisement in *The Stage* seeking new plays on contemporary themes and particularly new plays by new writers. George Devine's response to key sections of the dialogue was instinctive and immediate, for he recognized a view of society and personal relationships with which he could identify, and an abrasive use of language which was of the present and theatrically alive: 'I thought it must be said on a stage to a public.' Devine, as actor, director, manager, was primarily concerned with theatrical impact: social, moral and political commitments were only made active for him through the practice of theatre. It transpired that the author was a young out-of-work actor, and *Look Back In Anger* is in effect a very thinly disguised young middle-class actor's relationship with his profession and society at large. Insecurity is inherent in the economic, commercial, and social structures of English theatre, giving, it is sometimes argued, a stimulus to creative energy and achievement, but bringing with it potentially destructive tensions. A haphazard system of casting, adverse working conditions, and the lack of a clearly defined career structure, makes the actor vulnerable in the community, limits his aims and capacity for growth in his craft and creativity, and gives to the profession as a whole a sense of wasted material resources, and human skills. This general condition of English theatre was particularly evident in the early 1950s. The 1944 Education Act had for the first time provided grants for a limited number of working-class and lower-middle class students at schools of acting. Conscious of developments in post-war European cinema, and alternative kinds of theatre exemplified in England by Theatre Workshop, these actors felt enormous potential within themselves and within theatre, which no one wanted – in fact they had been trained for a theatre which did not exist. Establishment theatre was rolling along quite happily in its old patterns, and what was worse, film, radio and early television had no use for the vocal and physical 'signals' of the lower and middle class except as 'other ranks' in war films and 'below stairs' stereotypes in Loamshire comedy with little or no exploration in depth of character or social context. The new society which everyone had looked forward to in 1945 seemed, in 1956, to be picking up the threads from the thirties. As a result genuine feelings of anger and resentment were generated, reinforced by new-wave critics led by Kenneth Tynan, who were themselves challenging an old-style mandarin journalistic establishment, and distilled by John Osborne in *Look Back in Anger*.

Waste is the keynote of *Look Back in Anger*, whose central character, Jimmy Porter, has come to the realization that the brave new society promised to his generation and class in 1945 was mindlessly grinding to a halt. The strengths of the play are only revealed in performance. Its shabby attic setting, drab atmosphere, and lack of serious physical action dramatize themes and involvements outlined above. Jimmy's rhetoric articulated for a small but growing area of society a feeling of complete uselessness, and of being excluded from any position of real power by 'all the old guard'. Osborne brilliantly sustains mood and rhetoric but there are grave structural weaknesses. There is no real probing of Jimmy's working life, or of social reality outside his flat, and a justifiable feeling of exclusion becomes in Jimmy total paranoia. The play collapses in anticlimax when Jimmy and Alison retreat into their private fantasy play-world of teddy bears and bushy-tailed squirrels.

But the details and stature of *Look Back in Anger* are not important here. John Osborne was a prophet for a young generation demanding to be heard, and given a sense of purpose. Osborne's subjective scream contained a truth which found an immediate response in George Devine and the Court directors, in a disaffected but talented theatrical minority including some influential critics, and in the Court's special-ized audience. And its success with theatre people found a response in other disaffected groups in society who wished to dramatize them-selves as 'outsiders', and who until this moment could find no public forum for their views. Osborne's play found itself linked together with a new-wave of socially conscious novelists, under the collective label of 'Angry Young Men', and critics and public became con-vinced that post-war Britain had at last found a voice, whatever its timbre. Like Osborne, the Court was intensely theatre-based, looking inward rather than outward to the community. As a result, the main early playwrights (Wesker, Arden, and then to some extent Bond) moved away from their Court base, because of their overriding interest in political theatre. Alongside the Court, was Joan Little-wood's Theatre Workshop Company at Stratford East, whose pro-ductions had far greater political and theatrical significance. Also Peter Brook was making an important impact at the Phoenix with Paul Scofield in *Hamlet* and Graham Greene's *The Power and the Glory*. Yet it was the Court, with its dissident middle-class audience for *Look Back in Anger* and its 'Angry Young Man' label, which stepped into the limelight with a programme of less imaginative quality. Ironically many of Osborne's later plays, though stronger than *Look Back in Anger*, never had the same impact.

During these years, Devine gauged the trajectory of a gathering momentum and exploited it to the full:

The 'kitchen sink' and 'angry young man' labels, and the myth of an exclusively proletarian repertory, were desperate attempts to pin down an unclassifiably various output. The only safe generalization about the Court's first authors is that they were inventing their own kinds of play and drawing on firsthand experience, rather than following literary models. And that the

English stage, for so long 'hermetically sealed off from life' (in Arthur Miller's famous phrase of 1956), was now grabbing it in handfuls.[2]

Devine had two objectives which took precedent over every other activity and transaction – to keep the Court open and alive, and to maintain its identity as a 'writers' theatre'. In pursuit of these basic determinations Devine gave the Court an impetus and direction which endures, and which arose from his complex character – compounded of idealism about theatre verging on the mystic, insecurity which could induce ruthless fixity of purpose, and practicality – on first nights he carried pipe and screwdriver. Above all he had, in Irving Wardle's words, 'the capacity for conducting a pioneer enterprise without cutting its lifeline to the past'.

To achieve a measure of independence within our English system of theatre management in which government subsidy is closely locked into commercial interests at all levels (and therefore subject to continual unforeseen crises), Devine and succeeding directors have had to play every trick in the management book to keep solvent, to take on board and contain unexpected successes which distorted their general policy: and even to abandon what were to them important principles. Three serious attempts to establish a permanent company of actors failed: and it will be argued that some compromises seriously damaged potential progress (and enrichment). But a measure of their success is that, twenty-five years and 450 productions later, there still appears to be a flickering flame readily distinguished as Royal Court policy. And certainly, during the late fifties, the Court made a growing impact on British theatre. Directors, actors and craftsmen who had come into contact with Devine's ideas and course of action, began to circulate to other theatres; and the Court's visual austerity in staging, which reinforced Berliner Ensemble traditions, set an example later to be taken up by the Royal Shakespeare Company and National Theatre.

One author whose early plays were originally put on at the Coventry Theatre was Arnold Wesker. When these plays were moved to the Court, they brought with them an authentic East End Jewish voice, which was quite unfamiliar to Devine, and not much liked by him. Wesker's success resulted in London managements developing an interest in plays written in genuine working-class or middle-class idiom and nuances of speech. Bernard Kops's *The Hamlet of Stepney Green* was brought in from Oxford to the Lyric, Hammersmith; and Harold Pinter's *The Birthday Party* was staged at the same theatre. In its original run, despite outstanding performances by Beatrix Lehmann and Richard Pearson, *The Birthday Party* was a commercial and critical disaster. The implications of this failure were registered and reacted to by the Court: and also illustrate the complex and contradictory influence of journalist critics: 'Harold Pinter . . . has lately been understudying at the Royal Court. No doubt it was under its intellectual influence that he wrote this baffling mixture.'[3]

With one exception, the critics were genuinely unable to absorb Pinter's language and world at a first hearing. Harold Hobson in the *Sunday Times* (published after the play had closed) praised the high quality of writing, acting, and presentation:

I am willing to risk whatever reputation I have as a judge of plays by saying that Mr Pinter, on the evidence of this work, possesses the most original, disturbing and arresting talent in theatrical London.[4]

Hobson's review established the integrity of the Lyric production, but to theatre workers at the time the failure of *The Birthday Party* was a serious blow to new-wave thinking, and resulted in redoubled efforts by the Court to consolidate its bridgehead. Strategy demanded two kinds of action: immediate achievement of front-line successes, and to secure the future by forming a new generation of playwrights.

Following Osborne's success there was no simple line of development, and audience figures varied, the peaks being *The Entertainer* (100 per cent), *Roots* (66 and later 93 per cent), and *One Way Pendulum* (87 per cent). *Sergeant Musgrave's Dance*, which later achieved the dubious status of an A-level set-text, at first drew 21 per cent at the box office. These front-line plays, together with regular Sunday Night presentations, were the visible parts of a closely-knit complex of intense practical activity and argument about theatre. 'Sunday Night Productions Without Decor' began in 1957, primarily to allow new playwrights to see their work in performance, and get the feel of working in a theatre: but they became a centre for growth. Sunday performances included first plays by John Arden (*Waters of Babylon*, 1957), N. F. Simpson (*A Resounding Tinkle*, 1957), Wole Soyinka (*The Invention*, 1959), and Edward Bond (*The Pope's*

Wedding, 1962). Among directors to get their first work at the Court through Sunday theatre were John Dexter, Lindsay Anderson, William Gaskill and Anthony Page – each of whom were to become policy makers at the Court. Three weeks careful rehearsal in a small church hall off the King's Road led to a performance at the Court with minimum furniture and props, so that costs were low. Actors were paid two guineas for performance, and nothing for rehearsals; but for an actor there was the unfamiliar stimulus of appearing in a new play for one performance before an audience composed of the London theatrical élite. John McGrath gives a sardonic, but accurate, description of such a Royal Court 'post-Osborne' audience:

In the centre of the front row of the circle sits George Devine, the benign headmaster ... Around him in the circle are the associate directors, already in demand for bigger, more commercial projects, together with a few chosen writers and friends, plus the designers, casting director, dramaturge, etc. Amongst them sit the businessmen, solicitors and their wives who 'support' the theatre, who raise and contribute money – for this is before the time of realistic Arts Council subsidies. In the stalls are found the agents for plays and actors, the smart radio and television producers, the directors of other theatres, the film company casting directors, the brighter young film producers and directors – and of course the other actors and aspiring writers and directors who wish to catch the eye of some or all of the above. Plus the critics, poised to flee the theatre, the more quickly to create a new reputation, to destroy an ambition ... Behind the *cognoscenti* in the front rows of the circle, and up in the upper circle, are the unknown public – the students, young actors, technicians, schoolmasters, theatre freaks, the innocently interested and the green-eyed aspirant who on the whole create the throng necessary to admire, first of all, the rest of the audience, and then even the play itself. From their ranks will come the future, and the approval that justifies the present – and pays for it.

McGrath continues:

The work of Osborne, Pinter, Bond, Wesker, Arden, and their heirs – Stoppard, Griffiths, Brenton, Hare and Keeffe – may now seem to have developed beyond, say, *Saved*, or *The Dumb Waiter*, or *The Kitchen*. But it is important to realize their aesthetic/social roots. The audience has changed very little in the theatre, the social requirements remain constant, the values remain firmly those of acceptability to a metropolitan middle-class audience, with an eye to similar acceptability on the international cultural market.[5]

In 1958 George Devine wished to give his new writers confidence in presenting new and untried ideas to others, without the initial shock of attending open rehearsals – to prepare them for work in action at the Court. He therefore set up an informal Writers' Group in an old paint shop off the King's Road. Soon the leadership passed to William Gaskill and Keith Johnstone, and the group of about fifteen individuals included John Arden, Arnold Wesker, Ann Jellicoe, Wole Soyinka, David Cregan, and Edward Bond. The aim was to explore the nature of theatre through action; and in so doing to unravel writing problems which could not be resolved at a desk. The partial failure of plays like Jellicoe's *The Sport of My Mad Mother* (withdrawn after fourteen performances) and Arden's *Live Like Pigs*, and the attack on Pinter (although not at the Court) caused the Writers' Group to redouble its creative effort and will to make the new drama succeed. As always, at the Court, any positive action on the part of some members was resisted by others. Tension between individuals seemed to release energies for creativity. But the work achieved by the group had long-term effects – particularly on Arden, Wesker, and Bond.

The early 1960s was a time of uncertainty where processes of change interacted at many levels, and where Harold Macmillan's recipe for superficial prosperity arose from an assumption of steady growth, which could not be fulfilled. Major economic and social problems also failed to respond to the 'white heat of technological revolution' during Harold Wilson's administrations after 1964, and eventually came to a head in the 'events' of 1968. The most startling and direct effect on people's day-to-day lives came from the new architecture. Admiration for excellent design at the top end of the market conflicted with a general sense of anger and vulnerability as major city centres were devastated, through the unhappy union of public and private interest and property developers; and whole communities were dispersed to make room for tower-blocks, underpasses, windswept pedestrian ways, and tourist hotels. And above all was the growth of television, for this was the age of image-makers. The affluent society thrived on a profusion of hire-purchase consumer goods, and in particular markets were created by the new spending power of young people. As image became more important, advertising in fashion became highly competitive. Traditional British

preoccupation with appearances, became preoccupation with commercial image.

These changes had an effect on British theatre in general. Audiences
lost their sense of identity and were dispersed, through a combination
of urban development and tourism. Changes in architecture were
translated in theatre into a fascination with non-traditional perform-
ing-spaces, so that companies moved into new buildings, or old
buildings with the right image. In 1958 the Mermaid Theatre
heralded a change in theatre architecture, and coincided with the
critical growth of a theatrical 'fringe' using pubs, clubs, warehouses –
anywhere that was available. In Sloane Square the changes were
especially significant. Unlike the City, which had lost its ancient
pattern of streets, and its vertical scale and dimension, Sloane Square
and the King's Road still approximated to pre-war London, and had
become a centre for the new lively and colourful international culture
and fashion.

It was difficult for the Court to adjust to these contemporary
trends. A writer's theatre, in which austere design and staging were
used to extend theatre through the power of words, and informed
by a quasi-social and moral commitment, could not easily move
towards an emergent style of theatre based on action and spectacle,
nor express the mores and aspirations of 'swinging London'. George
Devine's solutions for survival in the present shaped the future more
than his careful long-term planning and strategy. A basic stumbling-
block was the shortage of new plays of substance, which would be
successful at the Court box-office, and might be exploited elsewhere.
John Osborne, with *Luther* and *Plays for England* (1962), *Inadmissible
Evidence* (1964) and *A Patriot For Me* (1965), provided a dynamism
which gave credence to a continuing Royal Court policy; Arnold
Wesker's liberal socialist ideals gave an authentic ring to the Court's
vaguely left-wing commitment, and made money; and John Arden's
vigorous theatricality gave an edge of defiant engagement with new
forms, and had George Devine's total support even in the face of
financial disaster. (*The Happy Haven* (1960) brought only 12 per cent
box-office receipts.) But apart from the works of these and a few
other dramatists, there was a dearth of new talent. As a result, the
Court fell back on old formulae – 'star' attractions, modern French
drama, and classical revivals. Devine's ability to attract and present

known 'stars' met with varied results. Laurence Olivier's success in *The Entertainer* (1957) had demonstrated how established actors might readjust to modern theatre; but Noel Coward's version of Feydeau, *Look After Lulu* (1959), in which Vivien Leigh appeared in white frilly drawers, was blatant commercialism. It provoked near mutiny within the English Stage Company, riled its regular audience, and packed the Court with an unrepresentative 'Daimler' audience (Devine's phrase). In contrast, *Rosmersholm* (1959) starring Peggy Ashcroft, and Chekhov's *Platonov* (1960) with Rex Harrison, were both substantial critical and box-office successes, and well within Court policy. However, *August for the People* (1961) by Nigel Dennis, intended to be Rex Harrison's rehabilitation to contemporary theatre, was a miserable failure in which author and star failed to find a common purpose. Harrison bought himself out of his contract after two playing weeks at the Court, the author was humiliated, and Devine retired to France with a severe nervous breakdown. The project, which had a right-wing flavour, had been initiated by Kenneth Tynan who by 1961, and by now well into his campaign for a National Theatre, had come to realize that the future of British theatre lay not wholly with the working class:

Too many of our younger playwrights have forgotten, in their passion for novelty of content, the ancient disciplines of style. Rightly determined to look beyond the drawing-room for their subject matter, they have poured the baby out with the bath-water. In the battle for content, form has been sacrificed.

What I look for in working-class drama is the sort of play that is not ashamed to assimilate and acknowledge the bourgeois tradition, which includes a multiplicity of styles, not all of them wholly despicable ... nothing is more crucially stupid than to deride the artistic achievements of a social class because one deplores its historical record.

... lacking a National Theatre, London has no playhouse in which the best of world drama is constantly on tap, available for immediate ingestion by spectators of eclectic tastes. One function of such a theatre would be to bridge the gap between those elements of bourgeois theatre that lean towards the future and those elements of the new drama that extend a hand towards the past.[6]

It was not the playwrights who had poured the baby out with the bath-water but Kenneth Tynan and those journalists who had created and fostered theatrical fashions. The rediscovery of 'style' arose when they, as spokesmen for an old élite, were in danger of being replaced by a new élite which they themselves had helped to nurture. *Look Back in Anger*, an expression of discontent among the new bourgeoisie, opened the door for a rediscovery of working-class consciousness which threatened to go beyond what was required by the closed circles of London theatrical trend-setters. In its turn the vanguard of 'working-class culture' as represented in London theatre and the media was in danger of becoming its own new élite. Jeremy Seabrook, in his book *What Went Wrong* (1978), makes the point clearly: 'There has developed a sub-culture that is not working-class, so much as a freemasonry of those who have come from it; a quite distinctive sensibility.' The ramifications of this attitude were to be felt progressively through the theatre and its associated arts during the seventies, and are even more evident today.

Peter Brook's experimental 'Theatre of Cruelty' in 1963 instigated an anti-verbal school of theatre based loosely on the theories of Artaud, the Polish mime Grotowski, various expatriate Americans, and a longing for the ultimate in primitive experience. This powerful movement, which threatened rational theatre throughout the late sixties and seventies, was well characterized by Simon Trussler: '*The Ik* was the stuff of which successful colour-supplement features are made.' At its worst, according to Eric Bentley, this kind of theatre disabled serious criticism, for 'There's no function for a critic where intellect has no status'; contrariwise its central preoccupation with words caused Glenda Jackson to describe the Court as 'an albatross round the neck of British theatre'.

During the sixties Devine took steps to secure, as he thought, the Court's long-term future. Like Tynan, he sensed that Laurence Olivier would be somewhere near the centre of development in British theatre. There were plans to join with Olivier in a project at the old Metropolitan Music Hall in Edgware Road (1960), panic measures to amalgamate with the Old Vic in 1961–2; and an attempt to become a part of the National Theatre in 1963. All these plans failed to mature. Although the Court's artistic and commercial success had arisen through the 'Angry Young Man' image, Devine was not political, hated overt propaganda, and under his management the Court did not specialize in social drama. He was interested in the advancement of civic freedoms and individual talents, not through abstract rhetoric or manifestoes, but through the practice of theatre. And even here there was inconsistency, for his companies were hierarchical, exclusive, and dismissive of outsiders. His prime objective at the Court was expressed to Irving Wardle in 1963: 'This place must stand or fall by its plays, because that is the only *raison d'être* that we have.'

Tynan's new-found theory of 'style' in his 1961 review, quoted above, corresponded to George Devine's long-established practice derived from 'La Compagnie des Quinze' and set out by Michel Saint-Denis in *Theatre: The Rediscovery of Style*, published in 1960 with a foreword by Sir Laurence Olivier. In his book Saint-Denis attempts to define 'style' in theatre; but it remains a vague concept, difficult to put in words, but a leaven which may emerge in performance. It has something to do with fitness for purpose, economy of means, and generosity: with finding the truth of a text, or a plain way of carrying out a significant action. To quote John Osborne on Devine: 'Strength, gaunt lines, and simplicity always excited him.' In classwork Devine's approach to style in acting was achieved through the use of masks and half-masks, intended to release an actor from the tyranny of naturalistic gesture, to release instincts and energies lying beneath his conscious persona. Acting and theatre for Devine 'was not simply the effect of dramatizing ideas. It was a question of using texture, sound, colour and other theatrical elements as a means of 'orchestrating the senses' and thus influencing human relationships'.[7] What Devine's preferred playwrights had in common was that an intuited meaning, over and above moment-by-moment narrative, only emerged when the stage action was finished. This explains why despite opposition, and a fierce exchange between Tynan and Ionesco on the value of Ionesco's world-view and mode of theatre, where words take on a life of their own, modern French dramatists (Genet, Giraudoux, Sartre, Ionesco and, above all, Samuel Beckett) formed a distinct core of work during Devine's tenure as director.

George Devine announced his retirement as Artistic Director of the English Stage Company early in 1965, and later in the year collapsed while playing in John Osborne's *A Patriot For Me*. He died on 20 January 1966. It is ironic that through single-mindedness, and enlightened self-interest on behalf of his company, he pioneered

increased grants and the abolition of censorship, which laid foundations for Alternative and left-wing theatre in the seventies.

The activity of making plays and the role of the writer in that
process have changed crucially in Great Britain between the 1950s
and today. The Court has played a paradoxical role in what amounts
to a revolution in theatre practice. Theatre Workshop, following
Piscator and Brecht, put plays together in action as a group activity,
a practice which was later extended by Alternative theatre groups:
and by Peter Brook who led changing fashions in Artaud-based
experimental aesthetics, movement, sound and spectacle. The Court
as a writers' theatre set out to interpret given texts; and its 'two-tier'
system of star actors and supporting company restricted other equally
valid approaches to theatre. Irving Wardle reports Angus Wilson's
experience of rehearsals for his play *The Mulberry Bush*, starring Gwen
Ffrangçon-Davies, which gives a sense of the writers' theatre in action
in 1956:

> Encouraged by Devine, he attended every rehearsal and made friends with
> the cast ... What did surprise Wilson, after the fraternal introductions and
> Devine's invitation to the cast to discuss their parts with the author, was the
> fact that only Ffrangçon-Davies was permitted to ask questions. When
> Kenneth Haigh tried to do it, Devine squashed him flat.[8]

In time, almost in spite of itself, Court policy became involved with
socio-political causes (CND, abolition of censorship, womens'
rights, Third World problems) which gradually informed and
changed its intentions and theatre practice, though never its basic
organization. Yet from its early days the Court provided the initial
impetus for politically-committed writers as different in outlook and
method as Arden, Wesker, McGrath, and Bond, who said of London
theatre in the middle fifties: 'what mattered and what intrigued one
was what was happening at the Court. There was some relevance
there that was lacking in other theatres.' But even in the late fifties
when the momentum of Osborne gave the Court a strong sense of
identity, there was no straight line of development.

An important change in trajectory came when William Gaskill
took over as Artistic Director in 1965 after Devine's resignation and
tragic death. Gaskill had worked with Devine since 1957, and had
directed several plays at the Court. At first there was no obvious

change in repertoire, for Ann Jellicoe, N. F. Simpson, Arnold Wesker, and John Osborne were staged again. However, Gaskill (following Devine's policy of encouraging new writers) presented plays by Edward Bond, David Cregan, Keith Johnstone, Christopher Hampton and the novelist David Storey, who in partnership with his director Lindsay Anderson became central figures of the 1970s. Also during Gaskill's regime three little known plays by D. H. Lawrence were staged in repertory, in a brilliant evocation of life in Lawrence's mining community.

The crucial change was in Gaskill's approach to work with actors. New writing required a new approach to acting. Since the closure of the Old Vic School (where Devine had been a director), theatre training had relapsed into its old haphazard pattern, except for isolated pockets of enterprise such as the work of Harold Lang, an actor/ teacher at the Central School. Lang knew Helene Weigel personally, and was much influenced by the work of the Berliner Ensemble. Lang's work was brought to a wider audience by John Schlesinger's BBC television-film called *The Lesson*, which was much discussed and argued about in the acting profession and by an interested general public. Gaskill, who ran his own Writers' Workshop group and acting classes at the Court and at the Jeannetta Cochrane Theatre, was also greatly influenced by the work of the Berliner Ensemble. Later, while Associate Director of the National Theatre (1963–5) he directed a production of Farquhar's *The Recruiting Officer* in the style of Brecht, and then *Mother Courage*. His Brechtian *Macbeth* at the Court in 1966, with Alec Guinness and Simone Signoret, although savaged by the critics, set a new standard of Shakespearean production and design. The play was bathed in brilliant white light with no attempt to suggest night scenes, nor establish mood through colour or changes in intensity of light. There are vital connections between Gaskill's work on Brecht, and his associations and work with Edward Bond. In 1965, as one of his first productions as Artistic Director, Gaskill directed Edward Bond's *Saved*, which the press greeted with an hysterical outburst; so much so that Gaskill was immediately caught up with the question of the abolition of censorship, which became a central objective for his management, and a media affair which brought the Court into national prominence. For the first time the

Court was fighting a battle with support from other areas (some perhaps uneasy allies); but powerful voices including Tynan and Olivier had a vested interest in the Court's battle and eventual success. What had been done for publishing (with *Lady Chatterley's Lover*), had to be done for theatre, and Gaskill organized a Bond Season in 1969, with revivals of *Saved*, *Early Morning*, and *Narrow Road to the Deep North* to celebrate the end of the Lord Chamberlain's powers. Gaskill has continued to direct and promote Bond's plays, including *Lear* in 1971, and *The Sea* in 1973.

During his years at the Court, and later with Joint Stock, Gaskill has explored new ways of making plays with actors. Although he works with his actors in immense detail, he does not favour a deeply psychological approach:

... the actor has become a much more independent, analytical and critical person than he or she ever was before ... Of course some directors work very closely with the actors on psychological viewpoints and they go very close and they whisper to the actors about their inner lives. But I've never done that. I don't really approve of that ... Because it's not objective. You're not really in an outside position. It's very important for a director to represent, as it were, some kind of objective viewpoint from outside rather than the inner workings of the psyche.[9]

A closely argued paper by Peter Holland traces the development of new political and theatrical consciousness in Bond and Gaskill in relation to their individual and joint study and practice of Brecht, and their work on Bond's plays:

The 'epic approach' of the plays is Brecht's, yet it would be wrong to search for detailed echoes; what Bond has achieved is primarily rooted in the Royal Court and the work of William Gaskill. That is the reason why his work fails to use significant parts of Brecht's theory of a Marxist drama; Bond does not make full use of alienation effects in the acting since such effects have never been a part of the English acting tradition, nor have they been particularly well understood in England. In spite of such omissions, Bond is achieving the recreation, in the context of British theatre, of the theatrical practice that Brecht outlined.[10]

Bond illustrated the trend between the fifties and the eighties of play-wrights becoming more directly involved with the whole theatrical undertaking. For Bond, inside the Court, and Arden, outside the whole establishment theatre, this change has strong political and social implications.

The problems of Max Stafford-Clark and the Royal Court in the 1980s are fundamentally economic, and spring from a longstanding refusal on the part of government and Arts Council to base their funding of the arts on the support of artists and people concerned, and the quality of the experience. In 1981 the Court was in danger of losing its Arts Council grant. Decisions made by the Council in the early and middle fifties had resulted in a change of focus in their activities away from the actual experience of theatre (by stopping their own tours to theatreless towns) to the encouragement, with the help of local authorities and other interested parties, of building new theatres. At Coventry and Nottingham, where enthusiastic and growing audiences packed ramshackle halls, new theatres were essential. But the consequences for London, largely unforeseen, became evident in the 1970s, when the maintenance of large theatres and overheavy administrations, in Robert Hutchison's words,

gobbled up much of the increased subsidy that the Government and local authorities have made available. For example, the total revenue costs of the National Theatre in the year ending April 1980 were £8·2 million. Of this, £1·5 million went on the building (cleaning, security, safety, electrical, mechanical and systems engineering, repairs and maintenance, depreciation, rates, insurance).[11]

But government and the Arts Council will always support the monolithic national institutions (Covent Garden, The National Theatre, and the Royal Shakespeare Company), for sponsors of all kinds and visitors of State are bemused by glitter, spectacle, and size, and tend to value experiences which are frequently achieved by the sacrifice of intellectual content. Under pressure from the new free-market economy, and looking for substantial cuts a little further down the scale, the Arts Council had prudently reversed its earlier aims, and put support into activities rather than buildings. So that by the 1980s the Royal Court was caught in a trap of its own making. Having pioneered the campaign for theatrical subsidy for studio and alternative theatre, the Court itself was now regarded as expensive plant. And, with some notable exceptions, the Court found little support from the critics, trained in the same traditions as the sponsors, and also dazzled by packaging. As Eric Bentley observed, criticism can become

a celebration of the personal superiority of the critic . . . I think that today, contrary to the snobberies of the past, and particularly in England, where an intellectual could once be put down by an aristocracy, snobbery is universitarian.[12]

Stafford-Clark's concentration on new plays actually works against his own and his theatre's best interests, in that theatrical reputations in this country are made in classics. Critics are on the whole incapable of perceiving the work that goes into a new play. The result is that longstanding work by dramaturges, the encouragement of new writers, and all the hidden activities which have been continuous at the Court have been going on unperceived and largely disregarded.

Detailed work on the craft and quality of acting has been practised over the years through workshops set up by Devine, developed by Gaskill as director and then with Max Stafford-Clark in their Joint Stock productions, to be fed back into core work at the Court. This work cannot be evaluated in histories of theatre and theatre policy, for a theatre lives in its day-to-day activities, particular productions, and moments within those productions. Stafford-Clark considers the most important play in two-and-a-half years as director was Andrea Dunbar's *The Arbor*, given in the Theatre Upstairs as one of four events in the 1980 Young Writers' Festival. And there remains the difficulty of finding new plays of substance for the main auditorium. With the National companies wallowing in the current fashion for musicals, and their experimental theatres attracting the best small-scale plays, the Court is left with a limited range of possibilities. Bond's *Restoration* (1981), described as 'an unsuccessful attempt to weld a musical superstructure on a fine foundation of a play', was an attempt to bridge the gap, but it pressed the Court to its limits, costing more to run each week than the box-office took. Reflecting on Devine's days, Stafford-Clark recently remarked: 'it is now beyond our resources to contemplate, as they could, plays with sixteen in the cast.'

Good theatre depends on intensity of experience, the scale of performance, and contact with a varied cross-section of the general public. Irving Wardle in its defence argued that:

PART THREE

The Court remains the one regular platform where this can happen; where totally unknown writers like Andrea Dunbar and Paul Kember can experience full professional exposure, where large-scale work can be mounted, and where the living playwright can make his voice heard in the world at large. If it goes, we shall be losing the single most important organ in the body of the British theatre.[13]

For an age in which opinion is increasingly formed by image-makers and critics, and subject to the hit-and-miss trends of fashion, the English Stage Company by continuing to remodel and redefine George Devine's original idea of a 'writers' theatre' affirms a principle expressed, in another context, by Hugo Ball: 'Every word that is spoken and sung here says at least this one thing: that this humiliating age has not succeeded in winning our respect.'[14]

NOTES

1. Kenneth Tynan, *A View of the English Stage 1944–63* (London, 1975), 147.

2. Irving Wardle, *The Theatres of George Devine* (London, 1978), 198–9.

3. Cecil Wilson, *Daily Mail* (20 May 1958), reprinted in John Elsom, *Post-War British Theatre Criticism* (Henley-on-Thames, 1981), 83–4.

4. Harold Hobson, *Sunday Times* (25 May 1958), reprinted in John Elsom.

5. John McGrath, *A Good Night Out* (London, 1981), 13–15.

6. Kenneth Tynan, 320–21.

7. Irving Wardle, 245–6.

8. Irving Wardle, 177.

9. William Gaskill, 'Working with Actors', in *Exploring Theatre Education*, ed. Ken Robinson (London, 1980), 53, 69–70.

10. Peter Holland, 'Brecht, Bond, Gaskill, and the Practice of Political Theatre', in *Theatre Quarterly*, Vol. VIII, No. 30 (1978), 33.

11. Robert Hutchison, *The Politics of the Arts Council* (1982), 101–2.

12. Eric Bentley, 'Portrait of the Critic as a Young Brechtian', in *Theatre Quarterly*, Vol. VI, No. 21 (1976), 8.

13. Irving Wardle, *The Times* (21 September 1981).

14. Hugo Ball, diary note, reprinted in John Willett, *The New Sobriety 1914–1933* (London, 1979) 26.

TED HUGHES AND GEOFFREY HILL:
AN ANTITHESIS

MARTIN DODSWORTH

English poetry of the 1980s is still a Romantic poetry, one that prefers individual insight to the conventional values of its society, and that tends to see itself as a privileged, indeed sovereign and unique, way of looking at life and judging it. Both aspects of this proposition are reflected in the poems of Ted Hughes (b. 1930) and Geoffrey Hill (b. 1932), who, despite their considerable differences, are at once very English and seriously concerned with the question of the poet's role in society. They represent an antithesis in quality and in mode of poetic achievement, which can better be understood once the basic pattern of their work and its development has been grasped.

When some time in the early sixties Ted Hughes gave a radio talk for schools on writing in general and on his own in particular, he called it 'Capturing Animals'. He emphasized, in a way that would not have offended Coleridge, that a good poem was an organism, 'an assembly of living parts moved by a single spirit'. He had started to write poetry, he said, just at the time when he had given up his childhood interest in collecting animals, and suggested that there was a vital relationship between these facts:

The special kind of excitement, the slightly mesmerized and quite involuntary concentration with which you make out the stirrings of a new poem in your mind, then the outline, the mass and colour and clean final form of it in the midst of the general lifelessness, all that is too familiar to mistake. This is hunting and the poem is a new species of creature, a new specimen of the life outside your own.[1]

He did not write his first poem about an animal until some time after he had started writing. In fact, in his talk he quotes it and discusses it. Early Hughes is, among other things, a poet of the world of animals. *The Thought-Fox* is the first of his animal poems and in many ways representative of what is to be found in his first two books, *The Hawk in the Rain* (1957) and *Lupercal* (1960):

> I imagine this midnight moment's forest:
> Something else is alive
> Beside the clock's loneliness
> And this blank page where my fingers move.
>
> Through the window I see no star:
> Something more near
> Though deeper within darkness
> Is entering the loneliness:
>
> Cold, delicately as the dark snow,
> A fox's nose touches twig, leaf;
> Two eyes serve a movement, that now
> And again now, and now, and now
>
> Sets neat prints into the snow
> Between trees, and warily a lame
> Shadow lags by stump and in hollow
> Of a body that is bold to come
>
> Across clearings, an eye,
> A widening deepening greenness,
> Brilliantly, concentratedly,
> Coming about its own business
>
> Till, with a sudden sharp hot stink of fox
> It enters the dark hole of the head.
> The window is starless still; the clock ticks,
> The page is printed.

It is a beautiful, slightly mysterious poem. Seamus Heaney, a poet who has been much influenced by Hughes, has drawn attention to the way in which Hughes's poems depend on the noise of consonants, whispering, clicking, exploding and clotting the poem at the expense of any broad harmonious music of the vowels, and has in this poem noted especially 'the monosyllablic consonantal shooting of the bolts'[2] on the fox in the last stanza: 'with a sudden sharp hot stink of fox/ It enters the dark hole of the head'. In his talk, Hughes says that 'words that live are those which we hear ... or which we see ... or which we taste ... or touch ... or smell'. *Click, chuckle, freckled, veined, vinegar, sugar* are some of his examples. The pronounced quality of sound in his poems is part of the way in which they engage with livingness through the five senses: and many of them are directed, as perhaps *The Thought-Fox* is, at a renewal of the senses.

Yet this poem is not quite as simple in effect as Hughes would have us believe. He says of it

... in some ways my fox is better than an ordinary fox. It will live for ever, it will never suffer from hunger or hounds. I have it with me wherever I go. And I made it.[3]

The emphasis on possession, in the very idea of 'capturing' the poem, in the thought of the poem as a 'specimen', is reflected in *The Thought-Fox* itself, in the way in which the fox is *held* between the opening and closing lines of the poem. Heaney's metaphor of shooting bolts is apt: there is a sense in which this poem imprisons its livingness – just as there is a sense in which the livingness is not there at all. The fox emerges from darkness and disappears into darkness. The poem substitutes itself for the fox. We are left with 'the clock's loneliness' and an awareness of the gap between what we see in the poem of ordinary living and the heightened experience of imagining the fox. It seems that Hughes's need to possess, embodied in the idea of 'capturing', is the reflection of a lack in him and in his sense of ordinary life.

Indeed, he is apt to depict the life of men in the aggregate as a nasty business, as in the story 'Sunday' in *Wodwo* (1967), or as an empty one, as in the poem *A Motorbike* in *Moortown* (1979):

... the shallowness of the shops and the shallowness of the beer
And the sameness of the next town.

The wholesale negative behind Hughes's positives is distressing, and it diminishes the stature of his poems. He is famous for 'violence' in style and subject-matter; the violence is a good deal exaggerated, but it is undoubtedly present, as a desperate wish to be out of the human altogether. Hughes is a poet who finds the human condition too much to take.

Thrushes, from his second book, illustrates this: it compares the 'terrifying' thrushes who live at the quick of instinct, as it were in an eternal present, with time-bound, self-divided men. Man is at a distance from the world of commanding energies, weeping and orgy and hosannah, evoked at the poem's end, and in which we must understand the thrushes to exist.

In *Thrushes* the careful control manifest in the enclosed form of *The Thought-Fox* is absent, as though the forces of 'darkness' have grown too much for the poet to handle. We may take this as a development that was just about unavoidable, given that Hughes had so little to say on behalf of the state of mind with which 'control' was associated; but it was a development that, because it opened up the gap between where his sympathies lay and what might keep him in contact with his fellow men, made writing more and more difficult for him: 'Almost all the poems in *Lupercal* were written as invocations to writing. My main consciousness in those days was that it was impossible to write.'[4]

There is no change in direction after *Lupercal*, but there is a change in style. In his radio talk he recommended a spontaneous writing process, yet spontaneity is what is lacking in the willed poetry of *The Hawk in the Rain* or *Lupercal*: a phrase like 'bends to be blent in the prayer' in *Thrushes* is, in its 'literary' quality, quite alien to the poem's positive values. Hughes's task was not exclusively stylistic: to achieve the release required he needed to resolve the conflict implicit in the possessiveness of his early poems. The logical step was to look further into the 'darkness' out of which the thought-fox had stepped.

In 1959 Hughes and his first wife Sylvia Plath devised exercises in meditation and invocation based on the 'whole body of magical literature'.[5] This reflects the example of Yeats, but also of Robert Graves's 'historical grammar of poetic myth', *The White Goddess* (1948), a book which declares all true poetry to celebrate some incident or scene in the story of 'the birth, life, death and resurrection of the Spirit of the Year', son and lover of 'the capricious and all-powerful Threefold Goddess',[6] who figures in Hughes's work largely as the numinous force of nature itself. When Hughes talks about using poetry to 'capture a spirit' he is not speaking altogether metaphorically.

In the early sixties also Hughes developed his idea of the poet as a kind of shaman. The shaman, he has said

... can enter trance at will and go to the spirit-world ... he goes to get something badly needed, a cure, an answer, some sort of divine intervention in the community's affairs. Now this flight to the spirit-world he experiences as a dream ...[7]

Hughes's interest in dreams and his recourse to occult symbolism are in line with the practice of many other modern poets. Lawrence comes to mind, because of Hughes's interest in a cleansing of the senses and Lawrence's own fantasy of a recreated paganism in *The Plumed Serpent* (and elsewhere). The question must be to what extent it has been a good thing for Hughes's poetry. Does the poetry stand clear or not from the system of belief and speculation to which it is related? Can we enjoy it without assenting to ideas about white goddesses and spirits of the year? Is access limited to believers only? Is the poetry better or worse for Hughes's heavy commitment to myth and archetype?

In one way at least there has been gain. The poems now have none of the imprisoning quality of *The Thought-Fox*, nor does one find the infelicities of diction that mar, say, *Lupercalia* – things like 'worn witchcraft *accoutrement*/Of proverbs' for the wisdom of the dead, or 'their eyes' golden *element*' for the iris of the goat's eye. The desired spontaneity is felt in the casual rhythms and unself-conscious audacity of many poems dealing more or less directly with natural phenomena – the beautiful *Season Songs* (1975, revised 1976) and the animal poems of *Under the North Star* (1981), primarily for children (for whom Hughes has written much else – plays, poems and stories), and the more savage record of farm life in the first section of *Moortown*, and the quasi-descriptive poems of *Remains of Elmet* (1979).

The books that show directly the influence of Hughes's primitivism take the form of myths or allusions to myths: *Crow* (1972), *Gaudete* (1977), *Cave Birds* (1978) and the sequences *Prometheus on his Rock* and *Adam and the Sacred Nine* in *Moortown*. These are more problematic. One difficulty is that they all have a certain shapelessness: *Crow* (which to some extent derives from tales of the

Winnebago Indians about a trickster-figure, tales which interested Jung) is sub-titled 'From the Life and Songs of the Crow': the complete set, which should be held together by a prose narrative, has never been published and has probably never even been put together. Poems from the 'Crow' series tend to wander from one context to another. This indecisiveness reflects an inability to come to terms with the cruelty and destructiveness to which so many of them give expression. Modernist ideas of art's impersonality and its allusiveness here flatter the artist's, and the reader's, disinclination to see brutalizing emotion for what it is; the result is radically flawed.

Gaudete is better organized than the other myth books: it has a bizarre story about a changeling vicar who attempts to found a new, primarily sexual religion of love but who is inadequate to the task he has set himself. His story is contrasted with a set of poems dedicated to Hughes's white-goddess-Nature-figure, supposed to be written by the man whose place the changeling took. These poems are indeed impressive in their freedom and assurance of expression, though not helped by their marginal relation to the rest of the book:

> What will you make of half a man
> Half a face
> A ripped edge
>
> His one-eyed waking
> Is the short sleep of aftermath
>
> His vigour
> The bone-deformity of consequences
>
> His talents
> The deprivations of escape
>
> How will you correct
> The veteran of negatives
> And the survivor of cease?

The parallelisms suggest primitive ritual forms, the gnomic quality in association with absoluteness of statement is much like what is to be found in the work of East European poets admired by the poet – Vasko Popa, Miroslav Holub or Janos Pilinszky – but there is a marked feeling of Hughes in such an expression as 'the survivor of cease'. The phrase evokes the speaker's exhaustion and alienation. One might speak justly of a renovation of poetic language here.

It could be said of such a poem that its character is fragmentary. It does not explain itself nor is it adequately explained by the narrative of which it is part. Yet this does not necessarily imply an adverse judgement. The fragment is a recognizable form of Romantic verse – *Kubla Khan*, for example. The fragmentary quality of Hughes's poems is part of their livingness. Whatever doubts we may have about the theories of myth and archetype that underlie them, this continually impresses itself on us in felicity and audacity of phrase.

On the other hand, the comparison with *Kubla Khan* is very much in Coleridge's favour, because his poem identifies itself with its culture: it looks to other poems and it imagines an audience, not merely in the way it sets out, but within itself. It locates its mystery within the community of readers. The *Gaudete* poem does not appeal to a sense of community. Like most of Hughes's poems it embodies fundamentally isolated experience. The advance on *The Thought-Fox* has been an advance in fluency, in confidence and in spontaneous feeling, but the split between poet and world in that poem remains as the basis of the *Gaudete* poems and their kin. About them all there hovers the spirit of retreat. The simplicity and primitivism of Hughes's poetry are only apparent: they overlay an unacknowledged element of fear and self-division. Hughes's poems remain symptoms of an illness they cannot heal.

As I have suggested, Geoffrey Hill is a very different kind of poet from Ted Hughes, though still firmly within the Romantic tradition. He is as willing as Hughes to think of poems in terms of organism, but his view of the poet's relation to the society in which and for which he writes eschews ideas of shamanism for a less exotic moralism scrupulously defined. This scrupulosity is reflected in a denser and more highly organized poetic style than Hughes's. It is also a difficult style.

Hughes can be difficult, too; but his difficulty derives from a reluctance or inability to articulate fully the structures on which his fragments of myth depend. Hill is difficult because he says so many things at once. The contradictory impulses of feeling within a poem by Hill are likely to leave his reader at one level perplexed, whatever sense or promise of resolution hangs over it, and this is so because there is something fundamentally ambiguous in his view of human experience. Take for example the sonnet *Idylls of the King*, one of a set in Hill's fourth book *Tenebrae* (1976):

> The pigeon purrs in the wood; the wood has gone;
> dark leaves that flick to silver in the gust,
> and the marsh-orchids and the heron's nest,
> goldgrimy shafts and pillars of the sun.
>
> Weightless magnificence upholds the past.
> Cement recesses smell of fur and bone
> and berries wrinkle in the badger-run
> and wiry heath-fern scatters its fresh rust.
>
> 'O clap your hands' so that the dove takes flight,
> bursts through the leaves with an untidy sound,
> plunges its wings into the green twilight
>
> above this long-sought and forsaken ground,
> the half-built ruins of the new estate,
> warheads of mushrooms round the filter-pond.

This is at once appealing and baffling. The qualities of the natural scene are given with Keatsian sensuousness, silver and gold shining out from a living landscape observed with a care and detachment which we might parallel from *To Autumn*. Yet, unlike Keats's, this landscape is curiously unstable. Within the space of the first line the wood which is solid enough for a pigeon to sound in disappears, and then in the tenth line reappears. The physical details – fur- and bone-smell, wrinkling berries, heath-fern scattering its rust – co-exist with a strange insubstantiality. It is characteristic of this poem that the leaves and orchids and heron's nest are both present and not present, transformed into light, the shafts and pillars of the sun. The physical world, the basis of life, becomes in a moment mysterious: its solidity is not denied but it is called in question. The poem's opening lines admit us to an experience something like what Wordsworth must have felt, when as a child he had to grasp at a wall or tree 'to recall myself from this abyss of idealism to the reality'.

The poem is characteristic of Hill in going beyond a concern with the world's physical mystery. The fifth line plunges us into a new kind of uncertainty, one that is enhanced by the obscurity of its own expression. 'Weightless magnificence upholds the past' is at once a description of the sunlit autumnal trees holding up their own past of dying leaves to the sun and a general statement which makes the wood symbolic of a present moment suffused with the spirit of a past at once magnificent and ghostly – 'weightless'. The poem's title implies that this past is that of Tennyson's *Idylls*, where the Arthurian dream gave dubious sanction for Victorian imperial ambition, now in its turn past, but still ambiguously glamorous. Its survival in human consciousness is contrasted with the dying and withering that in nature is always new, always of the instant – 'fresh rust'.

The clapping of the hands with which the sestet begins has, then, a dramatic force: it provokes change, it brings the moment alive and puts nostalgia, a yearning for the Tennysonian idyll, behind, as though it were exorcized. And yet the gesture does not present itself as successfully dismissing the past. On the contrary: for 'O clap your hands' is the opening of the forty-seventh psalm which bids us sing in praise of the King of Kings. The dove takes flight but not necessarily away from us: we stand in this poem's 'green twilight' in a place which may have been 'long-sought and forsaken' not merely by the speaker or his fellow creatures, but also by the dove of the holy spirit. 'The half-built ruins of the new estate' may reproach God equally with man for failure to complete what was begun, and the quotation from the psalms, a keeping faith with the past, may be used as part of the reproach directed at us: we have not kept faith with the God of the past, who now benignly and untidily, because unpredictably, tears into the life of the poem. The simply phenomenological doubts of the beginning of the sonnet have become moral and religious by the close.

A great deal more could be said in explication of this poem; explication is not, however, an end in itself. The force of the poem rests in its peculiar ordering of experience, not in what can be abstracted from it. What is striking about the poem from this point of view is the way in which the poem develops simultaneously as a certain kind of sensuous experience in which ear, eye, smell and touch participate and as an intellectual experience also, in which feelings and ideas grow one out of another. The contrast with

Hughes's lopsided anti-intellectualism is strong and surely much in Hill's favour.

It might be objected that Hughes is decisive where Hill simply does not know his own mind, that, for example, *Idylls of the King* simply expires in a welter of ambiguous expressions. Argument of this kind depends, however, on the assumption that the world is really a very simple place, about which it is not difficult to make up one's mind. The basic human experiences, it may be said, do not change, after all: love, hate, guilt, forgiveness. None of these, however, is necessarily simple, nor has historical change made it easier to see the objects of our love, hate, guilt or forgiveness clearly. Hill's poetry is a modern poetry because it takes into itself the dubieties of our own time. *Idylls of the King* acknowledges the instinct to simplify but does not allow that it is possible to go back to Tennyson's relaxed, imperious, imperial commerce with the past. The poem's development is into a complexity entirely characteristic of Hill but also one which is characterized as a complexity of our time: '*warheads* of mushrooms round the filter-pool.' The word points to *our* familiarity with threat, and with an absolute threat, to existence, and its association here with innocent mushrooms returns to the paradoxes of the opening quatrain in a way that deepens their significance, our evanescent sense of nature's real existence brought into line with the sense that it is in our nature to make nature evanesce.

Idylls of the King is characteristic of Hill not merely in its way of identifying ambiguity of experience with an immediate apprehension of the world, but also in its impersonality. The first person pronoun does not figure in it; it is as though we were presented with a registering consciousness somehow detached from purely private concerns. The poem is at once meditation and an invitation to meditate, because in no sense is there a claim to possess the experience of the poem on the part of the poet: the contrast with *The Thought-Fox* is striking, as is the paradox whereby Hughes's poem which deals explicitly with liberation is an affair of bolts and enclosure whilst Hill's, forbidding in the demands it makes on the reader's pitch of attention, nevertheless does open into a free space for thought. 'Possession' is a fundamental term in Hughes's shamanistic poetry, and its equivocal values are never clearly faced by him. Hill is the adept of an art that renders such questions irrelevant.

Impersonality, in fact, is more important to him than the complexity of attitude and style represented in *Idylls of the King*. *Tenebrae* opens with a set of poems called *The Pentecost Castle*, based on the subject-matter and style of Spanish ballads of the sixteenth century and earlier. Their folk purity purges the first person singular of any suggestion of exclusively private concern, and paradox and contradiction appear more nakedly and distressingly than in *Idylls*: 'as he is dying/I shall live/in grief desiring/still to grieve//as he is living/I shall die/sick of forgiving/such honesty'. Although the form and subject-matter are different, the repetitions and intensity of this look back to Eliot's *Ash Wednesday*; neither poet is impoverished by the comparison.

Eliot in fact is the determining modern master for Hill as Lawrence is for Hughes. F. R. Leavis has said that a proper understanding of English literature in the first half of the twentieth century must be based on an understanding of the opposition of these two geniuses.[8] Hughes and Hill demonstrate the continuity of that opposition up to our own day, and at the same time suggest that the balance of achievement did not fall quite so decisively in Lawrence's favour as Leavis thought. Lawrence's personalism provides a much more difficult model for the poet to follow than Eliot's impersonalism, since it tends to magnify any self-division, as it does in the poetry of Hughes. Eliot's cult of impersonality, however it may have reflected a need on his part to escape something in his own personality – not a view to which we have to assent – found expression not in a poetry without feeling but in one where the feeling attached itself primarily to specific topics rather than to a personality whose felt presence was to unify the poem. Hill's poetry is of this kind, and implies a constant invitation to share in the poet's business of understanding and creation.

This is borne out by what I have said of *Idylls of the King*, but the point could be made with reference to almost any other of Hill's poems. It has been said of him that his poetry is never bad poetry:[9] the compliment is excessive, but it is true that from the first book, *For the Unfallen* (1959) to the latest the qualities of intense feeling, thoughtful scrupulosity and packed, ambiguous expression are present with remarkable consistency. Stylistically, *Mercian Hymns* (1971) stands out, Hill's only sequence of prose poems. They bring into relationship the life of Offa, eighth-century king of Mercia, with scenes from a twentieth-century childhood, the focal point being an egoism ambiguously charged for good or evil. In subject-matter, then, they are not far from the concerns of *Idylls of the King*, where past and present meet, or the brilliant sonnet-sequence *Funeral Music*, on the Wars of the Roses, in *King Log* (1968); that deals with the relation between late medieval piety and the brutality of those wars, and is in turn connected with a number of impressive poems throughout the oeuvre which contemplate the Nazi holocaust.

In *Idylls of the King* it is a Christian dove that takes flight, and in *Funeral Music* Christian spirituality is violently juxtaposed to the destructive force of war: ' "In honorem Trinitatis". Crash.' Hill is a religious poet throughout his work, though his encounter with Christianity is baffled and painful, most powerfully conveyed in the sequence *Lachrimae* in *Tenebrae*, in which he addresses Christ:

> I cannot turn aside from what I do,
> you cannot turn away from what I am.
> You do not dwell in me nor I in you
> however much I pander to your name ...

Simplicity of diction does not here remove Hill's fundamental ambiguousness of utterance, and the sonnet-form produces a characteristic effect of stress and intensity. He prefers such forms.

In this, as in other respects, he may be compared with Hughes. Hughes's free forms are of a piece with the belief that all true poems deal with the same story, that of the goddess and her servants. Such poems must wear their individuality in an unmannerly fashion; their 'strange torn edges' distinguish one from another, but always in the same way, and belong to a 'whole body' somehow predicated above and beyond them.[10] Hill's manner of packing his sentences with meaning and of concentrating meaning by use of a tight form makes a 'whole body' of each poem itself, and shows as well as implies that the perplexed ambiguities and symmetries of the experience which sustains his poetry do not cancel out the aspiration to grace and simplicity of utterance as of life that is part of that experience.[11]

Geoffrey Hill and Ted Hughes are both greatly gifted poets, but a comparison of the two suggests that giftedness is not enough to make a poet equal to the circumstances in which he finds himself.

Hughes's indebtedness to Lawrence and the revived importance of myth in twentieth-century thought turns out to entail a weakness that Hill, the follower of Eliot's impersonality, does not exhibit. The fact that Hill's poetry is, however, so much more difficult to grasp than Hughes's suggests something of the cost of writing, indeed one might say of living, at this late stage in the Romantic era. Yet the cost is hardly crippling if, as I believe is the case, Hill's poetry embodies an affirmative truthfulness to match with that of his master, Eliot.

NOTES

1. *Poetry in the Making: An Anthology of Poems and Programmes from 'Listening and Writing'* (London, 1967), 17.

2. Seamus Heaney, *Preoccupations* (London, 1980), 154.

3. *Poetry in the Making*, 21.

4. 'Ted . lughes and *Gaudete*', interview with Ekbert Faas, in Faas, *Ted Hughes: The Unaccommodated Universe* (Santa Barbara, California, 1980), 209.

5. On this and related matters see 'Ted Hughes and *Crow*', interview with Ekbert Faas, in Faas, *Ted Hughes* (1980) 197–208, first published in *The London Magazine* (January 1971), 5–20.

6. Robert Graves, *The White Goddess* (3rd edn, amended and enlarged, London, 1952) 24; 1st edn (1948). Hughes's English master at Mexborough Grammar School gave him a copy of this book.

7. 'Ted Hughes and *Crow*', in Faas, 206.

8. Cf. F. R. Leavis, *English Literature in our Time and the University* (London, 1969).

9. 'There are no bad poems in Hill's three books'; Harold Bloom, *Figures of Capable Imagination* (New York, 1976), 235.

10. Cf. D. H. Lawrence, 'Preface to *Collected Poems* (1928)', in *The Complete Poems of D. H. Lawrence*, eds Vivian de Sola Pinto and Warren Roberts, 2 vols (London, 1964) I, 28.

11. Hill's essay ' "Perplexed Persistence": The Exemplary Failure of T. H. Green', in *Poetry Nation*, 4 (1975), 128–45 is very pertinent to what is said here.

PHILIP LARKIN AND CHARLES TOMLINSON: REALISM AND ART

MICHAEL KIRKHAM

Baudelaire gives us our terms of comparison. He contrasted the 'man of imagination', for whom the 'whole visible universe ... is a sort of pasture which the imagination must digest and transform', with the photographic realist who, thinking to 'represent things as they are', depicts them 'as they would be, supposing that I did not exist: in other words, the universe without man' (*The Salon of 1859*). Philip Larkin sees himself, evidently, as a realist of this kind. Charles Tomlinson's poetry cannot be assigned to either of Baudelaire's categories, but his conception of reality and art is a conscious repudiation of both positions and an attempt to transcend their contrariety.

The premise of all Larkin's poetry is that reality is existence without man: we have no place, and our feelings have no meaning, in it. Time irresistibly separates the poet from the young lady addressed in *Lines on a Young Lady's Photograph Album* (1955) as, in her photographs, she recedes into the past, and it is indifferent to his grief: 'We know *what was*/Won't call on us to justify/Our grief, however hard we yowl across/The gap from eye to page'. We are victims both of 'things as they are' and of our desires yowling across the gap. Only 'suffering is exact' – strict, precise, accurate – and only passive apprehension of our common helplessness tells the exact truth; 'but where/Desire takes charge, readings will grow erratic' (*Deceptions*, 1955). In *Lines on a Young Lady's Photograph Album* photography and art are confronted. Photography, ignoring, as the universe ignores, how we want life to be, records the truth of it with unselective candour:

> But O, photography! as no art is,
> Faithful and disappointing! that records
> Dull days as dull, and hold-it smiles as frauds.

> ... what grace
> Your candour thus confers upon her face!
> How overwhelmingly persuades
> That this is a real girl in a real place,
>
> In every sense empirically true!

The 'grace' surprisingly ascribed to photography – and 'candour', we note, is a kind word for truth – can only be the *pathos* of what it reveals, the pathos of being 'a real girl in a real place' overtaken by time; for Larkin, as for Owen, 'the poetry is in the pity'. The sigh in the apostrophe is sadly and self-mockingly eloquent: art, it tells us, is wishful thinking, necessarily unfulfilled desire. Desire – ridiculed in a clownish mime of impotent lust, 'My swivel eye hungers from pose to pose' – is linked by the word 'hunger' to religion's (and art's) search for unitary meaning described in *Church Going* (1955): 'A serious house on serious earth it is/In whose blent air all our compulsions meet', where consequently 'someone will forever be surprising/A hunger in himself to be more serious'. This has a kind of diffident solemnity, but 'surprising' makes us aware that the hunger for meaning is quixotic and no less incongruous with reality than love's craving for some inaccessible perfection. Photography captures the truth of the moment, miscellaneous and uncoherent; unwittingly it gives the lie to the artifice of art – those 'hold-it smiles' and 'poses'. But poetry, for Larkin, is the desire 'to preserve things I have seen/thought/felt', and as memory's (photography's) images become the past, they themselves, by seeming timeless and unchanging, take on the poignant falsity of art:

> to condense,
>
> In short, a past that no one now can share,
> No matter whose your future; calm and dry,
> It holds you like a heaven, and you lie
> Unvariably lovely there,
> Smaller and clearer as the years go by.

Balancing the lyricism of desire against the punning accusation in 'lie', the dispassionate recognitions in 'calm and dry', and the clash of 'unvariably lovely' with 'smaller and clearer', these lines, that teeter on the edge of sentimentality, avoid it and become instead a diagnosis of sentimentality. It is not enough then to say that Larkin is a realist. His poetry is, rather, the marriage of 'faithful and disappointing' realism with disappointed romanticism.

In Larkin reality is a given, unquestionable fact, excluding man; life is something that happens *to* him. Realism catches the random facts but at the centre of a poem is the poet's emotional response – resignation, disappointment, pain, bitterness, compassion, fellow-feeling – in face of the irremediable. His theme is the disparity between reality and desire. Charles Tomlinson's theme is not self and its emotions but the reality that exceeds but includes man, the reality of nature and of history and man's accommodations with it; poetry, for him, is exploration by the senses and the mind of the world before them. Self is discovered in the 'act of attention' (Lawrence's phrase) to what is not-self; feeling is what accompanies or is awakened by the act. His conception of man's relation to what he perceives, as when he imagines, in *A Prelude* (1963) to *A Peopled Landscape*, a land and 'The agreement of its forms, as if it were/A self one might inhabit', is the poetic counterpart of Cézanne's, who said: 'The landscape thinks itself in me, and I am its consciousness'.[1] It is neither Larkin's passive realism nor the cannibalizing of the natural world practised by Baudelaire's man of imagination. There are subjects and objects and boundaries between them, but the categories of subjectivity and objectivity are inapplicable. The self being conscious and the things it is conscious of make one (fluid) whole. Objects exist and the meeting between self and not-self is a relationship, one of inter-penetration, not a Whitmanesque merging. There is a further boundary, between what the mind can assimilate and those things which, like Cézanne's mountain, are 'irreducible' (*Cézanne at Aix*, 1960) or, like the mountain interior in *The Cavern* (1966), 'elude the mind's/Hollow that would contain' it. They constitute the unknowable but this is not the unthinkable 'emptiness' that, for Larkin, 'lies just under all we do ... So permanent and blank and true' (*Ambulances*, 1964): it is the larger whole that contains man and is still 'the self's unnameable and shaping home'. 'How it happened', the last of *Four Kantian Lyrics* (1963), provides an image of our relationship with that larger whole. It describes the manner in which the distant sound of a churn being grounded

> chimed for the wedding of the mind
> with what one could not see,
> the further fields, the seamless
> spread of space,

and calls it 'a whole/event, a happening, the sound/that brings all space in/for its bound'. The poem ends: 'No absolute of eye can tell/the utmost, but the glance/goes shafted from us like a well'. There is no absolute of knowledge and Tomlinson is no less aware than Larkin of 'evanescences' (*The Way of a World*, 1969) and 'disparities' (between the mind's image of reality and the thing itself), but 'to love' (to marry the world) 'is to see' (to be content with appearances), 'to let be this disparateness/and to live within/the unrestricted boundary between' (*Face and Image*, 1966). Freedom and scope are conditional upon accepting the terms of living. In the world of space objects are 'a given grace' – we are 'challenged and replenished by' them (*A Given Grace*, 1966); in the world of event, if we 'consent to time', 'Time in its fullness, fills us/As it flows' (*In the Fullness of Time*, 1969). Consent does not mean passive surrender: Tomlinson's is a poetry of negotiations (between subject and object) and resistances (subject and object maintaining their separateness). Alternatively we may say, using the title of his first book, that it is a poetry of reciprocal 'relations' (truces, treaties, leases – a vocabulary which, used equally for historical and perceptual phenomena, implies the whole civilizing enterprise of man in the world) and 'contraries' (between inner and outer, the human and the non-human, the possible and the impossible). Larkin 'watches the hail/Of occurrence clobber life out/To a shape no one sees' (*Send No Money*, 1964): man and poet, in Tomlinson, are finders and makers of shapes. Even water and wind, instances of the ungraspable fluidity of existence, have shapes: 'there is a geometry of water' (*Swimming Chenango Lake*, 1969) and there are 'shapes of change'[2] (*The Way of a World*). Not out of place in the world, as the speakers and characters of Larkin's poems are, Tomlinson's swimmer makes 'a where/In water', though it is 'a possession to be relinquished/Willingly at each stroke', in acknowledgement that the images he makes are momentary 'Where a wind is unscaping all images in the flowing obsidian/The going-elsewhere of ripples incessantly shaping'. Larkin writes poems, he says, to preserve things seen, thought and felt, but adds that he has no idea why he should want to do this – a gratuitous, meaningless act. The act, as Tomlinson images it in *The Way of a World*, is at once a flowing with and a countermovement to time. Art is the effort to find (rather than impose) meaning, value, order; its task is to discover in order to celebrate the terms of man's dwelling on earth.

Larkin's description of a train journey south in *The Whitsun Weddings* (1964) has most of the elements of his poetic world. It is characteristic, too, that all converge on a final pathos. At each station he notices the wedding couples; 'fresh couples climbed aboard' and 'A dozen marriages got under way'. Life becomes, in a half-facetiously reclaimed metaphor, a voyage, but one without significant coherence: the sights of Odeon, cooling tower and cricket match go by in random sequence; their destination is something as blankly impersonal as a map of London's postal districts. Comparing the districts to 'squares of wheat', a harvest neatly packaged, the poet, out of charity, conjures the ghost of a possible fulfilment, but withholds the reality in a concluding stanza all along delicately poised between hope and failure. The gathering expectancy as the train approaches London – 'we/Pick up bad habits of expectancy' (*Next, Please*, 1955) – is but a 'frail/Travelling coincidence'; the couples do not even think, as the poet sadly does, of their partnership in a vague, featureless future.

The frequent complement to pathos in Larkin's poetry is horror. Death-in-life is as much his preoccupation as it was Eliot's; exemplified by bedsitter living in 'one hired box', it is the theme of *Mr Bleaney* (1964). Critics who speak with qualified praise of such portraits – lonely, empty lives in rooms that are sad travesties of a home – as the definitive expression of a 'special localized moment: post-war provincial England in all its dreariness' (this is A. Alvarez reviewing *The Whitsun Weddings*) miss the point of these poems and misconceive the nature of poetry. *Mr Bleaney* is no more social realism than are Eliot's *Preludes*: its 'dingy urban images', corresponding to something in the poet, are, as they were for Eliot, who used the phrase in reference to his own work, the language of his feelings and perceptions. They are a language of the 'prison-house' in the same sense as Tomlinson's imagery is a 'language of water, light and air'

(*Marl Pits*, 1974) – a language of release from the 'blocked' views of the same industrial prison.

Poetry, Larkin has said, is emotional in nature, but frequently it is for him, rather, a means of exorcizing emotion. The photographic images 'lacerate', 'strike at [his] control' and photography, he sighs, 'overwhelmingly persuades' us of the reality of what it reveals. The strategies for maintaining control adopted here are a balancing self-mockery and a show of impartial reasoning ('Yes, true; but in the end, surely . . .'); but the aim of several poems is not so much to curb as to belittle or reduce or evade emotion. The jeering note in 'yowl' – 'we yowl across/The gap from eye to page' – becomes a sado-masochistic belittlement of pain in *Wires* (1955): the cattle are taught the lesson of life's limits by electric fences, 'Whose muscle-shredding violence', it is noted with apparent (vindictive or self-castigating) relish, 'gives no quarter'. The voice is too emphatic; life has been cut, and cut down, to a predetermined size. Better poems than *Wires* yet betray a similar bias. In order that, in the confrontation of realist and romantic, the romantic shall be the loser, love has to be portrayed, in *Love Songs in Age* (1964), reductively as a simpleton: 'Still promising to solve, and satisfy,/And set unchangeably in order'. Other poems show the constraining, constricting effect of a guiding voice – pedagogic, admonitory, authoritative – directing our responses, denying the experience room to expand. Many poems are dramatic impersonations, the motive for which is not infrequently evasion. Behind the various poses of *Toads Revisited* (1964), for instance, lies no identifiable feeling or attitude: mock-numbness to the attractions of idle hours spent in the park and mock-revulsion from the blank lives of the out-of-work are complemented by the mock-complacency of the man with his secretary and completed fittingly, but not resolved, by the mockery of death in the macabre Darby and Joan routine of the last couplet: 'Give me your arm, old toad;/Help me down Cemetery Road.'

Life is 'unsatisfactory'. Larkin does not, however, offer it the re-sistance, as his admired Hardy does, of contrary expectations. Perhaps the only unqualified positive emotion he expresses is one that he has remarked in Betjeman, a poet he also admires: 'a yearning for a world, as it were, unburdened by himself'; out of this he has created pastoral worlds blessedly emptied of himself, 'attics cleared of me' (*Absences,*

1955). The park scene in *Spring* (1955) is such a paradise – a child's picture, it seems, of ordinariness, the poet's entry into which is a comic 'indigestible' intrusion. *Here* (1964) is in effect a series of pastorals. The distanced tranquil view of the landscape described in the first stanza and the entrancement of the journey itself, reproduced in the repetitions of 'Swerving east ... swerving through fields ... swerving to solitude', restore the muddle and crowdedness of England to the simplicity of a sparsely settled land; the 'harsh-named halt that shields/Workmen at dawn' recalls in the name a simple barbaric ancestry and in the bare condensed phrasing (by way of Auden) the elemental word-relationships of Anglo-Saxon verse. The last stanza gives us the pastoral of nature, 'unfenced existence ... out of reach'. That 'leaves *unnoticed* thicken' and '*neglected* waters quicken' is the essence of their attraction, defining a place undisturbed by human – specifically Larkin's – restlessness. That there 'removed lives/Loneliness clarifies' is more pastoral wish than fact. But the word itself is reserved, unironically, for Hull and its shops, a 'fishy-smelling/Pastoral of ships up streets, the slave museum,/Tattoo-shops, consulates, grim head-scarfed wives', where 'the cut-price crowd, urban yet *simple*' meet and 'Push through plate glass swing-doors to their desires'. The intimation of contempt for the crowd in 'their desires' is, I think, no more than a miscalculation. If Larkin were asked to define happiness, the disappointed romantic might well answer in Yeats's words that 'we are happy when for everything inside us there is an equivalent something outside us'; the 'pastoral' of the urban shoppers is that in their simplicity their desires are 'matched' (cf. *The Large Cool Store*, 1964) by what the world has to offer. Whether this supposition is naïve or cynical is, of course, a matter of opinion.

Larkin the passive realist, the disappointed romantic, the deviser of strategies for depriving emotion of the power to hurt, is a minor poet; his poetic world of death-in-life, defeat, disenchantment, pathos, rendered exactly and poignantly, is a confined world in which self is a sufferer not a maker. Within or despite these limits, however, he has written several impressive poems. The poised control of *No Road* (1955), for example, is achieved without defensiveness or bias; the voice of reason and the voice of feeling live together in easy assurance:

> Since we agreed to let the road between us
> Fall to disuse,
> And bricked our gates up, planted trees to screen us,
> And turned all time's eroding agents loose,
> Silence, and space, and strangers – our neglect
> Has not had much effect.

The first three lines are a winning blend of the homely, the matter-of-fact and the gravely dignified, and the transitions from them to the slight literary swell of 'all time's eroding agents' and back to the almost bathetic informality of the ending (pointed by the rhyme) – inflation corrected by deflation of emotion – are finely managed. The poised tone owes much to the poet's resolute yet, in its paradoxes, painful confession of at least partial responsibility for the wintry reality he inhabits: time drafts a world 'where no such road will run/From you to me', but

> To watch that world come up like a cold sun,
> Rewarding others, is my liberty.
> Not to prevent it is my will's fulfilment.
> Willing it, my ailment.

Larkin's usual stance of helpless bystander in life has been slightly but decisively modified. This is not reductive realism but truth-telling without reservations. In *Deceptions* the poet is the untransmuted passive observer and fellow-sufferer of the Victorian girl, drugged, raped, and inconsolable, who tells her story in Mayhew's *London Labour and the London Poor*; but the poem is no less impressive than *No Road*. Its achievement is to let empathy subdue moral knowingness to diffidence ('I would not dare/Console you if I could .../For you would hardly care/That you were less deceived') and to imbue language and tone with a compassion that has no taint of self-pity in it:

> The sun's occasional print, the brisk brief
> Worry of wheels along the street outside
> Where bridal London bows the other way,
> And light, unanswerable and tall and wide,
> Forbids the scar to heal, and drives
> Shame out of hiding.

Sound, movement and imagery express the consciousness of someone who awakes to find herself an outcast – not only a social outcast but, like the poet, banished from life. The window stands between her and the sun (as it does in *Here*, 1955) and *The Whitsun Weddings* between the poet and the landscape), making only a faint 'occasional print' in the room of her mind; busy (brisk and worrisome) life, preoccupied with itself, touches her briefly and then, passing on, leaves her to a loneliness made more desolate by the contrast; the pomp of stately, respectable, unSamaritan London is there in the rhythm of that line and in the densely suggestive 'bridal', condensing into a word all that she has lost of sanctioned love, social acceptance, ceremony and beauty. I will not even try to 'translate' the effect of the next line. It perhaps sufficiently indicates the source of its power to say that, while staying within the girl's mind and making us feel the wretchedness of that specific experience in that time and that place, it also provides Larkin's most haunting image of 'the universe without man' and man's estrangement within it. These lines are characteristic of Larkin's writing at its best: by turns compactly suggestive and indefinitely resonant.

Both these poems are from *The Less Deceived* (1955); my list of his best poems would also include *At Grass* and *Here*, *MCMXIV* from the same volume, and the title-poem from *The Whitsun Weddings*. The only poems in his latest collection, *High Windows* (1974), to approach their standard without quite equalling them are *To the Sea*, *How Distant*, and *The Explosion*; this is a bleaker collection than its predecessors. Larkin's outstanding – his richest and most generous – poems, *Ambulances* and *An Arundel Tomb*, both appear in *The Whitsun Weddings* (1964).

Ambulances depicts life, predictably, as shapeless and unmalleable, whether seen in 'children strewn on steps or road' or as a dehumanized commodity on a stretcher 'stowed' into an ambulance; but 'strewn' also suggests the casual bounty of scattered seed, and even in the randomness there is a tenuous coherence, something to be cherished, if only 'the unique random blend/Of families and fashions' ('families' weighed down on either side by its assonantal rhymes 'random' and 'fashions'). Even as the poet presents the 'solving emptiness' of the end as the 'blank' underlying truth of life, his language supplies the love that is lacking:

> Closed like confessionals, they thread
> Loud noons of cities, giving back
> None of the glances they absorb.

What is latent in the comparison – unlike ambulances, confessionals are mediators of love – is made explicit in the last stanza:

> Far
> From the exchange of love to lie
> Unreachable inside a room
> The traffic parts to let go by
> Brings closer what is left to come,
> And dulls to distance all we are.

Love at last has its place in Larkin's world. It is here in the anxious sympathy of those 'glances' and the courtesy of the traffic, and finds its counterpart in the grave tenderness of the verse. *An Arundel Tomb*, a meditation on the voyage through time of two effigies, similarly balances negation and affirmation, in superbly resonant language and verse:

> Snow fell, undated. Light
> Each summer thronged the glass. A bright
> Litter of birdcalls strewed the same
> Bone-riddled ground. And up the paths
> The endless altered people came,
> Washing at their identity.

The single, neutral light (pitiless in *Deceptions*) is at the same time prodigal, varied and eager with life; 'litter' – both waste and natural profusion – repeats the doubleness of 'strewed'; sameness co-exists with difference; the process of change is solemnized in the altered/altared pun. Time here is far more than a resented enemy; the vision of its endlessness is a rapt, awed celebration of its mystery. Indeed, it is Larkin's vision, transformed, stripped of its wistfulness, of a world 'unburdened with himself': life in time viewed as a changeless frieze of everlasting change.

The antithetical but complementary early influences in the formation of Tomlinson's style were the clear line and phrasing of certain

American poems, by Pound, Stevens and Marianne Moore (Williams was added later), and the reasoned structures, civilities and conceptual diction of the eighteenth-century English poets. Occasionally the imitation of Augustan verse is too faithful. The Johnsonian judicious assurance of this sentence from *Northern Spring* (1960) – 'To emulate such confusion/One must impoverish the resources of folly/But to taste it is medicinal' – borrows, along with the civilly superior tone, the implausible assumption of minority attitudes and values shared with the reader. But such lapses are rare.

Tomlinson is also a painter and part of him thinks like a painter, but the point to emphasize is that he thinks – 'it is the mind sees' (*Skullshapes*, 1964). His poetic terrain is, in the first place, sense experience but his aim is not immersion in sensation, not the illusion of the 'thing itself' – not transcription of discoveries made by the eye, or the ear, but reflection upon the world perceived and how one perceives it. Recollecting his artistic beginnings as a poet and painter in the industrial midlands, he writes:

> It was a language of water, light and air
> I sought – to speak myself free of a world
> Whose stoic lethargy seemed the one reply
> To horizons and to streets that blocked them back
> In a monotone fume, a bloom of grey.
>
> (*Marl Pits*)

Art is at once a cleansing of the senses and an alternative to spiritual inertia.

The suitability of *Winter Encounters* (1960), a poem of the late fifties, as an introduction to his work is indicated by its title. 'Encounter' is a keyword in Tomlinson's vocabulary. It bridges opposite kinds of awareness (corresponding, roughly, to the American and Augustan aspects of his poetic personality), awareness of crowded, diverse particularities, on the one hand, and of order and pattern on the other; it describes the way things are connected, as parts of a fluid whole, without forfeiting their separate identities.

> House and hollow; village and valley-side:
>   The ceaseless pairings, the interchange
> In which the properties are constant
>   Resumes its winter starkness. The hedges' barbs

> Are bared. Lengthened shadows
>   Intersecting, the fields seem parcelled smaller
> As if by hedgerow within hedgerow. Meshed
>   Into neighbourhood by such shifting ties,
> The house reposes, squarely upon its acre
>   Yet with softened angles, the responsive stone
> Changeful beneath the changing light:
>   There is a riding-forth, a voyage impending
> In this ruffled air, where all moves
>   Towards encounter.

The achievement of these lines is to convey precisely and vigorously a reality that is at once constant and changing, simple and complex, single and multiple ('*all* moves/Towards *encounter*'). The theme is the nature of reality, but the poem is presenting it as both fact and ideal: this is how perception organizes things, how the world appears to the eye that really sees, but, since clear seeing is rare, we are also invited to recognize in these lines an interpreted paradigm, and to share the poet's experience, of a world ungraspably various and yet made to cohere. Tomlinson's language reflects the polarities of his vision: concrete description blends with abstract analysis; firmness of substance and relationships (a consequence as much of sound and rhythm as of the meaning in, for example, lines 7–11) accompanies a rich sense of movement and diversity; tension is expressed not only in paradox – 'shifting ties' – but also in such precisions as 'ceaseless pairings', which identifies a condition of fluctuant constancy; the balances and echoes in the first line seem to embody complementary opposites.

In the last three lines quoted the poem passes from description to open celebration. The transition is unforced – 'impending' is the same kind of word as 'resumes' – but, if the factual and analytic precision indicates affinities with modern American and Augustan poets, these lines employ a rhetoric of aroused expectancy, affirmative grandeur, that when brought to bear on this subject-matter recalls, if anyone, Wordsworth rather than Johnson. The contrast, in its attitude to expectancy and its positive use of the voyage metaphor, with Larkin's *disappointed* romanticism is exact.

The true size of the theme is to be glimpsed first in such words as 'interchange', 'neighbourhood', 'responsive', which describe human relationships but without violation to the literal sense can be stretched to include relationships seen by the eye. There is no imposing of a metaphorical connection: correspondences are dis-covered that already exist and are reflected in the language. Thus the natural and the human worlds are made one; or, rather, the phenomenal world is inevitably a human world, for eye and mind involuntarily organize what they perceive into shapes and categories. To acknowledge this is to discard the notion of man as a misfit in the universe. The second half of the poem is explicit:

> Inanimate or human,
> The distinction fails in these brisk exchanges –
>   Say, merely, that the roof greets the cloud,
> Or by the wall, sheltering its knot of talkers,
>   Encounter enacts itself in the conversation
> On customary subjects, where the mind
>   May lean at ease, weighing the prospect
> Of another's presence.

The language systematically demonstrates an interchange of qualities between the human and the inanimate and between mind and body. Opposition and agreement constitute the double principle governing what the eye sees, the relation of man to nature, and – a further extension of his theme – the social encounters of man and man in his dual capacity as an individual and the inheritor of a common tradition (the individual strands meet in a 'knot'; the talkers *exchange* views but on '*customary* subjects').

The voyage is 'towards encounter', which brings all together, and that is sufficient reason for the sense of exhilaration in the poem. But the note of celebration responds to something beyond encounter, hinted in that unexpected word 'prospect'. Presence points also to what is undisclosed: in conversation individuals meet without merging, but in doing so a further prospect opens and 'one meets with more/Than the words can witness'. Beyond the known and definable lie future possibilities undefined (the abstract sense of 'prospect') and (in the physical sense) an unbounded, wider, larger view (cf. 'the glance/Goes shafted from us like a well', quoted earlier).

'Encounter enacts itself' in a world observed by an eye alert to diversity and pattern. In *Snow Fences* (1966) it is also a moral stand taken by the human participant confronting winter and death. It defines the heroism of being human. The struggle against wind and cold as you climb the hill to a view of 'the church's dead-white/ limewash' and a graveyard with 'its ill-kept memorials' is an image and an instance – it makes comparable moral and physical demands – of man's struggle against time and nature. The conditions of life are the same here as when the Saxons 'chose/these airy and woodless spaces/ and froze here before they fed/the unsuperseded burial ground'. (The 'long perspectives' of time which in Larkin compose the pathos of life – see *Reference Back* (1964) – are for Tomlinson, as much as his spatial prospects, the means of understanding and coming to terms with it.) 'Fencing the upland against/the drifts' is an activity characteristic of man's determination to hold off the inevitable.

> The bitter darkness drives you
> back valleywards, and again you bend
> joint and tendon to encounter
> the wind's force and leave behind
> the nameless stones, the snow-shrouds
> of a waste season: they are fencing
> the upland against those years, those clouds.

The 'frosts have scaled' the grave stones of their names, as time has erased signs of human occupation, but the verse here, in the last stanza, continues to make its unflinching gesture of resistance to final defeat, denying itself the pathos of discouragement and *Waste Land* elegiacs over the ruins of civilization. The scene is as bleak as any to be found in Tomlinson, yet the poem is an act of human assertion; its effect is invigorating, rallying the forces of will and courage in the reader. The mood is more positive than stoicism, as these lines, in paying tribute to man's opponent, reveal:

> brow and bone
> know already that levelling zero
> as you go, an aching skeleton,
> in the breathtaking rareness of winter air.

Death the leveller strips you to the skeleton but 'breathtaking rareness' means both life-taking and life-giving – the phrase combines the extremes of danger and privilege. Fencing against the devastations of winter and time is not the same as fencing *out* the non-human:

fences maintain separateness (until death drags them down) but do not prevent encounter, and, though the struggle is grim and necessary, even more it is bracing and exhilarating.

The otherness of the outer world is always in Tomlinson's poetry a source of inner nourishment. Even the *Arizona Desert* (1966) flowers to the eye – ironically it is true, but the irony, conceding what it does, nevertheless enforces another point: the eye, animating what it sees, makes us denizens of a country not ours.

> Eye
> drinks the dry orange ground,
> the cowskull
> bound to it by shade:
> sun-warped, the layers
> of flaked and broken bone
> unclench into petals,
> into eyelids of limestone.

'Eye/drinks': the satisfaction of sight, the quenching of a visual thirst, is enacted in the surprise of the synaesthesia and the line-division's protraction and enhancement of that surprise. The weaving of alliteration, assonance, rhyme and especially internal rhyme reflects, as often in Tomlinson's verse, the 'shifting ties' between things and the interpenetration of inner and outer. *Actual* occupation of this arid land, signs of which are noted, merely extends the ironic message:

> Villages
> from mud and stone
> parch back
> to the dust they humanize
> and mean
> marriage, a loving lease
> on sand, sun, rock and
> Hopi
> means peace.

Though in style this is at the opposite extreme, the thought recalls Wordsworth. Tomlinson is not a Romantic but one measure of his achievement is that he has succeeded in reclaiming for the modern sceptical intelligence Wordsworth's theme, man in nature, and in creating a related substitute for Romantic affirmation of the relationship. Wordsworth contends, in his Prospectus to *The Excursion*, that 'Paradise, and groves/Elysian, Fortunate Fields' were not 'a mere fiction':

> For the discerning intellect of Man,
> When wedded to this goodly universe
> In love and holy passion, shall find these
> A simple produce of the common day.

(He also notes 'how exquisitely ... The external World is fitted to the Mind'.) In Tomlinson's variation of the theme, 'peace' is temporal and temporary; 'Hopi/means peace' exactly as extinct villages 'mean/ marriage' – it is a precarious *hope* in ironic tension with the actuality of 'unceasing unspoken war' between growth and decay; therefore it is not the product of holy simplicity but of unremitting labour. Death, as also toil, is conspicuous in, and necessary to, Tomlinson's paradise. The distinctions between the human and the non-human, the possible and the impossible (the second stanza), are sharp; words have sharp edges – there is no Romantic blurring of their semantic outlines. For the poem celebrates not myth but the fact of human resilience, patience, tenacity: the dust is transformed but by human effort not miracle. The verse has nothing of Wordsworth's exaltation – it is hard and spare – but its affirmation, though not absolute, is unqualified.

Tomlinson's poetry avoids the singular personal pronoun: 'Eye [not I] drinks the dry orange ground'. The poems thereby embody Tomlinson's conviction that we live in a composite human–natural world and we have that world in common. Man is extended into the world of objects and at the same time objects are humanized. This is one implication of the larger message conveyed by the suspended present participles in *The Well* (1966). The well is in the grounds of a Mexican convent damaged by the revolution; the participles help to reproduce a single act of attention by the senses and the historic imagination working together, centred on the well, in which sights and sounds of a past turbulence and the peaceful here-and-now are given simultaneous presence. The poem is one long utterance without periods, its stages marked only by the capitalization of the participles.

Listening down
the long, dark
sheath through which the standing
shaft of water
sends its echoings up
Catching, as it stirs
the steady seethings
that mount and mingle
with surrounding sounds
from the neighbouring
barrack-yard: soldiery ...
strollers in khaki
with their girls Aware
of a well-like
cool throughout
the entire, clear
sunlit ruin, ...
Hearing the tide
of insurrection
subside through time
under the still-
painted slogans ...

The mind and its objects form one whole, but its inclusiveness is larger than this suggests. Tomlinson's poetry is full of vistas, prospects, tunnels, shafts, wells, all images for the self's entry into further lengths and breadths of vision; 'the glance/Goes shafted from us like a well', whether to the furthest horizons of space or back through the long perspectives of time. *The Well* is an astonishing representation of that total vision the 'prospect' of which was opened, in *Winter Encounters*, by 'another's presence'. Contraries flow into and mingle with each other: 'here' by the well mingles with 'there' in the barrack-yard; sounds of the present – 'here' and 'there' – blend with echoings from the past; and all is movement which yet, in the continuous present of attention, subsides into the stillness of the normality that time creates, the cool sense of what always is.

One of the strongest reasons, surely, for esteeming Tomlinson's poetry, though critical convention discourages this kind of talk, is the originality, the surprise, of what it shows and says. Content and form are, of course, not separate categories in a poem; it goes without saying that the content exists only as realized in an appropriate style and form. Having paid due tribute to this truism, however, one must insist that to be debarred from *treating* them separately is to devalue poetry as a medium of thought. *Surprise*, which Poe and Eliot after him considered a supremely important element in poetry, is a moderate term for what I mean. Larkin is full of local verbal surprises: Tomlinson's work as a whole surprises – with a new, transformative perception of the world, effecting (what Owen Barfield ascribes exclusively to metaphor) 'a change of consciousness'. It has been noticeable in his poems since *The Necklace* (1955), the volume in which he first created an individual style – characteristically exemplified, indeed, on the first page by the visual reversal in the opening lines of *Venice*:

> Cut into by doors
> The morning assumes night's burden,
> The houses assemble in tight cubes.

Much of Tomlinson's work invalidates the distinction generally drawn, in discussions of it, between poems about sense experience and poems on human themes. The misleadingness of this distinction has been apparent in the preceding examination of poems focused on landscapes and places. It is more startlingly demonstrated by a poem like *Assassin* (1969), in which human actions are in the foreground. The poem is the self-revelation of Mercader, the fanatical assassin of Trotsky, as he mentally re-enacts the murder. The first surprise is the deployment of a morality of right perception, right relations with phenomena, to judge the mental state of a revolutionary idealist acting according to the logic of his beliefs. His sin is the will to exempt himself from time and place, from sounds and sights, and substitute for sensory reality the abstract world of a Marxist future, 'the deed's time, the deed's transfiguration', ruled by a theoretic intelligence. In imagination he had anticipated and steeled himself against the visual horror – 'I had put by/The distractions of the retina' – but not the dimension of sound, the unnerving rasp of papers or 'the animal cry' of the dying Trotsky:

> Fleshed in that sound, objects betray me,
> Objects are my judge: the table and its shadow,
> Desk and chair, the ground a pressure
> Telling me where it is that I stand.

The surprise is doubled in intensity by the device of the dramatic monologue: the poet's judgements are reflected in the reversed mirror-image of the assassin's mind. What is by Tomlinson's standards the restoration of wholeness and proportion is for Mercader a 'fall' into the world of phenomena:

> But the weight of a world unsteadies my feet
> And I fall into the lime and contaminations
> Of contingency; into hands, looks, time.

Observer and interrogator of appearances, judge, advocate, energetic participant, celebrant – all are strenuous parts to play. In a comparison with Larkin these are the aspects of Tomlinson's work that most sharply define their differences. But he has a larger range than this brief sampling of his poetry can suggest. He indeed writes a strenuous poetry – the product of (and cultivating in the reader) sensory alertness, scrupulous intelligence and will – but at the centre of his energy is a still point of 'repose', like that of the house in *Winter Encounters* at the centre of intersecting forces. It informs his style: its civil diction, the plotted relations of its syntax, the reasoning inflections of the poet's voice. A flowing ease, a courtesy and grace of demeanour are, in more recent volumes especially, a noticeable feature. In *Hill Walk* (1974), which commemorates a walk in the Provençal countryside with friends, part of the meaning lies in the civil decorum of the language.

> Innumerable and unnameable, foreign flowers
>   Of a reluctant April climbed the slopes
> Beside us. Among them, rosemary and thyme
>   Assuaged the coldness of the air, their fragrance
> So intense, it seemed as if the thought
>   Of that day's rarity had sharpened sense, as now
> It sharpens memory....
>   In our walk, time used us well that rhymed
> With its own herbs.

The poem celebrates not just the physical experience but the *sharing* of its pleasure with friends and, we are to believe, with time and nature: time that 'used us well', and herbs, that '*assuaged* the coldness of the air', are equally, it seems, considerate companions. The language of relationship is a civil one, as it were persuading nature into a 'reluctant' accord with the human image of it. It is a fragile harmony – the playful conceit of 'rhymed' admits as much – but when they reached the plateau and looked back over an 'unending landscape' long associated with human history, 'Where space has labyrinthed past time',

> Fragility seemed sufficiency that day
>> Where we sat by the abyss, and saw each hill
> Crowned with its habitations and its crumbled stronghold
>> In the scents of inconstant April, in its cold.

Another quality to remark, in a poet who often aims at minute explicitness, is the uninsistence of the analogical life in such words as 'unnameable' (naming is man's humanizing of nature), 'abyss' (calling our attention to the precariousness of man's achievement), 'reluctant' and 'inconstant' (reminders that ultimately nature is not amenable to man's persuasions). Neither the comparatively relaxed style nor the relaxed treatment of metaphor is new in Tomlinson: the latent correspondences were there, as I have noted, two decades earlier in *Winter Encounters*. They perhaps seem new only because in *Hill Walk* the poet's mastery is such that the art has become invisible. Relaxed not lax: the poem is as tightly organized as ever, and carries the same weight of meaning.

NOTES

1. Quoted by John Berger in 'The Sight of a Man', reprinted in *Selected Essays and Articles: The Look of Things* (1972), an essay to which I am indebted for one or two other observations.

2. 'Shapes' is correct. 'Shape of change' in *The Way of a World* and *Selected Poems* is a misprint.

V. S. NAIPAUL AND THE POLITICS
OF FICTION

GĀMINI SALGĀDO

To assert that V. S. Naipaul is among the two or three most important living English novelists is almost a critical commonplace. It is more than twenty years since Anthony Powell spoke of him as 'this country's most talented and promising writer', and since then a chorus of critical praise has endorsed that judgement and saluted the blossoming of promise into achievement in over ten novels and many short stories as well as a number of distinguished works of non-fiction in a variety of modes – autobiography, travel writing, literary criticism, history and political journalism among them. Naipaul has won almost every major literary award in England, beginning with the John Llewellyn Rhys Memorial Prize for his first novel *The Mystic Masseur* (1957), also a Book Society choice. His books are published in most countries where books are published at all, at least three full length critical studies have appeared, the bibliography of essays, articles and theses on him is an oppressively fat volume and he is a major component of the 'Commonwealth Lit.' sections of many university English courses. He was among the eighteen authors chosen to represent the 'Best of British' publicity campaign which recently shook the book world not at all (though characteristically Naipaul was one of the handful of literary figures who refused to appear in the publicity photograph by Lord Snowdon). The assimilation of V. S. Naipaul into the academic and cultural pantheon seems to have been effortless and complete.

It is precisely for this reason, of course, that some effort is necessary to understand the nature and quality of his success. For Naipaul is far more interesting and various a writer than the parade of achievement and accolade I have listed suggests, certainly one whose true scope and importance cannot be straitjacketed within the academic pieties of 'Commonwealth Literature' or the comfortable confines of media exploitation. Indeed, to call him an 'important

314

English writer' is already to beg some of the central questions about his work. If the phrase is looked at closely, each of its three terms invites examination. I intend in this chapter to outline the broad features of such an examination and to support my general view of Naipaul's development and achievement by reference mainly to four novels – *A House for Mr Biswas* (1961), *The Mimic Men* (1967), *In a Free State* (1971) and *Guerrillas* (1975). I have chosen these novels not simply because they illustrate and clarify my argument but because each of them is a fascinating work in its own right. Whatever retrospective pattern a critic sees or thinks he sees in the successive works, Naipaul is the last writer of whom an alert reader can feel that each work is written with a definite and pre-conceived notion of exactly where it is going and how it is going to get there. As Naipaul himself has noted:

> The novelist works towards conclusions of which he is often unaware; and it is better that he should. To analyse and decide before writing would rob the writer of the excitement which supports him during his solitude, and would be the opposite of my method as a novelist.
>
> (Foreword to *The Middle Passage*, 1962, p.5)[1]

Each of these novels is closely related to the others, but each has its freestanding strength as a genuinely independent exploration.

To begin with the most inclusive term, that of 'writer', one may note the faint but unmistakable assertiveness of the last sentence in the biographical note which Naipaul contributed to the Penguin edition of his works:

> V. S. Naipaul was born in Trinidad in 1932. He came to England in 1950 to do a university course and began to write, in London, in 1954. He has followed no other profession.

The bald statement not only seems to mock by implication those many autobiographical 'blurbs' wherein authors recount their brief and colourful careers as lumberjacks, dishwashers and part-time quantity surveyors, but conceals a depth and single-mindedness of intention which goes back at least to Naipaul's adolescence. Landeg White quotes from an essay on Somerset Maugham's *Liza of Lambeth* contributed in 1948 by the young Vidiadhar Naipaul to his school magazine, the Trinidad Queen's Royal College *Chronicle*. 'The faults in this work are obvious,' writes the youthful critic, 'but it is full of promise. Most young writers will take a little comfort from reading it.'[2] The standpoint of the aspiring writer is revealing and characteristic, as is the measured commendation. From the time he became aware of himself and his place in the world about him, Naipaul has never thought of his future except as a writer. 'I never wanted to be anything else' he told me on the only occasion we met. The ambition and its realization define not only the course of his development but provide the themes and raw materials of much of his work. It is inextricably involved with literacy and education, the principal avenues of escape in the mid century from the provincial culture of Trinidad, as they were for another scholarship boy, D. H. Lawrence, from a very different provincial culture at the beginning of the century. (Today, politics, sport and popular entertainment seem to provide other escape routes.) Up to and including *The Mimic Men* every one of Naipaul's heroes is an actual or aspiring writer for whom writing is a central act of self-definition. Even in *Guerrillas*, the narrative makes it clear that the naming of the commune Thrushcross Grange is no mere piece of literary whimsy on the author's part or that of Jimmy Ahmed. It is literature, or the politically reductive distortion of literature which has called that particular institution into being and which leads directly to the violence and outrage perpetrated within it.

In *A House for Mr Biswas* writing and literacy are presented on the whole benignly though without the comic condescension accorded to the poet B. Wordsworth in *Miguel Street* (the first work Naipaul wrote, though the third to be published, in 1959) or to Pundit Ganesh in *The Mystic Masseur*. The danger, when presented with biographical material about a writer, of substituting such material for a firsthand response to what the novelist has created, is especially great when the material relates to a comparatively unfamiliar or 'exotic' background. In the case of *A House for Mr Biswas*, the knowledge that the central figure is derived from Naipaul's father, a journalist and short story writer, and that most of the important events in the novel actually took place is likely to lead the unwary reader into seeing the author as a 'realistic' novelist in the limiting sense. It is therefore important to emphasize the shaping and unifying elements which impose coherence and clarity on such richly diverse biographical 'stuff '.

In an interview published over twenty years ago, Naipaul said:

The writing that has mattered most to me is that of my father, which has never been published. It taught me to look at things which had never been written about before, and seemed dull in life, yet when transferred to paper became very surprising. A great deal of my vision of Trinidad has come straight from my father.[3]

The reader of Seepersad Naipaul's *Gurudeva and Other Indian Tales* (which was in fact published in Trinidad in 1943 and has since been reissued in this country and the United States) will soon realize that Naipaul's acknowledgement of a debt to his father is no mere gesture of filial piety. Naipaul senior's stories, for all their occasional sentimentality and stilted rhetoric, do show an observant eye, a sceptical but sympathetic imagination and a shrewd sense of humour. But what is more important than occasional affinities of style and viewpoint is the example set by the father to the son, the demonstration that the life around them was a possible source of creative writing. In the same interview, Naipaul goes on to say that while other writers of fiction depicted traditional ordered and established societies, his father's work 'showed me that one could write about another kind of society', one that was raw, chaotic, and centreless. Naipaul's father could however, only write of that society under the auspices of a liberal English newspaper editor and, till his son's rise to fame, the father's work reached a small and comparatively indifferent regional public.

For Mr Biswas, the act of writing begins quite literally as that, the writing of signs which leads not only to his first job but, through his marriage, determines the shape of much of his future life:

He thought R and S the most beautiful Roman letters; no letter could express so many moods as R, without losing its beauty; and what could compare with the swing and rhythm of S?

The sensitivity to the physical shape of letters is a portent of the continuous sensitivity to rhythm and idiom which is as much a mark of the novel's hero as of its author. When 'at the end of a long and uncertain week' of idling, Mr Biswas gets his first commission, to paint a sign reading 'Idlers Keep Out By Order' for a local café proprietor, Naipaul presents the scene in dialogue and leaves the reader to see the joke for himself. But we laugh with, not at, Mr Biswas, for he has, untypically and almost unwittingly, cashed in on his difficulties. From one point of view it is his literal gift for writing which draws Mr Biswas into the trap – marriage into the Tulsi *ménage* – from which for the rest of his life he attempts, more or less in vain, to escape. But it is also his only means of evading the relentless grind of laborious poverty which was his father's lot. The limit of possible achievement in this society for the uneducated is marked by the modest dwelling of the yardboy who elopes with Mr Biswas's sister. The irrelevance of traditional literary models to the situation in which he finds himself (already clearly implied in Mr Biswas's first sign) is hilariously presented when Mr Biswas takes a correspondence course from London on How to Write Articles, just as it is reflected in the jolly outings to the seaside in motor cars bearing 'hampers –laden hampers' which feature in Anand's school compositions. Mr Biswas's stories, with their recurrent fantasies of escape from the marriage trap, bear an obvious relevance to the novel's wider theme and link up interestingly with its major structural metaphor, the building of a house. For the house represents not only a recognizable location and identity for the displaced second-generation colonial out of sympathy with his Indian roots and unable to identify with his new surroundings. It also stands for the acceptance of the roles of husband, father and breadwinner which both circumstance and temperament invite Mr Biswas to resist for so long. It is only when that resistance is abandoned that Mr Biswas succeeds in attaining a home which survives him and can become a point of growth for the new generation of Savi and Anand.

Throughout that long, continuously comic and sometimes heroic quest, writing represents the vision of an ampler life as well as the means to its partial fulfilment. It is not only in his 'escape' stories with their permanently alluring barren heroines that his dreams and inner life are revealed, but in the features he contributes to the *Sentinel*, as in his reports on the 'wife and four kiddies' with its reference, inescapable for the reader and perhaps for the hero too, to the family he has temporarily abandoned. Like his creator Mr

Biswas is aware of the incongruity between the situations in which he finds himself and the language available to him for their expression. When Mr Biswas sardonically refers to his wife as 'Mrs Samuel Smiles' he is registering, among other things, his own rejection of the appropriateness to his situation of the poor-boy-makes-good myth he himself had once so strenuously adopted. Just as it was his gift for signwriting which first started him on the road to freedom, so it is his gift for words which enables him finally to achieve that freedom. But it is important that the reader recognizes precisely what kind of freedom it is and what its limits are. It is free-dom in the first place from the humiliating tyranny of the extended Indian family as depicted in the casual and chaotic brutalities of Hanuman House (the 'Monkey House' as Mr Biswas refers to it, with a characteristic awareness of the different associations of 'monkey' and Hanuman, the monkey god). It is freedom too, from the ignorance, superstition, cruelty and downright laziness repre-sented by Pundit Jairam and Hari. It is freedom for the hero to establish himself at last as an independent individual, however pathetically shored up that individualism is with the fragments of modern materialism – Ford Prefect, hatrack, and the like. But finally it is a freedom which recalls Lawrence's lines 'Thank God I am not free, any more than a rooted tree is free'. Mr Biswas finds himself only in finding others, his wife and children, and out of that recognition of responsibilities comes the capacity to love and be loved that reminds us, in the last touching letters to Anand and in Anand's own later Proustian involuntary memories, that the hero's first name – Mohun – means 'beloved'. Mr Biswas himself dies after writing 'hysterical, complaining, despairing' letters to his son, perhaps in the frame of mind in which he looked on his own mother's corpse 'oppressed by a sense of loss: not of present loss, but of something missed in the past'. The house he finally succeeded in getting may have been jerry-built, ugly and debt-ridden, but his lasting memorial is *A House for Mr Biswas*.

For all its appearance of being a substantial work in the tradition of 'the realistic novel' and without being in the least flashily 'experimental', *A House for Mr Biswas* is as artfully constructed as any piece of problem-solving fictional virtuosity. The following authorial comment, which occurs early in the novel when Mr Biswas returns home after being ignominiously ejected from Pundit Jairam's household, is typical:

> He did not see at the time how absurd and touching her behaviour was: welcoming him back to a hut that didn't belong to her, giving him food that wasn't hers. But the memory remained, and nearly thirty years later, when he was a member of a small literary group in Port of Spain, he wrote and read out a simple poem in blank verse about this meeting. The disappointment, his surliness, all the unpleasantness was ignored, and the circumstances improved to allegory: the journey, the welcome, the food, the shelter. (p. 57)

Mr Biswas may 'improve' his experience in writing but there is no doubt in his creator's mind about the ability to order and interpret experience through writing. In *The Mimic Men*, which appeared six years later, both the prospect of escape from the confinements of philistinism, parochialism and superstition of Trinidad society which works such as *The Mystic Masseur* and *Miguel Street* had taken for granted, and the ability of writing to give order to experience and offer a release from it, are subjected to intense imaginative scrutiny. In re-examining these themes, Naipaul makes us more fully aware of what it means to speak of him as an English writer; even the apparently trivial literal sense of the words is not without ambiguities.

The narrator, Ralph Singh, is a failed politician from the West Indian island of 'Isabella' now exiled in suburban London and attempting to write his memoirs. The novel is the result of that effort. The first thing we note is that the London which was the dreamed-of Eldorado of the early Trinidad novels and stories (even Mr Biswas vicariously escapes to it through his son's scholarship) is the drab here and now of the book, seen with that harsh, empty-eyed evocation which so often in Naipaul reminds us of Graham Greene. The narrator speaks of

> the injury inflicted on me by the too solid three-dimensional city in which I could never feel myself as anything but spectral, disintegrating, pointless, fluid. The city made by man but passed out of his control: breakdown the negative reaction, activity the positive: opposite but equal aspects of an accommodation to a sense of place which, like memory, when grown acute, becomes a source of pain. (p. 52)

In *A House for Mr Biswas*, memory was the source of order and solace – 'The mind, while it is sound, is merciful.' Now memory itself needs the shaping imagination and there is no guarantee of clarity or coherence, only the faint possibility of the alleviation of pain. The narrator makes three abortive attempts to cast his narrative in chronological order before abandoning sequence and beginning in the middle, in the London of his student days, with glances backwards and forwards. At the outset he has Gibbonian pretensions of august and authoritative cadences comprehending a magisterial vision:

These are not the political memoirs I saw myself composedly writing in the evening of my days. A more than autobiographical work, the exposition of the malaise of our times pointed and illuminated by personal experience and that knowledge of the possible which can only come from closeness to power. This, though, is scarcely the book to which I can now address myself.
(p. 8)

Both the pretensions and their abandonment make their own comment on the appropriateness of the traditional narrative forms to the new and chaotic material of third world politics and society. The wished-for composure is unattainable and in its place come other and more disturbing imperatives. The 'evening' of a colonial politician's days, if it arrives at all, is often unlikely to be marked by leisured ease – 'The career of the colonial politician is short and ends brutally', as Ralph Singh tersely notes at the very beginning of his account. At any rate both the scope and the purpose of the narrative have narrowed and darkened, as the reader has noted well before the narrator makes the point explicitly a third of the way through the book:

My first instinct was towards the writing of history ... It was an urge that surprised me in the midst of activity ... when with compassion for others there came also an awareness of myself not as an individual but as a performer, in that child's game where every action of the victim is deemed to have been done at the command of his tormentor ... It was the shock of the first historian's vision, a religious moment if you will, humbling, a vision of a disorder that was beyond any one man to control yet which, I felt, if I could pin down, might bring me calm. It is the vision that is with me now. This man, this room, this city; this story, this language, this form. It is a moment that dies, but a moment my ideal narrative would extend.   (p. 81)

But the ideal narrative is no longer possible, though the effort towards it is unremitting. The plural of the title makes the claim for representativeness which the narrator articulates more than once and which rests not only on the narrator's subjective perception of being a performer mechanically rehearsing irrelevant and imported cultural routines, but on the established historical context in which, at this period, third world politicians were not agents but victims, puppets yanked on distant strings.

The Mimic Men is Naipaul's encounter with the reality of England, both in terms of the form of the English novel and the adequacy of the language to embody new and alien experience, and in terms of the vision of England, not from across a wide gap but as the solid-three-dimensional London of post-war politics which saps by its very solidity the individual's sense of himself. The continual false starts and new attempts seem to enact a central political theme, that the colonial politician is bound to destroy the structure which he takes over:

> The commonest type of political ambition is the desire for eviction and succession. But the order to which the colonial politician succeeds is not his order. It is something he is compelled to destroy; destruction comes with his emergence and is a condition of his power.   (p. 36)

Similarly, the politician's gift of success is characterized in terms equally applicable to the novelist's – 'When we are in the middle of success nothing seems so easy or natural; in failure nothing seems so unlikely.' The individuality which Mr Biswas struggled for so indomitably and which in his world was seen as admirable and even heroic now turns out to be fraught with peril and uncertainty. It is difficult – and the difficulty highlights the near-impossibility of separating narrator from author – to say whether the 'gift' described here is the politician's or the writer's:

> But the gift which falls on us is also an intolerable burden. It sets us apart; it distorts us; it separates us from the self we recognize and to which we remain close.   (p. 61)

That self is identified through the narrator's bleak and unfulfilling sexual adventures, with the body's humiliating needs – 'Through poor hideous flesh to have learned about flesh; through flesh to have gone beyond flesh.' It is a moment which recalls a similarly austere insight in that strange and insufficiently appreciated novel *Mr Stone and the Knights Companion* (1963). It must be confessed that the Swiftian disgust sometimes comes over as a spinsterish finickiness, recalling Naipaul's disarmingly frank confession nearly twenty years ago:

I cannot write Sex ... I would be embarrassed even at the moment of writing. My friends would laugh. My mother would be shocked, and with reason.[4]

The narrator of *The Mimic Men* moves beyond his bare and bitter perception, if not to his ideal narrative, at least to an order which if narrow and withdrawn offers its own satisfactions and is specifically related to the art of writing:

It never occurred to me that the writing of this book might have become an end in itself, that the recording of a life might become an extension of that life. It never occurred to me that I would have grown to relish the constriction and order of hotel life, which previously had driven me to despair.   (p. 244)

The relation between writing and living is brought even closer:

This is the gift of minute observation which has come to me with the writing of this book, one order of which I form part, answering the other, which I create. And with this gift has come another, which I least expected: a continuous, quiet enjoyment of the passing of time.   (p. 245)

And so we leave the narrator rejoicing over having constructed something upon which to rejoice, poised for fresh action, 'the action of a free man', reflecting without a trace of irony to cloud his satisfaction on a life that has fallen into the traditional fourfold Aryan pattern of student, householder, man of affairs and recluse.

Both *In A Free State* and *Guerrillas* explore many of the themes found in *The Mimic Men* – the nature and conditions of freedom private and political, the relationship between political activity and sexual activity, revolution as theatre and so on. They also show an increasing preoccupation with the question of the adequacy of the novel form to deal with contemporary political experience. In an interview in 1973 Naipaul suggested that the modern world may need 'another kind of imaginative interpretation'.[5] Since *Guerrillas*,

Naipaul has published one other novel *A Bend in the River* (1979) a powerful account of African politics rightly compared with Conrad's *Heart of Darkness*. But he has continued to produce reportage and travel writing of distinction and one of his latest works *Among the Believers* (1981) is a study of the impact of Islam on contemporary politics. *In A Free State* has a central story which gives the whole book its title and deals with two white people, Bobby and Linda, driving back to the uneasy security of their expatriates' compound through an African state devastated by civil war. Bobby's liberal humanism is gradually exposed by Linda's onslaughts as little more than a cover for his homosexual exploits, while Linda arouses the antipathy provoked by those who are always right. The 'free state' in which they dwell is a precarious and perilous territory.

The central tale is flanked by two shorter ones, both of which are linked to it thematically though not in any other way. 'One of Many' recounts, in the central character's own words, the story of an uneducated Indian who exchanges the comradeship and sense of belonging he had as a servant in Bombay for a similar position in New York in which he is totally lost. He achieves a free state at the cost of becoming anonymous and finally struggles out of it into a half life of community through marriage to a Negro woman. 'Tell Me Who to Kill' tells, in first-person dialect, of a West Indian who attempts unsuccessfully to achieve 'freedom' by vainly spurring his untalented brother towards educational success. The Prologue and Epilogue to the volume present excerpts from Naipaul's travel journals, the first dealing with a tramp hounded in a steamer by a motley group of fellow passengers, the second with Naipaul's indignant reaction to a group of Italians in Luxor throwing morsels of food to urchins outside a restaurant in order to film the Egyptian keeper whipping them when they come to pick up the food. However loose and episodic the structure of the book, the overwhelming impression is not one of diffuseness but of unity and intensity, as well as of an extension in the writer's range.

In *Guerrillas*, Naipaul succeeds in presenting his native Trinidad almost entirely through the eyes of a group of transient whites. The writer who in 1958 said that sex and race were not possible subjects for him and who denounced the device of 'introduc[ing] an English or American character and writ[ing] the story round him' as 'good business but bad art' not only does all three things but manages to combine them into a powerful and original exploration of the motives and pressures behind revolutionary politics and sexual aggression. Perhaps he was aided by the fact that the plot is based on a series of sensational events which took place in Trinidad in 1972 and which he reported on for the *Sunday Times*. *Guerrillas* contains no character of Indian extraction and all the characters are perceived with chilling detachment as they alternate, in public activity and private fantasy, between the impulse to dominate and the desire to be dominated. It is an appalled and appalling vision of a world we recognize as our own, set in the Caribbean but no longer confined to it. *Guerrillas* gives depth and meaning to Naipaul's dismissals of novels about race as 'chronicles of oppression' and his truism that 'the race issue is too complicated to be dealt with at best seller, black-and-white level'.[6]

It also shows an increasing uncertainty about the ability of the detached, highly intelligent and sceptical writer to confront adequately the complexities of modern political reality, whatever gifts of imagination and insight he may bring to that confrontation. With a little exaggeration one could say that in the later novels there is a quasi-masochistic punishing of the writer figure for his pretensions to detachment and understanding. It is noteworthy that whereas in the earlier work, from *The Mystic Masseur* through *Mr Biswas* to *The Mimic Men*, the central figure is a writer and the act of writing itself of great importance, the later novels focus on figures who are either agents or victims rather than observers or commentators. When they are narrators, as in the case of Salim in *A Bend in the River*, the narrative springs from the harshness of experience unmediated by any conscious narrative artifice (on their part, not, of course, on Naipaul's). When, as in *Guerrillas* a writer is prominent, as with Roche, it is not his role as writer which is stressed but his experiences as a political prisoner. Naipaul's remarks on the possibility of the modern world needing a kind of imaginative interpretation different from that provided by the novel is obviously relevant to this diminution of emphasis on the writer as hero.

Thus to call Naipaul an important English novelist is to understand anew each of the terms in the description. 'Englishness', no longer taken for granted, becomes not only a matter of definitions and exclusions, but affects the writer's relation to his medium. (Naipaul plays many variants on his father's linguistic device of using West Indian dialect English for ordinary dialogue and a rather more formal English for Hindi.) To call Naipaul's later works (from, say, *The Mimic Men* onwards) 'novels' is to raise questions about fictional form which are not desiccated into laborious theoretical formulations but excitingly grappled with by an outstandingly original craftsman. And to define his importance is to register a steadily widening awareness of the terrors and tensions, private and political, of a world that is intensely individual yet inescapably public.

Sooner or later in any discussion of V. S. Naipaul the term 'elitist' or its equivalent is bound to rear its elegant head, though the discussion it prompts is as likely to be futile as helpful. In the sense of consciously rejecting the brutal materialism and confined horizons both of the displaced Indian background from which he comes and of the wider Trinidadian society of which it forms a part, Naipaul is undoubtedly elitist. Perhaps he is elitist too in consciously addressing himself to an imagined centre, a metropolis in the Arnoldian sense. Finally there is the strain of Brahmin fastidiousness which may as well be called elitist. Beyond this, the charge of elitism merely serves to give undeserved respectability to vexation with Naipaul for not being crudely 'committed', a charge to which he has already replied both in theory and in the practice of such novels as *In A Free State*, *Guerrillas* and *A Bend in the River* (1979). No writer from the third world can avoid being political in a fairly narrow sense of the term, especially if he is writing in English. His subject matter, however 'domestically' or 'privately' focused, will almost certainly involve direct reference to far-reaching political, social and economic changes. His very choice of language and medium has political implications and his intended audience is likely to be primarily the English and American reader. Naipaul has never shown any reluctance to avoid this confrontation. His distinction lies in the force, subtlety and penetration which he brings to it.

NOTES

1. All page references are to the Penguin edition of the novels.
2. Landeg White, *V. S. Naipaul: A Critical Introduction* (London, 1973).
3. *Sunday Times Magazine* (26 May 1963).
4. Article in *The Times Literary Supplement* (15 August 1958). Reprinted in *The Overcrowded Barracoon* (London, 1972).
5. Interview with Ronald Bryden, *The Listener* (22 March 1973).
6. *The Times Literary Supplement* (15 August 1958). *The Overcrowded Barracoon*, 14.

TWO NIGERIAN WRITERS:
CHINUA ACHEBE AND WOLE SOYINKA

GILBERT PHELPS

The emergence of a strong and independent English literature from black Africa has been one of the most exciting post-war cultural developments. This chapter, however, concentrates on Nigeria, and in particular on Chinua Achebe and Wole Soyinka, the two writers of that country who (by western standards) seem most obviously to be of international stature.

This narrowing of focus has some justification quite apart from considerations of space. Admittedly it involves grievous exclusions, the most obvious of which is that of powerful black South African writers like Peter Abrahams and Ezekiel Mphahlele. But the special features of the situation in South Africa, historical and racial, differentiate their work in several important respects from that of Africans elsewhere. For one thing, the fact that most of them have been cut off from their cultural roots and brought up in an urban environment where English is often their first language has meant that their work has generally been closer in form, language conventions and narrative modes to that of Europe than is the case with writers from tropical Africa.

The concentration on Nigeria, however, also means the omission of such distinguished writers as James Ngugi (Ngugi Wa Thiong'o) of Kenya, Ayi Kwei Armah of Ghana, Okot p'Bitek of Uganda, and others who would demand attention in any comprehensive survey of the subject. On the other hand most of their work postdates the first wave of Nigerian literature in English and in most cases has been considerably influenced by it. In addition, the case of Nigeria pinpoints the common linguistic problem. Of the 1,000 or so different languages and dialects in the African continent no less than 250 of them are to be found in Nigeria, and Nigerian writers quickly realized that if they wished to communicate not only with the English-speaking world at large, but also with considerable numbers of their fellow-countrymen, it would have to be (at any rate for the forseeable future) in English.

It was, moreover, the publication in 1951 of the Nigerian Amos Tutuola's *The Palm Wine Drinkard* that really made the West aware that new literary developments were taking place in Africa. In many respects it was an unfortunate introduction. It was Tutuola's curious English that excited his first English critics – Dylan Thomas, for example, referring to it as 'young English by a West African'. These reactions embarrassed educated Nigerians at the time, both because they realized that such responses missed the real interest of Tutuola's novel, which resides above all in his fluent and imaginative use of Yoruba folk-lore, and because they knew that the 'young' language which Tutuola (whose education had ended shortly after primary school) was using was, quite simply, incorrect English. They were very much aware that the English of the new Nigerian literature could not avoid being coloured by their own cultural backgrounds, any more than could that of India and the West Indies (or, if it comes to that, of Canada and Australia). But they were also conscious of the fact that a more sophisticated and self-aware English usage than Tutuola's was necessary, at any rate *at that stage*, if African literature in English was to assume world stature. *The Palm Wine Drinkard* merely encouraged western emphasis on quaintness, novelty, and exoticism.

Since then, in fact, Nigerian estimates of Tutuola (though he is still the centre of a good deal of critical debate) have changed considerably. To many young Africans he now seems the most truly representative example of contemporary African writing in English, the only completely original African talent, almost totally uninfluenced by the West. Certainly those western critics like Anthony West, who saw *The Palm Wine Drinkard* as 'an unrepeatable happy hit', have been proved wrong. Not only was that novel successfully translated into a number of foreign languages, but Tutuola has gone on, in much the same style, to write (in addition to short stories) five other novels, the most recent of which, *The Witch-Herbalist of the Remote Town* was published in 1981. But Tutuola's work, though full of his exuberant fantasy and a kind of spontaneous surrealism, is perhaps linguistically something of a cul-de-sac. At any rate no one has attempted to imitate his idiosyncratic idiom, and as far as English usage is concerned the central problem facing African writers continues to be that summed up by Chinua Achebe:

> For an African, writing in English is not without its serious set-backs. He often finds himself describing situations and modes of thought which have no direct equivalent in the English way of life. Caught in that situation he can do one of two things. He can try and contain what he wants to say within the limits of conventional English or he can try to push back those limits to accommodate his idea. The first method produces competent, uninspired and rather flat work. The second method will produce something new and valuable to the English language as well as to the material he is trying to put over. *But* it can also get out of hand. It can lead to simply *bad* English being accepted and defended as African or Nigerian. I submit that those who can do the work of extending the frontiers of English so as to accommodate African thought-patterns must do it through their mastery of English and not out of innocence.[1]

There could be no better introduction to Chinua Achebe's own work, for one of his greatest achievements was the creation of a staple prose style which while incorporating African usages and thought patterns is fluent, lucid – and impeccably good English. The achievement is the reverse of innocent. It is, on the contrary, the product of a sophisticated mind thoroughly educated in English language and literature. Achebe's mother-tongue is Ibo, but he began learning English at an early age, and in 1953 he became one of the first students to graduate, in English Literature, from University College, Ibadan. *Things Fall Apart*, his first novel, was published in 1958. The choice of a phrase from W. B. Yeats's poem *The Second Coming* is itself symptomatic. Its aptness is not the result of thumbing through a Dictionary of Quotations (as with the titles of so many modern novels), but is indicative of a profound pondering on Yeats's vision of history as a succession of civilizations, each containing the seeds of its own destruction because no single enclosed social order has so far succeeded in containing the whole range of human impulses and aspirations.

In a limited sense, indeed, the whole provenance of this very African story which is both about a man, Okonkwo, who rises to a high position in his village society of Umofia until a disaster drives him into a seven-year exile during which white missionaries, followed by white colonial administrators, move in, and (even more so) about Umofia itself, was thoroughly English. In fact the hardback publication of *Things Fall Apart* in England at that time in effect excluded a large African readership, for the simple reason that it was too expensive. This situation changed when, after independence in 1960, a cheap paperback edition was published in Nigeria itself – and in 1964 when the old English-orientated School Certificate was in process of being Africanized, it became the first novel by an African writer to be included in the required syllabus for African secondary schools, not only in Nigeria but (excluding South Africa) throughout the English-speaking parts of the African continent. It was realized, that is, that *Things Fall Apart* was in effect the archetypal African novel, in that the situation it describes – the falling apart of a traditional African rural society as a result of the coming of the white man – was a traumatic experience common to all the colonial or former colonial territories.

Later Achebe came to see his function as a novelist in terms more directly related to specific African needs of the moment. In an address to the Conference on Commonwealth Literature held at Leeds University in 1964 he declared:

> I would be quite satisfied if my novels (especially the ones I set in the past) did no more than teach my readers that their past – with all its imperfections – was not one of a long night of savagery from which the first Europeans acting on God's behalf delivered them ... Perhaps what I write is applied art as distinct from pure art. But who cares? Art is important, but so is education of the kind I have in mind.

In truth, though, in *Things Fall Apart* Achebe was not only educating his African readers but his western ones as well – and doing so without any damage to his artistic integrity. One of Achebe's achievements in fact was that he communicated meaningfully both with his western readers who were for the most part ignorant of the material he was handling, and with those who knew it inside out. He is perhaps the only African writer to have bridged the gap with complete success. Doing so, moreover, with quite remarkable delicacy and tact. Take, for instance, the way in which he helps his western reader to understand why his characters rely so much on traditional proverbial usage in their exchanges:

Having spoken plainly so far, Okoye said the next half a dozen sentences in proverbs. Among the Ibo the art of conversation is regarded very highly, and the proverbs are the palm-oil with which words are eaten.

The explanation of the use of proverbs is itself neatly conveyed by means of a proverb. At the same time their occurrence is perfectly balanced between the needs of the western reader, for whom the proverbs are new, and those of the African reader who has always been familiar with them, or others like them. At the same time, there is nothing didactic about their introduction. On the contrary, they are adapted to an artistically functional purpose, establishing for western and African readers alike the sense of an immemorial wisdom underlying and sustaining a stable and cohesive society.

A similar tact and sureness of touch accompany the use of social or anthropological material. For example, in the same scene where the use of proverbs is commented upon, there is this passage:

Unoka went into an inner room and soon returned with a small wooden disc containing a kola nut ...
'I have kola,' he announced when he sat down, and passed the disc over to his guest.
'Thank you. He who brings kola brings life. But I think you ought to break it,' replied Okoye passing back the disc.
'No, it is for you, I think,' and they argued like this for a few moments before Unoka accepted the honour of breaking the kola ...

A whole world of traditional ceremony and courtesy is conjured up there with just that single word 'honour' by way of explanation for the western reader, and there are dozens of similar small scenes, each of them occurring with the same unobtrusive naturalness, in addition to the big set-pieces describing the turning-points of the agricultural cycle, with their elaborate, age-old ritual. All of these combine to create a complete picture of a rich, complex and fundamentally humane society – and one that certainly fulfils Achebe's aim of teaching his African readers that their past 'was not one of a long night of savagery'. It has the same effect, moreover, on his non-African readers. The calm, objective narration succeeds in robbing even those cultural aspects which a western mind might find most difficult to accept – the head-hunting, the exposure of twins, and the killing at the command of the Oracle of the hostage Ikemefuna

– of their power to shock, because they are seen to belong in a whole social and religious context which is essentially the reverse of savage. Achebe, in fact, makes the western reader *understand*, in a way that contrasts ironically with the utter incomprehension of the British District Commissioner in the novel itself. Even with him, however, Achebe preserves his objectivity and coolness of tone, so that the irony of the final passage, after Okonkwo's tragic end, following his return from exile and his clash with the Christians who have desecrated the gods of Umofia, is all the more effective. The District Commissioner's main thought is about the book he is writing:

> The story of this man who had killed a messenger and hanged himself would make interesting reading. One could almost write a whole chapter on him. Perhaps not a whole chapter but a reasonable paragraph, at any rate. There was so much else to include, and one must be firm in cutting out details. He had already chosen the title of the book, after much thought: *The Pacification of the Primitive Tribes of the Lower Niger*[2].

Some western critics have suggested that the African novel (Achebe's work included) is mostly situational, allowing little scope for character development and analysis. It is true that Okonkwo at the end of *Things Fall Apart* is almost exactly the same as he was at the beginning. But that is precisely where his personal tragedy lies. His is a static personality, incapable of bending or changing, but he is far from being a two-dimensional cut-out. He is first and foremost a man of action, and each of the actions in which he is involved throws fresh light on his basic character. The forces that moulded it are, moreover, fully represented – above all his determination to put as great a distance as he can between himself and his lazy, improvident father Unoka, who was utterly lacking in the virile, warlike qualities so highly prized in his society. It is this that lies behind Okonkwo's drive to success, behind his rigid adherence to the rules and traditions, and his desperate concern for their preservation, because for him they are both reassurances that he has indeed succeeded, and barriers against feelings that might throw doubt upon those reassurances. Okonkwo is by no means immune to gentler promptings, as is apparent in his grudging love for his daughter and his gruff affection for the young hostage Ikemefuna, who has been brought up by Okonkwo and regards him as his father. The repression of this side of his nature is evidenced in his sudden rages. Okonkwo, in spite of his genuine achievements and genuine manliness, which have rightly earned him the respect of his fellows, is obsessed by a kind of machismo. This is conveyed in particular, with Achebe's usual economy and concreteness, in the scene of Ikemefuna's slaughter in the forest, following the Oracle's edict:

As the man who had cleared his throat drew up and raised his matchet, Okonkwo looked away. He heard the blow. The pot [which Ikemefuna was carrying] fell and broke in the sand. He heard Ikemefuna cry, 'My father, they have killed me!' as he ran towards him. Dazed with fear, Okonkwo drew his matchet and cut him down. He was afraid of being thought weak.

It must be emphasized, though, that Okonkwo is not a mere puppet, manipulated either by his unconscious personal drives or by the impersonal ones of tradition and custom. He does not *have* to take part in the killing. One of the village elders in fact tells him: 'I want you to have nothing to do with it. He calls you his father.' In other words, there is, both in Okonkwo's character and in his situation, sufficient room for the play of free-will to make him a genuinely tragic figure. In any case Okonkwo is also a representative of the tragic elements in his society. In many respects it is Umofia itself which is the main protagonist, and Okonkwo's defects reflect those of Umofia itself. It, too, is revealed as insufficiently flexible to deal with unexpected crisis, unable to contain certain types of personality. It is not only that it has its *Osu*, or caste of outsiders, but also that it has its gentle, unaggressive characters like Okonkwo's son, Nwoye, for whom there is no real place in Umofia's scale of values, and it is shown that for all such people Christianity (in the spirit if not the letter) inevitably had a powerful appeal. It is no accident on Achebe's part that the crime for which Okonkwo had been exiled earlier is categorized by Umofian tradition as a female one. Not only is it ironically apt for Okonkwo himself, but the implication is that Umofia had not allowed sufficient play for the feminine principle in its way of life.

The actual instrument of Umofia's destruction is the advent of the white man. But with remarkable artistic objectivity Achebe (although in other contexts he has made his abhorrence of colonialism quite clear) does not present the intruder so much as villain as catalyst – or even as the Fates or Furies, in the classical sense. Achebe's triumph in this novel was to have adapted a western literary genre into something that was authentically African in content, mode and pattern, and at the same time to have created a dual tragedy – of a man and of his society – of universal significance.

Achebe's second novel, *No Longer at Ease* (1960) also takes its title from an English poem – T. S. Eliot's *The Journey of the Magi* – and it is again apt in a particularly profound, and bitterly ironic way. In the poem, after their journey to Bethlehem, with its disturbing and enigmatic challenge, the magi return to their homes:

> But no longer at ease here, in the old dispensation,
> With an alien people clutching their gods ...

In Achebe's novel, Obi, grandson of Okonkwo (and son of Nwoye, the convert to Christianity) is no longer at ease either in the old dispensation of tribal society, or in the new one of Lagos in the 1950s. Educated in London he has become Umofia's first graduate and its 'only palm fruit' in the government service. His ideals of probity and justice are soon corrupted, he is arrested for taking bribes and sent to prison. Caught between the old values of Umofia, and the temptations of modern Lagos, Obi's situation, too, is potentially a tragic one. The novel does not quite attain that level. It is a brave failure, however: Achebe was deliberately eliminating the kind of flawed greatness which made Okonkwo a tragic figure in an Aristotelian sense, in order to show that in a modern materialistic urban society there *are* no noble failures, only drab and sordid ones. But Obi's fall takes place too easily to be fully convincing. Nevertheless *No Longer at Ease* is a sombre and compelling work. It is one, moreover, which displays further linguistic resources of the most subtle kind. The flow of Ibo proverbs is still there. Sometimes they reassert the old traditional values. At other times, and especially among the Umofians now living in Lagos, they seem too slick, tainted sometimes by a tone of opportunism and cynicism. There are other linguistic variations. The semi-educated in Lagos use pidgin-English: the university educated use an ultra-correct

English, except when they wish to be matey or patronizing, and all these idioms are intimately related to nuances of character or social striving, and to a sense of values irretrievably lost.

In many ways, though, it is Achebe's third novel, *Arrow of God* (1964) that is the real sequel to *Things Fall Apart*. It, too, is about tribal society and its proverbs, full of pith and humour, again register its richness and reality. But it is now the early 1920s, with the colonial administration and the Christian churches no longer startling intrusions but accepted facts of life. The destruction of the traditional culture is again the main theme, but Achebe is too cunning a writer simply to carry the indictment of the white man a stage further. He is again the catalyst of tragedy, but this time the real causes lie back in the history of the six villages of Umuaro, long before the coming of the white man. These villages had originally united in self-defence against an aggressive neighbour, and (according to custom) had created a new clan god, named Ulu. But the old village gods still maintain their following, and there are ambitious men prepared to take advantage of the fact. Instead, therefore, of the initial unity of purpose that had distinguished Umofia in the earlier novel, there is now an internal political factor at work, and this inevitably throws more emphasis on individual characterization and especially that of the main protagonist, Ezeulu, the old and immensely dignified High Priest of Ulu. In some respects he is not unlike Okonkwo. He has the same stiff, unbending nature, and he is as unswervingly dedicated to the upholding of the old traditions. But the fact that he is from the start surrounded by disruptive elements within his own society throws him in upon himself. Whereas Okonkwo seldom thought before he acted, Ezeulu is more inward and introspective.

The reality and extent of Ezeulu's power as High Priest is the central psychological issue of the novel. As it happens his position is strengthened by factors outside the clan. Some years before he had tried to prevent a war, which he considered unjust, between Umuaro and a neighbouring community, thus earning the approval of Captain Winterbottom, the District Commissioner, who had put a stop to the hostilities. In addition, Ezeulu has sent his son to the mission school, so that he can spy out for him the white man's secrets. His enemies in the clan seize this opportunity to attack him as a friend of the white man and to scoff at Ulu, the god he serves. When, however, Captain Winterbottom peremptorily summons him to Government House, without explanation but in fact to make him Paramount Chief, Ezeulu's sense of his own and the clan's dignity is so outraged that he refuses to go. He is arrested and detained. When he returns he sees himself as the arrow of his god piercing the heart of Umuaro for its disrespect towards Ulu and his Chief Priest. So he refuses to make the ceremonial announcement of the feast of the New Yams, without which the harvest cannot be gathered. The yams rot in the ground, and hunger and suffering follow. When Ezeulu's son collapses and dies during a ritual ceremony, the clan regard it as Ulu's punishment for his High Priest's presumption. Grief and public humiliation unhinge Ezeulu's mind, and he lives his last days 'in the haughty splendour of a demented high priest'. He is at least unaware of the final irony that large numbers of the clan forsake Ulu to join the Christians – whose harvest of yams has been a particularly good one.

Arrow of God displays the same dramatic and linguistic control as *Things Fall Apart*, and its more psychological mode produces just as compelling a tragedy. With *A Man of the People* (1966), however, Achebe returned to the Lagos scene, and to an entirely different approach. Odili Samalu, the narrator of the story, is determined to get even with Chief Nanga, a corrupt politician who has stolen his girl-friend, by competing with him for his parliamentary seat and so destroying his political career. The political chaos that ensues is brought to an end by a military coup. This was probably Achebe's first novel to be addressed primarily to his Nigerian readers, and it contains a number of references to events in Nigeria in the 1960s which can only be fully appreciated by those who had first-hand experience of them. The characters are almost entirely stereotypes designed to illustrate various aspects of the political and social corruption of the times, and there is not a single one of them whose motives are disinterested. But this suits the starkly satirical mode Achebe has adopted, and *A Man of the People* is probably the most powerful of all the African novels that registered the widespread disillusionment following the initial euphoria of independence. It is, once more, the command of linguistic resources that gives the satire its bitterness and bite.

Since the Biafran war Achebe has written a number of poems and

essays and a long short story for children, but *A Man of the People*
was his last novel.

Wole Soyinka is a considerable poet and novelist, but it is as a
dramatist (and frequently a verse dramatist) that he is best known
in the West. He was another of the brilliant group of young writers
at Ibadan University College in the period leading up to independence (in addition to Achebe and himself it included, at different
times, Cyprian Ekwensi, Christopher Okigbo, and John Pepper
Clark, to name a few of the most outstanding). From Ibadan Wole
Soyinka went to Leeds University, where he worked with Professor
Wilson Knight, whose philosophical and metaphysical approaches
to literature he found particularly congenial. He wrote his first plays
while he was in England, and between 1958 and 1960 he read plays
for the Royal Court Theatre in London. Thus he is as thoroughly
steeped in English language and literature as Achebe. Indeed his style,
especially in his early plays, is even more Anglicized. The main
influences behind *The Lion and the Jewel* (1958), for example, both
as regards plot and language, are those of Ben Jonson's *Volpone* and
Restoration comedy. But the flow of comic invention in *The Lion
and the Jewel* is personal and original. Sometimes it resides in the
exchanges, as in this one between the village girl Sidi and the
schoolmaster Lakunle, who prides himself on his modernity (as well
as on his command of English) and for whom the whole concept
of the bride-price is anathema:

LAKUNLE. A savage custom, barbaric, out-dated,
     Rejected, denounced, accursed,
     Excommunicated, archaic, degrading,
     Humiliating, unspeakable, redundant,
     Retrogressive, remarkable, unpalatable.
SIDI.   Is the bag empty? Why did you stop?
LAKUNLE. I own only the Shorter Companion
     Dictionary, but I have ordered
     The Longer One – you wait!

At other times the comedy lies in the combination of language and
situation, as in the boisterous and swift-moving section of the play
in which the lecherous old chief Baroka gives out that he is impotent.
His first wife rushes in to tell the other women and cries:

So we did for you too, did we? We did for you in the end. Oh high and mighty lion, have we really scotched you? A – ya–ya–ya . . . we women undid you in the end!

When, however, Sidi goes into Baroka to laugh at him, he expertly seduces her and so overawes her with his virility that she agrees to become his latest wife, proclaiming: 'It was the secret of God's own draught, A deed for drums and ballads.' But from the point of view of sheer theatre the highlight of the play is a scene in which Sidi and the other village girls, to the accompaniment of drums, dancing, and Yoruba songs, force Lakunle to take part in a mime depicting a recent visit to the village of a photographer in his motor-car. This fast and furious scene is completely African in inspiration, and a reminder that Soyinka is not merely adding local colour to a basically English form, but is also soaked in the ritual traditions of Yoruba drama and masquerade, and after his return to Nigeria he conducted a scholarly research into them. These traditions are rooted in Yoruba mythology, and the part that chiefly underlies Soyinka's theory and practice of drama is the story of Ogun, the hero-god who created out of the primordial chaos a passage between gods and men. As a result, Ogun was persuaded to become king of the ancient African kingdom of Ife; later, however, in a great battle, he slaughtered not only the enemies of Ife but his own followers as well, thus demonstrating that although his was the heroism that had created a world shared by gods and men, he could belong to it only as both Destroyer and Creator. From that time human history must be a never-ending cycle of destruction and creation, in which, although new beginnings can and must be made by heroic action, they are all doomed to ultimate failure. Soyinka has described the Ogun story as 'the first rite of passage', and for him drama represents the 'passage-rites of hero-gods, a projection of man's conflict with forces which challenge his efforts to harmonize with his environment'.[3]

To some extent it can be said that, Ogun-like, Soyinka himself has sought to build a bridge between the philosophy of the West and the Yoruba religion and cosmology, in order to demonstrate the latter's universality. The key play in this development is *A Dance of the Forests* which he was commissioned to write as part of the celebrations of Nigerian independence in 1960. The dance involves human representatives, among them the Council Orator, and Demoke the artist who has carved a great totem pole in honour of the occasion (in the course of it killing a fellow-craftsman); non-human denizens of the forest, including (in addition to a representative of the Ants) a tree-imp and various spirits; purely symbolic creations, like the Half-Child (presumably those human aspirations which struggle perpetually to be born); Forest Head, symbol of Oludumare, the overlord of all the Yoruba deities; Eshuoro, the god of chance and disorder – and Ogun himself, the patron of artists, and therefore of Demoke; and in flashback, members of the court of Matu Kharibu, a famous twelfth-century African ruler – two of whose victims, the Warrior Captain and his wife, have risen from the dead to take part in the celebrations.

At one level the play is a debunking of the nationalistic fervour of the times, with its romanticizing of what the Council Orator (mouthpiece of the kind of platitudes expected on such an occasion) refers to as 'The accumulated heritage ... Mali, Chaki, Songhai, Glory, Empires', whereas the flashback shows Matu Kharibu, one of the most 'glorious' of the emperors, as a blood-thirsty tyrant who kills his servants or sells them to slave-traders, and wages unjust wars. The present is portrayed in no better a light. Various corruptions are exposed, among them the death of scores of people crammed, against the regulations and as the result of bribes, into a ramshackle old bus which catches fire and receives the grim nickname of the Incinerator. The Half-Child laments that once again she will be 'born dead', as in the past. The modern idealists and intellectuals are alike found wanting. What is needed to break the cycle and make independence a positive reality is, it is inferred, heroic action of a kind beyond conventional notions of good and evil. But there is little hope that it will be forthcoming. The Spirit of Darkness foresees that those who expect too much of independence will be misled, and Forest Head declares 'nothing is ever altered'. Only Demoke the artist-murderer and follower of Ogun, can be said to have learned anything – that he must accept his destructive as well as his creative instincts. And only his offering to the celebrations – the totem pole which, soaring upwards, symbolizes the passage which Ogun had once made between the gods and Man – has any real validity.

A Dance of the Forests must have dismayed those officials who had expected something more conventionally appropriate to the occasion. In some of Soyinka's subsequent plays the mythology (never entirely absent) takes precedence over contemporary political comment. For example, *The Road* (1965) contains, as part of the action, an Egungen masquerade – in which the masquerader becomes possessed and apparently undergoes the agonies of Ogun's first heroic journey from heaven to earth – and is throughout closely linked to it.

But in *Kongi's Harvest* (1967) the religious background was more directly related to current African politics. At the time it was taken to be primarily an attack on Nkrumah and his tyrannical rule in Ghana, but it is clear that it was intended to point just as much to the political situation in Nigeria itself. It was the last of Soyinka's plays before the outbreak of the Biafran war. Soyinka supported the Biafran cause and was imprisoned by the Lagos authorities in 1967, spending two years in solitary confinement. Much of his work in the years following his release reflected his experiences. There have been several important plays, including *Madmen and Specialists* (1970), but his greatest creative effort of recent years, perhaps, has gone into his poems, among them the powerful and topical *Ogun Abibimañ* (1976), in which Ogun becomes, in addition to his other functions, the restorer of rights, inspiring an in-gathering of all the African tribes to liberate black South Africa.

In all his work (the fiction as well as the drama and poetry) Soyinka has consistently applied his Yoruba mythology, believing that it provides a truer and more comprehensive vision of reality than anything the West, suffering from the fragmentation that (in Soyinka's view) is the inevitable result of its rationalist and materialist intellectual traditions, can now offer. (His two most important novels are *The Interpreters*, 1965, and *Season of Anomy*, 1973.) It is not always easy perhaps for the western mind to grasp or respond to either the content or the metaphysical implications of the Yoruba religion. Quite apart from the fact that its vision of the inevitable failure of all human ideals and endeavours at permanent regeneration must, to some, seem desperately pessimistic, it sometimes seems bewilderingly remote to western modes of thought and feeling. On the other hand, the plays of Wole Soyinka constitute a rare modern example of a drama which succeeds in embodying religion and ritual, with complete conviction and without strain or artificiality, as it did once in medieval Europe and in ancient Greece. And to *see* a Soyinka play on the stage is to have any misunderstanding of its symbolic or metaphysical content swept aside. For Wole Soyinka is first and foremost a man of the theatre. Merely to read part of the first stage direction in *A Dance of the Forests*, for example, is to feel that tingling of the nerves which can only be experienced in a theatre which is being put to its proper use by someone who thoroughly understands it:

An empty clearing in the forest. Suddenly the soil appears to be breaking and the head of the Dead Woman pushes its way up. Some distance from her, another head begins to appear, that of a man. They both come up slowly. The man is fat and bloated, wears a dated warrior's outfit, now mouldy. The woman is pregnant. They come up, appear to listen. They do not seem to see each other ...

A few general points must be added in view of a narrowing of focus in this essay, which necessarily excludes discussion not only of writers from other parts of Africa but other interesting Nigerian ones like Cyprian Ekwensi, whose *People of the City* (1954) was the first modern realistic novel published in English-speaking West Africa, and the first to depict the chaotic effects of rapid urbanization, and T. M. Aluko, whose *One Man, One Wife* (1959) was another exposure of the contrast between tribal and western values, mainly comic in intention (it includes parodies of Achebe's *Things Fall Apart*) but also containing serious warnings of the dangers of corruption and demagogy. The first of these general points is that all of the new African–English literatures began at approximately the same time, have shared similar styles and approaches, have dealt with much the same basic themes, and gone through much the same phases of development – from initial revulsion against colonialism and passionate reassertion of indigenous cultural values, through disillusionment with the fruits of independence, and thereafter either to a growing sense of alienation, or to silence, or to further explosions of anger and radicalism. One of the main justifications in fact for concentrating on Chinua Achebe and Wole Soyinka (apart, that is, from the literary value of their work) is that between them they illustrate the whole course of the new literatures of English speaking Africa – and, indeed, in many respects those of other parts of the world which have also emerged from the colonial experience.

Another important general point which these two writers illustrate is that the rate of change in Africa has been so rapid and drastic that political issues are present in a more urgent and immediate sense than is the case in the more settled countries of the west. The new African–English literatures, in consequence, have not yet, on the whole, displayed the same degree of interest either in introspection and psychological analysis of character or in elaborate experiments in language and structure, for the obvious reason that they have not seemed of overriding importance. As Nadine Gordimer has said of the situation in South Africa, there are times when even the most naturally apolitical writer *has* to confront politics, because personal relationships are being shaped, restricted and maimed by them. In many respects this is applicable to the former colonial territories of Africa as well, and although the work of Achebe and Soyinka serves to demonstrate that there is no lack of literary and imaginative resources for other kinds of exploration, the political and social issues are likely to exert considerable pressure on African writers in English for some time to come.

NOTES

1. Chinua Achebe, *The Role of the Writer in a New Nation*, in *Nigeria Magazine*, No. 81 (June 1964).

2. As it happens I can throw some light on the novel's genesis: I was working for the BBC Staff Training Department in London when Achebe was attending a course there: Achebe showed me his typescripts, and I was immediately struck by their quality. I advised him to divide his material into several separate novels (at that stage Achebe was contemplating one very long one) and when the first part (*Things Fall Apart*) was finished, I introduced it to his London publisher.

3. Wole Soyinka, *Myth, Literature and the African World* (1976).

CREATIVITY IN CHILDREN'S WRITING
AND CONTEMPORARY CULTURE

DAVID HOLBROOK

One feature of modern life must surely give us grounds for hope: our increased understanding of children. The study of the infant's growth in language and of the older child's creative work with language is not only important educationally but also for the light it can throw on the creativity of adult literature. One of the major insights in this field of study has been into infant fantasy, and the role of this in the development of the personality, of the reality-sense and of a personal culture. In D. W. Winnicott's work and notably in *Playing and Reality* (1971), culture is seen as taking a foremost place in human make-up, and especially in the development of the child as he moves from play to the language of rich cultural life of the adult.

In English teaching the investigation of the nature of the child has contributed enormously to our understanding of the relationship between literature and life. For one thing, the very ability to use language, symbols and culture is seen to represent a tremendous and mysterious achievement by the child, in which achievement his mother and family play a significant part. Moreover, this achievement is natural to the child, because he is the offspring of the *animal symbolicism* (as Ernst Cassirer called us, in *An Essay on Man*). A primary feature of man is his pursuit of meaning through the exercise of a symbolic culture. We have come to recognize man's need for meaning, his *natural* dimensions of culture and morality, and his 'intentionality', that is, his need to be continually groping towards new possibilities – his creativity. This creativity, as Winnicott points out, examining the origins of culture, is exercised towards answering the questions, 'What is it to be human?' and 'What is the point of life?' Children and adolescents respond at once, and gladly, to being given the opportunity to ask those two 'existential' questions, through art. What first needs to be established with them is a certain atmosphere of trust, and a recognition that what are involved here are 'tacit' or 'ineffable' powers of knowing, experiencing and expressing. This may sound like a mystique, but it is rather the recognition of a mystery. Though I can improve my creative work by study, the ability to create 'comes by nature' and is so complex an interaction between self, world and symbol, that it could never be 'explained' or 'controlled'. To develop one's art, one must both practise it 'unconsciously' or tacitly: and at the same time subject it to exacting attention and discrimination.

Culture always has a dual aspect: it unites us to all those who have used this language, or have seen the world in these ways. And it also enables us to be alone with our inner resources. Our fantasy life is exerted continually, as from the baby at the breast, in sustaining and developing a sense of what is real, and a creative interaction with reality (what F. R. Leavis called 'the living principle'). However 'practical' our problems, then, in the modern world, we need to recognize that our effectiveness even in the utilitarian sense depends upon the exercise of fancy and imagination: and, where education is concerned, our effectiveness depends upon the 'childhood of the mind' (a profound phrase from Dickens, in *Hard Times*). Especially does our moral sense depend upon a rich imaginative life, because in this we find the capacity to know what goes on inside others. An imaginative and human experience, as in the good primary school, is often the one redeeming experience in a child's life, in a world which is often physically ugly and inhuman, amid a culture, as on television, film, and in 'pop', which is often barbaric. It is remarkable that what is involved in providing for 'the childhood of the mind' is so widely understood at ground level in the schools. Many good teachers know exactly what they are doing, and have a marvellous confidence, in creative writing, drama and in teaching the other arts.

What is most fascinating about children's writing is the way in which it demonstrates how natural it is for young human beings to use symbolism. It is also natural for them to respond to the adult's expectancy, and to 'give' cultural gifts to her, to the teacher *in loco parentis*. This means, of course, that the teacher will get the kind of poems she likes to have, just as a Freudian analyst gets Freudian dreams and a Jungian analyst, Jungian dreams, but this is something we have to live with. There is a quite uncanny empathy between teacher and children, which D. H. Lawrence was aware of, when he wrote:

> ... sweet it is
> To feel the lad's looks light on me,
> Then back in a swift, bright flutter to work;
> Each one darting away with his
> Discovery, like birds that steal and flee.
>
> (*The Best of School*)

Lawrence also knew the dangers of such a relationship, on bad days!

> I came to the boys with love, dear, and they only
>   turned on me;
> With gentleness came I, with my heart 'twixt my
>   hands like a bowl,
> Like a loving cup, like a grail, but they split it
>   triumphantly,
> And tried to break the vessel, and violate my soul.
>
> (*Discipline*)

The experienced teacher survives, by maintaining order even in informality, and by keeping to that 'third ground', of that culture which has its dual aspect of union and separateness: where real-life problems can be engaged with. So, at the end of a session in a good primary school, it is possible to have thirty pieces of writing, each of which is well enough organized to be fit to be read aloud. It is important to recognize that most will be pleasant, articulate reports on experience:

> *My Baby Brother*
> He runs and plays for most of the day
> With not a care or a worry to display.
> He sits down at lunch and has a good munch
>
> – That's my Baby Brother.
>
> He takes me by the hand and makes me sit down and play
> I tell him I must take my coat off
> But he will not let me go
>
> – That's my Baby Brother.

When my dad comes in at night
Simon should be sleeping tight:
But not for long. He screams for Dad
And Daddy goes up and tells him to go to sleep like a good lad,

– That's my Baby Brother.

(Julia Lane, aged 10)

This is a characteristic, successful, simple small child's poem. One hears in it a 'voice', which has no pretentiousness, but reports with pride and affection on family life. It is perfectly literate, and plays a little with rhymes to raise it above the level of normal speech: the refrain adds a touch of drama, as refrains do in the ballad. The point of such writing could be discussed in the terms used by Peter Abbs in his useful book *Autobiography & Education* (1979): our contemplation of our ordinary experiences, especially in childhood, helps us to see our place in the scheme of things. It pursues, indeed, those two questions about being human, and 'the point of life'. The writing even of such a simple poem, moreover, helps the teacher to understand the child: who, having been amused by such glimpses of family life, could beat or ill-treat a child? How could such a child, having given such a glimpse, become alienated?

Winnicott shows us how culture is both a dynamic of our inner resources – enabling us to be 'alone' in separation; and yet belongs to 'union' – uniting us with all others who share it. So, doesn't a child in finding his own true voice understand better how to respond to each special 'voice' in writers in literature? In our time we have had a long and very valuable discussion of what 'sincerity' means in literary judgement, and because of this certain voices have become highly valued in teaching: Lawrence's own; Edward Thomas's, Huckleberry Finn's, 'Pip's' self-critical voice in *Great Expectations*, 'Nick's' voice in Hemingway's stories about his childhood, the voice of stoical Chinese poetry in translation, Jane Austen's and Emma Woodhouse's, and that of Shakespeare in his *Sonnets*. There are many implications here, about the way literature can assist our sense of 'authenticity'. What is particularly interesting in consequence, is the possibility of 'matching' a child's work with a 'voice' from literature, and this helps the English teacher to see how to help the child's whole development in English. The great problem in creative writing is to judge what it is the child has done – to see the achievement, and to respond. When we perceive in what way a child's poem is both like and unlike a poem in literature, we can appreciate it so much the better. We can also see that the creative writer who comes to be published and recognized is but exercising a common human capacity to use language in the way of art – but does it in an exceptional way.

Thus, when we read a young person's poem (written in an English lesson, like all the poems in this chapter), we may immediately recognize that the child has used a kind of dramatic manner that we have noted elsewhere:

Love?

He looked at me,
A strange, piercing stare.
'Something's wrong.'
'No.'
'Cup of tea?'
'No. Thanks.'
He leaves the room.
When he returns,
A weird, mystical smile
Has removed the grimness
And look of hatred
From his face.
'That's better,'
'What?'
The secrets have removed themselves
From his mind.
The uncertainty has once again
Lodged itself in my brain;
It swirls around with so many others
Like a whirlpool in the blackness.
I wonder.
Once he said he loved me.
Did he mean love,
Or was that just an excuse
To relieve the loneliness of everyday?
I love him,
And that, I'm sure is a fact.

(Girl, age 15)

D. H. Lawrence uses the same 'dialogue' manner in his ironic *Intimates*:

> Don't you care for my love? she said bitterly.
> I handed the mirror, and said:
> Please address these questions to the proper person! . . .

For the adolescent, the poem itself represents a formal way of looking at an incident and a relationship – at that question about what it is to be human – which could very well contribute insight to the next stage in a relationship: as, indeed, Lawrence's wry humour may well have done for him. This effect of literature, of possibly promoting sympathy and understanding between human beings is, I believe, one of the most important things we have learnt from the study of children's writing. One can see how their writing plays a part in their growing up. Where we adult practitioners are concerned, we may not be able to 'shed our sicknesses in books' as Lawrence confidently proclaimed we could. But it is not true to say, as Auden pessimistically declared, that no poem ever saved anyone from the gas chamber. Hatred and antipathy are often a sign of weakness, in the sense that we tend to project the shadows we fear in ourselves over others, and attack it in them. Once we have heard the inner voice of another human being who shares our troubles, we are much less able to reject them: so, poetry-writing by adolescents has an evident value, in promoting sympathy during those difficult years when the growing young adult feels that 'no one understands'. On the verge of adulthood there may come a new realization of the inner life of the adult, with whom the adolescent has earlier come into unconscious conflict, as here:

> ### Father
> He cares more than he cares to show.
> Sharing,
> Grieving, sympathizing in my disappointment.
> Happy, pleased in my joy.
> Pride in my achievement, but caring more when I fail.
>
> Striving all the time to please him, gain his attention,
>   win his praise.
> Ashamed to reveal to him my weaknesses,

Not wanting him to be disappointed in me,
If he is it never shows.

Sometimes needing his comfort, wanting to turn to him.
He's not always there; not just me relying upon him.
Wrapped up in responsibilities of job, wife, other children.
Feeling neglected, wanting his love.

Listens to me achievements. Do I appreciate his?
When I've cried, he's been there,
Helped me when pets have died, friendships died.
His handkerchief to dry my tears –
Does he cry?
Do we answer our fathers' cries for help as they do ours?

(Frances Quirke, age 16)

It seems to me that this poem itself represents a step towards new insights: a deeply sincere appraisal of the father, seen as an equal adult human being, perhaps for the first time.

Such an insight can be purely imaginative: in *English in Australia Now* I quote a poem written by an eleven-year-old for a student teacher of about twenty: it is about the predicament of a mother whose children have all left home. Comparison of the poem with the notes preparing it show that the child quite definitely uses the poetic device of 'movement' to give pauses in which the mother-protagonist is 'listening' – a device which enhances the dramatic power to do what it says:

Now the children have gone.
I walk into their old rooms,
Full of memory now.
Just a moment, I thought
I could hear their happy voices.
But it could never be again
For they have gone, gone for good.

The house feels so lonely,
It seems as if it is calling them back, like I have done,
But they take no notice of what I say.

This poem is strikingly similar, in many ways, to Edward Thomas's

The New House, and this is so because it approaches the two existential questions referred to above in a similar way. It is a human experience we all face, to be in a place contemplating past and future, a new stage. It is of course of enormous value for a child to contemplate the experience of late middle age – valuable both for adults and children. But the play with time in both poems, so that the realized 'felt life' of the moment in the room illuminates past and future, and opens up that question 'What is the point of life?' All those events – cries of children, tormented nights, hopes – which took place in the room, or are going to take place: what do they add up to? The play on memory and time focus on this question.

In a society as difficult as ours, it is just this kind of question that we need to ask. The 'control' by which the question is explored, by which it is kept to the particular living experience, is manifest in the art – which is delicate and exact, in each poem. The economy is as remarkable in the child's as it is in Edward Thomas's. The child who wrote the poem, and others in his class, and the teacher, all gained enormously from the recognition that what the outstanding poet Edward Thomas was doing is also being done superbly by the child, using the common language and natural poetic modes.

One further effect the widespread use of creative writing in schools may have on English teaching is in reducing pretentiousness. Any English teacher is aware of a large gap, between what is implied in syllabuses and examinations, and the actual level of literacy in his pupils. In creative writing we hear the child's true voice, and with luck this may develop in a real way, in this humanities subject, to become an individual way of speaking about the world.

So, a poem which moves us by its genuineness reminds us of the actual level of sensibility and the language capacities of the kind of young person we are dealing with. Incidentally, it may suggest to us the kind of literature which is suitable for such a youth, because it expresses problems of identity of a parallel kind.

To say that there is a certain kind of simple, direct poetry which one can use as a stimulus is not, I hope, to be patronizing, or to suggest that everything must be kept at the level of naïvety or callous inexperience. The most remarkable thing anyone discovers who works in this way with children is that an 'open' expectancy, 'allowing' poems in which they 'write better than they know', often yields remarkable, if perplexing results. This can often be an important, if mysterious experience.

Recently I went to a very good middle school, to work with children who were already well versed in creative writing. It is impossible to prove, but I am sure that it was because I had listened the night before to Mahler's *Kindertotenlieder* that I suddenly saw, in the almost incomprehensible writing of a disturbed child, held for a moment in front of my eyes, the record of deep suffering. Pulling her out of the queue, as it were, I went over her poem with her, helping to 'fix' it on the page in an accessible form. Eventually, it was printed in a class collection. Only afterwards did I hear of the severe family difficulties which lie behind this poem, which has that folk-song-like quality of 'anonymous suffering' that one often comes across in children's poems.

> *The Folk that Wept and Sorrowed*
> For though I think of my beloved one
> How I wonder!
> How I dream of you, Jonathan.
> Tears do I weep
> Children come, say to me
> 'When will Dad come back?'
> 'I don't know, my dears.'
> Dreams that I have
> Horses' deafening cries,
> Cannons banging off everywhere
> People get hit by arrows
> And daily blood comes rushing down hill
> Rivers, streams and all cannons bang loudly.
>
> There I sit with my baby son
> Staring in the fire
> It has been two years
> Jonathan! Come back!
> And those brave men
> But not my beloved Jonathan
> Together we cry with my son
> So do folks in our village.
> Come back! Come back! Jonathan!

> Please let me see you!
> The tears never stop
> The dreams and thoughts of you
> Many a folk have the same feelings.
>
> (Girl, age 10–11)

Igor Stravinsky, discussing the difference between live music performance and recorded music, said that in live performances what we value is, 'in the highest sense, the risk'. The 'risk' goes with the 'other' kind of knowing, noted philosophically by Polanyi, who emphasized that *knowing* requires a *change of whole being*. The only kind of education that matters in a humanities subject is that which changes the whole being. (Peter Abbs quotes Coleridge's idea of 'growledge'.) Creative writing is one way in which this happens: the children sit there, often in attentive silence, and at the end of the hour there are newly-created works of art which speak, each in a different voice, of their unique experience as beings. Whatever the teacher has read to them will be digested and taken into their symbolizing capacities. So, if you have read them Blake or Han Shan, the tone or rhythms or symbolic modes or voice of Blake or Han Shan will appear somewhere in their work. (See *Cold Mountain*, 100 poems by the T'ang poet, ed. Burton Watson. Arthur Waley's translations from the Chinese are ideal for children). How much of the music of this century has been influenced by the mind and sensibility of Nadia Boulanger! In children one can nearly always trace the influence of voices which have excited them.

Then, when children who have written a good deal of creative work turn to Yeats or Rosenberg, they will understand that *Among Schoolchildren* or *Returning we Hear the Larks* once didn't exist – they will realize what kind of struggle took place to set it on the page 'out there', between the poet and the public world. They will understand the element of 'risk' in art – and this will colour all their response to literature, which will be seen as a valuable complex of achievements of the human soul on which we can draw, to understand others, ourselves and 'life'.

The point is not that they, our students, or even a small minority of them, will ever become adult poets. But at least they may join the community of respect for all the arts, and sympathize with the often lonely struggle of the artist. Often, in literary studies, one has to pinch oneself to remember that it is an *art* one is dealing with, that is directed at joy in life and meaning. The point of teaching English is not keen discrimination, or abstract formulae or theory, or even to 'change society': nor is it merely therapeutic. It is to be articulate about humanness. Alas, very little of school is devoted to the Arts, and only a small amount of time is given in many schools to creative English if any. But there is much work done of this kind, and at best it provides a training in thinking about 'the point of life' as much 'religious' education fails to do. There is a kind of seriousness that is common to (say) Li Po, Chaucer, Mahler, the great English folksongs like *O Waly Waly*, Keats, Mozart, Dickens, George Eliot and Lawrence, which has to do with the need to ponder the nature and meaning of human existence. It is a seriousness about being – and about those questions 'What is it to be human?' and 'What is the point of life?' The child writing his own simple poem naturally tends, even writing in fun, to be as serious as this, because he is the *cub symbolicum*, and this gives him a taste of meditative contemplation often sadly lacking from his 'religious education', and from the culture all around outside school.

The 'creative' movement may have been confused by sloppy ideas of self-expression, and by national writing competitions (though the standard in these is often surprisingly high). The amount of creative work done in ordinary British state schools, however, is enormous and marks a genuine advance in the cultural life of the British child, on which literary studies at the higher levels of education ought to be able to build.

The teacher of English may be secure in his awareness of what he is doing, in trying to get his pupils to attempt creative writing. But even while they are still at school, problems arise as they encounter quite a different culture. The novel they are reading in the sixth form may be *The Rainbow*: down the road a novel by the same author appears as an 'X' film with an actress who has been chosen to play Lady Chatterley because of her activity in previous pornographic films. A sixth former may be reading the poems of Sylvia Plath for A-level – and who is to help him evaluate seductive poems which idolize suicide and child murder?

Though many in education probably shrug their shoulders and

cling to the last shreds of educational hope, the truth must surely be recognized that we can no longer even share the assumptions of a writer like George Sampson, who, in his remarkable book *English for the English* (1921), declared that it was the task of a subject like English to educate *against* the needs of industry and the claims of society: children needed to discover their best human qualities, and it might well be that they would discover that these were being thwarted by the civilization they lived in. Sampson was much influenced by Matthew Arnold, for whom the true remedy, for the defects of all classes in the society of his time, was culture: 'a pursuit of our total perfection by means of getting to know, on all the matters which most concern us, the best which has been thought and said in the world'. Culture, declared Arnold, leads us to conceive of human perfection as 'a *harmonious* perfection, developing all sides of our humanity, and as a *general* perfection, developing all parts of our society'. Culture was embodied in and was to be imparted through literature: the whole advance towards making English a humanizing and civilizing force, culminating in the great advances of creative work in the arts in British schools, had behind it the assumption that culture should have a beneficent social effect, which in turn would contribute to the health of democracy.

Obviously, we cannot simply make this kind of assumption any longer. Ours is a time when an elderly literary figure in America, Henry Miller, can declare:

The word 'civilization' to my mind is coupled with death. When I use the word, I see civilization as a crippling, thwarting thing, a stultifying thing. For me it was always so.

This is, says *Chronicles of Culture*, a conservative American journal, the 'philosophy' that guides America's reigning literary establishment:

'Up with art and down with civilization' chant the literati who have boosted to fame such writers as Norman Mailer, Edgar Doctorow and William Styron. In a replay on a now-familiar cultural ritual, America's claimants to literary immortality have grown fat and rich while indulging themselves in *nostalgie de la boue* and disdain for the bourgeoisie.

As M. B. Kinch writes, in the novel

a combination of technical facility and fashionable cynicism or brutality or sexual explicitness (often all three) seems to constitute a reliable formula for the achievement by a late twentieth-century novelist of critical as well as commercial success.[1]

The most fashionable novels of our times often represent a complete rejection of the English tradition – they 'admire the brutally selfish, and anti-social man' and even 'a militant philistinism'. Q. D. Leavis, speaking of 'moral stupidity' in her Cheltenham Lecture, 'The Englishness of the English Novel', quotes Samuel Johnson, 'want of tenderness is want of parts, and no less a proof of stupidity than depravity'.

But, as both these writers make clear, the new brutalities and developments of nihilism in contemporary works are fully endorsed by a vigorous criticism. So, for the educationist who continues to believe in the refining power of literature, there is a dilemma – which is part of the whole problem of culture discussed by Saul Bellow in *Mr Sammler's Planet* (1969) – 'who has made shit a sacrament?' If one feels (as I do) that Ted Hughes' *Crow* poems represent a destructive act of vandalism inflicted on language, poetry and the sensibility, one is aware that there are a number of solemn critical books and essays endorsing it as if it were comparable to the *Book of Job*. University professors commend literary pornographers: university examination boards set nihilistic poetry which requires recourse to insights into psychopathology for anyone to begin to understand it and to defend themselves against its persuasions.

This explains, I hope, why I turn from the positive dynamics to be found in every child, learning to exercise his or her power to symbolize in a creative way, to ask what happens to each young person's literary interests as they grow into adulthood. Here, as any teacher of literature knows, one meets with embarrassment – students becoming enthusiastic for literary figures whose postures and works fill one with dismay and even anger: what can one say? Of course, there are benign figures – a Geoffrey Hill here, a Charles Tomlinson, a Dannie Abse there.

In teaching one sometimes has to grasp the nettle. One most baffling example is the poetry of Sylvia Plath. The problem arises continually in discussions of her poetry, that a work which is entrancingly beautiful, like the poem *Edge*, may also offer the conclusion that it can be a kind of 'perfection' to kill oneself and to kill one's children: that suicide and infanticide are inevitable and proper 'tragic' 'necessities', given the author's attitude to existence. *Edge* seems a peaceful poem: but examined closely it has a vengeful undercurrent, and the end conceals a ferocious hostility (to the mother). When one knows Sylvia Plath's work through and through, and has penetrated her inner topography, the confusions, hate and madness become frighteningly apparent. Other poems by this same poet, like *Medusa, Daddy* and *The Applicant*, flip over into an energy which offers no redemptive or benign power. The same is true of many poems by Sylvia Plath's widower, Ted Hughes, and here the problem takes on a profound significance, because Hughes is also a sensitive and delicate poet. His poem about his little daughter Frieda, *Full Moon and Little Frieda* is full of symbolism of the child's fragile web of expectancy, her vibrating sense that she will find meaning in the night, and in the universe. Like the farmyard pail of water in which the image of a star is reflected, her soul is the

mirror
To tempt a first star to a tremor ...

And when she cries out at the moon, naming it, she gives a humanizing meaning to the universe:

'Moon!' you cry suddenly, 'Moon! Moon!'
The moon has stepped back like an
artist amazed at his work
That points to him amazed.

In this lovely poem, the child seems a product of the creative power of the universe itself – a manifestation of love. It seems impossible that the same poet could have produced the sequence of 'hate' poems, *Crow*, in which every value is trampled on, and in which the excitement is that of giving oneself up to nihilism: to a feeling that the brutal indifference of the (Newtonian, matter-in-motion) universe can never be overcome, that all values and meanings are tricks, while 'mere survival' is but a painful endurance. And perhaps even worse – worse than the coarse reduction of a great tragic myth to a coarse ballad in *Song for a Phallus* in *Crow* – is the galloping assault by Hughes on creativity itself, as in the poem *Gog* in *Wodwo*. In this, even

The atoms of saints' brains are
swollen with the vast
bubble of nothing ...

– that is, even the most visionary products of human consciousness
are no more than the epiphenomena of an atomistic universe,
operating by blind chance, with no sense or purpose. In response
to this terrible sense of the randomness, indifference and meaninglessness of the universe, the poem *Gog* gives itself up to a fantasy of
bloody mental rage, assaulting and denouncing woman, the womb,
new life, 'being' and meaning: everything, indeed, that poetry, as
the central discipline of literary engagement with meaning, ought
to cherish is relinquished in favour of mental rage. The hero of the
poem, the 'horseman of iron' tramples raucously over these tender
growing points. Must one conclude that much of Hughes' recent
popularity as a poet has been due to this indulgence in an abandonment to hate? With it has gone the coarsening of language and feeling
to a degree that spoils the atmosphere for poetry in general. Characteristic are lines like these:

> Once upon a time there was a girl
> She tried to give her breasts
> They were cut from her and canned
> She tried to give her cunt
> It was produced in open court
>   she was sentenced

Words like 'stabbed', 'flogged', 'blood' and the sexual expletives
colour the pages of Hughes' later work, and the reader retires exhausted – or giggles. Without recourse to a Johnsonian critical indignation, it is surely permissible to wonder how again it will ever be
possible to respond to 'Cupid and my Campaspe played/At cards for
kisses' innocently again, or even to Marvell's *To His Coy Mistress*,
without a spoiled cynicism in the reader's response? It seems to me
it has now become a central problem, to foster the capacity for tenderness in response to literature.

The word 'tenderness', not least because it is now such an embarrassing word to use, gives us a clue to a solution to our problem.
It was Ian D. Suttie who used the phrase 'the taboo on tenderness'
in *The Origins of Love and Hate* (1935), an important critique of

Freudian psychology. The human problem is not that of being a creature struggling with his 'instinctual urges' (as Freud thought) but of being afraid of our needs, not least the need to love and to be loved. Later theorists in psychoanalysis, like Harry Guntrip, have found the fundamental human problem to be that of our fear of inner emptiness, of weakness of the identity, and a fear of the meaninglessness of our existence: the schizoid problem.[2]

If one studies carefully the 'black' poetry of Sylvia Plath and Ted Hughes, what one discovers, buried deep down in the identity, is an unborn baby. In Plath's *Poem for a Birthday* it is 'Fido Littlesoul', 'Mumblepaws' a 'mouth hole' crying under the stones of the city. This symbol is illuminated by the dreams, which Guntrip reports in *Schizoid Phenomena* (1968), of schizoid patients who dream of the unborn self they cherish in the depths of the identity, as a little puppy which they will one day bring to life. In the strange phenomenology of Sylvia Plath's poetry, her delusion was that this unborn baby-self (which, disturbingly enough is a *boy*) could be brought into new life by the act of suicide, an ultimate regression. When she displays machismo, as in *Lady Lazarus* or *Daddy*, the hate disguises the anguish of feeling unborn at the heart of being: it is a raucous posture which denies a primary need. The reason is that the unborn self, source of existential hope as it is ('here's a cuddly mother'), is hated because it threatens to undermine the whole identity.

In Ted Hughes, the unborn self, the 'regressed libidinal ego', as Fairbairn calls it, appears as *Littleblood* and in *Gog* the machismo is turned fiercely against it. The black fascistic horseman, whose horse is shoed with vaginas of iron (an expression of contempt for feminine weakness), turns his lance against the womb, the foetus in the womb – against creativity and, ultimately, meaning.[3] The seductiveness of this kind of machismo lies in the way it hides the whole problem of the perplexity of being human, and the responsibility to being human. The mental rage, and the abandonment to hate, is a posture that hides existential weakness. Instead of the 'taboo on tenderness' we might speak of the 'taboo on being' (Saul Bellow speaks of 'a longing for non-being').

This is the truth of the schizoid problem that lies behind many problems of today's culture.

The clues to the logic of schizoid moral inversion is given in complex detail by W. R. D. Fairbairn, in *Psychoanalytical Studies of the Personality* (1952), in a chapter on 'Schizoid Factors in the Personality'. The schizoid individual already distrusts love, because it has failed him: he has never had the love due to him, so he feels unreflected, and psychically unborn. Because love is so dangerous to him in consequence he decides that he must try to live by hate: he suffers a taboo on weakness and opts for 'strength'. Hate is not the opposite of love, which is indifference: hate is the attempt to compel the other to give what is due, and represents a reversal of all those qualities which belong to love.

When we encounter demonstrations of a 'black' strength, righteous truculence and moral inversion in politics or culture today, we are seeing the expression of a pathological form of 'masculine protest' on these lines which can easily turn into sadism and destructiveness, and represents a failure to achieve the capacity to be fully human. So the seductive nihilism in contemporary culture is a barrier to the discovery of full humanness – which is the first step towards trying to find a meaning in life. If we examine Dickens's concern for the pursuit of authenticity in Pip, for the pursuit of goodness and the ideal in David Copperfield, for the possibility of redemption of Jo in *Bleak House*, or even with the human decency of a Pickwick, we shall find Dickens evidently inspired by the New Testament, deeply aware of Shakespeare's work, and even aware of the long quest for truth, since the original *telos* of Greek civilization.

What is seriously lacking in modern literature – indeed, in modern art in general – is this passionate conviction of the truth about man, and the compassion that one must feel for each man's (and woman's) life-quest for a meaningful existence. What Dickens shares with his readers, a love of good qualities, of striving, in man, is today all too seldom to be found.

What is found too often in contemporary literature is contempt for man, and its concomitant, that 'contempt for the audience which is the death of art', as James Baldwin, the black American author, has put it. Instead, what the audience is too often invited to enjoy is the humiliation of man, and especially of woman, Emmanuelle replacing Little Emily as if this were a liberation.

I believe Dickens belongs to that urge, which is that of a whole tradition of our civilization, of humanity struggling to understand itself, in existential terms, in the pursuit of truth. But we have become, as Edmund Husserl puts it, 'in the greatest danger of drowning in the sceptical deluge and thereby losing our hold on our own truth'. This sentence is from his *The Crisis of European Sciences* (1970), in which he seeks to draw our attention once more to that stream of thought which originated in Ancient Greece, and which was directed at probing both the inward or subjective truth as well as the outward or 'objective'. Talking to philosophers, Husserl sees them obliged to take on a task: 'our inner personal vocation bears within itself at the same time the responsibility for the true being of mankind ...' I want to employ Husserl's emphasis to insist that the artist is obliged, too, by the civilization to which he belongs, to be a 'functionary of mankind'. He is concerned to ask what can be believed and he is concerned with man's being and becoming. Art is (or was) a matter of passionate commitment to this 'socially and generatively united civilization,' to the means, ends and values implicit in Greek thought and its inheritance, and the tradition which followed. Dickens's greatness was that he belonged (whether he knew it or not) to that tradition.

That the arts are obliged by their historical role to take on these responsibilities is made even more evident by the findings of the subjective disciplines themselves, which are today confirming the truths towards which art used to strive. Psychoanalysis, in its post-Freudian development, has gradually ceased to see culture as mere sublimated instinct, and now sees it rather as a primary activity. In the theory of Winnicott a person cannot begin to be human until he develops the capacity to symbolize, in order to work on those existentialist questions which are the preoccupation of culture.[4] In post-Kantian philosophy, Ernest Cassirer and Susanne Langer find man to be the *animal symbolicum*, so that symbolism is a primary human need.[5] Existential philosophy, not least in its influence in psychotherapy, places the need for meaning to the forefront of man's needs, as in the work of Rollo May, Viktor Frankl and Abraham Maslow. Philosophical biology finds man to be an animal with an extra cultural dimension, closely related to his need for freedom.[6] From all these disciplines, which I will include under the heading 'philosophical anthropology', we see that one of man's primary needs is for symbolism, for culture, as a means towards truth about 'being', and towards 'becoming': that is, towards the release of new potentialities, in response to the life-tasks which the world may or may not offer us.

The primacy of cultural need is clear in the creative work of children and young people. Given the opportunity to employ the disciplines of creativity, they gladly use them to try to make sense of their lives at the deepest level. I think here of a girl of fourteen whose mother had died, all of whose writing was related, phenomenologically, to her problem of bereavement.[7] I also think of a poem like the following, revealing a personal voice, in relation to a reconsideration of experience:

FAÇADES

In my dreams, I dream of open spaces,
Where I run unfettered, in a world without restrictions
Where life is just a cake, segmented,
And simply choose my desire.

But when I return to reality, all I see is order,
Sometimes I think I am a square peg in the round
Hole of existence, without identity or individuality,
A misfit.

Here in my room is where I find my solace,
Here, surrounded by my possessions,
Pieces of me.

My life is like a flower, now in youth
But soon to blossom,
And for what?
Just to wither and die and be forgotten?

People, when they see me in the street or in the town
They don't know me,
They just think they know me.
If only they knew that this was just the superficial me.

When I'm dead
That's when they will really know me,
When they see my possessions, the photographs, the pressed flowers
And the diary.

They will say – 'So that's what she was really like, well I never!'
But then it will be too late.

(Catherine Lancaster, age 16)

In all my experience as an English teacher, I have found that where
human beings are offered an opportunity to exercise their powers
to use creative symbolism they energetically make use of it, to explore
inner experience, and to establish order and beauty there. In *English
for the Rejected* I hope I showed that even the least able children did
just this: and I believe I was able to show how 'outward' effectiveness depends upon the achievement of inner harmony and order,
by creative effort.

If the relationship between culture and personal existence is as
crucial as I have been trying to suggest, then there is a good case
for the disciplines of the humanities, in education. But there is also
an implicit assumption, surely, that this concern should continually
consider the degree to which the arts are devoted to human truth
and the realization of human potentialities. I do not say, it should
be noted, that one should expect the arts to contribute to a 'healthy
psyche' or to 'right living'. But what I do say is that the arts ought
to offer nourishment for that kind of need which is emphasized in
existentialist psychotherapy, especially what is called *Daseinsanalysis*,
under the influence of Martin Heidegger.[8] In his concept of 'being
unto death' every human being is preoccupied with finding some
way in which he can feel the *Dasein*, literally, the sense of 'being
there', of *having meaningfully existed* in the face of death and nothing-
ness. What we all need to feel is that we have at some time, or perhaps
at many times, in many ways, established some meaning in life which
death cannot take away from us. That I believe is as much as Gustav
Mahler ever achieved, in his Ninth Symphony and *Das Lied Von
der Erde*, in his quest for meaning without God.

Whether one takes the vision of a child's poem, of Mahler's 9th
and 10th Symphonies, or Dickens's novels about Pip or David
Copperfield, of Jane Austen's depiction of the anguish between
Elizabeth and Darcy, or Coleridge's struggle with depression in the
Dejection Ode – what these embody is a kind of art which has a deeply
serious value in human experience – how much less life would be
without them! *Pickwick Papers* surely shows this view to be equally

PART THREE

applicable to comedy. The note in that benign book changes darkly
when we enter the Fleet, and thereafter Sam Weller's loyalty becomes
a radiant human capacity, in the midst of the perspectives of what
man can do to a man, and of the dreadful fate which overtakes so
many. (By the way, surely Dickens must have encouraged many
to practise benignity and benevolence, as a way to find a sense of
meaning in existence, just as Jane Austen and George Eliot must have
illuminated for thousands the value of love.)

But what happens if we apply these criteria I have offered to
much of today's art? Too much of it reminds me of a maddening
undergraduate who used to tell me 'what we need is more meaninglessness'. I have asked for attention to human truth, to human potentialities, to the creation of meaning, that can be upheld against death,
and by implication to deep questions of morality – man being recognized as one whose humanness lies in his capacity *to be moral*, to concern himself with right choices. Only an art embodying these
concerns can satisfy that hunger for symbolic meaning which modern
philosophical anthropology has found to be fundamental to our
nature, whether as adults or children.

NOTES

1. M. B. Lynch, Q. D. Leavis, An Appreciation (Nottingham, 1982), 11.
2. H. Guntrip, *Schizoid Phenomena, Object-relations, and the Self* (London,
1968); also R. D. Laing, *The Divided Self* (London, 1960), and R. May, *Love
and Will* (New York, 1969).
3. See my detailed analysis in *Lost Bearings in English Poetry* (London 1977).
4. See D. W. Winnicott, *Playing and Reality* (London, 1971), chapter 7,
'The Location of Cultural Experience'.
5. See E. Cassirer, *An Essay on Man* (Yale, 1944); and *Philosophy in the
New Key* (Harvard, 1942).
6. See M. Grene, *Approaches to a Philosophical Biology* (New York, 1968).
7. See 'June' in my *English for the Rejected* (London, 1964).
8. See *Existence – a New Dimension in Psychiatry*, ed. R. May *et al.* (New
York, 1958).

LITERATURE FOR CHILDREN:
A RADICAL GENRE

BERNARD T. HARRISON

Here is a long passage – what an enormous perspective I made of it! – leading from Peggotty's kitchen to the front door. A dark storeroom opens out of it, and that is a place to be run past at night, for I don't know what may be among those tubs and jars and old tea-chests, when there is nobody in there with a dimly burning light, letting a mouldy air out of the door, in which there is the smell of soap, pickles, pepper, candles and coffee, all at one whiff!
(Charles Dickens, *David Copperfield*, 1850)

Some of the best treatments in literature of entry into children's experience and visions of living are, we know, to be found in books that were written not for children but for adults – or usually, rather, for 'readers of all ages'. David Copperfield's acuteness of touch and smell, as he looks into the 'blank of my infancy' and recalls his earliest impressions of home; the quality of Jane Eyre's resistance against older oppressors; Seriozha's insistent efforts in *Anna Karenina* to make sense of the confusion caused by his mother's absence; the brief, yet extremely distinct portrayal of Mamillius' strange precocity in *The Winter's Tale*; Stephen Daedalus' recollecting of first memories in *The Portrait of an Artist as a Young Man*; Henry James' fresh resilient Maisie, who thrives against the odds, among adult deceit and selfishness; Paul Morel's emergent awareness of the battle-lines drawn between his mother and father; Maggie Tulliver's intense experiences of childhood joys and pain: these and many other examples come quickly to mind, as classic examples of the portrayal of states of childhood. And while these works may not have been addressed to children, their art is characterized by a respect for the child's existence, and for what Dickens termed in *Hard Times* as 'the dreams of child-hood – its airy fables; its graceful, humane, impossible adornments of the world beyond'. Furthermore, the art of these writers, and the quality of their concern for children has had a powerful influence on the best among the many writers who have written exclusively, or especially for children, in the nineteenth and twentieth centuries. There are now, it is agreed, a considerable number of high quality books in the genre. Children's literature – in particular, children's fiction – has 'come of age' in our times, as a distinct branch of literature's great tree. Should we acknowledge its maturity by appraising its products, then, on essentially the same terms as other literary works?

Children represent such a special kind of reading public, and children's books such a special kind of literature, that several unusual questions raise themselves for criticism. A main one is: what can an adult critic of children's books possibly have to say to a child reader? Debate over the uses of critics has come not least from the authors themselves. John Rowe Townsend, a prolific writer and critic of children's fiction, has sought to enhance the status of the genre, in proclaiming the morally educative qualities of good children's fiction. As a writer, and in a spirit of some resistance to the differing viewpoints of 'psychologists, sociologists and educationists', he has emphasized that children's literature should, like all literature, offer enjoyment. But enjoyment of the best is, he claims, no easy pleasure; it ought to involve a stretching of imagination, a deepening of experience, and a heightening of awareness. He quotes with approval the view of Edgar Friedenberg, that the writer's task lies in 'the respectful and affectionate nurturing of the young, and the cultivation in them of a disciplined and informed mind and heart'.[1] By way of contrast Joan Aiken, while acknowledging the educative moral powers of a well-told tale, has dwelled on the iconoclastic, liberating, subversive qualities that a good children's book and a healthy child-reader should have in common: 'They can see through the adult with some moral axe to grind almost before he opens his mouth – the smaller the child, the sharper the instinct.'[2] Joan Aiken, who acknowledges Blake, Dickens and Charlotte Brontë among the main influences on her own ample production of fiction-writing for children, provides us here with a useful clue to an appropriate critical approach with children's books, which we might link with a view of innocence as being in itself a mode of insight.

In our criticism it would be foolish to ignore the good sense behind Townsend's remarks on the quality of enjoyment which apply to children's literature as to all literature; but for a touchstone, we might follow that first instinct which Joan Aiken identifies in children, to discern the honest from dishonest, plain from pretentious, delightful from depressing, kind from callous, amusing from dull, free from captive. We may then aim towards fine, but not needlessly sophisticated standards of discrimination. For as parents or relatives, and as teachers who are involved in the choosing and presenting of books for children, we shall clearly need some standards. Even as critics we write, eventually, on behalf of children. Thus, as with all our relations with children – direct or indirect – our criticism should never be stuffy, insincere or dull. Yet it ought essentially to be serious, it ought to offer a watchful attention, lest fun and celebration lapse into mere triviality, and thence to disrespect and contempt for the genre – and even for its readers.

In short, there are issues of taste to be discussed in children's literature, but they will be somewhat different from those in adult literature. Naïvety for instance, far from being condemned as a vulgarity, is to be acknowledged as a 'mode of insight'. Of course, there are different qualities of naïvety, of innocence to be discerned, as children are themselves capable of recognizing.

The state of innocence waits to be educated; but if innocence is to become a true 'mode of insight' and is not to be effaced by adult know-how, it will keep alive its connections with the earliest memories and events of childhood. It is hard to imagine a better way of promoting such insight, than by introducing the children to the best – especially the best – among the genre. In offering to make such choice our own qualities of imaginative depth and range, sense of humour, empathy for childhood and quickness of intuitive judgement, must be fully active, if we should wish to be reunited with Maggie Tulliver's 'triple world of reality, books and waking dreams'.

Our modern concept of childhood is built largely on the intelligent, anti-determinist concern for children that has long been enshrined in folk-lore, and which was highly developed by Blake, Dickens, Charlotte Brontë and others. One book in particular, *Jane Eyre*, has had a very special influence on the development of children's literature, particularly perhaps through women writers and through girl characters in their books. For in *Jane Eyre* the late eighteenth/early nineteenth-century version of the perfectly innocent 'romantic' child is transcended, through this first full study of an 'all-round' child. Jane reveals the typical 'romantic' virtues (of innocence, vulnerability, patience, and transparent truthfulness, honest laughter and grief), but is also capable of anger, stubbornness, pride and tantrums (in a good cause) as well as possessing other conventionally inadmissible properties such as beautiful long hair. Above all, Jane has courage and good sense – radical virtues which are incorporated directly into T. H. White's young heroine in *Mistress Masham's Repose* (1947), into Joan Aiken's robust heroines, and into those of many other modern writers.

These virtues and other qualities of ordinary, inner and outer normality are also to be found in what is virtually the earliest classic (i.e. still widely read) text written especially for children, Lewis Carroll's *Alice's Adventures in Wonderland* (1865). This claim would seem to ignore such pioneers in children's writing as Maria Edgeworth, the Lambs and Catherine Sinclair, whose *Holiday House* (1839) offered enough enjoyment – included as a deliberate antidote to mere 'improvement' – to be published until 1939. Less fairly still, it overlooks Charles Kingsley's influential *The Water Babies* (1856); but these works have now fallen beyond their readership as living texts, into literary history. As for linking *Alice* with *Jane Eyre*, the two books are indisputably quite unlike in many essentials. Each is a highly individual, original work in its own direction, and each asks to be read with quite different kinds of attention; but the clue to their extraordinarily strong common influence is given, perhaps, in a tribute paid to Carroll by Harvey Dalton in 1932, who saw a Copernican force in the celebration of childhood that the *Alice* books provide:

> The directness of such a work was a revolution in its sphere. It was the coming to the surface, powerfully and permanently, for the first unapologetic, undocumented appearance in print for readers who rarely needed it, of liberty of thought in children's books. Henceforth fear had gone, and with it shy disgust.[3]

Play, fantasy and enjoyment came now to be plainly justified in themselves, in children's literature. Yet Jane Eyre had to fight for the liberty of thought that Alice could take for granted. When Jane proclaims the truth of her Aunt Reed's hypocrisy ('*you* are deceitful!'), it is 'as if an invisible bond had burst, and that I had struggled for an unhoped for liberty'; yet she acknowledges too the 'dreariness of my hated and hating position', now that she has tasted the 'warm and racy' poison of vengeance. Jane's story proclaims the identity of a girl-child as a full human being, capable of independent choices and acts, and deserving of the same respect that is due to human beings of any age or status. *Jane Eyre* represents perfectly the best kind of infusion from adult literature into the genre; while *Alice* might be seen as the outstanding (and still very much living) work among nineteenth-century books written especially for children.

Towards the end of the nineteenth century children's books became established as a distinct market for writers, and many of the different classes within the genre could now be discerned – boys' adventures (Marryat, Kingsley, Stevenson); school tales (Hughes' *Tom Brown's Schooldays*, 1857; T. R. Reed's *The Fifth Form at St Dominic's*, 1887; Kipling's *Stalky and Co.*, 1899); animal stories (Anna Sewell's *Black Beauty*, 1877; Kipling's *Jungle Books*, 1894, 1895); fairy tales (Charlotte Yonge, E. A. Knatchbull-Hugessen); and fantasies (Lewis Carroll, Frances Hodgson-Burnett). A talent such as Richard Jefferies (especially *Wood Magic*, 1881, and *Bevis*, 1882) cannot be easily classified, although his contribution has been notable, especially in the quality of his depiction of landscape and spirit of place.

Many of the nineteenth-century writers were still active during the so-called Edwardian 'Golden Age' of children's writing, and were joined by several more talents – notably Edith Nesbit (whose *The Railway Children*, 1906, remains a firm classic), Kenneth Grahame (*The Wind in the Willows*, 1908), J. M. Barrie (*Peter Pan and Wendy*, 1911) and Beatrix Potter, whose quite original tales and illustrations over a publishing span of more than thirty years from the first *Tale of Peter Rabbit* (1902) provided an initial art experience and enjoyment for the very youngest readers and lookers at books.

John Buchan (1875–1940) carried, but cannot be said to have developed, the late Victorian–Edwardian boys' adventure patterns, throughout a publishing career of over forty years; there was never to be as good a tale of its kind again as Stevenson's masterpiece *Treasure Island* (1883). After the Edwardian era, the interesting advances were made, rather, in tales for the young (A. A. Milne, Alison Uttley, Eleanor Farjeon and most notably, perhaps, John

Masefield's *The Midnight Folk*, 1927 and *The Box of Delights*, 1935).
New kinds of adventure stories emerged, which involved both girls
and boys, usually on holiday in the hills or by the coast, and usually
with adults included only on the fringes of action. This kind of story
owes a good deal to E. Nesbit's achievement in *The Railway Children*;
but foremost among writers of children's holiday adventure stories
is Arthur Ransome. Notable among many good books by him are
Swallows and Amazons (1930), *Winter Holiday* (1933), *Pigeon Post*
(1936), *The Big Six* (1940) and *Great Northern?* (1947); while his best
book, *We Didn't Mean to go to Sea* (1937) is one of the outstanding
works of children's fiction. In this tale especially there are Conrad-
like layers of interest and metaphoric suggestion which deserve the
attention of readers of any age. Ransome's tales have substance and
subtlety; yet he succeeds too in ensuring that his stories never become
too complicated for the young readers to whom they are addressed.
His work achieves the specifications that were demanded of the
children's writer by one of his best contemporaries, Geoffrey Trease:

> It must be a genuine book at all levels. When he is choosing his theme
> and doing his research his standards can be as adult, indeed as academic, as
> he likes. When he is writing then he must let the child in himself dictate
> much of the form. He should be a children's writer because he still retains
> inside himself, perhaps more vividly than the average adult, the vestigial child
> he once was ...[4]

It might be added merely, that there are different qualities of child,
as there are different qualities of adult. Only Geoffrey Trease himself
bears comparison with the quality of Ransome's achievement in the
thirties and early forties; yet Ransome has also remained an unusually
successful writer in terms of actual sales figures – a heartening fact,
when the extraordinary mass success of Enid Blyton's abysmal
holiday-adventure stories are recalled. She too writes with a kind
of child's view of the world – but that view is too often acquisitive,
snobbish, sentimental or bullying. The popularity of this kind of story
has indeed attracted some of the worst as well as some of the best
kinds of children's writing. But then, why should children be
expected to be any less vulnerable than their elders in opting for pulp
fiction?

Since the end of the Second World War there has been a further abundance of children's fiction, produced by a very wide range of writers. Inevitably, much of this new fiction has been written in mere imitation of previously tried and successful formulas, and deserves no special attention in terms of its intrinsic qualities. Such fiction has helped often at best to fill that endemic gap between comics and classics which so many teachers report among their young readers. It may be claimed, at least, that like comics they encourage a reading habit which might then spread to the many books of better quality that have emerged among all the established, as well as some important new varieties of children's books. Notable among the updated store of school stories are Kathleen Peyton's *Pennington's Seventeenth Summer* (1970), William Mayne's *No More School* (1970) and Jan Mark's comically iconoclastic view of schools in *Hairs on the Palm of my Hand* (1981). Successful variations of the traditional adventure story have been developed by such writers as Richard Church (*The Cave*, 1950), Brigid Chard (*The Shepherd's Crook*, 1977) and Leon Garfield's robust, if sensational neo-Dickensian tales (*Smith*, 1967, *Black Jack*, 1968). Among historical tales, Rosemary Sutcliff's work has been notable (*The Hound of Ulster*, 1963, *Warrior Scarlet* 1958); while Barbara Leone Picard (*Ransom for a Knight*, 1956), Penelope Lively (*The Ghost of Thomas Kempe*, 1973; *A Stitch in Time*, 1976) and Clive King (*Stig of the Dump*, 1968) have each made their individual impact on this popular variety of story. Output of animal stories has also continued to be prolific, with horses, dogs and foxes as clear favourites (Peyton's *Fly-by-Night*, 1968; Church's *Dog Toby*, 1953; Ellis Dillon's *A Family of Foxes*, 1977). Animal stories have taken more unusual directions in such works as Richard Adams' neo-Darwinian fantasy of survival struggles among rabbits in *Watership Down* (1972); or Jan Needle's *Wild Wood* (1981), which transposes *The Wind in the Willows* into an amusing socialist satire aimed at the idle-rich Edwardian bank-dwellers; or the strange, disturbing tale of clockwork toys in Russell Hoban's *The Mouse and his Child* (1969). These books have attracted justifiably a good deal of attention from adults, as well as from children.

The two most important developments since 1950 are the rise of the 'teenage' novel, and the exceptional growth of works of fantasy (including science fiction, which might now be seen as a variety in its own right). Books for teenage readers have introduced such

themes as politics, social problems, parent–child and sexual relationships, which have been traditionally excluded from children's fiction.
Understandably, the quality of writing and sense of audience have
been less certain in this field, than in the better established areas for
younger readers (some examples of fiction for older teenage 'reluctant' readers have been truly dismal in terms of sensitivity and
taste). But among many successful ventures have been Kathleen
Peyton's *Flambards* series (1969–81) about the fortunes of a family
over several decades; adventures in social realism by Nina Bawden
(*Carrie's War*, 1973); Joan Lingard's *Across the Barricades* (1972), and
Robert Westall's *The Machine Gunners* (1975). As will be seen in
the discussion of Alan Garner's work below, there has also been an
important twin development of books for teenagers with the growth
of interest in fantasy.

Fantasy is, of course, root and stem of much of children's fiction.
In Carroll's *Alice* the many opportunities to enjoy fantasist escape
are presented in clear tension with the actual experiences and constraints of a child's real world. In short the fantasizing spirit is never
given complete licence to evade confrontation with real events.
Carroll recognized, as did Coleridge, that without such a disciplining
tension there is a danger that fantasy might feed parasitically on the
store of the imagination, weakening its capacity to give shape to
actual experience. In children's books, works of fantasy since 1950
proliferated to such a degree that they prompted scrutiny – not to
say alarm – from writers, critics and teachers. C. S. Lewis's *Narnia*
books (1950–56) and J. R. Tolkien's three volume *Lord of the Rings*
(1955) are among the best known of these; they are widely read by
children, and have achieved almost cult status among many adults.
Yet it is arguable that both of these writers are thorough-going
fantasists, in the terms that Coleridge feared: each betrays a need to
control, to manipulate their would-be myths and legends to a degree
which can make a reading of their work a most dissatisfying experience, for an adult reader – although both adult and child in me
can at least enjoy Tolkien's *The Hobbit* (1937) and the delightful short
story 'Leaf by Niggle' (1939). The limitations of fantasy are explored
in C. N. Manlove's illuminating critique *Modern Fantasy* (1975),
which includes a study of Lewis and Tolkien. Manlove reveals
how such works typically lack the 'inner consistency of reality'.

Tolkien, Lewis and others use fantasy to wall off any actual experience that proves to be inconvenient to their vision, with the result that

> they are often lacking in the unconscious creative imagination, and their's work without the inscrutable depth – and, incidentally, any potentially mythic power – that comes from the loss of self experience and art alike.

Many names and titles would deserve inclusion in a full account of developments in children's fantasy writing since 1950; but in order to offer some closer appraisal of these, and of books for teenagers, it is best to select just two writers who might reasonably be taken as representative of the field. In fact without undue disregard of such other talents as Ursula Le Guin, William Mayne, Joan Aiken, or others mentioned above, two names emerge from among a good field – Philippa Pearce and Alan Garner.

Philippa Pearce writes mainly for younger children, say, up to twelve years. Compared with story-makers like William Mayne or Russell Hoban the output of Philippa Pearce has been modest, if consistent; reflecting on her composing of *A Dog So Small* (1962), she declared of her own writing that

> from the very beginning – perhaps even before you think of writing a story at all – the story must grow. The idea of a story is a seed, and it grows with the slowness of natural growth.[5]

Her best known book is a work of fantasy which draws deeply on traditional modes of children's writing, yet is also strikingly original in its telling – *Tom's Midnight Garden* (1958). The book dwells in the ideal inner world of a young boy; its magic garden theme echoes other kinds of past classics, in particular Frances Hodgson-Burnett's *The Secret Garden* (1911). Unlike the haughty, sour-seeming Mary of *The Secret Garden* ('People never like me and I never like people'), Philippa Pearce's Tom weeps in the very first sentence of the book, though in would-be manly spirit ('If, standing alone on the back doorstep, Tom allowed himself to weep tears, they were tears of anger'). But like Mary, Tom creates the garden out of his extreme loneliness – in his case, while exiled from his family and beloved brother Peter (who has measles). He has been sent to stay in the 'oblong, plain, grave' house of Aunt Gwen, with her heavy, over-rich cooking that keeps Tom sleepless until he hears the clock strike thirteen, and he finds his way by moonlight as bright as daylight through the door into the secret garden. In entering the garden, Tom enters several different dimensions. For one thing, he is invisible when in the garden – except to Hatty, the youngest daughter of the great house to which the secret garden belongs; for another, he is taken back to late Victorian times and to different phases of Hatty's child-hood – Hatty, who is now old Mrs Bartholomew living alone upstairs in his aunt's vast house, and who had 'conceived' Tom as her own imaginary childhood companion.

The excellences of this subtle (yet very accessible) book are many; but one brief passage might serve to convey a flavour of Philippa Pearce's fine blending of fantasy and 'commonsense' experience. In chapter six, Tom realizes that he is not only invisible, but he can also put his hand through 'solid' objects. When he decides to venture his whole body through a door, Tom speculates on the comically embarrassing consequences that might occur – especially the possible upset that the gardener might suffer, to see a 'very thin slice of a boy, from shoulder to foot, coming through a perfectly solid wooden door'. And more than that, there is the prospect of unknown dis-comforts as the moment arrives for his head to go through:

'I'm just resting a minute,' said Tom's head, on the garden side of the door; yet he knew that he was really delaying because he was nervous. His stomach, for instance, had felt most uncomfortable as it passed through the door; what would the experience be like for his head – his eyes, his ears?

On the other hand – and the new idea was even worse than the old – supposing that, like a locomotive engine losing steam-pressure, he lost his present force of body and will-power in this delay? Then, he would be unable to move either forwards or backwards. He would be caught here by the neck, perhaps for ever. And just supposing someone came along, on the far side of the wall, who by evil chance *could* see him – supposing a whole company came: they would see an entirely defenceless stern sticking out – an invitation to ridicule and attack.

Such a prospect prompts Tom into a 'convulsive effort' to drag himself through the door, where he emerges 'dazed, but whole'. Compared to Alice's perfunctory entry through the looking-glass ('in another moment Alice was through the glass . . .') the acuteness of Tom's perfectly natural, understandable anxieties are fully exploited and resolved, in an enjoyably comic context; and that, we recall, is a familiar achievement of Lewis Carroll's elsewhere in the *Alice* adventures.

Philippa Pearce's gift of conveying a landscape, an object, a presence with sharp yet economic firmness of detail is a strength in all her books. It is there, for instance in 'Guess' (in *The Shadow Cage*, 1977) a very different kind of fantasy of the supernatural, where the ghostly Jess Oakes moves disconcertingly between two identities, first as an unkempt, smelly schoolgirl and eventually as a tree-spirit. Within a few pages, Philippa Pearce conveys memorably an outlandish sense of place and of character in this tale. And as with *Tom's Midnight Garden*, these stories manage to keep one foot firmly on the ground of familiar, commonsense living.

Despite her modest overall output, Philippa Pearce has had success in several different areas of children's fiction. Her first book *Minnow on the Say* (1955), for instance, is a treasure-hunt which echoes the work of Jefferies and Ransome, as well as revealing her own already distinctive gift for rendering the particulars of a scene. *The Children of the House* (1968, written from a manuscript by Brian Fairfax-Lucy) reveals further her capacity to inherit influences such as Lucy Boston (*The Children of Green Knowe*, 1954) as well as her co-author, and to extend them. She has also written 'animal' stories of merit, including *A Dog So Small* (1962) and *The Battle of Bubble and Squeak* (1978).

In contrast to Philippa Pearce, Alan Garner is noted as a 'difficult' writer. His books have been mainly in lists for teenage readers, although he himself has denied that he writes with any particular age-group in mind. Furthermore, despite his considerable standing as a children's writer, he is, in some essential respects, singular rather than representative. More than any other 'children's' writer he has received the kinds of very mixed responses of high praise, bewilderment and downright hostility that are usually reserved for exceptionally innovative artists. He has also revealed himself as one of the most attentive, intelligent thinkers about the craft of fiction in our times. He has declared that his main aim has been to write in his *own* language – not 'modern standard English', the language of Education:

I have not expressed myself in a direct and concrete way in order to write for a child – I have used this language, which is concrete and direct ... So it's a very relaxed and un–teacher-like way of talking. I want to get back the richness and freshness of a language which was beaten out of me by teachers so that I could get on in the rest of the world.[6]

The teacher and the writer have inevitably different aims, claims Garner: the teacher's is to conserve the received language, while the writer's essential task is to change it, through inserting his own experience into it. Leaving aside emergent protests at the too-menial role assigned to teachers here, it is clear from his own works of fiction that Garner has made extreme demands on himself as a writer, to meet his own high claim that the writer should change the language. And with Garner, this concern with language cannot be separated from his attention to the quality of the fantasy on which so much of his work is based.

Garner established an early success with *The Weirdstone of Brisingamen* (1960) and *The Moon of Gomrath* (1963) as a skilful interweaver of legend, dream and myth elements with ordinary, everyday events and characters. While these early fantasies proved popular, Garner has himself deplored his own disposition to work according to a recipe-formula in these early tales: he was writing not for himself but 'for children, and the result was the usual condescending pap'. Having decided to write for himself, he discovered that happily he was still writing for children too.

Elidor (1965) and *The Owl Service* (1967) benefit from this change of attention, in that the children-protagonists become involved in events which demand more genuine kinds of moral choices and action than is required in the usual parent-free 'goodies versus baddies' fantasy.

Elidor offers as a living nightmare the processes of slum-clearance in the desert areas of Manchester, while its citizens blankly watch their television screens. There is little wonder that the children are drawn into the imaginary, highly dangerous world of Elidor; though once they are in this, there is a tendency for the book to revert to the fantasy formula of earlier works. *Elidor* might be seen in fact as a kind of halfway house between his development from scholarly, self-indulgent researching into strands of myth and legend, to a more genuine artistic-moral contemplation of story patterns.[7]

In *The Owl Service* (1967) Garner's struggle to achieve living mythic power is successful; and judging from its popularity with eleven-to fourteen-year-old readers, he has managed to retain good accessibility with his young audience. The appeal of the tale is very direct, for all its tense delays of action and its symbolic loadings. The possessive loves and conflicts among the adults Huw, Nancy and Bertram, and among the teenagers Gwyn, Alison and Roger are magnified strangely through the tragedy of murderous demands made among the legendary characters Lleu, Blodeuwedd and Gronw. As in *Red Shift* (1973), adolescent extremities of feeling are conveyed with disturbing sharpness: this points to a power in Garner's writing whose fact the adult reader is tempted to resist, perhaps, as any discomforting truth is at first resisted. *Red Shift*, indeed, presents an even stronger challenge in this respect; it is a daring, exceptional novel, which remains problematic in as much as its admittedly considerable difficulties make it unattractive to many adolescent readers. Here there is no omniscient novelist at work, who might have intervened on the reader's behalf to help unravel the many shifts of time, of plot, of character's feelings and motives. Yet the book is anything but perfunctorily written. Especially where feelings are concerned, its extreme spareness of language obliges the reader to be an active interpreting witness of the novel's events, however discomforting; the reader must bear witness, for instance, to the overwhelming need to communicate, through any sexual expression that is worth having – a need which Jan and Tom enact with chaste intensity in their story. *Red Shift* is written with a Hobbesian vision of human untenderness in a harsh world. It presents the brute facts of conflict among rival tribes in fifth-century Roman times, or in the seventeenth-century Civil War, or in the twentieth-century nuclear family; yet it broods throughout on the quality of human love. In doing so, Garner must reach beyond current fashionable interest in violence; indeed, he must dare to risk sentimentality as well as over-severity of statement, in order to write with compassion and truth. As mediated through the varying characterizations of the hero Tom, the author's stance is that of the 'artist – Fool', who must be outraged by human-induced suffering, yet who cannot visualize without pity; he cannot be purely judge. *Red Shift* is bound to dent some preconceptions about what children's books ought to

be, including the criteria of accessibility and enjoyableness that have
underwritten this present chapter; if that is so, a book of this quality
must, I think, require an adjusting of our existing viewpoint, in order
to include it.[8]

In the *Stone Book Quartets* (1976–8) Garner reverts from fantasy
to personal family history. The *Stone Book Quartets* dwell on craftsmanship as a major theme; yet this theme itself is only a dimension
stone for larger religious preoccupations about what lives and is holy:

> Now the quarry seemed so small, and the church so big. The quarry would
> fit inside a corner of the church; but the stone had come from it. People
> said that a church was only a bit of stone round a lot of air.
>
> (*The Stone Book*)

The prose of the *Quartets* tends to be self-conscious, literary
– especially, perhaps, in *The Aimer Gate*; but overall these deliberately
'poetic' stories are well composed. It may be noted how Garner's
concern for 'valid metaphors of reality' is extended in *The Lad of
the Gad* (1980), where he turns his attention from fiction to the retelling of folklore, in order to present the reader with stories written
'in poet's words'.

In their different ways, Pearce and Garner provide important
touchstones for appraising the quality of children's books. They both
reveal a heartfelt belief in the worthwhileness of their chosen genre;
they both take their readers wholly seriously, and devote their craft
to this end; they both acknowledge in their writing that while
children may have limited experience this provides no excuse for
dodging or for distorting the truth of things and events. In choosing
to write for older children, Garner has taken greater risks, of course:
the emotional and psychological complexity of adolescence cannot
be as neatly separated from adult experience, as can the events of
younger children's lives. Yet Garner's experiments in a novel such
as *Red Shift* may have opened up new possibilities for a kind of fiction
which, by its nature, must take a rather special account of its readership.

NOTES

1. See 'Standards of Criticism for Children's Literature', ed. N. Chambers, in *The Signal Approach to Children's Books* (Harmondsworth, 1980).

2. See 'The Author as the Ally of the Reader', eds M. Meek *et al.*, in *The Cool Web* (1974).

3. Quoted in Green, R. L. *Tellers of Tales: Children and their Books from 1800 to 1964* (1965).

4. See 'The Historical Novelist at Work', ed. G. Fox, in *Writers, Critics and Children* (1976).

5. See 'Writing a Book', ed. M. Meek.

6. See 'An Interview with Alan Garner', ed. N. Chambers (Penguin Books, 1980).

7. See Neil Philip's accounts in *A Fine Anger* (1981) of Garner's substantial researches prior to writing, in his novels. Philip shows how Garner's investigations into the talk of Salford demolition gangs and children in the early sixties had a considerable impact on the quality of dialogue in *Elidor*. Furthermore, the attention he gave to Britten's *War Requiem* during his *Elidor* researches was a good deal more than scholarly: he listened to it 'nearly every day' (Philip, 63).

8. Its high quality is identified in Neil Philip's attentive commentary (1981), but it has received much unsympathetic appraisal. Fred Inglis, for instance, dismisses it in a few sentences as a failure (in *The Promise of Happiness*, 1981): 'It comes over clumsily ... cliches of teenage tantrums ... His novel is all theory ...' (286–7). Dr Inglis' judgements are usually well-based enough to be taken seriously; but in this instance his stance against the book seems ungenerous (especially so, perhaps, in the light of the embarrassing eulogy that P. G. Wodehouse receives in a later chapter of the same book).

JOHN MONTAGUE, SEAMUS HEANEY
AND THE IRISH PAST

GRAHAM MARTIN

John Montague (b. 1929) and Seamus Heaney (b. 1939), both growing up in farming communities in Catholic Ulster, draw in different ways upon 'versions of pastoral' hardly accessible to English poets of similar age, and perhaps not to Irish poets today. Their work is equally influenced by 'the matter of Ireland', and a struggle to come to terms with the Irish past, so it has seemed useful to concentrate on these themes, the last especially.

Though born in New York, as a child Montague was brought up on his aunt's farm in Co. Tyrone, educated at a Catholic boarding school, and University College, Dublin, where he began to write. But, as he explains in the Introduction to the 1977 reprint of *Poisoned Lands* (1961), with the exception of P. J. Kavanagh he found Dublin literary circles unsympathetic. Going to America, he met more congenial writers – Snodgrass, Bly, Snyder and Ginsberg – to whom poetry was a craft and a vision (p. 9). He returned to Ireland in the later fifties when his poems, he remarks, reflected 'a fear of emotion, of deliberate Irishism, of ruralism' (p. 10), themes which nevertheless surfaced in his next two collections, *The Chosen Light* (1967) and *Tides* (1970). His first substantial volume was *The Rough Field* (1972), which assembled into a coherent plan poems separately published in these earlier volumes and in periodicals during the previous decade.

'An epic,' wrote Pound, 'is a poem which includes history.' This very Poundian account of the genre illustrates a general difficulty experienced by twentieth-century poets preoccupied with 'history' yet without the support of an adequate poetic form. The novel having taken over many concerns of 'epic', and narrative verse as such discounted for serious purposes, how can the poet overcome the constraints of 'lyric' and engage the world of impersonal historical events? Pound's solution was to include, not so much 'history' as the stuff from which it is constructed: historical documents. Yeats' solution was to compose Sacred Books out of a series of personal poems which carried an implicit narrative or linking debate engaging a contemporary historical crisis. In *The Rough Field* Montague adopted both methods. Graphic woodcuts reproduced from an Elizabethan account of campaigns against the O'Neills of Montague's native Ulster, along with extracts from historical writing and sectarian pamphlets, are incorporated into a series of mainly personal poems meditating the province's troubled history. The chronology is selective: the Elizabethan conquest; the flight of the earls; the siege of Derry; his own forebears, grandfather a Catholic J.P. in post-Famine years who supported Home Rule; father a Northern Republican who emigrated to Brooklyn; some events of the sixties in the Republic and again in Derry. The narrative frame is provided in poems about Montague's return after long absence to childhood scenes near the family farm at Garvaghey, Co. Tyrone. Garvaghey derives from the Gaelic for 'rough field', allusion to the difficult farming land which Ulster's defeated Catholics had to learn to cultivate, to the history of Ulster, finally to the human condition. Beginning thus as a poem of place, parochial in Kavanagh's honorific sense, hallowed by personal memory and family connection, its scope widened and deepened by long historical perspectives, *The Rough Field* moves in its concluding sections beyond the Ulster location, and its Epilogue concedes that there is no return to the past, personal or historical. Technological, economic and social changes have superannuated a way of life once found from 'Ulster to the Ukraine', the small farming community of which Garvaghey was a local instance; so that the pastoral 'dream of man at home/in a rural setting' (p. 83), its roots in such history, is finally gone for good.

It will be clear that in the light of most contemporary poetry *The Rough Field* is a work of unusual ambition; and as one critic has remarked, it is 'elaborately mounted . . . varied and sure in structure and verse; its viewpoints are attractive and humane, passionate at times, never strident'.[1] A central strength derives from Montague's ability to balance description against symbolism, observation against allusion, present or remembered scenes and people against the history which the poet perceives in them. The well-known 'Like dolmens round my childhood, the old people' begins:

> Jamie MacCrystal sang to himself
> A broken song, without tune, without words;
> He tipped me a penny every pension day,
> Fed kindly crusts to winter birds.
> When he died his cottage was robbed,
> Mattress and money box torn and searched,
> Only the corpse they didn't disturb.

Several verses follow, in this manner, of bare observation and simple anecdote, couched in skilfully unemphatic rhythms; but the poem concludes in a stanza of Yeatsian eloquence:

> Ancient Ireland indeed! I was reared by her bedside,
> The rune and the chant, evil eye and averted head,
> Fomorian fierceness of family and local feud.
> Gaunt figures of fear and of friendliness,
> For years they trespassed on my dreams,
> Until once, in a standing circle of stones
> I felt their shadows pass
>
> Into that dark permanence of standing stones. .
>
> (p. 17)

The care with which Montague keeps these two styles distinct is one key to his achievement. Yeats's celebrated mythologizing of friend and foe all too often is made to serve a history of his country, characteristically wilful and eccentric. Montague's fidelity to the sparse and impoverished reality of such lives as Jamie MacCrystal's, his refusal to invest them with an imposed significance even of the Wordsworthian variety, is matched by his concern for the impersonal history stretching beyond them. And like the people who inhabit the landscapes of Garvaghey, the scenes themselves are undramatic, making no claims to the sublime or picturesque, the rhythms subdued, the observation exact and lucid:

> The well
> Is still there, a half-way mark
> Between two cottages, opposite
> The gate in Danaghy's field.
> But above the protective dry-
> Stone rim, the plaiting thorns
> Have not been bill-hooked back
> And a thick *glaur* floats.

> ... Croziered
> Fern, white scut of *canavan*,
> Spars of bleached bog fir jutting
> From heather, make a landscape
> So light in wash it must be learnt
> Day after day, in shifting detail,
> Out to the pale Sperrins.
>
> (pp. 33–4)

Seamus Heaney has written of Montague's sense of place that it is primarily cultural and historical, 'redolent ... of the history of his people, disinherited and dispossessed'.[2] His relish in local place-names and the legends that attach to them bear this out, or as he puts the point himself:

> The whole landscape a manuscript
> We had lost the skill to read,
> A part of our past disinherited;
> But fumbled, like a blind man,
> Along the fingertips of instinct.
>
> (p. 34)

But the effect here also depends upon the landscape having been first presented to the reader as an actual place, which the poet knew as a boy, as an adult is revisiting, and which now guides his exploration of the determining past:

> *Tír Eoghain:* Land of Owen,
> Province of the O'Niall;
> The ghostly tread of O'Hagan's
> Barefoot gallowglasses marching
> To merge forces in Dun Geanainn
>
> Push southward to Kinsale!
> Loudly the war-cry is swallowed
> In swirls of black rain and fog
> As Ulster's pride, Elizabeth's foemen,
> Founder in a Munster bog.

The masterly dramatic compression of these verses gains much of its power from the more reticent language of the preceding poems.

Montague's historical sense is, in the main, elegiac; yet a similar stylistic contrast is also deployed to address a more contemporary process of change, from the rural past to the mechanized future.

> From the quarry behind the school
> the crustacean claws of the excavator
> rummage, to withdraw a payload,
> a giant's bite ...

> 'Tis pleasant for to take a stroll by Glencull Waterside
> On a lovely evening in spring (in nature's early pride);
> You pass by many a flowery bank and many a shady dell,
> Like walking through enchanted land where fairies used to dwell

> Tuberous tentacles
> of oak, hawthorn, buried pignut,
> the topsoil of a living shape
> of earth lifts like a scalp
> to lay open

(p. 60)

Here, neither idiom defeats the other, and no easy judgement of the transformation being worked by modern technology is possible. A further set of contrast plays upon the central series of descriptions, anecdotes, imaginary reconstructions of the past, from the historical material set in the margins. Thus, juxtaposed with the description of a fiddler playing traditional reels, hornpipes and laments for the pillaging of Ulster after Kinsale, we find in the margin:

We have killed, burnt and despoiled all along the Lough to within four miles of Dungannon ... in which journeys we have killed above a hundred of all sorts, besides such as we have burned, how many I know not. We spare none, of what quality or sex soever, and it had bred much terror in the people who heard not a drum nor saw not a fire of long time.

Chichester to Mountjoy, 1607 (p. 38)

This history is thus documented, as well as recalled. Montague has written of the importance of visual effects, the spacing of verses down a page, the valuable tension between the printed words and the silence that surrounds them, provided the poet makes good use of it.[3] *The Rough Field* offers some brilliant instances of his own practice in this vein.

Yet the poem is in other ways less satisfactory. In *Patriotic Suite*, Montague touches on Irish history since 1916: Pearse, Connolly, the

Rising, Yeats, and the modern Coole Park receive brief allusions in a series of sketchy poems. The Irish Republic of the sixties, more prosperous, rising in international regard ('exemplary in the Congo,/ Rational in the U.N.' (p. 68)), the sexual puritanism of the Catholic church losing its hold (*'Puritan Ireland's dead and gone, A myth of O'Connor and O'Faolain'*) – such changes are granted a qualified praise. But both praise and qualification lack energy, as if this history, disconnected from childhood and family association, with no roots in the landscape of Co. Tyrone, fails to engage the poet's deeper sources of attention. Equally superficial is his direct assertion of nationalist feeling. *The Fault* includes two fine poems about Montague's father, the Northern Republican, for whom the 1921 treaty made exile to America the only acceptable choice. But slotted between them, another poem declares the poet's hatred of Anglo-Saxondom and Westminster:

> This bitterness
> I inherit from my father, the
> swarm of blood
> to the brain, the vomit surge
> of race hatred,
>
> (p. 45)

Hatred in such terms (*vide* Swift or Yeats) must be thought either a token affair, or the sign of more complex feelings insufficiently articulated. Finally, *The New Siege*, an impressive interweaving of the first Derry Siege and the events of 1969 (the poem is dedicated to Bernadette Devlin) attempts also to link the Ulster Civil Rights movement with events in other countries.

> Lines of protest
>   lines of change
> a drum beating
>   across Berkeley
> all that Spring
>   invoking the new
> Christ avatar
>   of the Americas
> running voices
>   streets of Berlin
> Paris, Chicago

seismic waves
zigzagging through
a faulty world
(p. 74)

'Lines' becomes the weakly metaphorical link between these world-wide matters and the 'lines of suffering' imposed by poverty amongst the Belfast working class, those of 'action and reaction' of Stormont politics, and more metaphysically with the 'lines of loss/lines of energy' which constitute 'the rough field/of the universe'. Singling out one aspect of a complex poem, one moreover in which visual layout plays an important part, has its dangers. Yet the sense of abstract connections imposed upon so many contrasting histories is difficult to escape. The general perspectives which emerge so effectively from some parts of the poem, through delicate symbolisms, or compressed historical reference, seem in such lines asserted rather than disclosed. And this points to a deeper division of feeling within the poem as a whole. 'One explores an inheritance to free oneself and others,' remarks the poet in his Preface (p. 7), yet the effect of *The Rough Field* is less than liberating. The 'pastoral dream' may have indeed gone, but it still inspires a powerful nostalgia, the stronger for excluding all Georgian sentimentalization of the rigours of rural labour. The 'rough field' of the modern world is a lonely place. Whatever community it offers is not welcomed by the poet, and 'the lines of loss' seem more memorably etched than those of the 'energy' reaching towards the future. It seems no accident that the two most beautifully realized characters in the poem, the poet's mother and the old hag in *The Wild Dog Rose*, are equally images of lonely, patient and devoted suffering.

In Montague's later writing (*A Slow Dance*, (1975), *The Great Cloak* (1978)), more personal themes dominate: the rupture of a marriage, sexual happiness, and its concomitant jealousy; or a nature no longer pastoral. 'The matter of Ireland' is virtually absent, and with the exception of a few place-poems (*Herbert Street Revisited*, *Walking Late*), modern Ireland receives no recognition. Slighter in ambition, if also surer in technique, these poems show that Montague has achieved the quality of language which in an earlier poem he had set as his aim:

> Not the accumulated richness
>   Of an old historical language –
> That musk-deep odour!
> But a slow exactness
>
> Which recreates experience
>   By ritualizing its details.
>   (*A Chosen Light*, p. 36)

Poets must write what they can, of course, but admirers of *The Rough Field* will regret this current restriction of scope. As we shall see, Heaney's work shows some points in common, perhaps sketching the general constraint of a still-forming historical moment.

Seamus Heaney is probably the most widely admired of a group of talented Ulster poets (Derek Mahon, Tom Paulin, Michael Longley, Paul Muldoon among them) whose work has achieved reputation during the last fifteen years or so, and now figures representatively (so the editors argue) in the *Penguin Book of Contemporary Verse* (1982). This collective literary event owes something to the long political crisis in Ulster, but it also belongs in a wider context, as one manifestation of that shift in the balance of cultural power away from the Oxbridge–London centre, commanding the immediate post-war situation, to the 'provinces' – a movement encouraged, if not actually initiated by, the 1944 Education Act and the expansion of higher education in the 1960s. In his own case, Heaney has acknowledged the special importance of Ted Hughes' poetry.

> It's a voice that has no truck with irony because the dialect is not that ... I mean the voice of a generation – the Larkin voice, the Movement voice, even the Eliot voice, the Auden voice ... the manners of that speech, the original voice behind the poetic voice, are those of literate English middle-class culture, and I think Hughes' great cry and call and bawl is that English language and poetry is longer and deeper and rougher than that.[4]

It was this voice which challenged the authority of the voice emanating from 'The Movement', and speaking to 'the scripts written into [Heaney's] being' gave him access to his formative childhood experiences as the son of a Co. Derry farmer. We can also add, more generally, that English poetry had already offered the young Heaney a cultural territory invitingly free from two forms of potential oppression, the Ulster Protestant 'state' and the Roman Catholic Church.

> Ulster was British, but with no rights on
> The English lyric: all around us, though
> We hadn't named it, the ministry of fear.
> (*North*, p. 65)

For an Ulster Roman Catholic, the political tension was doubtless to be expected, but the same poem also registers the immediate cultural power of the Church. Confronted with his rural charges, the strap-wielding Father at Heaney's Catholic boarding-school evidently brought to bear one powerful version of 'English middle-class culture', a conception of correct speech. Heaney quotes him as remarking that:

> Catholics, in general, don't speak
> As well as students from the Protestant schools.

Heaney's Derry 'voice' nevertheless appears to have survived this educative process. Indeed, his adult relationship with Roman Catholicism seems entirely genial. The 'puritanism' of the Irish Catholic church, so formidable an obstacle for the young Joyce, if present in Heaney's education, left no scars. His sense of the Catholic tradition derives more from family living than from theology or ethics, absorbing (he has suggested) such features as the 'Marian quality of devotion', and an admiration for 'a religion that has a feminine component and a notion of the mother in the transcendental world',[5] and not just of the father.

Hughes' catalytic effect on Heaney's early writing is, of course, evident in its subject-matter – frogs, bulls, eels, rats – generally in the poet's fascination with 'the slime kingdoms' (*North*, p. 41) of non-human existence. But where the creatures in Hughes' bestiary signify an abstract natural energy, alien or at least indifferent to man, Heaney's poems in this vein speak of what men and Nature share, a life of the earth, Lawrentian but without Lawrence's idealizations. Nowhere is this so marked as in Heaney's emphasis on human work: the father's skill in ploughing, the mother's in butter-making, the muscular ache of the potato pickers, the daily risk to life and limb for the fishers of eels. Cumulatively, such poems render as no English poet in our industrialized century could render, the truth that 'agriculture' is laborious. The admired sensuous immediacy of these poems is more than Keatsian. The poet's concern with touch and grasp and immersion points towards the physical demands of farming work. 'Labour,' wrote Yeats, 'is blossoming or dancing where/The body is not bruised to pleasure soul.' Labour in Heaney's poems has no such visionary character, but it is not alienated labour; it is felt as productive; it carries its own satisfactions. In one poem, Heaney equates his poetic endeavour with that of his digging and delving forefathers: as they dug with the spade, he will dig with the pen (*Death of a Naturalist*, pp. 13–14). The analogy, contrived though it may seem, points to his 'natural' relationship with writing. Many of his poems, he has remarked, are a product of 'trance',[6] a welling-up of inner speech, a negotiation of experience into language remarkably free of any signs of the composing will, whatever subsequent revision they also required. In his essay 'The Makings of A Music', he adopts Valéry's distinction between *les vers données* and *les vers calculés*, discussing Wordsworth as a writer of the first, and Yeats of the second. Heaney's own skill in the making of poems belongs, on balance, to the Wordsworthian category, though his admiration for Yeats' poetry of 'control' sufficiently expresses a determination to achieve success of another kind.[7] In skilled agricultural work, both response to and imposition upon 'Nature', we may glimpse a model for both endeavours.

'Description is revelation!' So Heaney quotes the advice of a fellow writer (*North*, p. 71) at the outset of his career, and the accessibility of his poems, not the least reason for their popularity, suggests that he followed it. Yet 'description' implies a disengaged observing eye that accounts for only one element in Heaney's characteristic effects. In *At a Potato Digging*, he writes:

> Flint-white, purple. They lie scattered
> like inflated pebbles. Native
> to the black hutch of clay
> where the halved seed shot and clotted
> these knobbed and slit-eyed tubers seem
> the petrified hearts of drills. Split
> by the spade, they show white as cream.
> (*Death of a Naturalist*, p. 31–2)

Descriptive detail matters, but so does the aural interplay. We sense the pickers' hands groping in the earth, as well as the earthy process

of growth that produced the potatoes from seed; while the series
of metaphors introduce an effect of phantasmagoria, which works
against the impression of an observed external world. In *Gifts of Rain*:

> A man wading lost fields
> breaks the pane of the flood:
>
> ... His hands grub
> where the spade has uncastled
>
> sunken drills, an atlantis
> he depends on. So
>
> he is hooped to where he planted
> and sky and ground
>
> are running naturally among his arms
> that grope the cropping land.
> *(Wintering Out*, pp. 23–4)

We see the man in 'hooped', and simultaneously grasp the metaphorical implication that he is 'bound tight' to the field he cultivates.
The earlier 'pane', equally visual, also anticipates the final image of
the mirroring water which unites sky, earth and the man's arms
thrusting through to the flooded crop. Description and metaphor
here blend in the evocation of an 'atlantis', concrete enough to be
grubbed for, yet retaining the elusive character of a human dream.
The poem offers less an observed scene than a complex interplay
between natural process and laborious human hope.

Metaphorical vitality, in fact, is as striking a feature of Heaney's
poems as his skill in evocative description. An eel is 'a gland agitating/
mud ... a scale of water on water ... a muscled icicle' (*Door into
the Dark*, p. 39). Derrygarve, the name of a place, is 'a lost potent
musk' and another, Anahorish, 'a soft gradient/of consonant, vowel-
meadow' (*Wintering Out*, pp. 16, 33). The conductor of the Ulster
Orchestra is 'our Jacobite'

> who marched along the deep
> plumed in slow airs and grace notes.
> O gannet smacking through scales!
> Minnow of light.
> Wader of assonance.
> *(Field Work*, p. 30)

Such play of analogy is one of the pleasures of Heaney's writing, affectionately extravagant as in the last quotation, but also the medium of a gravely contemplative searching, as in these lines about Irish bogland:

> Ruminant ground
> digestion of mollusc
> and seed-pod,
> deep pollen-bin.
>
> Earth-pantry, bone-vault,
> sun-bank, embalmer
> of votive goods
> and sabred fugitives.
>
> Insatiable bride.
> Sword-swallower,
> casket, midden,
> floe of history.
>
> (*North*, p. 61)

It is a remarkable salutation. As if modelled on an Anglo-Saxon riddle, the alliterative 'estranging' set of variations present the bog first biologically, then as the grave of prehistoric and more recent corpses, then as the mythic earth-mother ('insatiable bride'), then taking in the wit of 'sword-swallower', as the encompassing impersonal movement of history, the geological 'floe' (which is also 'flow') insisting on how far back this history reaches. Language here seems to evolve out of itself in a pondering associative movement of interlocking sound-patterns, each phrase representing a further stage in the poet's deeper and deeper penetration of the bog's meanings, in the final verse to be suddenly internalized as 'nesting ground,/outback of my mind'.

Heaney's first three collections are miscellaneous. They show a talented poet developing an individual style, but only a small number would merit inclusion in a selection of his best work. More considerable are the two recent books, *North* (1975) and *Field Work* (1979), reflecting (he has said) a conscious decision to put poetry at the centre of his life.[8] The individual poems are linked by theme, and in both cases the crisis in Ulster is never far away. *North* addresses it directly; *Field Work* offers an elegiac meditation on some of its consequences. In *North*, the poet struggles with the question of his immediate responsibility. What can he say, *qua* poet, which betrays neither his sense of the political issues, nor a conception of his art which rules out the merely rhetorical taking of sides? In *Field Work*, he writes from a condition of pastoral withdrawal, lamenting the deaths, seeing only a political deadlock, defending a prior loyalty to the poet's vocation. The last poem in *North* offers his celebrated self-definition, that of the 'inner emigré, grown long-haired/And thoughtful: a woodkerne/Escaped from the massacre' (p. 71). *Field Work*, then, is the product of this inner emigration, but though more 'personal' in emphasis than its predecessor, historical issues are hardly less important.

North has two sections, the first a meditative exploration of aspects of the Irish past, the second focused on the immediate conflict in Ulster. This latter group of poems, epistolary, documentary, sardonic and exasperated, circles round the conflict of loyalties Heaney experienced. As a 'liberal papist' (p. 58), he shared in the sense of helpless revulsion at the slide from the early Civil Rights marches towards urban guerilla warfare amongst the feuding sects and forces of the state. Yet also, *as* a 'papist', his deepest sympathies pulled towards one side of the dispute. Cutting across both attachments, there is also his loyalty to the poetic vocation for which the political conflict allows no expression.

> Yet for all this art and sedentary trade
> I am incapable. The famous
>
> Northern reticence, the tight gag of place
> And times: yes, yes. Of the 'wee six' I sing
> Where to be saved you only must save face
> And whatever you say, say nothing.
>
> (p. 59)

These poems in themselves may be said to give up 'history' as a bad job, beyond the poet's grasp. Placed as they are in the volume, they become the reader's retrospective clue to the earlier section, whose poems meditate reasons for the intransigence of the conflict, and search tentatively beyond it.

The Part I poems engage the historical questions in two ways: in a representation of the land as historical in its very texture, defended, cultivated, as source and grave of life, 'possessed and repossessed' (p. 47) in a history of successful conquest; and in a pre-occupation with language, both as instrument of cultural domination, and as a historical deposit central to the poet's activity. The 'person' uttering these poems, unlike the engaged polemicist of Part II is a meditative, wondering and self-critical presence, less 'person' than medium through whom contradiction and conflict can find a voice. As poet, his language is English, which in the Elizabethan *iamb*, consonantal rather than guttural, conquered the native Irish and vocalic medium, and he identifies with this language in the long perspective of its philosophical and cultural roots in Norse, Provençal French and Anglo-Saxon (p. 28). (The Norsemen, we recall, first ruled in Dublin; then as Norman-French, conquered England, before later as Plantagenet English rulers, they began the long struggle to possess Ireland.) A sexual metaphor occurs here: England in the person of Raleigh possessing a female Ireland (pp. 46–7); and the Hamlet-like poet broods erotically over the buried Bog Queen (pp. 31–2). Yet his loyalty is also to the land, and to its victims, whether sacrificial in the Iron Age fertility religions of the Danish Bog People, or victims of more recent history, of the modern, political 'religion' of the 'matter of Ireland' whose tribal imperatives override the claims of the liberal conscience. And it is in this context that the poems invite a communal human affirmation: that we are all of the earth, earthy, mutually involved in a dependence on the earth goddess, Nerthus, properly speaking all mourners and cele-brators of the tribal deaths. The unearthed corpses of the Bog People attract a quality of tender and humbling attention; in some cases, they seem the poet's *alter ego*, finally discovered and recognized. Such poems, give unjudging access to the power of a history which cannot easily be gainsaid. They are political poems, addressed to questions of power, achieved in the past, struggled for in the present, and it is through the poet's 'personal' response to land and language that this history and politics can directly speak.

Considered in this light, the poems of *Field Work*, more accom-plished and self-confident than many in *North*, are often less complex. The active history rendered in the earlier volume is now seen as occasion for elegy and lament, though also in sombre recognition that the history will not go away (*Triptych, The Toome Road, In*

Memoriam Francis Ledwidge). There is a higher proportion of 'personal' poems and, as has been pointed out, a tentative Romantic disengagement from the 'tribe' and an assertion of the prior claim of the poetic vocation.[9] When, as in *Casualty*, these merge with elegiac lament for a specific death (contrast the generalized deaths in *North*), a memorably impressive poem results. Central to *Field Work* are the Glanmore Sonnets, which speak from a Wordsworthian withdrawal into the pastoral mode, quite literally *poetic* ('Vowels ploughed into other: opened ground'; 'it was all crepuscular and iambic' (pp. 33, 35)), and this retreat becomes a source of rural imagery to set against the intransigence of history (*After a Killing, The Strand at Lough Bog*). The land is now simplified, unproblematic, with none of the difficult political reverberations of the land in *North*. Yet there are signs that a different historical process, sufficiently evident in an Irish Republic that belongs to the European Economic Community, may be addressed in this revived pastoral mode. In *Triptych*, the oracle speaks of imminent catastrophe:

> I think our very form is bound to change.
> Dogs in a siege. Saurian relapses. Pismires.
>
> Unless forgiveness finds its nerve and voice,
> Unless the helmeted and bleeding tree
> Can green and open buds like infants' fists
> And the fouled magma incubate
>
> Bright nymphs... My people think money
> And talk weather. Oil-rigs lull their future
> On single acquisitive stems. Silence
> Has shoaled into the trawlers' echo-sounders.
>
> (p. 13)

In the ecological issue touched here, there is a glimpse of contemporary forces presently influencing many European lands and societies. While in *Oysters*, *Field Work*'s opening poem, Heaney identifies the imperialist 'glut of privilege' (p. 11) with our generalized human predatory relationship with nature.

Field Work, nevertheless, scarcely addresses the developing society of the modern Irish Republic, and it remains to be seen whether the volume's emphasis on the private and the personal charts the future development of Heaney's work. What is certain is that this development, for any reader of contemporary poetry, will be a matter of keen interest.

NOTES

1. D. E. S. Maxwell, 'The Poetry of John Montague', *Critical Quarterly*, XV (2) (Summer 1973), 185.
2. 'The Sense of Place', *Preoccupations: Selected Prose, 1968–1978*, (1980), 141.
3. *Agenda*, nos. 10–11, Special Issue on Rhythm, 1972–3, 41.
4. John Haffenden, 'Meeting Seamus Heaney', *London Magazine* (new series), XIX (3) (June 1979), 27.
5. Haffenden, 11–12.
6. Haffenden, 23.
7. *Preoccupations*, 71–8.
8. Haffenden, 16.
9. Blake Morrison, *Seamus Heaney (Contemporary Writers)* (1982), 78–80. For my comments on *North* I owe a particular debt to this excellent survey of Heaney's work.

LOSING THE BIBLE

DENYS THOMPSON

The Bible is not a book but a library. It contains the sacred texts of Christianity and the complete literature of an ancient people; it was composed for a variety of purposes over hundreds of years. It includes myth and history; ballads, lyrics and hymns; legal documents and priestly codes; prophecy and meditation; biography and exegesis. It has features in common with other early literatures. Much of it was composed for oral delivery, often in verse recited to a group which had a close relationship with the speaker. The Hebrew creation story resembles the Babylonian at several points; the *Proverbs*, shrewd and commonsensical, sound very like the wisdom literature that was once common property in the Middle East. The prophets have affinities with those bards of western Europe who were leaders of men as well as poets. The old narratives are skilfully told, their success being that of folktales, which evolve through constant retelling.

What distinguishes the Hebrew from other ancient literatures is that it centres on the growth of religion. The first advance was the rejection of idols in favour of a single god. As well as controlling natural forces, this deity reflected a society wherein a tribal chief, through whom his people lived and had their being, held supreme power. The god was military and jealous; he protected his people if they behaved themselves. This anthropomorphic conception was replaced by the prophets, the conscience of their community, with a loving and merciful being, a true partner with whom men could make agreements, almost on equal terms. Finally in the Old Testament, the god of Isaiah was revealed as an ideal personality, to whom his worshippers would wish to be acceptable. Thus the notion of the divine developed towards the god of Christianity and other religions. For whatever the name – Brahman, Tao, Nirvana,

Christ — it stands for a vision of human potentiality at its full development. The prophets moreover believed that it was the duty of Israel
as his chosen people to announce to all nations that Jehovah was the
true god, and so to establish peace throughout the world. Their dream
of universal harmony was revolutionary; so too was their insistence
that god was one who took pity on the poor, the bereaved and the
oppressed.

The content of the Bible was settled by about A.D. 400, and from
then onward it joined the literature of Greece as the shaping force
of European civilization. The first translation from the original
Hebrew and Greek was St Jerome's (340–420) Latin version, the
Vulgate; and it was from his rendering that the first complete
English Bible was produced, under the supervision of John
Wyclif (1320–84). Official Christendom, however, was ferociously
hostile to vernacular Bibles, lest people should read it (as Wyclif
wished them to) and interpret it for themselves. Accordingly his Bible
was banned and burned, and the greatest of the reforming translators,
William Tyndale, was burned for heresy in Belgium in 1536. Like
Erasmus, and in his words, Tyndale wanted the plowman at his plow-
beam, the weaver at his loom, and the traveller on his journey to
beguile the time by reciting texts from the Bible. His New Testament
(1525) and his few renderings from the Old (1535) were the first
in English to use the Greek and Hebrew texts; he was faithful to
them, putting into currency such Hebrew expressions as 'die the
death' (which Shakespeare picked up), while giving play to his own
inventiveness and lively English. He settled once for all the kind of
language later to be the staple of the Authorized Version. Between Tyndale and 1611 the main individual translator was Miles
Coverdale (1488–1569), who gave his name to a complete Bible of
1535, compiled from earlier versions. The Psalter in the Anglican
Prayer Book is mainly his work.

In 1604 seven hundred and fifty reforming members of the Church
of England petitioned James I for a new translation. He saw the
possibilities of prestige for himself; and by 1607 six committees had
been set up, two each at Oxford, Cambridge and Westminster. They
worked to a common set of rules, and used every version they could
lay their hands on. The separate groups then met and listened to the

397

reading aloud of their members' drafts, which were then submitted to the other groups. This method must have contributed much to the success of the Authorized Version.

And it did succeed. Though it was never officially prescribed, it made its way steadily, and within a generation had replaced other Bibles. For two hundred years it was an invigorating part of English culture, in a way unapproached by the vernacular Bible of any other country. The names of people and places in the book unlocked meanings to those who heard them in new contexts: jeremiad, Job's comforter, philistine, gadarene, judas, prodigal. Expressions were taken from everyday speech, and the debt was repaid by the contribution of many phrases to the common stock: the apple of his eye, signs of the times, a thorn in the flesh, a labour of love, a broken reed. The Bible supplied words for the expression and relief of powerful feelings; at the crises of life emotion flowed in verbal channels formed by men of intelligence and sensitivity. Many authors, Langland and Shakespeare before 1611, and later Bunyan, Kipling, T. F. Powys, T. S. Eliot and David Jones, for example, have used Biblical references to set resonances ringing in their readers' minds, rather as Greek writers touched off echoes of Homer. But too much should not be made of its influence on style to the exclusion of other features of the Bible. Bunyan is often cited in this connection. Certainly the splendid ending of Part 1 of *The Pilgrim's Progress* owes much to the Bible, but the simplicity of his prose is the product of an artist, unlike the folktale quality of the Old Testament stories. Teachers have long been complaining that their students fail to pick up the kind of allusions we have cited, and they certainly lose a great deal in this way. More importantly they are deprived of the pleasure and profit which the abundance of the Bible has to offer.

The excellence of the King James Bible stems first from the moral fervour of the translators. It was their wish that people should be able to read the best possible version, in order that 'God's holy truth be yet more and more known'; the intensity of their feeling was akin to that of the generations who had suffered for their beliefs. Admittedly they were dealing with the work of Jews who themselves were moved by a powerful moral imperative, yet as one reads the English version the impression is inescapable of men carrying out a task in which they believed with the utmost ardour and devotion. They approached their undertaking with humility and a sense of responsibility. As scholars they were in full sympathy with the original languages; as writers of English they were possessed of a medium that was already expressive and growing in clarity; and the speech of their fathers had had much in common with Hebrew. They did not hesitate to use the resources of English, its colloquialism and rich vocabulary; in translating a single Hebrew word they would choose one of several English synonyms, as the context required; and the improvements made in the rhythm of earlier translations suggest that they were fully seized of the meaning. They were conservative, and restored many of Tyndale's renderings; they introduced syntax and turns of phrase that had gone out of use by their day, so that their language sometimes sounds archaic. Like earlier translators they were influenced by the Vulgate, from which came the cadences of various types that characterize the Authorized Version. *Ecclesiastes* xii offers several examples in which after a key word there comes a falling away at the end of a sentence: 'nor the clouds return/after the rain', 'or the wheel broken/at the cistern', 'the spirit shall return unto God/ who gave it'. These cadences, read aloud, cause the listener to feel that a final statement has been made, and that for the moment there is no more to be said. How well Tyndale translated, and how even so the revisers improved his versions may be judged from a comparison of his rendering of St Paul, writing on love to the Christians at Corinth. The spelling of both has been modernized.

Though I spake with the tongues of men and angels, and yet had no love, I were even as sounding brass: or as a tinkling cymbal. And though I could prophesy, and understood all secrets, and all knowledge: yea, if I had faith so that I could move mountains out of their places, and yet had no love, I were nothing. And though I bestowed all my goods to feed the poor, and though I gave my body even that I burned, and yet had no love, it profiteth me nothing.

Love suffereth long, and is courteous. Love envieth not. Love doth not forwardly, swelleth not, dealeth not dishonestly, seeketh not her own, is not provoked to anger, thinketh not evil, rejoiceth not in iniquity: but rejoiceth in the truth, suffereth all things, believeth all things, hopeth all things, endureth in all things. Though that prophesying fail, other tongues shall cease, or knowledge vanish away, yet love falleth never away.

For our knowledge is unperfect, and our prophesying is unperfect. But when that which is perfect is come, then that which is unperfect shall be done away. When I was a child, I spake as a child, I understood as a child, I imagined as a child. But as soon as I was a man, I put away childishness. Now we see in a glass even in a dark speaking: but then shall we see face to face. Now I know unperfectly: but then shall I know even as I am known. Now abideth faith, hope, and love, even these three: but the chief of these is love.

(I *Corinthians* xiii: Tyndale, 1534)

Though I speak with the tongues of men and of angels, and have not charity, I am become as sounding brass, or a tinkling cymbal. And though I have the gift of prophecy, and understand all mysteries, and all knowledge; and though I have all faith, so that I could remove mountains, and have not charity, I am nothing. And though I bestow all my goods to feed the poor, and though I give my body to be burned, and have not charity, it profiteth me nothing.

Charity suffereth long, and is kind; charity envieth not; charity vaunteth not itself, is not puffed up, doth not behave itself unseemly, seeketh not her own, is not easily provoked, thinketh no evil; rejoiceth not in iniquity, but rejoiceth in the truth; beareth all things, believeth all things, hopeth all things, endureth all things. Charity never faileth: but whether there be prophecies, they shall fail; whether there be tongues, they shall cease; whether there be knowledge, it shall vanish away.

For we know in part, and we prophesy in part. But when that which is perfect is come, then that which is in part shall be done away. When I was a child, I spake as a child, I understood as a child, I thought as a child: but when I became a man, I put away childish things. For now we see through a glass, darkly; but then face to face: now I know in part; but then shall I know even as I am known. And now abideth faith, hope, charity, these three; but the greatest of these is charity.

(Authorized Version, 1611)

Tyndale's translation shows how he set the style for his successors, so that the King James scholars needed to make only a few, but those masterly, improvements. They replaced 'love' with 'charity', thus retaining the three syllables of the Greek 'agape' for its rhythm, as well as permanently enlarging the meaning of the word. They were more accurate, substituting the literal 'childish things' for Tyndale's abstract 'childishness'; and their decisive 'Charity never faileth', with the following clauses, is both nearer the Greek and more positive than Tyndale's rearrangement of the original.

The revisers' accuracy with Greek suggests that they were equally faithful to the Hebrew; their version gives an impression of the original which tallies with what we are told by those who know Hebrew. Much of the Old Testament is the product of a pre-literate culture; people spoke of what they saw and heard and felt, and their vocabulary dealt with the concrete, never with abstractions. Thus psychic qualities were attributed to physical organs, and emotions expressed in physical terms, as in Psalm 69:

> Save me, O God;
>> for the waters are come into my soul.
> I sink in deep mire,
>> where there is no standing;
> I am come into deep waters,
>> where the floods overflow me.

There was no language for analysis and generalization; it is noticeable that Christ never used philosophic deduction, but always metaphors and similes, and perhaps actual verse forms to impress his words in the memory of his hearers.

Like other early literatures the Bible contains much poetry. Very old and primitive is the savage war song of Deborah (Judges v: 19 ff.): 'the stars in their courses fought against Sisera'. Three other poems are specially worth looking up. David's elegy on Saul and Jonathan (2 Samuel ch. i, 19–27) falls into three parts, each ending with the refrain 'How are the mighty fallen', like the toll of a bell, with the addition in the last verse of the wise reflection 'and the weapons of war perished.' The burden of Ecclesiastes is resigned acceptance of life and death; it ends with a sonorous and strongly rhythmical poem that presents the coming of old age, with its weakening, timidity and irritability. Symbols of life ('silver cord', 'golden bowl') are introduced before the reminder of man's fate, in cadences that enact its inevitability:

> Then shall the dust return to the earth as it was;
> And the spirit shall return unto God who gave it.

Finally, the *Song of Solomon* is a sequence of sensuous love poems, in which the rhythm (ch. ii: 10–12) insists on the certainty of the return of spring.

Not all the techniques of Hebrew verse can be reproduced in

English, but one device transfers successfully: the use of balancing sentences. There are several forms. In synonymous parallelism, the second of two lines repeats the idea of the first:

> The heavens declare the glory of God.
> And the firmament showeth his handiwork.
>
> (Psalm 19)

– this type is found in many Psalms. In contrasting parallelism, opposed ideas are balanced:

> The Lord knoweth the way of the righteous,
> But the way of the ungodly shall perish.
>
> (Psalm 1)

The revisers were aided by the affinity of Hebrew and English. Tyndale noted it, and so two hundred years later did *The Spectator* (405):

It happens very luckily, that the Hebrew Idioms run into the English Tongue with a peculiar Grace and Beauty ... They give a Force and Energy to our Expression, warm and animate our Language, and convey our Thoughts in more ardent and intense Phrases, than any that are to be met with in our own Tongue.

Like Hebrew, English was the speech of people living close to the land, in touch with the seasons and the weather; it was short on abstraction, but strong in references to what they knew, and full of lively idioms.

The value of the Authorized Version as the background of our religion and literature is rightly stressed. It is one of the great English books, but it is more than a treasury of allusions and an item on a reading list; the 'Bible as literature' implies too narrow a view of literature and of the volume itself. It is a living book, like Homer and Shakespeare, and like them is interpreted afresh every few generations. It embodies permanent truths, and deals with questions that have always engaged great writers – the meaning of the universe, life and death, the relationship of men with men and with their god. This preoccupation imparts a sense of proportion throughout. One question in particular weighed heavily on the Jews as a nation: why do the righteous suffer? But the Bible never grapples with the problem as do Greek and Shakespearean drama. It is true that *Job* approaches closely, but in the end the sufferer merely listens to God's exposition of his might, and so glimpses the power and wisdom of his creator:

> I had heard of thee by the hearing of the ear;
> But now mine eye seeth thee,
> Wherefore I abhor myself, and repent
> In dust and ashes.

Thus there is no answer to the problem of suffering; the only solution is a statement of the impotence of man.

One of the Jewish contributions to the civilization of the West is the sense of history that developed from their notion of god and their relationship with him. The prophets assure us that a heavy doom falls on those who neglect the warnings of history; and as they thunder against nations which behave as if they were divine, we cannot help being reminded of our own century's exaltation of the state. There are other lessons. For example in Psalm 137 the Jews enslaved at Babylon weep over their plight and curse their oppressors:

> Happy shall he be, that taketh and dasheth thy little ones against the stones.

In other words, if people are treated as sub-human, as was Shylock by the Christians in *The Merchant of Venice*, they will become sub-human and be happy to repay their tormentors in the same coin.

The Bible, however, contains more than warnings. There is a shift from the prohibitions of the Decalogue (Exodus xx) to the New Testament positive 'Thou shalt love ...' (Matthew xii). But even among the primitive taboos and the vindictive penal code of Leviticus we can find in essence the ideal of love that marks all great and mature religions:

> Thou shalt love thy neighbour as thyself ... the stranger that dwelleth with you shall be as one born among you ...

> (Leviticus, xix:18,34)

Much of the Old Testament has no interest for today's reader: the rules and codes of Leviticus, Exodus and Deuteronomy, the census reports and the genealogies that served as a dating system, accounts of cattle raids, and some of the minor prophets. The New Testament is another matter. Though some of the letters are limited and domestic, the civilization of Greece underlies the quality of much of the writing, which at its best leaves the reader in no doubt that something of import is being said. The translators produced an accurate, rhythmical and memorable version that was near perfection in its day. Thus readers of English have a full and clear picture of the New Testament's central figure. In our perspective today we can see Christ appearing at roughly the same stage in the growth of human consciousness as Buddha, Confucius and Socrates, four men who opened up fresh possibilities for humanity. None of them had any programme or ritual; all spoke in metaphor or parable; they are (in Karl Jaspers' words) 'beacons by which to gain an orientation, not models to imitate'.

The Bible began to lose its place as a popular possession as priest and people parted, and the Industrial Revolution sucked workless country people into the slums. In our day it is a bestseller, but unread, a dust-thick classic, partly because our half-baked 'scientific' notions dismiss the Bible as a religious text, and partly because there is no manageable selection from its great bulk. The usual complete edition is hopeless, an unedited, unarranged, unintelligible muddle, warranted to deter all but the most dedicated and well-equipped explorers. Sir Arthur Quiller-Couch pronounced the final condemnation of such volumes in his essay 'On Reading the Bible' – an excellent knockabout polemic.

The *New English Bible* (1960; *Apocrypha* 1970) does not of course remedy this state of affairs. It is a translation only, and valuable as the most accurate version yet produced. With the benefit of modern research and criticism, it is at many points an essential supplement to anyone reading the Bible for its content. As D. H. Lawrence concluded, after a lively consideration of modern versions (*Phoenix*, 1936, p. 302): 'Reading the Bible in a new translation, with modern notes and comments, is more fascinating than reading Homer.' Its rendering for example of St Paul on death and resurrection (1 Corinthians xv:20 ff.) makes most impressive sense when spoken aloud; it reads like an original text in a way that the Authorized Version of the passage does not. The NEB has understandably been the target of hostile criticism; its style at times is evidently the product of an age the language of which is influenced by commerce, applied science and the entertainment industry. The churches too have been castigated quite unfairly for using it, and so 'losing' the Bible.

The Authorized Version is literature. That is to say, there is something impressive and memorable in most of its varied styles which signifies that what is being said with such force and clarity and vitality is worth attending to. If it is 'lost', it will not be the fault of the church-going minority. All of us will be culpable, including the critics just mentioned, and especially those engaged in education at every level. Through neglect, aggravated by the traditional baffling presentation of the Bible, we are losing a piece of our history and forgoing what should be an element of our consciousness.

THE BOOK MARKET

PER GEDIN

The modern literary market developed in parallel with the growth of the capitalistic market economy. From a technical point of view, the spread of books on a large scale was made possible by the invention of the printing press in the middle of the fifteenth century, but up to 200 years later there were still a very limited number of books printed, mainly religious writing or books with a largely utilitarian emphasis. In a very few cases these were published in many editions – such as essays of Martin Luther and Erasmus, of which thousands of copies were printed – but generally speaking an edition consisted of only a few hundred copies.

The printer usually functioned also as both publisher and bookseller. The first Shakespeare folio, for instance, bears no publisher's name on the title page, only, 'Printed by Isaac Iaggard and Ed. Blount. 1623'. In some countries, though, the printer was not permitted to sell bound books; this privilege belonged solely to the bookbinder.

With the rise of the industrial revolution in the beginning of the eighteenth century, the book market rapidly developed the structure it maintains to this day. The publisher came to an agreement with the author and took over the manuscript. The printer printed it, and soon too became responsible for binding it, while special booksellers were established to sell the ever larger editions required by the steadily growing number of readers.

The author, who earlier had often been anonymous and had to be content with being a gentleman, or was paid a very modest settlement, had no legal copyright protection until 1709, with the establishment in England of The Copyright Act of Queen Anne, the first such law to be passed anywhere in the world. Thereby too his position improved both socially and financially.

The most important factor in the development of the book market at that time was, however, the emergence of a reading public. In an earlier period books, especially the possession of them, were largely the concern of monasteries or the aristocracy, who seldom had any intellectual interests and bought books primarily to furnish their palace libraries. With the rise of industrialism a new class appeared within the society: the bourgeoisie, which, with its newly acquired wealth, assumed the privileges of birth and education of the aristocracy and set new social patterns. One of these was social intimacy – the great halls of palaces were replaced by salons and drawing-rooms, the palace chapel by the family altar, the orchestra by a chamber ensemble or piano in the home. An aspect of this transformation was the growing interest in books, frequently read aloud round the evening lamp. An important element in the lifestyle of the bourgeoisie was that culture now had social value; it became highly respectable to be seen at the opera or the theatre, to own paintings by famous contemporary artists, and to have read the latest books.

The reading interests of the bourgeoisie influenced in turn the development of literature. The most popular literary form among the new social classes was the novel – which was easily comprehended by bourgeois readers though, at the same time, frequently describing them in critical terms. The book market reached its apex in the middle of the nineteenth century when writers such as Dickens, Thackeray, Walter Scott, Balzac and Dumas wrote masterpieces that were read by hundreds of thousands of people – editions of 50 to 60,000 were not unusual. The rising number of daily newspapers and periodicals also contributed to this phenomenon by publishing the works of well-known writers in serial form. The publishing houses became rich and powerful family companies and a network of booksellers spread throughout the whole country – not least among these was W. H. Smith, which was founded in 1848 and opened bookshops in most of the newly-built large railway stations.

The structure of the book market, established during the early days of industrialism, remained largely unchanged until the Second World War. The enormous social and technological changes that have taken place since then have, of course, also affected the book market. In most of the western world living standards have risen rapidly and leisure time has doubled within the last hundred years, while magazines, radio and television have brought passive entertainment and effortless culture into the home.

The new ideologies of the industrial society not only aimed at a greater measure of economic equality, but also they made available to workers a culture that had previously been the preserve of the bourgeoisie. The rise in education, the higher living standard and the increased leisure time we have today should thus have created excellent conditions for a greatly expansive book market. At the same time, however, these recent changes have brought about the dissolution of the bourgeois society and a transformation into what we may call mass-society, in which the old class structure has more or less disappeared and new values and lifestyles have emerged.

The culture of mass-society is different from that of bourgeois society, and it does not occupy the same central *social* position it once did. While the new millionaires of the last century, such as the Rockefellers, the Rothschilds and the Fords surrounded themselves with great collections of art and books and donated vast sums to cultural causes, the new rich of the mass-society prefer to symbolize their status almost exclusively with material objects such as sailing yachts, luxury automobiles and large houses. It is no longer important to be seen at the opera or theatre (except on opening nights), or be able to discuss the latest novel; what counts now is to be named in the gossip columns of magazines and newspapers in association with some superstar or the opening of a new nightclub.

This changed attitude towards culture, and thus towards serious literature, influences not only the status of books but also their form and subject matter. During the apex of the bourgeoisie, art and literature remained in permanent touch, as it were, with their public. Dickens changed the character of *The Pickwick Papers* so that Sam Weller was given considerably more space than was originally intended, in response to the wishes of his readers, and Balzac described himself as 'the Secretary of the French society'. The critics too played a different and more central role than they do now. The most famous critics could determine an artist's or author's future with a single article – the great French critic Sainte-Beuve was called, not without reason, the Emperor. The power of the critics and passionate public interest fostered an atmosphere of creativity, its influence strongest perhaps in the face of negative criticism. Writers and artists became avant-gardistes, particularly from the beginning of the twentieth century onwards. They desired always to be ahead of their times and they also had a growing need to challenge the bourgeoisie. During this period of growing tension the various art forms were revolutionized and this in turn brought about the creation of some of the most important experimental work of our times, such as the music of Stravinsky and Schoenberg, the painting of Picasso and the poetry and prose works of T. S. Eliot and James Joyce.

This tension is totally lacking in mass-society. The various art forms have themselves become a part of the mass-market in which virtually anything is accepted. Literature has been deprived of what philosopher Herbert Marcuse termed 'the Great Refusal':

> The efforts to recapture the Great Refusal in the language of literature suffer the fate of being absorbed by what they refute.

The literary form most adversely affected by these changes is, of course, the novel, the development of which was so intimately associated with the bourgeois society. The great period of the novel lasted until the Second World War. Since the war the bourgeoisie has no more been able to adjust to the new society than has the novel itself; it is a society that is culturally dominated by the mass-media and socially and economically by the dissolution of the class structure and increasing pressure from the Third World, with its gigantic problems.

The problem of the novel's literary and formal adjustment is clearly illustrated by *le nouveau roman* during the fifties in France, in which writers like Robbe-Grillet or Nathalie Sarraute attempted, through endless monologues and the presentation of non-events, to break off all communication with the reader by making the novel anti-psychological and anti-subjective. That is to say, they adopted a position diametrically opposed to the great novels of the nineteenth century. Another, more successful, attempt to find a form that responds to the recent changes in society is exemplified by factual novels or 'faction', in which the borderline between fiction and reality has been erased. The later work of Truman Capote and Norman Mailer is typical of such an adjustment, caused perhaps by the seeming impossibility of writing conventional novels in our time. Both writers have used factual accounts of condemned murderers, who describe themselves – their life and death becoming an integrated part of the author's story. Alexander Solzhenitsyn, too, chose a form somewhere between fact and fiction to describe the terror of the Stalin years; and that Doris Lessing has deserted traditional milieux in her latest novels and turned to science fiction may be seen as a symptom of the same tendency.

It is also interesting to note that the novel has not proved a successful form for Third World writers, whereas drama and poetry would appear to be a far more natural means of self-expression for them. An English critic has said of the Nigerian novelist Chinua Achebe, who ceased writing prose after the Nigerian civil war, that: 'He was hurt into poetry.' And it is a fact that surprisingly few novelists have emerged from either Africa or Asia recently, despite great efforts from the new nations to affirm national cultures within the Third World.

A central factor in the problems of the novel is also the changes that have taken place in language during the transformation from a bourgeois society to the mass-society. During the nineteenth century there existed both a common language, founded largely upon the ubiquity of the Bible, and a common frame of reference in knowledge and readership. Today the language has become superficial, on the one hand, through its misusage in the mass-media, and, on the other, much more specialized through the enormous developments within bureaucracies, technology and science. Writers have reacted against this schism in an erstwhile homogeneous language either by isolating themselves in a progressively more private and experimental writing, or they have employed a slick, simplified language in an effort to reach a public of millions.

The literary marketplace has, of course, also made adjustments to these changes in the society. In the bourgeois society there was an obvious connection between all parts of the literary circuit – authors, publishers, booksellers, critics and readers. There was, in a sense, a feedback at all levels. Authors wrote for a given public, publishers could prosper for generations on their successful authors, critics were in close touch with their readers, and book-buyers had their favourite booksellers. This situation remained relatively unchanged for over a hundred years. Since the war the market has changed rapidly. Many publishing houses, often old family firms, have either gone bankrupt in the stiff competition or been bought up by larger concerns in which they subsequently contribute only an insignificant percentage of the financial turnover. Bookshops have been forced to reduce their stock and their service, and here too many family firms have gone into bankruptcy or been purchased by larger conglomerates. The critic's power is now practically non-existent: it is exceptional to sell a book on the basis of a review today. In the diminishing number of newspapers less and less space is devoted to reviews, since culture 'doesn't sell'.

However, the new mass-media are able to sell specific books in vast editions. Classics such as John Galsworthy's *The Forsyte Saga* or Evelyn Waugh's *Brideshead Revisited*, for which normal annual sales would be a few hundred or perhaps a few thousand copies, may suddenly sell by the hundreds of thousands when a popular TV series is based on one of these books. Unfortunately the effect of this mass-media influence is to create an imbalance in the market, which is decisive for its whole economy. Since book sales are relatively constant, these enormous editions of a few titles tend to affect adversely the sale of other books, which sell less and less. This is also true of backlist sales, that is to say, the sale of books that date back beyond the year of publication, which of course includes the classics. The effect of this is negative both from a cultural point of view and for the publishers, since it weakens their financial position and forces them to publish more and more new books in order to survive.

Obviously the publishers have not been content merely to avail themselves of the opportunities provided by the mass-media for selling huge editions of a few titles; they too have actively influenced the market. The mass-market in paperbacks is a typical example. This particular form of book was created for the mass-society and has developed very rapidly since the war to become, perhaps, the most important source of income for both writer and publisher. The idea behind this method of publication is that a small number of titles are chosen from the ordinary hardcover books and then printed in very large editions (generally not less than 100,000) to be sold at an extremely low price. (These mass-market paperbacks should not be mixed up with quality paperbacks, which are printed in much smaller editions to a notably higher price.) The income from these relatively few titles is subsequently needed to finance the publication of new books, among which once again a few of the most successful are chosen to be circulated on a mass-scale.

Yet another method of selling books is through book clubs, which have become increasingly important from the seventies on. The basic idea behind the book clubs is the same: to sell a small number of titles to a large number of people. The book clubs exploit the passiveness and lack of knowledge that exist within mass-society: the members of book clubs receive a book every month without having to make the choice themselves, and the delivery of books does not cease until they leave the club. The comparatively few titles which are published are very much the same as those that appear on the paperback market.

The competition to achieve 'bestsellerdom' affects both writer and publisher to the extent that, rather than just sit back and hope for the best, they actually try to create such books. The most common means of doing this is to use pre-publication publicity and modern marketing techniques. Peter Benchley's *Jaws*, which was among the greatest sales successes of the seventies, is a typical example of this method of marketing. The publishers decided to publish the book on the basis of a brief outline, when the film rights to this material were sold to a film company. The huge sums paid to the author by the publisher and the film company were made public. This in turn created something of a sensation and much more money was then paid out for the paperback rights. Thus both the book and the film were famous before they even existed and in this way they got a tremendous start in world-wide publicity. The success that resulted from this 'hyping' encouraged those responsible to try and repeat it, by the simple means of commissioning the author to write a sequel, which was given the hardly imaginative title, *Jaws II*; this too was a great success.

Another example of how it is possible to gain vast profits from successful authorship is the revival of the *James Bond* books, the greatest publishing success of their time. Since the author was dead, the company that had acquired the rights to the literary figure commissioned another writer to write new *James Bond* books. The owners of the rights also provided the writer with detailed directions as to how the hero should be changed to gain the greatest number of sales to a new generation: he should now drive a more modest car, smoke low-tar cigarettes and treat women as equals.

This rather revolutionary change in the book market has been described as a division of the old homogeneous market into two circuits: the cultivated circuit and the popular circuit. The cultivated circuit is what remains of the book market of the bourgeois society, where writers, publishers, critics, booksellers and readers belong to the same circuit. This circuit tends to grow smaller as the society changes and there is thus a decline in the financial rewards of catering to it. This means that the publisher must exercise greater constraint in his choice of manuscripts, that the bookseller will choose fewer of the books published and that the critic will praise a limited selection of these books, from among which the reader will finally make his choice.

The other part of this increasingly polarized book market – the popular circuit – is, however, ideally suited to mass-society. Some elements of this circuit have long existed within the book market – such popular fiction as Westerns and Romances etc. and their distribution channels, kiosks, department stores and supermarkets. This part of the book market has become increasingly dominant and imposed itself upon traditional channels. The bestseller, particularly in mass-market paperbacks, is a typical example, while another is the increasing success of books written directly for the mass-market. These are sold internationally in a variety of series; Harlequin Romances, for instance, enjoy the widest distribution in the world. The authors of such books were not long ago anonymous and badly paid but are now famous and millionaires. It is not entirely a coincidence perhaps that Barbara Cartland, one of the best-known writers of romances, is through marriage related to the Royal Household. These books are now not only sold in kiosks but to a growing extent in bookshops too, and they even occasionally gain the attention of critics. A typical example is Danielle Steele, who started as an unknown author of mass-market romances. Now her paperbacks are published in expensive hardcover editions, getting reviews in leading newspapers. Finally, the readers of these books, who were once found among the servants and lower social classes, now belong to all classes. Since it is no longer important socially to read good literature, the reading of popular literature has become socially acceptable.

However, quality literature may also be found in the popular circuit. The present-day book market does not discriminate in any direction, due to the social attitudes mentioned above. There are a number of books and writers that have succeeded in making the jump from the cultivated circuit to the popular circuit. In general terms this has been caused by the exigencies of the mass-market or mass-media and has little to do with a book's quality. Film and TV tie-ins have already been mentioned; literary prizes can also produce a mass-media effect. The Nobel Prize is probably the best known of these awards that can suddenly make virtually unknown authors world famous and thereby turn their books into bestsellers in the popular circuit – their books are printed in paperbacks, filmed, dramatized on TV etc. Isaac Bashevis Singer was seventy-four when he was awarded the Nobel Prize in 1978. Until then he was almost unknown outside New York, making a living on writing short stories for Jewish–American magazines. The Prize made him one of the best-known authors both in Europe and America. His books were from then on reviewed on the front page of the literary weeklies and he became a very wealthy man. The same happened to Elias Canetti – also in his seventies when he won the Prize in 1981 – where his books, having been virtually unknown, became bestsellers overnight. The Goncourt Prize in France is another such award. This latter is so highly valued that book-buyers often ask for 'the new Goncourt' rather than the book's title or author's name. It has taken a long time to establish a literary prize in Britain. Though several prizes existed for many years, such as the Whitbread and the Booker prizes, they were not marketed in a proper way until the beginning of the eighties. In 1981 there was a breakthrough for the Booker Prize which for the first time put the winner, *Midnight's Children* by Salman Rushdie, on the bestseller list. At last the vigour of the prize was so strong that the other finalists also, like D. M. Thomas, became bestsellers with highly literary books. This was greeted in some media as a sudden breakthrough of the serious novel; in fact it was an example of a jump to the popular circuit through strong media interest created by a literary prize.

This polarization has had far-reaching consequences for the book market as a whole, both culturally and financially, and may be witnessed in its rapid restructuring since the war. The financial stability of general publishers has always been very dependent on the novel. Through the decades they built up a stable of increasingly well-known writers – such as, for example, Somerset Maugham, Evelyn Waugh, Graham Greene and J. B. Priestley – to mention names from the last generation of authors who turned in new manuscripts year after year that sold steadily and well. This pattern has become increasingly rare. Most literary novels now sell fewer and fewer copies, since they fail to make the jump over to the popular circuit. Thus, not only do the sale of these authors' books remain at a low level – often only a few thousand copies – but in the stiffening competition sales are actually declining. Even in the case of serious authors who have achieved wide popularity with a single book, there is no guarantee that their future books will be bestsellers. Alexander Solzhenitsyn is one example. He first became famous after his persecution and subsequent deportation from the Soviet Union and after he had been awarded the Nobel Prize, and his books had sold hundreds of thousands of copies. Since his exile he has received little publicity and the sale of his books has declined to the level of the cultivated circuit.

It has therefore become more difficult for serious writers to make a living and many have reacted either by withdrawing into more private experimental writing, or they have resorted to a simpler slicker style or applied their talents to film and television. Thereby the risks have become greater for the publishers. The profits from ever-fewer titles must be used to finance a growing number of hard-to-sell books. One consequence of this is that it is more difficult for new authors to find publishers: first novels are becoming a rarity. One method of dealing with these problems is that publishers try to gain control of distribution outlets. They attempt to buy or establish chains of bookshops, but primarily they form their own book clubs and mass-market lines where they themselves can determine which books are to be channelled into the popular circuit. This too, however, provides only a very limited outlet for serious literature.

Obviously bookshops are also affected by the changes in the market. As long as there existed a homogeneous book market most booksellers were able to stock a wide selection of the latest books published, for which there was also a steady demand. Since more and more copies are being sold of fewer and fewer books, the choice of titles available in the bookshops grows smaller. It is simply not profitable to stock thousands of titles when only a few hundred actually sell. This problem has been made more serious by rising rents and salaries. What counts is turnover per square metre, and the publication of classics and poetry do not give a profitable turnover, whereas bestsellers and paperbacks do.

It seems likely that this polarization and the need to adjust to the mass-society will become more firmly marked in the future. But of course there will still be a need for serious literature, although probably on a smaller scale. All the elements of the traditional book market will continue to exist, but in a more restricted and perhaps isolated form. That is to say, special bookshops will be established for serious literature, small publishing houses with low overheads will publish such books, and they will be reviewed in specialized journals and magazines. This specialization is not entirely negative. It will be easier for readers with these interests to find their favourite books and the economic pressure will be less harsh. The dominant factor in the operation of a large publishing house or chain of bookshops is profitability; among small publishers and specialized bookshops the norm is quality, the aspiration survival.

However, it is most probable that in the future the State will have to subsidize the cultivated circuit. After all, serious literature is virtually the only remnant of bourgeois culture that does not receive heavy financial support from the State. Serious music, opera and theatre, and the graphic arts are now all greatly dependent on government grants, seemingly without detrimental effects. There have been fears that freedom of expression could be at risk once the State is involved in such matters. However, it has been shown that where State support for literature has been tried, in Scandinavia for instance, it has stimulated a much more varied and manifold literature than is produced under the yoke of harsh economic laws. The important thing, of course, is to find an appropriate form for such support.

THE POST-WAR ENGLISH NOVEL

GILBERT PHELPS

When we recall the scope and variety of English fiction in the earlier years of this century in the hands of such writers of genius as Henry James, Joseph Conrad, E. M. Forster, D. H. Lawrence, Virginia Woolf and James Joyce, it is difficult not to feel that there has been a decline. The trend of the English novel since the Second World War has, on the whole, been analogous to that of the poetry – a turning aside from the mainstream of European literature and a tendency to retreat into parochialism and defeatism – attended, it is true, by outstanding moments of protest, defiance, honesty or insight, as well as by a proliferation of genuine talents, but rarely approaching a unified vision or the sustained solidity of achievement that rises from it. It is doubtful, for example, whether any single English novel of the period can bear comparison with Boris Pasternak's *Dr Zhivago* (English translation, 1957) or with Alexander Solzhenitsyn's *Cancer Ward* (English translation, 1972), either in profundity of theme or power of creative imagination (and these themselves are at a lower level of attainment than the greatest of the nineteenth-century Russian novels). At the same time, despite a number of gloomy prognostications, the English novel is far from dead.

In a limited space it is impossible to do more than indicate some of the more characteristic works of fiction written during the period (nearly half a century), and inevitably this means distortion and over-simplification, considerable licence to individual preferences, and an exclusion, in consequence, of many names and titles that may well strike the reader as inexcusable. Moreover, many of the more cele-brated writers are treated elsewhere in this volume, and so are omitted from this chapter.

In attempting, therefore, what is meant to be a very general picture of post-war developments, it is convenient to divide novelists roughly into six main categories: the survivors of the thirties (that is, writers who were already in the forefront of the literary scene between the wars); novelists who were already writing during the same period, but who either did not achieve maturity or failed to gain full recognition until after the Second World War; the so-called 'Angry Young Men', or those related to them in theme or approach; a group of women writers of more or less 'feminist' persuasion; a group of anti- or at least post-imperialist writers; and a few writers who have also achieved considerable reputations in the period under consideration but have little in common with any of the other categories.

The general point to be made about the first of these groups is that the majority of them found it as difficult to make the transition successfully to the post-war world as they had done to meet the challenge of their formidable predecessors or near-contemporaries. D. H. Lawrence's revolt against 'the old skin and grief form' of the English novel, Virginia Woolf's reaction against the 'materialism' of writers like Arnold Bennett and H. G. Wells, and James Joyce's linguistic and narrative innovations, had all seemed to be pointing in the direction of greater experimentation and a break-up of the familiar fictional moulds. By 1939, however, it had been pretty generally accepted that *Finnegans Wake* (published in that year) marked the *ne plus ultra* of that particular line of development. That it was a mistaken assumption is evidenced by the case of Samuel Beckett, but most of the writers of the earlier post-war period were, on the whole, still writing comfortably within the basic conventions of the traditional English novel, and it was some time before signs of doubt or anxiety began to appear.

The impact of the war itself, of course, affected those already writing in very different ways. There were, inevitably, some whose intellectual and emotional commitments belonged so unequivocally to the 1920s and 1930s that they never really adapted themselves with any degree of ease or conviction to the post-war world. This was especially the case, perhaps, with the politically confused or disillusioned, who sometimes give the impression that the mat had been pulled from under their feet. Rex Warner, for example, retreated to the distant past for his subject-matter and his later novels somehow do not possess the same vitality as his left-wing political fable *The Wild Goose Chase* (1937). Similarly, Christopher Isherwood's stories of pre-war Berlin carry more imaginative conviction than, say, *A Meeting by the River* (1967) with its excursions into Oriental philosophies, and the most successful of his later novels was *Down There on a Visit* (1962), largely because with the return of 'Herr Issyvoo' as narrator and the return visit, too, to Berlin, some of the 'I am a Camera' sharpness of vision and rightness of tone of the earlier work also returned. But for the most part the private hells which Isherwood explores in many of his post-war novels have little universal human significance.

To some extent much the same might be said of Aldous Huxley. His ideas and speculations continued to flow. *Ape and Essence* (1949) envisaged a California after a nuclear war, in which nothing remains of human civilization apart from its squalor, taboos, and worship of evil. The first part of *Island* (1962) shows a genuine Utopia, where the good life really does exist – before it is destroyed by a brutal, materialistic dictator. But on the whole there is more vitality in Huxley's novels of the thirties – *Brave New World* (1932) among them – largely because they succeeded in capturing a part, even if it was a particularly negative and destructive part, of the spirit of the times.

It was, however, the 'writers of sensibility' like Charles Morgan, Rosamond Lehmann and (in some respects at any rate) Elizabeth Bowen, who were exploring personal relationships, usually among the upper-middle class or the intelligentsia, within an already dead or dying social ambience, who found it most difficult to make the transition, and who seemed to many of the post-war young to be like denizens of Chekhov's *Cherry Orchard*, hanging on long after the trees had been chopped down, and retreating into nostalgia and fine writing. The dilemma of many of the more uneasy and recalcitrant survivors of the thirties is admirably symbolized by Evelyn Waugh's novel *The Ordeal of Gilbert Pinfold* (1957), especially in the first chapter entitled 'Portrait of the Artist in Middle Age', where Pinfold confesses that little of passion is left to men like him beyond a few testy prejudices:

> His strongest tastes were negative. He abhorred plastics, Picasso, sunbathing and jazz – everything in fact that had happened in his own lifetime.

Of the second group of novelists, the most idiosyncratic was also the one who most obviously and deliberately reached back to the past for her subject-matter. From her first mature novel, *Pastors and Masters* (1925) to her last, *A God and His Gifts* (1963), Ivy Compton-Burnett dealt almost exclusively, and with an astonishing consistency of method and tone, with upper-middle class Edwardian society, calmly declaring:

> I do not feel that I have any real organic knowledge later than 1910. I should not write of later times with enough grasp or confidence.[1]

The kind of highly-stylized effects she achieved lent themselves to a cult following and easily invite parody. She has a genuine wit, however – as distinct from smartness and stylistic ornament – proceeding from a critical but humane assessment of the standards and values of her creations. But the comparison with Jane Austen, which has often been made, immediately emphasizes the differences. Jane Austen was writing, after all, about a way of life that was a present and stable reality: her vision was both more profound and more vital, and her humour has a radiance, a redeeming quality that Ivy Compton-Burnett's lacks. Nevertheless, the fictional world the latter presents is consistent with its own laws of being and has its own credibility; and she had a good deal of justification in believing that the Edwardian country house and the patriarchal families that inhabited it provided her with a kind of laboratory in which she could examine human behaviour under closed conditions. The theme of all the novels is, in fact, summed up by the eldest daughter in *Parents and Children* (1941) when she sardonically exclaims:

> Dear, dear, the miniature world of the family! All the emotions of mankind seem to find a place in it!

It is a theme, though, that offers little in the way of normal human relationships and affections, and less still for romantic passion. Many of her novels are about domestic tyrants; sometimes men – as in *A House and Its Head* (1935) and *Parents and Children* (1941); sometimes women – as in *Daughters and Sons* (1937) and *Elders and Betters* (1944). The plots usually depend upon violent climaxes, either the actual committing of a crime or the revelation of some skeleton in the cupboard: incest in *Brothers and Sisters* (1929), sundry thefts and fornications in *Darkness and Day* (1951), and attempted suicide in *The Present and the Past* (1953). There is here an interest in violence that in a lesser writer could have degenerated into sensationalism or unconscious farce. She is saved from both by her sureness of touch and the complete freedom from sentimentality in her view of human nature. As she said:

> I think there are signs that strange things happen, though they do not emerge. I believe it would go ill with many of us if we were faced with temptation, and I suspect that with some of us it does go ill.[2]

But a sympathy and understanding for the victims of human wickedness – the evil-doers included – emerge unmistakably from the drift and texture of the conventionalized dialogue and the tensions they generate. Most of the human passions with which Ivy Compton-Burnett deals in her novels, moreover, belong to no particular age or society, and in depicting them she was fully aware of the modern world: her handling of family passions and jealousies makes it evident, for example, that she was conscious of a cultural background that included Ibsen, Dostoyevsky and Freud.

A review of L. P. Hartley's first novel, *Simonetta Perkins* (1925), in the *Calendar of Letters* accurately assessed his basic equipment — a cool and lucid style, firm intelligence, the 'observant, neat, and graceful exercises upon a "situation"', the 'ironic and comprehensive attitude'.[3] In many respects these qualities are also seen at their best in dealing with an Edwardian past. *The Shrimp and the Anemone* (1944), for instance, is about the childhood of the gentle, imaginative and rather ineffectual Eustace and his vivid, passionate and possessive sister Hilda, set against the background of an East coast seaside resort at the turn of the century. *The Go-Between* (1953) recalls a long hot Edwardian summer, and its violent events, as witnessed by the boy Leo Colston. In both cases the evocation of time and place is outstanding in its rich and sensuous detail and in the kind of shimmering brilliance that belongs to memories of childhood, at the same time that it is directly and concretely related to the experiences of the characters. Both novels also bring out with particular poignancy the theme that is central to Hartley's best work — the individual's search for a meaning to his existence, an existence that is usually full of disappointments, frustrations and apparent waste.

The Shrimp and the Anemone was the first of a trilogy: the second of the novels, *The Sixth Heaven* (1946) is not as convincing, but the third, *Eustace and Hilda* (also 1946) powerfully reveals the dangerous and potentially destructive nature of the relationship between brother and sister (with strong Jungian undertones of the Animus–Anima clash as well as the obvious quasi-incestuous one) and ends with Eustace discovering a sort of meaning to his life by choosing to die in order to release his sister. Leo Colston in *The Go-Between*, looking back in later life, lonely and unfulfilled, sees the boy he then was as 'a foreigner in the world of the emotions, ignorant of their language but compelled to listen to it', and realizes that the experience blighted his whole life, but in realizing this he begins to understand and accept. And in *The Hireling* (1957) a very different kind of character, the hard-bitten, cynical Steven Leadbitter dies with a sense of something accomplished after he has admitted to himself that he loves the widowed Lady Franklin (for whom he acts as chauffeur) and has taken the further step of admitting it to her, thus helping to free her from the guilts and depressions of her past.

Unlike the earlier trilogy *The Hireling* is fairly placed in post-war England. Hartley now tended to concentrate on rather narrow, closely-observed contemporary milieux – the film world in *My Fellow Devils* (1951), for example, and artistic Bloomsbury in *Poor Clare* (1968). The individual search for meaning continues to be the dominant theme, but increasingly it takes on metaphysical implications. The most obvious instance is *Facial Justice* (1960) a fantasy of a future state ruled by a more or less benevolent dictator who tries to impose a regime of equality, non-violence and conformity. The attempt fails, in circumstances that are too complex and often too enigmatic to be sure what exactly Hartley was getting at, but the general moral – that imagination and idealism, no matter what the cost, are vital to mankind's wellbeing and the suggestion that these are related to a higher order of being – emerges clearly enough.

Neither Ivy Compton-Burnett nor L. P. Hartley, in spite of the inherent vitality that carried them beyond the thirties where so many of their contemporaries had in effect remained transfixed, set out to be 'historians of their times' in the same way as Anthony Powell and C. P. Snow, the two best-known post-war exponents of the large-scale fictional sequence. Anthony Powell launched his long series *The Music of Time* in 1951, but as a whole it has revealed little in the way of a commanding structural design or pattern, especially when set beside Proust's *À la recherche du temps perdu* with which it has been compared. The plots, locations, and attitudes change, but there is always the feeling that the books, in spite of slightly different shapes and flavours, have all been cut, roughly to the same size, from the same interminable length of material, and that they depend rather too much on cast-marks and passwords that are sometimes meaningless outside a closed circle. Nonetheless the sequence does convince us that it is based on values that are fundamentally decent and humane, and that it is a genuinely created world of the imagination.

C. P. Snow began his *Strangers and Brothers* sequence with the title-novel in 1940. *The Light and the Dark* followed in 1947, but it was perhaps *The Masters* (1951), a study of the in-fighting at a Cambridge college over the election of a new Master, that first brought Snow's over-riding preoccupation – the analysis of the centres of power in post-war English society, in both their public and private manifestations – into sharp focus. The more closed the society, the more effective the approach usually is: certainly after *The Masters*, one of the most gripping of the novels was *The Corridors of Power* (1964), which is about the workings of the upper echelons of the Civil Service in Whitehall, and the clashes between private consciences and the interests of the state.

The sequence did not dodge the major challenges of the times: in *The New Men* (1954), for example, the narrator–participant Lewis Eliot shares the horror of many of his fellow-scientists at the implications of official policies on the nuclear deterrent, and in *A Sleep of Reason* (1968), Eliot returns to his home-town to find a horrifying child-murder trial in progress, and is in consequence brought up against the whole question of the spirit of violence that had attended so many of the events of the 1960s, permeating the whole of society. These are all big and important issues, and Snow was perhaps the only novelist of the period who consistently set out to explore them. At the same time his topicality does not possess the sense of urgency inherent and so effective in that of Graham Greene. Neither do the private lives of his characters always offer satisfactory correlatives to the public themes. This is in part the result of a lack of any passionate political commitment on the part of Lewis

Eliot, who is fundamentally a neutral observer, alert to all the issues but on the whole a figure of compromise. It is also, however, the result of a lack in Snow's novels of what Henry James called 'felt life', although this criticism applies less to the final novel of the sequence, *Last Things* (1970), than to the more overtly political novels.

A preoccupation with the 'facts' of history, and their proper use and interpretation, is one of the salient features of the work of Olivia Manning in her two trilogies about the Second World War. Her pre-1939 novels were marked by irony, detachment and a fastidiousness that verges on the chilling. These qualities, however, stood her in good stead when she came to work on *The Balkan Trilogy* (1960–65), because they so exactly defined and placed the central consciousness of the novels – that of Harriet, the young wife of Guy Pringle, whose work as lecturer takes them to various storm-centres in Eastern Europe and the Middle East during the war. The central consciousness operates on two levels. It is the filter through which the political events themselves are transmuted into something which is both factually correct and imaginatively true. Harriet is almost totally unpolitical, a stranger in a violent and exotic world, both naïve and shrewd, and it is this combination that gives the account of the decline and fall of Rumania in *The Balkan Trilogy* its almost Defoe-like air of authority and authenticity, the pervasive sense of unease and impending disaster being highlighted every now and then by flashes of violence and horror. The other level is that of Harriet's troubled personal relationship with her over-gregarious husband, and it is the troubled balance between these two levels of the central consciousness that makes *The Balkan Trilogy* genuine historical fiction, enabling Olivia Manning to reveal the workings of historical processes in living, human terms.

In her second sequence, *The Levant Trilogy* (1977–80), Harriet, Guy, and some of the other characters who had escaped from Greece at the end of the first trilogy, are living in Egypt. For Harriet marital stresses have become more severe, but this time they are not perhaps as successful in providing a unifying principle: they have become repetitive and even a little obsessive. More important, however, at the point when Harriet seems to have lost her personal battle, Olivia Manning turns to another one, and in doing so adds a new dimension to her stature as a war novelist. She introduces a new centre of consciousness, Simon Boulderstone, a young army officer who acts as a direct link between the fleshpots of Cairo and the desert campaigns. For the first time the war is now presented not from the civilian sidelines but through the experiences of a combatant. The description of the long and confused battle of El Alamein, in which Simon serves as a liaison officer, is probably the finest evocation of battle to emerge from the war.

These novelists, at varying levels of achievement, established their reputations in the post-war world, and had something of real value to say to it. It is doubtful, though, whether any of them could be thought of as a 'growing point' in the English novel. At one time it looked as if Joyce Cary, whose work in the 1940s and 1950s conveyed a strong sense of fresh energies released, might be just that. The dedication and enormous industry with which he pursued the search for rightness of style and form certainly qualified him for the role. His first novel, *Aissa Saved* (1932), was the result of ten years of continuous reshaping and redrafting. The manuscripts of the unfinished *Cock Jarvis* (edited after Cary's death by A. G. Bishop and published in 1974) comprise nearly a million words, and the fifteen published novels represent only the tip of the iceberg.

Aissa Saved is set in Nigeria where Cary had served six years in the colonial administration, as is the more accomplished *Mister Johnson* (1939), the story of an ill-fated African clerk, told with humour and compassion and already displaying that power of absorption into the aspirations and motivations of his characters that constituted one of his main strengths. The peak of his achievement, however, is represented by two trilogies. The first of these consists of *Herself Surprised* (1941), the story of Sara Monday, one-time model and mistress to the artist Gulley Jimson; *To Be A Pilgrim* (1942), about Thomas Wilcher, the retired Evangelical lawyer, to whom Sara becomes housekeeper and mistress; and *The Horse's Mouth* (1944), which is about Gulley Jimson himself, the relentlessly dedicated artist.

Cary's professed aim in writing this trilogy was to deal, according to Henry Reed, with 'English history, through English eyes, for the last sixty years' and a similar purpose lies behind the second trilogy, consisting of *Prisoner of Grace* (1952), the story of Nina, more or less married off to Chester Nimmo, the rising young politician of humble Nonconformist background; *Except the Lord* (1953), about Chester

Nimmo; and *Not Honour More* (1955), told from the point of view of the soldier James Latter, father of Nina's children and eventually (though tragically) her husband. In both trilogies the grasp of historical processes is remarkable; and in both the sense of gradual change within the social structure, of the interlocking of political events with sectional and individual destinies, of subtle shifts in public and private morality with their accompanying changes in dress, idiom and *mores*, are conveyed in vivid and concrete detail. Cary's other main aim continued to be the presentation of his characters through their individual habits of thought and feeling, and the search for techniques of impersonation lay behind his continuous writing and rewriting. In these respects alone Cary's achievement is an outstanding one.

In spite, however, of Cary's ability to eliminate himself as storyteller (and he achieves it more thoroughly than Joyce did in *Finnegans Wake*), judgements are inevitably implied, and it is here perhaps that there is a flaw in his work. In the last resort we *are* called upon to make a choice between those who are fundamentally hypocrites and those who are fundamentally outside accepted codes and conventions – and there are few variations in between. Our sympathies flow inevitably towards the victims of Evangelical self-righteousness because they, manifestly, are the ones who stand for life. But Cary tends to overdo their inadequacies in the face of the world: we feel that the odds are too heavily weighted against the victims. Not that the victims ever complain: their courage remains undimmed, and perhaps what Cary meant to convey was that although the forces of convention and respectability will always be too strong for the innocent, there is also a sense in which the former can never win.

Another (and perhaps the oddest in this context) of the survivors from the 1930s, was J. R. R. Tolkien, the Professor of Anglo-Saxon at Oxford who in the 1960s suddenly became the centre of a highbrow cult. He had taken a special interest in the Old English poem *Beowulf* and in the whole subject of the dragon in legend, seeing it as 'a potent creation of man's imagination', and an equally potent symbol of evil. Some of these ideas entered into *The Hobbit: or There and Back Again* (1937). But although the quest theme is treated with some seriousness, this is basically juvenile literature. After the war

Tolkien began to rework the same material in adult form. The result, after twelve years' labour, was the massive *The Lord of the Rings* (1954-77). The sequence, with its perilous quest, magical ring, elves, hobbits, and all kinds of other fabulous creatures (as well as humans) – together with the brooding presence of Sauron, Lord of Darkness – is an extraordinary *mélange* of adventure story and Nordic and Arthurian legend. Inevitably it has been seen as an allegory, inviting all kinds of interpretations from the historical and political to the religious and psychoanalytical, all of which Tolkien himself denied. He did believe, though, that the modern world was parched for the lack of viable myths, and the intensity of the Tolkien craze in the 1960s and beyond suggests that he was right in this respect.

There is one other novelist in this older group who is of relevance here. Lawrence Durrell published two novels before the war and several shortly after it. But it is on *The Alexandria Quartet* (1957-60) that his reputation mainly rests. The story told by these four novels is frequently melodramatic and erotic, and far too complicated for any kind of summary. But 'plot' in *The Alexandria Quartet* is really of minor importance. So in many respects is characterization as such. For the most part the protagonists remain flat surfaces upon which are inscribed, in ornamental profusion, all kinds of gestures, habits, sayings, but they never become three-dimensional creations. There is, too, a startling gap between the professedly brilliant ideas ascribed to the characters and their actual human behaviour. Purse-warden, for instance, is described as 'a great novelist', but there is nothing about him to convince the reader that he has the equipment, the responses to life, or the personality (as Joyce Cary does convince with Gulley Jimson) to make an artist of any kind at all. And although the novels purport to analyse 'Love', where are the profound human relationships that alone could support the claim? The erotic subtleties that are offered are almost entirely those of the intellect or of sexual behaviour divorced from love in any significant sense of the word. To some extent perhaps this is intentional insofar as it is Alexandria itself which is the main character. It is upon Alexandria that Durrell lavishes all the resources of his highly poetic style, evoking its exotic sights, sounds and smells, its splendours and decays, and its cosmopolitan, polyglot culture. Although this style is overdone (Durrell himself has described it as 'too juicy'), his purpose was to suggest that human character and behaviour are in large part controlled by the ambience in which they move. Thus Pursewarden argues in *Balthazar* (1956):

Our view of reality is conditioned by our position in space and time – not by our personalities as we like to think ... Thus every interpretation of reality is based upon a unique position ...

This may not be a very inspiriting account of human behaviour, but it indicates one of those aspects of *The Alexandria Quartet* which are of interest in relation to the whole problem of reality in fiction. In a radio interview Durrell declared that his aim was to give the reader 'the stereoscopic feeling which raised question marks – like: "What is reality?", and "Do you think that human personality is an illusion?".' Does this suggest one reason at least why Durrell's experiment in *The Alexandria Quartet* should have aroused a particularly enthusiastic response on the Continent? Another, no doubt is his evident debts to Proust, Musil, and Mann.

The reputation of Henry Green (the pseudonym of Henry Vincent Yorke) has also always stood higher on the Continent than in his own country. Realism and reality in his work, from his first novel, *Blindness* (1926), to his last, *Doting* (1952), have an oddly ambiguous, evasive quality. At first sight the outside contemporary world seems to play a crucial part: *Living* (1929) is ostensibly about workers in a Midlands factory; *Caught* (1943) is based on Green's own experiences in the Auxiliary Fire Service during the Blitz, which forms a vivid climax to the novel; and *Back* (1949) is about the problems facing a disabled prisoner-of-war on his repatriation and return to civilian life. But this contemporaneity is deceptive. The events, no matter how stirring, are really peripheral: there is no attempt to discuss their provenance or their implications: they are merely the given conditions, the conventions almost, for the evocation of the separate poetic entity that belongs to each novel. The single-word titles in part relate to Green's preoccupation with economy, precision and concentration: often, for example, he practises a near-Aristotelian compression of time and place, so that the action of *Party-Going* (1939) comprises only a few hours, while the whole of the action of *Loving* (1948) is confined to an Irish country house and its grounds. But the titles are also indicative of a concern with being rather than doing: the purpose of each novel is to evoke a state of being, that is, which exists in its own right, fundamentally independent of the envelope of fact and circumstance. It will be apparent from this that the titles have a symbolic significance: but it is symbol – used almost in an Imagist sense – strictly controlled by the necessities of each separate 'being' (or the more up-to-date 'happening'), very different from the clumsy and portentous symbolism common in so many other contemporary novels.

One more novelist might be mentioned in this group, though he really falls outside the scope of this chapter. Wyndham Lewis published *The Childermass* in 1928, but its sequels, *Monstre Gai* and *Malign Fiesta* (which together with the unfinished *Trial of Man* were to form a sequence entitled *The Human Age*), did not appear until 1955. Lewis published other works of fiction too after the war, including the novel *Self-Condemned* (1954) and a collection of short stories. But the date of *Childermass* has some significance, for Wyndham Lewis really belongs to the more robust ethos of the twenties. His vision of human society (in his painting as well as in his fiction) was formed in the explosion of anger that succeeded the First World War. It is pessimistic and largely destructive, expressed, as far as the sequence of novels is concerned, in terms of fable rather than realistic fiction, and marred by long digressions and clumsiness of technique. But at the same time it is a unified and dynamic vision of twentieth-century man and his predicament as a member of a mass civilization, as victim and participant in the Age of the Machine. It was the very scale of this conception that provided the impetus that carried it without any relaxation of purpose beyond the 1930s; but there was little development in Lewis's basic attitudes, most of which were already apparent in his early novel *Tarr* (1918).

If Joyce Cary can be seen as one of the few novelists to come into prominence after the war who responded deeply and imaginatively to the wider movements of contemporary history and their human implications, it is with a group of younger writers who were still children in between the wars, working at a far lower level of achievement and within much narrower limits, that we usually associate the typical mood and flavour of the 1950s. The label 'Angry Young Man', which became current after the presentation of John Osborne's play *Look Back in Anger* at the Royal Court Theatre in May 1956, is a rough-and-ready one to apply to writers who never pretended to form anything approaching a School. But it does signify an attitude of mind which they had in common at that stage of their careers.

The 'anger' they displayed was hardly of the kind we associate with D. H. Lawrence or with Wyndham Lewis in this century, or with such great eighteenth-century satirists as Swift and Pope, or with the Elizabethan social filibusters such as Nashe, because what is so clearly implicit in these cases is either a standard of moral reference passionately believed in or the background of a society and culture that still possessed a positive dynamic. The protest of the 'Angry Young Men' was of a far lower voltage, closer to a general dissentience or disgruntlement. It was part social and part cultural. Nearly all of them were too young to have seen war service, and were impatient of the war mystique cherished by their elders; most of them were mildly committed supporters of the Labour Government under whose dispensation some of them had received their educations; many had middle or lower-middle class backgrounds; and a number of them were college or university teachers. The main force of their anger was directed not so much against the survivors of the 1930s already discussed as against those who, it seemed to them, still constituted a powerful, though outdated, Establishment, the liberal-humane, largely upper-middle-class Bloomsbury intelligentsia – what Kenneth Allsop, in his lively little book *The Angry Decade*, called 'the old literati, the candelabra-and-wine *rentier* writers',[4] symbolized for them by the old Etonian Cyril Connolly and his magazine *Horizon*.

Lucky Jim remains the most vigorous and effective example of the protest, particularly in the passages that expose the academic racket, and the pseudo-culture and social pretensions that so often accompany it – notably in the hilariously funny scenes describing Professor Welch's musical evening and Jim Dixon's public lecture on 'Merrie England' – and Amis went on to explore other aspects of aesthetic cant and snobbery in *That Uncertain Feeling* (1955) and *I Like It Here* (1958). There were, of course, many other variations of the prevailing mood. In John Wain's *Hurry On Down*, for example (published in 1954, a few months before *Lucky Jim*) the picaresque hero Charles Lumley wishes both to stand outside society and to find a niche in it – provided it is one that carries no obligation of commitment, reflecting at the end of the novel:

> Neutrality; he had found it at last. The running fight between himself and society had ended in a draw.

In John Braine's *Room at the Top* (1957) Joe Lampton is presented as a typical product of the partial economic and social revolution of the Welfare State which, while providing opportunity for advancement, offers no real political dynamic, no incentives beyond the material ones, and a moral code summed up by the popular phrase of the period, 'I'm all right, Jack'. For all the novel's sensationalism and sentimentality, Braine made effective use of copywriter's English and a plethora of smart brand names to illustrate what Richard Hoggart in *The Uses of Literacy* (1957), one of the key books of the period, called the 'shiny barbarism' of the day. Yet Braine also successfully conveyed the small core of moral sensibility lurking behind the brashness and heartless go-getting of his main protagonist. The most fully realized of these anti-heroes, however, was Arthur Seaton, the factory worker of Alan Sillitoe's *Saturday Night and Sunday Morning* (1958), who perceives that the benefits of full employment are both partial and precarious, senses an unspoken comradeship between himself and his fellow workers directed against a vague 'they' of employer and State, and is dimly aware that all is not well either with the society in which he lives or with his own personal values.

Where, however, these novelists so often failed to live up to the standards represented by the great writers of the past, and some of those already discussed, was not in their subject-matter (which is a perfectly valid one for fiction) but in their lapses in artistic detachment and control. They were often too emotionally committed to the negative values they sought to illustrate. In their concern not to be associated in any way with genteel Bloomsbury traditions of fine writing, for example, some of these writers cultivated a deliberately slapdash, honest Jack style of writing, while the loose, picaresque structure often adopted was symptomatic of an emphatic rejection of the old Jamesian concept of form in the novel. Kingsley Amis deliberately pushed his counter-argument to its farthest extreme, depicting with evident relish characters who rail against 'filthy

Mozart' and 'all those rotten churches and museums and galleries';
and he was quite prepared to put himself out on a limb, as when,
in his review in the *Spectator* of Colin Wilson's *The Outsider* (1956),
another representative document of the period, he described Kierke-
gaard, Nietzsche, Dostoyevsky, Blake and others as 'those characters
you thought were discredited, or had never read, or (if you were like
me) had never heard of . . .' Such pronouncements from a university
lecturer in English were not, presumably, to be taken too seriously:
they were grapeshot discharged in the heat of battle. The fact, though,
that Amis had gone out of his way to tilt at foreign writers – again,
of course, because they loomed so large in the aesthetic of the literary
Establishment – is also significant. Behind the work of this group of
writers was a kind of defiant little Englandism, a reaction against the
cult of foreign experimentalism as evinced in *Horizon* (which had
contained articles on Proust, Genet, Cocteau and other contemporary
continental writers), and an assertion that the English fictional tradition provided all the nourishment that was needed to rejuvenate the
novel. In Amis's *I Like It Here*, for example, the hero, on a trip to
Lisbon, although contemptuous of the whole idea of 'abroad', visits
the grave of Henry Fielding, who could be seen as the exemplar of
the most healthy and characteristic strand in the English fictional
tradition.

Generally speaking the force of the protest tailed off after the 1950s.
Kingsley Amis continued for a time to direct his anger against a
variety of pretensions and hypocrisies. But on the whole his explosions modulated into a consciously satirical mode, accompanied
by a chilling but often effective distaste that recalls Evelyn Waugh
– as, in *I Want It Now* (1968), an acid comedy of sex, marriage and
money in the modern world, and *Jake's Thing* (1980), set in
Academia, with its joyless, cerebral sexual preoccupations. There is
no doubting the talent, but there are times when we feel that the
vitality of the talent has been sapped by a profound self-distrust
issuing in a wilful creative self-destructiveness. Alan Sillitoe, on the
other hand, after his long short story *The Loneliness of the Long
Distance Runner* (1959), an unsentimental but compassionate study of
a Borstal boy, tended to turn to a vaguely defined anarchism of 'the
rebel without a cause' type, as in *The Death of William Posters* (1965)
or to a more speculative mode, as in *Travels in Nihilon* (1970). During

the 1950s these anti-modernist writers dominated the English literary scene, whereas on the Continent and in America the novel was facing something of a crisis, increasingly preoccupied by the philosophical dilemmas of existentialism and absurdism. The re-affirmation in new and original terms of existing values, or, where old traditions have decayed, a passionate search for new ones, is surely one of the major tasks of the artist. The most disappointing feature of these writers is that so few of them have gone beyond merely stating the problem: the search hardly ever begins in earnest – or, where it does, usually peters out in defeatism, personal despair or mere cleverness. And yet, one cannot help asking, when has there been an age which more desperately needed novelists to undertake the task?

David Storey's fictional career has been marked by his recurrent doubts about the viability of the novel form, and at one stage he declared that it was 'no longer a reliable metaphor for what's going on' and that 'the whole social context' was inimical to the writing of fiction. Hence his abandonment of the novel, after the publication of *Radcliffe* (1963), in favour of the theatre. His first three novels, though, represented a profounder exploration of the contemporary human condition than anything attempted by the Angry Young Men, absorbed as they were with their more localized filibuster. Storey's novels are organized round a concept – the incompatability of body and soul – which in the hands of a less serious writer would appear pretentious. *This Sporting Life* (1960), in which Arthur Machin is plunged into the corrupt world of professional Rugby League football, concentrates of course on the world of the body, and the way in which Storey creates an atmosphere of physicality around both players and spectators is one of the novel's outstanding achievements. Another is the presentation of the story through the limited mind and outlook of the gladiator-style hero, with the minimum of author's comment, while at the same time conveying a passionate protest against the inherent violence and ugliness of twentieth-century life which recalls D. H. Lawrence. *Radcliffe* (1963), about a stormy, obsessive, and ultimately tragic homosexual relationship between a working-class man and an idealistic member of an upper-class family, explores the violent clash between body and soul, and their apparent irreconcilability. At one point Radcliffe, in a moment of visionary near-insanity, realizes that the love–hate conflict between

433

himself and Tolson, which must result either in union or destruction, represents 'the split in the whole of Western society ...'. and 'the division that separates everything in life now, *everything*'. *Radcliffe* is a rich, powerful and complex novel with characters and incidents unashamedly standing for the most profound human and metaphysical issues. Its literary provenance, moreover, was the reverse of insular and included especially Dostoyevsky and Flaubert, evidence of what A. S. Byatt has called 'the absorbing literary greed of huge talent'.[5]

Storey's highly successful plays were centred on two recurrent themes: breakdown and neurotic withdrawal, usually involving a crisis in marriage; and the stifling demands made by parents for their children's duty, obedience and love. These themes also predominated when he returned to fiction. In both *Pasmore* (1972) and *A Temporary Life* (1973) the main protagonists find that their careers and their marriages have suddenly turned sour, and are in bitter conflict with their working-class parents. Although the detailed, hypnotic intensity with which these themes are presented argues that Storey is drawing on personal experience of mental anguish, his main concern is to get closer to fundamental truth about human existence itself, in the context of the emptiness, anarchy and brutality of contemporary society. All this applies with special force to *Saville* (1976). It is the longest of Storey's novels and the most autobiographical. Until at least halfway through it reads like an old-fashioned chronicle about a miner named Saville, his early struggles, his marriage and his children, in a South Yorkshire mining village. Storey evokes his native milieu with impressive detail and concentration – the smoky, ravaged landscape, the poverty-stricken dwellings, the surrounding countryside, the rich gallery of neighbours, and the gang to which Colin, the hero, belongs as a boy. Sometimes the detail seems too painstaking, even monotonous. Yet the very richness and density of the ties which hold Colin to the past make his efforts to break out into some new and more meaningful kind of life more difficult, and more urgent. An additional difficulty for him is that whereas in most of the previous work parents are depicted as greedily demanding, in *Saville* they are fine characters, unselfishly devoted to their children's well-being. Colin's rebellion, in consequence, is directed not so much against them as against the system which had degraded them by poverty and caused them to try and propel their children towards their inevitably limited concept of a better life. Eventually he does break free, not only from his family but also from his career as a teacher and from a love affair which had once seemed full of promise. Again, there are no grand conclusions, but Colin has at least succeeded where the earlier protagonists had failed:

As the world faded all about him, as the people faded, as the bonds faded with his family, he felt a new vigour growing inside.

Saville was undoubtedly one of the most thought-provoking novels of the 1970s in the way it grappled with the challenges and dilemmas of the modern world. J. M. Newton has said of David Storey: 'His is a genuinely creative gift and his separately conscious ideas about life wait on his art, not *vice versa*', and has contrasted him in this respect with William Golding, Iris Murdoch, and Muriel Spark, whose complex ideas, in his view, lie 'too obviously on the surface of the uncreated works'.[6]

William Golding is an altogether more sombre and pessimistic writer. The four novels which he published in the 1950s were so completely out of key with contemporary realism and provincialism that *Lord of the Flies* (1954) was initially not at all successful, so unfamiliar and unfashionable was its whole tone and approach, though before long it became a best seller on both sides of the Atlantic. In effect it is a present-day reconstruction at an adult level of R. M. Ballantyne's famous nineteenth-century adventure story, *Coral Island*. But whereas the shipwrecked boys in Ballantyne's book soon organize themselves into a reasonable imitation of Victorian God-fearing British society, most of those in Golding's novel just as quickly relapse into savagery, and the worship – in the form of the decaying fly-blown corpse of a parachutist – of Beelzebub, one of whose traditional descriptions is 'lord of the flies'. In essence the novel is a moral fable exploring the innate evil in man beneath the veneer of civilization, driven home by vivid, naturalistic narration, the realistic characterization of the boys, and the sensuous descriptions of scenes and objects convincingly filtered through their perceptions.

Arthur Koestler described Golding's *The Inheritors* (1955) as 'an earthquake in the petrified forests of the English novel' because it restored the fable to a place in English fiction. It shows homo sapiens overrunning and corrupting the innocent world of Neanderthal man and, like the boys in *The Lord of the Flies*, turning naturally to the worship of Beelzebub because of the evil in them. This indeed is the dominating theme of all Golding's best work. In *Pincher Martin* (1956) its communication is attended by a kind of narrative double-take. Most of the book appears to be a realistic account of a shipwrecked sailor, cast up on a jagged rock in mid Atlantic heroically struggling to survive. But as he summons up his physical resources, Pincher Martin begins to realize that in the past he had used them in order to lie, cheat, and exploit his fellows, so that his physical struggle turns into a spiritual exploration. And then at the end of the book, when his body is picked up by another ship, it transpires that he had been drowned almost immediately, never reaching the rock the reader has come to know in such painful detail; so that the whole experience must have been an illusion, in which case Pincher Martin's ordeal perhaps took place not in time but in eternity, and the rock constitutes a kind of Purgatory in which his courage and endurance are merely an obstinate refusal to accept God's existence and his offer of redemption.

Considerations of original sin and free will must also enter into the reading of Golding's subsequent novels, which also carry the implication that man's propensities for evil are far more powerful than their opposites. Then, after a long gap, he returned to fiction with *Darkness Visible* (1979) and apparently to a new phase in his development and a somewhat different emphasis. The title is taken from Milton's description of Hell (in Book Two of *Paradise Lost*). Here evil is even more terribly present, in the angelic-looking but psychopathic twins Toni and Sophy. Set against them, however, is Matty, horribly disfigured as a child by fire during the London Blitz, who after many sufferings discovers a meaning to his life in the Bible, and in whom the possibility of innate goodness as well as innate evil is posited, shining with its own genuine and visible light. In this novel a modern realistic setting embodies the moral fable with its suggestions of spiritual dimensions. In *Rites of Passage* (1980) the time is the early nineteenth century. On a sea voyage to Australia, young Talbot, good-natured but cockily self-confident of his superior class and privilege, has to undergo his rites of passage in the bitter realization that he has dodged his human responsibilities towards Colley, a young clergyman persecuted by the tyrannical captain of the ship. But Colley experiences rites of passage of another kind when, in the traditional frolics of crossing of the line, he is made drunk and, sexually debauched by a crew member, literally dies of shame. Talbot's gradual development into manhood and a genuine sense of responsibility and justice, makes him the most psychologically satisfactory of all Golding's characters.

Most of the novel is in the form of a diary kept by Talbot, and it is a remarkable period recreation: Talbot, for example, is convincingly presented as a typical gentleman of his period, still three-parts an Augustan; but at the same time references to and quotations from the earlier Coleridge reveal his awareness of the new currents of thought and feeling. In a sense *Rites of Passage*, in spite of the realism of plot and characterization, by depending on 'the documents of the case' and carefully researched pastiche, can be seen as an example of Golding's concern over fictional reality.

Realism for Muriel Spark is only useful insofar as it can communicate her main preoccupations. At the same time she does not equate this with any inadequacy in the novel form as such:

> 'I don't claim that my novels are truth, I claim that they are fiction, out of which a kind of truth emerges. And I keep in my mind specifically that what I am writing is fiction because I am interested in truth – absolute truth …'[7]

The conciseness and precision of her style to some extent relates Muriel Spark to a number of younger women writers, but although most of her characters are women they are certainly not singled out for any special sympathy. Muriel Spark is sceptical about the motives and behaviour of *all* her characters. She feels that most people live lives of self-deception, evasion and lies. Hence the presence in her novels of various manipulators, from teachers and film makers to blackmailers and con men; and also of cameras, tape-recorders and other mechanical gadgets for recording and reproduction, elements which themselves serve to underline the essentially fictive nature of so much of modern experience. In a sense, of course, all Catholic writers must be sceptical of the 'reality' of their characters' actions in that they believe all human beings operate within a greater reality,

· to which they struggle to conform, or (more often) from which they deviate, with results that are either ludicrous or tragic. A metaphysical view of the universe, that is, provides these writers with a framework of reference which in turn assures, no matter what kind of novel they are writing, a basic underlying and unshakeable central theme. They can, therefore, indulge in all kinds of structural and linguistic games without losing touch with the only reality that, ultimately, matters to them.

Muriel Spark is very much aware in all her novels of this sustaining framework – and in *The Mandelbaum Gate* (1964), there is a direct reference to 'a supernatural process going on under the surface and within the substance of all things'. The effects are most obvious in the novels which, coolly and unemotionally, introduce suggestions of the supernatural. The old people in *Memento Mori* (1959), for example, receive mysterious telephone calls, warning them of death; in *The Prime of Miss Jean Brodie* (1961) the heroine exercises a mysterious influence over her pupils, and so on. But it is just as evident in her handling of evil. In *The Girls of Slender Means* (1963), set in the bizarre May of Teck Club – with an unexploded bomb in the garden – the wicked Selina is just as important in the divine scheme of things as the virtuous Joanna, because she provides Nicholas with the means of grace. In other novels it is the perversion of God's purpose by self-willed actions that moulds the plot. In all cases events are adventitious, even arbitrary, subordinated to the spiritual drama. In all this there is very little psychological analysis of the inner lives of the characters, and practically everything is conveyed by action and dialogue with the absolute minimum of comment and emotion. It is, though, *The Driver's Seat* (1970) which reveals the external world in its bleakest aspects. In this novel Lise, without parents, children, husband or lover, neurotically obsessed by outward forms and patterns of behaviour, drives to meet a man whom she knows will murder her. The underlying purpose of the novel, of course, is to reveal the desolation attending a life controlled entirely by adherence to the external world, and at the end Muriel Spark allows herself to speak the words 'fear and pity, pity and fear'. But that is the only authorial intrusion, and for the rest it is Lise herself who is, so to speak, the author of her own text. Clearly, Muriel Spark has produced a body of highly original work. Yet it seems to have little solidity, warmth or inherent moral content, and her people seem physically and spiritually anaemic, while the coolness and restraint frequently produce an effect of aloofness and disdain. It is difficult, too, to understand how some critics have related Muriel Spark's work to folk-lore, fairy-tale or myth, which surely have a power and strength derived from positive traditions, aspirations or psychological truths. Muriel Spark's fantasy is delicately handled and enjoyable, but sometimes one cannot help wondering what it all adds up to, what it is *about*, even if this is an apt enough reflection of the spiritual emptiness of modern society.

Margaret Drabble is certainly not aloof. The subject-matter of her novel *The Ice Age* (1977) was basically historical in that it was a determined attempt to capture the facts, flavour, and shifting sensibility of the era of Rachman and the Poulson scandal, in the story of Anthony Keating, TV producer turned property speculator, who has a heart attack as the market begins to crumble in the early 1970s and who, finally landing up in an East European prison camp, reflects 'I am nothing but a weed on the tide of history.' In essence, though, *The Ice Age*, is a 'condition of England' novel similar in intention to those of the 1840s (like Mrs Gaskell's *Mary Barton*), seeking to rouse the nation from its greed, materialism and selfishness. In any case Margaret Drabble is probably still best known for her earlier novels about 'the condition of women' in the modern world, and especially the young, highly-educated and articulate who are faced with what another novelist, Margaret Forster, has called 'the predicament of being a "new" type woman and yet as trapped by the "old", by the same old snares'.[8] Thus in *The Millstone* (1965) Rosamund Stacey, a dedicated scholar completing a Ph.D thesis on Elizabethan poetry, becomes pregnant after a single brief encounter, decides to have the baby, and is forced by the experience out of the enclosed world of scholarship and into an awareness of ordinary female lives. One of the complaints made by the critics of Drabble's work has been that the milieux of her characters are more realized than the characters themselves. In *The Needle's Eye* (1972), though, the lush but characterless furnishings of Nick's and Diana's sitting-room aptly reflect the characterless nature of their marriage, just as the untidy, cosy, domestic interior in which Rose is placed reflects her personality – and her attraction for Nick. And *The Middle*

Ground (1980) takes a sardonic look at a group of well-to-do intellectuals who, having reached middle age are rapidly losing the left-wing idealism of their youth in pursuit of their careers, their empty affairs, and their empty, clever talk.

In one sense it is obviously ludicrous to speak of women novelists as if they formed a different compartment of literature. But the radically changed situation of women in society, the advent of women's presses, and the creation in some universities of departments of women's studies suggest that perhaps special conditions have to some extent constituted a separate phenomenon. Certainly one of the most striking features of contemporary English fiction has been the large number of talented women novelists. Among these must be included two who have enjoyed notable revivals. After the rediscovery of Jean Rhys and the subsequent success of her *Wide Sargasso Sea* (1966), her long-forgotten pre-war novels and short stories, also reflecting a bitterly sad woman's-eye-view of women's lives, were reissued. And Barbara Pym, who had published six of her dry, stylishly ironic, and very 'English' novels of middle-class 'churchy' and professional life between 1950 and 1960, and who had then been without a publisher for sixteen years, was also rediscovered. The success of *Quartet in Autumn* (1977) and *The Sweet Dove Died* (1978) brought her earlier novels, too, back into print and ensured the posthumous publication of *An Unsuitable Attachment* (1982), a rejected novel of the 1960s. Jean Rhys's voice was one from the 1920s and early 1930s, recognized as still fundamentally modern; Barbara Pym's work, no less vital and relevant and thoroughly contemporary in its character types and social provenance, belonged unashamedly to the tradition that reaches back to Jane Austen.

Among other older women writers Doris Lessing, who has perhaps been the most innovative, both in her explorations of women's situation in the modern world and in her awareness of the problems of the modern artist in relation to the self and to the nature of fictive reality, is discussed elsewhere in this volume. Such themes as the exploration of the ways in which modern society appears to offer freedom and equality to women, without any really worthwhile context in which these can operate – and which still, in point of fact, involve both injustice and violence to women's natures and talents – have been the special concern of novelists like Penelope

Mortimer, Brigid Brophy, Edna O'Brien, and A. S. Byatt. All of them have dealt with various aspects of the modern woman's dilemma with insight, honesty, and an unsentimental realism. Their novels often succeed without any false heroics in moving us, and convincing us of their closeness to authentic human experience; they release feelings in a way which makes many of the novels of their male contemporaries seem forced and faked.

There can be no question of the vital importance, for a society so confused in its sexual values and objectives, of this whole field of exploration. On the adverse side it could be said that a kind of tiredness and defeatism sometimes enters into the work of this group of writers. Thus the coolness and detachment that distinguished Edna O'Brien's *The Country Girls* (1960) gradually faded through *The Lonely Girl* (1962) and *Girls in their Married Bliss* (1964) into something which is at times not far removed from bitterness and stridency in *Casualties of Peace* (1966). The woman reviewer of this novel who tartly pointed out: 'Being a woman is fairly normal' was perhaps drawing attention to the fact that there are times when these writers seem to be reverting to the more arid aspects of 'the sex war', becoming 'angry' in the negative, stultifying manner of so many of the 'Angry Young Men' of the 1950s. And in order to keep our literary perspectives, it is worth asking ourselves whether we don't still learn more about the dilemmas, physical, social and spiritual, facing twentieth-century women from the novels of D. H. Lawrence (and notably *Women in Love*), and more perhaps of 'universal woman' in those of Jane Austen or even George Eliot.

Some younger women novelists, however, have evolved original fictional modes which enable them to render their own and other women's experience with a free play of intelligence accompanied by a strongly marked ironic detachment. Beryl Bainbridge, for example, often incorporates sensational newspaper stories in drab domestic settings, with equally drab heroines, rendered in a calm, economic style, so that the sudden intrusions of violence have an almost Gothic horror, part tragic, part manically comic. Thus *The Bottle Factory Outing* (1974) begins as a comedy about two girls working in a wine-bottling factory in London run by Italians, continues with uneasy undertones, and then almost before the reader is aware of it, so controlled is the style, slides into squalid tragedy and death. Angela Carter in novels like *Fireworks* (1974) explores with similar detachment the havoc wrought by passive, accident-and-violence-prone women, and similar though even more horrific irruptions of Gothic horror. In *Puffball* (1980) Fay Weldon inserts passages that might have come from a medical text-book describing the biological drives and processes of Liffey's mating and pregnancy, which cut down to size all the unreal expectations, all the illusions and rationalizations, attending both processes. There is a Gothic element here too, in the machinations of Liffey's witch-like neighbour Mabs (as a result of her own biological drives) to destroy Liffey's baby, which, in a horrifying climax, almost succeed. Liffey, always touchingly vulnerable and likeable, emerges into maturity, but in a sense it is the baby, from embryo to birth, who is the 'real' character.

It was no doubt as a side-effect of the Suez fiasco of 1956 that a number of novelists turned to the exploration of Britain's imperial past, especially in India. The outstanding examples are Paul Scott's *Raj Quartet* (1966–75) and its moving coda *Staying On* (1977), and J. G. Farrell's *The Siege of Krishnapur* (1970). The first novel in Scott's sequence, *The Jewel in the Crown* (1966), centres on the rape of an English girl, Daphne Manners. Inevitably this recalls E. M. Forster's *A Passage to India* (1924), but as inevitably emphasizes the great differences. In Forster's novel the liberal, humane criticisms of British behaviour in India are in the context of an imperial confidence still barely shaken. Scott's quartet is about the British Raj in decline, and there is in consequence a whole new set of political, social and psychological motivations and reactions. At the same time the racial issue lies at the core of the whole work (Indian critics have found Scott the most honest of the English novelists who have written about India in this respect). The construction of the quartet, though, is not traditional, especially in its handling of time. It comprises some 800,000 words in all, but the time-span is only five years – from 1942 to 1947, the year of British withdrawal, of independence and partition. The novels, moreover, are not sequels in the usual sense and the progression is not chronological: Scott moves backwards and forwards in time and switches from first person to third person narration, using a large number of British and Indian narrators, and latticing the main incidents and especially the rape (which is in effect the *leitmotiv*) over and over, first from one point of view, then another. And at the end of the quartet everything is firmly placed in an historical perspective as, with the outbreak of inter-communal rioting, the passengers on a train are massacred – with the exception of the British, not out of respect but because they are no longer relevant.

J. G. Farrell's *The Siege of Krishnapur* is just as firmly placed in a historical past, though at another crisis of British imperial rule, the Indian Mutiny of 1857. It can be read at one level as an exciting Victorian adventure story, and its narrative mode is at first sight uncompromisingly realistic and traditional, almost in an antiquarian sense. The historical and social details – clothes, objects, books, manners and so on – are carefully researched and placed. The language and imagery are for the most part in period, and Farrell does not scruple to intervene, in the manner of earlier novelists, as the omniscient narrator. All this was carefully calculated, and in a note on his earlier novel *Troubles* (1970), set in Ireland during the 1919–21 struggle for independence, he explained his purpose in terms that are equally applicable to *The Siege of Krishnapur* (and also to his last novel, *The Singapore Grip*, 1978), as being 'to show people "undergoing" history, to use a phrase of Sartre's ... What I wanted to do was to use this period of the past as a metaphor for today ...'[9] In these novels, that is, Farrell was consciously aware of the demands of history, of a shared reality between past and present, and of the conventional nature of fiction making.

Finally in this brief and necessarily incomplete survey of the post-war English novel, what of the tricky epistemological issues that some contemporary philosophers, strongly influenced by French and American writers, have discovered in the writing of fiction? The American critic Robert Alter has referred to 'the problematical relationship between real-seeming artifice and reality',[10] and the extreme position is that of those structuralists for whom there is no such thing as 'fictions' but only 'texts', for whom the lexical surface is everything – and who argue that since all human experience is grounded in language and its various codes, it is in fact pointless to try and distinguish fiction and reality, because 'reality' too (even our innermost thoughts and desires) is just another text.

Although few modern English novelists have accepted the implications of these ideas in full, several have set out to write 'anti-novels', based on the premise that all the traditional modes of realistic narrative are now valueless, and many have been affected by them. An unpretentious example is David Lodge's 'problematical' novel, as he has called it, *The British Museum is Falling Down* (1965), in which a research student in modern literature is so soaked in his subject that, as Lodge himself has explained, 'everything that happens to him comes to him moulded by some master of modern fiction', and the novel in large part consists of pastiche or parodies of the novelists he is studying. Lodge's novel, in consequence, is a series of interlacing texts, and has at least some similarities to the methods of the French practitioners of the *nouveau roman*. There have been a number of other instances, too, of novels in which the actual act of writing is part of the subject, thus exemplifying doubts as to the reality both of fiction and, by implication, of human experience itself, in an exploration of the paradoxical relationship between art and life.

The most determined and extreme onslaught on traditional realism, however, came from B. S. Johnson who in 1973 insisted that the old kind of novel was 'finished', and that 'No matter how good the writers are who now attempt it, it cannot be made to work for our time, and the writing of it is anachronistic, invalid, irrelevant and perverse.' For Johnson, indeed, the whole rationale behind novel writing was suspect:

A useful distinction between literature and other writing for me is that the former teaches one something true about life; and how can you convey truth in a vehicle of fiction? The two terms, *truth* and *fiction* are opposites.[11]

Nevertheless Johnson wrote highly talented novels himself in an attempt to put across his ideas. In *Albert Angelo* (1964), in particular, he played all sorts of games with the novel format in order to demonstrate that it is merely an artefact. On one of the pages there is a hole made by a knife, which a few pages later is revealed as the death of Christopher Marlowe. At the end of the novel Johnson asserts that his purpose in making the hole was 'didactic: the novel must be a vehicle for conveying truth, and to this end every device and technique of the printer's art should be at the command of the writer ...' – though he had precedents for this of course in Sterne's

Tristram Shandy. In the posthumous *See the Old Lady Decently* (1975), the most humanly satisfying of his novels, he sets out to tell the story of his mother's life up to the moment of his own conception, sticking as far as possible to verifiable facts, supported by journalistic vignettes about the period, and distancing the theme by inserting what are apparently edited extracts from guide-books or history text-books in order to illustrate the decline and fall of Britain and her empire.

There are two contemporary novelists in particular, however, who seem to offer what is, perhaps, a more balanced response to current challenges to truth in fiction. In one way it is unfair to select Anthony Burgess, another Catholic, in that he is bound to find some of the philosophical implications of structuralism unacceptable. His Catholicism, however, is of rather a special narrowly Augustinian stamp, and he has said: 'The God my religious upbringing forced upon me was a God wholly dedicated to doing me harm ... A big vindictive invisibility'[12] – and at times he regards himself as a renegade Catholic. But nearly all his important novels are preoccupied with the problems posed by the religion of his youth, and particularly with those of Original Sin and the prevalence of evil, accompanied by the apparent conviction that human depravity far outweighs the instances of transcendent goodness. At the same time Burgess is deeply suspicious of idealistic plans for the betterment of society or the individuals in it. In *A Clockwork Orange* (1962), Alex is a young hoodlum in a nightmarish England of the future who, paradoxically, has a passion for classical music; he is caught and sentenced to be cured of his violence by a species of aversion therapy. The cure succeeds, but the new docile Alex, besides losing his love of music, has become something that only has the appearance of organic life. Science, that is, has deprived him of his most precious God-given gift, his free will – even, it is implied, if it is will to evil. Obviously there are dangerous implications in this attitude – which has something in common with the 'theatre of cruelty' and other contemporary explorations of the idea that evil, as an authentic source of energy, is preferable to a purely negative passivity. Burgess's vision is certainly a pessimistic one. In *The Wanting Seed* (1962) he sees human history as for ever swaying between the contrary poles of Augustinian severity and Pelagian tolerance, with no hope of any final resolution, and in *Earthly Powers* (1980) Toomey encounters at every turn of his life nothing but evidence that evil has triumphed everywhere.

In conveying his disturbing themes Anthony Burgess has been ready to try out any fictional or linguistic mode that might suit his purpose. In *Nothing Like the Sun* (1964), which he wrote as a tribute for Shakespeare's quatracentenary year, he experimented with Elizabethan English, and in *A Clockwork Orange* he invented a new language called 'nadsat' for Alex and his 'droogs' (mates). *MF* (1971) is built around an Algonquin Indian myth, cited by Claude Lévi-Strauss in *The Scope of Anthropology* – at the very centre of Structuralist theory. Miles Faber, the central character of this very complex novel, experiences every aspect of the myth as he makes a long and roundabout journey on the way to an incestuous marriage with his sister. There are all kinds of mysteries and puzzles, which the reader is expected to solve if he is to discover some sort of order, and the narrative consists of a whole series of 'fictions' which seem to take place entirely at random, imposed from the outside rather than growing out of the central quest. And then, at the end of the book, Burgess suddenly reveals that Miles is a negro, so that the reader has to reexamine some of the solutions he thought he had arrived at. There is a good deal of tongue-in-cheek in all this, though. The truth of the matter is that Anthony Burgess, like any other genuinely original and creative writer, is quite prepared to play with any contemporary ideas, in part, one suspects, to please or tease the academic critics, in part out of genuine curiosity to see where they might lead, but mainly because they happen to be there. They are caught up, like all his other materials, in the sweep of his creative vitality, but they differ from the controlling perspectives of his religion in that they are not central and inherent. In the last resort it is the creative vitality itself that is the reality.

All the novels of John Fowles display an interesting technical resourcefulness. The first of them, the horrific *The Collector* (1960) is presented in part through the diary kept by the victim, which also contains passages of formally set-out dialogue. *The Magus* (1964, with a revised edition in 1977) is to some extent an elaborate literary game with the writer as puppet-master; and *Daniel Martin* (1977) alternates between first person and third person narration, frequently switches the tenses, and incorporates 'contributions' from Jenny, Daniel's young mistress left behind in California. But it is *The French Lieutenant's Woman* (1969) which has achieved the most fashionable success. The basic plot, the love affair between Charles and Sarah, is conveyed in the style of a traditional nineteenth-century novel, with its solid characterization and scene-setting, attended by carefully researched contemporary details. There are, however, various warning hints quite early on. There are, for example, the epigraphs at the head of each chapter. At first sight they support the nineteenth-century illusion. Significantly, though, they are not taken from those works which represent the full confidence of the Victorian era, but from those which in one way or another throw doubt on it. Then suddenly, at the end of chapter 12, Fowles begins to step down from his Victorian rostrum to demand: 'Who is Sarah? Out of what shadows does she come?' And the next chapter begins:

> I do not know. This story I am telling is all imagination. These characters I create never existed outside my own mind. If I have pretended until now to know my characters' minds and innermost thoughts it is because I am writing in a convention universally accepted at the time of my story: that the novelist stands next to God. He may not know all, yet he tries to pretend that he does. But I live in the age of Alain Robbe-Grillet and Roland Barthes ...

From that point onwards there are other authorial intrusions – in one of them Fowles himself appears in person, as a bearded figure sitting opposite Charles in a railway carriage. One chapter is in effect a separate essay, mainly on Victorian sex, written with all the benefits of post-Freudian hindsight, but drawing attention also to what has been lost in modern sexual mores as well as what has been gained. Historical facts and figures also enter the story directly when Charles rediscovers Sarah living with the Rossetti ménage in the house they actually occupied in Cheyne Walk, Chelsea. As for the authorial intrusions, there is of course nothing new about them as such; Henry James, for example, had upbraided Trollope for his 'suicidal satisfaction in reminding the reader that the story he was telling was only, after all, a make-believe'.[13] But Fowles is deliberately and programmatically committing this kind of suicide, and there is an even more startling instance in the last two chapters, when, after bringing the novel to a satisfactorily romantic Victorian conclusion, he offers an alternative ending, more in tune with 'modern' expectations.

What Fowles has set out to do in *The French Lieutenant's Woman*
is to blend a self-questioning post-existentialist modern text of the
1960s with a traditional one of a hundred years earlier. In spite of
this ambitious programme the novel is still, to put it at the lowest
level, 'a good read', the ordinary reader taking the author's interpola-
tions in his stride, carried along by the sheer impetus of the story-
telling to the conclusion he prefers. The novel, that is, operates at
two quite different levels, available both to the general reader and
to the one who is interested in the various epistemological issues
associated with the nature of 'fictions'. This is not to say that the
novels of John Fowles and Anthony Burgess are better or more
successful than those written before the *nouveau roman* and other
related influences began to make themselves felt in England. But it
is to suggest that they illustrate how creative vitality can carry along
with it elements that are apparently, in part at least, inimical to the
writing of fiction; they show how a compromise can be arrived at
– and is it possible that it is along the lines of some such compromise
that the English novel will develop in the future?

This particular survey has merely tried to pick out some of the
main trends of post-war fiction with reference to the names that most
naturally come to mind in connection with them. The opinions it
contains are, of course, personal ones; some of the omissions were,
however, dictated not so much by personal taste as by pressure of
space*: among the more obvious of them are such younger writers
as Keith Waterhouse, Sid Chaplin, Nigel Dennis, Thomas Hinde,
and Christine Brooke-Rose; and no survey could be complete
without some mention of such older writers as Richard Hughes,
Storm Jameson, V. S. Pritchett, William Sansom, Pamela Hansford-
Johnson, R. C. Hutchinson, and Gabriel Fielding, each of whom
has made appreciable contributions to modern English fiction. In a
limited survey, too, there has been no attempt to include interesting
and sometimes important novelists from other parts of the English-

---

* And modesty. One of the names that might have been included is that of Gilbert
Phelps himself. His novels, and especially *The Centenarians* (1958), *The Winter People*
(1963), and *The Old Believer* (1973) have been highly praised by writers and critics such
as Graham Greene. *Tenants of the House* (1971) was also particularly well received. His
most recent novel is *The Low Roads* (1975). *Editor.*

speaking world, some of whom are in any case dealt with in other chapters of this volume. Where genuine talent exists, too, there is always the possibility of new developments and surprises in the future. There may even be novels more important than many discussed here still awaiting publication, or which have not yet worked their way through the reviewers' sieve. But in the last resort the fact remains that, taken as a whole, English fiction since the war does not measure up to that of the earlier part of the century, with its handful of truly major novelists.

NOTES

1. Quoted by Robert Liddell in *The Novels of I. Compton-Burnett* (London, 1955), 23.

2. Liddell, 36.

3. *Towards Standards of Criticism: Selections from the Calendar of Letters (1925–1927)*, ed. F. R. Leavis (London, 1933).

4. Kenneth Allsop, *The Angry Decade: A Survey of the Cultural Revolt of the Fifties* (London, 1958).

5. A. S. Byatt, 'People in Paper Houses', in *The Contemporary English Novel*, Stratford-upon-Avon Studies, 18, ed. Malcolm Bradbury and David Palmer (London, 1979).

6. 'Two Men Who Matter? David Storey and Edward Dorn', by J. M. Newton, *The Cambridge Quarterly*, Vol. 1, No. 3 (Summer 1966).

7. 'The House of Fiction', interview with Frank Kermode, repr. in *The Novel Today*, ed. Malcolm Bradbury (London, Manchester, 1977).

8. Margaret Forster, 'What Makes Margaret Drabble Run and Run?', *The Guardian*, 28 February 1981.

9. In *Contemporary Novelists*, ed. James Vinson (London, 1972), 399–400.

10. Robert Alter, *Partial Magic* (Berkeley, London, 1975). An interesting study of the modern novel from a structuralist point of view is *The World and the Book*, Gabriel Josipovici (London, 1971).

11. B. S. Johnson, *Aren't You Rather Young to be Writing Your Memoirs?* (London, 1973).

12. Quoted in *The Situation of the Novel*, Bernard Bergonzi (London, 1970).

13. Henry James, 'Anthony Trollope' (1883), repr. in *The House of Fiction*, ed. Leon Edel (London, 1957).

SOME ASPECTS OF
POETRY SINCE THE WAR

CHARLES TOMLINSON

Anyone attempting to write on the poetry of today must inevitably feel the shifting of the ground under his feet: tomorrow is already here, and the arrival of a new poet or the republication of a neglected one has altered the sense of priorities. That modification of an accepted order 'by the introduction of the new (the really new) work of art', which Eliot speaks of in 'Tradition and the Individual Talent', accounts for one of the difficulties. Another lies in the fact that 'the silent celerity of time' is itself needful for a true perspective on the present moment. An earlier draft of this chapter was prepared in 1959. It was composed polemically from a standpoint that felt itself challenged by the publication, in 1955, of a number of verse manifestoes, from the group known as the Movement, in D. J. Enright's *Poets of the 1950s*. These included Kingsley Amis's:

... Nobody wants any more poems about philosophers or paintings or novelists or art galleries or mythology or foreign cities or other poems. At least I hope nobody wants them.

and Philip Larkin's:

[I] have no belief in 'tradition' or a common myth-kitty or casual allusions in poems to other poems or poets.

English empiricism had narrowed with a vengeance: if this was to be the whole extent of a poet's wisdom, then a counter possibility had to be established. In his introduction to *New Lines* (1956), Robert Conquest announced that the poetry of the fifties, at least that part of it represented by the Movement, 'is empirical in its attitude to all that comes'. But how much was *allowed* to come before the poet? Hadn't the deliberate narrowing – in some part a healthy reaction against the gestures of neo-romantic poetry of the forties – been merely an excuse, one asked oneself, for the British philistine and was not the need still the Arnoldian one – 'to pull out a few more stops in that powerful but at present somewhat narrow-toned organ, the modern Englishman'? Years later, in 1964, Philip Larkin was still saying:

... to me the whole of the ancient world, the whole of classical and biblical mythology means very little, and I think that using them today not only fills poems full of dead spots but dodges the writer's duty to be original.
('Four Conversations', *The London Magazine*, Vol. 4, No. 8.)

So Eliot, Pound, Cavafy, Seferis, Pasternak had dodged their duty? England seemed, in all senses, to be becoming an island, adrift from Europe and the past.

Yet it was precisely in the fifties that David Jones, Hugh Mac-Diarmid, Austin Clarke and Basil Bunting were beginning a re-emergence. To take first MacDiarmid and Clarke, one could say that it was only in the fifties that one came to be aware of work they had accomplished as far back as the late twenties and thirties, though not until *Collected Poems* (1962) in MacDiarmid's case and *Later Poems* (1961) in Clarke's was their work readily available. MacDiarmid had fought Scottish philistinism (even more single-minded than English) from the beginnings of his career and perhaps it left him with something of its own steely intransigence. MacDiarmid's *Collected Poems* revealed, particularly in its early stretches, something of what may be won by conscious determination supported by poetic ability. Mac-Diarmid does not resemble Eliot technically, but like the latter he has retained in his best verse the presence of 'the mind of Europe' and like him he has worked in the full knowledge of what he was about. His aim has been to resurrect the Scottish tradition that petered out with Burns; his achievement has been to forge a Scots verse, neither antiquarian nor provincial, but one in which a modern aware-ness can nourish itself on the Scottish past, and that can absorb into itself Chaucer, Dunbar, Villon. The *Second Hymn to Lenin, The Seam-less Garment, The Parrot Cry*, a body of lyrics which would include the early *Sangschaw, Penny Wheep, A Drunk Man Looks at the Thistle* (particularly, *O Wha's Been Here Afore Me Lass*) represent something of MacDiarmid's harvest. All this in 1962, was largely forgotten work – from the twenties and thirties. His range extends from the short lyric as in *The Eemis Stane* (1925):

I' the how–dumb–deid o' the cauld hairt[a] a nicht
The warl' like an eemis[b] stane
Wags i' the lift;
An' my eerie memories fa'
Like a yowdendrift.

Like a yowdendrift[c] so's I couldna read
The words cut oot i' the stane
Had the fug o' fame
An history's hazelraw[d]
No' yirdit[e] thaim.

to rich and strange explorations of unfamiliar words as in *On a Raised Beach* (1934):

All is lithogenesis – or lochia,
Carpolite fruit of the forbidden tree,
Stones blacker than any in the Caaba,
Cream-coloured caen-stone, chatoyant pieces,
Celadon and corbeau, bistre and beige,
Glaucous, hoar, enfouldered, cyathiform,
Making mere faculae of the sun and moon,
I study you glout and gloss, but have
No cadrans to adjust you with, but turn again
From optik to haptik and like a blind man run
My fingers over you, arris by arris, burr by burr,
Slickensides, truité, rugas, foveoles,
Bringing my aesthesis in vain to bear,
An angle-titch to all your corrugations and coigns,
Hatched foraminous cavo-rilieva of the world,
Diectic, fiducial stones. Chiliad by chiliad
What bricole piled you here, stupendous cairn?

Subsequent collections of MacDiarmid (*A Clyack Sheaf*, 1969, *Selected Poems*, 1970, *Complete Poems*, 1978) still leave one with the impression that, for all the interest and ambition of late poems like *In Memoriam James Joyce* (1956), the essential work was done in the twenties and thirties. It was thirty to forty years later that its nature was assimilable because re-available. A comparable time-lag affects Austin Clarke.

(*a* harvest; *b* insecure; *c* snowdrift; *d* lichen; *e* buried.)

Another reason for juxtaposing the later poetry of Austin Clarke and MacDiarmid would be to illustrate the way a sense of nationality can deepen a comparatively narrow talent. Clarke is Irish. Yeats wrote of one of his prose romances to Olivia Shakespear in 1932: 'Read it and tell me should I make him an Academician.' Clarke was made an Academician, but Yeats's subsequent hesitations about him and his backing of the far weaker poetic abilities of F. R. Higgins have resulted in his neglect. *Later Collected Poems* (1961) – these, in fact, contain a selection from the *Collected Poems* of 1936 – show Clarke, particularly in *Ancient Lights* (1955) and *Too Great a Vine* (1957), to be an epigrammatist, satirist, and autobiographer of remarkable individuality. *Flight to Africa* (1963) confirmed all this; *Mnemosyne Lay in Dust* (1966) attempts to extend the range into narrative, *Tiresias* (1972) into myth. *Twice Round the Black Church* (1962) and *A Penny in the Clouds* (1968) fill out the picture in prose. A sense of not only what Ireland is, but what it was, enables Clarke to speak with a national voice that, like MacDiarmid's at his very fragmentary best, represents not the inertia of chauvinism, but a labour of recovery. Clarke's skill in using traditional Irish rhyming patterns is similarly not merely a technical recovery, but the measure of a worked-for relation with the past. His poem on the death of orphanage children by fire (the third of *Three Poems About Children*, 1955) accomplishes what in intention Dylan Thomas sets out to do in *A Refusal to Mourn the Death, by Fire, of a Child in London*:

> Martyr and heretic
> Have been the shrieking wick.
> But smoke of faith on fire
> Can hide us from enquiry
> And trust in Providence
> Rid us of vain expense.
> So why should pity uncage
> A burning orphanage,
> Bar flight to little souls
> That set no church bell tolling?
> Cast-iron step and rail
> Could but prolong the wailing;
> Has not a bishop declared
> That flame-wrapped babes are spared
> Our life-time of temptation?

Leap, mind, in consolation
For heart can only lodge
Itself, plucked out by logic.
Those children, charred in Cavan,
Pass straight through Hell to Heaven.

The work of Ezra Pound continued to appear throughout the fifties, and it was then that a gradual reassessment of his achievement began with that first, courageous study of his poetry, Hugh Kenner's *The Poetry of Ezra Pound* (1951). To pass from the assured, narrow national strength of Clarke to the vaster resources of an expatriate like Ezra Pound is to realize, as in the case of MacDiarmid, the extent to which the *déracinement* of our century can ultimately entail great unevenness and loss of creative power and balance of tone, even in the finest writers. The continued appearance of Pound's Cantos – *The Pisan Cantos* (1949), *Section: Rock-Drill* (1957), *Thrones* (1959), *Drafts and Fragments of Cantos CX-CXVII* (1969) – return one to that criticism which Yeats made of Pound in his preface to *The Oxford Book of Modern Verse* in 1936:

When I consider his work as a whole, I find more style than form: at moments more style, more deliberate nobility and the means to convey it than in any contemporary poet known to me but it is constantly interrupted, broken, twisted into nothing by its direct opposite, nervous obsession, nightmare, stammering confusion; he is an economist, poet, politician, raging at malignants with inexplicable characters and motives, grotesque figures out of a child's book of beasts.

Yeats's criticisms, when due qualifications have been made, are still often valid after the passage of many decades, but having endorsed them we should do wrong to follow common English opinion and to relegate the Cantos to that total neglect they by no means deserve. As Ronald Bottrall contended in one of the first lengthy appraisals of *A Draft of XXX Cantos* in 1933 (*Scrutiny* II) and as Donald Davie has since argued, the finest work in the Cantos is both nobly impressive and of extraordinary beauty. 'More deliberate nobility and the means to convey it ...': Yeats's words still apply to those passages of processional magnificence in *The Pisan Cantos* – 79 (O Lynx keep watch on my fire .../O puma sacred to Hermes),80 (the lyric, Tudor is gone and every rose), 81 (Yet/Ere the season died a-cold .../all

in the diffidence which faltered) – and in *Rock-Drill* – Cantos 90–93
– where Pound evokes the paradisal elements of myth and folk-
memory, as in the earlier and splendid Cantos 17 and 47. Cantos
99 and 106 in *Thrones* are relevant here. This recurrence to the
ceremonial aspects of past cultures (see Canto 52, Know then:/
Toward summer when the sun is in Hyades . . .) links the Pound
of the Cantos to Pound the translator (*The Classic Anthology Defined
by Confucius*, 1955). A reader who experiences the rhythmic tact of
the 'Envoi' in *Mauberley* will recognize that a comparable power is
at work in this later volume:

1

For deep deer-copse beneath Mount Han
hazel and arrow-thorn make an even, orderly wood;
A deferent prince
seeks rents in fraternal mood.

2

The great jade cup holds yellow wine,
a fraternal prince can pour
blessing on all his line.

3

High flies the hawk a-sky,
deep dives the fish,
far, far, even thus amid distant men
shall a deferent prince have his wish.

4

The red bull stands ready, and
clear wine is poured,
may such rite augment the felicity
of this deferent lord.

5

Thick oaks and thorn give folk fuel to spare,
a brotherly prince shall energize
the powers of air.

6

And as no chink is between vine-grip and tree
thick leaf over bough to press,
so a fraternal lord seeks abundance
only in equity;
in his mode is no crookedness.

Sensuous exactness becomes in this translation the defining equivalent for a moral distinction: 'And as no chink is between vine-grip
and tree/thick leaf over bough to press ...' And not only have we
the power of the sensuous image: the first of these lines, riding
forward on its stresses, enacts the vigour of the moral directness which
is being recommended. The didactic element and the poetic element
are at one, whereas in the weaker sections of the Cantos the morals,
whether economic or political, are too much a matter of *a priori*
formulation, nakedly and shrilly dogmatic without organic relation
to their context. The Cantos can degenerate into abuse; whereas the
moral scheme of the Confucian translations unites compellingly with
imagery and rhythm. In Pound's *Classic Anthology* is to be found
some of the most impressive verse of the fifties. Of his contribution
to modern dramatic verse in *Women of Trachis* (first published 1954),
a 'version' of Sophocles' *Trachiniae*, suffice it to say that Pound has
given us one of the very few readable (and actable) translations of
Greek drama.

Pound remains a looming presence, an active irritant in a way
that only the major figure can. Thus it is not my intention to deal
here with those smaller but excellent poets of an older generation,
Robert Graves and William Empson. The best work of Graves has
long been a model for poems that combine formal grace and
masculinity of expression. Empson's compressed and inimitable
poems *were* imitated by several members and fellow-travellers of the
Movement, that miscellaneous group chiefly united by their rejection
of the neo-romanticism of the 1940s. Empson has himself expressed
the opinion that it is his criticism which stays 'developable' and not
his verse. I share that opinion. Nor is it my intention to recreate
the poetic climate of the forties against certain tendencies of which
period several poets, today in their maturity, forcefully reacted. A
fair account of this phase exists already in John Press's *A Map of
Modern English Verse* (1969). A critical book, very pertinent to the
reaction of the fifties, was Donald Davie's *Purity of Diction in
English Verse* (1952): it sought primarily to cleanse diction of excess
and inanity and it pointed us back to the achievements of the great
Augustan figures. In a postscript to the edition of 1967, Davie admits
the existence of that streak of philistinism I have noted among the

Movementeers, but attempts to measure what was seriously in question:

In my book this vulgar streak shows up where I declare myself in-different to any poem or poetic effect that cannot be shown to be moral. Nowadays this strikes me as strident and silly. And yet I can see clearly enough how it came about, as an angry reaction from the tawdry amoralism of a London Bohemia which had destroyed Dylan Thomas, the greatest talent of the generation before ours, and had helped some journalists to cast a facile glamour over the wasted squalor of Thomas's last years. Some years later, in his learned and mordantly witty poem, *Antecedents*, Charles Tomlinson wrote of the Bohemianism which grew up around the figure of Thomas as only a vulgarized reach-me-down version of the more justifiable Bohemias of the nineteenth century in France. Tomlinson was a poet right outside the Movement and opposed to it, though not opposed, I am glad to say, to the thesis of *Purity of Diction in English Verse*. It seems to me now that the poems of Tomlinson, the poems of Amis and others, my own poems and this essay in poetics, have at least this continuing relevance and impor-tance – that they represent an originally passionate rejection, by one genera-tion of British poets, of all the values of Bohemia ... That there is no necessary connection between the poetic vocation on the one hand, and on the other exhibitionism, egotism and licence – this was what my book was con-tending for, even when it seemed most 'technical'. The Bohemians hit back by calling it 'puritan' or, more cleverly, 'genteel'.

The poet whom common consent has chosen as the most signifi-cant of the Movement is Philip Larkin (*The North Ship*, 1945, *The Less Deceived*, 1955, *The Whitsun Weddings*, 1964, *High Windows*, 1974). His work is dealt with at greater length elsewhere in the present volume. My own feeling is that Larkin's talents work hand in hand with a wry and sometimes tenderly nursed sense of defeat. In poem after poem, one waits for the dying fall – 'Nothing to be said', 'It had not done so then, and could not now', 'Never such innocence again' – as it closes off poetry that is clearly individual, often beautifully phrased and yet where the possibilities of fulfilment seem almost wilfully short-circuited. Not that one is asking for facile optimism – defeat can also come to seem facile. Larkin's narrowness suits the English perfectly. They recognize their own abysmal urban landscapes, skilfully caught with just a whiff of English films *c.* 1950. The stepped-down vision of human possibilities (no Renaissances, please), the joke that hesitates just this side of nihilism, are national vices.

One attempt to confront Larkin's poetry occurs in Davie's *Thomas Hardy and British Poetry* (1972). In the same volume Davie argues the merits of Roy Fisher (*Collected Poems*, 1980). Fisher's *City*, a work consisting of poems in verse and prose, first appeared in 1961: Larkin, facing the urban scene, smothers both its vulgarity and its warmth in his own dejection; Fisher recognizes its lacks, but his vision of Birmingham has a factuality and geographic exactness that give it a more than personal authority:

> In the century that has passed since this city has become great, it has twice laid itself out in the shape of a wheel. The ghost of the older one still lies among the spokes of the new, those dozen highways that thread constricted ways through the inner suburbs, then thrust out, twice as wide, across the housing estates and into the countryside, dragging moraines of buildings with them. Sixty or seventy years ago there were other main roads, quite as important as these were then, but lying between their paths. By day they are simply alternatives, short cuts, lined solidly with parked cars and crammed with delivery vans. They look merely like side-streets, heartlessly overblown in some excess of Victorian expansion. By night, or on a Sunday, you can see them for what they are. They are still lit meagerly, and the long rows of houses, three and four storeys high, rear black above the lamps enclosing the roadways, clamping them off from whatever surrounds them. From these pavements you can sometimes see the sky at night, not obscured as it is in most parts of the city by the greenish-blue haze of light that steams out of the mercury vapour lamps. These streets are not worth lighting. The houses have not been turned into shops – they are not villas either that might have become offices, but simply tall dwellings, opening straight off the streets, with cavernous entries leading into back courts.

A poet who has ridden alongside Larkin in Movement anthologies is Thom Gunn, a very different kind of writer, and one early resolved to seek out the heroic in the experience of nihilism. Gunn startled poetry readers by writing, while still an undergraduate, *Fighting Terms* (1954). His uneasy energy and admiration for a Hemingway-like muscularity in situations of a Sartrean tortuousness (the spirit of the age seemed as consciously courted as all that implies) left one uncertain whether he would develop a moral sensitivity equal to his concerns. *The Sense of Movement* (1957) and *My Sad Captains* (1961), for all their range and skill, still left one, as do more recent collections, with unresolved doubts. In an early poem he writes of those who, like Byron and like 'strong swimmers, fishermen, explorers', 'Dignify death by thriftless violence – /Squandering all their little left to spend.' Precisely the same uncritically rhetorical gestures turn up in later poetry where, in those symbols he draws from the world of James Dean and Marlon Brando, Gunn often seems committed to a kind of nihilistic glamour for which he cannot always convincingly apologize. Elsewhere, as in *In Santa Maria del Popolo*, the poet's stance is far more convincing and so is his diction. Yvor Winters has compared him with Donne while admitting that 'as a rule, he has a dead ear, and the fact makes much of his work either mechanical or lax in its movement ...' Gunn continues to add to an uneven but always individual body of work (see *Moly*, 1971, *Selected Poems*, 1979) and in *Jack Straw's Castle* (1976) the nakedly human will seems, at last, to have entered into negotiation with less tense areas of the psyche, resulting in a poetry that represents Gunn at his most unified and comprehensive.

Peter Redgrove is a poet who failed to find the early acceptance accorded to Gunn and to subsequent and tamer talents. It is no easy task to take his measure. Prolific, inventive, grotesque, with a vision of cosmic unity that is optimistic without being shallowly so, he is still in full career. One sees what Peter Porter means when, in *Poetry Review* (September 1981), he writes of him as

the most gifted poet working in British poetry today. Not always the most successful or accomplished – he can be over-strenuous, hypertrophied or obsessional – but the poet with the largest vision.

The hypertrophy shows in a style which, reliant on the force of the surprising image, seeks to build itself into an idiom of philosophic conviction, yet lacks both the supple diction and the argumentative *charpente* to succeed. The result is a certain sameness of tone – the Whitmanian failure – and a vocabulary of vitalism whose repetitiveness often has the appearance of merely treading water. All the same, one goes back to Redgrove with the feeling that here is a writer whose presence on the scene is sanitive and joyous. A good way in is *Sons of My Skin: Selected Poems 1954–74*.

I have mentioned already the criticism of Donald Davie. Its impact on our day and our own sense of poetry is comparable in scope to that of William Empson's at the height of his powers. Some time ago Davie was writing verse close to that of Yvor Winters and, though he is to return to this earlier mode (see *Against Confidences* in *New and Selected Poems*, 1961, and compare it with *Creon's Mouse*, one of his best pieces from *Brides of Reason*, 1955), he has developed since then a more various and ample style. Indeed, one of the effects of reading Davie's *Collected Poems* (1972) is to be reminded of the many styles in which he has written. The variety of attack and the pulsation of energies ranging from tenderness to anger leave one in no doubt of the demands Davie makes on his craft: he is not the merely careful, 'academic' poet some critics have mistaken him for. Rather, he is incautious, drawn to extremes of fret and exacerbation, always in search of forms adequate to contain and qualify his troubled feelings. *Collected Poems* contains a note by the poet himself which defines the sort of writer he is:

It is true that I am not a poet by nature, only by inclination; for my mind moves most easily and happily among abstractions, it relates ideas far more readily than it relates experiences. I have little appetite, only profound admiration, for sensuous fullness and immediacy; I have not the poet's need of concreteness. I have resisted this admission for so long, chiefly because a natural poet was above all what I wanted to be, but partly because I mistook my English empiricism for the poet's concreteness, and so thought my mind was unphilosophical, whereas it is philosophical but in a peculiarly English way.

Most of the poems I have written are not natural poems, in one sense not truly poems, simply because the thought in them could have been expressed – at whatever cost in terseness and point – in a non-poetic way. This does not mean however that they are worthless or that they are shams; for as much can be said of much of the poetry of the past that by common consent is worth reading and remembering ...

Since *Collected Poems*, Davie has continued with *On the Stopping Train* (1977) and *Three for Water Music* (1981) to consolidate a range that is at once traditionalist and modern.

Some of the stylistic virtues that Davie admires were anticipated in the work of an earlier poet, Keith Douglas, but a poet who was not readily obtainable until *Selected Poems* (1965) and is available once more in *Complete Poems* (1979). Douglas, who was killed in the war at the age of twenty-four, belonged to the generation of Sidney

Keyes. It was Keyes who received the public recognition which in terms of comparative achievement is so evidently the due of the other poet. For that of a poet who died in his twentieth year, Keyes's work, self-consciously over-literary as it was, showed a great deal of promise (see *Paul Klee*, *Kestrels*, *Seascape* in *Collected Poems*, 1945), but more than that one cannot say. Douglas's *Collected Poems* did not appear until 1951. The wartime poetry boom which had made possible three editions of Keyes was over. The fashion was on the point of change – from the excessive verbal luxuriance of neo-romanticism to the slick formalism of Empson's successors. Douglas, like any original poet, did not fit the picture and although his collection was well received, it has taken the better part of thirty years for his true importance to be acknowledged. His work despite the immaturities, suggests that here was a poet whose death was a serious loss for English literature. Take, for example, these lines from *Time Eating* (1941):

> But as he makes he eats; the very part
> Where he began, even the elusive heart,
> Time's ruminative tongue will wash
> and slow juice masticate all flesh.
>
> That volatile huge intestine holds
> material and abstract in its folds:
> thought and ambition melt and even the world
> will alter, in that catholic belly curled.

Here one has something of the linguistic compactness and steady cumulative attack Douglas brings to his awareness of mutability. Death may be the chief factor behind his verse, but it focuses rather than blurs the vision. Sensuous detail grows compact in its presence; life takes on an edge, as in *The Sea Bird*, *Syria I*, *Egyptian Sentry*, *Cairo Jag*, *Words*, and as in the view of the wrecked houses in *Mersa* (all except *Words* which came a year later, written in 1942):

> faces with sightless doors
> for eyes, with cracks like tears,
> oozing at corners. A dead tank alone
> leans where the gossips stood.
> I see my feet like stones
> underwater. The logical little fish

> converge and nip the flesh
> imagining I am one of the dead.

What one finds impressive in Douglas, even in those poems where the idiom is not yet equal to the vision, is the intrinsically poetic nature of that vision. In *The Marvel* (1941), for instance, a dead sword-fish has 'yielded to the sharp enquiring blade/the eye which guided him' past dead mariners 'digested by the gluttonous tides'; and a live sailor, using the eye for a magnifying glass, burns into the deck of his ship the name of a harlot in his last port. The incident welds into a poetic unity the worlds of life and death, of time and nature.

'To be sentimental or emotional now is dangerous to oneself and to others,' Douglas wrote in 1943, and the fruit of this realization is the firm yet malleable tone which can encompass the charmingly satirical *Behaviour of Fish in an Egyptian Tea Garden*, the satiric yet good-natured *Aristocrats*, and the ironically ambitious *Vergissmein-nicht (all of 1943)*. The refusal to *force* himself into stylistic neatness (which in effect was the attempt of many of the poets of the fifties) meant a certain unevenness and want of finish in his later poems; yet even this is evidence of Douglas's integrity.

It was a subsequent poet, Ted Hughes, who, in a fine selection of Douglas's work, *Selected Poems* (1965), isolated most succinctly the latter's qualities and their relation to the war:

The war brought his gift to maturity, or to a first maturity. In a sense, war was his ideal subject: the burning away of all human pretensions in the ray cast by death. This was the vision, the unifying generalization that shed the meaning and urgency into all his observations and particulars: not truth is beauty only, but truth kills everybody. The truth of a man is the doomed man in him or his dead body. Poem after poem circles this idea, as if his mind were tethered. At the bottom of it, perhaps, is his private muse, not a romantic symbol of danger and temptation, but the plain foreknowledge of his own rapidly-approaching end – a foreknowledge of which he becomes fully conscious in two of his finest poems.

Hughes comments on this achievement:

... he has invented a style that seems able to deal poetically with whatever it comes up against. It is not an exalted verbal activity to be attained for short periods, through abstinence, or a submerged dream treasure to be fished up when the everyday brain is half-drugged. It is a language for the whole mind, at its most wakeful, and in all situations.

It is no accident that Ted Hughes was a poet who recognized Douglas as potentially one of the most powerful writers of his generation. Hughes also circles the idea of death in poem after poem:

> I drown in the drumming ploughland, I drag up
> Heel after heel from the swallowing of the earth's mouth,
> From clay that clutches my each step to the ankle
> With the habit of the dogged grave, but the hawk
>
> Effortlessly at height hangs his still eye.
> His wings hold all creation in a weightless quiet,
> Steady as a hallucination in the streaming air.
> While banging wind kills these stubborn hedges,
>
> Thumbs my eyes, throws my breath, tackles my heart,
> And rain hacks my head to the bone, the hawk hangs
> The diamond point of will that polestars
> The sea drowner's endurance: and I,
>
> Bloodily grabbed dazed last-moment-counting
> Morsel in the earth's mouth, strain towards the master-
> Fulcrum of violence where the hawk hangs still.
> That maybe in his own time meets the weather
>
> Coming the wrong way, suffers the air, hurled upside down,
> Fall from his eye, the ponderous shires crash on him,
> The horizon trap him; the round angelic eye
> Smashed, mix his heart's blood with the mire of the land.
>
> *(The Hawk in the Rain)*

He emerged, already an impressive talent, with *The Hawk in the Rain* (1957), a book where his own voice blends a little too easily at times into that of Dylan Thomas. Two experiences seem to have dominated him – firstly, the mythos of the First World War and that sense of dislocation it brought to 'the mind of Europe', secondly an awareness of nature, of that other England which the London-bound writer has forgotten about. *Lupercal* (1960) and *Wodwo* (1967) extend these two worlds of violence – that of men and that of animals. Hughes' tensions and generosities, his struggle to live through and beyond the broken world of *Crow* (1970) occupy a large body of work. At times, he seems like a one-man psychic circus. Whatever he does commands attention as few other poets can, because he surprises us after stridencies and unevenesses with moments when his poise is equal to his power. Two instances of this have shown themselves in Hughes' interest in translation – his *Oedipus* (1969), a free version of Seneca's play, and perhaps more compellingly, because more chastely and compactly achieved, his *Selected Poems: Janos Pilinszky* (1976) where Hughes puts his own voice into the service of another, a Hungarian poet, and out of the demands of that meeting of minds, produces translated verse where violence is often present but everywhere in check.

Since the time of Sir Thomas Wyatt many English poets have given us in their translations work which equals or even surpasses their original verse. The post-war phase is no exception to this refusal to make of translation a mere line by line crib, poets reaffirming Rossetti's dictum that,

> The life-blood of rhymed translation is this, – that a good poem shall not be turned into a bad one. The only true motive for putting poetry into a fresh language must be to endow a fresh nation, as far as possible, with one more possession of beauty.

Michael Hamburger, a poet who moved from neo-romantic beginnings (*Flowering Cactus*, 1950) to a poetry of fine sobriety (*Travelling*, 1969, marks the onset of an interesting phase of his work), has been for years one of our most prolific translators of German poetry. He has almost always found a convincing voice in English for his importations (this is true also of his work on Franco Fortini and Philippe Jaccottet), but his *Paul Celan: Selected Poems* (1972) contains altogether exceptional evidence of Hamburger's ability to excel himself and shows that translation can call forth inventiveness and new linguistic power.

One would not have immediately thought of Hamburger as the pre-destined translator of Celan (after all, their basic styles are worlds apart). Judging, perhaps with hindsight, the poetry of Elaine Feinstein, one sees how the author of the early *In a Green Eye* (1966) and *The Magic Apple Tree* (1971) was morally and psychologically equipped to render into English *Marina Tsvetayeva: Selected Poems* (1971). Feinstein illustrates uncannily Roscommon's contention that the translator in identifying himself with his original must become 'No longer his Interpreter, but He.' A common ground of impending inner chaos seems to have drawn Feinstein to Tsvetayeva – a degree of identification quite unlike Hamburger's with Celan, but once more permitting the poet to surpass herself and to challenge contemporary British poetry by confronting it with this very unEnglish sensibility that has found for itself at last a style in English. Is not this kind of confrontation far more important than the so-called 'original work' of poets resolutely and impeccably minor?

To say that a poet has done some of his best work as translator is not to demote him; after all, one can say this of Dryden's Ovid and Pope's Homer. Thus *War Music* (1981), Christopher Logue's series of adaptations from Homer's *Iliad* – translation in a much looser sense than Hamburger's or Feinstein's – contains some of his most striking contributions to contemporary verse. These adaptations do not always work. Indeed, there are moments of cinematic exaggeration that make one feel that, if Orson Welles had ever written poetry, it would sound like this. All the same, Logue succeeds (to adopt his own words) in making the voices of the protagonists come alive and in keeping the action on the move. He quotes in his own defence Johnson's words to Boswell: 'We must try its effect as an English poem, that is the way to judge the merit of a translation.'

A continuous tradition of excellent translations has rounded out the work of a number of poets over the past few years: Christopher Middleton, an interesting experimentalist in his own right and frequently a co-worker with Michael Hamburger in the presentation of modern German poetry; Peter Whigham, who has finally given us a readable Catullus (1966) and an outstanding version of that long poem which has bothered scholars but intrigued poets from Landor to Blok and Bunting – Catullus's *Attis*; Edwin Morgan, who among his versions of the Hungarian poet Sándor Weöres has again met the challenge of 'a poem of some length', namely Weöres's *The Lost Parasol*, and has provided us with something of the measure of the presence of a mysterious poet who might have seemed intractable to the translator. Along with his versions of Weöres (1970), one must also mention Morgan's *Wi the haill voice* (1972), perhaps his most successful single volume: this consists of a selection of poems by the Russian Vladimir Mayakovsky rendered into Scots. They are brusque, brutal and entirely convincing and stood Morgan in good stead when in *Rites of Passage* (1976), another book of translations – these from several languages – he translated into Scots from Shakespeare *The Hell's-Handsel o Leddy Macbeth*, i.e., her first two soliloquies. Among this same company of poet–translators one must also place Alan Neame whose *Leoun* (1947–57), an 'Englishing' of Jean Cocteau's extensive poem *Léone*, brings into the range of poetic possibilities an extraordinary mixture of the heroic, the surreal, the colloquial and the ballad-like. Save for extracts in *The Oxford Book of Verse in English Translation* (1980), this dashing achievement seems to have been almost wholly forgotten and it invites quotation:

> 'Twas Renaldo fallen prey to Armida's devices
> Sleeping in the fragrance of his dewy fleeces.
> Biceps shoulderblade breastbone thigh and hip
> Littered the warm snow where the heroes sleep.
>
> Armida in the veil of a lawful bride
> And taller than a shot-tower surveyed fallen pride.
> Chaste after love, her great body locked up,
> She slept on her feet by her own true love.

Geoffrey Hill appears as a translator in his version of Ibsen's *Brand* (1978) but unlike, say, Neame or Logue, it is as an original poet that he has made most mark. He reflects on men's awareness of divinity and its reverberations in history. It is as if he had taken a route proposed by Hughes' own *The Martyrdom of Bishop Farrar* in *The Hawk in the Rain* – a route Hughes did not follow. There the resemblance ends. Hill's own style is dense and, at its least effective, clotted, yet the clotting seems less the result of an easy rhetoric than the failure of a magnificent attempt to notate the antiphonal ironies of history: the attempt stretches Hill's resources and the reader's capacities defeatingly in many poems. His successes in *For the Unfallen* (1959) number the fine *Martyrdom of Saint Sebastian* and *Requiem for the Plantagenet Kings*:

> For whom the possessed sea littered, on both shores,
> Ruinous arms; being fired, and for good,
> To sound the constitution of just wars,
> Men, in their eloquent fashion, understood.

Relieved of soul, the dropping-back of dust,
Their usage, pride, admitted within doors;
At home, under caved chantries, set in trust,
With well-dressed alabaster and proved spurs
They lie; they lie; secure in the decay
Of blood, blood-marks, crowns hacked and coveted,
Before the scouring fires of trial-day
Alight on men; before sleeked groin, gored head,
Budge through the clay and gravel, and the sea
Across daubed rock evacuates its dead.

The vindication of Hill's methods appears in the sequence *Funeral Music*, 'a florid grim music broken by grunts and shrieks', in *King Log* (1968). *Mercian Hymns* (1971) is a book of poems in prose in which King Offa, who reigned over Mercia in the eighth century A.D., is taken as a recurrent psychological type of human tyranny, reappearing in the schoolboy bully and the twentieth-century magistrate.

In a characteristically rich and subtle essay, 'Redeeming the Time' (*Agenda*, Vol. 10, No. 4) Hill reflects on Coleridge's attachment to what he called 'the moral copula', by which he meant the action of the humanizing intellect as against the merely prudential or circumstantial reasoning of those who judge history by what is termed results. The moral copula, according to Coleridge, would 'take from history its accidentality and from science its fatalism'. Hill himself is concerned to keep vivid our sense of that moral copula in face of the brutalities of history which he so painfully records. Thus, he will have none of the scholarly detachment that sees in the Wars of the Roses merely dynastic skirmishes 'without much effect on the economic routines of the kingdom'. In the essay which accompanies *Funeral Music* he retorts: 'Statistically, this may be arguable; imaginatively, the Battle of Towton itself commands one's belated witness.' The poem provides the witness of imagination as against statistics, in accordance with the Coleridgean imperative. Again, Coleridge defends his use of parentheses for their enactment of 'the drama of reason', one thing held in balance over against another. Hill, by a typical flight of mind, makes us see this drama in terms of the uses of rhythm and even the antiphonal responses of the Anglican church service. This sense of 'the other voice' demanding to be heard is central to Hill's own poetic style in its renovation of clichés, its punning density and its grim humour.

Hill's *Mercian Hymns* are headed by an epigraph from C. H. Sisson: 'The conduct of government rests upon the same foundation and encounters the same difficulties as the conduct of private persons ...' The quotation is from Sisson's privately printed *Essays* (1967). Sisson did not begin to receive his due as a poet until the appearance of his collected poems, *In the Trojan Ditch* (1974). Both he and Hill are deeply responsive to the traditions of Christian thought, Sisson far more doctrinally so than the other. Wry, haunted, unexpectedly bleak for an Anglican, Sisson's poetic character is puzzlingly divided between the savagely saturnine and the Hardy-esque. His admirable prose (see *The Avoidance of Literature*, 1978) is sometimes (almost) genial, his poetry never. His confessed inability to believe in the reality of the human self – and thus his own – too often runs aground on the sands of a familiar Waste Land. Yet in poems like *The Usk* and *Insula Avalonia* (1974) and in those vale-dictory and humane pieces that form the second part of *Exactions* (1980), Sisson adds something unforgettably individual to recent poetry. He has also given much thought to translation – including Horace, Heine and Virgil, besides a complete *De Rerum Natura* of Lucretius (1976) and Dante's *Divine Comedy* (1980).

Almost simultaneously with the delayed recognition of Sisson, a much younger poet, Seamus Heaney shot to rapid fame during the seventies. Conor Cruise O'Brien's 'the most important Irish poet since Yeats' seems an exaggerated way of welcoming the per-suasively fluent talents of Heaney and an excuse for shunting out of sight much Irish poetic history of the intervening years, including the contribution of John Montague. These two poets are examined in more detail elsewhere in this volume of the *Guide*.

Peter Porter whose *Preaching to the Converted* (1972) brought a new dimension into his work, bears witness, like C. H. Sisson, to the persisting strength of a Christian imagination, though Porter's Christianity seems residual rather than that of the regular believer. *An Exequy* from '*The Cost of Seriousness*' (1978) has some claim to being his most impressive single poem. Porter is an outstanding 'performer', technically adept, morally conservative. We are always being told of the death of Christianity and yet Christian belief and ethics temper the imagination of a number of poets, from Sisson to the minor, but justly admired, R. S. Thomas. It is evidently still easier to be a Christian than a Jew in present English society: the strain shows in some of Jon Silkin's committed poems. Silkin seems to me almost invariably at his best when he is least self-conscious of his Jewishness. Michael Schmidt has written well on Silkin in *Poetry* (Vol. 120, No. 3) when he says:

> Many, if not most, of his poems are technically flawed. There are recurrent obscurities of diction – an elaborate, often archaic or poetical diction; there is excessive punctuation, a blurred syntactical line. These qualities make the poems hard reading, but what is flawed in Silkin is still substantial. The humanity of the poems, their concern with situations of relationship, suffering, and death, and the strong tone of voice with an 'I' not self-assertive but perceptive, redeem the frequent clumsiness.

A useful choice of Silkin appears in *Poems New and Selected* (1966). He is to be found at his most ambitious in *Amana Grass* (1971).

The most remarkable re-emergence of our phase was that of Basil Bunting. *The Spoils*, written in 1951, was not generally available until 1965; *Briggflatts* (1966) is a poem that makes contact with our traditions at a level that had not seemed possible in many years. For too long Bunting's work had been lost to all but a few readers and was to be found in any bulk only in the rare Cleaners Press edition of *Poems* (1950). His verse, now united in *Collected Poems* (1968), should clearly have penetrated the anthologies long ago: *The Well of Lycopolis, Chomei at Toyama, Vestiges, The Orotava Road, Villon, Attis* often confess their Poundian provenance, but they are intricate and interesting poems. *The Spoils*, with its experiences of semitic culture and its return to 'Cold northern clear sea-gardens' leads directly to the richness of *Briggflatts*, the most authoritative long poem of the sixties. Here Bunting comes back to the Northumbrian landscape and tongue ('Southrons would mawl the music of many lines in *Briggflatts*') where monosyllables combine to produce a music new to modern verse. The sense of mortality, the vision of landscape, the repeated motifs are densely but lucidly orchestrated in a

> Flexible, unrepetitive line
> to sing, not paint: sing, sing
> laying the tune frankly on the air.

The music of Byrd, Monteverdi, Scarlatti and Schoenberg are some of Bunting's analogies for what he is after in terms of structure. One of the measures of the poem's success is his right to such analogies.

Bunting instances the sixth-century bard, Aneurin, who celebrated in *Y Gododdin* the deaths of warriors at the battle of Catterick. Aneurin is also a central instance for another poet, David Jones. Jones has produced a striking series of poems on the Roman–Celtic past (written 1955–65). The most readily approachable of these is perhaps *The Wall* (1955), the most recent, *The Fatigue* (1965) and *The Tribune's Visitation* (1969). All are a further growth beyond the exasperating and intriguing *Anathemata* (1952), a poem of great ambition and often impenetrable scholarship. 'The work of David Jones,' wrote T. S. Eliot, 'has some affinity with that of James Joyce ... and with the later work of Ezra Pound, and with my own.' Indeed, as Eliot points out, Jones belongs to the literary generation of these men and his ambition marks him as one of their fraternity. What remains impressive about *The Anathemata* is its penetration of pre-history, and to my own mind its opening section, *Rite and Fore-Time*, is unique in post-war writing. A difficult work to assess with finality, *The Anathemata* points us back to Jones' incontrovertible masterpiece, the prose book *In Parenthesis* (1937). Here he was able to convey a range of reference without burying the text in footnotes, as too frequently happens later on.

ENGLISH PHILOSOPHY SINCE 1945

MICHAEL TANNER

The greatest influence on English philosophy since the Second World War has unquestionably been Ludwig Wittgenstein, one of the surpassing geniuses in the history of the subject. For various and rather complex reasons the nature and consequences of that influence are not easy to specify. In the first place, he almost always wrote in German, though fortunately his works have been mainly translated with extraordinary brilliance by G. E. M. Anscombe, one of his closest associates. Second, the fact that, apart from the *Tractatus Logico-Philosophicus* of 1921, all his writings have been posthumously published, beginning with the *Philosophical Investigations* (1953), and are still continuing to appear, means that there was a period during which he was known to be engaged in extremely important work, of a revolutionary kind, but that the substance of that work was largely a matter for conjecture. From his return to Cambridge and philosophy in 1929, after an absence from both of more than a decade, he was energetically engaged in both writing and teaching; but he was too dissatisfied with what he wrote to publish it, and too insistent on secrecy from his disciples – almost all of whom were only too happy to keep what they heard to themselves – for his views to have any significant impact. And if a pupil dared to publish an account of what Wittgenstein was saying, or to write philosophy which was avowedly heavily influenced by him, as John Wisdom did from 1936 onwards – insisting both on the extent of Wittgenstein's influence and on the degree to which he felt unsure of having fully understood and assimilated what Wittgenstein was saying – he was liable to be banned from future contact: it was a very characteristically Viennese set-up.

The situation was, then, a decidedly odd one. Wittgenstein's reputation stood so high that few could doubt that when his views were finally published they would have a tremendous impact, but it was largely unclear what they would turn out to be. The best idea could be gathered from two typescripts which Wittgenstein had dictated to some pupils in the early thirties, and which enjoyed wide clandestine circulation. For many philosophers who read them in that form (they were finally published, as *The Blue and Brown Books*, in 1958), they were, as P. F. (now Sir Peter) Strawson has written, the most moving intellectual experience of their lives. Ranging widely over many of the most difficult and disputed areas of traditional philosophy in a most untraditional manner, they were uniquely liberating in the claustrophobic philosophical atmosphere of the thirties and forties. The power and grace of their language, the amazing fertility of their ideas, and the freshness of approach were precisely what was needed to effect a major change. But there remained the unnerving fact that they *were* work in progress – and obviously the work was progressing fast – and they left their readers at least as intrigued and perhaps even apprehensive as to where Wittgenstein had moved on to as astonished at where he had arrived.

When, finally, the *Philosophical Investigations* was published, the effect was not as sudden or drastic as might have been expected. It turned out to be obscure in a unique way. Written in numbered paragraphs, usually between two and twenty lines in length, the impression was of a jigsaw puzzle. Many individual pieces were clear; but the relationship among them was baffling. Not only were the sections clear, they were often beautiful and memorable. Wittgenstein is one of the great German prose writers[1] and, thanks to Miss Anscombe, could be said to have contributed to great English discursive prose too. On the other hand, quoting individual remarks was soon seen to be dangerous, though it was scarcely discouraged by Wittgenstein's false statement in the Preface that 'this book is really only an album'. Actually it is constructed with remarkable care. But other claims that Wittgenstein makes in it, such that he holds no philosophical views, that 'if one tried to advance *theses* in philosophy, it would never be possible to debate them, because everyone would agree to them', and much else to similar effect, tended to lead people into quoting isolated aphorisms more as unanswerable put-downs than as part of a sustained philosophical discussion.

So the *Philosophical Investigations* entered English philosophy as something both baffling and exhilarating, on account of its extreme hostility to system-building, and its apparent demonstration of what an anti-system might be. And the philosophical climate was such that an anti-system, especially one expressed in so impressively lapidary a style, was to be welcomed. For there had been so many systems, and they had all manifestly failed. In England, so far as any system commanded widespread loyalty in the early fifties, it was the radical empiricism otherwise known as 'logical positivism', which had been brilliantly popularized by A. J. (now Sir Alfred) Ayer in his youthful *tour-de-force* (inevitable characterization) *Language, Truth and Logic* (1936). In fact that book, which took the placid philosophical world by storm, might wisely have had as its epigraph the words that Wittgenstein chose for the *Investigations*, from the Austrian playwright Nestroy: 'In general progress has this about it, that it appears to be much greater than it really is.'[2] For Ayer did little more than express with enormous verve the traditional doctrines of British empiricism as they had been most strongly formulated by Hume: only statements susceptible of verification by the senses had literal meaning, the propositions of logic and mathematics being merely tautologies. This, the notorious Verification Principle, was naturally a source of endless debate among philosophers since it meant that the would-be propositions of ethics, indeed any value-statements, of metaphysics as traditionally conceived, and of theology, were 'cognitively meaningless'. The fact that Ayer withdrew from this extreme position in his long Introduction to the Second Edition of *Language, Truth and Logic* in 1946 did not prevent many philosophers, especially young ones returning from the war, embracing it with the greatest enthusiasm; and it was probably more responsible than anything else for the almost total lack of interest in ethics, aesthetics, political philosophy and philosophy of religion, let alone 'Continental philosophy', which prevailed in Britain for two decades after the publication of his book. That fact provides a striking indication – one which should not be needed, but perennially is – of the superior power of slogans, fashions, 'temperament', over reasoned argument in philosophy. For Ayer had never *argued* for the Verification Principle. It is merely dogmatically asserted and reiterated in *Language, Truth and Logic* and in many articles and books by other philosophers since. Not even the acknowledged fact that no one has ever achieved a strict formulation of it which succeeded in including just what was desired and excluding everything else deterred people from accepting it. And it is fair to say that in 1953 the British philosophical scene was divided between those who accepted it, even if they didn't say as much, and those whose principal cause was to reject it – and Wittgensteinians, whose attitude to it was obscure.

Evidence for this claim is provided by the appearance and reception of Gilbert Ryle's *The Concept of Mind* (1949), the most striking contribution to the post-war philosophical scene until the *Investigations*. That book set the tone of British philosophy to an extent that was only made possible by the continued impact of Ayer's first book. For what Ryle aimed to do, and was widely thought to have achieved, was to give an account of the mind, that notoriously recalcitrant item, which made it seem less anomalous in a climate where the physical sciences were taken to be the paradigm of knowledge; that was the underlying creed of logical positivism. The title of Ryle's book in its Italian translation, *Lo Spirito come Comportamento* (The Mind as Behaviour) is a fair one, though Ryle was sardonic about being labelled a behaviourist ('inevitable but harmless'). The first striking thing about it is that it is a rather long book; the prevalent tendency was much more towards articles, hence the enormous and significant proliferation of philosophical journals since the war. Ryle aimed systematically to consider all the chief mental attributes – intelligence, emotion, will, sensation and so on – and show that they are to be understood in terms of what would normally be thought to be only their manifestations. Thus in a characteristic passage he writes:

> The chess-player may require some time in which to plan his moves before he makes them. Yet the general assertion that all intelligent performance requires to be prefaced by the consideration of appropriate propositions rings unplausibly, even when it is apologetically conceded that the required consideration is often very swift and may go quite unmarked by the agent. I shall argue that the intellectualist legend is false and that when we describe a performance as intelligent, this does not entail the double operation of considering and executing.

The writing is fluent, free from technicality, contains hints of mockery, and the tone is forthright; the example at the beginning of the passage is typically homely. If one is inclined to ask: 'But what about considering, reflecting, when they don't issue in action?' one gets no clear answer. Ryle says that he is concerned to attack 'the dogma of the ghost in the machine', and that he will do so 'with deliberate abusiveness'; and he is as good as his word. His view is that everything about a person is in principle discoverable by others, and he goes so far as to claim, without any sense of being outrageous, that people 'are relatively tractable and easy to understand'. They would be if his analysis of them were correct. Rylean man is typically concerned to *do* things, even if the doing is speaking or writing. There are no inexpressible torments, no aesthetic or emotional ecstasies separable from their behavioural correlates (as we would normally take them to be), nor, it would seem, unproductive periods of reflection. It is a desperately limited and palpably false view of man which was eagerly accepted by many expert readers. And indeed, granted their general philosophical outlook, it is hard to see how it could have been otherwise. What makes *The Concept of Mind* beguiling is its ministering to the temper of the times so perfectly, yet in a way so innocently. Written as it is with an absence of technicalities – by no means complete: Ryle has quite an armoury of 'informal' distinctions, but they tend to have charming names and to be illustrated by example rather than provided with necessary and sufficient conditions for their use – with an overwhelming accumulation of cases disguised as themes with variations, it gives an apparently total account of the mind, and eases the removal of anxieties about such frightening issues as free will ('the bogey of mechanism') and the opacity of persons. Ryle's prose is the perfect vehicle for his views; manner and content are extraordinarily close, and if one is seduced by the style and eager for those conclusions, warm gratitude expressed with suitable British restraint is inevitable. Once again temperament, tone and a sense of 'where it's at' are what determined the astonishing success of a book whose arguments are often as preposterous as its conclusions, and were rapidly, if respectfully, shown to be so.[3]

Ryle was, to the point of self-caricature, an Englishman, as Stravinsky noted with amusement when he visited him in Oxford.[4] By the sharpest contrast Wittgenstein was, as I have already noted, a highly typical Viennese figure. The difference of tone of his magnum opus from Ryle's is instantly arresting: 'It is not impossible that it should fall to the lot of this book, in its poverty and in the darkness of this time, to bring light into one brain or another – but, of course, it is not likely' is a note inconceivable in Ryle or virtually any of his British contemporaries. Nonetheless, in spite of the grand manner which separates the *Investigations* sharply from anything that could be *expected* to emerge in the England of the Welfare State, it was taken in the first place as a contribution to the British philosophical tradition, a book which was fundamentally sound in spite of having been written by a bizarre, by then legendary foreigner (Ryle is reported as saying that 'Every generation or so the progress of philosophy is set back by the appearance of a "genius" '). Wittgenstein was seen as producing fascinating and difficult new arguments – despite all his disclaimers – on behalf of a view which, broadly speaking, was coincident with Ryle's, and as being engaged in the rebuttal of epistemological scepticism.

This seemed to bring him close to a further strand, at that time dominant in English philosophy: the defence of common sense, which had always been a central tenet of G. E. Moore. But while Moore conducted his defence in a style reminiscent of a cumbersome legal document, replete with inelegant and elaborate sentences with a plethora of jargon, Wittgenstein not only wrote with elegant profundity, but with profound elegance. Actually his writings contain a good many more terms of art than one might expect given his views but he is at pains to use them loosely, so that expressions, some of which have become celebrated (relatively speaking) – such as 'language-game' and 'form of life', used in highly idiosyncratic ways – are very difficult to pin down. In this respect he *is* comparable to Ryle; and it is not surprising that they came to be thought of as the leaders of 'ordinary-language philosophy'. That term has a twofold significance: not only do both Ryle and Wittgenstein insist that our quotidian language, uninfected by philosophical jargon, is perfectly adequate to its purposes. They both also view with the strongest suspicion the introduction into philosophy of new terms. Up to a point, they were thoroughly justified in doing so. For philosophers who introduce terminology often have done so under the impression that they had discovered features of the world which had previously been overlooked. In twentieth-century English philosophy the chief culprit has undoubtedly been 'sense-datum'. Coined about 1912 by Moore and Russell, it was thought for a long time to denote the immediate objects of sensation, or even of perception, and there were many disputes about, e.g. the relationship between sense-data and the surfaces of physical objects (Moore's last piece of philosophical writing, produced in 1954, returns to this subject which he had been pondering for forty years). Both Ryle and Wittgenstein insisted that philosophers can never discover entities, especially not mental ones, such as 'volitions', alleged by some philosophers including the young Ryle to be explanatory of how we perform free actions. And one of the first fruits of Wittgenstein's later teaching, a brilliant paper produced in 1936[5] demonstrated that if such a term as 'sense-datum' was to be used, it was only for purposes of linguistic convenience.

Nonetheless, as both Wittgenstein and Ryle discovered, it is impossible to do philosophy for long at a stretch without introducing some at least quasi-technical vocabulary. And a similar discovery was made on a much larger scale by J. L. Austin, the arch-defender of ordinary language, who died in 1960 at the age of forty-seven. If he had lived, he would almost certainly have become one of the practitioners of the Philosophy of Language as it is pursued today – a wholly different enterprise, though this is seldom registered outside the profession, from the 'ordinary-language philosophy' practised most intensively in Oxford during his lifetime, and not much heard of since. That activity can be seen in retrospect to have achieved very little, and part of its prestige was due to confusion with the almost wholly different enterprise of Wittgenstein. Not only his practice, either; it is now much clearer, thanks partly to the availability of a much larger part of his oeuvre, that Wittgenstein's work was animated by an ethical purpose, in a broad sense. He philosophized in order to gain a clarity which would release him and others from the pointlessness of pondering philosophical issues. 'The real discovery is the one that makes me capable of stopping doing philosophy when I want to', he wrote in the *Investigations*, and he was desperately concerned that his pupils should not become philosophers. He wanted to inculcate respect for 'forms of life', for the ways in which we non-philosophically think and act, and which he said were 'what had to be accepted, the given'. Philosophers futilely try to answer the question 'Why should I believe that anyone else has a soul [mind]?' whereas they should realize that 'My attitude towards you is the attitude towards a soul' (the *Investigations* again), where belief and hence justification do not enter in. One central thing that he was trying to do was to show the hopelessness of the traditional enterprise of founding our most general ideas about the world on self-evident truths, from which we move upwards and outwards.

Given the ethos in which the *Investigations* made its appearance, as that had been established by Ayer, and later by Ryle, it was inevitable that at first the *Investigations* should be seen as a kind of Humean work – at least the work of someone who, like Hume at the end of Book I of the *Treatise*, found the speculations of philosophers 'so cold, and strain'd and ridiculous' that he turned his back on them. Scepticism could be seen in one way as unconquerable, but in another as completely absurd. Wittgenstein did not deny that philosophical problems expressed 'deep disquietudes', indeed he harped on it, but nonetheless they were based on confusions and often on the illicit assimilation of one kind of knowledge to another, the preferred kind being most frequently mathematics. Since he saw the task of philosophy as destructive (of 'houses of cards') and corrective, the anti-systematic bent of the *Investigations*, together with the piecemeal tackling of philosophical issues advocated by Austin, led the majority of English philosophers to set a modest goal for themselves. It was at this time that collections of articles dealing with discrete problems, culled from the journals for the most part, began to appear, something new in philosophical publishing. Soon such collections proliferated at a tremendous rate, and became one of the most familiar, enduring and useful features of the philosophical scene.

But philosophy never remains anti- or unsystematic for long. One of the driving impulses of philosophers is to organize, if not knowledge itself, then the ways of knowing, and the conditions under which knowledge is possible. By the end of the fifties this more ambitious urge, the constructive as opposed to the merely restorative, was beginning to be felt strongly again by some figures who inaugurated much of the philosophical work of the sixties. The first book in which the new tendency was unashamedly manifest was Strawson's *Individuals* (1959), subtitled 'An Essay in

Descriptive Metaphysics'. He went to some lengths in the Introduction to stress the modesty of his endeavour, writing that 'up to a point, the reliance upon a close examination of the actual use of words is the best, and indeed the only sure, way in philosophy', but added immediately that 'the discriminations we can make, and the connections we can establish, in this way, are not general enough and not far-reaching enough to meet the full metaphysical need for understanding'. And it was the latter demand that he tried to fulfil in the first half of his book. It has an imaginative boldness and sweep which had been absent from English philosophy since the death of the neglected Collingwood in 1943 (neglected then and largely neglected now). But though Wittgenstein's name is not often mentioned in it – nor is anyone else's, that absence being characteristic of ambitious philosophical works – *Individuals* does build, especially in its most important and influential chapter, 'Persons', on the *Investigations* and is inconceivable without it.

From that releasing point onwards, philosophers began to see Wittgenstein's later work in a new light – specifically, a Kantian light. When Strawson published his next book *The Bounds of Sense* in 1966, it was explicitly as a highly selective critical–creative commentary on *The Critique of Pure Reason*. Generality had come back with a vengeance, and the undercutting arguments of the *Investigations* were seen as working against scepticism not so much by showing up its futility, but by showing how we can build up from certain indubitable facts, primarily from the existence of language, the most general beliefs we have about the world – a much more traditional-sounding enterprise than it had previously been taken as engaged upon, but given a new authority by the radical nature of its techniques. I have no doubt that Wittgenstein would have seen both the Humean and the Kantian ways of regarding his work as abject misunderstandings. But there is no doubt that that *is* how it came to be viewed. Even his closest associates embarked on metaphysical enterprises. And at the same time it was seen that his work could equally be a source of inspiration and direction in the philosophy of religion, of anthropology, even of aesthetics, always the Cinderella among the intransigently philistine English. His own deep and life-long concern with mathematics stimulated huge endeavours in the philosophy of that subject. And finally, his consuming interest in the nature of language was one key element in the philosophy of language becoming the major concern of British philosophers, who also saw, as he had done, that that subject was inseparable from the philosophy of mind.

Until the early sixties, British philosophy, with Wittgenstein of course counting as an honorary Englishman, was self-sufficient. But during the sixties the initiative passed to a very large extent to the United States, where many of the traditional claims of British empiricism – the separation of the empirical from the logical, of philosophy from science therefore, the whole notion of philosophy as a totally separate discipline – had always been viewed with suspicion. The formidable figure of W. V. O. Quine, a great logician whose interests had moved increasingly towards philosophy, especially to ontology ('On What There Is' is the title of one of his most famous papers), crossed the Atlantic several times and had an immense impact on Oxford; by this stage Cambridge was widely regarded as a backwater, a place that had had far more than its ration of geniuses, all of whom were dead or had ceased to do any new work. The excitement of building up, partly on the basis of the discoveries of modern logic, a fully-fledged philosophy of language meant that the speed of changing interests accelerated yet further. And once the centre of philosophical activity had moved to the other side of the Atlantic, it remained, and still does, decisively there.

Temporal myopia is bound to affect one's judgement at this point. But now the most imposing figures in contemporary philosophy, at least in its central concerns with language and the nature of mind, appear to be Donald Davidson and Saul Kripke, quintessentially American in their obsessive attention to detail, whilst they strive for the larger view. In England, only Michael Dummett at Oxford, dauntingly prolific and influential in the philosophy of language and of mathematics, commands the kind of attention that half-a-dozen English philosophers had a generation ago. And Wittgenstein? It would be grotesque to imply that he is forgotten; but, naturally enough, in a subject where there is frequent change even if not progress, contemporary philosophers approach him in their own spirit, not in his. And they are deeply incompatible. Philosophy has become during the last twenty years a subject for professionals and experts, armed with an impressive set of conceptual gadgets.

Anxiety, insight and concern about the moral function of philosophy – except for the application of moral philosophy – are at a discount. Philosophers want results, so that they can feel at home in a society even more scientifically and technologically oriented than the one in which Wittgenstein lived. If Ryle's dictum about the progress of philosophy being impeded by genius was correct, that is a hazard we need no longer fear.

NOTES

1. Erich Heller, the most distinguished prose writer in English at the present time, states of Wittgenstein: 'Perhaps only talent is needed for writing such prose in any other language, but certainly genius for writing it in German' (*The Artist's Journey into the Interior*, Harvest edn, 201).

2. This epigraph has been dropped in recent English reprints of the book.

3. See especially S. N. (now Sir Stuart) Hampshire's critical notice of the book in *Mind* (1950).

4. See the account of their meeting in Robert Craft, *Stravinsky: Chronicle of a Friendship* (London, 1972), 223–5.

5. G. A. Paul, 'Is there a Problem about Sense-Data?', in *Proceedings of the Aristotelian Society* (supplementary volume, 1936).

For some further reflections on the topics treated in this essay, see my article 'The Language of Philosophy', in *The State of the Language*, eds Leonard Michaels and Christopher Ricks (Univ. of California Press, 1980).

CRITICISM NOW:
THE ABANDONMENT OF TRADITION?

MARTIN DODSWORTH

T. S. Eliot's essay of 1919, 'Tradition and the Individual Talent', together with those on Elizabethan dramatists and the English poets of the seventeenth century, had an enormous influence on literary and cultural criticism in his lifetime. George Williamson's book *The Donne Tradition* (1930) was not much more than academic elaboration of what Eliot had already written, but later work – for example, Cleanth Brooks's *Modern Poetry and the Tradition* (1939) and F. R. Leavis's *The Great Tradition* (1948) – set out to extend the meaning of 'tradition' in specific literary terms and made it a central idea of criticism in the middle of the century. Its centrality can easily be demonstrated by a simple list of titles. Richard Chase's study of *The American Novel and its Tradition* (1957), Harold Rosenberg's essays on *The Tradition of the New* (1962), the weighty anthology compiled by Richard Ellmann and Charles Feidelson, Jr, to demonstrate *The Modern Tradition* (1965), even Frank Kermode's collection of essays, *Continuities* (1968) all – and many more could be cited – testify, sometimes in a paradoxical fashion, but still indisputably, to the importance of an idea of 'tradition' for criticism in their time.

The word has not suddenly vanished from the lips and pens of critics; but it is no longer a key-word for those who believe themselves to be reshaping literary thought and who are felt to be challenging orthodoxies now supposedly stale. In a wider sphere than that of literary criticism the word has fallen into disrepute; indeed the sociologist Edward Shils takes that fact as the starting-point for his own attempt at a rehabilitation, *Tradition* (1981).

The fall in the stocks of 'tradition' goes along with a sense of 'crisis' in English literary criticism. It is a false sense of crisis, but it is undeniably present. One expression of this is the symposium, *Re-Reading English* (1982), compiled by its editor, Peter Widdowson, in the belief that 'an increasing number of people teaching and studying in this field are aware that their subject is in the midst of some kind of crisis'. Widdowson and his associates represent various points on a left-wing spectrum, and their effort to redefine the subject 'English' is motivated by political idealism. But the same view, that English studies have reached the threshold of some new and radically different form of existence, is offered by writers with no political axe to grind. The emphasis may be slightly different; when David Lodge opens his preface to a collection of essays, *Working with Structuralism* (1981), by declaring that 'literary criticism is at present in a state of crisis which is partly a consequence of its own success' there is an obvious attempt to minimize the proportions of the crisis, as though his readers were being encouraged to make the best of a bad job and remember they had brought it on themselves.

The supposed 'crisis' derives from the incursion upon the English literary scene of a host of more or less new ideas from France and elsewhere. This chapter will not attempt an extended exposition of what is involved in formalism, structuralism and post-structuralism. Ronald Hepburn's chapter (pp. 494–508) supplements what is to be found here, and those who are interested can easily move on, perhaps by means of the by now numerous introductions and readers, to the works of Barthes, Derrida, Lévi-Strauss and Foucault themselves. They have little to say, it will be found, about English literature or, indeed, about much of their own literature: their status is that of philosophers and theoreticians, with the possible exception of Roland Barthes, whose mercurial intelligence played more often with specific works of literature than is the case with the others. The question to which this essay is addressed is how it should come about that a crisis in English studies should be provoked by thinkers so little concerned with the traditional subject-matter of those studies. The 'abandonment of tradition' to which its title refers is not merely the fall into disrepute of an idea; it is also a threatened discontinuity, of a marked kind, in practices of reading and study: and therefore in literary criticism.

The positive attractions of formalism, structuralism and post-structuralism must be understood. All three forms of thought turn upon a conception of language, and so promise more accurate descriptions of literary creation. As far as the French thinkers are concerned, the starting-point is in the posthumously published *Course in General Linguistics* (1915) of the Swiss linguist Ferdinand de Saussure. Instead of focusing on the historical development of languages, Saussure chose to consider language in atemporal terms, as a system of differentiated signs which could only have meaning within the system of which they were part. The nature of the signs themselves was indifferent; language is a system of differentiated *sounds*, but what Saussure had to say could apply just as well to a system of differentiated gestures, shapes or colours. Language was constituted in the relationship *between* signs, not in the signs themselves. *Bag* takes its meaning from the fact that we recognize it as not *beg, big, bog* or *bug*, as not *receptacle, container, wallet* or *purse*. Language is a system or structure of relationships.

This may not sound very exciting, but there is more to it than first seems. Saussure's abstract notion of a system of differentiated signs is capable, as he himself understood, of application to many other phenomena than language as such. The anthropologist Claude Lévi-Strauss applied Saussure's ideas in his studies of kinship, totemism and myth, in order to make intelligible apparently meaningless sets of prohibitions or sequences of events, providing them with a rational basis in what he posits as universal qualities of mind. In so doing he promoted a new interest in Saussure and became a focal point for the structuralist movement of the 1960s. Structuralism takes Saussure's idea of the sign as a union of signifier – the sound 'bag' – and signified – the idea of a bag distinct from other ideas, associated with other signifiers in a given language-system – and then extends it, so that a sign can be anything, and anything can be a sign. Roland Barthes's relentlessly entertaining and finally superficial *Mythologies* (1957, English translation 1972) is a collection of essays on various phenomena of modern life – all-in wrestling, striptease, a *Paris-Match* cover, a new car – which seek to show how these are all parts of 'language'-systems which present us with a mediated vision of the world, though they appear to belong to a natural, unmediated world of objects.

As applied to literature, structuralism tends to work in two opposite directions. Saussure's ahistorical systematization of language points towards hypotheses about the universal qualities of mind. As Roland Barthes asks in a rhetorical question,

Is not structuralism's constant aim to master the infinity of utterances (*paroles*) by describing the 'language' (*langue*) of which they are the products and from which they can be generated?[1]

In particular, writers like Tzvetan Todorov, Gerard Genette and most contributors to the journal *Poétique* have sought to describe the 'language' of which works of literature may be supposed to be part

discourse itself ... is organized and ... through this organization, it can be seen as the message of another language, one operating at a higher level than the language of the linguists.

Most emphasis has been put on the development of theories of narrative, and these studies revived an interest in the writings of the Russian formalist critics, Shklovsky, Tynyanov and others,[2] among them the folk-lorist Propp whose own work had been an inspiration for Lévi-Strauss in his studies of myth.

The positive attractions of this side of structuralism are clear. By focusing attention on the relations between parts in a given work of literature, identified by reference to a universal typology, it can induce a keener appreciation of what the work presents, though, as in the case of Todorov's *The Fantastic* (1970, translated 1975), the kernel of insight may seem to require more effort in the getting at than it quite justifies. On the other hand, the use of a linguistic model for such analyses fosters the illusion that they are somehow 'scientific' in a way that other literary studies are not. This cannot be the case, as Barthes himself has made clear.[3] Furthermore, the conception of 'narrative' or 'literature' as coherent sign-systems tends to leave out of account the social and historical element within literature itself. This was a trap into which the Russian formalists also fell, though it was not inevitable that they should do so: the work of Mikhail Bakhtin stands as a model of how the formalist method could come to terms with historical development.[4] Pure formalism, of course, allowed for an evolution of literary forms in history, but by refusing to value some aspects of development at the expense of others de-vitalized the relation between literature and its historical setting. The twin tendency in structuralism to abstract 'rules' from literature and to abstain from evaluation – studies of narrative theory, because they aim at universality, are uninterested in differences of quality between narratives – makes much of its literary theory dry and dusty – a new scholasticism.

The second tendency in structuralism, towards post-structuralism, is complementary to that towards formalism. Its starting-point is Saussure's notion of a plurality of coexistent language-systems. The old school tie, the preference for hard rock music, the taste for beer rather than spirits, these and similar phenomena can be seen as statements within various unspoken codes of language, and these codes themselves will be reflected within the spoken language in so far as it relates to the physical and social world. It follows that a structuralist critic may view the work of literature as a kind of meeting-place for different systems of meaning. Barthes's *S/Z* (1970, English translation 1974) analyses a long short story by Balzac in terms of interrelated 'codes' of meaning.

> The text is not a line of words releasing a single 'theological' meaning (the 'message' of the Author-God) but a multi-dimensional space, in which a variety of writings, none of them original, blend and clash.[5]

The author is either good or bad at constructing texts on the basis of the several codes at his disposal; Barthes denies him any responsibility beyond this. He will not allow that the author expresses feeling or insight in what he writes; such things are generated by the codes with which he works, not by him. Barthes is especially scornful of the Romantic idea of the genius, the 'Author-God'; his ideal for literature is not remote from that of Mallarmé whose 'entire poetics consists in suppressing the author in the interests of writing'; 'for him, for us too, it is language which speaks, not the author'. As for the writer who still has the hardihood to think in terms of expression, he ought at least to know, says Barthes, that

> the inner 'thing' he thinks to 'translate' is itself only a ready-formed dictionary, its words only explainable through other words, and so on indefinitely.

The author who imposes himself on his work by this means only impoverishes the play of meaning that constitutes, for Barthes and those like him, the ideal work of literature – something like *Finnegans Wake*.

It is only a little step from here to post-structuralism, whose most distinguished representatives are Michel Foucault and Jacques Derrida

(Barthes is both structuralist *and* post-structuralist). The idea of 'words only explainable through other words, and so on indefinitely' suggests a philosophy of complete relativism in which all affirmation of value becomes arbitrary. Derrida's major critical undertaking has been to 'de-construct' the work of various writers, mostly philosophical, in order to show how in each case it depends on internal contradiction, that is, on the affirmation of a value which is in effect undermined if the full implications of the extended argument are taken into account. 'Deconstruction' is an activity in line with that debunking of middle-class myth and especially the myth of the author as genius that takes place, for example, in Barthes's *S/Z*.

French structuralists and post-structuralists have in common a style of writing that is frequently turgid and obscure, reacting in part against a lucidity which they regard as suspect, because they believe it to be the final disguise of that bourgeois ideology which they have made it their chief business to expose.

To challenge familiar assumptions and familiar values in a discourse which, in order to be easily readable, is compelled to reproduce these assumptions and values, is an impossibility,

an English exponent of the new and foreign ways argues,[6] and the argument is sound, as far as it goes. If, however, we feel disinclined to commit ourselves to an absolutely relative view of the world, the lack of definition in post-structuralist prose, along with its disinclination to deal with specific literary texts, is likely to pall. It does not follow that post-structuralism has nothing to offer the reader; it certainly does, in the work of Derrida and Foucault, grapple with real problems, though they are more strictly philosophical than literary. In so far as their work and that of their associates enhances our sense of ideological bias and internal contradiction within the work of literature, it must be a force for the good.

However, much of what we find within structuralist, formalist and post-structuralist criticism is already in existence within the Anglo-Saxon and more particularly the English literary tradition. Barthes's declaration of the 'death of the author' makes no reference to the discussion by Wimsatt and Beardsley of the 'intentional fallacy', but it is plainly in line with it, as it is with Eliot's statement of the necessary impersonality of great literature more than fifty years ago. Eliot's scorn for the 'inner voice' anticipates Barthes's attack on 'expression', though Eliot does not, as Barthes does, reduce the writer's responsibility to a mere craftly generation of messages from codes. Barthes's attack on the 'genius' and an effusive criticism that treats language as a transparency giving direct access to the writer's emotions at some point beyond the text does not advance us much beyond the point at which I. A. Richards had arrived in his attack on Vernon Lee in *Principles of Literary Criticism* (1924). Barthes's homilies on the plurality of meaning in literature are not at all ridiculous, but lack their force in a literary world that has been familiar with William Empson's *Seven Types of Ambiguity* (1930; never translated into French) for more than fifty years now. Empson's study of semantic change, *The Structure of Complex Words* (1951), is a radical challenge to Saussure's account of language as a 'system': one chapter has been translated into French, but there is little sign that its import has been grasped. More to the point, writers advocating structuralism to the Anglo-Saxon have not recognized the places in a continuing argument where their arguments would help; but then, the essay in which, as long ago as 1941, Allen Tate investigated the foundations of modern semiotics ('semiology' in the French tradition) and found them wanting[7] is never, as far as I have been able to see, cited in the many footnotes of the new New Criticism. When Barthes wrote (in 1966) that

everything suggests ... that the mainspring of narrative is precisely the confusion of consecution and consequence, what comes *after* being read in narrative as what is *caused* by ...[8]

he was presumably ignorant that this was a fundamental idea in the writings of the American critic, Kenneth Burke, whose thought often anticipates structuralist insight.[9] Barthes is not to be blamed for this; his English exponents are. The objection to much structuralist criticism is that, once stripped of its linguistic–scientist rhetoric, it proves either unrewarding or, within the English tradition, redundant.

That can hardly be argued very thoroughly in an essay of this length; the point that has been made, I hope, is the extent to which there has been a failure on either side of the critical divide (in Great Britain – things are rather different in the United States) to assess the situation and discover whether there might not be a common inheritance. David Lodge, it is true, has tried 'working with structuralism' and seems likely to continue the practice, but his structuralism is largely the linguistic descriptive technique of Roman Jakobson, on the formalist side of the movement, applied to particular works in an English empirical spirit and, to my mind, with little success. The 'crisis' in English studies is an illusion if it is supposed that two parties are engaged in momentous controversy of a kind that must be decided only in favour of one of them.

Talk of 'crisis' is part of the rhetoric by which the new school of critics would accede to what they imagine as 'power'. French structuralism was very much a new-wave movement, an attack on an old guard in French academic life, the most powerful burst of which is represented by Barthes's *Critique et Vérité* (1966; untranslated). It is the glamour of this moment in French cultural history that proponents of the 'crisis' transfer to themselves. There is, however, more to it than that. British proponents of this form of literary thought have understood better than its American epigones – Harold Bloom, Geoffrey Hartman, J. Hillis Miller and others – that it carries a strong social and political implication. Talk of the 'crisis' is part of a political rhetoric whose function is to bring about the change which it suggests is already taking place. The idea of 'tradition' is abandoned, for example, in an attack on the 'critical discourse' of *The Great Tradition*, and this abandonment is associated with a desired change in society itself, a change that will end 'hierarchy':

> What is inscribed in the Leavisian model is the making of hierarchies through judgements of relative human value, not just in literature but in life. The discourse of *The Great Tradition* helps to guarantee relations of inequality by the endless production of discriminations between subjectivities. Hierarchy is not seen to be produced by an external ordering of society which is subject to change. On the contrary, it is created through the affirmation of one identity at the expense of another, and maintained by the rejection of any rational criticism of the process itself.[10]

The clarity of this statement is welcome; 'the major sin in criticism,' said Barthes, 'is not to have an ideology but to keep quiet about it'. There is no such keeping quiet here. Nor is the 'ideology' unmasked in Leavis's writing altogether untrue to its spirit, for Leavis endorsed Lawrence's concept of 'disquality' ('spiritually, there is pure difference and neither equality nor inequality counts').[11] On the other hand, it is not obvious that Leavis was wrong to endorse it. The denial of subjectivity, with the ensuing 'death of the author', naturally leads to the suppression not merely of individualism but also of individuality. That is a high price to pay for philosophical consistency, and we need to have a very secure base if we are to pay it.

In the passage just quoted, Catherine Belsey points to a 'rejection of any rational criticism of the process' of judgement in Leavis's writings, thinking not only of his refusal to engage in philosophical debate, but also of his reliance on intuitive assent as the basis for value-judgement. For her it is objectionable that Leavis should say of George Eliot that in her creation of Gwendolen Harleth

she is exhibiting what we recognize from our own most intimate experience to be as much the behaviour of a responsible agent . . . as any human behaviour can be.[12]

It is not 'rational' to make the test of a novel's quality some unsophisticated response of 'our own most intimate experience'. 'Subjectivity' and 'idealism' rule here, to our detriment, she says. 'If we know it already,' she asks of such discoveries as George Eliot might, in a Leavisian way, be said to make, 'in what sense can we be said to learn it?' This is the point of internal contradiction in her deconstructing account of Leavis's work.

But does not even Barthes offer us something akin to this kind of contradiction? For if 'it is language which speaks, not the author', whose is the illusory subjectivity that constructs its 'messages' from 'codes'? how is it that 'codes' can be perceived by an illusory subject? It is perhaps unfair to move from Leavis to Barthes, leaving Belsey out of the argument; for her, then, the question would be: what constitutes the rationality of her denial of hierarchy? what privileges one mode of life (without hierarchy) over another? what privileges 'rationality' over other forms of discourse? The relativism inherent in post-structuralism leads to *impasse*, the conclusion that meaning is impossible, hiding behind an infinite recess of word upon word, or to the incoherence of political messianism linked to the revolutionary turmoil of nihilism. It leads to a great deal of talk and the inability to believe that knowledge can be anything *but* talk, hence the denial that there can be an unarticulated knowledge which we recognize and comprehend when articulated for us, as it were by George Eliot, but which nevertheless we did in a sense have before it was articulated.[13]

The opposition of Leavis and Belsey, I wish to suggest, is an opposition of beliefs about human nature to which we can only respond by an intuitive leap one way or the other: to deny 'subjectivity' and 'individuality' or to accept them as prime facts in human existence. A future based on the expungement of individuality seems to me not only uninviting but an impossibility. Hence my belief that there is no 'crisis' induced by structuralism and its like.

There is, however, another crisis in English studies which is real, and exists on the other side of the rhetoric and abstractions of the structuralist 'revolution'. English literature is running out of readers.

The signs of this are various and too many. One sign is the physical nature of the book whose characteristic paper binding marks it out as 'disposable', that is, not designed to last. Another is the short time that modern accounting methods allow a book to remain on sale; far more than ever used to be the case, saleability determines whether and for how long a book remains in print. Another is the host of introductions, guides and casebooks which imply a gap between the reader's interest and aptitude and what the books introduced, poems, plays or novels, have to say, a gap that has to be bridged by the indefatigable introducers. English literature is ceasing to be read; it is increasingly only studied. It follows that the ordinary-language criticism of the English tradition, which is represented by writers like C. S. Lewis or A. J. Waldock or William Empson as well as by F. R. Leavis or T. S. Eliot, is being left behind: for that was, and still is, in so far as it survives, written from within the experience of English literature as a living thing, a form of pleasure whose roots lay both in a sense of historical and social reality and in an ethical being which shaped the future in accord with its sense of the past. The continuance of an English tradition of literary criticism depends on the continuance of an English literary tradition.

The significance of the false 'crisis' in English studies lies here. The uneasy sense that many teachers of English have that they should really be learning about language-systems and the 'inscription' in them of 'ideologies' rather than talking about plays, poems and novels is a sign that they are less than sure that imaginative literature exists for their students as anything more than a complex of data to be analysed. The philosophical and scientific pretensions of the new style of talk flatters that view and helps make the change in the subject of study an irreversible one: poetry dies as 'poetics' takes over. It dies, that is, as a form of pleasure challenging judgement. The new forms of talk about literature have virtually nothing to say about either pleasure or judgement.

The prospects for English literary criticism are, then, not very healthy. The courage to affirm value is sapped by the very circumstances of modern life, its specialization, its fragmentation, the hostility that it shares with structuralist thought to any but the most theoretical individuality. These are, however, circumstances that will put to the test the underlying principles of that tradition which is being left behind. 'No poet, no artist of any art, has his meaning alone.' As long as poetry and the other arts have a meaning we may expect those principles to survive. Just as the individual self preserves its identity in time, so do institutions depend on a sense of tradition that is analogous. Traditions are not, however, forms of rigid armature; they are as flexible as the spirit they serve.

NOTES

1. 'Introduction to the Structural Analysis of Narratives' in Barthes, *Image – Music – Text*, selected and translated by Stephen Heath (London, 1977), 80. See the same essay, p. 83, for the other quotation in this paragraph. Heath's selection makes an excellent introduction to the range of Barthes's thought.

2. See Tzvetan Todorov's anthology, *Théorie de la litterature: Textes des formalistes russes* (Paris, 1965). The best anthology in English is *Readings in Russian Poetics: Formalist and Structuralist Views*, eds Ladislav Matejka and Krystyna Pomorska (Cambridge, Mass., 1971).

3. '... in structural analysis there is no canonical method as there is in sociology or philology, such that by automatically applying it to a text will cause its structure to appear ...' Barthes, 'Par où commencer?', in *Poétique*, 1 (1970), 3.

4. P. N. Medvedev and M. M. Bakhtin, *The Formal Method in Literary Scholarship*, translated by Albert J. Wehrle (Baltimore, 1978), is powerfully and subtly argued: it was published in Russian in 1928.

5. Barthes, 'The Death of the Author', in *Image – Music – Text*, 146. Other quotations in this paragraph come from the same short essay.

6. Catherine Belsey, *Critical Practice* (London, 1980), 4–5.

7. 'Literature as Knowledge' (1941) in Tate, *Essays of Four Decades* (London, 1970).

8. 'Introduction to the Structural Analysis of Narratives', in *Image – Music – Text*, 94.

9. On 'consecution and consequence', see Burke's account of 'syllogistic and qualitative progression' in the 'Lexicon Rhetoricae' in *Counter-Statement*, first published 1931; (2nd edn, Chicago, 1953), 124 ff.; and *The Philosophy of Literary Form* (Baton Rouge, 1941), 74–5.

10. Catherine Belsey, 'Re-reading the great tradition', in *Re-Reading English*, ed. Peter Widdowson (London, 1982), 129–30.

11. See F. R. Leavis, *Nor Shall My Sword* (London, 1972), 20, 54, 127, for example.

12. F. R. Leavis, *The Great Tradition* (London, 1948), 109.

13. Leavis's admiration for D. W. Harding's essay 'Aspects of the Poetry of Isaac Rosenberg', in *Experience into Words* (London, 1963; first published in *Scrutiny*), is significant here; see my 'Thought, Literature and Criticism', in *English*, XXV (1976), 176–81.

LITERATURE AND THE RECENT
STUDY OF LANGUAGE

RONALD HEPBURN

This has been a period of intense activity in the study of language, whether from the point of view of linguistics or philosophy. During this time, indeed, some philosophers have been tempted to see the traditional problems of philosophy as themselves essentially linguistic in nature, to be unravelled only by better grasp of the complexities of language. Meaning, sense and reference, naming and describing, 'speech acts', the varied functions of language, have been topics of special (and specialist) attention, all of them having a bearing – indirect if not immediate – upon how we understand language to work in literary contexts. The outcome of such studies may affect how – for instance – reader and critic see the relation of a literary work to its author, and whether they see literature as essentially communication or as essentially texts for the freest play of 'creative' interpretation.

Nevertheless, not all the explorations of language in literature have had helpful results for either readers or critics. For example, although there have been good reasons for theorists to reject some rather naïve accounts of literary works as giving direct expression to authors' intentions, or as plain statements of the 'truth' about the human condition, it does not follow that we can profitably abandon every account of the author's communicational aims (even more sophisticated accounts), or support fashionable non-mimetic views of literary works, in an unqualified way. In some cases, again, the role of interpreter and critic has become pretentiously inflated. Implausible esoteric background material is sometimes being introduced as necessary to the understanding of a work of literature. Too often attempts to assimilate the vocabularies of linguistic theory, of the structuralist and post-structuralist movements, and the language of Freudian and post-Freudian psychoanalysis, have led to a congested prose in which few expressions are not technical, and all too few of the technical terms themselves are lucidly introduced. As obscurity increases, so the possibility of rigour, and of any confirmation or falsification of claims, drastically declines. Certainly, clarity is not everything; but it remains a major ideal, intellectual and moral.

With the attraction of its prestigious and scholarly standing, language study, not surprisingly, has tempted some writers into imagining that it can do more for the understanding of literature than it really can.

The 'New Criticism' and the philosophical writing on aesthetics most in tune with it made a memorable contribution to our understanding of a work of literary art, importantly qualified though their claims have to be. A literary work, on that account, approaches the ideal of a self-sufficient microcosm: it constitutes a proper object of criticism to the extent that all major interpretative clues lie within the work, and not, for instance, in the author's biography. Density of meaning is the distinctive feature of literary language – many-levelled, controlledly ambiguous, through and through metaphorical. Further, the criteria for *appraising* a literary work must relate to qualities internal to the work: imaginative and dramatic vividness, vitality, ironical tension, 'presence', the coherence of the 'world' of the work rather than truth as correspondence to the world beyond the work. It is a 'well-wrought urn'; or, in MacLeish's extreme formulation, 'a poem should not mean but be'.

This view, though attractive, involves simplification and idealization – most evidently so in that last formulation. I do not myself believe that there can be a linguistic structure capable of being a serious work of art, that does not mean at all, that makes no reference to the world, that does not rely on tacit importation of notions from other times and other places. I doubt, too, if the thought of recovering the author's communication in the literary work is ever *altogether* unhelpful; or that the reader can do without the resonances of comparison and contrast with other literary works, genres, movements in art – whether these are being pursued or rebelled against. Do not these qualifications totally erode the view of a literary work as a self-sufficient object of contemplation? Not altogether: external references won't remedy deficiencies and thinnesses in a work itself. They will only alert us to potentially rewarding ways of approaching it, and furnish the relevant background of thought against which to set it. Whether our resulting experience is actually rewarding depends on the senses, associations, images, emotional qualities that those words in their very complex combination in the work can be made to bear and evoke.

To study a literary work is to see language functioning at the highest pitch of its power to *connect* – to connect subtly discriminable and often mutually remote, endlessly numerous, areas of experience. Empson's *Seven Types of Ambiguity* and *The Structure of Complex Words* made readers aware in a permanently important way of the great degree of complexity to be looked for behind a literary effect. Moreover, the reader looks for the interpretation that integrates the lower unities (small-scale images, metaphors etc) in higher inter-mediate unities, and all these ultimately in a single overarching view.[1] This yields also an appraising criterion, the extent to which a particular poem or other literary work proves responsive to such integrative attempts, or turns out to be no more than episodic, its components failing to determine jointly a single overall character to the work. The criterion cannot, however be applied mechanically or in a facile way. Resistance to being displayed as an unmysterious transparently intelligible structure can itself be a positive aesthetic feature of a poem.

How a competent reader approaches a work of literature, his attitudes and expectations, depend importantly upon the genre he sees it as exemplifying. A work that rebels against genre-conventions equally relies on the reader's recognition of the conventions being rejected. Aesthetically relevant features of a work may stand out only if its reader has a background awareness of the historical development of the genre, or of the style, that the work is transforming in its distinctive way and perhaps without direct allusion within the text itself. The work may demand to be seen against the foil of the whole tradition from which it stems, and which it modifies by its very existence. (Eliot's *Tradition and the Individual Talent* remains a seminal essay.)

If the literary work must be seen not simply as a self-contained object of contemplation, so equally must the reader be seen not as an innocent contemplative eye but as enabled by literary education to bring to bear on a work the complex set of attitudes and ex-pectations that literary understanding presupposes, and to play the part, even if a minor part, of collaborator in reconstructing the richness of meaning in the text.

Language in literature – especially in poetry – often deviates markedly from its everyday use. Metaphor is a kind of deviant language, where a literal interpretation of an utterance is precluded because normal rules of use are violated. Violations set our minds into a lively search for alternative, novel, illuminating meanings, consistent with meanings already hazarded for other sections of the literary work. Context is the determiner, or counsellor, of choice of possible new meanings. On a large scale, what is true of individual metaphors is true also of a complete poem. It may, with obvious deliberateness, break language-boundaries or the ordinary conditions of meaningfulness, in a way that initially checks the reader. Of course, it may be a bad poem and be hiding its badness in its convoluted obscurity. If it is not, then the reader, recovering, takes it as 'up against the boundaries of language': seeking to say what language (in general, or this particular language) cannot say easily or directly. The structure of a given language makes some things easy to say, and some very difficult. The poet more than any other language-user is always seeking to prevent the grain of language from coaxing him into saying what he never wished to say, and is always striving against the clichés and stale idioms that would wrest the distinctiveness from his thought.

No poetic theory has convincingly argued that any boundary can be put round the vocabulary and the legitimate subject-matter of literary art. Not even the concrete or the particularized or the sensuously realized provides a demarcation between literature and non-literature: a poem or novel may properly take as its subject styles of thinking, complex relationships, alternations of perspective, as much as concrete objects and persons. Literature exhibits or displays or celebrates its subject-matter, whatever that is, and gives vivid presence to it, whatever its mode of being.[2] It may do more than that, but that at least it must achieve. Its subject-matter can be highly elusive, hard to hold in the focus of attention. The density of metaphor, the poet's syntactical deviations, signal the difficulty of his task – signal the ultimate inability of language directly to recreate or duplicate the author's experience; and yet these same means, simultaneously, go an astonishing way towards effective expression.[3]

The Expression Theory of art is one of the ever-revivable options in aesthetics. Dominant in a Romanticism that sees literary art as the expression of a writer's inner and affective life, it has recently been damped down, at least by writers who wish to minimize biographical reference in criticism. Yet the communication of emotion, with precision and discriminatory power, cannot be denied to be one of the achievements of language in literature.

Recent analysis of emotion has made this communication much more intelligible than before. Part of what it is to have an emotion is to interpret and appraise one's situation – for instance, as threatening, humiliating, or full of promise. Emotions contain an essentially cognitive element. For the most part, too, they necessarily involve (describable) *objects*. So to express a particular emotion is not to have the impossible task of transfusing to the reader a unique mode of inner excitation, but primarily to communicate a way of seeing an object, a person or a view of the world.

It becomes intelligible how a writer may give a new precision to inchoate emotional responses and even facilitate new responses. Compare Eliot: the poet makes possible 'a much greater range of emotion and perception for other men, because he gives them the speech in which more can be expressed'.[4] Moreover, the intimate relation between emotion and language means that our everyday emotions are very much at the mercy of the language we hear and make our own. Slipshod, cliché-ridden, stereotyping language makes for imprecision and a sentimentalizing distortion in our emotions themselves. To read, heeding all the nuances, a passage from Thomas Hardy or George Eliot can be to discover a particularity, a complexity in emotion that slipshod language denies. The unity-in-complexity that makes for formal integration in a literary work makes also for *emotional* creativity, fashions a finely-regulating instrument enabling a precise emotional response to complex elements normally beyond our powers to hold together.

There may also be a spill-over from literature to life. Literature can educate the emotions by showing up the clichés, and showing that they can be avoided. It gives us thereby a measure of *freedom*, freedom not to be conditioned into conforming to a narrow, con-stricting set of emotional possibilities for life-situations, conditioned, i.e. by current popular social models and stereotypes of what 'one' does and does not feel. The discriminatory power of literature *vis-à-vis* the emotions can also be a reproach to sentimentality, and help towards its reduction. For sentimental emotion is undiscriminating emotion, emotion that blurs differences in the objects of feeling.

We have been moving some way from the work of literature as an object of contemplation, to the humanly important but very general effects of communion with it. There is no guarantee that those effects will invariably be benign and never harmful. A literary work may displace current stereotypes of feeling, only to create new ones, no more adequate to the complexities of life as we live it. More fairly, the writer condenses certain possibilities of feeling into a vivid and memorable image (or statement, or dramatic action). And a reader may be tempted to seize upon that image as thereby conferring unique 'authority' on this form of feeling. It alone is authentic, sanctioned, necessary. Only a wide exposure to the diversity of emotion expressed in contrasting works of art can prevent the arts imposing new emotional tyrannies instead of enhancing emotional freedom. With these caveats, the conclusion ought to be this: that we can understand better, because of recent work on language and emotion, how creativity in literature includes, importantly and literally, the creation of new and highly individualized forms of emotion; and that the relevance of literature to the life of the emotions does not end there, but extends from experience of the work itself to the educating of the reader's own emotions, his critique of his own socially conditioned or confused forms of feeling.[5]

In the present climate of literary theory, to ask whether the role of language in literature is primarily the revealing of truth about the world is to invite contradictory and sharply-contested answers. It is obvious, first of all, that no simple criterion of truth-to-reality can be legitimately applied to the detail of a literary work. Lack of 'fit' between the real world and a historical or topographical description in a novel are quite compatible with the greatness of that novel as literature. Exactness of fit is compatible with mediocrity. Secondly, there can be no legitimate inference from imaginative coherence or vividness or a wide range of subject-matter to the 'truth' of a work in an extra-literary sense. All these are compatible with misrepresenting the real world.

Yet our human interest in, and need for, the truth about ourselves and our world are so constant and so serious, that we cannot be indifferent to the power that literature undoubtedly has to present the truth – power to make us aware of it with unusual vividness, to *realize* it in an unusually intense degree. Its way of revealing truth may be oblique, and may gain in efficacy from being oblique. For instance, in a country where a totalitarian ideology is dominant, the bare refusal of a poet to have any truck with the official 'newspeak' may itself be a powerful (and personally costly) witness to the falsifying tendency of that jargon, and thus to a truth that it obscures. (Nadezha Mandelstam observed that 'Stalinism sought not only to blot out those who rejected the official ideology, but "above all those who rejected its phraseology"'. 'If the language of poetry, the language of reality as opposed to socialist realism, is annihilated, then there's no hope.'[6]) The concern with truth can also be very direct. No literary works could be further from quasi-objects for contemplation than the writings of Solzhenitsyn; and with such works it is least plausible to suggest that our appraisal should be limited to the purely internal articulation of their component parts.

With other writings again we are indifferent to the matching of fictional detail with extra-literary detail, but we are by no means indifferent to implicit truth-claims at another level. Through the fictional detail can be revealed such matters as the immense difficulty of acquiring self-knowledge, or the near-pervasiveness of self-deception, or the nature of the struggle against egoistic degradations of love.[7] The importance of a work may rest chiefly on these disclosures. They are literary, in that a disclosure is enacted, brought to realization, in the fabric of the work itself, and by distinctively literary resources; but the confirming or rebutting of its implied affirmations is *not* internal to the reading of the text. It relies on (perhaps often repeated) testing against the reader's funded experience of life. If he does not find them wanting, they may eventually be appropriated in a close personal assimilation, their key images and phrases coming to be adopted in the articulating of his own intimate experience.

Of high interest to serious students of literature and of the language of literature is a range of explorations that have gone on throughout the period under review in this volume (in philosophy, linguistics and related movements such as structuralism) on the relations be-

tween language, thought and our picture of the world. It may reasonably be claimed that the language made available to a person regulates
in very considerable detail the distinctions he can make, the qualities
he can heed, the appraisals he can make, of self as well as of others,
the intellectual operations with which he conducts his reflective, inner
life. The topic, so extended, carries us beyond literary use of language
to language-use in general; though we may expect that the force
and memorableness of works of literature may make their contribution peculiarly important. To the naïve view that thought is one
thing and language quite another, and that perception too is independent of language and concepts, retorts will come from recent
students of language belonging to diversified traditions. Whorf and
the like-minded claim that 'the forms of a person's thoughts are controlled by inexorable laws' – the laws of his own language. Language
furnishes the categories by which he 'builds the house of his consciousness'.[8] To Derrida, it is 'metaphysical' in a derogatory sense
of the word to assume that there is an identifiable thought, distinct
from its expression.[9] Benveniste argued that it is impossible to communicate ideas which do not fit the conceptual framework of the
relevant language.[10] Language is not 'compliant to individual intention and meaning': 'all thought presupposes language'.[11]

Shunning the naïve view, some influential theorists go quite to
the opposite pole. They do not simply and justifiably reflect on, e.g.,
the 'radically linguistic' nature of such fundamental features of our
experience and social life as the sense of past and future, sex and
kinship,[12] yet leaving room for linguistic and literary creativity; but
they affirm a thoroughgoing linguistic determinism. We are never
really the masters of words: they master us, impose tight restrictions
on our ability to think, understand, interpret against their grain.

There is material here of very different degrees of plausibility.
Some is highly plausible and yields important insights: for instance
arguments against concepts totally independent of language. Again,
it is entirely plausible and important to urge that the systematically
interrelated set of available meanings that constitutes a language has
a semi-autonomous existence of its own: a writer cannot assume that
it will be compliant to the communicating of his immediate, willed,
personal intention.

But the extreme linguistic deterministic position cannot, I think, be sustained – cannot even be coherently stated. The knowledge that language puts pressures upon my thought – facilitates one way of seeing and blocks others, this knowledge has itself to be put on the map, and *it* cannot be taken as simply more determination of thought by language. Rather, in this very insight about my predicament there lies the intimation of a limited but real freedom – freedom to transcend, to escape being wholly immersed in, any particular language-dominated view, even if the escape is partial, fitful and painful. What literature, notably, offers here are astonishingly many *alternative* language-and-concept schemes. I am not altogether a prisoner in a cage of language, if I can inhabit markedly different linguistic homes, as I turn from author to author, from period to period.

Strong witness against the deterministic extreme is also provided by the frequent testimony of poets to their struggle against the boundaries of available language – their strenuous efforts, therefore, to think 'up-speech' (Friedrich Waismann). Though obliquely and often uncertainly (and with characteristic strenuousness), communication is possible by pushing against linguistic limits. A truer picture emerges of language as (a) the entirely indispensable condition of the articulating of perception and thought, and (b) equally the agency by which thought and perception are constricted. Language has its own persistence, inertia to will and to instant change: paradoxically it is itself the medium in which both the need for and the projects of change have to be embodied.

Second: the pressures of experience itself constantly call in question the adequacy of current linguistic resources to express it. Our life is not simply language-use; and though our experience is profoundly influenced and moulded by language, there is no adequate reason to see that experience as exhaustively determined in its nature and qualities by language alone.

For several related and already noted reasons, many literary theorists of the period have tended to give the author a diminished role in their account of literature, a role in sharp contrast to that given, say, by Romantic theorists who were centrally concerned with his 'genius' and saw his works as primarily his triumphs of expression.

Admit essential reference to the author, embed the literary work in a biographical context, then at once the unity, completeness and givenness of a literary work are violated. Criticism has then no determinate object, and it cannot (lacking that) establish precise meanings.

Similarly, writers in philosophical aesthetics argued that only confusion results when author and work of art are not clearly kept apart. The 'voice' of the work cannot be identified with the voice of the author: the expressive and emotional qualities of the work cannot be identified with the author's own feelings and emotions.[13]

Thirdly: we could cull further arguments against taking a work as its author's personal statement, and against giving him unique authoritativeness as its expositor, from the writings of the 'semiotic', structuralist and post-structuralist traditions. A literary text, again, is primarily an independent public object in a public language governed by conventions and rules. Its author, though causally related to it, is no more than one of its interpreters. For some bolder theorists the interpreter, far from being obliged to reconstruct the author's intention, may experiment creatively with an indefinite number of ways of freely producing meaning on the basis of the text.[14]

Obviously, if the author is eclipsed in any of these ways, the reader, critic and theorist of literature are not going to be involved, as often they have been, with questions about the author's 'sincerity' or 'authenticity'.[15] No one could claim that the ideals of authenticity and sincerity are simple and clearly applicable, whether in life or literature. Our twentieth-century knowledge of the labyrinths of self-deception or 'mauvaise foi' — of the devious self-protective strategies of the unconscious mind, of ways in which even the arts themselves can be appropriated to furnish second-hand life-patterns for inauthentic self-presentation — gives excuse enough to give up the ideals in cynicism or see them as already far discredited. Nevertheless, to do that decisively may well strike us as an unacceptable, unwarranted moral diminishing of man. For the possibility of mitigating the inauthenticity is necessarily open, in principle, so long as we can stand sufficiently back from ourselves as to discern and identify some aspects of it. With that modest amount of self-knowledge, enough insight is already given into the possibility of limited, partial shifts towards authenticity. The ideals show themselves as, perhaps unexpectedly, alive. It is not, then, too surprising if, when a literary work forcefully presents a view of the human situation carrying moral implications, the reader does have a serious concern whether the author of the work consistently and undeceivingly affirms the view his text presents, whether it is the product of a disciplined acquisition of experience that can be matched, or responded to, with an appropriate gravity in the reader. To discover the author's actual indifference to his subject-matter would have an analogy with (as Colin Lyas has put it) the discovery that 'someone we took to be a dear friend has been planted on us as a spy'.

The attempt to 'contain' the work of appreciation and criticism to the text on the page is, as we saw earlier a hopeless one, for all its attractions. Once that closed and contained ideal is abandoned the radical alternative is certainly open – to treat any and every text as a field for completely free reader-interpretation or re-creation. Many readers, however, would have well-founded doubts whether, in terms of sheer literary rewardingness, they are likely often to find a more worthwhile poem emerging from their free, creative interpretations than from effort on more traditional lines to reconstitute the author's intentions as realized in the poem. The successes and failures in a poem's wrestle with syntax, and its energetic marshalling of multiple meanings are the successes and failures of some individual human being, *vis-à-vis* the existing system of meanings. We have not simply the text to reconstitute, but we can also imaginatively extrapolate to that personal struggle. It seems safe to conclude that the author can neither be simply identified with particular voices and characters in his works, nor can his *obiter dicta* be given authority to pronounce on what his *literary* intentions were – supposing these are not realized in his work itself. But no more can he be discounted without inflicting a gratuitous loss of intelligibility and of human importance upon the work.

Critics and literary theorists have taken widely diverging attitudes to the ability of linguistics to illuminate literature. Some, like F. R. Leavis, have claimed that linguistics 'has nothing to contribute to our understanding of literature'. Others see it as for the first time enabling a systematic and scientific understanding of how language, including language in literature, really functions; and how could that be irrelevant to literary studies? We have already noted how writings like Empson's *Seven Types of Ambiguity* and *The Structure of Complex Words* alert a reader to undoubtedly vital features of literary communication, whose full complexity was unlikely to have been grasped

without such analysis as he provided. Linguistics, as it has systematically developed in very recent decades, however, is a specialist, technical inquiry, its theoretical elaboration requiring the skills of a
formal logician and philosopher of mathematics. The degree of
rigour and thoroughness that linguistics requires of its own analyses
has meant that far more attention has been given to understanding
the meaning of sentences enormously simpler than those in works
of literature. In even a short poem, the relevant interactions of meanings still far exceed our analytical resources. There is thus today a
strongly promissory element in the application of linguistics to
literary language.

Further, when a linguistic theorist like Jakobson does attempt a
highly detailed analysis of a poem,[16] he skilfully draws attention to
symmetries, minute correspondences of structure and theme
throughout the poem. But which of these contribute, and contribute
most, to the aesthetic qualities of the work, this only the reader's
individual judgement can determine: language-analysis by itself cannot. Nor can such analysis show that it is only in a meritorious literary
work that structural complexity of that order can be found.

There is no doubt, however, that literary theory and criticism
would be very ill-advised to ignore linguistics. Literature *is* language;
and the systematic study of language is the study of its own substance.
The most obvious and incontrovertible value of linguistic study for
literature is a heuristic, attention-directing one. In stylistics, attention
is focused on a writer's language-choices from the options open to
him, and the effect of his choices, actual and possible. Among
authorial choices are choices of syntax and rhetorical figures: and
a renewed and useful concern with the syntactical and rhetorical
analysis of literary writing is due, in part, to linguistics.

Yet the thrust of this chapter is against our being able to give a
wholly self-contained and self-sufficient account of literature in terms
of its distinctive range of language-uses alone. Additional to these
are the general imputation of intention to an author, the background
knowledge necessary to flesh out and make intelligible his communication as realized in the work, and the reader's own expectations,
directed by his knowledge of the conventions and practices of
literature and of the relevant genres in particular.

Far more vigorously contested is the contribution to literary understanding of the loosely connected set of arguments and attitudes known as structuralism. Structuralism is again fundamentally linguistic in its inspiration and orientation. It has focused its attention (disproportionately so, to its critics) on the Swiss theorist Ferdinand de Saussure; also on the programme of developing a general theory of signs, semiology. Characteristic of structuralism is its applying of an explanatory model, based on a view of the nature of language, to subject-matters beyond that of the natural languages themselves, for instance to myth, to fashion in dress, to menus, as well as to the structures great and small in the arts.

In its application to literature, a structuralist may see an entire literary work as analogous to a single, vast sentence. The task of the theorist becomes the excogitating of the rules by which the various components of meaning, from the most elementary (individual words) upwards, are integrated to form the 'sentence' constituting the total work. Critics of the approach have shown, however, that the analogy is misleading if applied at all strictly and seriously; and if it is applied only loosely (so as to express the claim that all the components in a fine literary work are organized hierarchically to achieve through their interaction a unified total effect), then the claim is true but unoriginal and imprecise.[17]

In reaction to the prevalence of 'diachronic' language-study (the study of the successive states of a language through time), structuralists have emphasized the importance of the *synchronic* – the state of a language at a given moment.[18] The meaning of the signs that make up a language are determined by the system of interrelated elements at a particular time, by oppositions and their implied 'phonic and conceptual differences'. Applied to literary studies, however, an emphasis on the synchronic is one-sided. Although it would be unrealistic to suggest that a poet intends all his words to be read with an awareness of their whole history, it is not at all unrealistic to claim that he may rely on a widely diachronic understanding of certain key words. Current senses may be counterpointed with earlier senses; and an openness to, and knowledge of, the history of the language may distinguish the sensitive from the shallow reader.

The more general criticism has to be made of structuralist (and some post-structuralist) analyses, as of other linguistic and formalist analyses mentioned above, that to discern structures, recurrent patterns, binary oppositions in literature is not necessarily to discern what makes literature great or significant. Members of the *Tel Quel* group, for example, rejected any principles of discrimination by which to distinguish plausible from quixotic readings: *any* configuration that can be discerned has a right to consideration. Once again, this insistence on the interpreter's freedom, on unrestricted improvisatory play, may indeed 'liberate' from the constrictions of ideology and from cultural pressures; but it liberates from *too much*, and risks making the literary work a plaything.

Following Saussure's analysis, structuralism accepted that language does not 'directly' latch on to the facts, but that all expressions in a given language acquire their meaning through contrast with the meanings of other expressions. But it is post-structuralists ('deconstructionists') who have been fully exploiting the implications they (rightly or − more probably − wrongly) see in this, for a more radically sceptical view of language in general and at all levels (literary, critical, philosophical). They stress the irreducible elusiveness and the instabilities in meanings, the illusions generated by metaphorical and other figurative strategies. '... the meaning of meaning is infinite implication,' wrote Jacques Derrida, 'the indefinite referral of signifier to signifier ... its force is a certain pure and infinite equivocality which gives signified meaning no respite, no rest ...'[19]

So far as this amounts to a strenuous effort to uncover the concealed incoherences and unestablished assumptions of a piece of discourse: well and good.[20] But there is room for serious doubt whether the underlying philosophy of language is really well-founded: and it is far from clear, again, that some particular 'deconstructive readings' of literary texts can escape the charge of being ingenious but wilful and arbitrary linguistic games.[21]

NOTES

1. Cf. S. H. Olsen, *The Structure of Literary Understanding* (Cambridge, 1978), particularly ch. 4.

2. See Justus Buchler, *The Main of Light* (New York, 1974).

3. Cf. K. Harries, 'Metaphor and Transcendence', in *On Metaphor*, ed. S. Sacks (Chicago, 1978). Essays by other contributors are relevant also.

4. T. S. Eliot, 'Dante', in *T. S. Eliot, Selected Prose*, J. Hayward, ed. (Penguin Books, 1952), 101.

5. For an attempt at a fuller discussion of this topic, see my 'The Arts and the Education of Feeling and Emotion', in *Education and the Development of Reason*, eds. Dearden, Hirst, and Peters (London, 1972).

6. D. M. Thomas reviewing R. Hingley, *Russian Poets in Revolution* (Akhmatova, Pasternak, Osip Mandelstam and Marina Tsvetaeva), *The Observer* (24 January 1982).

7. In 'Against Dryness' Iris Murdoch counselled a turning away from the 'temptation' of form, away from the 'self contained', 'the dry symbol', 'the false whole', towards the 'real impenetrable human person' (in *The Novel Today*, ed. M. Bradbury, 30).

8. B. L. Whorf, *Language, Thought and Reality* (London, 1956), 252.

9. See also the discussion in ch. 3 of G. Strickland's *Structuralism or Criticism* (Cambridge, 1981).

10. 'Ce contenu [de pensée] reçoit forme quand il est énoncé et seulement ainsi. Il reçoit forme de la langue et dans la langue ...; il ne peut s'en dissocier et il ne peut la transcender. La forme linguistique est donc ... la condition de réalisation de la pensée' (Emile Benveniste, *Problèmes de linguistique générale* (Paris, 1966), 63 f.

11. 'Catégories de pensée et catégories de langue', in Benveniste.

12. Steiner's plausible examples: *Extraterritorial* (London, 1972), 'The Language Animal', Penguin edn, p. 69-73.

13. The now classic paper in the debate over this was W. K. Wimsatt and M. C. Beardsley, 'The Intentional Fallacy', *The Verbal Icon* (Kentucky, 1954).

14. See Jonathan Culler, *Structuralist Poetics* (London, 1975), 247 ff.

15. Lionel Trilling vividly chronicled the vicissitudes of these concepts in his *Sincerity and Authenticity* (London, 1972).

16. e.g. R. Jakobson and L. G. Jones, *Shakespeare's Verbal Art in 'Th'Expence of Spirit ...'* (The Hague, 1970).

17. Olsen, *The Structure of Literary Understanding*, 19 ff.

18. F. de Saussure, *Course in General Linguistics* (London, 1974), 81 ff.

19. J. Derrida, *Writing and Difference*, 25.

20. Derrida's deconstruction, writes J. V. Harari, is 'the tracing of a path among textual strata in order to stir up and expose forgotten and dormant sediments of meaning which have ... settled into the text's fabric' (*Textual Strategies*, 37).

21. See, for instance, Christopher Norris, 'Deconstruction and the Limits of Sense' in *Essays in Criticism*, Vol. XXX (October, 1980), 281-92.

AUTOBIOGRAPHY: QUEST FOR IDENTITY

PETER ABBS

While autobiographies have been long written and read by vast audiences, their study is recent and uncertain and, particularly in Britain, still badly neglected. As a preparation to writing this chapter I found myself examining the autobiographical section of a good university library. There were less than a dozen titles on autobiography placed between books on genealogy, history and biography, neighbouring such massive and unreadable works as *The Irish Landed Gentry* and *The Peerage of the People*. I found the experience depressing. I felt a substantial injustice had been unwittingly recorded. The meagre collection on the nature of autobiography – mostly American studies, for reasons that will become clear in due course – told me that the university, like nearly all other British universities, had accorded little importance to such inquiry or, perhaps more truly, had not even considered the value of such writing.

It is a sobering reflection that until about 1960, the year in which Roy Pascal's *Design and Truth in Autobiography* was published, there had been in Britain virtually no significant appraisal of the actual nature of autobiography. The somewhat earlier publication of H. N. Wethered's study *The Curious Art of Autobiography* (1956) illustrates the poverty of English analysis before this period. There, in the very opening sentences of the Foreword of the book, the author blankly states:

This is a book about autobiographies. As a literary form these have passed through many phases in history and supplied us with many works combining considerable quaintness and much useful information.

Considerable quaintness. Much useful information. If these were the defining qualities of autobiography from St Augustine to Rousseau, from Rousseau to Edwin Muir, their absence from humanist and literary studies would be amply justified. However, such superfluous observations reflect not on autobiography per se but upon the quality of the critical analysis and, beyond the individual study, to the general lack of any tradition in our culture for the evaluation of auto-biography. For every hundred books published on the novel, there must be one on autobiography and, I believe, a definitive study of the form still remains to be written. Nevertheless, it would be entirely misleading to suggest that there are no important studies. Since Roy Pascal's book, the study of autobiography has shifted to America. In 1972 James Olney published his pioneering *Metaphors of Self: the Meaning of Autobiography* and in the years following that work there has been a steady flow of books from American scholars. Indeed by 1980 the tone of American critics in the study of autobiography had changed from that of strident proclamation to that of gentle apology. William Spengemann, for example, in his introduction to *The Forms of Autobiography* published in 1980 writes almost defensively:

Had I written this introduction even five years ago, I could have begun, as was then the custom among critics of autobiography, by lamenting the scholarly neglect of this worthy literature. Now ... the genre has become critically respectable, not to say fashionable.

Alas, what has been firmly established in America has hardly begun to take root in our own culture. American pop culture has an in-finitely greater velocity than that of American criticism and scholar-ship.

And yet, particularly in autobiography, our own literary tradition could have much to contribute. The high abstractions of continental speculation such as the German philosophical studies of Dilthey and Misch and Gusdorf and the breezy generalizations of American criticism need not only to be modified, but, as it were, anchored down by that more detailed method of critical analysis which derives from the Cambridge School of English. Here, also, that exacting synthesis of psychoanalytical, anthropological and literary ap-proaches which David Holbrook has called for might find its most appropriate subject-matter. The study of autobiography is still in its infancy and we may have to wait some years before the truly seminal book on this genre has been written. At the moment, the most sensitive studies have been written by Pascal, Shumaker and Olney.

However, the lack of an adequate theory of autobiography has not inhibited the writing of autobiography. Quite simply, autobiography thrives. Writers write autobiography. Readers read it. Publishers publish it. Libraries stock it. Is it that in an age which so ubiquitously threatens our sense of personal meaning, we become preoccupied with the question of identity and, consciously or unconsciously, turn to autobiography to see how others have managed to secure their sense of a self, hoping, also, that from their struggles we may find clues to our own uneasy quest for identity? I think there is considerable truth in such a reflection. Certainly autobiography, at its best, is engaged with ontological questions, with true and false modes of being in the world. Virginia Woolf in her fragment of autobiography *A Sketch of the Past* establishes some of the necessary terms when she refers to 'moments of being' and 'moments of non-being' and claims that the moments of non-being prevail. Part of the task of autobiography, it is suggested, is to locate those moments of being in which the self, as it were, coincides with self and intuitively recognizes an existential rightness and an underlying pattern. Herbert Read in the Preface to the 1962 edition of his autobiography, *The Innocent Eye*, claimed that to establish one's individuality (in the writing of autobiography) was possibly the only effective protest against what he saw as the permeating power of the collective death wish. Perhaps, then, we as readers turn to autobiography for the images and narratives of struggling existence, wanting to contemplate the hidden forms of inwardness, wanting to discover the concealed springs of life. Whatever the interpretation, the fact remains that the genre thrives. It is not easy to get a precise figure for autobiography alone, but at the present time over 1,300 new biographies and autobiographies are published in Britain every year. The following list I hope will give the reader some indication of the extent to which writers use the form. It is not intended as a definitive list; it begins with Virginia Woolf and closes with Patrick White, who published his own full-scale autobiography at the end of 1981.

Virginia Woolf, *A Sketch of the Past* (written 1939–40). Enid Starkie, *A Lady's Child* (1941). Elizabeth Bowen, *Seven Winters* (1943). Osbert Sitwell, *Left Hand, Right Hand* (1945). Jack Clemo, *Confessions of a Rebel* (1949). Sean O'Casey, *I Knock at the Door: Swift Glances Back at Things that Made Me* (1949). Arthur Koestler, *Arrow in the Blue* (1952). Stephen Spender, *World Within World*

(1953). Edwin Muir, *An Autobiography* (1954). C. S. Lewis, *Surprised by Joy* (1955). Richard Church, *Over the Bridge* (1955). David Daiches, *Two Worlds: an Edinburgh Jewish Childhood* (1956). James Kirkup, *An Only Child* (1957). Leonard Woolf, *Sowing* (1960). Cecil Day-Lewis, *The Buried Day* (1960). Janet Hitchman, *The King of the Barbareens* (1960). Frank O'Connor, *An Only Child* (1961). J. B. Priestley, *Margin Released* (1962). Herbert Read, *The Contrary Experience* (1963). Compton Mackenzie, *My Life and Times*, Volume I (1963). Ronald Duncan, *All Men are Islands* (1964). P. J. Kavanagh, *The Perfect Stranger* (1966). V. S. Pritchett, *A Cab at the Door* (1968). Storm Jameson, *Journey from the North*, Volumes I and II (1969 and 1970). Dannie Abse, *Ash on a Young Man's Sleeve* (1971). Lois Lang Sims, *A Time to be Born* (1971). Graham Greene, *A Sort of Life* (1971). Malcolm Muggeridge, *Chronicles of Wasted Time*, Volume I (1972). Kathleen Raine, *Farewell Happy Fields* (1973). Winifred Foley, *A Child in the Forest* (1974). Colin Middleton Murry, *One Hand Clapping* (1975). Charles Hannam, *Boy in Your Situation* (1977). Edward Blishen, *Sorry Dad* (1978). John Osborne, *A Better Class of Person* (1981). Patrick White, *Flaws in the Glass: A Self Portrait* (1981).

Of course such a list only represents a tiny fraction of autobiographies published during the last four decades. It does not include the innumerable autobiographies written by those who have distinguished themselves in other fields: by composers, artists, dancers, singers, politicians, philosophers, industrialists, academics, film stars, journalists, pop-stars, media pundits etc. Nor does it include obvious autobiographical novels (like Raymond Williams' *Border Country*, 1960, or David Holbrook's *A Play of Passion*, 1978) nor all those cultural studies with an essential autobiographical base (like Richard Hoggart's *The Uses of Literacy*, 1957, or those made by the Oral History Society). Yet for all the wealth of material, for all the abundance of published life-stories, it must be frankly admitted that while nearly all are of some general human interest, only a few possess the artistic power and the depth of good imaginative literature. Too many autobiographers evade the full challenge of the form: they elect to shape only the external elements. The temptation is to establish, as it were, a public portrait which, ultimately, exists to flatter both author and reader.

The problem with many English autobiographers is that they refuse to break the national vice of protective reticence and social urbanity. One of the great strengths of Lois Lang Sims' *A Time to be Born* is that it is prepared to shock the reader with the almost inhuman intensity of the hatred for her mother, even when her mother is dying. Social form demands that such feeling is repressed: but good autobiography must express it, especially when it is crucial to the full understanding of the author's experience. (Anthony Rossiter's *The Pendulum* and Jack Clemo's *Confessions of a Rebel* have the same quality of an all but explosive emotional honesty.)

In the autobiographical act it may not always be clear what the position of the reader is. In reading an autobiography, though, he can find himself being more than a passive spectator. Quickly, even reluctantly, he becomes implicated. He is addressed sometimes as sympathetic witness, sometimes as objective judge. Frequently he is appealed to as independent listener. The reader, it could be argued, is the objective 'other' which makes the autobiographer's confession a reality and not an act of solipsistic introversion.

An analysis of the historical development of autobiography confirms such a concept of its nature. It is pertinent to note that the word 'autobiography' was first employed in 1809 – at the height of the Romantic period – and that the first formal use of the word 'autobiography' in publishing was in 1834 when W. P. Scargill's volume *The Autobiography of a Dissenting Minister* was printed. But the form of autobiography goes back through fourteen centuries to St Augustine's *Confessions* written in the second half of the fourth century. These words 'autobiography' and 'confessions' – and the particular historical tides on which they bob – are charged with meanings which we must not overlook. The Confessions of the Christian period can be viewed from one perspective as the sacrament of confession metamorphosed into literary form; the Autobiographies of the Romantic and Modern periods can thus be understood as those Confessions secularized. In their transformed state acknowledgement (confession derives from the Latin: *confiteri*, to acknowledge) of past failures is made first to the self (not God) and then to the reader (not priest). Confessions, in their traditional form, crave forgiveness; autobiography desires understanding. Confessions are devoted to salvation; autobiographies to individuation.

As with the sacrament of confession so with St Augustine's *Confessions*; it begins with a prayer taken from the tradition, 'Can any praise be worthy of the Lord's Majesty? How magnificent his strength! How inscrutable his wisdom!' The author submits himself to tradition. His opening invocation taken from the Psalms is one of many forming a persistent thread in the tapestry of the writing. He addresses his self-analysis not to himself or to the reader but directly to God.

My soul is like a house, small for you to enter, but I pray you to enlarge it. It is in ruins, but I ask you to remake it.

The work is a passionate examination and recreation of the author's past before his Maker and Judge; the motivating force comes from the desire for inner renewal. As in the sacrament of confession, the failings of the past are brought consciously to mind in the present for the securing of the future – the quintessential autobiographical rhythm.

Although there were many significant movements in the development of self-reflection and self-recreation between St Augustine and the eighteenth century – in the writings of, for example, Petrarch and Montaigne, or, to take a closely related medium, in the self-portraits of Rembrandt (who all but obsessively recorded himself at every significant stage of his own life) and Dürer (who with a new found audacity painted himself in the image of Christ) – it is yet commonly accepted that it was Rousseau who was to take the form of autobiography dramatically further, or, more precisely, to give it its modern shape. His *Confessions* is a great and original work sounding a new key:

I have resolved on an enterprise which has no precedent, and which, once complete, will have no imitator. My purpose is to display to my kind a portrait in every way true to nature, and the man I shall portray will be myself.
Simply myself.

Here lies the character of true *auto*biography, its characteristic mood and predisposition. The writing describes the unfolding life of the unique self (*auto-bios-graphein*). And does so without apology. Even if in the third paragraph there is, as in the confessional manner, reference to 'my Sovereign Judge', the tone is gently mocking and the author – staying firmly at the centre of the stage – retains authority. In Rousseau we find the traditional confessional style transposed into a new key, that of autobiography as a quest for self-definition and for authenticity of being.

After Rousseau the autobiographer addressed himself directly and had for his listener not priest or congregation but the individual reader. The new context, the evolving form, the formation of a more precise word placing the burden on identity, manifested (as did the parallel emergence of the novel) a deepening concern for psychological truth, for the infinitely subtle processes of individuation rather than the definitive one-and-for-all matter of salvation. The number of writers employing autobiography after Rousseau – Goethe, Wordsworth, Herzen, Mill, Ruskin, Tolstoy, Gorky, Gosse, Darwin, Newman – demonstrate that the form had come of age. Our own century and our own times continues to testify to its indispensable place in the act of self-exploration and actualization. As Ronald Duncan put it, in the first sentence of his own autobiography, *All Men are Islands*: 'We settle down to write our life when we no longer know how to live it.' During a period of tremendous confusion in beliefs and values we have evolved autobiography to secure some sense of order and inner identity.

It is not possible to embark here upon a lengthy evaluation of three of the more remarkable autobiographies published in our times: Herbert Read's *The Contrary Experience*, Kathleen Raine's trilogy beginning with *Farewell Happy Fields* and Edwin Muir's *An Autobiography*. But I bring them together because in literary style and guiding predisposition they seem to me to stand together. They possess the same literary strengths – they are all remarkably eloquent testaments – and they raise simultaneously a cluster of awkward questions about identity and authentic being.

'Perhaps the best autobiography in our language.' So claimed Graham Greene of Herbert Read's *The Innocent Eye* and, initially, one is tempted only to modify that judgement to '*one* of the best'. It is incomparably the best section of *The Contrary Experience*, a volume made up of four discrete autobiographies written at different times and under different circumstances and brought together as late as 1962. *The Innocent Eye* is a precise poetic recreation of Read's

childhood memories of his father's farm. There are twelve sections
each named after a particular place or object, e.g. the Vale, the Green,
the Orchard, the Cow Pasture, the Church, the Mill, and each section
concentrates on the memories which the place elicits. The book
begins with the birth of the writer and ends with the death of his
father. The object of the last section is explicitly titled 'Death' and
refers also to the death of the child's vision, the termination of his
visionary world.

The work has the classical formality of a Baroque concerto. It is
free of sentiment. As there is no self-consciousness in the memories,
so there is no self-consciousness in the writing. Like Wordsworth's
Prelude with which it has much in common, it presents the experience
of immediate vision, the 'thereness' and 'thatness' of the child's un-
premeditated consciousness yet paradoxically caught in a language
quite beyond the range of the child: the first person singular is used
most sparingly for the objects perceived and recreated through the
autobiographer's memory define his nature. Where the innocent I
is the innocent eye, vision is identity. For Herbert Read such experience is definitive:

> All life is an echo of our first sensations, and we build up our consciousness,
> our whole mental life, by variations and combinations of these elementary
> sensations. But it is more complicated than that, for the senses apprehend
> not only colours and tones and shapes, but also patterns and atmospheres,
> and our first discovery of these determines the larger patterns and subtler
> atmosphere for all our subsequent existence.

All the bright moments of ecstasy derive, Read insists, from 'this
lost realm'. We progress only to repeat, with less resonance, what
has already been given.

But the great bulk of *Contrary Experience* is made up of three
other volumes (*The Innocent Eye* comprises only forty pages of a
substantial volume). These volumes simply do not possess the same
extraordinary power of verbal enactment of the first volume. From
a literary point of view *The Contrary Experience* moves from highly
condensed expression to conceptual generalization; moves from
metaphor to abstraction; from poetic embodiment to the tinkle of
'ideas'. Is it possible that the literary failure is a direct consequence
of the informing concept of self which is seen, as it moves away

from childhood, to enter exile and unreality? Does the failure of the work to develop cumulatively through time expose a prior failure in a conception of identity which cannot move through time from childhood without diminution? Is it farewell to those happy fields of which, at best, one can only ever capture a dying echo?

The first volume of Kathleen Raine's trilogy, *Farewell Happy Fields*, recreates her childhood and adolescence; the second volume, *The Land Unknown*, describes her experience as a student at Cambridge University in the thirties, her two short-lived marriages and her various reactions to Positivism, Marxism and Catholicism, all of which she partially embraced only to disown as distorting commitments, distracting her from her own authentic vocation. The third volume, *The Lion's Mouth*, is largely and courageously confined – although that is quite the wrong choice of verb for such a volcanic experience – to the author's attachment to Gavin Maxwell. Of the three volumes *Farewell Happy Fields* is the masterpiece, a sustained piece of autobiographical recreation on a par with *The Innocent Eye*. The language is simultaneously lyrical and precise; it is able to embody the most elusive and haunting of childhood memories:

> A little hand of flame, blue tipped, thin, labile, without substance or constant form, dancing gently on a gas-jet from the wall. In my warm cot gently laid to sleep I watched those luminous fingers dancing for me, for me. I found a song to rise and fall with the hand of the flame, glimmer and glum, glimmer and glum, glimmer and glum, and so on and on. The living flame was a being strange and familiar, familiar and strange. My father would turn it out, send the little hand away.

The rhythms there convey exquisitely the mesmerized moment in which object, self and symbol flow together only to disappear out of the stream of consciousness. Kathleen Raine also, but much less frequently, captures the moment of childhood trauma which has its root in the child's spontaneous identification with the world. In the following passage she narrates the death of the bull:

> There was a long waiting; the butcher, alone, crossing the yard, gun in hand; a muffled blow, and as in a Greek tragedy the king is slain behind the heavy doors of his palace, so we waited for the shot, and knew that the great one of our small world, the creature of power, had once again been slaughtered; the strong by the weak, the great by the small. Presently, as from those

palace doors, the great body was dragged out of the byre and on to the dray, limp and powerless. I saw his pepper-and-salt purplish-brown hide with a sense of infinite compassion: I *was* him. My body suffered in itself the death of the beast, my skin mourning for his skin, my veins for his veins, my five senses for his; and when from that anus slipped a mass of faeces, I was ashamed for the abasement of his death.

The death of the bull is presented as the death of a god. This, too is characteristic of Kathleen Raine's instinctive approach. The isolated event is taken down into its deep archetypal structure and so made universal. Thus simple places are converted into spiritual conditions – Ilford becomes Hades, Scotland becomes Paradise, London a kind of Purgatory ('but now, in London, in order to survive at all, I must simulate some other person, or perish') – and her journey becomes, at best, the journey of Everyman. Her life becomes her 'story'; her story becomes her 'myth'; her myth, in as much as myth is always representative, becomes that of our own experience. No sooner does she name an object than it becomes a symbol of the imaginative life. And it is here that one is able to identify both the great poetic strength and the possible existential failing of the trilogy. When the myth-making propensities of her imagination are converting childhood memories into a living symbolism – when the childhood experiences recalled are meeting the needs of the present and leading to transformation and renewal – one feels the essential rhythm of good autobiography. But when she takes her later experience, experience in which she seems unable to encounter 'the other' even as it gives birth to vision, we find ourselves, as readers, perplexed. We cannot help asking: is the vision attained at the expense of self-knowledge? Is the mythic narrative at the expense of the psychological? Does this numinous world of the imagination depend upon the dissolution of the full impinging actuality of many diverse worlds which nevertheless come together in any one experience? Does the predisposition to see self as child-like visionary innocence inevitably lead to a trilogy which begins with a literary masterpiece (where childhood is evoked) and yet which, in spite of all its honesty and passion, fails to culminate in any comprehensive significance? Is the author's concept of self adequate to the full task of autobiography?

In Edwin Muir's *An Autobiography* there is a greater sense of growth; there is repetition and return, certainly; but there is also development and integration. The first part, *The Story of the Fable*, was published in 1940 and then incorporated into the complete autobiography first brought out in 1954. The autobiography takes us in chronological order through Muir's childhood in the Orkneys, his experience as an adolescent and young man in Glasgow and Fairport; it narrates his activities and relationships as an emerging writer, in London, Prague, Dresden, Helleran, Italy, Austria, France, Prague again (this time under a Communist regime), and lastly in Rome where his commitment to Christianity finally crystallizes. The places are important because they mark the stations of an inner journey. Rather like Ilford in Kathleen Raine's *Farewell Happy Fields*, so Fairport (where Muir works in a bone factory of unbelievable squalor) represents the negation of all positives. In Virginia Woolf's terms Fairport symbolizes Non-Being – and in its hideous machinery Muir is tragically entangled for many years. The Orkneys symbolize a prior Eden before Fairport. The two visits to Prague, in part, represent two versions of politics, the liberal and the totalitarian, the open and the closed. While, at one level, the reflection takes the reader deep into archetypal structures – into 'the fable' and those moments of being 'liberated from the order of time' – it is open, at another level, to the fact of historical and biological process, of relationship and social obligation. Individual being is seen as the reel on which the radically different strands of life are wound. There is both a sense of exile (therefore a movement backwards) and a sense of indivisible unfolding (with a forward motion) and such a dialectic allows for individual growth and pain and anguish.

The opening chapter of *An Autobiography*, describing Orkney, has an all but visionary intensity. The reader is gently taken through a sequence of vast still-life images, of childhood memories which have become primordial. The incidents remembered have become so slowed down they imperceptibly slip into a kind of eternity. The power of the writing depends on paragraphs rather than sentences but the following account, describing his father sowing seeds in the spring is characteristic:

I would sit watching him, my eyes caught now and then by some ship passing so slowly against the black hills that it seemed to be stationary, though when my attention returned to it again I saw with wonder that it had moved.

The sun shone, the black field glittered, my father strode on, his arms slowly swinging, the fan-shaped cast of grain gleamed as it fell and fell again; the row of meal coloured sacks stood like squat monuments in the field.

These childhood images were later to form the primary material of Muir's poetry:

A little island was not too big for a child to see in it an image of life; land and sea and sky, good and evil, happiness and grief, life and death discovered themselves to me there; and the landscape was so simple that it made these things simple too.

Yet it is a measure of Muir's growth as a poet and as a man that he is able to employ the childhood images to convey not the world of a child but the hidden import of the most catastrophic events of our era (as, for example, in his great poem *The Horses*). It is also to be observed that Muir's imagination is as capable of presenting the experience of unreality and nausea as of glory and innocence. His chapters on Glasgow and Fairport are so disturbing to read for they recreate, in the way that Herbert Read's War Diary in the *Contrary Experience* fails to, the weird phenomena of dislocation and psychic disease. In fact, Muir has an all but frightening ability to define with a poetic precision the lineaments of pure emotional states. He is the William Blake of autobiography.

His comprehension of depth and complexity is further recorded in his attention to dreams. Should the autobiographer present the streaming images of the unconscious as well as the events and circumstances of everyday experience? Muir writes:

It is clear ... that no autobiography can confine itself to conscious life and that sleep, in which we pass a third of our existence, is a mode of experience, and our dreams a part of reality. In themselves our conscious lives may not be particularly interesting. But what we are not and can never be, our fable, seems to me inconceivably interesting.

For this reason Muir describes many dreams in his autobiography I have read, even Jung's. But surface and underground are not forced to inhabit the same level; they are allowed to co-exist. The fable is not the life; mythic time is not historic time. These very distinctions, I believe, make possible a development and comprehensiveness missing in the other autobiographies. Yet, they in turn create their problems. For where is the self which would mediate between the diverse and distinguished worlds? And how can the nature of that self be known when many of its truths are out of reach, for much of the time, in the darkness of the unconscious? There are only fragments, memories, elusive movements and 'in a great number of dreams ... a few glints of immortality'.

To consider the three autobiographies together is to detect certain similarities. The writers belong to the same generation; they are poets; they have deep roots not in the urban but in the rural order; they suffer exile; they leave their social class and background; they devote their lives, in different ways, to the truths of the imagination. In their autobiographies, at least in their most memorable and haunting sequences, one becomes aware of the common quality of the language which, while it remains wholly contemporary, still has behind it the gravity and grandeur of the Authorized Bible and the sinew and pulse of Shakespeare. They also have that unusual power to lift ordinary experience up into the symbolic dimension where it is given an enduring significance, becomes, in Muir's phrase, part of the fable. At the same time, they present the reader with concepts of self which require the most delicate scrutiny. In the case of Herbert Read and Kathleen Raine we find the image of the visionary child which lies deep in the Romantic tradition, yet can the child ever act as metaphor for comprehensive existence? I have suggested that the comparative failure of their work to accumulate, to grow, to deepen, indicates not, in the first place, a literary failure, but a partiality of conception which derives from an inability to fully integrate the human dialectic and the appalling complexity of existence. In Edwin Muir's autobiography we find a similar commitment to what he called the child's 'original vision of the world'. But, at the same time, there is an authoritative recognition of its opposite state; a tacit appreciation of the role of negative experience in the ecology of consciousness. Hence *An Autobiography* has a forward movement. The book develops as the author develops.

The problem which Muir's work raises relates to his persistent sense of the elusiveness and uncertainty of identity. The central preoccupation of autobiography with realization of self is cast into doubt. Perhaps identity is only ever a partial fragment of something larger and, forever, unknowable? Muir states emphatically: 'I can never know myself.' We are always and forever more than we can symbolically grasp. Such a view could be taken to define the limitations of the form. Alternatively, it could be seen as a further challenge to the dominant convention in autobiography in its use of the chronological and historical narrative. Is it not possible to write an autobiography which captures the truth of experience, with its uncertainties, gaps, aspirations, visions and banalities, without relying on the method of linear chronology? Does this hint at the next development in autobiographical recreation? If so, Muir's autobiography, with its sense of human life camped precariously on the border between the ordinary and the fabulous takes us, at points, very close to the new ground. Muir, at any rate, leaves us with the sense that self-knowledge must serve something other than itself. In this deep insight, autobiography, once again, finds its ontological source; moves us deftly from the certainty of knowledge into the mystery of being.

BROADCAST DRAMA

ROGER KNIGHT

When David Mercer died in 1980 at the age of 52 the BBC re-ran a selection of his plays for television. Most of those plays had been published. For once, the proverbial 'ephemerality' of the medium for which they were written had been defeated. Effectively television and radio work that is neither published nor regularly repeated evaporates. When his regular producer says of the radio dramatist Rhys Adrian that he would 'rank him with Pinter'[1] the challenge to criticism cannot be taken up. What little of Adrian's work has been published is difficult to locate and there are no recordings to rectify the omissions: 'ephemerality' is here the product of neglect.

Part cause and part effect of this familiar and frustrating situation is the failure to establish a serious criticism of television and radio drama in this country. Moreover, the absence of such a criticism is not generally felt to matter. The implications are serious for media where there is inevitably an 'archive problem': what shall be preserved; where are the standards that shall help us decide? The years 1961–6 saw the rise and fall of *Contrast*, a quarterly founded in the recognition that in the field of television criticism there were standards to be articulated and a public to be educated – a public that might, for instance, have saved David Mercer's *A Suitable Case for Treatment* (1962) from its ironic fate: the play won a Writers' Guild award for the year; by the time Mercer received it the BBC had obliterated the tapes! There have undoubtedly been small advances since that time – though *Contrast* has had no successors. Reputations *have* been established; there is probably now sufficient consciousness that judgements change with time and that the eventual interpretation and valuation of an author's work may benefit from his total oeuvre being available for viewing: presumably it is now unlikely that a new play by, say, Dennis Potter or Jim Allen will be summarily removed from the record. With radio drama there are the beginnings of critical activity in the universities. Such activity, urgently needed in the field of television too, will thrive only if it can promote a common acceptance of Henry Reed's argument in favour of the printing of radio plays:

> As soon as a form of entertainment becomes a vehicle for serious thought and speech we cry for a permanent record of it which we can return to and of which we can regulate the tempo to our own understanding and enjoyment.[2]

The situation being what it is, it would be difficult (even if space allowed) to do justice here to the best that has been done in radio and television drama. What is more, it is obvious that neither has a history totally separate from that of the other or of the theatre. However, we are not for the most part concerned here with the many writers whose first commitment is to the theatre but who have also written for radio and television. The purpose of this chapter is to suggest the nature of the field that is there to be critically explored and to glance at a few writers who have discovered their authentic voices within it.

In his introduction to *The Dark Tower and Other Radio Scripts* (1947) Louis MacNeice admitted that before he joined the BBC he had been 'like most of the intelligentsia, prejudiced not only against that institution but against broadcasting in general'.[3] A generation later it was possible for P. H. Newby, himself an author and Managing Director of BBC radio, to claim that the Corporation was 'the biggest single market for the writer in Great Britain'.[4] However, the movement from rejection to acceptance of the BBC's encompassing patronage has not been the uncomplicated matter that the juxtaposition of these two quotations might suggest. In MacNeice's case a high measure of success and the experience of working with people who believed in the expressive possibilities of the young medium quickly eradicated his prejudice. The prefaces to his plays for radio are the critical statements of a practitioner who knows that he is working in a field where standards have still to be set and the potentialities of a new medium explored. But to become convinced that radio (and, in turn, television) presents such a challenge is one thing; to produce a critical climate in which it is accepted that serious writers might reasonably take up the challenge, quite another. Giles Cooper, probably the best, certainly the most distinctive of radio dramatists, said that it took him 'a long time to live down the slur of being a radio writer'.[5] The notion that a serious writer might find the proper ambience for his imagination in a mass medium was (and in some quarters still is) offensive to many people. Certainly in the early days of radio there was strong warrant for such scepticism. Popular taste favoured the adaptation of already well-known stage plays and, inevitably in what was until the fifties *the* popular medium, there were pressures making for compromise and against the advance and acceptance of original writing for radio.

As a stimulus to such writing the eventual emergence of the 'Third Programme' was equalled in importance only by the rise of television, the new popular medium. Many writers responded to the idea of the 'Third' with a sense of relief that its prospective audience, axiomatically a minority, would be assumed, in Mac-Neice's words, to be ready to 'work at its listening'. Somewhat intemperately, Henry Reed applauded the 'blunt, crude acknowledgement of the fact that some listeners are fools, and some are not, and that we cannot wait for the fools to catch up with their betters.'[6] Within a few years television had usurped the role of radio as the principal medium for drama and while, in its turn, it struggled to produce work of which it could be said that it was truly *of* the medium for which it was written, radio drama entered its most authentic phase. 'Any movement towards the creation of good radio drama should be away from the theatre, and in another direction altogether,' said a writer in the *BBC Quarterly* in 1950.[7] In 1964 MacNeice declared that 'Sound radio can do things no other medium can and if "sound" dies, those things will not be done.'[8] The years that separate these two statements are particularly rich in radio drama; reputations were established and the reach of the medium explored with unprecedented vigour. Dylan Thomas's 'play for voices', *Under Milk Wood*, was first heard in 1954; all but four of Giles Cooper's radio plays belong to the period as does most of Henry Reed's work. Beckett's seminal *All that Fall* was broadcast in 1957 and in 1959 its producer, Donald McWhinnie, brought out what is still the most persuasive and rigorous study of *The Art of Radio*.

In describing radio drama as 'an expression in voices of something which cannot be exteriorized'[9] McWhinnie indisputably accounts for only a tiny, but nonetheless distinctive, proportion of what is generally covered by that term. The most distinguished work for radio is inadequately served by the conventional headings under which it is presented: the words 'play', 'drama' and 'theatre' persist not only to advertise the dependence of the great bulk of radio drama on work originally conceived for other media but as a token of what in general its public looks to radio to provide. What the words obscure is that we experience some of the best work as we experience fiction: the interior monologue, the centrality of the narrator – staples of traditional fiction – are the stuff of much good radio drama too. It is salutary to be reminded by a German critic that 'as a genre the radio play in England is composed not simply and solely of the radio play proper, nor of the feature, nor of the show. It is identical with none of these forms but comprises all three.'[10] Indeed, the dominance of theatrical vocabulary in the presentation of radio drama tends to obscure the origins of some of its most distinguished and directive work: MacNeice's *The Dark Tower* and Thomas's *Under Milk Wood* are two celebrated examples of work produced within the Features Department of the BBC; two of many that might be adduced in support of Henry Reed's claim that the feature is 'radio's most natural expression'.[11] Reed speaks as an outstanding practitioner: the conventions of the feature are the backbone of his splendid series of comedies published in 1971 as *Hilda Tablet and Others*.

It is one of the signal strengths of radio that it can concentrate the mind with unparalleled intensity on the inward power of words, on their capacity to generate a substantial reality that has no equivalent in the physical world. 'When a man knows he will soon be blind what he looks at stays looked at,' says Charles Lefeaux in introducing R. C. Scriven's series of autobiographical plays, *The Seasons of the Blind*.[12] And yet these are plays in which 'the *inward* eye, as the outer ear rejoices'; in *All Early in the April* (1970) Scriven evokes the ordinariness of family life on the one hand and, powerfully, the intense, sensuously receptive and private world of the child on the other. Again, *The Seasons of the Blind* recalls the structure of the radio feature: each play is a series of lyrical interludes in a loose narrative. The narrator, the lyric poet, is the key feature. They are ideal radio: nothing comes between the fullness and immediacy of the words and their reception in the mind of the listener.

This directness of contact with the listener seems to promote a special tolerance. 'One can do anything at all with the juxtaposition of events in time and space.'[13] Donald McWhinnie's association with the most original radio drama has been a crucial factor in our understanding of what the best writers can achieve with the form. Through his production of Beckett's *All that Fall* and many of Giles Cooper's plays we are the better able to see the justice of Frances Gray's claim that 'radio's reality is never consistent; it is perfectly adapted to the portrayal of an absurd universe'.[14] Visual support might not always destroy but it would certainly much reduce the impact of Cooper's characteristic work, as of Don Haworth's. Both writers have a fine ear for verbal mannerism and cliché; Cooper in particular for speech as 'a stratagem to cover nakedness'.[15] Cooper's is frequently a world in which the routine shades into nightmare or farce with disturbing ease. We come away from his best plays with a heightened sense of the ways in which through common speech men and women negotiate a path that is all the time threatening to lead them into absurdity, of the precarious balance between the trite and the lunatic. What Cooper gives us is an image of ourselves where we struggle, often lamely and ineffectually, often hilariously, for however modest a sense of coherence and self-reliance. 'You've been doing too much thinking,' says Jane to Desmond in *Before the Monday* (1959). 'How does one stop?' replies Desmond, a man obsessed and immobilized by the relentless detailed inconsequence of ordinary living, unable to contemplate a razor or a tin of sardines without being assailed by a vivid appreciation of the multiplicity of processes that have finally washed it his way. There is no holding off the world's absurdity however minute the territory one claims as one's own – even when it has shrunk to the limits of one's bathroom (*Under the Loofah Tree*, 1958).

In Giles Cooper's plays men and women speak in perfectly credible voices in mostly incredible situations. So they do in the work of Don Haworth, a master of a radio genre that includes the Goon

Show and the best radio 'light comedy'. His characters lead lives of quiet desperation; Haworth discovers the farce in the desperation. He can be both surreal and realistic, crazy and earthy. (One thinks of *There's no Point in Arguing the Toss* (1967) in which two brothers attempt to take home by bus the body of their father who has died on the ghost train at the fair.) Haworth has an ear for the common-place saw and the banality of ordinary conversation – for its decency as well as its frequently hilarious inconsequence. The ex-hilarating effect of his plays is due to his ability to endow them with an internal plausibility that has only a tenuous relation with the 'real' world that we think we know. It is a plausibility possible only within the medium of radio.

Like radio before it, television in its early days appealed to an audience that in sitting down to 'Armchair Theatre' could be fairly confident that the title accurately described the experience that awaited it. In their early days both media were more remarkable for familiarizing a mass audience with established plays and authors than for presenting original work. Both have of course continued to broadcast plays written for the theatre. Indeed even now most authors have usually written first for the stage. The example of David Mercer who wrote 'four or five plays' for television before he 'got into live theatre'[16] is as rare as the special relationship with the BBC that allowed him to do so. Nevertheless Dennis Potter – one of the very few writers to have established a reputation specifically as a television dramatist – was undoubtedly speaking for many when he described television as 'the biggest platform in the world's history' and said that 'writers who don't want to kick and elbow their way into it must be disowning something in themselves'.[17] Once that platform had begun to attract writers (like Potter himself) with a primary interest in the small screen it was natural that they should be eager to incorporate elements from non-theatrical traditions in their work.

The television screen, like to some extent radio, is hospitable to dramatic images of an immediacy and an intensity common in the cinema but technically impossible on the stage. At the present time it is common to find what is advertised as a play offered on the screen as 'a film for television'. Frequently since the mid sixties, and the more urgently as technological advance has sharpened the issue, writers and directors have argued the merits of filmed and studio-based drama respectively. The argument can be barren. The current fashion in 'films for television' frequently calls for the sharp – and early – reminder of Don Taylor that it would be 'very silly of a writer to be so pleased with his new glasses that he cuts out his tongue'. 'In an ironic way,' said Taylor in 1964, 'it may well be that creative thought about picture making is partly responsible for the terrible superficiality of television drama.'[18] However constricting the studio-based television play may be found by some writers,[19] however considerable the freedoms made available through film, the exploration of human relationships still requires the kind of sensitivity with words that is at a premium in the theatre. Which is not to say that studio-based drama cannot benefit from the stock-in-trade of film making. It has often been observed that the most powerful expressive resource in television drama is the close-up; it exploits the peculiar intimacy of the domestic screen; it impresses us as being to scale in a medium that is clearly less well-adapted to the broad canvas than is the cinema screen. In close-up we are privy to the most expressive, the most immediate projection of the individual soul. The effect is however most striking, most full-blooded, when the expressive power of the human figure is complemented by that of the words: a truism many 'films for television' seem to overlook. John Hopkins' quartet *Talking to a Stranger* (1966) shows us a writer working within this understanding. The plays document the emotional history of a divided family, evoking the impelling intensities of emotional life that the clichés and evasive verbal counters normally disguise. That history of misunderstandings, deluded hopes, hatreds and resentments is active in every line and image. His quartet is a triumph of words *and* images; within the intimate confines of the small screen the viewer feels almost as trapped as those he watches.

The most conspicuous and controversial attempts to sever television drama from its theatrical roots can best be indicated by reference to BBC television's 'Wednesday Play' and such individual examples as Jeremy Sandford's *Cathy Come Home* (1966) and *Edna the Inebriate Woman* (1971). The flexibility of the modern film camera – as against relatively cumbersome video-recording apparatus – gave the makers of such work the opportunity to blur the

distinction between art and life,[20] to go out into the streets to gather
in images of ordinary, recognizable, day-to-day living and return
to the cutting room to organize the material into some kind of
dramatic unity: in the two cases mentioned, into a unity shaped by
a clear proselytizing purpose. The importance of such works may
be seen in the long term not so much in their impact upon
popular feeling or their success in changing 'official' attitudes as in
the stimulus they have given to the all but moribund English
documentary tradition. In its most distinctive expression in the films
of Humphrey Jennings and (of most immediate influence) the television documentaries of Dennis Mitchell, it is a tradition that
discovers the drama latent in the ordinary, the tragic and the comic
locked up in the banal. The movement represented by the television
work of such writers as Jack Rosenthal, Peter Nichols and Alan
Bleasedale extends that tradition in terms of television drama. These
are authors who have contributed to making the variousness of the
English people more visible. Like so many of the best English writers
they are acutely aware of the drama inherent in differences of class
and culture. Specifically they represent working-class speech and
behaviour with compelling authenticity.

The documentary tradition, when allied to a political or ideological stance, has certainly inspired writers to engage with public
issues and open out areas of the national life normally invisible or
obscure to us. The most notable attempts to combine the elements
of documentary with drama *tout court* have come in the politically
committed work of Jim Allen (*The Big Flame*, 1966, *United Kingdom*,
1981). Such plays, however (like much of the television work of
Trevor Griffiths), rarely get free of their commanding theses; the
inner lives of their characters rarely engage our interest as compellingly as the overriding political analysis they are there to endorse.
Writers such as Jeremy Sandford and Jim Allen nonetheless credit
television with the kind of importance Martin Esslin attributes to
the theatre when he calls it 'the place where the nation thinks in
public in front of itself'.[21] From 'the biggest platform in the world's
history' (contrasted by Sandford with working in radio where he
had 'the impression of shouting something very important down
a deep well'),[22] they work to alter popular consciousness in
immediate and politically significant ways. No television dramatist

has been more exercised by the formative power of the medium within which he works than has Dennis Potter. The audacity and technical adventurousness of much of Potter's work is that of a writer who recognizes that power and is determined that his plays shall survive in the 'landscape of indifference' against which all television drama takes its chance – 'bullets on one side and football on the other'.[23]

Appropriately the power of the popular media is the focus of some of Potter's most arresting work. Potter is the passionate puritan. He scorns the shallowness and inanity of the age's representative imagery as he observes it, for instance, in advertising, popular music and cheap entertainment of many kinds. He knows the power of television to give that imagery a steady and pervasive currency. Disgust with a civilization which allows it to invade the private self is active, sometimes extravagantly so, in many of Potter's plays, from *The Yellow Brick Road* (1972) to *Pennies from Heaven* (1978). The latter, a series of six plays, is Potter's tour-de-force. The principal expressive device – dialogue is periodically displaced by miming to popular songs of the 1930s – is powerfully deployed. 'Oh God I wish I was good with words,' says Arthur Parker, the songsheet salesman and quintessential common man of the plays. For Arthur the words of the songs are the truth he lacks the power to express for himself. To his cost he cannot see that the romantically sanitized world they evoke is hollow and unreal. In the crises of his personal life the romantic twaddle of the songs is quite inactive. Arthur is *l'homme moyen sensuel* and needs a culture that will give a degree of grace and expressive subtlety to his sensuality. It may seem problematic to talk of *Pennies from Heaven* as literature. But whatever we may want to say about the balance of its elements, verbal, visual and musical, it is clearly the work of a writer with a powerful sense of the limitations that clichés of behaviour and feeling place on those ill-equipped to resist them. The problem that Potter on the whole so impressively overcomes is the one inherent in naturalistic drama: how to display the shape of people's inner lives whilst remaining true to the way they ordinarily express themselves.

Potter's continuing interest in 'technical' experiment within television drama (one thinks of *Blue Remembered Hills*, 1979, in which, very effectively, adults play the parts of children) is to be expected in a writer for whom 'the single play is one of the last areas of television where the irritating cadences of the individual voice can be heard'.[24] David Mercer's pursuit of technical advance arose from a similar persuasion. Mercer too was a conscious innovator. If in many of his plays one is inescapably conscious of technique, one is equally aware that the evident virtuosity is imaginatively controlled, indeed necessitated by the character of his thought. Characteristically the various 'devices' of *On the Eve of Publication* (1968) subserve the presentation of what, reviewing Mercer's work as a whole, we can see was for him a representative modern sensibility, a sensibility haunted by the dislocation of private and public worlds. Such dislocation is the urgent theme of his trilogy *The Generations* (1961–3), the plays that established him as an important voice. Now, with anxiety and debate about nuclear war again at a high pitch, the plays retain their illuminating power. But that power is not due to the persistent relevance of the political issues. If the artist is a man fully alive in his own time, Mercer's aliveness is of a quality to go beneath the abstractable issues, beneath the larger politics of decision-making. His is a sensibility for which the lives of individuals constitute an inescapable arena within which the most urgent meanings of those politics are enacted. In *The Generations* the family is the microcosm within which the larger transforming agencies of the culture are most clearly and painfully seen at work. It is at the level of personal relationships, of the search for self-respect, of a way of living that will be worthy of the gift of life in an insane phase of man's development that Mercer sees the crucial drama of our time being played out. In the third play, *Birth of a Private Man*, the young man Colin retreats into the privacy of despairing impotence and insanity; and that is a social disaster because it signals a withdrawal in the face of horrendous odds for which no previous experience of human conflict has prepared us. What is the right way to live when annihilation is both imminent and unimaginable? As Colin says:

There are people in every generation who act out some of its hopes and needs. The subjective reasons for their actions hardly matter. In some way they define a generation to itself.

It is of course Mercer who defines the generations. The remarkable strength of the plays is in the breadth of his sympathies: there is no propaganda, no thesis, no solution – just an urgent sensitivity to what the unnameable and unimaginable is doing to the ill-prepared human psyche. Most disturbingly Mercer makes the ultimate horror plausible: that man may be waiting to embrace his fate with a half-paralysed, half-welcoming fascination. If the theatre is 'the place where the nation thinks in public in front of itself', David Mercer's plays provide a standard by which we may judge the quality of the thought in what is the first truly 'national theatre' of the twentieth century.

NOTES

1. John Tydeman, in *Radio Drama*, ed. P. Lewis (Harlow, 1980), 18.

2. Henry Reed, 'What the wireless can do for literature', *BBC Quarterly*, Vol. III (1948–9), 218–19. (Accordingly, the plays discussed or referred to in this chapter are for the most part available in printed form.)

3. Louis MacNeice, *The Dark Tower and Other Radio Scripts* (London, 1947), 11.

4. Howard Newby, *Radio, Television and the Arts*, BBC Lunch-time Lectures (1976), 12.

5. 'Radio writing: Giles Cooper, talking to Michael Billington', *Plays and Players*, Vol. XIII, No. 3 (December 1965), 10.

6. Henry Reed, 218.

7. Sewell Stokes, 'Radio drama as I hear it', *BBC Quarterly*, Vol. V, No. 3 (Autumn 1950), 165.

8. Louis MacNeice, *The Mad Islands and the Administrator: Two Radio Plays* (London, 1964), 7.

9. *The Art of Radio* (London, 1959), 59.

10. Horst P. Priessnitz, in *Radio Drama*, 36.

11. Henry Reed, 219.

12. R. C. Scriven, *The Seasons of the Blind and Other Radio Plays* (London, 1974).

13. Susan Hill, 'Introduction' to *The Cold Country, Five Plays for Radio* (London, 1975). The dreamers and seers of Susan Hill's plays, men and women with access to spiritual insights denied to the more pedestrian minds amidst which they move, are at home in a medium hospitable to the creation of private worlds.

14. Frances Gray, in *Radio Drama*, 16.

15 Harold Pinter, 'Introduction' to *Plays: One* (London, 1976), 15.

16. 'The Birth of a Playwriting Man', *Theatre Quarterly*, Vol. III, No. 9 (January–March 1973), 47.

17. *The New Priesthood*, eds N. Garnham and J. Bakewell (Penguin Books, 1970), 82.

18. Appendix to *The Generations*, by David Mercer (London, 1974), 243. Don Taylor produced the plays.

19. Cf. David Hare, 'Guardian Weekend', *The Guardian* (15 August 1981).

20. The role of the writer becomes problematic. For Tony Garnett, speaking as a television producer, the important question was: 'Had a person got something to say about the world and their relationship to it – it didn't matter whether they could write plays or not.' *Theatre Quarterly*, Vol. XI, No. 6 (April–June 1972), 19.

21. Martin Esslin, *Anatomy of Drama* (1976), 101.

22. In Alan Rosenthal, *The New Documentary in Action* (University of California Press, 1971), 167.

23. In *The Television Dramatist*, selected by R. Muller (London, 1973), 305.

24. Dennis Potter, 305.

THE SPRINGS OF LIFE:
A THEME IN THE OPERAS OF BRITTEN AND TIPPETT

WILFRID MELLERS

Opera is not usually considered to come within the range of literary history, though drama is. Yet throughout the centuries theatre has often, indeed usually, had a musical and terpsichorean dimension, which fell into abeyance only during the nineteenth century, under the weight of a 'realism' that ultimately sank into the kitchen sink. In the second half of the twentieth century British opera has made an impressive comeback; and two composers of genius, not just talent, have created a sequence of operas of which the musical distinction is inseparable from their dramatic effectiveness. In various ways they are parables of our time, their literate meanings being projected into musical sound and stage action. It is difficult to think of any purely theatrical works created during these years which can challenge the operas of Britten and Tippett in range and relevance.

The impact made by the operas of Benjamin Britten (1913–76) cannot be separated from his precocity. It is unlikely that any nineteen-year-old composer, even Mozart and Mendelssohn, has produced a piece of greater technical brilliance and imaginative power than Britten's *A Boy was born* (1932). In so far as it is a choral work based on the traditional Christmas theme, it is part of the heritage of Holst and Vaughan Williams, through whom our music was itself reborn, after two centuries of relative darkness, in returning to the roots of our musical consciousness in folk song and in medieval and renaissance liturgy. Where it differs from other returns to a relatively remote past is in the absence of either nostalgia or inhibition. The 'youthfulness' of Britten's music seems to spring from a direct realization of what it felt like to live in an age dominated by faith. It is not necessarily a religious piece; it is simply about the growth of life in innocence. A boy is born indeed; and the affirmation is inseparable from the technical virtuosity. This is not merely a matter of contrapuntal skill. It also involves an element that one might call theatrical projection: an ability to discover, as did composers of the Baroque age, aural images that musically, even physically, *enact* the visual and psychological images of the poem.

It does not follow that Britten's *A Boy was born* is a better piece of music than Bax's sumptuous *Ora Mater Filium* or Warlock's haunting *Corpus Christi Carol* on the one hand, or Holst's gaunt *Hymn of Jesus* on the other; but it does follow that in Britten's work there was the germ of future evolution, whereas the works of Bax and Warlock, and of Holst, were two very different kinds of dead end. For the theatrical projection in *A Boy was born* – its unprovincial cosmopolitanism, notwithstanding its English roots – led Britten instinctively to opera: so that he took up the problems of English music not in a remote past but precisely at the point when our traditions lapsed at the end of the seventeenth century. Purcell's failure to create an English operatic tradition was not a personal failure but the deficiency of a society. That had something to do with the division epitomized in the Civil War, as a consequence of which mind and senses, body and spirit, were in England more rapidly and more radically split than elsewhere. Perhaps that breach had to be healed, and the heart reborn in innocence, before an English opera could be achieved.

The breach *was* healed in *A Boy was born*; and the fact that this work is so much more impressive than the instrumental pieces Britten had written in his teens is related to the fact that it is conceived for the human voice. Yet Britten did not graduate direct from vocal polyphony to opera. Instead he began to explore the possibilities of operatic 'projection' by composing song cycles in the French and the Italian manners. Only when he had discovered how an English composer could exploit the heritage of European styles – as Purcell had exploited French and Italian conventions of his day – did Britten investigate the possibilities of an arioso and aria relevant to the English language. The *Serenade* for tenor, horn and strings (1943) resembles Purcell's music in being at once eclectic and almost aggressively personal. One can tabulate Britten's mannerisms – the melodies built on arpeggiated thirds, the expansive leaps, the pentatonic undulations – while knowing that his music has become unique, if not inimitable.

The creation of an English operatic idiom was not, however, a purely musical matter: the technical discovery also involved the discovery of the necessary myth. Looking back, we can see that all Britten's operas deal with the same parable: the renewal of innocence as the condition of human creativity. *A Boy was born* – almost literally a boy's work – could with dazzling innocence recreate innocence in our minds and senses; and the myth that was latent in it became patent a few years later when the composer left this country with W. H. Auden, possibly to settle in the United States. This suggests that genius knows where it is going long before it knows that it knows; for Britten's migration to America was not so much a rejection of moribund Europe as a discovery of a New World which, in being new, was a potential Eden. At a basic geographical level Britten was exploring his essential theme: out of which he produced his first musical–theatrical piece. Interestingly enough, the New York commission offered to Auden and Britten was for a music-theatre piece for *young people*. *Paul Bunyan* (1941) dealing with an American folk-hero, may be an unpretentious piece which Britten, after he became a fully fledged opera composer, would not admit to the canon of his works. Nonetheless, it is far from trivial, and its rather grand theme is the relationship between Nature and Nurture. The message of Auden's cleverly articulate text and of Britten's resourcefully simple music is that 'America is what you *do*; America is what you choose to make it': a message that still rings clear, in any country, through the forty years since the piece was created.

'In any country' may be the point: for Britten soon came to realize that his rebirth, his New World, could be discovered only at home. Unlike Auden, he was back in Britain by the end of the war, hard at work on the profoundly English opera, set in his native Suffolk, that was to make him internationally famous. *Peter Grimes* (1945), like almost all Britten's operatic works, is concerned with the Fool's simple heart and single mind, beset by the corruptions of the world. It turns on the ancient myth of the Savage Man who in Eden would be innate goodness: whom the depravity of the world renders destructive. Deprived of Ellen's love by a community that puts conformity to convention above the heart's truth, Grimes's innocence sours to cruelty and he destroys the Boy who is his own soul. Then the World rounds on him, harries him to his death.

Though Grimes may be an unheroic hero, his predicament is genuinely tragic, and *Peter Grimes* is the first genuinely grand English opera since Purcell's *Dido* (1689) – and that was a miniature affair intended for a girls' school. Grimes's progression from the Fool's innocence to exile, and from exile to persecution, is a theme as relevant to our times as Nahum Tate's and Purcell's rehashing of Dido's story was to theirs. Arioso – the human singing voice become dramatic enactment – is the core of Britten's opera as it is of Purcell's; and the element of theatrical projection in Britten's work ensures that no opera is more evocative, yet at the same time precise, in its creation of time and place. The tang of the sea, the hues of Suffolk light, the bustle of anonymous human activity, are revealed through that baroque instinct for the musical image that first appeared in *A Boy was born*. And this precise realization of the external world is inseparable from the music drama's insight into the mind and heart. Britten's music, in association with Slater's adaptation of Crabbe's poem, achieves its deepest insight through its operatic objectivity; and its Englishness is revealed through its eclecticism.

Albert Herring (1947) – not a 'grand' opera but a chamber opera written for Britten's own English Opera Group – has the same theme as *Grimes*, treated comically rather than tragically. Herring is again the Fool, a pathetic, not heroic figure; but although his exile and destruction by the world turn out to be only a charade, that does not deflate the almost-tragic potency of the threnody sung over him. These two operas convincingly balance the private and the public aspects of Britten's habitual theme. In the first of the chamber operas, *The Rape of Lucrece* (1946), wherein the virgin-victim is female or androgynous, there is much heart-felt and exquisite music and, in Tarquin-the-barbarian's night ride, a threat that gets under our skin, as it did under Lucrece's and Britten's; but the Christian overtones of the epilogue strike an uncomfortable, perhaps even slightly synthetic, note. The Christian crucifixion reappears, along with the theme of the scapegoat, in Britten's second 'grand' opera, to a libretto by E. M. Forster based on Melville's trenchant tale, *Billy Budd* (1950–51). Any true artist uses his art in part as therapy, resolving or alleviating what might otherwise be diagnosable as neuroses in his psyche. If he is a genuine artist, however, the personally therapeutic aspects of his art will become archetypal, revealing their general rather than specific human relevance. Only in one of his operas, *Gloriana* – composed for a ceremonial occasion, telling the story of the first Elisabeth as an act of homage to the second – did Britten attempt to escape from personal involvements that one might call obsessional; and this may explain why *Gloriana*, despite a plenitude of lovely music, doesn't 'tell' in the theatre as brilliantly as do the other operas. At the other extreme, only in *Billy Budd* is there any suspicion that Britten's personal obsessions were too strong to be artistically projected. Now that it is possible to speak openly of his homosexuality, we can recognize that it was always his own 'alienation' which was mythologized in his operas, though of course the personal involvement merely acted as a trigger and was not the total, or even the main, theme. In *Budd* the homosexual aspects of the tale may seem obtrusive; certainly one can object that Melville's womanless Man of War cannot, of its nature, be an adequate image for the Ship of Life. Grimes, though an unhero, is a tragic character, the Savage Man who in different circumstances might have grown to civilized consciousness. Billy is not a tragic character because we have no evidence that he has any capacity for growth. He is a child destroyed by his childishness, by a stammer that we cannot equate with *mea culpa* – with a, let alone *the*, tragic flaw. For this reason the crucifixion analogy – so stridently emphasized in the first production but modified in later ones – is illegitimate. Billy cannot be identified with Christ who, after all, did grow up, the hard way.

Yet it is not really helpful to compare *Billy Budd* with *Peter Grimes* since in *Budd* the drama is neither social nor moral, but almost entirely psychological. With deeper knowledge we may find *Budd* the more heroic achievement, since in it Britten has uncompromisingly faced his own obsessions and has achieved purgation through pity and terror. The ship isn't so much the World as the Mind; and the mind is that of Vere, the ship's captain and in that role a father-figure. Although he is outside the action, he is called upon to judge it; and in making his judgement he becomes the action itself, since he is the only human consciousness we're aware of. Guileless and guiltless Billy and the darkly will-driven officer Claggart are what they are: good and evil, white and black, active in the world outside. Yet they are also within the ship and within Vere's psyche, and Vere is also Britten, who 'foresuffered all'. So the opera tells us that growing up is a complex equilibrium of the contradictory impulses which Billy and Claggart don't 'stand for' but are. We cannot dispose of evil by a blind blow, provoked by the inarticulateness of the good within us. To accept destiny, in will-lessness rather than in passivity, is to be able to say 'This Thing of Darknesse I/Acknowledge mine'; and Britten's wondrous musical metaphor for this – the procession of major triads that (echoing and resolving the minor triads of Claggart's aria of destruction) initiates the death verdict – moves us so much precisely because we know that Billy cannot live to taste the fruits of experience. Yet the resolution is Vere's, not Billy's. It is Vere who has lived through his life to find peace in submission to a law that is 'beyond good and evil' because it recognizes their mutuality. The action of the opera is enclosed within the memory of this old man, whose name means truth.

So in a sense *Billy Budd*, if not specifically Christian, is a religious opera, as is *Noye's Fludde* (1958), Britten's most extended piece for children, based on the Chester Miracle play. It is hardly surprising, given his basic theme, that Britten should have composed so much music expressly for children; in this case the choice of the text itself is evidence of a self-knowledge that finds what is needful for each occasion. Thus the Chester Miracle play is medieval, and the common people with whom it deals are, despite the intellectual sophistication of medieval civilization, child-like at heart. On the other hand the story is a conflict, so that the piece can grow from ritual into music-drama, if not quite into opera. Indeed, it starts from a direct admission of human contrarieties; the congregation, including you and me, sing the well-known hymn, Lord Jesus, think on me. This hymn is an appeal to Christ to restore us to peace and innocence, which if we're adult we have lost, or if we're children are about to lose, in travelling through 'darkness', 'perplexity', and the Flood. We *start* with the consciousness of sin and earth-born passion, which we have to encompass before we can see 'eternal brightness'. Although the Flood is in one sense a destructive force, it is in another sense a necessary return to the unconscious waters. The innocence of Britten's technique in this truly miraculous score itself enacts the philosophical, even theological, theme. Seldom has so much been 'done', ritually enacting comedy, pathos, tragedy and sheer fun, with such childishly simple means.

What is here achieved in childhood experience is explored at adult level in Britten's later 'parable for church performance', *Curlew River*

(1964). The convention, halfway between theatre and ritual, is again related to the medieval miracle play, and the piece was first performed, on something like a medieval trestle stage, in a medieval church. Yet although the action takes place in church, in the English fens, Britten gives the convention a wider dimension by relating the English miracle play to that of the Japanese Noh play, which had deeply impressed him on a visit to Japan in 1956. He was emboldened to do this by the fortuitous (if such it was) fact that he lighted on a Noh play text which is close to Christian myth, and closer still to the personal myth that has dominated all Britten's work. A mother, desperate in grief, is searching for her lost son, slain by the barbarian; in a vision she sees him reborn. So Britten's myth of primal innocence, of persecution, and of the sacrificial scapegoat reappears, but with one significant difference: in *Grimes* the hero is the barbarian, the Wild Man who, having lost love, slaughters his own soul. In *Curlew River* the persecutor doesn't even appear, the story being narrated retrospectively. The central characters are the suffering mother (played by a masked man) and the boy himself who is, in momentary vision, restored from death. The duality of persecution and guilt is absolved.

This shift of theme entails a technical evolution. Each character has his own musical motives, auralized with the precision that typifies the earlier operas; but the conception is now almost entirely linear rather than harmonic. Britten effects an extraordinary equation between individual passion and universal lament; instrumental lines become disembodied extensions of half-articulate vocal cries that hurt too much to be borne. Such melodic-rhythmic techniques are common to many 'primitive' folk cultures as well as to oriental musics; in centring the musical and psychological action in them Britten discounts 'Western' harmony and employs timeless drones and ostinati as background to the action. The technical revolution *is* the Boy's and our rebirth; 'innocence outshines guilt' as Britten renews European music in a manner both new and immemorially ancient. So the orientalism of *Curlew River* has nothing to do with pastiche, but is a matter of spiritual discovery. In being easternized, plainsong is recreated in terms relevant to us. Britten's two other 'parables for church performance', *The Burning Fiery Furnace* (1966) and *The Prodigal Son* (1968), having biblical subjects, confirm the philosophical and psychological import of this mating of East and West. Britten has gone 'back', first to the Middle Ages, then to remoter and more savage antiquities, in order to go forward.

Nor had this entailed a *volte face* in his development. The complementary pair of chamber operas that precede *Curlew River* still deploy traditional tonality and harmony in the highly personal, post-Renaissance, neo-Baroque manner that Britten had evolved through the sequence of his earlier works; at the same time the technique is now far more reliant on ostinato patterns and on melismatic melodic line. In particular, the supernatural elements in both *The Turn of the Screw* (1954) and *A Midsummer Night's Dream* (1959–60) generate their magic by way of these new-old techniques. Henceforth such 'transcendence' will be the heart of the Britten experience.

The Turn of the Screw stands midway in Britten's career and is its pivotal point in that in this opera the supernatural first becomes irresistible. Like *Billy Budd*, it faces Britten's fundamental theme of innocence and corruption head on; but evolves from Budd's confrontation of good and evil to an apprehension of their metaphysical as well as psychological interdependence. Significantly it is, in its psychological dimension, based on a story by an American author who was voluntarily expatriated. Leaving behind the giant technocracy that America had spawned, Henry James settled in Europe, where he wrote of the American as an innocent reborn in the Old World. Britten's first theatre piece, *Paul Bunyan*, had concerned an American Eden, its advance into civilized sophistication, and its corruption. *The Turn of the Screw* starts from our modern hyper-consciousness, linked with what James called 'the black and merciless things that lie behind great possessions'; and explores its impact on the child within us all. The Governess's neurotic obsession opens her senses to psychic realities that are normally hidden, especially in the socially respectable world to which she belongs. In going mad she may have intimations of a deeper sanity; for although such terrors may be 'bad', to use Miles's word, they are not necessarily and only bad since in representing the daemonic they embrace the heights along with the depths of human potential. There are more things in heaven and earth, not to mention hell, than are dreamed of in the Governess's philosophy, or in Mrs Grose's lack of one. The children see these things out of the very perfection of their childishness: as Mrs Grose, innocent by natural limitations, never could. The Governess sees them too, from the maelstrom of her mental sickness. She is a victim of the daemonic's translation into the demonic; and destroys life in an attempt to save it. Unlikely though it seems as a basis for an opera, James's story proves an ideal vehicle for Britten's (strictly speaking) transcendent genius. As Myfanwy Piper's libretto tells the tale, Britten's music reveals the inextricable warp and woof of the natural and supernatural. In presenting the action in a series of cinematic flashbacks, sandwiched between instrumental variations on a single theme which embraces all the chromatic semitones, he encloses the story within a single obsessive psyche; at the same time he objectifies the depths which that mind thinks it sees with a precision pertinent to us all, in that we have most of us had momentary glimpses of them. Watching the opera as the 'screw' of the obsessional theme is remorselessly tightened, we ourselves suffer the awe-ful, fright-ful, unfathomable interplay of innocence and corruption which those differentiated innocents, the children, the Governess and Mrs Grose, undergo, until they find nemesis or expiation.

The Turn of the Screw is Britten's most tightly wrought score, its musical and its psychological meanings being inextricable; we, unlike little Miles, survive by desperate strategy and the skin of our teeth. *A Midsummer Night's Dream*, though about dream rather than night-mare, is no less cogently organized, and likewise indicates, as does Shakespeare's play, that the unconscious may know more of 'reality' than the conscious mind. Britten uses Shakespeare's text shortened, but virtually unaltered; and through the agency of his music manages the transitions between the natural and the supernatural no less adroitly than does Shakespeare in his most musical play. The action functions on three planes: the conscious or would-be conscious world of the sophisticated young Athenians; the pre-conscious world of the fairies; and the world of the 'rude Mechanicalls', which is halfway between the two, human yet brutish, and therefore intuitively in touch with natural and supernatural realms. Entering the magic wood, the humans encounter the supernatural beings, whose relation-ships to the humans parallels that of Greek immortals to mortals. If a divine hierarchy exists, the human mind cannot conceive it as much less muddled than our own. The difference lies in the faculty for wish-fulfilment; the fairies can sometimes put things right by magic, we can't. So the mortals suffer for their mistakes and the fuddled fairies help them to start afresh: which may be a synonym for learning by experience. Neither the human will nor fairy magic is infallible.

Although *A Midsummer Night's Dream* is a comedy and *The Turn of the Screw* most decidedly isn't, there are significant parallels between the two operas. As *The Screw* encloses its action within the reiterations of its obsessional row-theme, so *The Dream* embraces its action within a sequence of concords covering all twelve semitones: a cosmos of sleep from which all aspects of our being emerge. The aristocratic humans, the rude Mechanicalls and the fairies have different kinds of music associated with different groups of instruments; as the levels of experience interact, so each is wondrously transformed. Britten's opera is no more 'escapist' than is Shakespeare's play. Although at the end the occupants of the house may be 'ever blessed', it is Puck-Luck who speaks the epilogue, to his prickly trumpet fanfares. So although he asks for and receives our approbation, we recognize that his blessing is not an absolute, and tomorrow is another day. *A Midsummer Night's Dream* is a genuinely comic opera which nonetheless opens magic casements on *perilous* seas and fairy lands *forlorn*. If it is an accident that E flat, the pitch and key associated with the *Dream*'s immortals, is also that associated with Quint's 'evil' in *The Screw*, it's the kind of accident that happens only to genius: which helps us to understand why the comedy of *A Midsummer Night's Dream* is an achievement comparable with, and no less significant than, the tragedy of *The Turn of the Screw*.

Britten's operatic techniques are remarkably catholic. He began, in *Paul Bunyan*, with a cross between ballad opera and music-hall. In *Peter Grimes* and *Billy Budd* he assayed the convention of Verdian Grand Opera, reconciling it with the English baroque heritage of Purcell. In *Noye's Fludde* and the three parables for church performance he called on techniques derived from the medieval miracle play and from aspects of non-Western music theatre. Yet his most consummate achievements are surely within the chamber opera form that was his own invention; *Grimes* is a powerfully epic work that presents its private theme in universal terms, but *The Screw* and *The Dream* probe more deeply into the human condition, precisely because in them personal involvement is more truly sensitive, yet is at the same time objectified in the lucidity of Britten's art. If the chamber opera, in the context of Aldeburgh, may imply a coterie audience, that is the price one must pay for uncompromising intensity; and of course coteries disperse as the operas are presented around the world. It certainly seems significant that Britten should have ended his operatic cycle with a work, *Death in Venice* (1973), which is a grand opera in calling for full musical and theatrical resources, yet is at the same time as intimate in its techniques and as elaborately wrought in its form as the chamber operas.

Nor can it be an accident that *Death in Venice* is not only the last of Britten's operas but also the one in which his personal involvement is most patent. The central character of Mann's tale is an artist who, like Britten, is creating in the knowledge that he is seriously ill and may be under threat of death. He loves the mutely mythical Dream Boy, the *puer aeternus* whom he meets on the beach: an idealized, intangible metamorphosis of the earthy Suffolk boy whom Grimes loved but, driven to distraction, murdered; of the innocently suffering but perhaps corrupted boy whom the Governess stifled in *The Screw*; of the visionarily reborn boy of *Curlew River* and of the humanly redeemed boy of *The Prodigal Son*; and even of the little male child bandied between the frenzied fairies in *A Midsummer Night's Dream*. Our ultimate tribute to Britten must be that his most personal opera affects us as being the one closest to our own experience. Listening to it, we recognize that atonement, in the sense of at-one-ment, is a concept relevant to us all, and that if it can be encompassed only in dream, then dreams may be truer than truth.

Both as a musician and as a man of the theatre Britten was a 'natural'; in the mere act of creation, without resort to ratiocination, he knew intuitively what his theme was. Michael Tippett (born 1905) is not in that sense a natural; yet it is remarkable that he, who came to fruition at the same time as Britten, attained a similar goal by proceeding on a diametrically opposite path. He came to opera comparatively late and, one suspects, by conscious ratiocination, in an attempt to define the attitude to our multifariously perplexing world already implicit in his instrumental works. And although it wasn't an opera that brought him fame, it was an oratorio that used techniques derived directly from baroque opera. *A Child of our Time*

(1939–41) – the title is significant, and may be compared with Britten's *A Boy was born* – has a libretto by Tippett himself, which dramatizes a true story of Nazi terror, and deals with war, oppression, persecution and alienation. But the personal story becomes a twentieth-century myth: by relating the conception to Handel's *Messiah*, Tippett suggests a kinship with the oratorio-going British public; by substituting Negro spirituals for Lutheran chorales, he uses an oppressed people as a symbol for the stifling of the human spirit – with the advantage that the idiom is related to popular music with which his public is familiar. Tippett's awareness of the anguish inherent in experience, especially today, communicates itself to his technique which, compared with Britten's, is here strained and un-fulfilled. Yet the inward validity of feeling conquers. Without offering any solution to our social evils, without castigating us for our wickedness, the oratorio grows into a lyrical affirmation of life. In the thrilling final chorus the polyphony swells, the solo vocal writing burgeons into ecstatic arabesque. What keeps us alive, the music tells us, is the human impulse to sing and dance, whatever man's bestiality to man.

The end of the oratorio effects *The Heart's Assurance*: which is the title of the marvellous song cycle that Tippett wrote to a series of death-haunted poems by two young poets who were killed in the war. He reached that point, as did Britten, by an apprehension of the interdependence of 'light' and 'dark' forces; and this is the specific theme of his first and still (I believe) greatest opera, *The Midsummer Marriage* (1946–52). The libretto, again by Tippett him-self, starts from the affirmation of life with which the oratorio had ended. The marriage is the mating of the sense's joy with the spirit's ecstasy – a consummation more ambiguously sought for in Britten's *The Turn of the Screw* and *A Midsummer Night's Dream*, and more 'transcendently' sublimated in *Curlew River* and *Death in Venice*. Tippett's technique, though more complex than Britten's, is here no less fully 'realized'. The compulsive rhythm is a more extravagant version of the Purcellian tension between vocal inflexion and corpo-real dance movement; the polyphonically derived harmony intensi-fies the seventeenth-century partiality for modal variety; while the flowering of the lines into ever smaller note-values parallels the seventeenth-century technique of divisions on a ground. There's a baroque, sensuously exciting quality in the curling tendrils of Tippett's vocal lines; yet the sustained lift of the melodies gives the music a spiritual buoyancy also. It is relevant to note that all the features which make Tippett's idiom so distinctive – the sprung rhythms and lilting syncopations, the harmonic false relations, the technique of division – have counterparts not only in our seventeenth-century music, but also in the urban folk music of our time, jazz.

Technical limitations are always also imaginative limitations. In shedding his in this masterly score Tippett has done something very rare in our day: he has created an act of *celebration*. His libretto has often been criticized, in my view irrelevantly. In taking his operatic mythology from Jungian psychology Tippett was both intelligent and empirical, since such imagery must strike deep, to a twentieth-century audience, without need of intellectual explanation. We are aware of the archetypes, whether we know it or not, even if, living in a society that believes itself to be rational, we've grown out of the habit of allegorical thinking. Tippett's libretto is the only kind he could have set; through it he achieves fulfilment in the old magical sense, offering not illusion, but a revelation of the deepest compulsions from which our lives draw sustenance. The difficulty of Tippett's music is evidence of the struggle most twentieth-century people must undergo in order to learn to celebrate. *The Midsummer Marriage* demonstrates that, when we are free, the act of celebration is at once simple and sublime.

Britten's mature operas, I suggested, are an equation between reality and dream. One might say the same of *The Midsummer Marriage*; though it might be more on the mark to call it visionary, in Blake's sense, he being a poet–painter who rendered incarnate the archetypes which Jung merely rediscovered. Such a consummated celebration could perhaps happen once only. However this may be, for his next opera *King Priam* (1958–61) Tippett explored a technique of epic narration rather than of ritual celebration. In recounting the Trojan story he touched on many of his basic themes – the *conjunctio oppositorum*, the nature of the Hero, the meaning of Time – but in a musical idiom lean and spare, as compared with the *Marriage*'s luxuriance. The music preserves the typical Tippettan vibrancy, the electrical incandescence of sonority, but 'does coolly', as Berlioz put it, 'the things that are most fiery'. The two late operas – *The Knot Garden* (1966–9) and *The Ice Break* (1973–6) – again start from a ratiocinative process, for they are exploratory both in dramatic content (calling on the findings of anthropology and sociology as well as psychology), and in musical resource (adding to Tippett's habitual use of jazz electrophonic elements derived from rock and pop). The topicality of the libretti and of some of the techniques has already dated: which must be why though each opera fascinates and stimulates, neither totally satisfies – as does the 'enactment' of *The Midsummer Marriage* and the spontaneous identity of medium and message achieved in all Britten's mature operas.

Britten and Tippett are, as opera composers, complementary. Almost all Britten's music is concerned at some level with rebirth; Tippett, no less preoccupied with the pre-conscious springs of life, is more aware of the inevitablity of human failure. For Britten, technique is revelation; for Tippett, it is discovery, and if, in some of his works, he seems to 'fail', that is because he doesn't often claim to delineate more than beginnings. Britten's music has virtually no affinities with Beethoven; Tippett deeply admires Beethoven and, like Beethoven, awakens 'beginnings' which he must later explore further for himself, and which will in turn be beginnings for those who come after. Approaching his eightieth year, Michael Tippett is still a Child of our Time who is just *beginning* to be an old man. He's a vivid embodiment of Eliot's dictum that 'Old men ought to be explorers'. Britten's late works, on the other hand, have a Mozartian sense of total consummation.

PART IV

APPENDIX

VOLUME 8

COMPILED BY FRANK WHITEHEAD

ed.	edited
edn	edition
enl.	enlarged
comp.	compiled
pub.	published
repr.	reprinted
rev.	revised
trans.	translated
vol. (s)	volume(s)
b.	born
d.	died
c.	circa
?	probably

The lists which follow are intended as a guide to the literature written in the British Isles and Commonwealth since the Second World War. See also the bibliographies in Volume 7 of the Guide *for much of direct relevance to this period.*

FOR FURTHER READING
AND REFERENCE

The Social and Intellectual Setting

I. HISTORIES: GENERAL AND SOCIAL

Addison, P. *Now the War is Over: A Social History of Britain 1945–51*, 1985
Bogdanor, V. and Skidelsky, R. (eds.) *The Age of Affluence, 1951–64*, 1970
Calvocoressi, P. *The British Experience, 1945–75*, 1978
Davies, A. *Where Did the Forties Go?*, 1984
Gamble, A. *Britain in Decline*, 1981, rev. 1985
Kelf-Cohen, R. *British Nationalisation 1945–1973*, 1973
Marwick, A. *British Society since 1945*, 1982
    The Explosion of British Society 1914–1970, 1971
Middlemas, K. *Politics in Industrial Society*, 1979
Moran, M. *The Politics of Industrial Relations*, 1977
Perkin, H. *The Rise of Professional Society: England since 1880*, 1989
Sampson, A. *Anatomy of Britain*, 1962
    Anatomy of Britain Today, 1971
    The Changing Anatomy of Great Britain, 1982
Seabrook, J. *What Went Wrong? Working People and the Ideas of the Labour Movement*, 1978
Westergaard, J. Weyman, A. and Wiles, P. *Modern British Society: A Bibliography*, 1974, rev. 1977

II. SOCIAL AND ECONOMIC BACKGROUND

Bryan, B., Dadzie, S. and Scafe, S. *The Heart of the Race: Black Women's Lives in Britain*, 1985
Davenport, N. *The Split Family*, 1964
Goldthorpe, J. H. *Social Mobility and Class Structure in Modern Britain*, 1980
Gorer, G. *Death, Grief and Mourning in Contemporary Britain*, 1965
    Sex and Marriage in England Today, 1971
Halsey, A. H. *Change in British Society*, 1978, rev. 1981
Heron, L. (ed.) *Truth, Dare or Promise: Girls Growing up in the Fifties*, 1985
Kaldor, N. *The Causes of the Slow Rate of Economic Growth in the United Kingdom*, 1966
Klein, J. *Samples from English Culture*, 2 vols., 1965

Noble, T. *Modern Britain, Structure and Change*, 1975
Rowbotham, S. *Woman's Consciousness, Man's World*, 1973
Schaffer, F. *The New Town Story*, 2nd edn., 1972
Shrapnel, N. *The Seventies: Britain's Inward March*, 1980
Taylor, R. *Against the Bomb: The British Peace Movement, 1958–1965*, 1988
Titmuss, R. M. (ed.) *Essays on the Welfare State*, 1964
Walter, A. (ed.) *Come Together: The Years of Gay Liberation*, 1986
Williams, G. (ed.) *Social and Cultural Change in Contemporary Wales*, 1978
Worswick, G. D. N. and Ady, P. H. (eds.) *The British Economy 1945–1950*, 1952
    The British Economy in the 1950s, 1962

III. DIARIES, LETTERS AND MEMOIRS

Benn, T. *Out of the Wilderness*, 1987
    Office without Power, 1988
    Against the Tide, 1989
Butler, R. A. *The Art of the Possible*, 1971
Crossman, R. *The Diary of a Cabinet Minister*, 2 vols., 1975–6
Graves, R. *Between Moon and Moon: Selected Letters, 1946–72*, ed. P. O'Prey, 1984
Hayman, R. *Secrets: Boyhood in a Jewish Hotel 1932–1954*, 1985
Healey, D. *The Time of My Life*, 1989
Jacobson, D. *Time and Time Again: Autobiographies*, 1985
Lyttelton, G. *The Lyttelton Hart-Davis Letters, 1955–1962*, ed. R. Hart-Davis, 6 vols., 1978–86
Macmillan, H. *Memoirs, 1914–63*, 6 vols., 1966–73
Malcolm, N. *Ludwig Wittgenstein: A Memoir*, 1958
Medawar, P. B. *Memoirs of a Thinking Radish*, 1986
Nicholson, H. *Diaries and Letters 1930–1964*, ed. S. Olson, 1980
Russell, D. *The Tamarisk Tree, Vol. 3*, 1985
Scannell, V. *The Tiger and the Rose*, 1971
Thompson, D. (ed.) *The Leavises: Recollections and Impressions*, 1984
Woolf, L. *Autobiography, Vol. 5: The Journey Not the Arrival Matters (1939–1969)*, 1969

IV. PHILOSOPHY, RELIGION, SCIENCE AND EDUCATION

Ayer, A. J. *The Problem of Knowledge*, 1956
Coplestone, F. *Contemporary Philosophy*, 1956
Lewis, H. D. (ed.) *Contemporary British Philosophy, Personal Statements*, 3rd Series 1956, 4th Series 1976
Magee, B. *Modern British Philosophy*, 1971
Mehta, V. *The Fly and the Fly-Bottle*, 1963
Polyani, M. *Personal Knowledge*, 1958
Popper, K. *Conjectures and Refutations: The Growth of Scientific Knowledge*, 1963, rev. 1969

The Open Society and its Enemies, 1945, 2 vols., rev. 1966

Ryle, G. *The Concept of Mind*, 1949

Strawson, P. F. *Individuals*, 1959
  The Bounds of Sense, 1966

Williams, B. and Montefiore, A. (eds.) *British Analytical Philosophy*, 1966

Wittgenstein, L. *Philosophical Investigations*, 1953
  The Brown and Blue Books, 1958

Davies, H. *Worship and Theology in England*, Vol. 5: *The Ecumenical Century 1900–1965*, 1966

Gilbert, A. D. *The Making of Post-Christian Britain*, 1980

Hastings, A. *A History of English Christianity, 1920–1985*, 1986

MacQuarrie, J. *Twentieth-Century Religious Thought*, 1963, rev. 1971

Perman, D. *Change and the Churches: An Anatomy of Religion in Britain*, 1977

Robinson, J. A. T. *Honest to God*, 1963

Bernal, J. D. *The Natural Sciences in Our Time*, 1969

Blackett, P. M. S. *Military and Political Consequences of Atomic Energy*, 1952

Bowlby, J. *Attachment and Loss*: Vol. 1, *Attachment*, 1969; Vol. 2, *Separation: Anxiety and Anger*, 1973; Vol. 3, *Loss: Sadness and Depression*, 1980

Burnet, M. *Genes, Dreams and Realities*, 1971

Dawkins, R. *The Selfish Gene*, 1976

Eldredge, N. *Life Pulse*, 1987

Evans, C. *The Mighty Micro: The Impact of the Computer Revolution*, 1982

Hawking, S. W. *A Brief History of Time*, 1988

Lyons, J. (ed.) *New Horizons in Linguistics*, 1970

Medawar, P. B. *Advice to a Young Scientist*, 1970

Medawar, P. B. and Medawar, J. S. *The Life Sciences: Current Ideas of Biology*, 1977

Nora, S. and Minc, A. *The Computerisation of Society*, 1980

Rhodes, R. *The Making of the Atom Bomb*, 1986

Robins, R. H. *General Linguistics: An Introductory Survey*, 1966

Rose, H. and Rose, S. *Science and Society*, 1969

Sheail, J. *Seventy-five Years in Ecology*, 1987

Taton, R. *Science in the Twentieth Century*, 1966

Watson, J. D. *The Double Helix*, 1968; reviews, original papers, ed. G. S. Stent, 1981

Weizenbaum, J. *Computer Power and Human Reason*, 1976, rev. 1984

Bantock, G. H. *Education and Values*, 1965
  Education, Culture and the Emotions, 1967

Benn, C. and Simon, B. *Half-Way There: Report on the British Comprehensive School Reform*, 1970, rev. 1972

Bennett, N. *Teaching Styles and Pupil Progress*, 1974

Bullock Committee, *A Language for Life*, 1976

Cox, C. B. and Dyson, A. E. (eds.) *Fight for Education: A Black Paper*, 1969

Douglas, J. W. B. *The Home and the School*, 1964

Floud, J., Halsey, A. H. and Martin, F. M. *Social Class and Educational Opportunity*, 1957

Holbrook, D. *English for the Rejected*, 1964

Jackson, B. and Marsden, D. *Education and the Working Class*, 1962, rev. 1966

Plowden, B. *Children and their Primary Schools*, 2 vols., 1967

Pedley, R. *The Comprehensive School*, 1963

Perkin, H. J. *New Universities in the UK*, 1969

Simon, B. *Bending the Rules: The Baker 'Reform' of Education*, 1988

Whitehead, F. *The Disappearing Dais*, 1966

V. CULTURAL BACKGROUND

Appleyard, B. *The Pleasures of Peace: Art and Imagination in Post-War Britain*, 1989

Banham, M. and Hillier, B. (eds.) *A Tonic to the Nation: the Festival of Britain, 1951*, 1976

Bigsby, C. W. E. (ed.) *Approaches to Popular Culture*, 1976

Cornforth, M. (ed.) *Rebels and their Causes*, 1978

Hewison, R. *In Anger: Culture in the Cold War, 1945–60*, 1981
    Too Much: Art and Society in the Sixties, 1960–1975, 1986

Hoggart, R. *The Uses of Literacy*, 1957

Hutchinson, R. *The Politics of the Arts Council*, 1982

Melly, G. *Revolt into Style: The Pop Arts in Britain*, 1970

Middleton, R. *Pop Music and the Blues: A Study of the Relationship and its Significance*, 1972

Panek, L. L. *The Special Branch, The British Spy Novel, 1890–1980*, 1983

Pawling, C. (ed.) *Popular Fiction and Social Change*, 1984

Shaw, R. *The Arts and the People*, 1987

Sissons, M. and French, P. *The Age of Austerity*, 1963

Sutherland, J. *Fiction and the Fiction Industry*, 1978
    Offensive Literature: Decensorship in Britain, 1960–1982, 1982

Thompson, D. (ed.) *Discrimination and Popular Culture*, 1963

White, E. W. *The Arts Council of Great Britain*, 1975

VI. ARTS OTHER THAN LITERATURE

Ford B, *The Cambridge Guide to the Arts in Britain, 9. Since the Second World War*, 1988

Banham, R. *The Architecture of the Well-Tempered Environment*, 1969, rev. 1984

Esher, L. *A Broken Wave: The Rebuilding of England 1940–1980*, 1981

Curtis, W. J. R. *Modern Architecture since 1900*, 1987

Jencks, C. *The Language of Post-Modern Architecture*, 1977, rev. 1984

Lasdun, D. (ed.) *Architecture in an Age of Scepticism*, 1984

Lyall, S. *The State of British Architecture*, 1980
MacEwen, M. *Crisis in Architecture*, 1974

White, J. W. (ed.) *Twentieth Century Ballet in Britain*, 1985

Armes, R. *A Critical History of British Cinema*, 1978
Manvell, R. *New Cinema in Britain*, 1969

Foreman, L. (ed.) *British Music Now: a Guide to the Work of Younger Composers*, 1975
Griffiths, P. *New Sounds, New Personalities: British Composers of the 1980s in Conversation*, 1985
Kennedy, M. *Britten*, 1981
Pirie, P. J. *The English Musical Renaissance: Twentieth Century British Composers and Their Works*, 1979
Routh, F. *Contemporary British Music*, 1972
Shafer, M. *British Composers in Interview*, 1963
Trend, M. *The Music Makers: Heirs and Rebels of the English Musical Renaissance from Elgar to Britten*, 1985

Berger, J. *Permanent Red*, 1960
P. Fuller, *Images of God*, 1990
Lucie-Smith, E. *Art in the Seventies*, 1980
    Movements in Art Since 1945, 1975, rev. 1985
MacCarthy, F. *British Design Since 1880: A Visual History*, 1982
    A History of British Design, 1830–1979, 1979
Nairne, S. and Serota, N. *British Sculpture in the Twentieth Century*, 1981
Read, H. (introd.), *Henry Moore: Sculptures and Drawings Vol. 2 1949–1954*, 1955, rev. 1965 (continued as Bowness, A. (ed.), Vols. 3, 4, 5, 1965–83)
Rothenstein, J. *Modern English Painters: Hennell to Hockney*, 1974, rev. 1984
Shone, R. *The Century of Change: British Painting since 1900*, 1977
Spalding, F. *British Art since 1900*, 1986

VII. THE MEDIA

Baistow, T. *Fourth Rate Estate: An Anatomy of Fleet Street*, 1985
Briggs, A. *The History of Broadcasting in the United Kingdom: Vol. IV, Sound and Vision (1945–1955)*, 1978
Curran, J. and Seaton, J. *Power Without Responsibility: The Press and Broadcasting in Britain*, 3rd edn., 1988
Durgnat, R. *The Mirror for England: British Movies from Austerity to Affluence*, 1970
Goldie, G. W. *Facing the Nation's Television and Politics, 1936–76*, 1977
Hetherington, A. *News, Newspapers and Television*, 1985
Hood, S. and O'Leary, G. *Questions of Broadcasting*, 1990
Inglis, F. *The Imagery of Power: A Critique of Advertising*, 1972

Schlesinger, P. *Putting 'Reality' Together: BBC News*, 1978
Smith, A. C. H. *Paper Voices: The Popular Press and Social Change, 1935–1965*, 1975
Whitehead, K. *The Third Programme: A Literary History*, 1989
Williams, R. *Communications*, 1962
 Television: Technology and Cultural Form, 1974
Wilson, H. H. *Pressure Group: The Campaign for Commercial Television in England*, 1961

The Literature

VIII. REFERENCE WORKS

Adelman, I. and Dworkin, R. (eds.) *The Contemporary Novel: A Checklist of Critical Literature*, 1972
Barnes, P. *A Companion to Post-War British Theatre*, 1986
Borkland, E. (ed.) *Contemporary British Literary Critics*, 1977
Chevalier, T. (ed.) *Twentieth Century Children's Writers*, 3rd edn., 1989
Ellis, A. *How to Find Out About Children's Literature*, 1966, rev. 1968, 1973
English Association, *The Year's Work in English Studies* (annually from 1921. Separate chapters for 'The Twentieth Century' from Vol. 35, 1956 onwards)
Jones, B. *A Bibliography of Anglo-Welsh Literature, 1900–1965*, 1970
Kirkpatrick, D. (ed.) *Contemporary Dramatists*, 4th edn., 1988
Mikhail, E. H. *A Bibliograhy of Modern Irish Drama, 1899–1970*, 1972
 Contemporary British Drama, 1950–1976: an Annotated Critical Bibliography, 1976
Modern Humanities Research Association, *Annual Bibliography of English Language and Literature*, (annually from 1920)
Willison, I. R. (ed.) *New Cambridge Bibliography of English Literature, Vol. IV, 1900–1950*
Vinson, T. and Kirkpatrick, D. (eds.) *Contemporary Novelists*, 4th edn., 1986
 Contemporary Poets, 4th edn., 1985

IX. GENERAL STUDIES

Allsop, K. *The Angry Decade: a survey of the cultural revolt of the 1950s*, 1958
Bradbury, M. *The Social Context of Modern English Literature*, 1971
Lehmann, J. (ed.) *The Craft of Letters in England*, 1956
Maschler, T. (ed.) *Declaration*, 1957
Morrison, B. *The Movement: English Poetry and Fiction of the 1950s*, 1980
Sinfield, A. (ed.) *Society and Literature 1945–1970*, 1983

X. POETRY

Alvarez, A. *The Shaping Spirit: Studies in Modern English and American Poets*, 1958

Bedient, C. *Eight Contemporary Poets*, 1974

Brown, M. *Double Lyric: Divisiveness and Communal Creativity in Recent British Poetry*, 1980

Dodsworth, M. (ed.) *The Survival of Poetry*, 1980

Fraser, G. S. *Essays on Twentieth Century Poets*, 1977

Fulton, R. *Contemporary Scottish Poetry*, 1974

Haffenden, J. (ed.) *Viewpoints: Poets in Conversation*, 1981

Hamilton, I. (ed.) *The Modern Poet: Essays from 'The Review'*, 1968

Holbrook, D. *Lost Bearings in English Poetry*, 1977

Homberger, E. *The Art of the Real: Poetry in England and America since 1939*, 1977

Jones, P. and Schmidt, M. *British Poetry since 1970: A Critical Survey*, 1980

King, P. R. *Nine Contemporary Poets*, 1979

Martin, G. and Furbank, P. N. (eds.) *Twentieth Century Poetry: Critical Essays and Documents*, 1976

Pinsky, R. *The Situation of Poetry: Contemporary Poetry and Its Traditions*, 1977

Powell, N. *Carpenters of Light: Some Contemporary British Poets*, 1979

Schmidt, M. (ed.) *British Poetry Since 1960: A Critical Survey*, 1977

Thurley, G. *The Ironic Harvest: English Poetry in the Twentieth Century*, 1974

Thwaite, A. *Contemporary English Poetry*, 1959
　　Poetry Today, 1960–1973, 1973
　　Twentieth Century English Poetry, 1978

XI. FICTION

Adams, R. M. *After Joyce: Studies in Fiction after Ulysses*, 1977

Bergonzi, B. *The Situation of the Novel*, 1970, rev. 1979

Bradbury, M. and Palmer, D. (eds.) *The Contemporary English Novel*, 1979

Craig, D. *The British Working Class Novel Today*, 1963

Dowling, D. *Fictions of Nuclear Disaster*, 1987

Foster, J. W. *Forces and Themes in Ulster Fiction*, 1974

Gindin, J. *Post-War British Fiction*, 1962

Gray, N. *The Silent Majority: A Study of the Working Class in Post-War British Fiction*, 1973

Haffenden, J. (ed.) *Novelists in Interview*, 1985

Hanson, C. *Short Stories and Short Fictions, 1880–1980*, 1984

Hayman, R. *The Novel Today, 1967–75*, 1976

Karl, F. R. *A Reader's Guide to the Contemporary English Novel*, 1961, rev. 1972

Kennedy, A. *The Protean Self: Dramatic Action in Contemporary Fiction*, 1974

Kenyon, O. *Women Novelists Today: A Survey of English Writing in the Seventies and Eighties*, 1988

Lodge, D. *The Language of Fiction*, 1965
　　The Novel at the Cross Roads, 1971

McEwen, N. *The Survival of the Novel*, 1981

Newby, P. H. *The Novel, 1945–1950,* 1951

Parrinder, P. *Science Fiction, Its Criticism and Teaching,* 1980

Rabinovitz, R. *The Reaction against Experiment in the English Novel, 1950–1960,* 1967

Rippier, J. S. *Some Post-War British Novelists,* 1965

Smith, D. *Socialist Propaganda in the Twentieth Century British Novel,* 1978

Spacks, P. M. (ed.) *Contemporary Women Novelists,* 1977

Stacey, T. F. (ed.) *Twentieth Century Women Novelists,* 1981

Swinden, P. *The English Novel of History and Society, 1940–1980,* 1984

XII. DRAMA

Anderson, M. *Anger and Detachment,* 1976

Brandt, G. (ed.) *British Television Drama,* 1981

Brown, J. R. *Theatre Language,* 1972

Bull, J. *New British Political Dramatists,* 1984

Davison, P. *Contemporary Drama and the Popular Dramatic Tradition in England,* 1982

Drakakis, J. (ed.) *British Radio Drama,* 1981

Dutton, R. *Modern British Tragicomedy and the British Tradition: Beckett, Pinter, Stoppard, Albee and Storey,* 1986

Elsom, J. *Post-War British Theatre,* 1976, rev. 1979

Findlater, R. *At the Royal Court: 25 Years of the English Stage Company,* 1981

Gaskill, W. *A Sense of Direction: Life at the Royal Court,* 1988

Hayman, R. *British Theatre since 1955: A Reassessment,* 1979

Itzin, C. *Stages in the Revolution: Political Theatre in Britain Since 1968,* 1980

Lewis, P. (ed.) *Radio Drama,* 1981

Maxwell, D. E. S. *A Critical History of Modern Irish Drama, 1891–1980,* 1984

Roberts, P. *The Royal Court Theatre, 1965–1972,* 1986

Rodgers, I. *Radio Drama,* 1982

Taylor, J. R. *Anger and After,* 1962, rev. 1969
    The Second Wave: British Drama of the Sixties, 1971, rev. 1978

Trussler, S. (ed.) *New Theatre Voices of the Seventies,* 1981

Wardle, I. *The Theatres of George Devine,* 1978

Worth, K. *Revolution in Modern English Drama,* 1972
    The Irish Drama of Europe from Yeats to Beckett, 1978

XIII. LITERARY CRITICISM AND LITERARY THEORY

Abrams, M. H. *Doing Things with Texts,* 1990

Coveney, P. *The Image of Childhood,* 1957, rev. 1967

Culler, J. *On Deconstruction: Theory and Criticism after Structuralism,* 1983
    Structuralist Poetics, 1975

Harding, D. W. *Experience into Words,* 1963
    Words into Rhythm: English Speech Rhythm in Verse and Prose, 1976

Kermode, F. *The Romantic Image,* 1957

The Sense of an Ending: Studies in the Theory of Fiction, 1967
Knights, L. C. *Explorations*, 1946
　Poetry, Politics and the English Tradition, 1956
Leavis, F. R. (See entry under AUTHORS)
Lerner, L. (ed.) *Reconstructing Literature*, 1983
Olney, J. (ed.) *Autobiography: Essays Theoretical and Critical*, 1980
Parrinder, P. *The Failure of Theory*, 1987
Pascal, R. *Design and Truth in Autobiography*, 1960
Robinson, I. *The Survival of English*, 1973
Strickland, G. *Structuralism or Criticism? Thoughts On How We Read*, 1981
Walsh, W. *A Human Idiom: Literature and Humanity*, 1964
Williams, R. *Marxism and Literature*, 1977
　Politics and Letters: Interviews, 1979

XIV. LITERATURE IN ENGLISH FROM AFRICA, ASIA AND THE CARIBBEAN

Barnett, U. A. *A Vision of Order: A Study of Black South African Literature in English, 1914–1980*, 1983
Gates, H. L. (ed.) *Black Literature and Literary Theory*, 1984
Gilkes, M. *The West Indian Novel*, 1981
Killam, G. D. (ed.) *African Writers on African Writing*, 1973
　The Writing of East and Central Africa, 1984
King, B. A. (ed.) *A Celebration of Black and African Writing*, 1976
　Introduction to Nigerian Literature, 1971
　Literatures of the World in English, 1974
　The New English Literatures: Cultural Nationalism in a Changing World, 1980
Moore, G. *The Chosen Tongue: English Writing in the Tropical World*, 1969
Mukherji, M. *Twice-Born Fiction*, 1971
Narasimhaiah, C. D. (ed.) *Awakened Conscience: Studies in Commonwealth Literature*, 1978
Ngara, E. *Art and Ideology in the African Novel*, 1985
Ngugi wa Thiong'o, *Homecoming: essays on African and Caribbean Literature, Culture and Politics*, 1972
　Writers in Politics, 1981
Ramchand, K. *The West Indian Novel and its Background*, 1970, rev. 1983
Smith, R. (ed.) *Exile and Tradition: Studies in African and Caribbean Literature*, 1976
Walsh, W. *A Manifold Voice*, 1970
　Indian Literature in English, 1990
　(ed.) *Readings in Commonwealth Literature*, 1973
Zell, H. M., Bundy, C. and Coulon, V. *A New Reader's Guide to African Literature*, 1983

XV. WRITING FOR CHILDREN

Bettelheim, B. *The Uses of Enchantment: The Meaning and Importance of Fairy Tales*, 1976

Blishen, E. (ed.) *The Thorny Paradise: Writers on Writing for Children*, 1975

Butts, D. (ed.) *Good Writers for Young Readers*, 1977

Chambers, A. *Booktalk: Occasional Writing on Literature and Children*, 1985

Crouch, M. *Treasure Seekers and Borrowers: Children's Books in Britain 1900–1960*, 1962

Eyre, F. *British Children's Books in the Twentieth Century*, 1952, rev. 1971

Fisher, M. *Intent upon Reading: A Critical Appraisal of Modern Fiction for Children*, 1961, rev. 1964

Ford, B. (ed.) *Young Readers: Young Writers*, 1960

Hollindale, P. *Choosing Books for Children*, 1974

Inglis, F. *The Promise of Happiness: Value and Meaning in Children's Fiction*, 1981

Leeson, R. *Reading and Righting*, 1985

Leng, I. J. *Children in the Library*, 1968

Meek, M., Warlow, A. and Barton, G. (eds.) *The Cool Web: The Pattern of Children's Reading*, 1977

Moss, E. *Part of the Pattern: A Personal Journey through the World of Children's Books, 1960–1985*, 1986

Townsend, J. R. *A Sounding of Storytellers: New and Revised Essays on Contemporary Writers for Children*, 1979
    Written for Children, 1965, rev. 1974, rev. 1988

Trease, G. *Tales out of School*, 1948, rev. 1964

Whitehead, F. *et al. Children and their Books*, 1977

Whitehead, W. *Different Faces: Growing up with Books in a Multicultural Society*, 1988

XVI. BACKGROUND TO THE NEW ENGLISH BIBLE

Alter, R. and Kermode, F. (eds.) *The Literary Guide to the Bible*, 1987

Henn, T. R. *The Bible as Literature*, 1970

Hunt, G. (ed.) *About the New English Bible*, 1970

Martin, D. and Mullen, P. (eds) *No Alternative: The Prayer Book Controversy*, 1982

Partridge, A. C. *English Biblical Translation*, 1973

PN Review 13 (special issue on the new translation), 1979

AUTHORS AND WORKS

Collections and Anthologies

POETRY ANTHOLOGIES

Abse, D. *The Hutchinson Book of Post-War British Poets*, 1989
Allnutt, G., D'Aguiar, F., Edwards, K. and Mottram, E. *The New British Poetry*, 1988
Allott, K. (ed.) *The Penguin Book of Contemporary Verse*, 1950, enl. 1962
Alvarez, A. (ed.) *The New Poetry*, 1962, rev. 1966
Conquest, R. *New Lines*, 1956
Couzyn, J. (ed.) *The Bloodaxe Book of Contemporary Women Poets*, 1985
Enright, D. J. (ed.) *The Oxford Book of Contemporary Verse 1945–1980*, 1980
Hobsbaum, P. and Lucie-Smith, E. (eds) *A Group Anthology*, 1963
Larkin, P. (ed.) *The Oxford Book of Twentieth Century English Verse*, 1973
Lucie-Smith, E. (ed.) *British Poetry since 1945*, 1970
Morrison, B. and Motion, A. (eds.) *The Penguin Book of Contemporary British Poetry*, 1982
Schmidt, M. (ed.) *Eleven British Poets*, 1980
   Some Contemporary Poets of Britain and Ireland, 1983
Scott, D. (ed.) *'Bread and Roses': Women's Poetry of the Nineteenth and Twentieth Centuries*, 1982
Skelton, R. (ed.) *Six Irish Poets*, 1962
Summerfield, G. (ed.) *Worlds: Seven Modern Poets*, 1974
Wain, J. (ed.) *Anthology of Contemporary Poetry, Post-War to the Present*, 1979
Wright, D. (ed.) *Longer Contemporary Poems*, 1966
   The Mid Century: English Poetry 1940–1960, 1965

PROSE ANTHOLOGIES

Bradbury, M. (ed.) *The Book of Modern British Short Stories*, 1988
Davin, D. (ed.) *Short Stories from the Second World War*, 1982
   The Killing Bottle, 1958
Dorsch, T. S. (ed.) *Charmed Lives*, 1965
Gray, S. (ed.) *The Penguin Book of Southern African Stories*, 1985
Kohli, S. (ed.) *Modern Indian Short Stories: An Anthology* 1974, rev. 1983

Maclean, A. D. (ed.) *Best For Winter: A Selection from Twenty-five Years of 'Winter's Tales'*, 1979

Mutloatse, M. (ed.) *Africa South: Contemporary Writings*, 1980

Naik, M. K. (ed.) *The Indian English Short Story*, 1984

Ramchand, K. (ed.) *Best West Indian Stories*, 1982

Sharrock, R. (ed.) *The Green Man Revisited*, 1976

Authors

ACHEBE, CHINUA (b. 1930): Novelist, short-story writer and poet; born Eastern Nigeria; graduated from University College, Ibadan, 1953; worked for Nigerian Broadcasting Corporation, 1954–66; first novel *Things Fall Apart*, 1958; Professor of English, University of Nigeria, Nsakka, 1973–81; Emeritus Professor, 1985.

Other works include:

(novels) *No Longer at Ease*, 1960; *Arrow of God*, 1964; *A Man of the People*, 1966; *Anthills of the Savannah*, 1987

(short stories) *Girls at War*, 1972

(poetry) *Beware Soul Brother*, 1971, rev. 1972

(non-fiction) *Morning Yet on Creation Day*, 1975; *Hopes and Impediments: Selected Essays*, 1988

See:

C. L. Innes, *Chinua Achebe*, 1990

G. D. Killam, *The Writings of Chinua Achebe*, 1977

B. Lindfors and C. L. Innes (eds.), *Achebe*, 1978

A. Ravenscroft, *Chinua Achebe*, 1969

AMIS, KINGSLEY (b. 1922): Novelist, poet and short-story writer; educated St John's College, Oxford; army service, 1942–5; lecturer, University College, Swansea 1949–61; first novel *Lucky Jim* 1954 (filmed 1957); contributor to *New Lines* poetry anthology, 1956.

Other works include:

(collections) *Collected Poems, 1944–1979*, 1979; *Collected Short Stories*, 1980

(novels) *That Uncertain Feeling*, 1955 (filmed 1962); *The Anti-Death League*, 1966; *The Riverside Villas Murder*, 1973; *Ending Up*, 1974; *The Alteration*, 1976; *Jake's Thing*, 1978; *The Old Devils*, 1986 (Booker Prize, 1987); *Difficulties with Girls*, 1988; *The Folks that Live on the Hill*, 1990

(belles-lettres) *New Maps of Hell: A Survey of Science Fiction*, 1960; *What Became of Jane Austen?*, 1970; (ed.) *New Oxford Book of Light Verse*, 1978

See:

D. Salwick, *Kingsley Amis: A Reference Guide*, 1978

ANAND, MULK RAJ (b. 1905): Novelist and short-story writer; educated at Lahore, London and Cambridge Universities; first novel *Untouchable*, 1935.

Other works include:

(novels) *Coolie*, 1936; (trilogy) *The Village*, 1939, *Across the Black Waters*, 1940, *The Sword and the Sickle*, 1942; *The Big Heart*, 1945; *The Private Life of an Indian Prince*, 1953, rev. 1970; *The Old Woman and the Cow*, 1963; *The Power of Darkness*, 1966; *Morning Face*, 1968 (autobiographical novel in the series *Seven Ages of Man*); *Gauri*, 1981; *Bubble*, 1984 (fourth volume in *Seven Ages of Man*)

(short stories) *The Barber's Trade Union*, 1944; *The Tractor and the Corn Goddess*, 1947.

See:

M. Berry, *Anand: The Man and the Novelist*, 1970

S. Cowasgee, *So Many Freedoms: A Study of the Major Fiction of Anand*, 1978

G. S. Gupta, *Anand: A Study of the Fiction in Humanist Perspective*, 1975

ARDEN, JOHN (b. 1930): Dramatist; educated at King's College, Cambridge, where he studied architecture; first play *All Fall Down* performed Edinburgh, 1955; first London production *Waters of Babylon* at Royal Court Theatre, 1957; Fellow in Playwriting at Bristol University, 1959–60; after disillusionment with London West End theatre founded Corrandalla Arts Centre, County Galway, Eire, 1975.

Other works include:

(plays) *Live Like Pigs*, 1958; *Serjeant Musgrave's Dance*, 1959; *The Workhouse Donkey*, 1963; *Armstrong's Last Goodnight*, 1964

(with Margaretta D'Arcy): *The Happy Haven*, 1960; *The Hero Rises Up*, 1968; *Where is the Kingdom*, 1988

(novel) *Silence Among the Weapons*, 1980

(essays) *To Present the Pretence: Essays on the Theatre and its Public*, 1977; (with Margaretta D'Arcy) *Awkward Corners: Essays, Papers, Fragments*, 1988

See:

F. Gray, *John Arden*, 1982

M. Page (ed.), *Arden on File*, 1985

AUDEN, WYSTAN HUGH (1907–73): Poet and critic; educated at Gresham's School, Holt and Christ Church, Oxford; *Poems*, 1930; migrated to USA, 1939; from 1945 permanent home in New York, though spending spring and summer in Europe; Pulitzer Prize, 1948; Oxford Professor of Poetry, 1956–61.

(For publications before 1945 see Volume 7 of the *Guide*.)

Other publications include:

(poetry) *The Age of Anxiety*, 1948; *Nones*, 1951; *The Shield of Achilles*, 1956; *Homage to Clio*, 1960; *About the House*, 1965; *Thank You, Fog*, 1974 (criticism) *The Dyer's Hand*, 1963; *Secondary Worlds*, 1968

Life by C. Osborn, 1980; H. Carpenter, 1981
Collected Shorter Poems 1927–57, 1966
Collected Longer Poems, 1968
Collected Poems ed. E. Mendelson, 1976
See:
G. W. Bahlke, *The Later Auden*, 1970
J. W. Beach, *The Making of the Auden Canon*, 1977
B. C. Bloomfield, *W. H. Auden, a Bibliography*, 1985
E. Callan, *Auden: A Carnival of Intellect*, 1983
J. A. Fuller, *A Reader's Guide to W. H. Auden*, 1970
J. H. Haffenden (ed.), *W. H. Auden, The Critical Heritage*, 1983
A. Rodway, *A Preface to Auden*, 1984

BAINBRIDGE, BERYL (b. 1934): Novelist; b. Liverpool; actress in repertory companies, 1949–60.

Novels include: *A Weekend With Claude*, 1967, rev. 1981; *The Bottle Factory Outing*, 1974; *Sweet William*, 1974 (filmed, 1980); *Young Adolf*, 1978; *Watson's Apology*, 1984; *Filthy Lucre*, 1986.

BARSTOW, STAN (b. 1928): Novelist and short-story writer; b. Yorkshire; draughtsman in engineering industry, 1945–62; first novel *A Kind of Loving*, 1960 (filmed).

Publications include:
(novels) *Ask Me Tomorrow*, 1962; *Joby*, 1964; *A Brother's Tale*, 1980; *Give Us This Day*, 1989
(short stories) *The Desperadoes*, 1961; *A Season With Eros*, 1971

BECKETT, SAMUEL (1906–89): Dramatist, novelist and poet; b. Dublin; educated at Portora Royal School and Trinity College, Dublin; lecturer in English, Ecole Normale Superieure, Paris, 1928–30; lecturer in French, Trinity College, Dublin, 1930–32; from 1932 lived mostly in France, settling in Paris from 1937; first publication *Whoroscope* (verse) 1930; first novel *Murphy*, 1938; first play *En Attendant Godot*, 1952 (translated by the author as *Waiting for Godot*, 1954); Nobel Prize for Literature, 1969.

Other works include:
(novels) *The Trilogy*, 1956 (consisting of *Watt*, 1944; *Molloy*, previously published in French, 1951; and *Malone Dies*, previously published in French, 1952); *The Unnameable*, 1960 (previously published in French, 1953)
(plays) *All That Fall*, 1957 (radio play); *Endgame*, 1958; *Krapp's Last Tape*, 1959; *Embers*, 1959; *Happy Days*, 1960; *Breath and Other Short Plays*, 1972; *Not I*, 1973; *Company*, 1980; *Collected Shorter Plays*, 1984

Life by D. Bair, 1978
Collected Poetry, 1930–1978, 1984
Collected Shorter Prose, 1945–1980, 1984
Collected Shorter Plays, 1984
See:
H. P. Abbott, *The Fiction of Samuel Beckett*, 1975
R. Cohn, *Just Play: Samuel Beckett's Theatre*, 1980
B. S. Fletcher, *A Student's Guide to the Plays of Samuel Beckett*, 1978
J. Fletcher and J. Spurling, *Beckett the Playwright*, 1985
L. Graver, *Samuel Beckett: Waiting for Godot*, 1990
    (ed.), *Samuel Beckett: The Critical Heritage*, 1979
C. R. Lyons, *Samuel Beckett*, 1983
K. Worth (ed.), *Beckett the Shape Changer*, 1975

BOND, EDWARD (b. 1934): Dramatist; b. Holloway, London; left school at 14 to work in factories and offices; first play *The Pope's Wedding*, 1962 (Sunday performance at Royal Court Theatre); outcry over baby-stoning scene in *Saved*, 1965.

Other plays include: *Narrow Road to the Deep North*, 1968; *Lear*, 1971; *The Sea*, 1973; *Bingo*, 1974; *The Fool*, 1976; *The Woman*, 1978; *The Bundle*, 1978; *Restoration*, 1981; *The War Plays (Red, Black and Ignorant; The Tin Can People; Great Peace)*, 1985; *Human Cannon*, 1985
See:
T. Coult, *The Plays of Edward Bond*, 1977
M. Hay and P. Roberts, *Edward Bond: A Companion to the Plays*, 1978
    Bond: A Study of his Plays, 1980
D. L. Hirst, *Edward Bond*, 1985
P. Roberts (ed.), *Bond on File*, 1985

BRAINE, JOHN (b. 1922): Novelist; born and educated in Yorkshire; librarian in various public libraries, mainly in Yorkshire, 1940–1957. Novels include *Room at the Top*, 1957 (filmed); *Life at the Top*, 1962; *Stay With Me Till Morning*, 1970
See:
J. W. Lee, *John Braine*, 1968

BROOKE-ROSE, CHRISTINE (b. 1923): Novelist and critic; educated at Somerville College, Oxford; journalist, 1956–68; since 1975 Professeur, University of Paris, Vincennes.

Novels include: *The Language of Love*, 1957; *The Dear Deceit*, 1960; *Thru*, 1975; *Amalgamemnon*, 1984; *Xorandor*, 1986

BUNTING, BASIL (b. 1900): Poet; b. Northumberland; educated London School of Economics; gaoled as conscientious objector during First World War; lived in France, Italy and the US in the 1920s and 1930s; sub-editor

Newcastle Chronicle for twelve years; first general recognition with publication of *Briggflatts* in 1966.

Collected Poems, 1968, rev. 1978
See:
R. Guedalla, *Basil Bunting: A Bibliography of Works and Criticism*, 1973

BURGESS, ANTHONY (b. 1917): Novelist; educated at Xaverian College, Manchester and Manchester University; army service, 1942–6; Birmingham University extra-mural lecturer, 1946–8; grammar-school teacher, 1950–54; education officer Malaya and Brunei, 1954–9; first novel *Time for a Tiger*, 1956.

Other publications include:
(novels) *The Enemy in the Blanket*, 1958; *Beds in the East*, 1959; *The Clockwork Orange*, 1962 (filmed 1971); *The Wanting Seed*, 1962; *Inside Mr Enderby*, 1963 (published under pseudonym Joseph Kell); *Nothing Like the Sun*, 1964; *MF*, 1971; *Earthly Powers*, 1980. (First three novels repr. as *The Malayan Trilogy*, 1972, and as *The Long Day Wanes*, 1980); *The Piano Players*, 1986; *The Devil's Mode*, 1989
(autobiography) *Little Wilson and Big God*, 1987
See:
G. Aggeler, *Anthony Burgess: The Artist as Novelist*, 1979

CARY, JOYCE (1887–1957): Novelist; b. Londonderry; educated at Clifton College; 1907–9 studied painting in Edinburgh; 1909–12 Trinity College, Oxford (law); 1912–13 medical orderly in the British Red Cross attached to the Montenegrin army; 1913–20 Nigerian political service.

(For publications before 1945 see Volume 7 of the *Guide*.)

Later works include:
(novels) *A Fearful Joy*, 1949; Trilogy: *Prisoner of Grace*, 1952, *Except the Lord*, 1953, *Not Honour More*, 1955; *The Captive and the Free* (unfinished), 1959
(short stories) *Spring Song*, 1960
(criticism) *Art and Reality*, 1958; *Selected Essays* (ed. A. G. Bishop), 1976

Life by M. Foster, 1968
See:
C. Cook, *Joyce Cary: Liberal Principles*, 1981
M. J. C. Echeruo, *Joyce Cary and the Dimensions of Reality*, 1978
B. Fisher, *Joyce Cary, the Writer and his Theme*, 1980
M. Mahood, *Joyce Cary's Africa*, 1964
A. Wright, *Joyce Cary: A Preface to his Novels*, 1958

COMPTON-BURNETT, IVY (1884–1969): Novelist; read classics at Royal Holloway College, London, 1902–5; first novel, *Pastors and Masters*, 1925; CBE, 1951; DBE, 1967.

(For publications before 1945 see Volume 7 of the *Guide*.)

Other novels include: *Parents and Children*, 1941; *Elders and Betters*, 1944; *Mothers and Sons*, 1955; *A God and His Gifts*, 1964

Life by E. Sprigge, 1973; H. Spurling, *Ivy When Young*, 1974, and *Secrets of a Woman's Heart: The Later Life of Ivy Compton-Burnett*, 1984
See:
C. Burkhart, *Ivy Compton-Burnett*, 1965
R. Liddell, *The Novels of Ivy Compton-Burnett*, 1955

DAVIE, DONALD (b. 1922): Poet and critic; educated at St Catharine's College, Cambridge; Lecturer Cambridge University, 1958–64; Professor of Literature, University of Essex, 1964–8; Professor of Humanities, Vanderbilt University, since 1978; Clark Lecturer, Trinity College, Cambridge, 1976.

Works include:
(poetry) *Collected Poems 1950–70*, 1972; *Collected Poems 1970–83*, 1983
(criticism) *Purity of Diction in English Verse*, 1952, rev. 1966; *Articulate Energy*, 1957, rev. 1976; *Thomas Hardy and British Poetry*, 1973; *A Gathered Church*, 1978; *Trying to Explain*, 1980; *Dissentient Voice*, 1982
See:
Agenda, Summer 1976 (Donald Davie issue)
G. Dekker (ed.), *Donald Davie and the Responsibilities of Literature*, 1983

DENNIS, NIGEL (b. 1912): Novelist; b. in Surrey; educated in Southern Rhodesia and Germany; lived in America for many years; joint editor of *Encounter*, 1967–70; staff book reviewer, *The Sunday Telegraph* from 1961.

Publications include:
(novels) *Boys and Girls Come Out to Play*, 1949; *Cards of Identity*, 1959; *A House in Order*, 1966
(plays) *Two Plays and a Preface*, 1958

DRABBLE, MARGARET (b. 1939): Novelist, biographer, editor; educated at the Mount School, York and Newnham College, Cambridge; first novel *A Summer Birdcage*, 1962

Publications include:
(novels) *The Garrick Year*, 1964; *The Millstone*, 1966 (filmed); *The Waterfall*, 1969; *The Needle's Eye*, 1972; *The Ice Age*, 1977; *The Radiant Way*, 1987; *A Natural Curiosity*, 1989
(others) *Arnold Bennett: A Biography*, 1974; *A Writer's Britain*, 1972; (ed.) *The Oxford Companion to English Literature*, 5th edn 1985
See:
J. V. Creighton, *Margaret Drabble*, 1985
V. G. Myers, *Margaret Drabble, Puritanism and Permissiveness*, 1974

PART FOUR

DURRELL, LAWRENCE (b. 1912): Novelist, poet, travel-writer; b. India; has lived mainly abroad, working for the Foreign Office or the British Council.

Publications include:
(novels) *The Black Book*, 1938; *Cefalu*, 1947, repr. as *The Dark Labyrinth*, 1958; 'The Alexandria Quartet': *Justine*, 1957; *Balthazar*, 1958; *Mountolive*, 1958; *Clea*, 1960. Also: *Tune*, 1968; *Nunquam*, 1970; and 'The Avignon Quintet': *Monsieur, or The Prince of Darkness*, 1974; *Livid, or Buried Alive*, 1978; *Constance, or Solitary Practices*, 1982; *Sebastian, or Ruling Passions*, 1982; *Quinx, or The Ripper's Tale*, 1985
(travel-books) *Prospero's Cell*, 1945 (about Corfu); *Reflections on a Marine Venus*, 1953 (about Rhodes); *Bitter Lemons*, 1958 (about Cyprus)

Collected Poems, 1980
See:
G. S. Fraser, *Lawrence Durrell*, 1968

ELIOT, THOMAS STEARNS (1888–1965): Poet, critic, and dramatist; b. St Louis, Missouri; 1915 came to London; first volume of poems *Prufrock and Other Observations*, 1917; awarded OM and Nobel Prize for Literature, 1948.
   (For publications before 1945 see Volume 7 of the *Guide*.)

Works include:
(plays) *The Cocktail Party*, 1950; *The Confidential Clerk*, 1954; *The Elder Statesman*, 1959; *Collected Plays*, 1972; *Collected Poems and Plays*, 1969
(criticism) *Notes Towards a Definition of Culture*, 1948; *The Three Voices of Poetry*, 1953; *Essays on Elizabethan Drama*, 1956; *On Poetry and Poets*, 1957; *To Criticise the Critic*, 1965
(letters) *The Letters of T. S. Eliot, Vol. I, 1898–1922*, ed. V. Eliot, 1988

Life by P. Ackroyd, 1984
See:
E. M. Browne, *The Making of T. S. Eliot's Plays*, 1968
A. Calder, *T. S. Eliot*, 1987
L. Gordon, *Eliot's New Life*, 1988
M. Grant (ed.), *T. S. Eliot: The Critical Heritage*, 2 vols., 1982
F. B. Pinion, *A T. S. Eliot Companion: Life and Work*, 1986
G. Smith, *T. S. Eliot's Poetry and Plays, a Study of Sources and Meanings*, 1956

EMPSON, WILLIAM (1906–84): Poet and critic; educated at Winchester and Magdalene College, Cambridge; taught in Japanese and Chinese universities in the 1930s; worked for the BBC in London, 1941–6; Professor of English Literature at Sheffield University, 1953–71; knighted, 1979.

Publications after 1945 include: *Collected Poems*, 1955; *The Structure of*

Complex Words, 1951; *Milton's God*, 1961, rev. 1965; *Using Biography*, 1984; (ed. D. Pirie) *Essays on Shakespeare*, 1986; (ed. J. Haffenden) *Argufying: Essays on Literature and Culture*, 1988
See:
R. Gill (ed.), *William Empson: The Man and his Work*, 1974. (For longer entry see Volume 7 of the *Guide*)

ENRIGHT, DENNIS JOSEPH (b. 1920): Poet, critic and novelist; educated Downing College, Cambridge; lecturer in English, University of Alexandria 1947–50; from 1953 Professor of English at various Far Eastern universities, including University of Singapore, 1960–70.

Publications include:
(poetry) *Collected Poems*, 1981, enl. 1987; *Selected Poems*, 1990
(novels) *Academic Year*, 1955; *Figures of Speech*, 1965
(criticism) *The Apothecary's Shop*, 1957; *Conspirators and Poets*, 1966; *Shakespeare and the Students*, 1971; *A Mania for Sentences*, 1983; *The Alluring Problem: an essay on irony*, 1986
(ed. anthologies) *The Oxford Book of Contemporary Verse, 1945–80*, 1980; *The Oxford Book Of Death*, 1983; *Fair of Speech: The Uses of Euphemism*, 1985
See:
W. Walsh, *D. J. Enright: Poet of Humanism*, 1974

FARRELL, JAMES GORDON (1935–79): Novelist; educated at Rossall School and Brasenose College, Oxford; stricken with polio while at Oxford and partly paralysed; first novel, *A Man From Elsewhere*, 1963; drowned while fishing from the Irish coast.

Novels include:
The Lung, 1965; *Troubles*, 1970; *The Siege of Krishnapur*, 1973 (Booker Prize); *The Singapore Grip*, 1978
See:
R. Binns, *J. G. Farrell*, 1986

FOWLES, JOHN (b. 1926): Novelist; educated Bedford School and New College, Oxford.

Fiction includes:
(novels) *The Collector*, 1962 (filmed); *The Magus*, 1966, rev. 1977; *The French Lieutenant's Woman*, 1969 (filmed); *Daniel Martin*, 1977; *A Maggot*, 1985
(short stories) *The Ebony Tower*, 1974
See:
S. Loveday, *The Romances of John Fowles*, 1985
B. Woodcock, *Male Mythologies: John Fowles and Masculinity*, 1984

FULLER, ROY (b. 1912): Poet, novelist and critic; b. Lancashire; qualified as solicitor, 1934; served in Royal Navy, 1941–6; Professor of Poetry, Oxford University, 1968–73; CBE, 1970.

Publications include:
(poetry) *New and Collected Poems 1934–84*, 1985; *Subsequent to Summer*, 1985; *Consolations*, 1987; *Available for Dreams*, 1989
(novels) *The Ruined Boys*, 1959; *The Perfect Fool*, 1963
(criticism) *Owls and Artificers*, 1971; *Professors and Gods*, 1974
(autobiography) *Souvenirs*, 1980; *Vamp till Ready*, 1982; *Home and Dry*, 1984
See:
A. E. Austin, *Roy Fuller*, 1979

GARNER, ALAN (b. 1934): Children's author; born in Cheshire; educated at Manchester Grammar School and Magdalen College, Oxford.

Fiction includes: *The Wierdstone of Brisingamen*, 1960, rev. 1963; *The Moon of Gomrath*, 1963; *Elidor*, 1965; *The Owl Service*, 1967; *Red Shift*, 1973 (filmed); *The Stone Book*, 1976; *Tom Fobble's Day*, 1977; *Granny Reardun*, 1977; *The Aimer Gate*, 1978; *The Lad of the Gad*, 1980; *A Bag of Moonshine*, 1986

GOLDING, WILLIAM (b. 1911): Novelist; educated at Marlborough Grammar School and Brasenose College, Oxford; grammar-school teacher at Bishop Wordsworth School, Salisbury; first novel *Lord of the Flies*, 1954 (filmed, 1963); CBE, 1966; Nobel Prize for Literature, 1983; knighted, 1988

Works include:
(novels) *The Inheritors*, 1955; *Pincher Martin*, 1956; *Free Fall*, 1959; *The Spire*, 1964; *The Pyramid*, 1967; *Darkness Visible*, 1979; *Rites of Passage*, 1980 (Booker Prize); *The Paper Men*, 1984; *Close Quarters*, 1987; *Fire Down Below*, 1989
(essays) *The Hot Gates*, 1965; *A Moving Target*, 1987
See:
J. Carey (ed.), *William Golding's 75th Birthday Book*, 1986
M. Kinkead-Weekes and I. Gregor, *William Golding: A Critical Study*, 1967, rev. 1984
N. Page (ed.), *William Golding Novels 1956–67: A Casebook*, 1985

GORDIMER, NADINE (b. 1923): Novelist and short-story writer; born S. Africa; educated Witwatersrand University; first novel, *The Lying Days*, 1953.

Works include:
(novels) *A World of Strangers*, 1958; *The Late Bourgeois World*, 1966; *A Guest of Honour*, 1970; *The Conservationist*, 1974 (jointly Booker Prize); *Burger's Daughter*, 1979; *July's People*, 1981; *A Sport of Nature*, 1987

(short stories) *Six Feet of the Country*, 1956; *Friday's Footprints*, 1960; *Not For Publication*, 1965; *Selected Stories*, 1975; *Some Monday for Sure*, 1976; *A Soldier's Embrace*, 1980; *Something Out There*, 1984
See:
C. Heywood, *Nadine Gordimer*, 1984
M. Wade, *Gordimer*, 1978

GREEN, HENRY – Henry Vincent Yorke – (1905–71): Novelist; educated at Eton and Magdalen College, Oxford; first novel, *Blindness*, 1926; joined Auxiliary Fire Service, 1939.

Publications include:
(novels) *Living*, 1929; *Party Going*, 1939; *Caught*, 1943; *Loving*, 1945; *Back*, 1946; *Concluding*, 1948; *Nothing*, 1950; *Doting*, 1952
(autobiography) *Pack My Bag*, 1946

GREENE, GRAHAM (b. 1904): Novelist, short-story writer and dramatist; educated Berkhamsted and Balliol College, Oxford; on staff of *The Times* 1926–30; first novel *The Man Within*, 1929; first play *The Living Room* 1953; made CH, 1966; OM, 1986.
(For publications before 1945 see Volume 7 of the *Guide*.)

Other publications include:
(novels) *The Heart of the Matter*, 1948 (filmed); *The End of the Affair*, 1951; *The Quiet American*, 1955; *Our Man In Havana*, 1958 (filmed); *The Comedians*, 1966; *Travels With My Aunt*, 1969 (filmed); *The Honorary Consul*, 1973 (filmed); *The Human Factor*, 1978; *Monsignor Quixote*, 1982; *Getting to Know the General*, 1984; *The Tenth Man*, 1985; *The Captain and the Enemy*, 1988
(plays) *The Potting Shed*, 1957; *The Complaisant Lover*, 1959
(essays) *The Lost Childhood*, 1951; *Collected Essays*, 1969
(autobiography) *A Sort of Life*, 1971; *Ways of Escape*, 1980
See:
D. Lodge, *Graham Greene*, 1961
D. Pryce-Jones, *Graham Greene*, 1963, rev. 1973
R. Sharrock, *Saints, Sinners and Comedians: The Novels of Graham Greene*, 1984

GUNN, THOM (b. 1929): Poet; educated University College School, Hampstead and Trinity College, Cambridge (1950–53); has lived in California since 1954; Visiting Lecturer, later Associate Professor, University of California (Berkeley) 1958–66; Visiting Lecturer, University of California (Berkeley) since 1975.

Publications include:
(poetry) *Fighting Terms*, 1954, rev. 1962; *The Sense of Movement*, 1959; *My Sad Captains*, 1961; *Touch*, 1967; *Moly*, 1971; *Jack Straw's Castle*, 1976;

Selected Poems, 1950–1975, 1979; *The Passages of Joy*, 1982
(prose) *The Occasions of Poetry*, 1982
See:
W. C. Jack and G. Bixby, *Thom Gunn: A Bibliographny 1940–78*, 1979
A. Bold, *Thom Gunn and Ted Hughes*, 1976

HARTLEY, LESLIE POLES (1895–1972): Novelist, short-story writer and critic; educated at Harrow and Balliol College, Oxford; army war-service 1916–18; first novel, *Simonetta Perkins*, 1925; resumed novel-writing during Second World War with the trilogy *The Shrimp and the Anemone*, 1944, *The Sixth Heaven*, 1946, and *Eustace and Hilda*, 1947; CBE, 1946.

Works include:
(novels) *My Fellow-Devils*, 1951; *The Go-Between*, 1953 (filmed); *The Hire-ling*, 1957; *Facial Justice*, 1960; *Poor Clare*, 1968
(short stories) *Collected Stories*, 1968; *Mrs Carteret Receives*, 1971
(criticism) *The Novelist's Responsibility*, 1967 (Clark Lectures, Trinity College, Cambridge, 1964)
See:
A. Mulkeen, *Wild Thyme, Winter Lightning: The Symbolic Novels of L. P. Hartley*, 1974

HEANEY, SEAMUS (b. 1939): Poet and critic; b. County Derry; educated Queen's University, Belfast; since 1985 Boylston Professor, Harvard University; since 1989 Professor of Poetry, Oxford University.

Publications include:
(poetry) *Death of a Naturalist*, 1966; *Door into the Dark*, 1969; *Wintering Out*, 1973; *North*, 1975; *Field Work*, 1979; *Selected Poems 1965–75*, 1980; *Station Island*, 1984; *Sweeney Astray*, 1984; *The Haw Lantern*, 1987; *New Selected Poems 1966–1987*, 1990
(prose) *Preoccupations: Selected Prose 1968–78*, 1984; *The Government of the Tongue*, 1988
(anthology ed. with Ted Hughes) *The Rattle Bag*, 1982
See:
N. Corcoran, *Seamus Heaney*, 1986
T. Curtis (ed.), *The Art of Seamus Heaney*, 1982, rev. 1985
T. C. Foster, *Seamus Heaney*, 1987
B. Morrison, *Seamus Heaney*, 1982

HILL, GEOFFREY (b. 1932): Poet and critic; educated at Keble College, Oxford; member of academic staff of University of Leeds from 1954, Professor of English Literature, 1976–80; Fellow of Emmanuel College, Cambridge since 1981; Clark Lecturer, Trinity College, Cambridge, 1986.

Publications include:

Collected Poems, 1985; *The Lords of Limit: Essays on Literature and Ideas*, 1984

See:

H. Hart, *The Poetry of Geoffrey Hill*, 1980

C. Ricks, *Geoffrey Hill and the Tongue's Atrocities*, 1978
   The Force of Poetry, 1984

P. Robinson (ed.), *Geoffrey Hill: Essays on his Work*, 1985

V. Sherry, *The Unknown Tongue: The Poetry and Criticism of Geoffrey Hill*, 1988

HOLBROOK, DAVID (b. 1923): Poet, novelist and critic; b. Norwich; educated Downing College, Cambridge; war service 1942–5; tutor in adult education and schoolteacher 1951–61; Fellow of King's College, Cambridge, 1961–5; first poetry volume, *Imaginings*, 1961; Fellow of Downing College 1981–90.

Publications include:

(poetry) *Chance of a Lifetime*, 1978; *Selected Poems, 1961–78*, 1980

(novels) *Flesh Wounds*, 1966; *A Play of Passion*, 1978; *Nothing Larger than Life*, 1987; *A Little Athens*, 1990

(criticism) *Dylan Thomas and the Code of Night*, 1972; *Sylvia Plath: Poetry and Existence*, 1976; *Lost Bearings in English Poetry*, 1977; *Authenticity and the Novel*, 1987

(education) *English for Maturity*, 1961; *English for the Rejected*, 1964; *English for Meaning*, 1980

HUGHES, RICHARD (1900–76): Novelist; educated at Charterhouse and Oriel College, Oxford; first novel *A High Wind in Jamaica*, 1929; worked at Admiralty during Second World War; OBE, 1946

Other novels include: *In Hazard*, 1938; *The Fox in the Attic*, 1961; *The Wooden Shepherdess*, 1973

See:

P. Thomas, *Richard Hughes*, 1973

HUGHES, TED (b. 1930): Poet and children's writer; educated at Mexborough Grammar School, Yorkshire, and Pembroke College Cambridge; married Sylvia Plath, 1956; OBE, 1977; Poet Laureate since 1984.

Publications include:

(poems) *The Hawk in the Rain*, 1957; *Lupercal*, 1960; *Wodwo*, 1967; *Crow*, 1970, rev. 1972; *Cave Birds*, 1975, rev. 1978; *Season Songs*, 1976; *Remains of Elmet*, 1979; *Moortown*, 1979; *Selected Poems 1957–81*, 1982; *Flowers and Insects*, 1987, *Wolfwatching*, 1989

(for children) *Meet My Folks!* 1961; *The Earth-Owl and Other Moon People*, 1963; *How the Whale Became* (stories), 1963; *The Iron Man* (story), 1968; *Moon-Bells and Other Poems*, 1978; *Under the North Star*, 1981; *What is the*

Truth? (story), 1984; *Fangs the Vampire Bat and the Kiss of Truth*, 1986; *Tales of the Early World*, 1988

(anthology ed. with Seamus Heaney) *The Rattle Bag*, 1982

See:

T. Gifford and N. Roberts, *Ted Hughes: A Critical Study*, 1981

K. Sagar, *The Art of Ted Hughes*, 1975, rev. 1978
    (ed.), *The Achievement of Ted Hughes*, 1983

K. Sagar and S. Tabor, *Ted Hughes: A Bibliography*, 1983

D. Walder, *Ted Hughes*, 1988

JONES, DAVID (1895–1974): Poet and painter; served as private in the Welch Fusiliers, 1915–18; became a Roman Catholic, 1921, and went to work under Eric Gill; elected to the Seven and Five Society, 1928, where he exhibited paintings; first publication *In Parenthesis*, 1938; CBE, 1955; CH, 1974.

Other publications include: *The Anathemata*, 1951; *The Sleeping Lord*, 1974; *The Kensington Mass*, 1975

See:

D. Blamires, *David Jones*, 1971

T. Dilworth, *The Literary Parenthesis of David Jones*, 1979

R. Hague, *David Jones*, 1975
    A Commentary on 'The Anathemata', 1976

LARKIN, PHILIP (1922–85): Poet and novelist; b. Coventry; educated St John's College, Oxford; from 1943 worked in various libraries, becoming Librarian, Brynmor Jones Library, University of Hull, 1955; CBE, 1975.

Works include:

(poetry) *The North Ship*, 1945, rev. 1966; *The Less Deceived*, 1955; *The Whitsun Weddings*, 1964; *High Windows*, 1974; *Collected Poems*, ed. A. Thwaite, 1988

(fiction) *Jill*, 1946, rev. 1964; *A Girl in Winter*, 1947

(essays and reviews) *All That Jazz: A Record Diary 1961–68*, 1970; *Required Writing: Miscellaneous Pieces 1955–82*, 1983

(ed.) *The Oxford Book of Twentieth Century Verse*, 1973

See:

B. C. Bloomfield, *Philip Larkin: A Bibliography 1933–1976*, 1979

R. Day, *Larkin*, 1987

B. Dyson, *Essays in Memory of Philip Larkin*, 1989

G. Hartley (ed.) *Philip Larkin 1922–1985: A Tribute*, 1988

J. Hartley, *Philip Larkin, the Marvell Press, and Me*, 1989

A. Motion, *Philip Larkin*, 1982

A. Thwaite (ed.), *Larkin at Sixty*, 1982

T. Whalen, *Philip Larkin and English Poetry*, 1986

LEAVIS, FRANK RAYMOND (1895–1978): Critic and editor; b. Cambridge where he lived throughout his life; 1914–18 service on Western Front as stretcher-bearer with Friends' Ambulance Unit; from 1932 director of English Studies, Downing College; 1932 joined editorial board of *Scrutiny* with its third issue, thereafter editing it, in effect, until it ceased publication in 1953; 1936 Fellow of Downing College and half-time lecturer in English Faculty; 1959 appointed Reader; after retirement from Cambridge, Visiting Professorship at York University, 1965–8; 1978 made CH.

(For publications prior to 1945 see Volume 7 of the *Guide*.)

Publications include:

The Great Tradition, 1948, rev. 1960; *The Common Pursuit*, 1952; *Anna Karenina and Other Essays*, 1967; *English Literature in Our Time and the University*, 1969 (Clark Lectures); *Nor Shall My Sword: Discourses on Pluralism, Compassion and Social Hope*, 1972; *The Living Principle*, 1975; *Thought, Words and Continuity: Art and Thought in Lawrence*, 1976

(ed. G. Singh) *Valuation in Criticism*, 1986; *The Critic as Anti-Philosopher*, 1982

(with Q. D. Leavis) *Lectures in America*, 1969; *Dickens the Novelist*, 1970

See:

R. P. Bilan, *The Literary Criticism of F. R. Leavis*, 1979

F. R. Boyers, *F. R. Leavis: Judgment and the Discipline of Thought*, 1978

P. J. M. Robertson, *The Leavises on Fiction: A Historic Partnership*, 1981

D. Thompson (ed.), *The Leavises: Recollections and Impressions*, 1984

W. Walsh, *F. R. Leavis*, 1980

G. Watson, *The Leavises, the 'Social' and the Left*, 1977

LESSING, DORIS (b. 1919): Novelist and short-story writer; b. Persia; lived in Southern Rhodesia 1924–49.

Works include:

(novels) *The Grass is Singing*, 1950 (filmed 1981); five-novel sequence *The Children of Violence* (*Martha Quest*, 1952; *A Proper Marriage*, 1954; *A Ripple from the Storm*, 1958; *Landlocked*, 1965; *The Far-Gated City*, 1969); *The Golden Notebook*, 1962; *Briefing for a Descent into Hell*, 1971; *The Summer Before the Dark*, 1973; *Memoirs of a Survivor*, 1974 (filmed 1981); five-volume sequence, *Canopus in Argos: Archives* (*Shikasta*, 1979; *The Marriage Between Zones Three, Four and Five*, 1980; *The Sirian Experiments*, 1981; *The Making of the Representative for Planet 8*, 1982; *The Sentimental Agents in the Volyen Empire*, 1983); *A Sport of Nature*, 1987; *The Fifth Child*, 1988

(short stories) *Collected African Stories*, 2 vols., 1973; (*This Was The Old Chief's Country*; *The Sun Between Their Feet*); *Collected Stories*, 2 vols., 1978 (*To Room 19*; *The Temptation of Jack Orkney*)

(non-fiction) *Going Home*, 1957; *In Pursuit of the English*, 1960; *Prisons We Choose to Live Inside*, 1986; *The Wind Blows Away Our Words*, 1987

See:

L. Sage, *Doris Lessing*, 1983

J. Taylor (ed.), *Notebooks/Memories/Archives: Reading and Rereading Doris Lessing*, 1982

M. Thorpe, *Doris Lessing*, 1973
  Doris Lessing's Africa, 1978
R. Whittaker, *Doris Lessing*, 1988

LEWIS, CLIVE STAPLES (1896–1963): Children's writer, literary historian and writer on theological issues; Fellow of Magdalen College, Oxford, 1935–54; Professor of Medieval and Renaissance English Literature, Cambridge, 1954–62.

Publications include:
(children's fiction) *The Lion, the Witch and the Wardrobe*, 1950; *Prince Caspian: The Return to Narnia*, 1951; *The Voyage of 'The Dawn Treader'*, 1952; *The Silver Chair*, 1953; *The Horse and His Boy*, 1954; *The Magician's Nephew*, 1955; *The Last Battle*, 1956
(literary history) *The Allegory of Love*, 1936; *A Preface to 'Paradise Lost'*, 1942; *English Literature in the Sixteenth Century*, 1954
(autobiography) *Surprised by Joy: The Shape of My Early Life*, 1955; *A Grief Observed*, 1961
See:
R. L. Green, *C. S. Lewis*, 1963

LOWRY, MALCOLM (1909–57): Novelist, short-story writer and poet; educated at the Leys School and St Catharine's College, Cambridge; lived in USA and Mexico in the thirties, and from 1940–54 mainly in Canada; first novel *Ultramarine*, 1933.

Other publications include:
(novels) *Under the Volcano*, 1947; *Dark as the Grave Wherein My Friend is Laid* (ed. D. Day and M. Lowry), 1968; *Lunar Caustic*, 1968
(short stories) *O Lord, From Heaven Thy Dwelling Place*, 1961
(poetry) *Selected Poems*, 1962; *Psalms and Songs*, 1975
(letters) *Selected Letters* (ed. H. Brett and M. Lowry), 1967

Life by D. Day, 1973
See:
T. Bareham, *Malcolm Lowry*, 1989
R. Binns, *Malcolm Lowry*, 1984
G. Bowker (ed.), *Under the Volcano: Critical Essays*, 1987
M. Bradbook, *Lowry: His Art and Early Life*, 1974
J. H. Woolman, *Malcolm Lowry: a Bibliography*, 1983

MACDIARMID, HUGH – Christopher Murray Grieve – (1892–1978): Poet and prose writer; educated at Langholm Academy, Dumfriesshire, and as a pupil-teacher in Edinburgh; journalism in Scotland and South Wales, followed by army service 1915–1919; edited three anthologies, *Northern Numbers*, of current Scottish poetry, 1920–22; first volume of poems *Annals of the Five Senses*, 1923; first experiments in the revivial of Scots as a literary medium published as *Sangschaw*, 1925; founder member of National Party of Scotland 1927–8, but expelled from it, 1933; joined Communist Party of Great Britain 1934, expelled for 'national deviation' 1948, rejoined 1957; Civil List pension, 1950.

Works include:
(poetry) *Complete Poems 1920–1976*, ed. M. Grieve and W. R. Aitken, 1978
(prose) *Selected Essays*, ed. D. Glen, 1969; *Lucky Poet*, 1943 and *The Company I've Kept*, 1966 (autobiographies); *The Letters of Hugh MacDiarmid*, ed. A. Bold, 1984; *The Hugh MacDiarmid–George Ogilvie Letters*, ed. C. Kerrigan, 1988

Life by Gordon Wright, 1977 and by Alan Bold, 1988
See:
J. Baglow, *Hugh MacDiarmid: The Poetry of Self*, 1988
A. Bold, *Hugh MacDiarmid: The Terrible Crystal*, 1983
P. McCary, *Hugh MacDiarmid and the Russians*, 1988
E. Morgan, *Hugh MacDiarmid*, 1977

MARKANDAYA, KAMALA: Novelist; b. Southern India; educated Madras University.

Novels include: *Nectar in a Sieve*, 1954; *A Handful of Rice*, 1966; *The Coffer Dams*, 1969; *The Nowhere Man*, 1974; *Two Virgins*, 1975; *The Golden Honeycomb*, 1977; *Shalimar*, 1983
See:
M. Joseph, *Kamala Markandaya*, 1987

MERCER, DAVID (1928–80): Dramatist; educated King's College, Newcastle upon Tyne.

Publications include: *The Generations*, 1964; *Three TV Comedies*, 1966; *The Parachute and Other Plays*, 1967; *On the Eve of Publication and Other Plays*, 1970; *Collected TV Plays*, 2 vols., 1981

MONTAGUE, JOHN (b. 1920): Poet; b. New York; educated University College, Dublin.

Publications include:
(poetry) *Selected Poems*, 1982; *The Dead Kingdom*, 1984
(short stories) *Death of a Chieftain*, 1964

MURDOCH, IRIS (b. 1919): Novelist and philosopher; educated at Somerville College, Oxford; civil servant 1942–4; administrative officer with UNRRA, 1944–6; Fellow of St Anne's College, Oxford since 1948; first novel, *Under the Net*, 1954; C B E, 1976; D B E, 1987.

Other works include:
(novels) *The Flight from the Enchanter*, 1965; *The Sandcastle*, 1957; *The Bell*,

1958; *An Unofficial Rose*, 1962; *The Unicorn*, 1963; *The Italian Girl*, 1964; *The Nice and the Good*, 1968; *Bruno's Dream*, 1969; *A Fairly Honourable Defeat*, 1970; *An Accidental Man*, 1971; *The Black Prince*, 1973; *The Sacred and Profane Love Machine*, 1974; *The Sea, The Sea*, 1978 (Booker Prize); *The Good Apprentice*, 1985; *The Book and the Brotherhood*, 1987; *The Message to the Planet*, 1989

(non-fiction) *Sartre: Romantic Rationalist*, 1953; *The Sovereignty of Good*, 1970; *The Fire and the Sun: Why Plato Banned the Artists*, 1977

See:

A. S. Byatt, *Degrees of Freedom: The Novels of Iris Murdoch*, 1965

P. Conradi, *Iris Murdoch: The Saint and the Artist*, 1985

E. Dipple, *Iris Murdoch: Work for the Spirit*, 1981

D. Johnson, *Iris Murdoch*, 1987

R. Todd, *Iris Murdoch*, 1984

NAIPAUL, VIDIADHAR SURAJPRASAD (b. 1932): Novelist; b. Trinidad; educated at Queen's Royal College, Trinidad and University College, Oxford.

Publications include:

(novels) *The Mystic Masseur*, 1957; *Miguel Street*, 1959; *A House for Mr Biswas*, 1961; *Mr Stone and the Knights Companion*, 1963; *The Mimic Men*, 1967; *In a Free State*, 1971 (Booker Prize); *Guerrillas*, 1975; *A Bend in the River*, 1979; *The Enigma of Arrival*, 1987

(non-fiction) *The Middle Passage: Impressions of Five Societies in the West Indies and South America*, 1962; *An Area of Darkness: An Experience of India*, 1964; *The Loss of Eldorado*, 1969; *India: A Wounded Civilisation*, 1977; *Among the Believers: An Islamic Journey*, 1981; *Finding the Centre*, 1984; *A Town in the South*, 1989

See:

R. D. Hamner (ed.), *Critical Perspectives on V. S. Naipaul*, 1977

P. Theroux, *Naipaul, an Introduction to His Work*, 1972

L. White, *Naipaul: A Critical Introduction*, 1975

NARAYAN, RASIPURAM KRISHNASWAMY (b. 1906): Novelist and short-story writer; educated at Maharajah's College, Mysore, India.

Publications include:

(novels) *Swami and Friends*, 1935; *The Bachelor of Arts*, 1937; *The English Teacher*, 1945; *The Financial Expert*, 1952; *Waiting for the Mahatma*, 1955; *The Guide*, 1958; *The Man-Eater of Malgudi*, 1961; *The Sweet Vendor*, 1967; *The Painter of Signs*, 1977; *A Tiger for Malgudi*, 1983; *The Talkative Man*, 1987; *The World of Nagaraj*, 1990

(short stories) *An Astrologer's Day*, 1964; *Gods, Demons and Others*, 1965; *Lawley Road*, 1969; *A Horse and Two Goats*, 1970; *Under the Banyan Tree*, 1985

(autobiography) *My Days*, 1975

See:
P. S. Sundaram, *R. K. Narayan*, 1987
W. Walsh, *R. K. Narayan: A Critical Appreciation*, 1982

ORWELL, GEORGE – Eric Blair – (1903–50): Novelist, journalist and critic.

Publications include: *Animal Farm*, 1945; *Critical Essays*, 1946; *The English People*, 1947; *Nineteen Eighty-Four*, 1949; *Shooting an Elephant*, 1950; *England, Your England*, 1953; *Collected Essays* (ed. S. Orwell and I. Angus, 4 vols.), 1968 (For longer entry see Volume 7 of the *Guide*.)

Life by B Crick, 1980
See:
J. R. Hammond (ed.), *A George Orwell Companion*, 1982
S. Hynes (ed.), *Twentieth Century Interpretations of '1984'*, 1971
J. Meyers (ed.), *George Orwell: The Critical Heritage*, 1975
R. Wiliams, *Orwell*, 1971

OSBORNE, JOHN (b. 1929): Dramatist; from 1948 to 1978 pursued acting career, at first in touring and repertory companies, later in the West End, television and film, while writing plays at the same time; first London production *Look Back in Anger*, 1956 (filmed 1958).

Other publications include:
(plays) *The Entertainer*, 1957 (filmed 1959); *Luther*, 1960 (filmed 1971); *Inadmissable Evidence*, 1965 (filmed 1965); *A Patriot for Me*, 1966; *The Hotel in Amsterdam*, 1967; *West of Suez*, 1971; *A Sense of Detachment*, 1972; (with A. Creighton) *An Epitaph for George Dillon*, 1958
(autobiography) *A Better Class of Person*, 1981
See:
R. Hayman, *John Osborne*, 1968, rev. 1970
A. P. Hinchcliffe, *John Osborne*, 1983
M. Page (ed.), *File on Osborne*, 1988

PEARCE, PHILIPPA: (b. 1920) Children's writer; b. Cambridgeshire; educated Girton College, Cambridge; civil servant, 1942–5; worked for BBC Schools Broadcasting, 1945–58.

Publications include:
(novels) *Minnow on the Say*, 1955; *Tom's Midnight Garden*, 1958; *A Dog So Small*, 1962; *The Battle of Bubble and Squeak*, 1978; *The Way to Sattin Shore*, 1983; *The Toothball*, 1987; (with B. Fairfax-Lucy) *The Children of the House*, 1968
(short stories) *What the Neighbours Did*, 1972; *The Shadow-Cage and other Tales of the Supernatural*, 1977; *Lion at School*, 1985; *Who's Afraid? and Other Stories*, 1986

PINTER, HAROLD (b. 1930): Dramatist and poet; b. East London; educated Hackney Downs Grammar School; conscientious objector, 1948–9; actor, mainly repertory, 1949–57; first play *The Room*, 1957; Associate Director, National Theatre, 1973–83; CBE, 1966.

Plays include: *The Birthday Party*, 1958 (filmed 1968); *The Caretaker*, 1960 (filmed 1963); *The Collection*, 1961; *The Lover*, 1963; *The Homecoming*, 1964; *Landscape and Silence*, 1969; *Old Times*, 1971; *No Man's Land*, 1975; *Betrayal*, 1978 (filmed 1983); *One for the Road*, 1984

Collected Poems and Prose, 1986
See:
G. Almansi and S. Henderson, *Harold Pinter*, 1983
A. Bold (ed.), *Harold Pinter: You Never Heard Such Silence*, 1985
J. R. Brown, *Theatre Language*, 1972
B. F. Dukore, *Harold Pinter*, 1982
M. Esslin, *Pinter: The Playwright*, 4th edn., 1984
S. H. Gale, *Harold Pinter: An Annotated Bibliography*, 1978
A. P. Hinchcliffe, *Harold Pinter*, 1976
M. Scott (ed.), *The Birthday Party, The Caretaker, The Homecoming: A Casebook*, 1986

PLATH, SYLVIA (1932–63): Poet and novelist; studied at Smith College, Northampton, Massachusetts; 1955 Fulbright Fellowship to Newnham College, Cambridge; 1956 married Ted Hughes; 1957 moved to US to teach at Smith College; returned to Europe December 1959; her volume of poems, *The Colossus,* published in London 1960; separated from her husband October 1962; her novel, *The Bell Jar,* published (under the pseudonym Victoria Lucas) January 1963; committed suicide February 11th.

Other works include:
(poems) *Ariel*, 1965; *Crossing the Water*, 1971; *Winter Trees*, 1971; *Collected Poems* (ed. T. Hughes), 1981
(letters) *Letters Home, 1950–63*, 1976

Life by L. Wagner-Martin, 1988, and by A. Stevenson, 1989
See:
E. M. Aird, *Sylvia Plath*, 1973
D. Holbrook, *Poetry and Existence*, 1976
J. Kroll, *Chapters in Mythology: The Poetry of Sylvia Plath*, 1976
G. Lamb and M. Stevens, *Sylvia Plath: a bibliography*, 1978
G. Lane (ed.), *Sylvia Plath: New Views on the Poetry*, 1970
M. D. Uroff, *Sylvia Plath and Ted Hughes*, 1979

PORTER, PETER (b. 1929): Poet; b. and educated in Queensland, Australia; formerly journalist, bookseller, clerk; has worked in advertising.

Collected Poems, 1983; other poems in *Fast Forward*, 1984; *The Automatic Oracle*, 1987; *Selected Poems*, 1989; *Possible Worlds*, 1989

POWELL, ANTHONY (b. 1905): Novelist; educated Eton and Balliol College, Oxford; first novel, *Afternoon Men*, 1931; served in the Welch Regiment and the Intelligence Corps, 1939–45; CBE, 1956

Publications include:

(novels) *Venusberg*, 1932; *From a View to a Death*, 1933; *Agents and Patients*, 1936; *What's Become of Waring*, 1939; *A Dance to the Music of Time*, 12-volume sequence, 1951–75 (*A Question of Upbringing*, 1951; *A Buyer's Market*, 1952; *The Acceptance World*, 1955; *At Lady Molly's*, 1957; *Casanova's Chinese Restaurant*, 1960; *The Kindly Ones*, 1962; *The Valley of Bones*, 1964; *The Soldier's Art*, 1966; *The Military Philosopher*, 1968; *Books Do Furnish a Room*, 1971; *Temporary Kings*, 1973; *Hearing Secret Harmonies*, 1975); *O How the Wheel Becomes It!*, 1983; *The Fisher King*, 1986

(autobiography) *To Keep the Ball Rolling*, 4 vols., 1962–82; one-volume abridgement, 1983

See:

B. Bergonzi, *Anthony Powell*, 1971

H. Spurling, *A Handbook to Anthony Powell's 'The Music of Time'*, 1977

J. Tucker, *The Novels of Anthony Powell*, 1976

RAINE, KATHLEEN (b. 1908): Poet and critic; educated Girton College, Cambridge.

Publications include:

(poems) *Collected Poems 1935–80*, 1981

(autobiography) *Farewell Happy Fields*, 1973; *The Land Unknown*, 1975; *The Lion's Mouth*, 1977

(criticism) *Blake and the New Age*, 1979; *The Human Face of God: William Blake and the Book of Job*, 1982

RAO, RAJA (b. 1909): Novelist and short-story writer; born in Mysore into a Brahmin family; after graduating from Nizam's College, Hyderabad, 1928, went to France to study and research at the university of Montpellier and at the Sorbonne; began writing in Canada (short stories some of which he later translated into English); wrote also in French but ultimately chose English; in the 1960s taught at the University of Texas, USA

Works include:

(novels) *Kanthapura*, 1938; *The Serpent and the Rope*, 1960; *The Cat and Shakespeare* (novella), 1965; *Comrade Kirillov*, 1976

(short stories) *The Cow of the Barricades*, 1947; *The Policeman and the Rose*, 1978

See:

M. K. Naik, *Raja Rao*, 1972

C. D. Narasimhaiah, *Raja Rao*, 1987
K. R. Rao, *The Fiction of Raja Rao*, 1980

REDGROVE, PETER (b. 1932): Poet and novelist; educated Queen's College, Cambridge; formerly scientific journalist and editor; lives in Cornwall.

Publications include:
(poetry) *The Moon Disposes: poems 1954–87*, 1987; *In the Hall of the Saurians*, 1988
(novels) *In the Country of the Skin*, 1972; *The God of Glass*, 1979; *The Sleep of the Great Hypnotist*, 1979; *The Beekeeper*, 1980; *The Facilitators*, 1982

RHYS, JEAN – Ella Gwendolen Rees Williams – (1890?–1979): Novelist and short-story writer; b. Dominica and educated in the island's convent school; occasional theatre work until her first marriage and removal to France in 1919; from 1923 befriended and encouraged to write by Ford Madox Ford; first novel *Postures*, 1928; from early 1950s lived in isolation and was thought to be dead; in 1957 she 'reappeared' in answer to BBC advertisement asking for information about her; a new novel, *The Wide Sargasso Sea*, 1966, won acclaim, two awards, and the re-publication of all her earlier work; CBE, 1978.

Other works include:
(novels) *After Leaving Mr Mackenzie*, 1930; *Voyage in the Dark*, 1934; *Good Morning, Midnight*, 1939; *Quartet*, 1969; (re-publication of *Postures* with different title)
(short stories) *Tigers are Better Looking*, 1968; *Sleep it Off, Lady*, 1976
(autobiography) *Smile Please* (unfinished), 1979

Life by C. Angier, 1985
See:
E. W. Mellown, *A Descriptive and Annotated Bibliography of Works and Criticism by Jean Rhys*, 1984
H. Nebekev, *Jean Rhys: Woman in Passage*, 1981

RUSHDIE, SALMAN (b. 1947): Novelist; educated Cathedral School, Bombay, Rugby School, and King's College, Cambridge.

Publications include:
(novels) *Grimus*, 1975; *Midnight's Children*, 1981 (Booker Prize); *Shame*, 1983; *The Satanic Verses*, 1988
(non-fiction) *The Jaguar's Smile: a Nicaraguan Journey*, 1987
See:
T. Brennen, *Salman Rushdie and the Third World*, 1990

SCOTT, PAUL (1920–78): Novelist; joined the army in 1940, and travelled extensively in India, Burma and Malaya; first novel, *Johnny Sahib*, 1952; worked as literary agent, 1950–60.

Other novels include: *The Corrida at San Feliu*, 1964; *The Jewel in the Crown*, 1966; *The Day of the Scorpion*, 1968; *The Tower of Silence*, 1971; *A Division of the Spoils*, 1975; *The Raj Quartet* (the previous four novels in one volume), 1976; *Staying On*, 1977 (Booker Prize)
See:
P. Swinden, *Paul Scott*, 1983

SHAFFER, PETER (b. 1926): Dramatist; educated St Paul's School and Trinity College, Cambridge.

Plays include: *Five Finger Exercise*, 1958; *The Private Ear and The Public Eye*, 1962 (filmed); *The Royal Hunt of the Sun*, 1965 (filmed 1969); *Black Comedy, Including White Lies*, 1967; *Equus*, 1973 (filmed 1977); *Amadeus*, 1980 (filmed 1984); *Yonadab*, 1985; *Lettuce and Lovage*, 1987
See:
V. Cooke and M. Page (eds.), *File on Shaffer*, 1987

SILLITOE, ALAN (b. 1928): Novelist, short-story writer, dramatist and poet; educated at elementary schools in Nottingham; worked in Raleigh Bicycle Factory 1942–6; writer from 1948; acclaimed first novel *Saturday Night and Sunday Morning*, 1958 (filmed 1960); Hawthornden Prize for volume of short stories *The Loneliness of the Long-Distance Runner*, 1959 (title story filmed 1962)

Other works include:
(novels) *The Death of William Posters*, 1965; *Travels in Nihilon*, 1971; *The Open Door*, 1989; *Last Loves*, 1990
(short stories) *The Ragman's Daughter*, 1962; *Men, Women and Children*, 1973; *The Second Chance*, 1981; *The Far Side of the Street*, 1988
(drama) *Three Plays*, 1978
See:
S. Atherton, *Alan Sillitoe: A Critical Assessment*, 1979

SNOW, CHARLES PERCY (1905–79): Novelist; degrees in chemistry and physics at University College, Leicester, 1924–8, followed by research at Cavendish Laboratory, Cambridge; Fellow of Christ's College, Cambridge, 1930, and tutor from 1935–45; first novel, *Death under Sail*, 1932; *Strangers and Brothers*, 1940 (first title in the 11-volume sequence of that name); CBE, 1943; Civil Service Commissioner, 1945–60; knighted 1957; life peerage 1964.

Other writings include:
(novels) *The Masters*, 1951; *The New Men*, 1954; *The Affair*, 1960; *The Corridors of Power*, 1964; *Last Things*, 1970
(non-fiction) *The Two Cultures and the Scientific Revolution*, 1959; *Science and Government*, 1961; *Postscript*, 1962

See:

W. Cooper, *C. P. Snow*, 1959, rev. 1962
F. R. Leavis, *Two Cultures? The Significance of C. P. Snow*, 1962
D. Shesterman, *C. P. Snow*, 1975

SOYINKA, WOLE (b. 1934): Dramatist and poet; b. Abeokuta, Western Nigeria; educated at University College, Ibadan, and Leeds University; 1957–9 attached to Royal Court Theatre as Play-Reader; first play *The Swamp-Dwellers* produced London and Ibadan, 1959; 1961–2 Research Fellow, Ibadan University; 1962–4 Lecturer University of Ife; 1967–9 two years in gaol in connection with attempts to negotiate a truce in the Biafran War; 1969–72 Director of School of Drama at Ibadan; 1973 his adaptation of Euripides' *Bacchae* commissioned by National Theatre, London; 1975 Professor of Comparative Literature, University of Ife; Nobel Prize for Literature 1986.

Works include:
(plays) *The Lion and the Jewel*, 1963; *The Road*, 1965; *Kongi's Harvest*, 1966; *Madmen and Specialists*, 1971; *Death and the King's Horseman*, 1975; *Opera Wonyosi*, 1979
(poems) *Idanre*, 1967; *A Shuttle in the Crypt*, 1972; *Ogun Abibiman*, 1976; *Mandela's Earth*, 1989
(novels) *The Interpreters*, 1965; *Season of Anomy*, 1973; *Isara*, 1990
(autobiography) *The Man Died*, 1972; *Ake, the Years of Childhood*, 1982
(criticism) *Art, Dialogue and Outrage*, 1988

Collected Plays, 2 vols, 1974–5
See:
J. Gibbs, *Wole Soyinka*, 1985
     (ed.), *Critical Perspectives on Wole Soyinka*, 1980
E. D. Jones, *The Writing of Wole Soyinka*, 1973, rev. 1983
G. H. Moore, *Soyinka*, 1971, rev. 1978
O. Ogunba, *The Movement of Transition: A Study of the Plays of Soyinka*, 1975

SPARK, MURIEL (b. 1918): Novelist and short-story writer; educated Heriot Watt College, Edinburgh; General Secretary, The Poetry Society 1947–9; first novel *The Comforters*, 1957.

Works include:
(novels) *The Go-Away Bird*, 1958; *Memento Mori*, 1959; *The Ballad of Peckham Rye*, 1960; *The Prime of Miss Jean Brody*, 1961 (filmed 1969); *The Girls of Slender Means*, 1963; *The Mandelbaum Gate*, 1965; *The Driver's Seat*, 1970 (filmed 1974); *The Abbess of Crewe*, 1974 (filmed 1977); *Territorial Rights*, 1979; *The Only Problem*, 1984; *A Far Cry from Kensington*, 1988

(stories) *Collected Stories I*, 1967; *Bang-Bang You're Dead*, 1982; *The Stories of Muriel Spark*, 1987
See:
A. Bold, *Muriel Spark*, 1986
   (ed.), *Muriel Spark: An Odd Capacity for Vision*, 1984
R. Whittaker, *The Faith and Fiction of Muriel Spark*, 1982

STOPPARD, TOM (b. 1937): Dramatist and novelist; b. Czechoslovakia; worked as a journalist, 1954–63; first play *A Walk on the Water* produced on TV, 1963, rewritten for stage as *Enter a Free Man*, 1968; novel *Lord Malquist and Mr Moon*, 1965

Plays include: *Rosencrantz and Guildenstern are Dead*, 1967; *The Real Inspector Hound*, 1968; *After Magritte*, 1971; *Jumpers*, 1975; *Dirty Linen and New-Found-Land*, 1976; *Every Good Boy Deserves Favour*, 1978; *Professional Foul*, 1978; *Night and Day*, 1978; *Undiscovered Country*, 1980; *On the Razzle*, 1982; *The Real Thing*, 1983; *Hapgood*, 1988
See:
M. Billington, *Stoppard: The Playwright*, 1987
P. Delaney, *Tom Stoppard: The Moral Vision of the Major Plays*, 1990
R. Hayman, *Tom Stoppard*, 1977, rev. 1982
J. Hunter, *Tom Stoppard's Plays*, 1982
A. Jenkins, *The Theatre of Tom Stoppard*, 1987

STOREY, DAVID (b. 1933): Novelist and dramatist; educated Queen Elizabeth Grammar School, Wakefield, and Slade School of Fine Art; first novel *This Sporting Life*, 1960 (filmed 1963); first play *The Restoration of Arnold Middleton*, produced at Royal Court Theatre, 1967.

Other works include:
(plays) *In Celebration*, 1969; *The Contractor*, 1970; *Home*, 1970; *The Changing Room*, 1971; *Life Class*, 1974; *Mother's Day*, 1976; *Sisters*, 1978; *Early Days*, 1980; *The March on Russia*, 1989
(novels) *Flight into Camden*, 1960; *Radcliffe*, 1963; *Pasmore*, 1972; *A Temporary Life*, 1973; *Saville*, 1976 (Booker Prize); *A Prodigal Child*, 1982; *Present Times*, 1984
See:
J. R. Taylor, *David Storey*, 1974

THOMAS, DYLAN (1914–53): Poet: b. Swansea; educated at Swansea Grammar School; reporter for *South Wales Evening Post*, 1931–2; first poem published in *Sunday Referee*, 1932; first volume of poetry, *Eighteen Poems*, 1934; unfit for active service, lived in London during the war, writing scripts and reading poetry for BBC radio; three lecture-tours in US 1950–53, followed by a visit to New York for the first performance of *Under Milk Wood* in October 1953; died a few days later of alcohol poisoning.

Other publications include:
(stories) *Portrait of the Artist as a Young Dog*, 1940; *Adventures in the Skin Trade*, 1955; *A Prospect of the Sea* (ed. D. Jones), 1955 (includes some miscellaneous prose)
(radio play) *Under Milk Wood*, 1954
(film script) *The Doctor and the Devils*, 1953
(radio scripts) *Quite Early One Morning*, 1954

Collected Poems 1934–52, 1952
Dylan Thomas: The Poems (ed. D. Jones), 1971
Collected Letters (ed. P. Ferris), 1985
Life by P. Ferris, 1977
See:
J. A. Rolph, *Dylan Thomas: A Bibliography*, 1956
D. Holbrook, *Dylan Thomas: The Code of Night*, 1972
W. Y. Tindall, *A Reader's Guide to Dylan Thomas*, 1962

THOMAS, RONALD STUART (b. 1913): Poet; educated University College, Bangor; ordained 1936; curacies 1936–42; Rector of Manafon, 1942–54; Vicar of Eglwysfach, 1954–67; Vicar of St Hywyn, Aberdaron, 1967–78; first volume, privately printed, *Stones of the Field*, 1947; first recognition with *Song at the Year's Turning*, 1955.

Other publications include: *Selected Poems 1946–1968*, 1974; *Later Poems 1972–82*, 1983; *Experimenting with an Amen*, 1986; *Welsh Airs*, 1987; *The Echoes Return Slow*, 1989
See:
S. Anstey (ed.), *Critical Writings on R. S. Thomas*, 1982
W. M. Merchant, *R. S. Thomas*, 1979
D. Z. Phillips, *R. S. Thomas: Poet of the Hidden God*, 1985
J. P. Ward, *The Poetry of R. S. Thomas*, 1987

TOLKIEN, JOHN RONALD REUEL (1892–1973): Children's writer and philologist; Professor of Anglo-Saxon, Oxford University, 1925–45; Merton Professor of English Language and Literature, 1945–59; CBE, 1972.

Children's books include: *The Hobbit*, 1937; *The Lord of the Rings*, 3 vols., 1954–5; *The Silmarillion* (ed. C. Tolkien), 1977

TOMLINSON, CHARLES (b. 1927): Poet, critic and artist; educated Queen's College, Cambridge; first volume of poems *Relations and Contraries*, 1951; Lecturer, Bristol University, 1957–68, Reader, 1968–82, Professor of English since 1982; Clark Lecturer, Trinity College, Cambridge, 1982.

Publications include:
(poetry) *Collected Poems*, 1985 (expanded 1987); *The Return*, 1987; *Annunciation*, 1989

(prose) *Some Americans: A Personal Record*, 1980; *Poetry and Metamorphosis*, 1983

(graphics) *Words and Images*, 1972; *In Black and White*, 1975; *Eden*, 1985

(ed.), *The Oxford Book of Verse in Translation*, 1980

WAIN, JOHN (b. 1925): Novelist, poet and writer; educated St John's College, Oxford; lecturer, University of Reading, 1947–55; Professor of Poetry, Oxford University, 1973–8; CBE, 1984

Publications include:

(poetry) *Poems 1949–1979*, 1981

(novels) *Hurry on Down*, 1953; *Strike the Father Dead*, 1962; *Young Shoulders*, 1982

(criticism) *Samuel Johnson*, 1974; *Professing Poetry*, 1977

WAUGH, EVELYN (1903–66): Novelist; educated at Lancing and Hertford College, Oxford; studied art in London and began teaching; served with Marines and later the Commandos in Second World War.

(For publications before 1945 see Volume 7 of the *Guide*.)

Later works include:

(novels) *Brideshead Revisited*, 1945; *The Loved One*, 1948; *War Trilogy: Men at Arms*, 1952; *Officers and Gentlemen*, 1955; *Unconditional Surrender*, 1961 (these three revised as *Sword of Honour*, 1965); *Love Among the Ruins*, 1953; *The Ordeal of Gilbert Pinfold*, 1957

(autobiography) *A Little Learning*, 1964

Life by C. Sykes, 1980

See:

M. Bradbury, *Evelyn Waugh*, 1964

J. F. Carens, *The Satiric Art of Evelyn Waugh*, 1966

I. Littlewood, *The Writings of Evelyn Waugh*, 1982

M. Stannard (ed.), *Evelyn Waugh: The Critical Heritage*, 1984

WESKER, ARNOLD (b. 1932): Dramatist; educated Upton House School, Hackney, RAF, 1950–52; various jobs, including plumber's mate, farm labourer and kitchen porter, 1952–4; pastry cook, 1954–8; first play *The Kitchen* produced at Royal Court Theatre, 1959 (filmed 1961); Founder Director of Centre 42, 1961 (dissolved 1970).

Plays include: The Trilogy, *Chicken Soup With Barley*, 1959, *Roots*, 1959, *I'm Talking About Jerusalem*, 1960; *Chips With Everything*, 1962; *Their Very Own and Golden City*, 1966; *The Four Seasons*, 1966; *The Friends*, 1970; *The Old Ones*, 1973; *Love Letters on Blue Paper*, 1974; *The Journalists*, 1975; *The Wedding Feast*, 1977; *The Merchant*, 1978; *Caritas*, 1981; *Annie Wobbler*, 1983; *Yarsdale*, 1987; *Whatever Happened to Betty Lemon?*, 1987

Collected Plays, Vols. 1–4, 1980

See:

R. Hayman, *Arnold Wesker*, 1970

G. Leeming, *Wesker the Playwright*, 1983

    (ed.), *Wesker on File*, 1985

G. Leeming and S. Trussler, *The Plays of Arnold Wesker*, 1971

WHITE, PATRICK (b. 1912): Novelist, short-story writer and dramatist; brought up partly in England, partly in Australia; educated at Cheltenham College and King's College, Cambridge; first novel *Happy Valley*, 1939; 1939–45 war service with RAF as Intelligence Officer, mainly in the Middle East; returned to Australia after the war to a farm near Sydney; moved into Sydney 1964; supporter of Whitlam's Labour government, 1972–5; Nobel Prize for Literature, 1973.

Works include:

(novels) *The Aunt's Story*, 1948; *The Time of Man*, 1955; *Voss*, 1957; *Riders in the Chariot*, 1961; *The Solid Mandala*, 1966; *The Vivisector*, 1970; *The Eye of the Storm*, 1973; *A Fringe of Leaves*, 1976; *The Twyborn Affair*, 1979; *Memoirs of the Many in the One*, 1986

(short stories) *The Burnt Ones*, 1964; *The Cockatoos*, 1974; *Three Uneasy Pieces*, 1988

(plays) *Four Plays*, 1965; *Big Toys*, 1978; *Signal Driver*, 1981; *Netherwood*, 1983

(autobiography) *Flaws in the Glass*, 1981

See:

C. Bliss, *Patrick White's Fiction: The Paradox of Fortunate Failure*, 1981

J. Colmer, *Patrick White*, 1984

B. Kiernan, *Patrick White*, 1980

W. Walsh, *Patrick White's Fiction*, 1977

G. A. Wilkes (ed.), *Ten Essays on Patrick White*, 1970

WILSON, ANGUS (b. 1913): Novelist, short-story writer and critic; educated Westminster School and Merton College, Oxford; Foreign Office 1942–6; Deputy to Superintendent of Reading Room, British Museum, 1949–55; Professor at East Anglia University from 1966; CBE, 1968; knighted 1980.

Works include:

(novels) *Hemlock and After*, 1952; *Anglo-Saxon Attitudes*, 1956; *The Middle Age of Mrs Eliot*, 1958; *Old Men at the Zoo*, 1961; *Late Call*, 1964; *No Laughing Matter*, 1967; *As If By Magic*, 1973; *Setting the World on Fire*, 1981

(short stories) *The Wrong Set*, 1949; *Such Darling Dodos*, 1950; *A Bit Off The Map*, 1957

(play) *The Mulberry Bush*, 1956

(other) *Emile Zola*, 1950; *The Wild Garden, or Speaking of Writing*, 1963; *The World of Charles Dickens*, 1957; *The Strange Ride of Rudyard Kipling*,

1977; *Diversity and Depth in Fiction*, 1983; *Selected Critical Writings of Angus Wilson* (ed. K. McSweeney), 1983; *Reflections in a Writer's Eye*, 1985.

See:

P. Faulkner, *Angus Wilson: Mimic and Moralist*, 1980

J. L. Halio, *Angus Wilson*, 1966

ACKNOWLEDGEMENTS

For permission to reprint copyright material, either whole or in part, acknowledgements are made to the following:

George Mackay Brown, for one poem only from *Loaves and Fishes* to The Hogarth Press Ltd; Austin Clarke, for one poem only from *Poems 1955–1966* to The Dolmen Press Ltd; Keith Douglas, for poems from the *Complete Poems* to Oxford University Press; Thom Gunn, for poems from *The Sense of Movement* and *My Sad Captains* to Faber & Faber Ltd. Reprinted by permission of Farrar, Straus & Giroux, Inc. Excerpts from *Selected Poems 1950–1975* by Thom Gunn. Copyright © 1957, 1958, 1961, 1967, 1971, 1973, 1974, 1975, 1976, 1979 by Thom Gunn. Excerpts from *Moly* and *My Sad Captains* by Thom Gunn. Copyright © 1961, 1971, 1973 by Thom Gunn. Seamus Heaney, for poems from *North*, *Death of a Naturalist*, *Wintering Out* and *Field Work* to Faber & Faber Ltd. Reprinted by permission of Farrar, Straus & Giroux, Inc. Excerpts from *Poems 1965–1975* by Seamus Heaney. Copyright © 1966, 1969, 1972, 1975, 1980 by Seamus Heaney. Excerpts from *Field Work* by Seamus Heaney. Copyright © 1976, 1979 by Seamus Heaney. Geoffrey Hill, for poems from *For the Unfallen* and *Tenebrae* to André Deutsch Ltd; Ted Hughes, for poems from *The Hawk in The Rain*, *Lupercal*, *Crow*, *Wodwo* and *Gaudete* to Faber & Faber Ltd and Harper & Row Publishers Inc.; Philip Larkin, for poems from *The Less Deceived* to The Marvell Press; D. H. Lawrence, for poems from *The Complete Poems* to Laurence Pollinger Ltd, the Estate of Frieda Lawrence Ravagli and Viking Penguin Inc.; Norman MacCaig, for poems from *The Sinai Sort* and *A Common Grace* to The Hogarth Press Ltd; Hugh MacDiarmid, for poems from the *Complete Poems 1920–1976* to Martin Brian & O'Keeffe Ltd and Mrs Walda Grieve and from *The Hugh MacDiarmid Anthology* to Routledge & Kegan Paul Ltd; John Montague, for poems from *The Rough Field* to The Dolmen Press Ltd and Wake Forest University Press. 'A Chosen Light' was originally published by MacGibbon & Kee Ltd in the volume of that name and later in *Selected Poems* by The Dolmen Press Ltd; Edwin Muir, for poems from the *Collected Poems* to Faber & Faber Ltd and Oxford University Press Inc.; Alan Neame, for one poem only which was first published in *Edge, June 1957*, edited by Noel Stock. Reprinted by permission of the author; Ezra Pound, for one poem only from the *Collected Shorter Poems* to Faber & Faber Ltd, also to New Directions Publishing Corporation; Peter Redgrove, for poems from *Dr Faust's Sea-Spiral Spirit and Other Poems* to Routledge & Kegan Paul Ltd; Dylan Thomas, for poems from

ACKNOWLEDGEMENTS

the *Collected Poems* to David Higham Associates Ltd and New Directions
Publishing Corporation; R. S. Thomas, for poems from *Pieta, Not That He
Brought Flowers, Tares* and *A Song at the Year's Turning* to Granada Publishing
Ltd; thanks are also due to Julia Lane for 'My Baby Brother', Frances Quirke
for 'Father' and Catherine Lancaster for 'Façades' and to the authors of the
poems 'Love?', 'Now the children have gone' and 'The Folk that Wept and
Sorrowed'.

Every effort has been made to trace copyright holders but we would be
grateful to hear from anyone not here acknowledged.

NOTES ON CONTRIBUTORS

PETER ABBS Lecturer in Education at the University of Sussex. His books include *Autobiography in Education* (1974) and *Reclamations* (1979). He is the editor of the Falmer Press Library on Aesthetic Education, the first three volumes of which are *Living Powers* (1987), *A is for Aesthetic* (1988), and *The Symbolic Order*. He has also published three volumes of poetry, *For Man and Islands* (1978), *Songs of a New Taliesin* (1981) and *Icons of Time* (1991).

C. B. COX Professor of English, University of Manchester. His books include *The Free Spirit* (1963) and *The Great Betrayal: An Autobiography* (1992). He is editor of *Critical Quarterly* and was Chair of the National Curriculum Working Group. He has published two collections of verse, *Every Common Sight* (1981) and *Two-Headed Monster* (1985).

S. W. DAWSON Formerly Senior Lecturer in English at the University College of Swansea. Author of *Drama and the Dramatic* (1970).

MARTIN DODSWORTH Professor of English at Royal Holloway and Bedford New College, University of London. Editor of *The Survival of Poetry* (1970) and (from 1976–87) of *English*, the journal of the English Association; author of *Hamlet Closely Observed* (1985).

PER GEDIN Managing Director of Gedins Förlag Publishers, in Sweden. Author of *The New Book* (1966) and *Literature in the Market Place* (1977).

BERNARD HARRISON Reader and Dean of Education Faculty, University of Sheffield. Works include *Learning Through Writing* (1983), *English Studies, 11–18* (ed., 1983) and *Sarah's Letters* (1986).

RONALD HEPBURN Professor of Moral Philosophy at the University of Edinburgh. His publications include *Christianity and Paradox* (1958) and *'Wonder' and Other Essays* (1984).

DAVID HOLBROOK Emeritus Fellow of Downing College, Cambridge. His recent works include *The Skeleton in the Cupboard: the Fantasies of C. S. Lewis* (1991) and *Where D. H. Lawrence was Wrong about Women* (1992): also two novels, *The Gold in Father's Heart* (1992) and *Even If They Fail*.

JOHN HOLLOWAY Emeritus Professor of Modern English, Cambridge; publications in or largely in the Victorian field include *The Proud Knowledge* (1977), *Narrative and Structure* (1979) and *The Slumber of Apollo* (1983); numerous critical articles and tapes; editions of *Little Dorrit* (1962) and *Silas Marner* (1967, enlarged 1977), and *The Oxford Book of Local Verses* (1987).

GABRIEL JOSIPOVICI Professor of English at the University of Sussex. His books includen ten novels, two volumes of short stories; and also *The World and the Book* (1971), *The Lessons of Modernism* (1977), *Writing and the Body* (1982), *The Book of God* (1988) and *Text and Voice* (1992). His plays have been performed in the USA and Britain.

MICHAEL KIRKHAM Professor of English Literature at the University of Toronto. Among his publications are *The Poetry of Robert Graves* (1969) and *The Imagination of Edward Thomas* (1986). He has recently completed a book on the poetry of Charles Tomlinson.

ROGER KNIGHT Senior Lecturer in Education at the University of Leicester. Author of *Edwin Muir* (1980) and, with Ian Robinson, editor of *My Native English* (1988) and *English in Practice: English at A-level* (1989). He is the editor of *The Use of English*.

KRISHAN KUMAR Professor of Social Thought at the University of Kent at Canterbury. Author of *Prophecy and Progress: The Sociology of Industrial and Post-Industrial Society* (1978), *Utopia and Anti-Utopia in Modern Times* (1987), and *The Rise of Modern Society* (1988). He was a talks producer at the BBC, 1972–3.

GRAHAM MARTIN Was Professor of Literature at the Open University. Publications include O.U. Courses on Dickens, Lawrence, James Joyce, Eliot, Auden, Camus and Soyinka. Editor of *Eliot in Perspective* (1970), co-editor of *Twentieth-century Poetry: Essays and Documents* (1975), *Industrialization and Culture, 1832–1914* (1971), the *Book of Romantic Verse* and is currently editing the *Faber Book of 20th Century Criticism*.

WILFRID MELLERS   Formerly Professor of Music at the University of York. His books include *François Couperin and the French Classical Tradition* (1950), *Music in a New Found Land* (1964), *Bach and the Dance of God* (1981), *Beethoven and the Voice of God* (1984), *The Masks of Orpheus* (1986), *Vaughan Williams and the Vision of Albion* (1989) and *Percy Grainger* (1992).

OLIVER NEVILLE   After twenty-one years as a professional actor and director and working in Bristol University Drama Department as senior lecturer, he is now Principal of the Royal Academy of Dramatic Art.

GILBERT PHELPS   Formerly BBC Third Programme producer; is now a freelance writer, lecturer and broadcaster. Author of *The Russian Novel in English Fiction* (1956), *A Survey of English Literature* (1965) and *From Myth to Modernism: A Short Guide to the World Novel* (1988). His eight novels include *The Winter People* (1963), *The Old Believer* (1973) and *The Low Roads* (1975).

GĀMINI SALGĀDO (d. 1985)   was professor of English at the University of Exeter. His books include *Eyewitnesses of Shakespeare* (1975). *The Elizabethan Underworld* (1977) and *English Drama* (1981).

D. S. SAVAGE   Has held clerical and administrative positions in the T. & G.W.U., Christian Aid and Anglican Pacifist Fellowship. His books include *The Personal Principle* (1944), *The Withered Branch* (1950), *Hamlet and the Pirates* (1950) and *The Cottagers' Companion* (1975). His selected poems, *Winter Offering*, was published in 1990.

GEOFFREY STRICKLAND   Reader in French at the University of Reading. He is the author of *Stendhal: the Education of a Novelist* (1974) and *Structuralism or Criticism* (1981). He is an editor of *The Cambridge Quarterly*.

MICHAEL TANNER   Lecturer in Philosophy at the University of Cambridge. He has published articles on literature, philosophy and music, an extended piece on 'The Total Work of Art' in *The Wagner Companion*, ed. P. Burbidge and R. Sutton (1979); and a monograph on Nietzsche's *Daybreak*.

ROBERT TAUBMAN   Formerly Head of the Department of Humanities at Bristol Polytechnic. He has written on current literature in the *New Statesman*, the *Listener* and the *London Review of Books* and edited *The Penguin Book of Modern European Short Stories* (1969).

DENYS THOMPSON (d. 1988) Formerly Head of Yeovil Grammar School. He assisted F. R. Leavis with *Culture and Environment* (1933) and was one of the early editors of *Scrutiny*. Also the first editor of *The Use of English*. Author of innumerable books linked to the teaching of English, including *The Uses of Poetry* (1978) and *Change and Tradition in Rural England* (1980).

CHARLES TOMLINSON Emeritus Professor of English, University of Bristol. His most recent books are *Collected Poems* (1987), *The Door in the Wall* (1992) and *Poetry and Metamorphosis* (1982). *Eden* contains a selection of his graphics.

WILLIAM WALSH Professor of Commonwealth Literature and formerly Acting Vice-Chancellor at the University of Leeds. His books include *R. K. Narayan* (1971), *F. R. Leavis* (1980), *Introduction to Keats* (1980) and *Indian Literature in English* (1990).

FRANK WHITEHEAD was Reader in English and education at the University of Sheffield. He is the author of *The Disappearing Dais* (1966), and co-author of the Schools Council Research Study *Children and their Books* (1977).

INDEX

INDEX

READ MORE IN PENGUIN

In every corner of the world, on every subject under the sun, Penguin represents quality and variety – the very best in publishing today.

For complete information about books available from Penguin – including Puffins, Penguin Classics and Arkana – and how to order them, write to us at the appropriate address below. Please note that for copyright reasons the selection of books varies from country to country.

In the United Kingdom: Please write to *Dept. JC, Penguin Books Ltd, FREEPOST, West Drayton, Middlesex UB7 OBR*

If you have any difficulty in obtaining a title, please send your order with the correct money, plus ten per cent for postage and packaging, to *PO Box No. 11, West Drayton, Middlesex UB7 OBR*

In the United States: Please write to *Penguin USA Inc., 375 Hudson Street, New York, NY 10014*

In Canada: Please write to *Penguin Books Canada Ltd, 10 Alcorn Avenue, Suite 300, Toronto, Ontario M4V 3B2*

In Australia: Please write to *Penguin Books Australia Ltd, 487 Maroondah Highway, Ringwood, Victoria 3134*

In New Zealand: Please write to *Penguin Books (NZ) Ltd, 182–190 Wairau Road, Private Bag, Takapuna, Auckland 9*

In India: Please write to *Penguin Books India Pvt Ltd, 706 Eros Apartments, 56 Nehru Place, New Delhi 110 019*

In the Netherlands: Please write to *Penguin Books Netherlands B.V., Keizersgracht 231 NL–1016 DV Amsterdam*

In Germany: Please write to *Penguin Books Deutschland GmbH, Friedrichstrasse 10–12, W–6000 Frankfurt/Main 1*

In Spain: Please write to *Penguin Books S. A., C. San Bernardo 117–6° E–28015 Madrid*

In Italy: Please write to *Penguin Italia s.r.l., Via Felice Casati 20, I–20124 Milano*

In France: Please write to *Penguin France S. A., 17 rue Lejeune, F–31000 Toulouse*

In Japan: Please write to *Penguin Books Japan, Ishikiribashi Building, 2–5–4, Suido, Tokyo 112*

In Greece: Please write to *Penguin Hellas Ltd, Dimocritou 3, GR–106 71 Athens*

In South Africa: Please write to *Longman Penguin Southern Africa (Pty) Ltd, Private Bag X08, Bertsham 2013*

READ MORE IN PENGUIN

LITERARY CRITICISM

The English Novel Walter Allen

In this 'refreshingly alert' (*The Times Literary Supplement*) landmark panorama of English fiction, the development of the novel is traced from *The Pilgrim's Progress* to Joyce and Lawrence.

Sexual Personae Camille Paglia

'A powerful book ... interprets western culture as a sexual battleground pitting the Apollonian desire for order against the forces of Dionysian darkness' – *The Times*

The Anatomy of Criticism Northrop Frye

'Here is a book fundamental enough to be entitled *Principia Critica*,' wrote one critic. Northrop Frye's seminal masterpiece was the first work to argue for the status of literary criticism as a science: a true discipline whose techniques and approaches could systematically – and beneficially – be evaluated, quantified and categorized.

Art and Literature Sigmund Freud

Volume 15 of the Penguin Freud Library contains various writings that Freud intended mainly for the non-specialist reader. They include such topics as the theory of instincts, libido and repression, infantile sexuality, Oedipus complex, the sexual factor in neurosis and much more.

Modernism Malcolm Bradbury and James McFarlane (eds.)

'The Modern movement in the arts transformed consciousness and artistic form just as the energies of modernity transformed forever the nature, the speed, the sensation of human life' write the editors in their new Preface. This now classic survey explores the ideas, the groupings and the social tensions that shaped this transformation, as well as the literature itself.

The New Pelican Guide to English Literature
Edited by Boris Ford

**'The best and most lively general survey of English litera-
ture available to schools, students and general readers'**
– The Times Educational Supplement

Authoritative, stimulating and accessible, the original seven-volume
Pelican Guide to English Literature has earned itself a distinguished
reputation. Now enlarged to ten volumes and a readers' guide, this
popular series has been wholly revised and updated.

What this work sets out to offer is a guide to the history and traditions of English literature, a contour-map of the literary scene. Each
volume includes these standard features:

    (i)   An account of the social context of literature in each
            period.

   (ii)   A general survey of the literature itself.

 (iii)   A series of critical essays on individual writers and their
            works – each written by an authority in their field.

 (iv)   Full appendices including short author biographies, listings
            of standard editions of authors' works, critical commen-
            taries and titles for further study and reference.

The *Guide* consists of the following volumes:

  1. Medieval Literature:
      Part One: Chaucer and the Alliterative Tradition
      Part Two: The European Inheritance
  2. The Age of Shakespeare
  3. From Donne to Marvell
  4. From Dryden to Johnson
  5. From Blake to Byron
  6. From Dickens to Hardy
  7. From James to Eliot
  8. The Present
  9. American Literature
      A Guide for Readers